Genreflecting

Recent Titles in
Genreflecting Advisory Series

Diana Tixier Herald, Series Editor

Genreflecting

A Guide to Popular Reading Interests

Seventh Edition

Cynthia Orr and Diana Tixier Herald, Editors

Genreflecting Advisory Series

 LIBRARIES UNLIMITED

AN IMPRINT OF ABC-CLIO, LLC
Santa Barbara, California • Denver, Colorado • Oxford, England

4/13

Library of Congress Cataloging-in-Publication Data

Genreflecting : a guide to popular reading interests / Cynthia Orr and Diana Tixier Herald, Editors. — Seventh edition.

      pages cm. — (Genreflecting Advisory Series)

  Includes index.

  ISBN 978-1-59884-840-3 (Hardcover : acid free paper) — ISBN 978-1-59884-841-0 (paperback : acid free paper) 1. American fiction—Stories, plots, etc. 2. Popular literature—Stories, plots, etc. 3. English fiction—Stories, plots, etc. 4. Fiction genres—Bibliography. 5. Fiction—Bibliography. 6. Reading interests. I. Orr, Cynthia. II. Herald, Diana Tixier.

  PS374.P63R67 2013

  016.813009—dc23   2012051480

ISBN: 978-1-59884-840-3 (case)
     978-1-59884-841-0 (pbk.)

17 16 15 14 13   1 2 3 4 5

Libraries Unlimited
An Imprint of ABC-CLIO, LLC

ABC-CLIO, LLC
130 Cremona Drive, P.O. Box 1911
Santa Barbara, California 93116-1911

This book is printed on acid-free paper ∞

Manufactured in the United States of America

Contents

Chapter 15—Science Fiction 339
Maura Heaphy

Chapter 16—Mainstream Fiction 389
Hannah Jo Parker

Chapter 17—Nonfiction 425
Sarah Statz Cords

Preface

What self-respecting librarian doesn't love readers? And likewise, what self-respecting reader doesn't appreciate a good readers' advisor? Readers' advisory has been growing and flourishing in recent years, with many brilliant librarians taking it up as a career focus, and many new readers' advisory tools becoming available. There are now many avenues for readers to find the books they want to read, but the best remains an interested, knowledgeable readers' advisor who fortunately now has a full arsenal of tools to help. While the art of readers' advisory is still unknown to some, it is no longer ignored. Readers' advisory has come a long way!

I was fortunate early in my career to work as a library assistant in a branch headed by Loren Tabor at Denver Public Library. She valued my devotion to reading and started me on a plan to become an expert readers' advisor. She helped me devise a reading plan that took me into genres and subgenres I would have never ventured into, as well as assigning me a broad variety of book reviews to read to see how other readers viewed books. Loren knew that the branch's patrons were visiting the branch primarily for fiction, and trained her staff to help them find the books the patrons wanted to read but didn't know about.

I became involved with the *Genreflecting* books through a strange happenstance. Attending one of my first ALA conferences and having next to no money, I asked at the taxi stand where a long line of librarians were waiting for cabs at the airport, if anyone wanted to share one. A couple of women who were going to my hotel invited me to ride with them; and as we chatted on the trip from the airport, I discovered they worked for Libraries Unlimited. "You publish my favorite nonfiction book!" I gushed. I went on to confess that I was a fiction addict, and Betty Rosenberg's *Genreflecting* published by their company had been the first book I purchased with my first paycheck as a professional librarian. In library school, Dr. G. Edward Evans introduced me to *Genreflecting* in his Collection Development class. *Genreflecting* instantly made following a reading plan easy. I could just pick a title from each genre; and with every pass through, I would just go on to the next subgenre or theme.

I loved *Genreflecting* because it didn't treat the reading I enjoyed as trite, unimportant, or, heaven forbid, "trashy." Rosenberg obviously respected me as a reader. A few years later, when an editor at Libraries Unlimited called to ask if I would be interested in submitting sample sections for a new edition of *Genreflecting*, I jumped at the opportunity. My tattered copy of *Genreflecting* had notes on every page. The title of every book I had read since I bought it was penciled into the margins in the appropriate sections. The white space at the beginning and ends of chapters was used for new categories I had seen emerging as titles accumulated that didn't fit well into Rosenberg's categories.

I am so excited about this edition of *Genreflecting*. Cindy Orr, who has orchestrated this edition, is an amazing readers' advisor. As I read through the introductory chapters she wrote for this book, I found myself thrusting my fist into the air and shouting yes! Her research reinforces so many things I know instinctively, but she has found the data to back them up.

My personal mantra is "No two people ever read the same book." I came to that realization after booktalking *Snow Crash* by Neal Stephenson. I loved the protagonist, Hiro Protagonist (I could remember his name!), the pizza delivery, the self-adjusting skateboard wheels, the virus that could be transmitted to people via machine, the rip-roaring adventure of it all. My son Nathan, who happened to hear my presentation, had also read *Snow Crash*, but the book he read was quite different. For him, it was all about neurolinguistics and how language shapes thought.

So, since different people have varying experiences when reading, having the variety of accomplished readers' advisors contributing chapters in this edition opens up our world a little more. The more perspectives, the better. Cindy has assembled a terrific crew of experts to contribute chapters on the different genres. Their diverse perspectives offer unprecedented richness to this edition, filtering them through their own knowledge and history. This leads us, as readers' advisors, to think in other ways about books and how readers will experience them; and, as readers, it offers us a plethora of new titles to try.

Enjoy using this edition of *Genreflecting* as a personal reading guide for both pleasure and professional growth, and as a tool to help you connect people with the books they want to read. Above all, Happy Reading.

—*Diana Tixier Herald*

Acknowledgments

We would like to thank the contributors to this book, especially those of you who persevered through a long process and those who stepped in to help in the final hours. We are especially indebted to our wonderful, one-of-a-kind editor, Barbara Ittner, who shepherded this complicated undertaking with exceptional grace, expertise, and doggedness. She is, and has been, an indispensible ingredient for the entire *Genreflecting* series.

Introduction

Cynthia Orr

Genreflecting has a long and stellar history beginning with its first edition written by Betty Rosenberg and published in 1982. The fact that there is still demand for this, the 7th edition, nearly 30 years later, is a testament to the significance of its approach. The book resulted from Rosenberg's class on reading interests for UCLA's Graduate School of Library and Information Science in the late 1960s. While interest in readers' advisory service had largely gone underground from 1950 to 1980, Rosenberg believed in it, and its importance to the field of library science has grown significantly since her publication of the first edition of this book.

Part I of this book, "Readers' Advisory Service in the Library," is meant to place readers' advisory service into context. As detailed in Chapter 1, readers' advisory service is growing in importance, not only in public libraries, but also in school, university, and even special libraries, where pleasure reading is acknowledged to be a legitimate and positive part of people's lives. Training in the service has spread to other countries as well, with a significant movement in Great Britain and interest from around the world.

Librarians realize that reading for pleasure is an important part of the lives of many people, but that finding a good book to read is often difficult, and even overwhelming for the average reader. Adding to the pressure, choosing a good book is a crucial factor in developing new avid readers. After all, if a potential reader is struggling through a book that is not a good fit, why would he or she think that reading is pleasurable? Helping people find a good book is an essential piece of the puzzle if we are to successfully encourage reading.

Understanding readers is vital for librarians who expect to do readers' advisory work, and Chapter 2 covers the research and theories that relate to reading for pleasure. This includes general approaches to studying reading, as well as such topics as Catherine Sheldrick Ross' research with successful avid readers, what they say about how they choose books to read, and how they developed as readers.

In Chapter 3, you'll find guidance on understanding the literature. If readers' advisory service is a matter of understanding readers, understanding books, and then using professional techniques to match readers to books and books to readers, then you must understand the literature in order to be successful. *Genreflecting*'s traditional approach "maps" popular literature by genre, and this chapter explains how charting the landscape by genre plays a central role in readers' advisory service. This guides you through the landscape of literature, without which the librarian "scouting" for books to match with readers would be either hopelessly lost or, at best, flying by the seat of the pants.

As Arthur Asa Berger explains, "Writing about texts . . . without dealing with their genres is often too narrow, too focused. But writing about genres without dealing with texts that exemplify these genres is too abstract, too general" (Berger, p. xii). *Genreflecting* attempts to do both, using a simplified, quick reference approach to explaining each genre and also listing specific titles that fit each genre and subgenre.

Research has shown that readers looking for a good book look first for books by an author they have enjoyed. This kind of search is quite easily accomplished. But once readers have exhausted all the books by their favorite authors, where do they go next? The research shows that the next most common strategy is to search for a book in a similar genre (Ross et al.). This book provides a unique tool for those using the genre approach.

Part II, "Readers' Advisory Service Basics," offers an overview of the techniques used by current readers' advisors to provide good service to their patrons. Chapter 4 offers a basic introduction to the professional techniques used by readers' advisors when working with the literature. This includes a section on professional tools, one on further reading in the field, and current and future trends. Chapter 5 introduces basic professional techniques used by librarians when working with readers, such as the readers' advisory interview, the "Golden Rules for RA," and other tips for becoming a star readers' advisor, including working with difficult people. Chapter 6 covers the library's environment, how to build the library's brand, provide comfortable spaces for readers, do outreach, and find ways to allow readers to help themselves if they prefer.

Part III, "The Genres," contains genre-focused chapters contributed by experts in the field. Comments about each genre and its characteristics are followed by lists of currently significant titles in that genre organized so that users of the book can readily see a map of popular literature as it looks today. For each genre, you will also find a list of "Must Reads" for a place to start if you're not familiar with a particular genre. In order to help guide someone who is new to a particular genre, the chapters also include a list of "Five Fan Favorites," as well as 20 or 30 benchmark titles.

Genres come and go, and the depth of coverage in each of these chapters reflects their current popularity. Westerns, for instance, took up a large number of pages in earlier editions of this book, but interest in the genre has waned, and the current edition reflects that with reduced coverage.

For the first time, we have included a section on Nonfiction, which has become very popular among those reading for pleasure. Many readers enjoy reading nonfiction books, and it is exciting to be able to include this genre in the new edition. The addition of a chapter on Mainstream Fiction is also a first for *Genreflecting*. It was not covered in earlier editions because mainstream novels are not generally considered to be genre titles. It is included for the first time in this edition, because not to do so leaves a giant gap in the landscape we are attempting to map—and titles are increasingly crossing genres, defying labels, and generally becoming more difficult to pigeonhole. This edition of *Genreflecting* also includes sections on other reading interests—Christian Fiction, Urban Fiction, and Graphic Novels.

Understanding genres is important. As Ursula K. Le Guin explains, "If you don't know what kind of book you're reading, and it's not a kind you're used to, you probably need to learn how to read it. You need to learn the genre" (Le Guin, p. 63).

Our hope is that this book will be used by professors and students as a text for readers' advisory classes, classes on genres, or classes on popular adult-reading interests. In addition, library practitioners can use it as an introduction to the field of readers' advisory service, a general map of the terrain of literature, a tool with specific titles to suggest on the job or use for a genre study, and a source for readers to use themselves.

I would like to thank the contributors who stuck with this sprawling project as it seemed to take forever to pull it together and get it ready for the editors. Great thanks are owed to Betty Rosenberg for writing the early editions of this work, to Diana Herald, who has kept it going over the years, and to its editor, Barbara Ittner of Libraries Unlimited, whose vision, talent, and skills have insured its success. I hope that Di will be firmly back at the helm when it's time for the next edition.

- = The book or series has received one or more awards, listed in the entry.

- = A movie or television series has been made based on the book or series.

- = The book may be a good choice for a book discussion group.

- **YA** = The book may have been written for young adults, but has appeal for adults as well.

- ★ = The book is a benchmark title.

Books set off by lines are Must Read titles. Each book may be considered to be a benchmark, or a core title in this genre.

Further Reading

Berger, Arthur Asa. 1992. *Popular Culture Genres: Theories and Texts*. Thousand Oaks, CA: Sage.

Le Guin, Ursula K. 2004. "Genre: A Word Only a Frenchman Could Love," in *The James Tiptree Award Anthology 1: Sex, the Future, & Chocolate Chip Cookies*. San Francisco: Tachyon Publications, 61–69.

Ross, Catherine Sheldrick, Lynne McKechnie, and Paulette M. Rothbauer. 2006. *Reading Matters: What the Research Reveals About Reading, Libraries, and Community*. Westport, CT: Libraries Unlimited.

PART I

READERS' ADVISORY SERVICE
IN THE LIBRARY

Chapter 1

Reading and Libraries

Cynthia Orr

About 70 years ago, while digging along the Struma River in Bulgaria, a man made an incredible discovery—the world's oldest multiple-page book. The book consists of 6 bound sheets of 24-carat gold and is more than 2,500 years old, dating to about 600 BC. It is written in the lost Etruscan language, which has never been deciphered, so scholars have no idea what it says. I can't claim to be a scholar, but I believe strongly that we can make some assumptions about this precious artifact from its illustrations. The book, which is now in Bulgaria's National History Museum in Sofia, contains pictures of a horse and rider, a mermaid, soldiers, and a lyre.

It was important enough to be placed carefully into an ancient tomb, but it was not a list of assets of a powerful king, or a treatise on his genealogical heritage. No, with its mermaid and warriors and lyre, I maintain that this prized possession—this narrative important enough to be made of gold—is simply a story. Imagine that. The earliest known bound multipage book was fiction. This is quite a testament to the power of story (BBC News).

Story has been as precious as gold since our earliest ancestors received the gift of language and began sharing experiences around their fires at night. And have we outgrown that need? Not at all. Today, there are more stories shared throughout the world than ever before.

Just think about it for a minute. The oral storytelling that our ancestors used still makes up a large part of our everyday human conversation. But we've added printed stories on paper and screens, visual stories told through movies and television, and audio stories frozen onto discs or saved in digital files. We have live performances of plays by everyone from children in their schools, or in their garages at home, to amateurs who spend hours and hours of their own free time preparing to put on a show, to professionals who turn out enough content to fill hundreds of television channels in many languages.

Why is this? What makes story so important in our lives? Here are a few reasons.

WE LEARN BETTER FROM STORIES

Once upon a time there was a wise and revered woman who sat every day on the porch of her cottage weaving, as she responded to those who came to her with questions. People came from far and wide to learn from this woman whose wisdom was celebrated. The people from her village watched with pride as she helped all who came to her.

One day, a young boy asked a question. "Mother," he said, "Why do you always respond to the people's problems by telling a story? Wouldn't it be more efficient to simply give a direct answer when someone asks for your help?" She merely smiled and said, "Could you bring me a drink of water, my son?" The boy immediately hurried away, found a cup, filled it with water from the well, and brought it back to her.

Smiling at him fondly, she said, "Thank you. But why did you also bring me a cup, when I asked only for water?"

We can immediately recognize the truth contained in this folktale about story. The woman's tales were efficient containers of wisdom, just as the cup was an efficient container for water. She could have sipped water from her hands, but much of it would have leaked away. And we can learn from a recitation of facts, but it is also true that in merely memorizing facts we risk having some of the knowledge leak away.

Roger Schank says in his book *Tell Me a Story: Narrative and Intelligence*, "Stories illustrate points better than simply stating the points themselves because, if a story is good enough, you usually don't have to state the point at all; the hearer thinks about what you have said and figures out the point independently. The more work the hearer does, the more he or she will get out of your story" (p. 12).

STORIES ALLOW US TO WALK IN THE SHOES OF OTHERS

Stories let us share in experiences that we have not lived ourselves. In this way also, the story is an efficient container for truth, not just fact. Which is more powerful, reading an article listing the facts about the burning of Atlanta during the Civil War or living the experience along with Scarlett O'Hara in the novel *Gone with the Wind*? Arnold Weinstein in his book *A Scream Goes Through the House: What Literature Teaches Us About Life* says, "Literature . . . offers us access to, and a way to share in, the entire range of human feeling over the ages. This is a gift like no other" (p. xx).

Steven Covey, in his book *The Seven Habits of Highly Effective People*, uses a story to illustrate the power of the paradigm shift. He tells the story of his trip on a train with a father who ignored his disruptive children who were running up and down the car, jumping on the seats, and preventing Covey from working. When Covey asked the man if he could control his children, the father explained that they had just left the hospital where their mother had died. Covey's entire view of the situation changed immediately, of course, when he heard the man's story. Stories allow us to experience the lives of other people in a way that is impossible to do otherwise (Covey, p. 31).

STORIES CONNECT PEOPLE SOCIALLY

Even though reading seems like the ultimate solitary activity, stories, rather than isolating us, often bring us closer together, and even serve as a social connection between people. When we've finished reading a book that we've really enjoyed, our first reaction is to tell someone else about the book—and if they too have read it, a discussion of the book inevitably follows. How many times have you read an exceptional passage aloud to someone else?

Bestseller readers prefer to read books that are currently on the *New York Times* list so that they can participate in discussions about them at the next party where everyone else is reading the same titles as well. Reading the book later is simply not as much fun. As Gary Saul Morson explains in his Foreword to Roger C. Schank's *Tell Me a Story*, this is the same reason people are willing to pay high movie ticket prices to see the latest film, rather than waiting until they can see it in the comfort of their own homes at a much lower price—"the conversations are going on now." This also helps explain why so many people were willing to go out at midnight to buy the latest <u>Harry Potter</u> or *Twilight* book. It wasn't just the book, it was the social experience.

In contrast, Morson asserts that reading a classic is different, because this process is like a story exchange not only with contemporaries but also with people from other times and places. The attraction of a classic is that it is widely known and appreciated, and because many classics are from other areas of the world, they provoke "discussions" with people unlike ourselves.

STORIES BIND COMMUNITIES TOGETHER

Stories can also help create and perpetuate a feeling of community among people. Think of religious texts, for example. These sacred stories help a particular group of people understand their common religious heritage. Whether it's David versus Goliath or the story of the Bodhi tree, hearing these tales and sharing them with our family and community lets us know that we are part of a particular community.

Stories about our own families cement us to our relatives and ancestors, and help us define what it means to be part of this kinship community. How many times have you heard someone talk about the pressure they feel because there has not been an unsuccessful marriage in their family for many years, or that not one of their relatives has ever failed to go to college, or that they are expected to join the family business because that has been the case for several generations? These pressures are particularly strong because they are usually supported by a narrative of the family experiences—the stories told around the dinner table, at family gatherings, and during every crisis.

Other family stories serve to strengthen the ties between generations. A relative may say that a particular child has the gift of gab just like his grandfather, which leads someone else to launch into the story of the time Grandpa talked his way out of being arrested. These kinds of stories reinforce our membership in societal groups.

STORIES ROOT US TO A PARTICULAR PLACE

"She opened the door leading to the verandah and found the servants clustered there with their heads close together. When they saw her, they got quickly to their feet. The dust got instantly into her eyes, nostrils, between her teeth; it blew in gusts into the room. 'It's me!' cried a voice from the car. It was not the Nawab, but Harry. He hurried in with her and the door was quickly shut again. But already, even from that one moment, the desert dust lay in a thick layer on her piano and the yellow silk of her armchairs."

This excerpt from Ruth Prawer Jhabvala's *Heat and Dust* (p. 70) lets you feel as if you are in India with the dirt in your teeth and nostrils. Now compare the following description of India in this excerpt from the travel guide *Lonely Planet India* by Sarina Singh (p. 35): "India has a three-season year—the hot, the wet and the cool. . . . The heat starts to build up on the northern plains of India from around February, and by April or May it really hots up. In Central

India temperatures of 45°C and above are commonplace. Later in May, the first signs of the monsoon are visible in some areas—high humidity, violent electrical storms, short rainstorms and dust storms that turn day into night." These are helpful facts for the traveler, but do not offer the experience of a story.

Stories transport us, immerse us in other places, allow us to feel intensely, and thus understand better, the experience of places we may never visit.

STORIES FIX US IN A PARTICULAR TIME

In *The Doomsday Book*, Connie Willis transports a modern woman back in time to England during the Black Death epidemic in 1348. Historical novelists like Willis who pride themselves on authenticity can help us to experience the world in a particular time period in ways that history textbooks cannot.

Alternate histories show us what might have been. What if Lindbergh had been elected President? (*The Plot Against America* by Philip Roth) Science fiction lets us imagine a future based upon what has happened in the past (*Forty Years of Rain* by Kim Stanley Robinson). Authors who take us to a different time do the research for us, and let us simply experience that time through a story.

STORIES TAKE US FAR AWAY

"In a hole in the ground there lived a hobbit. Not a nasty, dirty, wet hole, filled with the ends of worms and an oozy smell, nor yet a dry, bare, sandy hole with nothing in it to sit down on, or to eat: it was a hobbit-hole, and that means comfort.

"It had a perfectly round door like a porthole, painted green, with a shiny yellow brass knob in the exact middle. The door opened on to a tube-shaped hall like a tunnel: a very comfortable tunnel without smoke, with panelled walls, and floors tiled and carpeted, provided with polished chairs, and lots and lots of pegs for hats and coats—the hobbit was fond of visitors" (Tolkien, p. 1).

So where are you right now? Sitting in a comfortable chair or at a desk reading this book? But where were you a few seconds ago? I'd wager that the opening passage of J.R.R. Tolkien's *The Hobbit* took you to a place far, far away. Stories can mean escape to another reality besides our own, and many readers read stories just for this purpose.

STORIES TEACH US TO BE HUMAN

How do we learn to be human? Children live their lives, ask questions, observe, grow, learn, and learn how to learn. And through their sometimes seemingly endless questions, what are they trying to do but get inside the heads of others, to learn what other people think, to find out about others' experiences, and to use that insight to learn how to be human themselves?

In Marge Piercy's novel *He, She and It*, we enter a story set in the near future—probably around 2060 or so—and find a world run by huge multinational corporations instead of nations. Those who aren't lucky enough to have a good job working for a multinational, thus qualifying to live inside one of their enclaves, usually live in the Glop—a megalopolis in the Boston to Atlanta corridor that is overcrowded, dangerous, and unprotected from the ruined environment. Some even live in the Black Zone—a supposedly uninhabitable area that used to be Jerusalem before it was hit by a nuclear attack in 2017. A few lucky ones live in free towns and struggle to keep from being taken over by the multinationals. People connect to the Net via a port in their neck, and that means that a hacker could kill them. And most of the hackers work for the multinationals, which aspire to take over the world—or at least any valuable parts of it.

In Piercy's world, human-formed cyborgs are illegal, but the residents of Tikva (one of the free towns) build one anyway, in order to protect themselves from hacker attacks. A cyborg's reaction time is so much better than a human's that he can save the town. But how can they teach the cyborg how to be human?

One of the cyborg's creators, Malkah, a woman in her 80s, begins telling him the legend of Rabbi Judah Loew, who in the early 1600s created a golem to protect Prague's Jewish ghetto from attacks by the Christians. In telling stories to the cyborg Yod about the golem Joseph, Malkah helps him to understand what it means to be human. Even though the scientists have used advanced technology to give him a body with incredible physical powers, and other scientists have built an advanced interface for him to react to the Net, she chooses old-fashioned storytelling as the way to transform Yod into a real person.

And after all, isn't that how we all have learned to be human? We supplement our firsthand experiences with stories that let us understand from others what it means to be a human being.

STORIES HELP US TO DEAL WITH PAIN

"This morning, before I came to Ruth's house, I made yet another casserole for my husband and my daughter" (Berg, p. 3). This is the first sentence of Elizabeth Berg's *Talk Before Sleep*, a novel that explores the importance of relationships, feelings, and the pain of dealing with a loved one's terminal illness, as a group of women rally around their friend who is dying of cancer. Stories often help us to see that others have gone through the same pain and trials that we face, and that life goes on, people do survive, no matter how difficult that may be. Stories let us see that we are not alone, and that the human race faces similar challenges all over the world—and has throughout time.

STORIES ARE RESERVOIRS OF WISDOM

In the book *The Call of Stories*, Robert Coles quotes his father as saying that novels contain "reservoirs of wisdom" from which he and his mother drank (p. xii). Coles, throughout his career as a psychiatrist and teacher, used works by such authors as Tillie Olsen, William Carlos Williams, Thomas Hardy, and others to encourage his students to connect with a character, evaluate the ethical issues the character faced, and to make decisions about their own lives and responsibilities. Each reader has a very personal response to a book, and even young children think about the moral significance of life. Stories of how other humans have met the challenges of tough decisions can help us to make our own decisions.

STORIES SHOW THE CONSEQUENCES OF ACTIONS

From the simple fable of "The Boy Who Cried Wolf" to the complex issues leading up to the Vietnam War explored in a novel such as *A Dangerous Friend* by Ward Just, stories teach us the consequences of our actions. When we see, through the power of this novel, how the "dangerous friend" puts horrible events into motion through his own naiveté and arrogance, we may ponder some of our own decisions and actions, and question our natural assumption that we know best. Storytelling makes this into a much deeper exploration that resonates in a way that merely making a rule cannot.

Research is beginning to show that reading fiction, as opposed to reading nonfiction or watching a movie, leads readers to be more empathetic. One study put it this way: "Bookworms, by reading a great deal of narrative fiction, may buffer themselves from the effects of reduced direct interpersonal contact by simulating the social experiences depicted in stories. Nerds, in contrast, by consuming predominantly non-narrative nonfiction, fail to simulate such experiences and may accrue a deficit in social skills as a result of removing themselves from the actual social world" (Mar).

Kendall Haven has summarized the research on the importance of story. He shows that using stories improves comprehension in learning, that stories motivate and create enthusiasm for learning, and that they create involvement and a sense of community. The research also shows that the use of story improves language skills and writing, enhances memory, and improves logical thinking (Haven, pp. 89–122).

STORY IS IMPORTANT TO LIBRARIES

So where do people get access to stories? Well, they can buy books, movies, and cable or satellite television subscriptions, but many thousands of people find story in their free public, school, or university library. Anyone who has worked in a public library sees those stories going out and then back in the door multiple times every day.

"There are more public libraries than McDonald's restaurants, and two-thirds of Americans use public libraries every year," says Professor Wayne Wiegand, an expert on public library history. Research has shown that more children participate in library reading programs than play Little League baseball in the summer. Americans make 3.5 billion visits to libraries each year—three times more than visits to the movies (Wiegand). More people borrow movies from libraries than from Netflix (OCLC).

We've all seen these happy readers in our libraries. Many of them come back every week to check out more stories. Satisfied customers support their libraries, vote for bond issues and tax levies, and protest when local government tries to close branches or cut services. So story is crucially important to libraries.

Research shows that library users consistently think of libraries as places to find books to read for pleasure. A January 2010 Harris poll showed that when asked about services used at the public library in the past year, 77 percent of Americans reported taking out books (e-books or books on paper or tape) as the number one use (American Library Association).

Earlier surveys and polls have similar results. Patron surveys show that 74 percent use the library to find a book to read. Circulation statistics show that about 60 percent of public library adult circulation is fiction (Herald, p. xviii). Patrons consistently rank books and reading highest in user surveys.

Avid readers love their library. Appreciative patrons vote for levies. More children participate in summer reading programs than play Little League baseball. Who else delivers "story" free to the public? In the last section, we argued that story is important in people's lives, but story is important to libraries as well.

Finding a good book to read is central to a successful reading experience. Catherine Sheldrick Ross has charted how "costly" the route is to a good reading experience. Each pleasurable reading experience reinforces the feeling that reading is fun, while each unsuccessful choice of a book makes it more likely that the potential reader will conclude that reading is not pleasurable. People who do not understand that reading is pleasurable will not read for pleasure (Ross, p. 206). Why would they?

CHOOSING A GOOD BOOK CAN BE OVERWHELMING

One evening, I was invited to dinner at the home of some people I didn't know well. Having been brought up to be polite, I naturally stopped to buy a hostess gift on the way to their house. Knowing that Emily Post says a small gift of food or wine is appropriate, I went to a local wine store to make my choice. I confess that I enjoy a glass of wine now and then, but I know very little about it.

I might be a bit like a person who reads what is put in front of her, but doesn't seek out reading herself. "Look at this article in the newspaper," someone says, and she dutifully reads it, finds it interesting (or not) and moves on. She may read the jokes her father sends her via e-mail, and the newsletter of her church, or the daily newspaper upon occasion, but she can take reading or leave it. This desultory reader, as I'll call her, is like me with wine. I don't dislike it, I have a glass when offered, can take it or leave it, and find it all pretty much the same—mostly pleasant, but nothing to get excited about.

When I arrived at the wine store, I was totally baffled as to where to begin. I was confronted by section after section of aisles, shelf after shelf containing rows of bottles of all sizes, shapes, and colors. Although I was sure there was an order to the overwhelming arrangement, I couldn't figure it out. Were they divided by price? That might help. No, it wasn't price. Color? Red, white, pink? No, not that either. I could make no sense of the arrangement at all and had no idea where to begin. I began walking up and down the aisles looking for something that might catch my eye. I tried looking at the labels, but I didn't understand what they meant. I could read the words of course, but had only a vague idea of their meaning. Okay, blanc—that means white. And the name of the wine is supposed to be related to the kind of grapes used, I think. Simple enough! But here is a Zinfandel that is red, and another one that's not. Uh oh!

Finally, running short of time, I went to the cash register and asked the clerk for help. Naming a price range, I took whatever he handed me and hurried off to dinner, at least relieved to know that Emily says a hostess gift is not to be opened that evening, but should be enjoyed later—by which time I would be safely back at home in case it turned out to be a ridiculous choice.

I think many people could sympathize with my plight in the wine store. If you are one of those erudite creatures who are perfectly at home browsing the wine cellars of the world, I envy you. But perhaps you could try to imagine yourself standing in the screw and nail aisle of a giant home improvement store looking at the little bins of fasteners and trying to figure out what they are all used for. The point is, when you don't know the criteria used to arrange products, you don't know how to decipher the labels, you don't know the key differences, the context, the uses, or even understand the vocabulary used, then you are reduced to pretty much asking the next person who comes along for a "good" choice.

The next time you walk into the stacks of your library, imagine that you don't see and understand the arrangement, look around with the eyes of that casual reader who doesn't hate reading, but who just hasn't done enough of it to understand what she likes and dislikes. If she were going to try to choose a good book for herself, how would she begin? Would she wander up and down row after row of books packed together spine-out on shelves up to seven feet tall until something catches her eye? And even if she did understand the Dewey Decimal System, which arranges nonfiction books by subject so that she could find an area of interest and browse, what is she to make of fiction, which is arranged simply by author? Chances are, she would be just as lost as I was in the wine store.

This is an overwhelming prospect for many readers, and it is an overwhelming prospect for many librarians faced with helping those readers. If story is important in our lives, and story is important to our libraries, if readers have trouble finding good stories that they will find pleasurable, and potential readers who never find a pleasurable book will never become avid readers, then it follows that successfully suggesting a book to a reader is extremely important work. And this work deserves attention, commitment, and training. So how do librarians learn about books and readers? Do graduate library programs measure up in the area of helping readers find books?

DO LIBRARIANS GET ENOUGH READERS' ADVISORY TRAINING?

Library schools have traditionally done a good job with readers' advisory training for children's and teen librarians, but not very well at all in the area of adult services, where, as Kathleen Mangan put it, "in revamped library schools, information trumps books" (p. A43).

Although a few library schools teach some form of readers' advisory service or literature for adults, most do not. And in the 1970s and 1980s, when many current practicing librarians received their degrees, this subject was largely unheard of. Many older librarians have struggled with readers' advisory service over their careers, learning how to suggest books from those with a knack for this kind of thing.

But demand for this service is not new. Readers have always wanted help in finding good books. Early in my career in a suburb of Cleveland, a well-known local journalist named Dorothy Fuldheim had a book review show on television every month or so. As soon as her broadcast was finished, the phone would begin to ring at public libraries in the area, as readers rushed to get the book she recommended. She was the Cleveland Oprah Winfrey of her day.

I distinctly remember once when she miscalculated the amount of time available for her program and had just a few seconds to fill at the end of her show. She said that she was reading another book that she just loved, that she couldn't remember the author or the title at the moment, but that the book was about Wales. The phone rang anyway, and it was a revelation to me that the readers who called didn't care if the book was on Wales or whales. If Dorothy liked it, they wanted it! (The book was *Green, Green My Valley Now* by Richard Llewellyn.)

The point is that readers' advisory service for popular materials has been a service that librarians have quietly provided for decades. But many of us learned this skill by modeling ourselves after the older librarians with whom we worked. Since the 1980s, librarians have been trying to codify this service to patrons who wish to read for pleasure and pass the skills along in a more formal way. Today's readers' advisory movement began with the publication of the first edition of this book by Betty Rosenberg in 1982.

Mapping the world of story by genre made sense to Professor Rosenberg back in 1982, and later research by Catherine Sheldrick Ross confirmed the usefulness of this approach for readers' advisors. Dr. Ross found in her interviews with avid readers expert at finding books they liked, that when attempting to find a good book to read, their first approach was to find other titles by the same author—a task that can easily be carried out using the typical library catalog.

When they had exhausted the writings of their favorite author, however, their second approach was to look through books in the same genre (Ross, p. 204). But this is no easy task in the typical library. Cataloging of fiction is improving now that libraries no longer have to worry about producing and filing (and then potentially unfiling) 3 × 5 cards, but it is still inadequate in identifying genre. Even in libraries that shelve fiction by genre or include genre in the OPAC record, choosing a title is difficult. Typical subject headings for genre fiction (if there are any at all) are geographic locations. But unless the reader has an all-encompassing interest in a location, this kind of subject heading is useless. An extremely violent Andrew Vacchs Burke mystery set in New York City is almost a polar opposite to a cozy Rhys Bowen Molly Murphy mystery, also set in New York. A sweeping historical novel may have more in common with a sweeping fantasy novel than a historical fictional biography. But these differences are typically not addressed in catalogs. The cataloging of fiction is horribly inadequate in most libraries.

Why is this the case? Why is fiction cataloging so poor? A bit of public library history should help us to put things into context.

THE "FICTION PROBLEM"

Once upon a time in the olden days, around the beginning of the 20th century, American librarians grappled with something they called "The Fiction Problem." Just what was this problem? Well, the Fiction Problem boiled down to this question: Should public libraries stock any fiction books? (Yes, you read that sentence correctly.)

Many librarians at the time argued that fiction had no place in the public library (Garrison, p. 65). Other librarians stocked fiction, but were wary of its addictive properties, and called it "mind-weakening," among other things. For years, the controversy raged, and while few libraries ended up with no fiction at all, several tried schemes designed to entice fiction readers into taking nonfiction books as well. Some libraries made rules that patrons could take one fiction book for every nonfiction book; some shelved nonfiction above and below the fiction in hopes of attracting readers' attention.

Eventually, the issue split into two theories: (1) fiction has no place in libraries or (2) libraries should have fiction because readers might be enticed to elevate their tastes (Carrier, p. 45). The truth is that from the very beginnings of this country, fiction has been popular with readers and looked upon with suspicion by others (Ross, pp. 6–15).

A book auction in 1744 in Boston had five bestsellers: three of which were fiction, one a poem, and the fifth a classic Puritan work of nonfiction (Shera, p. 122). The Library Company in 1783 wrote to their London dealer about what to send them once they could begin buying books again after the American Revolution, saying "We shall confide entirely in your judgement to procure us such books of modern publication as will be proper for a public library, and though we would wish to mix the utile with the dulce, we should not think it expedient to add to our present stock anything in the novel way" (Jewett, p. 118). Yet, the New York Society Library in 1789–1790 recorded statistics on its collection and circulation. Fiction had the highest turnover rate of all: 22.7 (Shera, p. 122). Readers loved fiction. Library officials did not.

While having fiction in libraries is no longer questioned, remnants of the old prejudices remain, particularly regarding genre fiction. And there are still those who would ask whether helping readers find good books to read is a worthwhile task.

HISTORY OF READERS' ADVISORY SERVICE

Historically, librarians have, of course, always had a relationship with reading. We've assumed that reading, in and of itself, is a good thing (Leigh, p. 12). We've participated in literacy projects, and we've encouraged reading—especially for children. We obviously have a history of buying materials for our customers to read. But our public service training—with the possible exception of youth services librarians—has for years emphasized reference service and technology at the expense of other services. We learned how to discern through the reference interview what the patron was really looking for, and we learned what sources could help us find the answers to their questions. But we really didn't pay much attention to reading for pleasure except in an informal way.

Early librarians saw readers' advisory service as an adjunct to, or part of, the adult education movement. In 1922, the Cleveland Public Library and Detroit Public Library each established a readers' advisory department, and five other urban public libraries followed suit, with Chicago, Cincinnati, Indianapolis, Milwaukee, and Portland establishing readers' advisors in the first wave. By 1935, 44 libraries offered the service in the United States (Saricks, p. 5). These early services consisted of a one-on-one interview session between a librarian (by appointment) and a patron, and they resulted in a written reading plan for each patron (Saricks, p. 5).

This kind of service was expensive, and the departments began phasing out during the Great Depression and merging into general reference departments. Librarians adhered to the "missionary spirit" and believed that their role was to educate readers. But several early librarians conducted sociological reading studies of their patrons. Examples of these studies include the following:

1929—*The Reading Interests and Habits of Adults* by William S. Gray and Ruth Monroe

1931—*What People Want to Read About* by Douglas Waples and Ralph Winfred Tyler

1932—*Fiction and the Reading Public* by Q. D. Leavis

1938—*The Geography of Reading* by Louis Round Wilson

1940—*What Reading Does to People* by Douglas Waples, Bernard Berelson, and Franklyn R. Bradshaw

After the 1940s, many librarians on the front lines attempted to help readers connect with books, but hardly any wrote about the subject. And with all the attention first on reference work, then on "closing the card catalog," automating the functions of the library, getting onto the "information superhighway," and struggling to keep up with the technology produced by amazon.com and Google, it's no wonder authors in the library field in the 1960s through the 1990s didn't write that much about readers' advisory service.

READERS' ADVISORY SERVICE TODAY

Today, libraries have moved past the Fiction Problem and no longer debate the necessity of including fiction in their collections, but the biases of the past (nonfiction is more useful than fiction), the widespread, ingrained feelings of guilt about reading for pleasure from early life messages (get your nose out of that book), and the lack of training in readers' advisory service (most library schools don't teach the subject—now or in the past) have made the timid request for help from a puzzled reader one of the most feared questions that many reference librarians ever face.

I once surveyed the public service staff of a library I was managing, in order to find out their most dreaded reference questions, thinking I would design a training program based upon their answers. Help them with their worst fears first—that was my motto—and then move on down the list from there. Imagine my surprise when "Can you help me find a good book to read?" was in the list of the top three most feared questions.

I wondered how this could be, when it seemed like such a natural question for patrons to ask in a library full of books. I had started my career in the fiction department of a library, and having had no formal training on the subject in library school, I learned how to suggest books from my mentors. This was my absolute favorite question. I had trouble understanding how it couldn't be just as much fun for someone else. But when I stepped back and looked at the careers of myself and others, it was easy to spot the reasons for this fear.

The people working at the public service desk were a mix of talented and smart professional librarians and people with bachelor's degrees. When someone was hired to work in reference, the manager of the department, a professional with a master's degree, took care of their training. But none of the managers I spoke to had ever had a course in readers' advisory service while they were in library school, so naturally their training programs did not include it. Most library schools still don't teach this skill. In fact, the trend for offering readers' advisory courses may be downward (Orr).

If a skill isn't learned in school, then most likely it is obtained through in-service training, workshops, or continuing education classes. At the time that I did this survey of my staff in the early 1990s, almost no one was teaching workshops in the area of readers' advisory service. I remember how excited my staff members were when a local consortium brought Joyce Saricks to do a workshop on the subject, and how much better prepared they felt when she finished her training. Even though there are many more practitioners teaching workshops now, I believe that most librarians still have not had sufficient training in this area.

An article in *Library Journal* a few years ago published the results of a "secret shopper" survey of library service, in which library school students posed as readers and asked staff of various libraries for help in finding a good book to read. Their study reinforces the assertion that this is one of the most feared questions, as librarians said things like "I hate this question" or "You know this is the query the reference desk dreads" (May, pp. 40–43). The study showed that fewer than half of the librarians consulted any professional tools and most simply recommended books they themselves had enjoyed. Only one librarian used standard readers' advisory interview questions, and overall, most librarians seemed very uncomfortable trying to answer this kind of question.

While many people assume that readers' advisors are born and not made, and that suggesting books to readers is a knack that some people just naturally have, readers' advisory techniques can absolutely be taught. There is hope.

WHAT IS A READERS' ADVISORY SERVICE AND WHAT DOES A READERS' ADVISOR DO?

Joyce Saricks says that readers' advisory service is "a patron-centered library service for adult fiction readers." In her words, the readers' advisor provides the "vital link between the library's fiction material and readers" (Saricks, p. 1).

S. R. Ranganathan, in his classic book of 1931, *The Five Laws of Library Science,* outlined his ideal of library service. Most library school students have been exposed to Ranganathan's laws:

- Books are for use.

- Every reader, his book.

in Personality 40: 694–712. www.yorku.ca/mar/Mar%20et%20al%202006_bookworms%20versus%20nerds.pdf

May, Anne K., Elizabeth Olesh, Anne Weinlich Miltenberg, and Catherine Patricia Lackne. 2000. "A Look at Reader's Advisory Services." *Library Journal* 125, no. 15 (September 15): 40–43.

OCLC. 2010. "How Libraries Stack Up: 2010." www.oclc.org/reports/pdfs/214109usf_how_libraries_stack_up.pdf

Orr, Cynthia. 2009. "Dynamics of Reader's Advisory Education: How Far Can We Go?" *Readers' Advisor News.* www.readersadvisoronline.com/ranews/sep2009/orr.html

Ranganathan, S. R. 1931. *The Five Laws of Library Science.* Madras, India: Madras Library Association.

Ross, Catherine Sheldrick, Lynne McKechnie, and Paulette M. Rothbauer. 2006. *Reading Matters: What the Research Reveals about Reading, Libraries, and Community.* Westport, CT: Libraries Unlimited.

Saricks, Joyce. 2005. *Readers' Advisory Service in the Public Library.* Chicago: American Library Association.

Schank, Roger C. 1995. *Tell Me a Story: Narrative and Intelligence.* Chicago: Northwestern University Press.

Shera, Jesse H. 1949. *Foundations of the Public Library: The Origins of the Public Library Movement in New England 1629–1855.* Chicago: University of Chicago Press.

Singh, Sarina. 2003. *Lonely Planet India,* 10th ed. Oakland, CA: Lonely Planet.

Tolkien, J.R.R. 1966. *The Hobbit: Or There and Back Again.* New York: Houghton Mifflin.

Waples, Douglas, Bernard Berelson, and Franklyn R. Bradshaw. 1940. *What Reading Does to People: A Summary of Evidence on the Social Effects of Reading, and a Statement of Problems for Research.* Chicago: University of Chicago Press.

Waples, Douglas, and Ralph Winfred Tyler. 1931. *What People Want to Read About.* Chicago: University of Chicago Press.

Weinstein, Arnold L. 2004. *A Scream Goes Through the House: What Literature Teaches Us about Life.* New York: Random House.

Wiegand, Wayne A. 2000. "Librarians Ignore the Value of Stories." *Chronicle of Higher Education* 47, no. 9 (October 27): B20.

Wilson, Louis Round. 1938. *The Geography of Reading: A Study of the Distribution and Status of Libraries in the United States.* Chicago: American Library Association and University of Chicago Press.

Chapter 2

Understanding the Reader

Cynthia Orr

Librarians have always paid attention to books—reading reviews, making bibliographies, creating displays, leading book discussion groups, posting bestseller lists, and learning everything we can about the literature—but we don't have much of a history of paying attention to readers. Meanwhile, research in reading for pleasure has developed into a robust field without us. This may largely be due to the fact that early librarians, especially Melvil Dewey, approached libraries through Francis Bacon's lens of providing "useful knowledge." His Dewey Decimal System dealt only with organizing books of nonfiction (Wright, p. 136). Over the years, librarians have largely focused on this same area—information, if you will. Library science and information studies have almost totally ignored research about reading, so most of us don't know much about the field.

It's shocking to know that over the entire history of libraries, users have pressed for more fiction, and yet library school researchers have ignored reading for pleasure, instead focusing on reading as an arm of adult education. To make it worse, experts on reading from other fields have done their research while largely ignoring public libraries. Because of this, we're woefully ignorant about pleasure reading and its readers.

So let's try to catch up a bit. Experts generally look at reading in the following ways: through literacy studies, the social history of print, reader-response theory, ethnographies of reading, and cultural studies (Wiegand, "On the Social Nature of Reading," p. 6 and "Critiquing the LIS Curriculum," p. 188).

Literacy studies, of course, look at the process of learning to read—what works best, who is literate, how do you define literacy, how people actually learn to read. It's important for librarians to know the highlights of this research in order to understand their part in the literacy equation. For instance, research has shown that library storytimes have a minimal effect on children's preliteracy skills, but they have a major effect on the adults who are the most important in helping children develop these skills—the adult caregivers of those children. Keeping up with the most current research at the national Literacy Information and Communication System (lincs.ed.gov/facts/facts.html) and other agencies can be very helpful.

Reader-response theory studies reading from the point of view of the reader rather than focusing on the writer or the work itself. This approach recognizes the reader as an active agent in creating the meaning of a particular text. This is totally opposite to the approach of literary criticism, which assumes that there is a fixed meaning to a text and that the reader is irrelevant. William Blake said in his poem *The Everlasting Gospel*, "Both read the Bible day and night, but thou read'st black where I read white." This is reader-response theory in a nutshell. Another example of a work on reader-response theory is *5 Readers Reading* by Norman Holland, in which he compares the reactions of five different students to the same passages and finds very different experiences among them.

Ethnographies of reading look at reading through the lens of anthropology and try to make sense of a culture as a whole way of life. They survey the uses of literature within a group or community in a particular time and place. A good example is Janice Radway's now classic *Reading the Romance: Women, Patriarchy and Popular Literature*, a study of the role of romance reading in the lives of a small group of women in the 1970s. Radway found that word of mouth was the most important factor in choosing titles to read for the women in the group. They trusted a local bookstore owner's judgment because she had a vast knowledge of different novels, and they found that they usually agreed with her recommendations. Though the romance novels reinforced patriarchal gender roles, the women saw reading them as almost subversive—a "gift to themselves" when they were tired of nurturing their husbands and children with no one to nurture them. They freely agreed that they read the novels for escape.

Cultural studies of reading focus on the political nature of reading and how it relates to social class, gender, sexuality, ethnicity, nationality, or ideology. One example of this approach is *Novels, Readers, and Reviewers: Responses to Fiction in Antebellum America* by Nina Baym, who studied all reviews of novels that appeared in American journals between 1840 and 1860. She discovered a large difference between novels and reviews written by or about women and those written by or about men. Further, she found that the reviewers defined the success of these early novels by their popularity with readers, noting that "the explanation for the success of the novel lies in the inherent power of the form to generate reader excitement" (Baym, p. 43).

Contrast that with critics of today, who belittle the "good read" as something beneath notice. For today's critics, good novels must be "serious." The success of novels in the 19th century was never based on deep interpretation of the text. And since most readers of the time were interested in story, the critics judged the works based upon the cohesion of the plot. Again, contrast that with today's "serious" novels that are rarely judged on plot. We have a lot to learn from cultural studies.

Social history is a branch of history that focuses on the reactions and experience of ordinary people and their methods of coping with life. The social history of reading covers such things as the invention of the codex, the transition from scribes to a print culture, and the rise of silent reading. Alberto Manguel's *A History of Reading* covers many of the highlights, and those wishing to dig deeper could also see *A History of Reading in the West* by Guglielmo Cavallo, Roger Chartier, and Lydia G. Cochrane.

Manguel covers such interesting topics as censorship, the preferred surroundings for readers, and the surprise that St. Augustine expressed when he saw that St. Ambrose read silently, unlike the other monks who mumbled aloud to themselves as they read. Learning about the social history of reading is an enjoyable project that can only help us to a deeper understanding of the field in which we work.

It's easy to see that the river of reading studies is wide and deep. We owe it to ourselves and our readers to learn more about it—even if library schools don't teach the subject.

READING AS A SOCIAL ACTIVITY

We tend to think of reading as an individual and isolating experience. After all, a reader sits staring at the page, oblivious to what goes on around him. At first glance, reading seems like something that is experienced by one person alone; and though one can say that it involves an interaction between the reader and the author, reading is even more social than that. The proliferation of book groups, author readings, social networks built around reading, and just discussing a new book with friends, shows that humans experience reading as a social activity as well as a solitary one.

What are the implications of this for librarians? One obvious conclusion is that reading the same book is a different experience for every reader. And the proliferation of online venues for discussing books just makes this even more evident than in the past. For example, within a very short time after the publication of the novel *Freedom* by Jonathan Franzen, a furious discussion ensued online and was evident in Amazon reviews, as readers talked about whether the novel was a great work or a self-indulgent, though well-written, cop-out. Library websites and catalogs are a natural place to conduct these discussions, and enabling patron comments in catalogs may help this to happen in the future.

Another factor is the power of word-of-mouth recommendations. Of course, recommendations can be via e-mail or social network as well, but readers do trust their circle of acquaintances to suggest titles. By talking to readers and suggesting titles, you, as their local librarian, can easily become one of those trusted sources just as Radway's bookseller was trusted by the women in the romance reading group. Many librarians tell stories of patrons who find that they often like the same titles as the librarian, and when this happens, they eagerly ask her what she's read and enjoyed recently.

People read for many different reasons, from pure escape to learning new things. Keep that in mind when making suggestions to readers. Novels were not always judged by how erudite they were, and just because some authors and scholars belittle genre works does not mean that they are correct.

The social history of reading takes us from the scroll to the codex to the Gutenberg press to e-books. But through that history, people coped and continued to read. It's the content that matters, not the container. And over that history, people's reading techniques evolved as well. Early readers read aloud. Silent reading later became the norm. Later came the audiobook. We're entering a new period where it is possible to read an electronic book with other earlier readers' comments attached. Who knows where reading will go in the future?

All of these issues point to the importance of building a relationship with readers. You can accomplish this in many different ways, such as discussing books with patrons on the floor of the library, conducting book discussion groups, making recommended book lists and displays, and answering readers' advisory needs through a Facebook page or an online form. These are all ways to build relationships, and that communication with readers is crucial for librarians.

Communicating with readers is easy in many ways, because readers like to talk about books, but you need to be aware of some common pitfalls as well. Since many readers have heard negative messages about reading their whole lives (reading is not cool, romances are trash, you're a nerd, why don't you do something useful), many have an underlying feeling of guilt about reading too much or reading what they enjoy rather than something educational. All this in spite of the fact that research shows that readers are more active in their communities than nonreaders are (National Endowment for the Arts, p. 5). But because of these negative messages, guilty feelings, and because reading for pleasure is not valued in society, many readers will not ask for help in finding a good book. If they do ask for help, they will often preface their question with disclaimers, such as "I know you're busy, but . . ." or "I hate to bother you, but. . . ." Knowing this is the case, make it a habit to wander the fiction stacks and offer to help browsers.

Research by Catherine Sheldrick Ross shows that mood is very important to a reader looking for a good book. Sometimes things are calm in our lives, and sometimes we go through stressful times. Ross found that the higher the stress level, the more likely the reader will want a "safe read" — a book they know they will like, or even an old favorite they've read before. When life is calm, readers are much more likely to experiment with something outside their comfort zone. This mood issue has nothing to do with the education level or sophistication of the reader. Ross found that the reader in her study who self-identified with reading "trash" had a PhD in literature.

So the same readers may read very different books according to their mood and at different stages of their lives. Even if this were not true, be careful not to pigeonhole readers or make assumptions about what they might enjoy reading. Just because a reader looks young does not mean that she belongs in the YA section. I remember a story that I was told in the early 1970s when I began my library career. In this particular public library, like many others, I suspect, decades earlier, the library kept what were considered racier books behind the checkout desk. Who used those books? According to the old timers who remembered those days, it was little old ladies. Be careful not to stereotype readers.

Studying Readers

Not enough studies have been published about pleasure readers, but we do have some research to draw from. In Milwaukee in 1927, a study of 1,207 adults and young adults who asked for help from the readers' advisor found that their self-described reasons for recreational reading included satisfaction of curiosity, relaxation, culture, emotional satisfaction and stimulation, vicarious experience, vivid description, background or atmosphere, to idle away time, or from a sense of duty (Gray and Munroe, p. 268).

In the early 2000s, Ross interviewed avid readers about their reading habits. These were not the 55 percent of people who said they had read a book in the past 6 months, or even the 10 percent of those who read a book a week. She interviewed people who said they could not imagine their lives without books and reading, those who had a book on their nightstand, and one in their car, and one in the living room, and one in their handbag. She operated on the premise that asking really avid readers about their reading history, and how they chose books to read, would lead to some insights that might be of use to librarians serving readers who were not so successful.

Ross found that many avid readers were read to as children, had books in their home when they were growing up, received books as gifts (often from a beloved relative), or went to the library as a child (Ross, p. 5). Many times they learned to read early, and she found that successful readers learned to read without being formally taught, much as a baby learns to talk. Many of them read series books as children, which is ironic, since librarians a generation ago traditionally frowned upon them. In their experience, series books helped them to "get into the book" more easily and not give up too soon. They often read dozens, sometimes hundreds of series books, reread them, shared them with friends, and traded them like baseball cards as a social activity. They liked that a heroine or hero was often successful without adult help. They felt that reading about these powerful children helped them to learn the ability to overcome real-life obstacles.

Series books helped them learn how a story works, such as who is the protagonist, what are clues, who are the bad guys, and so on. Sometimes they were given series books by adults, but sometimes they were discouraged from reading them, which only made them more attractive. They "moved up" to different series—first the Bobbsey Twins, for example, and then Nancy Drew as they got older.

Most readers pointed to successful reading experiences in their past: they were read to and decided books were fun, and then they learned to read themselves and decided books were still fun. They eventually learned what kind of reading they liked and disliked, and became even more successful at choosing good books to read.

So, how do these expert readers choose? First, they look at the author. If they have enjoyed other books by a writer, they read the rest of that author's work. Second, if they can't choose by author, they try genre. If they've liked mysteries in the past, they try other mysteries. Third, they use word of mouth—recommendations by people they trust. Fourth, they use lists. They check for award winners, read the Sunday book pages, and watch for other lists as they go about their lives. They also seek out and talk to other trusted readers, attend fan conventions, browse from displays, look in the "just returned" section at the library, read reviews and discussions in the media, and look for books that were made into recent movies. They always have their "antennae out," and if they hear of a likely book, they write down the title so they can look for it later.

When asked about libraries, they pointed out that they can take a greater risk in the library, choosing a book they're not sure they'll like, because it is free. When they buy a book, they are more careful to purchase titles they are more certain to enjoy. All these techniques helped them to learn their own preferences, and they explained that sometimes they were in different moods and read different things.

Avid readers often choose books by browsing in bookstores or libraries. How do they browse? They read the cues on the book itself. They may recognize the name of the author or the publisher's line. They pick up cues from the jacket, including the cover design, the blurb on the back, the jacket copy, and information about the author. They are attracted to catchy titles and cover art. If the book is a prize winner, that's a plus. And if these jacket cues are interesting to them, they often dip into the book itself and read a few paragraphs or pages to see if they might like the book.

Elements of the books that they say they consider when browsing for a good read are the genre for fiction, subject for nonfiction, or the treatment of the book—whether it is popular or literary, for instance. They consider elements of the characters in the book—their gender, whether they are sympathetic or not, their strength, or whether they are likeable. The setting may also be important. This includes the real-world geographic setting of the book and whether that is interesting or off-putting, and the kind of world depicted—a treatment of the upper classes, such as the world portrayed in F. Scott Fitzgerald's *The Great Gatsby*, or a novel set in the terrible poverty of Bombay, like *The Space Between Us* by Thrity Umrigar. Or, it could be an entirely created world, such as the one depicted by George R. R. Martin in his Song of Ice and Fire series, or that of *The Left Hand of Darkness* by Ursula K. Le Guin, set on a planet where, at various times in their lives, the adults can be either female or male, and have no control over the process.

The ending of a book is important to many people. Is it all tied up neatly, or does it have an open ending where the reader is not sure what happened? Does it have a happy ending? Readers of romance can be comfortable knowing that romances always have a happy ending, though it may not be the one that is expected. Is it a tear jerker with a sad ending? Is the ending predictable, or unexpected? One patron I know looks for books with several main characters whose lives intertwine. Her favorite ending is an epilogue that discusses what has happened to the characters in their lives after the novel ends.

Physical size may also be extremely important. We've all had the last minute request for a skinny book, from a panicked student, but some people prefer a nice, long, heavy book that they can settle into and live in for a good while.

These avid readers also stressed the importance of mood in making a reading choice. When things were going fine in their personal lives, they might feel more adventuresome in their reading choices. When their lives were stressful, they often gravitated to "comfort reads," or even to rereading old favorites. Stress in life means they want to read a book that they know they will enjoy. Interestingly, they said that mood is more important when choosing fiction than it is with nonfiction.

Other elements that are often important to readers depending upon their mood include factors such as whether a book is easy or challenging, upbeat or depressing, reassuring or stimulating, or "safe" as compared to risky. Another question is whether they want to read a book that challenges their beliefs or confirms the beliefs they already hold.

So how exactly do avid readers choose when they are browsing? They use the cues we have discussed to sort the books into a yes pile and a no pile, and then choose from that small range of "yes books."

Narrowing the range of choices is an important tactic that has implications for librarians. And this technique confirms what we learn from the book *The Art of Choosing* by Sheena Iyengar and the seminal 1956 article "The Magical Number Seven, Plus or Minus Two: Some Limits on Our Capacity for Processing Information" by George Miller. The research has shown that too much choice is overwhelming for humans. In one study, a display of a wide variety of flavors of various jams and jellies in a grocery store actually led to fewer purchases than a display of the same jams and jellies with fewer choices. Sharon Baker believes that many library browsers are frustrated due to information overload (Baker and Wallace, p. 277).

IMPLICATIONS FOR LIBRARIANS

All of this research is invaluable in providing some insight and implications for librarians who wish to encourage reading for pleasure. Since readers "give themselves lessons," as Ross puts it, we should trust their choices. We should be very careful not to belittle series books. Series books are actually allies in the development of confident readers, and children's librarians, especially, should reconsider the definition of a "good book" and broaden it. Since many readers are less practiced at choosing than avid readers, we should help make it easier for them to choose a good book. One way we can do this is by leaving the packaging on the book so that the cues can be read. If a book needs to be mended or bound, the jacket should be preserved and put back on.

Since many readers do not know how to choose a good book, it is part of the librarian's job to learn about books, authors, publishers, genres, jacket cues, and other knowledge about books and reading that they can pass on to readers as they suggest titles. One of the most important things you can do is to narrow readers' choices so that they are not overwhelmed by shelf after shelf of books. You can do that by creating displays on different themes and genres and changing them often.

Trying to change a reader's book preferences or "elevate their tastes," as librarians in the late 19th and early 20th centuries used to say, does not work. Instead, modern libraries should acquire a great variety of books that can fit every taste and mood, make these choices accessible, and let readers choose what appeals to them.

Helping readers find a good book to read—especially young readers who have not had time to develop good techniques for choosing titles they will enjoy—is essential work for librarians. And it is worth noting that one of the most important things teachers can do to encourage literacy is to provide time for free voluntary reading in the classroom. The main point to keep in mind is that a reluctant reader is one who has yet to find that book that is perfect for him—easy to read and a perfect match for his tastes. Until he reads his first enjoyable book, he will not consider reading to be pleasurable. And if a reader has not yet found that first enjoyable work, we can't expect her to know how to find it. The readers' advisor can absolutely change lives by matching a potential reader with a book that will make her a reader for life. What a privilege, but what a challenge.

NOTES

Baker, Sharon L., and Karen L. Wallace. 2002. *The Responsive Public Library: How to Develop and Market a Winning Collection*. Englewood, CO: Libraries Unlimited.

Baym, Nina. 1984. *Novels, Readers, and Reviewers: Responses to Fiction in Antebellum America*. Ithaca, NY: Cornell University Press.

Blake, William. *The Everlasting Gospel*. bartleby.com/236/58.html

Cavallo, Guglielmo, Roger Chartier, and Lydia G. Cochrane. 1999. *A History of Reading in the West*. Amherst: University of Massachusetts Press.

Coles, Robert. 1989. *The Call of Stories: Teaching and the Moral Imagination*. Boston: Houghton Mifflin.

Gray, William S. and Ruth Learned Munroe. 1929. *Reading Interests and Habits of Adults*. New York: Macmillan.

Holland, Norman Norwood. 1975. *5 Readers Reading*. New Haven, CT: Yale University Press.

Iyengar, Sheena. 2010. *The Art of Choosing: The Decisions We Make Every Day: What They Say about Us and How We Can Improve Them*. New York: Twelve.

Kimball, Melanie A. 2006. "A Brief History of Readers' Advisory." In *Genreflecting: A Guide to Popular Reading Interests*, 6th ed., edited by Diana Tixier Herald and Wayne A. Wiegand, 15–23. Westport, CT: Libraries Unlimited.

Manguel, Alberto. 2008. *A History of Reading*. New York: Penguin Books.

Miller, George. 1956. "The Magical Number Seven, Plus or Minus Two: Some Limits on Our Capacity for Processing Information." *Psychological Review* 63, no. 2 (March): 81–97.

National Endowment for the Arts. June 2004. "Reading at Risk: A Survey of Literary Reading in America." Research Division Report No. 46. nea.gov/pub/readingatrisk.pdf

Radway, Janice. 1984. *Reading the Romance: Women, Patriarchy and Popular Literature*. Chapel Hill: University of North Carolina Press.

Ross, Catherine Sheldrick, Lynne McKechnie, and Paulette M. Rothbauer. 2006. *Reading Matters: What the Research Reveals about Reading, Libraries, and Community*. Westport, CT: Libraries Unlimited.

Schank, Roger C. 1995. *Tell Me a Story: Narrative and Intelligence*. Evanston, IL: Northwestern University Press.

Weinstein, Arnold L. 2003. *A Scream Goes through the House: What Literature Teaches Us about Life*. New York: Random House.

Wiegand, Wayne A. 2006. "Critiquing the LIS Curriculum." In *The Whole Library Handbook, 4: Current Data, Professional Advice, and Curiosa about Libraries and Library Service*, edited by George M. Eberhart, 188–91. Chicago: American Library Association.

Wiegand, Wayne A. 2006. "On the Social Nature of Reading." In *Genreflecting: A Guide to Popular Reading Interests*, 6th ed., edited by Diana Tixier Herald and Wayne A. Wiegand. Westport, CT: Libraries Unlimited.

Wright, Alex. 2007. *Glut: Mastering Information through the Ages*. Washington, D.C.: Joseph Henry Press.

Chapter 3

Understanding the Literature

Cynthia Orr

CLASSIFYING PLEASURE READING

It is natural for human beings to classify things. Placing items in categories helps us to grasp the whole of what we are trying to understand. Pleasure readers tend to begin classifying by author. If I liked one book by this author, I will probably like another book by this author. While choosing works by author is often successful in fiction, it's more difficult with nonfiction. Some authors like James Herriot write similar nonfiction books, but others like Truman Capote do not. And looking on the library shelf by classification number can be problematic, because the nonfiction for pleasure readers is mixed in with encyclopedias, textbooks, and tutorials on the same subject. And in either case, when the reader is finished with an author or a subject, where can he go next for something similar?

Most readers' advisors talk about appeals (Saricks, p. 12) or doorways (Pearl)—the characteristics that readers enjoy, like setting, plot, characterization, and language. And sometimes we talk about the reading interests of the public we serve (Gray and Munroe, p. xx).

But even before we begin classifying title by title, how can we get an overview of the literature that exists for pleasure readers? Even if we narrow our subject to the novel, hundreds of thousands of novels have been written since the first one was published in England as a serial between 1740 and 1742.

How very minimal is the number of classics we study today compared to the number of books that have been published. As Franco Moretti puts it, "a canon of two hundred novels, for instance, sounds very large for 19th century Britain (and *is* much larger than the current one), but is still less than one per cent of the novels that were actually published." No one even knows exactly how many novels were published in the 19th century, but it is at least 20,000 or 30,000, and maybe more. Even if you could read a book a day forever, it would tales, Newgate novel, conversion novel, industrial novel, sporting novel, Chartist novel, mysteries, multiplot novel, Bildungsroman, religious novel, domestic novel, provincial novel, sensational novel, fantasy, children's adventures, school stories, imperial romances, invasion literature, utopia, Cockney school, regional novel, nursery stories, decadent novel, naturalist novel, imperial gothic, new woman novel, and Kailyard school.

It's fascinating that Moretti finds that gender issues relate to the ebb and flow of genres as well. Between 1750 and 1780, men published twice as many novels as women in Britain. But in the 1780s, the ratio reversed, with women novelists publishing more than men. A third shift occurred around 1820 toward male writers, and then again switched back to favor women around 1850 with the rise of authors such as the Bronte sisters, Elizabeth Gaskell, George Eliot, and Mary Elizabeth Braddon. Then, in the 1870s, women were edged out by men again. Even more interesting is the fact that these numbers seem to bear out in other countries as well.

While researchers each think they are describing something unique, Moretti believes they are "all observing the same comet that keeps crossing and recrossing the sky: the same *literary cycle*, where gender and genre are probably in synchronicity with each other—a generation of military novels, nautical tales, and historical novels, *à la* Scott attracting male writers, one of domestic, provincial and sensational novels attracting women writers, and so on."

Moretti cycles back to the central issue of genre. While most literary historians treat genre and subgenre almost as accidents and come up with literary theories that ignore them and discuss one basic form, whether it is realism or metafiction, or whatever fits their theory, he believes that the 44 genres show that the novel did not develop as a single entity but instead is the system of its genres: "the whole diagram, not one privileged part of it." Great theories of the novel that reduce it to one form leave out nine-tenths of the picture. Moretti's work is in progress. It will be exciting to watch it develop.

So what is happening now? What are the genre trends in the United States in 2012? Book industry statistics show the following dollar figures for sales in 2010:

Romance: $1.358 billion

Religion/inspirational: $759 million

Mystery: $682 million

Science fiction/fantasy: $559 million

Classic literary fiction: $455 million

(Romance Writers of America: Romance Literature Statistics)

It is difficult, if not impossible, to get detailed subgenre breakdowns of sales, so we are faced with trying to identify trends in publishing instead.

CURRENT TRENDS IN PUBLISHING

Genre blending is one of the largest current trends and makes organizing the titles in this volume impossible except as a very basic guideline. Michael Chabon in *Maps and Legends,* points to genre blending as a way to keep fiction new and fresh. By writing in the "borderlands" between genres, he believes writers are able to experiment with conventions and push genres forward.

A vice president for Barnes & Noble was quoted in the *New York Times* as saying that "sales of novels with vampires, shape shifters, werewolves and other paranormal creatures were 'exploding,' whether they were found in the romance, fantasy or young adult aisles." Graphic novels have increased in popularity, and young adult books are being read by more and more adults and are showing up on major bestseller lists.

Of course, one of the biggest trends in book publishing is the switch to digital publications. Circulation of downloadable e-books and audiobooks in libraries has more than doubled in early 2011; and that September, when OverDrive, the major vendor of downloadables for libraries, added Kindle compatibility, this number shot up incredibly higher. By the end of the year, the increase was 180 percent. In 2012, their network of 22,000 libraries around the world registered 70 million digital titles checked out.

More and more books will be published in digital form only. While this is a huge trend affecting libraries and bookstores, it is outside the scope of this book. Suffice it to say, though, that the main issues are availability (some Big Six publishers refuse to license their digital content to libraries, and others limit access to new titles or the number of checkouts allowed) and the affect on bricks and mortar stores and libraries. (Hundreds of independent bookstores have closed, and Borders went bankrupt in 2011.)

If this trend toward e-books continues, libraries will need to find ways to help readers browse digitally. Publishers themselves acknowledge that digital is the wave of the future. Libraries will need to figure out how to absorb this trend into the regular workflow of their selection, acquisitions, and cataloging departments.

Chapter 4

Working with the Literature

Cynthia Orr

PREPARING TO BE A STAR

Before we get into the nuts and bolts of readers' advisory (RA) skills, let's discuss a few things that can make a huge difference in your ability to improve yourself as a readers' advisor.

Of course, there are people who just appear to have the knack for recommending books to others. They seem to have read all the key books; they're comfortable chatting about them; and their minds work in such a way that they easily make connections between books. I won't try to convince you that there aren't people with a special talent for RA service, any more than I would assert that there aren't people with a special gift for music, or mathematics, or any other field. But, just as all of us can get better at music and math, we can improve our skills as readers' advisors. There are skills, and they can be learned.

Helping guide a reader to the next book is valuable work, and we're lucky to be doing that work. Faithful readers who come to the library regularly are the same people who make sure the library has the financial support it needs. We need to remember that we do important work and guard against any cynical judgment about either the work we're doing or the patrons and the books they read.

We need to be willing to read, so that we have a background upon which to base our work, and we need to be willing to work at improving our communication skills—both listening and speaking—in order to be better able to work with patrons.

We need to work at improving our understanding of readers and the reading experience, and we also need to work at improving our understanding of books and genres and their appeal factors, so that we can use this knowledge to make connections between books and readers. Of course, we'll need to familiarize ourselves with information sources available to readers' advisors, and when all is said and done, we can follow a simple routine in preparation for work each day.

To prepare, readers' advisors should keep up with currently popular authors and highlights of the best books of the past; we should understand genres and subgenres in order to have a concept of the lay of the land of literature; we should be trained in the art of the RA conversation; we should keep up with the current world of books; and we should read as professional readers' advisors, paying attention to the appeals of the books we are reading. Thus, good readers' advisors understand the landscape and appeal of literature, understand readers' tastes, stay up-to-date in the field, and use the RA conversation to match books with readers and readers with books.

We can't read everything, of course, or even all the popular things, but there are some other ways to learn more about books we haven't necessarily read. First of all, there are the reviews in the standard review journals that most libraries use, like *Library Journal*, *Booklist*, *Kirkus Reviews*, and *Publishers Weekly*, for example. When reading reviews, watch for words that will give clues to appeal factors. A term like "page turner," for instance, tells you about the pace of the book.

Another way to keep up is to leaf through new books as they arrive in your library. Cover art offers cues that indicate the contents, jacket copy is very helpful as well, and sampling a few paragraphs can reveal the author's style and pace. Even a quick glance at each book can help. For instance, lots of white space on the pages usually means a good amount of dialogue, which in turn can indicate a quick pace for the story.

Magazines for fans of reading can be quite useful for readers' advisors as well. A general magazine like *Bookmarks* gives an overview, but don't forget *Romantic Times*, *Locus*, *Mystery Scene*, and other specialized magazines for fans of various genres. Blogs can be helpful, and so can the book pages of major newspapers and magazines. Just like those avid readers, readers' advisors should have their antennae out at all times, scouting for book information and industry news.

An in-depth way of learning more about the literature is to do a genre study. The Adult Reading Round Table, a Chicago-area group of librarians interested in RA service, has been doing genre studies for years. They typically choose a genre and spend about a year studying its features, reading widely, and identifying key books. Their website, *ARRT Reads* (arrtreads.org/genre studies.html), features their past genre studies for all to use.

Another way to learn more about books is to write reviews of titles you have read, or at the very least, write annotations for the readers in your library. Posting lists of good books with good, short annotations is a great service to your patrons, and it will help you remember the books as well. Reading publishers' guidelines for writers can also be quite helpful. Harlequin, for example, has posted detailed descriptions of the requirements for each of their lines on their website *eHarlequin*.

But preparing to do RA service and keeping up with the literature are only a part of the process. We can't read everything, and just as we do with reference questions, we should cite our sources for RA questions as well. Many great print and online tools exist to help librarians do RA work, and a familiarity with these tools is especially important.

YOUR RA TOOLKIT

Generally speaking, the RA questions that come up in the course of regular work seem to fall into several categories. Here is an abbreviated list of some of the most useful RA tools arranged by the kinds of questions that occur most frequently and the types of questions you yourself may need to answer in order to perform well as a readers' advisor. We'll begin with tools you'll need in order to keep current with the RA field. (A much more complete list of regularly updated tools can be found at ww2. ikeepbookmarks.com/browse.asp?account=115961 or by searching *IKeep-Bookmarks.com* for Cindy Orr's RA Bookmarks.)

Tools for Keeping Up with the RA Field

Early Word (earlyword.com)

This blog by Nora Rawlinson, former editor of *Publishers Weekly* and *Library Journal*, is meant for public library collection development librarians. It tracks new popular books, lists movie tie-ins, reports on what's hot in various libraries across the country, and which titles seem to have been missed by librarians.

Fiction_L (webrary.org/rs/flmenu.html#subscribe)

This is a mail group for RA librarians, where 3,000 readers' advisors share tips, compile book lists, and answer tough questions for each other . . . in real time.

Library Journal (libraryjournal.com)

This well-known library magazine regularly publishes articles on RA service. Neal Wyatt's columns "Wyatt's World" and "The Reader's Shelf" are two examples. Library Journal often features editorials in support of RA service.

Publishers Lunch (http://lunch.publishers marketplace.com)

A publishing insider has all the latest book news, and he sends it out in a daily e-mail message.

PW Daily (publishersweekly.com/pw/email-subscriptions/index.html)

Subscribe to this daily e-mail update on publishing news from *Publishers Weekly*, the premier journal of the publishing world.

Readers Advisor Online Blog (readersadvisoronline.com/blog)

Every Monday morning, the RA Run Down section of this blog lists news of the week for RA librarians, and the New, Noteworthy, and No-Brainer entry features new titles that will be published in the upcoming week, plus a list of titles new to this week's bestseller lists. Consider it your one-stop Monday morning briefing. It is sponsored by Libraries Unlimited, the publisher of the *Genreflecting* series. (Full disclosure—Cindy Orr and Sarah Statz Cords are editors of this blog.)

RUSQ (rusq.org/category/issues)

Reference & User Services Quarterly is the journal of the Reference and User Services Association (RUSA), a division of the American Library Association (ALA). It often publishes full-length articles on RA service.

General Tools for Suggesting a Good Book to Read

Here are some of the best known and most useful general RA sites. These sites are more "full service" than the specialized niche sites listed further below in this chapter. Unfortunately, most of these general sites are not free, so you will be constrained by the subscriptions your library pays for.

Books and Authors (gale.cengage.com/pdf/facts/Books Authors.pdf)

This is a subscription, fee-based database from Gale and is the successor to their earlier *What Do I Read Next?* It includes over 100,000 fiction titles and more than 40,000 nonfiction titles, with information on genres and subgenres, and the ability to create unique landing pages for book groups. Not every title has read-alikes, but when they are there, they are very good.

Fiction Connection/Nonfiction Connection (fictionconnection.com)

Provided by *Books in Print*, these two RA tools—available by subscription only—use a visual interface to display read-alikes for known titles.

NoveList (ebscohost.com/uploads/novelist/pdf/ NovComplete_March2011.pdf)

Provided by Ebsco, *NoveList* is a subscription database begun in the early 1990s. It has continued to grow and enhance its services, and now includes over 180,000 fiction titles and more than 80,000 nonfiction titles with information on each title including reading level, searchable subject headings, read-alikes, and much more.

Overbooked (overbooked.org)

This site was created and is maintained by librarian Ann Theis. It has lots of great features, but one of the most useful is *Overbooked* Stars—a listing of books in various genres that have received starred reviews from standard library book review journals. Want to know the best books of the year in a particular genre? This free site will allow you to quickly scan the list of titles and spot which ones have the most stars.

Reader's Advice (readersadvice.com)

This free site is maintained by a retired librarian. It provides read-alikes and lists of authors and titles by genre and subgenre.

Reader's Advisor Online (readersadvisoronline.com/ lu/RAlogin)

Originally launched as a subscription database by Libraries Unlimited, the publisher of the *Genreflecting* series of reference books for readers' advisors, this site is now free. It covers fiction as well as nonfiction, and allows for multiple points of access and for narrowing searches and exploring connections. It contains hundreds of quick lists that contain read-alikes for specific authors and titles. Its strength is its flexibility and arrangement by genre, subgenre, and theme.

Which Book? (whichbook.net)

A refreshingly different experiment on how to choose a book, this British site allows you to pull sliders in a range between 12 choices such happy or sad, funny or serious, or larger than life or down to earth, and see what books turn up. Sliders exist for plot, setting, or character too.

Tools for Identifying Award Winners

Winning an award doesn't necessarily mean that a book is a great read . . . but it's a good indication. These sites will help you find the award winners easily.

Barnes & Noble Awards Page (barnesandnoble.com/awards/awards list.asp)

Bookseller Barnes & Noble lists links to most of the major awards.

Notable Books (ala.org/rusa/awards/notablebooks)

Since 1944, the RUSA division of ALA Notable Books Council members choose 25 notable books to honor each year.

The Reading List (ala.org/rusa/awards/readinglist)

In 2007, the RUSA division of ALA added the Reading List awards as a supplement to the Notable Books awards. The Reading List honors one book in each of eight genres of fiction each year. The eight genres currently included in the council's considerations are Adrenaline titles (Suspense, Thrillers, and Action Adventure), Fantasy, Historical Fiction, Horror, Mystery, Romance, Science Fiction, and Women's Fiction. These genres, however, may be adjusted in the future if contemporary reading tastes change.

Tools for Finding the Best-Loved Books

If there is one thing you can do to increase the odds of success in suggesting books, it is to know the best-loved books—the books that many people have read and loved. As the years go on, you'll hear about these books yourself from readers. When several people independently tell you how much they liked a particular title, you know you have a winner. Here are some sites that can help you identify best bets that others have identified.

BBC Big Read Top 100 (bbc.co.uk/arts/bigread/top100.shtml)

The BBC conducted a survey, and this list of 100 novels consists of the top vote-getters in Britain.

Modern Library 100 Best Novels—the Reader's List (modern library.com/top-100/100-best-novels)

The Board of the Modern Library chose the 100 best novels, and many readers disagreed, so they've also published the top readers' choices.

Nancy Pearl's Picks (nancypearl.com)

The most famous librarian in the world lists her favorite reads on her website. She also has published several books in her Book Lust series for adult reading and her Book Crush series for young adults.

Oprah's Book Club (oprah.com/book_club.html)

Yes, Oprah is still suggesting books—just not quite as often.

Readers' Advisory Guide to Genre Fiction by Joyce Saricks

In this book, Joyce Saricks lists sure bets in various genres. This is an excellent source.

Fiction Catalog

By definition, this book lists favorites. While it was probably the first RA tool ever, it's still going strong today. Each annual supplement lists about 2,000 titles, though, so it's not as selective as other tools.

Tools for Finding Read-Alikes

While some expert readers' advisors warn against simply using read-alike lists, they are, if done well, extremely helpful. The objection is that no book is an exact read-alike for another. Instead, the readers' advisor should find out what the reader liked about a particular favorite and match that information with other books. Still, read-alike lists can help narrow the choices.

Fiction_L Books by, or Similar to, a Particular Author (webrary.org/rs/flbklistauthor.html)

Here's an extensive list of read-alikes by author based on contributions by Fiction_L members.

Library Booklists Read-Alike Fiction (librarybooklists.org/fiction/adult/ ifyoulike.htm)

Library Booklists gathers read-alike lists from many libraries and organizes them by genre and by specific author. Very handy.

Read-Alikes at BookBrowse (bookbrowse.com/ read-alikes)

BookBrowse is a handy site that libraries can subscribe to for a very small fee. Even its free section contains read-alikes, though.

Tools for Finding Series Listed in Order

While it's not always necessary to read series books in order, many readers prefer to do so. And often it *is* important to read the books in order—especially in recent years. It doesn't matter in what order you read Agatha Christie's Miss Marple books, for instance. Things don't change much in St. Mary Mead, and while a few characters appear in more than one book, and even age over the years, reading the books in order is not crucial. But in many modern series—especially Mysteries—the characters develop and change, and later books contain spoilers for earlier books, so reading in order is more important. An example of this is Patricia Cornwell's Kay Scarpetta series where in the first nine books of the series, the main character has an ongoing love interest. In book 10, everything changes. I won't spoil things here by saying what happens, but if someone read one of the later 10 books before the earlier 9, their enjoyment of the series would be affected.

Another issue related to series books is whether to read them in the order in which they were published or in chronological order based on the plots of the stories. Most people would prefer to read Bernard Cornwell's Sharpe military series based on the dates of the battles that Sharpe participates in, rather than the dates of the publications of the novels, which is considerably different. This is one of the issues that makes it difficult for readers to figure out the order of the series books. Their first approach is usually to look in the front of a book by the author, but, surprisingly, publishers do not often worry about listing the books in order. Often there will be a list of titles previously published by the author, but if some of the author's books were issued by a different publisher, they are sometimes omitted. And, even if all the books are listed, it is difficult to tell from a list with no numbers attached, whether the book at the top of the list is the oldest or the newest.

Also surprisingly, this is difficult information to find in library catalogs, so it's necessary to have tools that list series and sequels in order.

What's Next (ww2.kdl.org/libcat/WhatsNextNEW.asp)

Kent District Library in Michigan has been adding to their *What's Next* database for several years. Search for a series and get a list of the titles in order.

Sequels: An Annotated Guide to Novels in Series by *Janet and Jonathan F. Husband*

This is a reference book–listing sequels, and while it is useful, it has the same problem as many print resources—it quickly goes out of date.

Wikipedia (wikipedia.org)

Believe it or not, Wikipedia is often a great source for sequels in order, as are authors' personal websites.

Tools for Finding a Forgotten Title Based on a Few Remembered Details

Maybe this is more like a reference question than an RA question, but it comes up quite often. A reader remembers reading a book but can't remember the author or title. How do you help her find the book? The first step, of course, is to ask her to tell you everything she can remember about the book. Here are some tools to help identify the title.

Fiction_L Query (Fiction_L@maillist.webrary.org)

One simple approach is to post the question on the Fiction_L mailing list. You must be a member to post to the list. Be sure when you sign up to choose individual messages rather than digest. Otherwise, you'll have to wait until the end of the day to get your answers. Quite often one of the other members will recognize the book you're looking for, and you often get an answer within minutes.

Google Search (google.com)

It's quite possible that you can find the title through a simple Google search. Be sure to include the word "novel" or "book" along with appropriate key words based on what the reader tells you. Then simply scroll down and look for hints in the results. It will usually take several pages before you find it.

WorldCat (worldcat.org)

The powerful searches allowed in WorldCat, the huge database that includes titles owned by thousands of libraries, makes this a quite useful search tool. Limit searches by format, year or range of years, subjects, and more.

Tools for Finding the Correct Pronunciation of an Author's Name

The question of how to pronounce an author's name actually comes up more often than you would think. Here are some tools that help answer that question.

Pronouncing Dictionary of Authors' Names (https://sites.google.com/a/soledadapps.org/susd-libraries/for-the-love-of-reading/pronouncing-dictionary-of-author-s-names-1)

This website is a collaborative effort from library listserv members of Soledad Unified School District.

Voice of America Pronunciation Guide (names.voa.gov)

This site provides sound files and pronunciation guides for more than 2,200 names of people, groups, places, and things in the news around the world.

Buzz Feed's How to Correctly Pronounce Authors' Names (buzzfeed.com/scott/how-to-correctly-pronounce-authors-names)

While this article doesn't list too many names, it is a guide to the pronunciation of some of the most difficult, and most often mispronounced, authors' names.

Tools for Finding Author Pseudonyms

A.K.A. (trussel.com/books/pseudo.htm)

While this site was created and is maintained by one person, it includes over 15,000 entries of author pseudonyms, aliases, nicknames, working names, legalized names, pen names, noms de plume, maiden names, etc. Steve Trussel, the owner, also has a handy database of Historical Fiction set in prehistoric times at this site (trussel.com/f_prehis.htm).

FictionDB's Pseudonym Search (fictiondb.com/author/pseudonym-lists.htm)

FictionDB's Pseudonym Search has thousands of entries arranged alphabetically by author and pseudonym. The click through entries also lists all of the author's pseudonyms on one page, which is very convenient.

Tools for Finding Books with No Sex, No Violence, or No Bad Language

One of the most difficult RA dilemmas is when a reader tells you what they *don't* want in their books. I once had a regular library patron who didn't want to read any books that referred in any way to World War II. Some people say they don't want any books where animals are killed. But by far the most common request is to exclude sex, violence, or bad language, and this can be tough to know.

No Sex, No Violence (commonsensemedia.org/book-reviews)

Common Sense Media, a not-for-profit corporation, says it doesn't believe in censorship, but rather is focused on age-appropriate media. They're all about filtering what people read—especially kids. But their reviews may help you find what your patron wants.

That All May Read (loc.gov/nls)

The catalog for the National Library Service for the Blind and Physically Handicapped includes the following notations if appropriate: contains explicit descriptions of sex, contains strong language, or contains violence. The site is useful for helping patrons who want to exclude certain kinds of works from their lists.

Tools for Making a Book Display or Book List

Something that comes up, if not every day, probably every week or month, is the need to produce book displays or book lists. Browsers in your library appreciate book displays that narrow their choices to a manageable amount. Here are some good tools for displays and book lists.

Fiction_L Book Lists (webrary.org/rs/FLbklistmenu.html)

This site has hundreds of book lists compiled from suggestions of about 3,000 RA librarians who belong to the Fiction_L mailing list. These lists are great for display ideas as well.

Library Booklists (librarybooklists.org)

This site, formerly published on a public library site, is now maintained by its originator, who arranges book lists posted by libraries into the categories of adult fiction, children's fiction, young adult fiction, and nonfiction. She also has several original lists and a calendar of author birthdays. You know these lists are good because they were done by libraries.

Flickr Book Displays in Libraries or Anywhere (flickr.com/groups/bookdisplays)

If you're a visual learner, take a look at these photos of book displays for some great ideas.

Tools to Help with Book Discussion Groups

Another common challenge for readers' advisors is leading library book discussion groups. While this may be daunting—especially if you've never belonged to a reading group yourself, below you'll find some handy tools to help get you through this.

Book Group Buzz (bookgroupbuzz.booklistonline.com)

This blog by ALA's *Booklist* covers anything of interest to book groups: best books for discussion, reviews of specific titles well suited to discussion, tips for groups, and more.

Reading Group Guides (readinggroupguides.com)

This is an essential site for book club leaders. It includes articles on how to start and run a reading group, plus much more. Perhaps the most valuable section is the reading group guides for more than 3,500 books. The guides include plot summaries and suggested discussion questions.

In short, arming yourself with powerful tools, preparing yourself by learning the skills needed by readers' advisors, reading widely, and keeping up with the field will help you to become a RA star.

Chapter 5

Working with Readers

Cynthia Orr

No book on the subject of advising readers would be complete without a mention of Rosenberg's First Law of Reading:

"Never apologize for your reading tastes."

Library school professor Betty Rosenberg first espoused this philosophy in her 1982 book *Genreflecting: A Guide to Reading Interests in Genre Fiction*—the first edition of this book. Since then, it has deservedly become the mantra for public library readers' advisors, is passed along at workshops and conferences, tacked onto the end of handouts, and appended to e-mail signatures.

Rosenberg called her book "the fruit of a blissfully squandered reading life," claiming unapologetically that, except for requirements for her formal education, she had read only what she enjoyed. Many readers follow this same path, reading only for enjoyment, but to many of us, this wonderful pleasure is dampened by a healthy dose of guilt left over from messages heard throughout our lives.

Which avid reader hasn't heard comments like these? "Get your nose out of that book and get some fresh air!" "What's that . . . another one of your bodice rippers?" "Do you need something to do? I'll give you something to do." "Why don't you read something worthwhile instead of that trash?"

These pervasive messages make it likely that if you're an avid reader, even though you might take every opportunity to squeeze a bit of pleasure reading into any spare moment, you still feel slightly ashamed of your reading habit. Somehow we can't get completely past those old messages, thinking that either we should be doing a chore or at least getting some fresh air instead, or that if we must read, we should be reading something "useful" rather than something enjoyable.

> Lady Peabury was in the morning room reading a novel; early train-
> ing gave a guilty spice to this recreation, for she had been brought up
> to believe that to read a novel before luncheon was one of the gravest
> sins it was possible for a gentlewoman to commit.
>
> —*Evelyn Waugh (p. 295)*

So, part of following Rosenberg's instruction to "never apologize for your reading tastes" is to remember that most readers struggle with this guilt and need to be treated with sensitivity. I believe this leads logically to the conclusion that Rosenberg's somewhat defiant law should have a corollary: "Be careful not to disparage anyone else's reading tastes." And, since many readers have that persistent guilty feeling that they should be doing something besides reading, they may be overly susceptible to anything less than our full-fledged support.

Terms like "sci-fi," "tearjerker," "bodice ripper," and "whodunit" are often used to denigrate genre fiction, implying that readers should read only "real literature" or "useful books." A disapproving facial expression can put a barrier between you (as a librarian) and the reader. Likewise, a smile at the wrong time can be very off-putting.

Try taking this corollary a step further by praising readers whenever possible. After all, most of them have a lifetime of negative messages to overcome, and they deserve to know that it's perfectly okay to read purely for pleasure and that it's perfectly okay to enjoy whatever kind of book they enjoy. This can be accomplished by looking for something positive to say about each particular reader. Here are some compliments to give you an idea of what I mean:

"You are one of our very best customers!"

"You read more than just about anyone I know."

"You are a real expert on that subject."

"I admire you so much for making sure your children have good books to read."

"You set such a good example by reading."

"You must have read hundreds of books over the years! That's so wonderful."

Any positive, sincere message will do, and don't worry too much about overdoing it, as long as what you're saying is heartfelt and sincere. After all, we'd have to work very hard to outweigh all the negative comments most readers have heard all their lives.

With that preamble, however, and with a nod to Betty Rosenberg, I propose 12 golden rules for readers' advisors.

THE GOLDEN RULES OF READERS' ADVISORY SERVICE

Rule #1—It's Not About You

Like any modern educated mother, I read to my children when they were small. Conscious of the tale of the shoemaker's shoeless children, I made doubly sure that this librarian's kids had a mother who read to them. My daughter became an avid reader at an early age, and like many of us, eventually ranged about the shelves at will, reading everyone from Jennifer Crusie to Ken Follett to the classics. She named our Labrador Retriever Lizzy Bennet. I breathed a sigh of relief. She would be okay.

My son was a good reader too, but I worried because he did not choose to read often. True, when he was a first grader, he asked for some *Goosebumps* books because the big third grade boys were reading them. But he mostly liked the *idea* of reading them and didn't get through more than one or two. I bought him books and talked about books and suggested audiobooks—all without much success. Reading was a chore for him—not that it was difficult—just that it felt like homework.

Then one day, some years ago, he was invited on a camping trip with his grandparents. I brought home *Harry Potter and the Sorcerer's Stone*. The book was popular in England and was just beginning to catch on in this country, and I thought he might like it. To my delight, he devoured it on the trip. His grandparents reported that he read in the back seat as they drove, at the picnic table in the campground, in his bunk at bedtime. When I let him know how happy I was, he said, "Well, duh, Mom, if you'd brought me a good book before this, I would have started reading a long time ago." I'm happy to report that he is now an avid reader in his 20s.

My point is that readers, especially novice readers, need a book that is right for them. And if you work hard enough to help them find that book, it can change their lives. After all, until a reader finds that first wonderful enjoyable book, she won't know that reading is pleasure, not work. And if she doesn't ever find that first book that's just right for her, she will never know the pleasure of being lost in a book. And that means she will live her whole life without one of the most profound and pleasurable experiences possible.

As tempting as it may be to talk about *your* favorite book or the book *you* are reading at the moment, Rule #1—It's Not About You—means that we have to put ourselves into our readers' shoes and try to understand what *they* might like, what *they* are in the mood for, what would appeal to *them*, and not necessarily what we ourselves enjoy—or even worse, what we think they *should* read.

It's amazing how many times bookstore or library employees respond to a request from a reader by giving them the last book they themselves have read. Secret shopper studies in libraries have shown that this approach is all too common. In the previously mentioned study published in *Library Journal*, where library school students went to several public libraries to see how typical RA questions were handled, one of the lessons they learned was that librarians often suggested the book they were currently reading, rather than trying to ascertain what the patron was really looking for in a reading experience (May et al). So learn to observe, to really listen, and to empathize, so that you can suggest titles that will take into account each reader's likes and dislikes. Use active listening skills and really focus on what the person is saying. And resist the temptation to turn the conversation to what *you're* reading, what *you* enjoy, and what *you* might like. Remember, it's not about you!

Rule #2—Attitude and Atmosphere Are Everything

Readers often approach the bookstore and the library much as they do a grocery store—with the assumption that they are expected to serve themselves. It is difficult for them to ask you for help, except possibly to request the whereabouts of a particular title. Somehow, asking this kind of specific question seems to feel okay—much like asking the grocery clerk for help in finding the green beans—but anything more than that often feels like an imposition. You've heard it before, "I hate to bother you, but. . . ."

Librarians these days are perpetually busy as they struggle to keep up with never-ending workloads. But if readers already have trouble understanding that it's okay to ask for help finding something to read, imagine how much harder it will be if you have your head down and look really busy. Remember also, that body language and facial expression can be even more important than words. You want to avoid sending out any messages that will put the reader off.

Be careful not to condescend on the one hand, but if you're feeling panicked on the other, you need to hide that as well. Readers hesitant to ask for help in the first place will be easily scared away if you make them uncomfortable, or if they feel that you are uncomfortable. And whatever you do, be careful of the reader's privacy. In fact, try not to merely guard against giving off unwelcome attitudes, instead, go to the other extreme and work to make the patron feel welcome and comfortable.

To overcome this obstacle, it's important to make eye contact, to smile, to offer to help, and to try not to look as busy as you really are. In the same vein, remember that you will look less busy if you are standing up—or at least sitting on a high chair that raises you up to the customer's level. At least one study has shown that staff members working at high desks that put them at the eye level of customers are more approachable than those sitting at low desks. I'd wager that in your library, patrons approach the checkout staff for help just as often, or more often, than they do the staff at the information or reference desk. Could it be because the people behind the circulation desk are standing up and the reference librarians are sitting down?

And speaking of sitting down, don't merely point to a section and send the patron off. Get up, go with them, and take the opportunity during this stroll to find out more about what they're looking for. Too many librarians either send the patron off to the mystery section unescorted, for example, or turn to the computer and begin typing, instead of giving patrons the attention needed to really do a successful interview. Worse yet is to send the patron to the catalog. Cataloging and classification of fiction is pretty uniformly inadequate in libraries. Referring a patron to the computer unescorted is most likely going to result in failure. As you work with professional tools, remember to disclose the process to your patron. Explain what you are doing as you go along so that they understand what's going on.

Wandering the aisles is a great technique and a good habit to get into if you want to serve readers. You'll be infinitely more approachable when it appears that you're not immersed in an important task. A desk, even though it's meant to be a central place to ask for help, creates a barrier between yourself and the person you hope to help.

Going back to the grocery store analogy—who would you ask about the green beans? Would you go up to the cashier area and ask someone at their work station, or would you ask the employee working in the aisles? The Disney Corporation, known for its great customer service, makes sure that their employees who are on litter patrol in their theme parks know the answers to the most frequently asked questions. They realize that customers feel more comfortable approaching someone pushing a broom than the official person ensconced behind a desk. How often do your patrons approach the person shelving books rather than the one sitting down?

Regularly taking a walk around the floor and approaching someone who looks lost can make a huge difference. Casually straightening a shelf near a browser and asking if they are finding what they need is an effective approach. Sometimes patrons are so taken aback by your offer that they refuse help at that moment, only to come back to you in a minute or two with a question. At worst, you've let them know that it's okay to approach you for help, and they may be less hesitant in a later visit.

The physical environment of your building is important as well. Try for an ambience that feels leisurely. Bookstores generally do a much better job of this than libraries, so make a few field trips and incorporate their best ideas. Readers will think they are bothering you or keeping you from your work in the best of situations. Hurrying them along will guarantee failure. Avid readers love to browse. Make sure they have the chance by creating book displays, shelving books with cover art facing outward, producing reading lists, and arranging print RA tools in a publicly accessible area, so they can flip through them. Let them know you value reading by inviting authors to speak and by sponsoring reading groups and programs. And anything you can do to give the customer permission to stop and chat is a good thing.

Chances are you have a sign over your desk that says "Information" or something similar, making it clear that it's acceptable for customers to ask for help in finding a title or an answer to a factual question. But why not have a sign or a button saying "Ask Me What to Read Next"? Remember those negative messages about how reading for pleasure is a waste of time? Chances are good that many patrons who see the "Reference Desk" sign will think that means they can ask for help in answering homework or research questions only.

Overcoming the perception of the library as a self-help store takes work— but it's worth it. Make sure your attitude and your library's atmosphere are a help, not a hindrance.

Rule #3—Don't Pigeonhole the Readers

For an assignment, a 20-something master's in library science student in one of my RA classes went to a public library anonymously and played secret shopper by asking for help finding a good book to read. Imagine her chagrin when the woman at the desk told her that "the young adult librarian is off today, but the books for teens are over there."

Looks can be deceiving.

A new library branch was built in a primarily African American neighborhood in my city. Librarians, with all good intentions, had purchased a compact disc collection that consisted mainly of rap, rhythm and blues, and gospel music. The very first reference question when they unlocked their doors on opening day was, "Do you have any opera on CD?"

While generalizations can be helpful, they can also be your downfall. Remember to use your skills to find out what the reader really wants, and never rely solely on assumptions or preconceptions that may very well be embarrassingly false.

Rule #4—Don't Pigeonhole the Books

To a person who doesn't read in a particular genre, all the books in that genre seem the same. Stop and think about that for a minute. Do you read mysteries? Many librarians do. If you do, you know that there are many subgenres within the mystery category. You'll find police procedurals that let you get inside the precinct and see how police do their work. There are cozy mysteries with amateur sleuths like Agatha Christie's Miss Marple, who cleverly solve the crime—sometimes in spite of the police. There are the books featuring hard-boiled private eyes—the tough guys (or gals) who are hired by a client to investigate something. Flip to the mystery section in Chapter 8 of this book to see even more subgenres.

Besides subgenre, there are differences among the books that include such factors as setting, level of violence, language, style of writing, and whether the book is funny or not. I could go on, but the point is that to a fan of a particular genre, there are obvious differences to consider within each genre when choosing a good book to read.

Forgetting this phenomenon and pigeonholing the books or grouping them all together can lead to poor service. To those who don't read mysteries, they are merely all those books shelved together "over there." The person who makes assumptions about genres they're not familiar with will tend to take a reader to the mystery section or the romance section or the science fiction section and just leave them there. Even though each genre by definition has similarities, each has subgenres that set them apart quite distinctly. We need to understand these differences— especially in genres we don't read ourselves—so that we can help guide readers.

Suppose a customer came into the library and said they'd read and loved all the Agatha Christie Miss Marple mysteries and were looking for another good mystery author. Would they necessarily enjoy *Silence of the Lambs* just because it also involves murder? Agatha Christie wrote cozy mysteries where the murder took place offstage—not bloody, horrifying psychological suspense.

One romance reader may like Regencies—historically accurate, usually slim works set in England exclusively between 1811 and 1820, when George III was the King, and his son, George IV, ruled as regent. Regency fans take their history seriously and are quite adamant about accuracy. Another romance reader may like long, sexually explicit romances set in contemporary times. Still another might want sexy, but not explicit stories involving time travel.

Use works such as this book to familiarize yourself with the subcategories of all the genres—especially those you don't read—so that you can understand the literally hundreds of different types of books that exist. The chapters in Part III of this book are intended to help you do exactly that.

And talk to the fans. You'll be amazed at how much you can learn from someone who absolutely adores a genre. If you don't hesitate to have these conversations, you'll begin to understand why they read, what they get out of it, how the genre is broken down, and who the best authors are. And you'll have fun doing it.

Remember, don't pigeonhole the books! If books in a particular category seem all alike to you, then you haven't learned enough about that genre.

Rule #5—Read, Read, Read

There's no substitute for reading books. You can't read everything, of course, but really—think about it. This is one of the most enjoyable assignments you could ever have—and a perfect antidote to any feelings of guilt you yourself may have left over from those old voices that told you to get your nose out of that book. It's a great excuse. You *need* to read—it's your job.

Having said that, I would suggest that you make sure to read with a professional attitude. Most people read as pure fans. They immerse themselves in the book and read for enjoyment, never sparing a thought for why they are enjoying themselves. At the other end of the spectrum, academics read with a critical viewpoint, dissecting, criticizing, and studying the work they are reading, going over it line by line to discern its meaning. Someone who aspires to help readers find books they will enjoy should be somewhere between these two extremes.

Readers' advisors can't afford to read in a totally abandoned carefree way, as fans do. Read critically enough to think about the author's style, the appeal factors of the books, what kinds of readers might enjoy the works, and what other books might be similar. Only by reading in this way—as a professional—can you understand enough to suggest books to readers.

Part of the responsibility to read professionally includes reading outside your personal preferences. If you don't normally read romance, for instance, find a list of the best or most popular romances and read a few in various romance subgenres. This will help you immensely the next time a romance reader approaches. The suggested titles in Part III are intended as an aid in finding titles typical of the subgenres or favorites with fans.

It's a mistake to fake it. If you are asked if you've read a book and you haven't, just admit the truth. One of the myths of RA service is that you have to have read a title before you suggest it to a patron. This just isn't so. There are book reviews and RA tools that can help you learn enough about a book to have an idea whether a patron might like it. You can learn about books by discussing them with colleagues and having conversations with patrons who have read them. You can test your suggestions by asking patrons to come back and tell you how they liked the books you gave them.

But there is no substitute for reading widely, so do enjoy yourself, and just remember, you now have permission to read, read, read—without guilt.

Rule #6—Keep a Reading Log

Many avid readers log what they read. This may seem like a lot of trouble at first, but keeping a list of the books you've read will help you to remember them. And it's fun to look back over the years and remember what you were reading at different periods of your life.

The format of your log is not as important as simply keeping one. I'd recommend including at minimum the author, title, and date you read the book. Anything else is a bonus, and elaborate annotations and categories and comments are great, but if your log is so complicated that it's a chore to fill out, you'll soon stop; so simplify it to something you will actually keep up in the future. You can log your books online at social media sites (like *GoodReads*, *Shelfari*, or *LibraryThing*), on your library's BiblioCommons site, in a spreadsheet, or on paper, or on your blog.

As you log your books, think about connections—what other books does this one remind you of, what kind of reader might like this book, what kind of feeling did it evoke, and was it a fast read or a book you immersed yourself in? These kinds of questions will help clarify your thinking when you use the book in your work with readers. Often, just looking back at the date that you read a work might bring it back vividly. You may have read it while on vacation, listened to it in the car on a trip to a conference, or you may remember it because you read it between two other titles that you recall well. You'd be surprised how much a reading log can help in your work.

Rule #7—Prepare, Prepare, Prepare; Then Use Your Skills and Tools

Matching books with readers deserves attention, commitment, and training. Imagine this scenario:

A man approaches one of your fellow staff members. "I've just been chosen to be the coach of a Little League baseball team. Can you help me find a book about how to teach baseball to six-year-olds?"

Now imagine this response from your coworker: "Sorry, but I don't know anything about baseball."

Or: "This is my least favorite kind of question!"

Or this one: "No, I can't recommend a book on coaching baseball, but I just finished reading a really good one on trout fishing. Let me show you that one instead."

These scenarios are almost impossible to imagine because no competent library employee would respond in such inappropriate ways. But research has shown that often when readers ask for help in finding an enjoyable book to read for pleasure, librarians respond either by trying to evade the question, by showing their discomfort with the situation, or by talking about what they themselves enjoy (May et al).

But if story is essential in our lives, it follows that helping a reader find a book that he or she will enjoy is important work, and that this work deserves as much attention and commitment to success as a reference question about baseball.

If you can't bring yourself to go that far, at least admit that a request for a good book is as important as a request to help settle a bar bet or answer a trivia question. We train our employees to answer these kinds of queries without a second thought. We teach them how to run the cash register and where the books on different subjects are shelved. Library schools teach future librarians interview skills to help them draw out what the library patron really wants. Libraries purchase important tools and resources to answer these kinds of questions. Continuing education classes and workshops at conferences keep staff up-to-date on the latest techniques.

Training on how to match readers with books deserves the very same level of attention and commitment. And, yes, it involves a certain knack, but the skills can be taught as well. Look for courses and workshops given by the closest library school or professional organization. Buy the essential tools and work out training programs for your staff. Take a few minutes before every staff meeting and ask each person to give a two-minute book talk on something they've recently read. Taking these opportunities regularly will result in a huge increase in the number of books your staff knows about.

And after training, remember to use those skills and tools. Research has shown that many librarians when faced with an RA question seem to panic and forget to use a professional interview or even print or electronic tools. Training is essential, but it's also important to make sure that RA service gets the respect it deserves so that staff members understand that they need to use professional skills and tools to answer these kinds of questions.

Rule #8—There Is No Perfect Answer

Don't put too much pressure on yourself! Since there truly is no one right answer to a reader's needs, don't worry too much. Spend the time needed on the interview, chatting with the patron about what kinds of things they've enjoyed in the past and what they're in the mood for today. Remember to discuss their choices in terms of appeal factors. Then suggest a range of titles instead of trying to find that one perfect book. Offering at least three books is good, and six or seven isn't too many. On the other hand, be careful not to overload the reader with too many options. I knew a librarian once who used to routinely bring 25 or 30 books in answer to a reference question. The looks on the readers' faces made it clear that they were overwhelmed, but since he wasn't watching for their cues, he never noticed.

Joyce Saricks (p. 89), one of the premier experts in the field, uses the word "suggest" rather than "recommend" when helping readers. Using the word "suggest" takes away a bit of the pressure by making it clear that you are not picking the one perfect read but are helping the reader by narrowing the range of titles for her to consider. The final choice of what to read belongs to the reader.

Think about the row after row of shelves of books facing a reader in a library. What an overwhelming choice! If you can select an armload of books that are good candidates, you are helping the reader immensely by increasing their chances of choosing a good match.

Rule #9—Invite the Reader Back

Research has shown that the success rate for answering reference questions can be greatly increased if the librarian asks one simple question at the end of the transaction—"Does this completely answer your question?" Since there is no one right answer when suggesting a good book to read, the RA transaction is more like a conversation. Ask the customer to come back sometime and tell you how they liked the books you suggested. If they come back again, you've been successful. Congratulate yourself! Even if they didn't like the choices, you can talk about what they didn't like and make better suggestions next time.

Remember to have fun, immerse yourself in the moment, and enjoy the people and the conversations. As you get to know the reader and they feel more comfortable with you, your success rate will improve. And doing this regularly with many people will help you to become a better readers' advisor. After all, conversations and feedback with many people can't help but enhance your skills as well as your knowledge of genres, authors, and titles. And inviting them back reinforces the fact that it really is okay to ask this type of question.

Rule #10—Keep Current

The RA field is constantly changing, of course, just like any other pursuit. But it is extremely important to keep up in this career—not only to improve your skills—but because the books, of course, are new every day. So make it your business to keep current by reading widely in the field; attending conferences; watching for articles by the best-known names in the field; subscribing to Fiction_L and electronic newsletters like *Publishers Lunch*, *Shelf-Awareness*, and *PW Daily*; and reading blogs such as *The Reader's Advisor Online*.

Rule #11—Enjoy Yourself

Being a readers' advisor is a privilege. It's fun. It allows you to work with the nicest people in the world—readers. And it immerses you in the life of books. As a bonus, it's important, uplifting work. So make sure you enjoy it. Revel in it.

Begin every day remembering that you could be flipping burgers instead, or working in the hot sun, or worse yet, you could be unemployed. Instead you get to spend the day talking about books. How lucky you are! This can be your favorite, most enjoyable part of the job. So remember to relax and enjoy it.

Rule # 12—Pass It On

My first job was in a suburban public library where I learned to suggest books by modeling myself on the other librarians who had been practicing this art for decades before me. They didn't learn how to do this in library school, and neither did I. While library schools of the time taught about children's literature, they did not address adult pleasure reading in any way. There were no books on the subject of RA service then either, and the catalogs were totally inadequate when it came to fiction. There were a handful of print tools to help readers' advisors, like lists of sequels and the *Fiction Catalog*, but not many.

Over the years, things have changed a lot, but too many library schools still do not teach RA service. And many of us who practice and teach and write about the RA art are now middle-aged and older. The torch must be passed on. If you're reading this book, I hope that means you share a passion for reading. If so, please consider not only learning from others, but also building on, and adding to, the knowledge that exists now.

The RA field is in its infancy. Pick a niche that you love and learn what you can. Then share it with others. Give workshops, write articles, teach a class, or train your colleagues. Be an evangelist. You can make a huge difference by suggesting a book that may change someone's life, but think how many more people you could affect if you help train new readers' advisors who will suggest books to thousands of readers during their careers.

It's true that this takes a bit of courage—and a lot of work. But the work is enjoyable, and the fear of failure is really unnecessary. Book people are the nicest people in the world. They will be very forgiving at the least, and most likely very appreciative and complimentary. And lest you question your qualifications to teach or write, remember that at this point in time, there are many more practitioners working in this area, giving workshops, holding training sessions, and speaking at conferences than there are library school professors. And practitioners were the ones who kept the skill alive while most library schools ignored it. Please swallow your fear and join their ranks in at least some small way.

This is vital work. Pass it on.

BEST PRACTICES

To summarize, let's review some best practices for RA services. First, read widely, not just at your own comfort level, and keep a reading log. Walk the stacks and ask "Are you finding what you need?" Don't forget to conduct RA service in a similar fashion to reference services. In other words, use the RA interview or conversation to elicit the information you need to help the reader. Listen actively. After that, don't forget to use RA tools to help you answer the question. Research has shown that too many librarians try to answer RA questions purely from their own experience, without using tools. Use the appeal factors of books to make good matches with readers. Invite the reader back to discuss the choices and how they liked them. Have a good attitude—enjoy people, be approachable, and discuss books with other staff members as well.

Prepare your library to receive readers and make them welcome. Adopt the best aspects of bookstores and retail stores. Display books, publish book lists for patrons, and sponsor reading-related activities such as book groups and author visits. Keep up with the field by subscribing to Fiction_L, reading blogs, and paying attention to local resources like the book pages of area newspapers. Develop yourself by taking advantage of training opportunities, but take it a step further. Find a niche, become expert in that area, and offer to do training in your specialty for others. Write articles and share information with other RAs at conferences.

THE READERS' ADVISORY CONVERSATION

Much has been written about the importance of developing the ability to conduct an effective reference interview as an essential skill for librarians. The RA interview is similar, though there are some definite variations. While the reference interview has the goal of determining the answer to a patron's exact question, which the librarian then finds by using the tools and skills of the trade; the RA interview is more of a conversation, and there is no one right answer.

In a nutshell, as a readers' advisor, make contact and try to discern the reader's tastes and the type of book their mood dictates; then, by thinking about books in ways that can lead to connections, come up with a list of possible suggestions. Link the appeal of books with interests of the particular reader, and then present these titles and articulate their appeal in ways the reader can understand. At the end of the conversation, invite the reader to return and give feedback after they've finished reading.

Initiating this conversation may very well require that you wander the stacks and strike up conversations with browsers. In the conversation, the readers' advisor must determine the readers' purpose and mood. Is he looking for something to read for pleasure or a school assignment? Is he in the mood to read something challenging, or something soothing, or something funny? Would he consider nonfiction as well as fiction? Eliciting answers to these questions without putting the reader on the spot, or being too vague, is a skill that takes practice, but relaxing and having fun with the encounter will help the reader feel relaxed too. The classic question suggested by Joyce Saricks (p. 172) is "Tell me about a book you enjoyed." But if the reader draws a blank, you can ask her to tell you about a movie she liked, or you can ask her to tell you about a book or movie she hated.

As the reader talks, use active listening skills, and be aware of cues. If he talks about what happened in the book he liked, he may be most interested in a book with a great plot. If she talks about the characters, that tells you something else. Paraphrasing what they say—repeating what you heard them explain, but in your own words—should keep them talking so that you get a good idea of what kinds of books they like.

One major mistake that many librarians make when beginning to provide RA service is to think they must know good read-alike titles off the tops of their heads. Reference librarians would not dream of answering a reference question without consulting a source. Readers' advisors should use sources as well.

Every person is different, of course. It's best to just be yourself, find your own comfort zone, and operate from there. We can all improve our communication skills with practice, and that's good, but don't think you have to have sterling acting skills or be a great public speaker in order to do great RA work. Making a genuine connection using your own style is all that's needed.

Just as all readers' advisors are different, all readers have different needs too, of course. But one special challenge to think about is that of serving patrons who came from countries where they either had no native libraries or where they used libraries with no concept of RA service. Explaining that this service is available can be a very uplifting experience when the patron is delighted to learn that this help is offered.

Learning what you can about diversity is also important. While every reader is an individual, various groups have special interests, whether they are Christians who want to read books that emphasize their faith or members of a particular group who want to read stories that have characters that look and sound like them; so as a readers' advisor it's important to have the sensitivity to deal with diversity issues.

DIFFICULT SITUATIONS, DIFFICULT PEOPLE

While RA service can be tremendously rewarding, it involves working with people, so of course it follows that some situations and readers require special handling. Let's discuss some common difficult situations and how to handle them.

Overcoming Panic

Let's be frank. Helping people can sometimes be scary—especially if you're a rookie. And, even if you know what you're doing, some people can be downright difficult. So here are a few tips that might help. Here's the first tip. Since readers are often interested in how to find good books to read for themselves, do the RA interview or conversation, then take the reader with you to an appropriate source, such as a display or one of the titles in the *Genreflecting* series by Libraries Unlimited. Show them briefly how the source works, tell them you're going to check something and you'll be right back. Then leave them to browse while you take a few moments to take a deep breath, clear your mind, and to use sources that will help you suggest a few books. Just that little bit of time away from the reader can help you gather your wits.

How to Begin Your Day

Spending a little time preparing at the beginning of the day can really help you to relax and be ready to give great service and make sure that you and your library are ready for those readers when they come in. Walk around, straighten the new book shelves and note what titles are available, fill the displays, wander up and down the aisles of fiction for a few moments, and note five or six good reads that are in today. If you have a poor memory, jot them down and put the list in your pocket for later. See what's on the bestseller list this week and which new books will be published by reading the weekly RA Run Down on the *Reader's Advisor Online Blog*, check your daily electronic newsletters and blog feeds, and be ready to make sure your attitude and the library's atmosphere are ready.

Difficult Patrons

No matter how well-prepared you are, some kinds of readers are just harder to help than others are. Here are a few of the most common difficult readers, with some tips on helping them.

The Clam

Some people just don't communicate well. No matter what you ask, they don't respond. This kind of reader may be shy, or they may not have the vocabulary to describe what they like. One trick that may help is to ask open-ended questions. If you ask a closed question like, "Do you like mysteries?" you risk the person answering with just yes or no. But what if they can't tell you about a book or movie they liked? All you can do in an extreme situation like this is to try to narrow the choices in any way you can—even if it's just asking them one by one about genres. You could ask if they enjoyed the *Star Wars* movies or if they are a fan of *Downton Abbey*, for example, and use their answers and the follow up conversation to settle on possible genres and subgenres. Then suggest a range of books in those areas that are sure bets—titles that many people have read and enjoyed. In fact, you'll find a list of fan favorites in each genre chapter of this book. The idea is that if a person generally enjoys a book in a particular genre and you can suggest some books in that genre that many people have raved about, you'll be more likely to succeed.

The Searcher

Sometimes individuals are looking for a very specific book, but they can't remember the author or the title. In this case, there are two or three tools that can really help. Of course, there's the good old Google search, and sometimes this works. Sometimes one of your colleagues will know the book. Another tactic is to use the Amazon search and see what turns up. The descriptions and reviews of the books may turn up with the key words you use. But often the best source for identifying a mystery title is Fiction_L, the discussion group with 3,000 readers' advisor librarians. If you post your question there, you will often get an answer in just a few minutes because these thousands of colleagues have read thousands and thousands of books, and many of them are at work and online and will be happy to help. You'll be amazed at how well this works.

The Fuss-Budget

Some readers are very picky. They may ask for a book with no violence, no swear words, or no sex. They might tell you that no animals may die in the books you suggest. Or maybe they want a great book, but only in large print. This can be one of the most challenging RA assignments. One source that can help with a violence, sex, or bad language limit is the online catalog for the

National Library Service for the Blind and Physically Handicapped of the Library of Congress (www.loc.gov/nls). Their catalog will say "contains descriptions of violence," "contains descriptions of sex," or "contains strong language." This can be a very helpful tool. This is another question that your Fiction_L colleagues may be able to help with too.

The Creature of Habit

Some readers are stuck in a rut and will only read one specific kind of book. If they read a lot, it can be very difficult to find enough titles to keep them happy. One thing that might help with this kind of patron is to watch for books they might like as you read reviews and note them down. Reviews are like gold mines of information about books, and sometimes they are key word searchable. The best approach for known, repeat patrons is to be proactive and think of them while you're reading reviews.

The Proxy

Here's another tough one. The Proxy comes into the library looking for books for someone else. It's very challenging to try to do an RA interview with someone who is not actually the reader. One thing that can help is to ask if the reader is available by telephone. If not, and if the Proxy does not know a lot about the other person's reading tastes, all you can really do is ask about their hobbies, favorite movies, or other interests, and try to find some sure bets that seem to fit so that they can take them to the reader and give them a few choices.

The Believer

Some readers depend upon the recommendations of others they trust—whether it be Oprah Winfrey or a friend or acquaintance—and many come into the library with partial or incorrect information on the book that was recommended. I'm sure you've heard some hilarious stories of misunderstood titles. Here is where your preparation pays off. If you've made sure that you know the popular books, and if you've kept current with new books, you may recognize the book they are describing. I once had someone ask for *Silent Ship, Silent Sea*, which of course turned out to be *Run Silent, Run Deep*. If you don't recognize it, though, again, remember Fiction_L, which is like having 3,000 colleagues to ask, "Do you recognize this book?"

The Pleaser

Pleasers agree with everything you say, and say that every suggestion sounds great. This is very frustrating because they can be so agreeable that you can't tell anything about their own likes and dislikes. One technique that can help with this customer is to give them comparative choices. For instance, you can ask which they prefer—a mystery or a romance. Or you can talk about a couple of titles and ask them which one sounds better. This is an unusual case where a closed question may actually help you get more information than an open-ended question.

The Regular

Regular, repeat customers can be difficult because when a reader comes in quite often, it may seem like they've seen everything you have. On the other hand, a Regular comes in so often that staff members have a chance to really get to know them. This makes it easier to suggest more outlier titles that may not be so obvious, but that your intuition tells you this patron may like because you know their tastes so well. A colleague once told me about a women's book discussion group that read only books related to being Jewish. They loved fiction—especially fiction about Jewish families. She knew them well, and just knew that they would like Amy Tan's *The Joy Luck Club*, a book about four Chinese women and their daughters. She said they were hesitant at first, but she convinced them to give the book a try, and they loved it. So remember that the Regular may be someone you know well, and because of that, you may be able to broaden their perspective a bit when it feels like they've read everything in their usual area.

The Lonesome

Anybody who has worked in public service knows about the poor soul who is lonely and really just wants some human contact. This person may just strike up a conversation, or they may come up with various questions that give them an excuse to chat. There's no foolproof way to disentangle yourself from the Lonesome. All you can really do is excuse yourself and say you have something you must do. If it's really a problem, make a deal with your coworkers to "rescue" each other after an appropriate amount of time. Sometimes you can turn this kind of person into a reader, but if you can't, don't beat yourself up. Just remember that they are very lonely.

The Double Whammy: Teens and Their Parents

It's very awkward when a parent comes in with their teenager and interrupts your attempt to conduct an RA interview with the teen. Sometimes they say negative things about their child's reading habits, and that doesn't help the situation either. Here it makes sense to pose your questions directly to the teen and avoid eye contact with the parent. Eventually, they may get the idea that you really need to talk to their child about what the child likes, rather than what the parent wants the child to like. This is a tough one, but you have to persist or you will have no chance to help the teen find a book that they will find enjoyable.

The Reluctant Reader

Students who come into the library with a reading assignment offer another challenge. If they have a specific title assigned, there's little you can do except try to be enthusiastic about the book or give them a few tips on how to read it. But often students are told to choose a book from a list of titles or to choose a book with certain characteristics. Ideally, you'll conduct an RA interview that gives you an idea of the student's likes and dislikes, and can find a qualifying book that is likely to appeal to him. Best of all is if you can find an appropriate book that fits their best loved categories and is also a teen favorite. This gives the student a much better chance to enjoy the book even though it is a school assignment. Another factor in helping students find a good book to read is reading level. Some assignments will specify Lexile or certain number values based on the Accelerated Reading Program. It is generally true, though, that a book will be more enjoyable if it is easy for the student to read. Think about it. If readers have to struggle to get through each page, there isn't much of a chance they will enjoy the book. Some teachers and parents don't understand this, and sometimes push the student to read a book that is too hard for her.

The Groupie

Serving book clubs is another challenge. Not only must you find a book they're likely to enjoy, but it also needs to be a "discussable" book. Many readers enjoy reading a good fast-paced thriller, for example, but there may not be much to say about the book in a discussion. Most times it's easier to discuss nonfiction books, but some fiction has complex characters facing difficult situations or choices, interesting themes, and fascinating settings or backgrounds. There are some exceptions to this, as some long-lasting book clubs discuss mysteries only, for instance, but generally speaking, discussable books are more complex. The second problem, of course, is finding enough copies to serve the book club's members. Many libraries and consortia have instituted book discussion sets for their public. Typically, this means that a librarian or committee chooses books that have been popular with other book groups or that they believe would be good for discussions, and then purchases a designated number of copies of the title to place in their book discussion collection. Often, then, the library publishes a list of the titles in the collection, with annotations, so that book clubs have a handy source for choosing their books.

In almost all of these difficult cases, it is worth taking the time to show readers the tools you are using so that they understand how the tools work. Making the process transparent will enable them to help themselves in the future if that is what they prefer, and it may help them to refine their own likes and dislikes by exposing them to the tools and vocabulary of RA service, which may help them frame their questions better in the future.

DISTANCE RA

Library patrons are becoming more and more accustomed to using online or mobile services to relieve them from the necessity of visiting the library in person. Libraries have done a good job of keeping ahead of their customers by offering RA service via live chat, by posting suggested reading lists on their websites, and by providing the opportunity to place holds online, even with mobile devices. A few libraries offer mail delivery of books, but most still require the reader to go to the library to pick up and return items.

But now, in the age of e-books and digital audiobooks, most libraries offer their patrons the chance to browse, choose a book, check it out, read it, and return it—all without leaving their home. What changes and adjustments will we need to make in order to adapt RA service to this new mobile world? Libraries have begun adapting by offering more finding aids for pleasure reading via their websites, by placing digital displays in their library buildings, and by offering download stations for those who may not have an Internet connection. But what more should we be doing?

The main barriers to library digital use are technical problems due to current cumbersome checkout methods, the difficulty of browsing easily, and the inability to provide RA service face-to-face. The technical barriers have steadily gotten better and are in the process of being solved as the software improves. Browsing easily is a bigger issue. Currently, anecdotal evidence supports the fact that many people browse for books in brick and mortar bookstores and then buy online—just because it is so much easier to browse physically. Readers' advisors will need to find ways to mitigate this problem, since research shows that many readers find their next book by browsing.

One obvious approach is to develop digital displays similar to the physical displays that readers' advisors already employ. Taking these displays to the next level is the challenge because it is easier to walk physically through a space and browse the books that are available than it is to navigate displays online. The answer may involve building a 3-D virtual library world that browsers could "walk through."

The issue of the need for face-to-face RA service is being addressed by the availability of live chat service provided by libraries, and other technologies such as Skype and videoconferencing may also be used.

It is difficult to predict exactly how librarians will deal with digital RA because the technology changes so quickly. But libraries have generally done a good job of keeping up with new trends in the technical world, and so it seems likely that we will cope with this new trend as well. It will be exciting to see what RA service looks like in 5 or 10 years.

NOTES

Byatt, A. S., ed. 1998. *Oxford Book of English Short Stories*. New York: Oxford University Press.

May, Anne K., Elizabeth Olesh, Anne Weinlich Miltenberg, and Catherine Patricia Lackne. 2000. "A Look at Reader's Advisory Services." *Library Journal* 125, no. 15 (September 15): 40–43.

Rosenberg, Betty. 1982. *Genreflecting: A Guide to Reading Interests in Genre Fiction*. Englewood, CO: Libraries Unlimited.

Saricks, Joyce. 2005. *Readers' Advisory Service in the Public Library*. 3rd ed. Chicago: American Library Association.

Chapter 6

The RA Environment: Building Your Library's Brand

Cynthia Orr

READING SPACES

Providing comfortable reading spaces in your library building is more important than ever. The thousands of bookstores that have closed in the past decade have left significant gaps in their communities. The closing of Borders stores across the country was a shock to the publishing community. The library may be the last place left for book lovers to browse and relax in many towns. Making your space attractive to browsers will attract even more readers. Comfortable chairs, attractive displays that change often, a clear arrangement of your collection, and use of merchandising techniques suggested in books like Paco Underhill's *Why We Buy* will make your library *the* place to go for readers in your community.

HELPING READERS HELP THEMSELVES

Part of building a space that's attractive to readers is making it possible for them to help themselves if they so desire. If your comfortable, browsable, reading space includes magazines and newsletters about books, displays filled with books arranged with their covers showing, handy bookmarks with lists of good titles, flyers advertising book-related events, and posters with the current bestsellers, readers will gravitate there. Consciously, look for new and better ways to make them even more comfortable.

HOW READERS BROWSE AND THE IMPLICATIONS FOR LIBRARIES

Library surveys have shown that the majority of readers use browsing as a major tool in selecting books to read. As modern life speeds up and people have less and less leisure time, libraries are finding that many patrons place holds on books from home, and when they come to pick them up, they often make a tour of the displays, choose a few things, then pick up their holds, check out, and leave. Often they don't go into the stacks at all. So the more you can do to encourage browsing, the better.

Sharon L. Baker, in her article "A Decade's Worth of Research on Browsing Fiction Collections," notes that, though there are few browsing studies, the ones we do have show that "a significant number of public library patrons choose their materials through browsing." One study showed that 86 percent of those who borrowed fiction had not used the catalog. One library did a small study that showed that putting books into a display increased their circulation by 90 percent (Seipp).

What are the implications of numbers like this? Obviously, public libraries should cater to browsers. And this approach makes even more sense when we realize that a huge majority of people would say that the library's brand is books.

Catering to browsers means narrowing the overload of vast library stacks to smaller displays of a few choices, as we discussed earlier. Research has also shown that all things being equal, most browsers look at the shelves at eye level. This means that shifting and rearranging books can make a difference in the titles that are browsed.

Another technique that helps browsers is to clearly identify the recent returns of the library. An astounding number of browsers are attracted to books that others have read. It's also true that browsers tend to browse more near the front door of the library, so making sure the prime browsing space is not taken up by unimportant objects like copy machines is a key point to remember.

But another important question is how to make browsing easier within the stacks. Studies have shown that more than half of browsers are looking for a book in a particular genre. This is true even if the library does not separate its fiction by genre. Research also shows that a large majority of readers prefer browsing a fiction collection that is separated by genre (Baker and Wallace). A second option is a collection that is interfiled with genre indicated by a sticker on the spine. Very few readers prefer to have all the fiction interfiled and arranged by author, but many librarians don't like the idea of separating genres because they believe it prevents cross-genre browsing, and that it saves the time of the library staff to have the books interfiled. (Note: Saving the time of the librarian was *not* one of Ranganathan's library laws.) Another reason not to separate by genre is that many books could be shelved in more than one genre, and separating by genre may cause an author's work to be shelved in more than one place.

How to arrange the fiction collection is a tough question. It's helpful to know that the bigger the collection, the more likely that your readers will feel overwhelmed; so it is even more important to consider separating genres if you have a large fiction collection. Another fact that may impact the decision is that separating genres increases circulation. So does interfiling with genre sticker markers, but not as much (Baker and Wallace).

I once weeded a tiny fiction collection in a branch that had experienced high turnover of branch managers with different philosophies. Sometimes I found an author's works shelved in general fiction and sometimes within a genre section. In almost every case, the author's titles shelved by genre had circulated more than the same author's titles shelved in general fiction. And this was a tiny collection—often just 10–15 shelves of a particular genre. This anecdotal evidence supports Baker's findings. Readers seemed to be browsing and choosing titles by genre. Imagine how much more difficulty they would have in a huge central library fiction collection that was not separated by genre.

Sharon Baker and Karen Wallace (p. 141) suggest that one compromise might be to check circulation records to determine which genres are most popular with your customers, and then separate those genres only. Larger collections could have more genres separated than smaller collections. In her research, she found that patrons experience some overload with collections with as small as 4,000 volumes.

BOOK CLUBS AND BEYOND: OTHER RA PROGRAMS

If books are the library's brand, many would say that's a good thing now that the Internet provides "good enough" answers to reference questions that, in days past, would have been asked by patrons at the library. Libraries have an opportunity to add to their brand by providing programs of interest to readers. These can include sponsorship of book clubs, book talks for groups, author visits and signings, or provision of a venue for meetings of writers' groups. Many libraries now answer readers' advisory (RA) questions through e-mail and Facebook, provide book programming for local radio and television stations, conduct summer reading clubs for adults as well as children, and even offer story times for adults. These kinds of programs can only enhance your library's brand.

COMMUNICATION TOOLS

Libraries have been using traditional communication tools for many years, such as providing a regular column in the local newspaper listing new books that the library has acquired, or printing flyers with the most popular books of the month, or bookmarks with read-alikes. But new technology offers new and exciting options for building the library's brand.

Social media offers an exciting new channel for libraries. Not only do many libraries maintain a Facebook page, but also sites such as *Shelfari*, *GoodReads*, and other social media for readers, provide an opportunity to share specific books with your readers.

Many library catalogs now allow readers to rate books and post reviews of books for other patrons to see. And, if we see the library catalog as the number one source of information for readers, and we should, then integrating RA tools with the catalog is an exciting new possibility. Ideally, if a reader searches for a particular title, he or she should see other similar suggested titles with no additional searching.

Librarians are adding content to their catalogs by recording podcasted book reviews, videos of staff booktalks, or creating their own book trailers to publicize titles they especially like. Since many browsers bypass the catalog, an RA section on the library's website can entice browsers with book lists, links, and offers to provide a tailored reading list via e-mail if the reader fills out a form about their reading tastes. Some catalogs also offer the chance for readers to make a reading log to keep track of their books.

This is an area of service that can only grow as creative librarians put themselves in the shoes of avid readers and let their imaginations run wild as they consider providing a service that patrons will love. And with the availability of e-books, libraries are attracting new users who prefer not to visit the library's buildings at all. This gives a whole new meaning to library outreach.

Working with readers online requires new skills, and just as most librarians had no training in RA service in library school, many also have had no training in using social media, downloading e-books, creating web pages, making videos or recording podcasts, or serving patrons via e-mail.

The first online 24 × 7 live chat RA service was launched in Ohio in 2004 and was part of the Know It Now service, which allows Ohio patrons to chat with a librarian 24 hours a day, 7 days a week. One of the challenges for this service is that during the hours that public libraries are closed, the questions are answered by "After Dark" librarians who work from home. The sources they use must therefore be online, unless they have their own print reference works that can help them answer questions. When the tools are not in the same room with the librarian, it's important to have reliable online tools readily bookmarked and annotated, based upon what kinds of questions the tool can best be used to answer, and this presents a new challenge for collection development.

Chat-based library service has its own limitations and requires the use of different skills. For example, the librarian should send frequent messages to fill the dead space, so that the patron knows they are still there. And a readers' advisor who first attempts service this way quickly realizes that it's tough, without body language and tone of voice, to understand the patron's likes and dislikes. Chat RA service offers a prime area for research.

Some libraries, like Williamsburg Regional Library in Virginia, Skokie Public Library in Illinois, and others, have instituted what they call form-based RA service online. In this model, the reader fills out a questionnaire about reading tastes, and librarians e-mail them a suggested reading list. Another fairly new attempt at using new tools to suggest books to readers has been used by Cuyahoga County Public Library in the suburbs of Cleveland, and others. In this case, the library announces a particular time period and readers submit favorite titles via the library's Facebook page, while librarians monitor the page and suggest titles the reader may like.

Other libraries have experimented with using technology to enhance book discussions. Many authors are willing to call in to a group discussing their book and answer questions, for instance. Other librarians blog a summary of their in-person group discussions, and others are trying online book discussion through e-mail or chat.

TRAINING STAFF

Since many staff members lack training in both RA techniques and technology, libraries are faced with a training challenge. Several libraries have addressed this problem by designing a long-term program of training for their public service staff (often including desk clerks, who receive many questions about books as they check out items for their readers). Some libraries have initiated plans for an entire year of training, bringing in expert readers' advisors like Nancy Pearl, former head of the

Washington Center for the Book and well-known media personality, to help design and lead their initiatives. But even with training, librarians need to keep up with the world of books in order to be effective. New titles are published every week, bestseller lists change, and new techniques are developed. How can we keep up?

KEEPING CURRENT

Techniques for keeping current are vital for readers' advisors. In order to be ready for the new stream of books each week, be sure to follow your local newspaper's book pages and check the *Reader's Advisor Online Blog* (www .readersadvisoronline.com/blog) from ABC-CLIO each Monday for a list of the books to be published each week and the titles that are new to the bestseller lists. The RA Run Down, also on Monday at the same site, is a roundup of links to news of interest to readers' advisors. *Early Word* (www.earlyword.com) is a blog for collection development and RA librarians, and features movie tie-ins, book news, book lists, chats about books, and more.

Several excellent blogs and journals are useful for their discussion of current issues in RA service. One good one is *RA for All* (raforall.blogspot.com), and *Citizen Reader* (www.citizenreader.com), which covers nonfiction, is another. *Library Journal* has been carrying an ongoing series of columns by Neal Wyatt on RA service, and is also available online (www.libraryjournal.com). *Reference and User Services Quarterly (RUSQ)* is the official journal of the Reference and User Services Association of the American Library Association. In recent years, this journal has been covering RA service often, and is also available online (www.rusq.org). Unfortunately, there is at this time no journal devoted entirely to RA service. *Readers' Advisor News* (www.readersadvisoronline.com/ ranews), sponsored by Libraries Unlimited, is a newsletter that has some very good articles, but it is not published regularly.

Subscribing to Fiction_L (www.webrary.org/rs/flmenu.html) is a great way to keep up with display ideas, to get help in answering RA questions, and to keep in touch with readers' advisors around the country. *Publishers Lunch* (http://lunch.publishersmarketplace.com/) is a book trade insider publication that often gets the gossip first. The Independent Booksellers Association (www .indiebound.org) features many useful tools on its site, like the IndieBound bestseller lists, printable shelf talkers (short book annotations that can be attached to a book shelf), and more.

Another great way to keep up is to be aware of magazines about books. These include *Bookmarks* (www.bookmarksmagazine.com), *Romantic Times* (www.rtbookreviews.com), *Locus* (www.locusmag.com), *Mystery Scene* (http:// mysteryscenemag.com), *The Believer* (www.believermag.com), *Fantasy & Science*

Fiction (www.sfsite.com/fsf), and *The Historical Novels Review* (www.his toricalnovelsociety.org/the-review.htm). This is, of course, in addition to traditional book review journals for librarians like *Library Journal*, *Kirkus Reviews*, *Booklist*, *Publishers Weekly*, and even *Entertainment Weekly* (ew .com).

There are hundreds of book blogs on the Internet, and finding a few favorites and adding them to your RSS feed is a good way to keep up with titles as well. Some are quite specific to particular genres, like *Smart Bitches, Trashy Books* (www.smartbitchestrashybooks.com), which covers Romance. Some post only reviews, while others publish industry news. Some of the top-ranked book blogs include *McSweeney's* (www.mcswee neys.net), *Blog of a Bookslut* (www.bookslut.com), *Omnivoracious* (www .omnivoracious.com), *Book Ninja* (www.bookninja.com), and *Jacket Copy* (http://latimesblogs.latimes.com/jacketcopy).

Keeping up means going to any workshops, author events, or training sessions that you can; attending conferences, especially the Public Library Association conference held every other year; and reading *about* reading to increase your knowledge.

But one last plea, if I may: Please give back by writing articles or books and doing presentations yourself. Many of the readers' advisors who contribute professionally are at, past, or nearing retirement age. Being able to keep up means that those interested in furthering the knowledge of RA service must step up and contribute to the profession. Remember that most library schools still do not teach this subject, so it's up to you. Keep up the good work, but please pass it on.

NOTES

Baker, Sharon L. 1996. "A Decade's Worth of Research on Browsing Fiction Collections." In *Guiding the Reader to the Next Book*, edited by K. Shearer, 127–47. New York: Neal-Schuman Publishers.

Baker, Sharon L. 1988. "Will Fiction Classification Schemes Increase Use?" *RQ* 27, no. 3 (Spring): 366–76.

Baker, Sharon L., and Gay W. Shepherd. 1987. "Fiction Classification Schemes: The Principles Behind Them, and Their Success." *RQ* 27, no. 2 (Winter): 245–51.

Baker, Sharon L., and Karen L. Wallace. 2002. *The Responsive Public Library: How to Develop and Market a Winning Collection*. 2nd ed. Englewood, CO: Libraries Unlimited.

Seipp, Michele, Sandra Lindberg, and Keith Curry Lance. 2002. "Book Displays Increase Fiction Circulation Over 90%, Non-Fiction, 25%."

Library Research Service Fast Facts (May 1): ED3/110.10/No. 184. www.lrs
    .org/documents/fastfacts/184display.pdf
Underhill, Paco. 2008. *Why We Buy*. Rev. ed. New York: Simon & Schuster.
Wyatt, Neal. 2008. "Take the RA Talk Online." *Library Journal*, February 15.
    www.libraryjournal.com/article/CA6529404.html

PART III

THE GENRES

Chapter 7

Historical Fiction

Sarah Johnson

Historical Fiction has exploded in popularity since the mid-1990s, achieving both a wide readership and critical acclaim. The trend shows no signs of slowing down, prompting declarations that we're currently experiencing a Historical Fiction renaissance. These books appear regularly on bestseller lists, with Ken Follett's *Fall of Giants*, Philippa Gregory's *The Red Queen*, and David Mitchell's *The Thousand Autumns of Jacob de Zoet* ranked prominently on *Publishers Weekly*'s list of the highest selling titles of 2010. In *Booklist*'s annual spotlight on historical novels for 2010, editor Bill Ott looked back on the 13 years since Charles Frazier's landmark novel *Cold Mountain* was published, attempting to put things in perspective: "Is it still a renaissance, or have we moved on to a new golden age? Either way, neither the quantity nor the quality of Historical Fiction seems to have abated one bit [since then]" (Ott). Readers often seek out historical novels as book club choices, discovering that they encourage thoughtful discussion on the characters, setting, and how day-to-day life has changed over time.

Not only do these novels continue to be popular on library and bookstore shelves, but the genre has also several new awards to call its own, demonstrating the respect it has been receiving in the literary community. The launch of the Walter Scott Prize in 2010 (with Hilary Mantel's revisionist look at Tudor-era statesman Thomas Cromwell, *Wolf Hall*, taking home the £25,000 award) gave additional exposure not only to the seven highly acclaimed novels on the short list, but also to the field as a whole. In describing the importance of the prize, historian and awards chair Alistair Moffat explained the reasons behind the boom in historical novels. "They [authors] are giving history back its stories," he said. "Historical fiction may have become more popular because at a time when the future seems terrifying to us, we need to refer back to and understand the past more fully" (Flood). *Wolf Hall* had also won the Booker Prize in 2009, a year in which all six books on that short list were historical novels. This caused some grumbling, though Booker Prize chair Lucasta Miller ably defended her committee's choices. "Some of the strongest historical and biographical writing at the moment is being done by novelists," she explained (Miller).

On this side of the Atlantic, the Reading List Award, inaugurated in 2007 by the Collection Development and Evaluation Section (CODES) of the Reference and User Services Association (RUSA) within American Library Association (ALA), celebrates outstanding genre fiction in eight categories, including Historical Fiction. The Langum Prize, honoring U.S.-set historical novels, has been gaining prominence since its inception in 2003, and other prizes are given for excellence in subgenres like Historical Mystery, Historical Romance, and Western Historical Fiction.

DEFINITION

On the surface, defining "Historical Fiction" seems simple: the term refers to novels set in the past. However, how far back should a novel take place in order to define it as historical and whose past are we talking about—the reader's or the author's? For example, does Jane Austen's *Pride and Prejudice* qualify, even though it was both written and set at the turn of the 19th century? Also, should novels set in Manhattan just before 9/11 be counted, because they depict a setting somewhat removed from today? Although books in both categories do provide details on society at a particular moment in time, by this definition, any work of contemporary fiction might be considered "historical" at some point in the future. When readers ask for Historical Fiction, this normally isn't what they mean.

Within this chapter, "Historical Fiction" is defined as fictional works (mainly novels) set before the middle of the last century, ones in which the author is writing from research rather than personal experience. This usually means that the novels take place before the author's life and times. Classic works of literature like Thomas Hardy's *The Return of the Native* and F. Scott Fitzgerald's *The Great Gatsby*, for example, may have great appeal for Historical Fiction fans due to their evocations of daily life in Victorian-era rural Dorset and New York during the Roaring Twenties, respectively. Also, novels taking place during the 1960s and Vietnam War years may be considered Historical Fiction by readers who weren't yet born at those times. These and other such novels are beyond the scope of this chapter, but librarians should be aware that readers may not have the same definition that they do and adjust their readers' advisory interviews accordingly. Chapter 16, Mainstream Fiction, provides information on novels set during and after the 1950s, such as Karl Marlantes' acclaimed Vietnam-era novel *Matterhorn*.

CHARACTERISTICS AND APPEALS

At its best, Historical Fiction can serve as a form of armchair time-travel. Its readers enjoy immersing themselves in the day-to-day lives and mindsets of people who lived during earlier eras. They seek out novels that evoke the past by including information on all aspects of life: customs, fashion, religion, cuisine, architecture, and more. In reading historical novels, readers can vicariously experience what it might have been like to be a young aristocratic woman living through the French Revolution (Catherine Delors' *Mistress of the Revolution*) or an adolescent boy fighting in a shield wall in Viking-era England (Bernard Cornwell's *The Last Kingdom*). These books let readers imagine all the sights, sounds, and even smells of an earlier era, and all of these little details can make the setting come alive. The historical frame should be presented in an authentic way, in order to convince readers that the world may have actually existed as described. At the same time, an accurate historical backdrop isn't nearly enough. If that were the case, readers would be satisfied with reading history books covering the same period. While there is a significant crossover readership between historical novels and nonfiction texts such as narrative histories and biographies, they provide a different type of reading experience. The "fiction" part of Historical Fiction adds emotional intensity, something that straight history can't easily provide.

Readers choose historical novels based on a variety of factors. Some hone in on specific time periods and settings, reading everything they can get their hands on about the people and events involved. Some enjoy reading about characters who actually lived, while others prefer an author's fictional creations. The type of historical content (political, social, economic, etc.) can play into readers' decisions on what to read next, as can the level of realism—which can vary considerably within the genre. The novels in Jean Plaidy's Plantagenet Saga, for instance, present a clean, somewhat romanticized version of English royal history, while Tim Willocks' *The Religion*, about the 1565 Siege of Malta, is unsparing in its violent detail. The pacing can also vary, with military adventure novels on one end of the spectrum and literary historical novels on the other. Traditional readers' advisory work has focused on making Historical Fiction recommendations based on time and place, but these additional appeal factors should be taken into account when assisting readers as well. For more details on the diversity of and subgenres found within Historical Fiction, see the section labeled "Themes and Types."

BRIEF HISTORY

Historical Fiction is one of the oldest forms of storytelling. Members of long-ago cultures, from Babylonia to ancient Greece and Rome, proudly re-counted tales of their forebears' heroism and defeats. Early works we consider to be classics—Shakespeare's *Hamlet*, Goethe's *Faust*, and even Homer's *Iliad*—were written as fictionalized, embellished retellings of events from long before the author's time. Modern historical novelists continue the tradition by revisit-ing the same characters and themes, often with a new twist (e.g., Jo Graham's *Black Ships* and Ursula K. Le Guin's *Lavinia* are feminine retellings of events from the *Iliad*). This demonstrates that the legacy of these ancient tales has endured.

Sir Walter Scott's *Waverley*, published anonymously in 1814, is generally credited as being the first historical novel. A recent book by Anne H. Stevens demonstrates that other historical novels had been written before that time, though *Waverley*, which attempted to accurately portray ordinary people in-volved in the 1745 Jacobite rebellion against the British crown, did much to pop-ularize the genre. Its subtitle, " 'Tis Sixty Years Since," established the original cutoff date for Historical Fiction, a definition the Walter Scott Prize uses today. To modern readers, Scott's prose seems old-fashioned and cumbersome, but *Wa-verley* inspired many followers and imitators. Among other successful historical novels of the 19th century are Nathaniel Hawthorne's *The Scarlet Letter* (1850, about Puritan New England), Charles Dickens' *A Tale of Two Cities* (1859, about the French Revolution), and Tolstoy's *War and Peace* (1869, about early 19th century Russia). Considered classics now, they were bestsellers in their day. The early 20th century continued this trend, and some of the most highly praised and enduring historical novels were written during this time. Sigrid Undset's *Kris-tin Lavransdatter*, a trilogy following a woman's entire life in medieval Norway, helped win her the Nobel Prize for Literature in 1928. Margaret Mitchell's *Gone with the Wind* (1936), the epic of Civil War and Reconstruction-era Georgia that made icons out of its romantic leads, won the Pulitzer Prize in 1937.

The dichotomy between popular and critically acclaimed historical nov-els began developing in the mid-20th century. This period saw the heightened popularity of Westerns as well as sweeping historical epics, such as those by Anya Seton and Gwen Bristow, that recounted the exploits of intrepid women from American and British history. Then Historical Romances exploded onto the scene in the 1970s, with their lavish tales of wild passion and star-crossed lovers set against vivid backdrops. The extreme popularity of Historical Fic-tion, in its many guises, contributed to its perception as a lowbrow form of lit-erature. Over and over again, authors and the media of the time implied that Historical Fiction was a genre rarely done well; these novels were either bad his-tory—costume dramas with modern-day characters wearing period garb—or bad fiction, in which the author's research overwhelmed the plot. Many acclaimed historical novelists like Rosemary Sutcliff, Howard Fast, and Zoe Oldenbourg made names for themselves in the 1950s through 1980s, but their novels were admired as exceptions to the rule.

Things picked up again in the mid-1990s, when literary writers began looking back to the past for inspiration, and historical novels began winning major prizes once again. Margaret Atwood's *Alias Grace*, about a housemaid tried for her employer's murder in 1843, won the Pulitzer in 1996, and Charles Frazier's *Cold Mountain* won the National Book Award for Fiction in 1997. In the realm of more commercially oriented fiction, Philippa Gregory's *The Other Boleyn Girl* (2002) became a breakout sensation, setting off a craze for other novels about royal women and Tudor-era settings. People's huge and growing interest in historical topics has been shown through the success of films like *Gladiator*, *Elizabeth*, *Girl with a Pearl Earring*, and even the TV miniseries *The Tudors*. In an appropriately named essay for the *Times* in 2010, best-selling novelist Sarah Dunant explained both the appeal and current popularity of Historical Fiction:

> It is the novel, possibly more than any other art form, that can explore complexity over sensation when it comes to the past. Here is a form of time travel in which, if the novelist has done the research, writer and reader can create a fiercely imaginative and challenging experience.
>
> —Dunant

CURRENT TRENDS

It has been said that Historical novels, because they attempt to recreate the past, have a certain timeless quality that novels in other genres lack. This isn't exactly true. Historical Fiction is subject to the same forces of change as other types of fiction (or nonfiction); writing styles, subjects, and other trends come and go. Although the past may seem fixed and unchanging, authors continually approach the same events and personalities in a new light. This ensures that the genre remains fresh and interesting.

Biographical fiction, with a focus on historical women (royal women especially), continues to be all the rage, with many authors—Susan Holloway Scott, Jeanne Kalogridis, Anne Easter Smith, and more—following ably in the footsteps of Philippa Gregory. Novels with strong women protagonists can be easy to spot on library shelves, as their covers frequently showcase female figures wearing beautiful period garb. Not surprisingly, these books have proven most attractive to women readers. Action-adventure novels such as those by Bernard Cornwell and Conn Iggulden are strong draws for male readers in particular (though their appeal isn't limited to men alone), and they are regularly found on bestseller lists. These books, described more fully in the "Historical Adventure" section in this chapter, bring to life the battles and military encounters of long ago.

Topics chosen for Historical novels often reflect trends in history. Beginning in the 1970s, social history came to the forefront in academic circles, with scholars delving into the daily lives of average women, minorities, and other people and topics that had previously remained in the background. The shift in focus away from great men in history—the rulers and conquerors of time past—has uncovered fertile ground for historical novelists, especially those who write literary fiction. Dolen Perkins-Valdez's *Wench*, for instance, depicts four slave women who meet while on vacation with their masters at a summer resort in pre–Civil War Ohio; Geraldine Brooks' *People of the Book* celebrates the Sarajevo Haggadah and the many seemingly average individuals (and religious perspectives) who contributed to its creation and survival.

The trend toward genreblending has expanded the market and audience for Historical novels. Multiperiod novels that alternate between modern and past storylines, such as Katie Hickman's harem novel *The Aviary Gate*, appeal to readers of both historical and contemporary fiction. The six novels in Sara Donati's best-selling Wilderness series have proven very popular with both Historical Fiction and Romance fans. Novels that reach across multiple genres are among the most successful examples of Historical Fiction.

Because of the genre's ability to incorporate many different themes, topics, and styles, it has something to offer almost every reader. Only time will tell how long the Historical Fiction renaissance will last, but fans are reveling in its popularity and thoroughly enjoying the large number of titles available.

Benchmark Titles

Benchmark historical novels encompass a wide range of subgenres, locales, and historical periods. Frequently cited on book jackets, they set standards by which newer novels are measured and are still popular in their own right. Within this chapter, benchmark titles are labeled with ★ in the left-hand column near their appropriate subgenres.

Novels for Book Discussion

Many Historical Fiction titles make good choices for book discussion groups. Literary Historical novels, for example, speak not only of the time period but also the human experience, which can raise many interesting discussion points. Other good choices are Historical novels that present social issues that resonate with today's readers. In this chapter, these titles are labeled with 📖.

Note: A portion of this introduction appeared in Johnson, Sarah L., *Historical Fiction II: A Guide to the Genre.* Copyright (c) 2009 by Sarah L. Johnson. All rights reserved. Reproduced by permission of ABC-CLIO, LLC, Santa Barbara, CA.

NOTES

Dunant, Sarah. 2010. "Historical Fiction Is the Genre of the Moment." *The Times*, June 11. entertainment.timesonline.co.uk/tol/arts_and_enter tainment/books/fiction/article7147658.ece

Flood, Alison. 2010. "Booker Rivals Clash Again on Walter Scott Prize Shortlist." *The Guardian*, April 1. www.guardian.co.uk/books/2010/apr/01/booker-rivals-walter-scott-prize-shortlist

Miller, Lucasta. 2009. "The Booker Prize's Historical Novels Aren't Living in the Past." *The Times*, October 3. www.timesonline.co.uk/tol/com ment/columnists/guest_contributors/article6859223.ece

Ott, Bill. 2010. "Special This Issue: Spotlight on Historical Fiction." *Booklist*, April 15, 2.

Stevens, Anne H. 2010. *British Historical Fiction before Scott.* New York: Palgrave Macmillan.

THEMES AND TYPES

Historical fiction is a wide-ranging category, incorporating novels as diverse as Edward Rutherfurd's 1,000-page multigenerational epic *New York*, Sarah Waters's postwar literary ghost story *The Little Stranger*, and Philippa Gregory's Wars of the Roses–era biographical novel *The Red Queen*. Although all of these books are Historical Fiction in its most basic definition, the writing styles are very different, and readers who like one of them may not automatically enjoy the others. Kate Quinn's female-focused epic *Mistress of Rome*, for example, may appeal to a different audience than Conn Iggulden's brawny, fast-paced *Emperor* Historical Adventure series about the exploits of Julius Caesar. Rather than arrange these books by time and place alone, this chapter takes a subgenre approach, looking at characteristics such as storyline, language, pacing, and other appeal factors.

In addition, Historical Fiction combines readily with other genres such as Mystery, Romance, Thrillers, Westerns, and Christian Fiction. Some of the most popular works of Historical Fiction (e.g., Ariana Franklin's award-winning crime novel *Mistress of the Art of Death*) fall into these categories. Due to the structure of this book, readers in search of historical novel genreblends should consult the chapter for the other category. Also, many historical novelists are quite prolific, though for reasons of space, only a selection of their works is included here. For a more comprehensive overview of Historical Fiction in all its forms, readers may wish to consult Sarah Johnson's *Historical Fiction: A Guide to the Genre* (Westport, CT: Libraries Unlimited, 2005) and its sequel, *Historical Fiction II* (2009).

Historical Fiction Key

Traditional Historical Novels

Prehistoric
Ancient Civilizations
Europe and the British Isles
The United States
The Middle East
Asia, Africa, and the Antipodes
Multiperiod Epics
Romantic Historical Novels
Sagas
Historical Adventure

Literary Historical Novels

Ancient Civilizations
Europe and the British Isles
The United States
Canada, Greenland, and the Arctic
Latin America and the Caribbean
The Middle East
Asia, Africa, and the Antipodes
Alternate History

Traditional Historical Novels

The novels in this section are those most commonly thought of as Historical Fiction: straightforwardly told tales with appealing protagonists, well-paced narratives, and plotlines in which the historical background plays a major role. Their authors are strong storytellers, and their goal is twofold: to portray a historical period as realistically as possible and to entertain. If these purposes happen to conflict, explanations are often provided in an author's note at the end of the book. The characters may be real-life figures whose lives are imagined against a vividly rendered historical backdrop, invented creations, or a mix, with historical characters interacting with fictional ones. Many of these novels are biographical, following one or more characters through the major events of their lives.

Prehistoric

Novels set before the time of recorded history that attempt to recreate life in prehistoric times accurately.

Must Read

★ **Auel, Jean M. *Clan of the Cave Bear*.** Crown, 1980. 468p. 0517542 021. Ayla, a Cro-Magnon woman living in Europe 30,000 years ago, searches for her place in a world populated by Neanderthals. First in Auel's six-volume Earth's Children Series; *Land of the Painted Caves* (2011) is the final volume.

Austin, Debra. *Daughter of Kura*. Touchstone, 2009. 310p. 9781439112663. The fictional recreation of a matriarchal system in prehistoric southeast Africa, based on the author's expertise in paleoanthropology.

Barnes, Steven. *Great Sky Woman*. Ballantine, 2006. 368p. 978034545 9008. Spiritually focused fiction set in the shadow of Africa's Mt. Kilimanjaro in prehistoric times.

Gear, W. Michael, and Kathleen O'Neal Gear

The Gears are professional archaeologists, and the novels in their 15-volume **First North Americans Series** are based on the latest archaeological findings about Native American civilizations and cultures. The settings range from prehistoric Siberia to the Iroquois tribes in the early 15th century. *People of the Wolf* (1990) is the first volume.

Hearst, Dorothy. *Promise of the Wolves*. Simon & Schuster, 2008. 341p. 9781416569985. Prehistoric fiction uniquely told from the viewpoint of the sentient wolves living in a wolf pack in Europe some 10,000 years ago.

Wood, Barbara. *Woman of a Thousand Secrets*. St. Martin's, 2008. 483p. 9780312363697. In this exciting adventure story, Tonina, an "island girl," searches for her true heritage through 14th century Guatemala and Mexico.

Ancient Civilizations

Novels set in biblical times or in ancient lands such as Greece, Rome, or Egypt.

Bradshaw, Gillian. *The Sun's Bride*. Severn House, 2008. 231p. 9780727866417. A beautiful woman rescued from pirates in 246 BC turns out to be a royal concubine.

📖 **Edghill, India.** *Delilah*. St. Martin's, 2009. 354p. 9780312338916. A feminine reinterpretation of the traditional Bible story, with Delilah as a devout temple priestess who refuses to betray the kindhearted man she loves.

George, Margaret. *Helen of Troy*. Viking, 2006. 624p. 0670037788. A sweeping recreation of the Trojan War and the legendary woman known as Helen of Troy, who narrates her tragic life story about beauty, fate, and destiny.

Must Read

★ **Graves, Robert.** *I, Claudius*. H. Smith and R. Haas, 1934. 494p. The Emperor Claudius wryly looks back on his life and his unlikely path to power in ancient Rome. *Claudius the God and His Wife Messalina* (1935) is the sequel.

Harris, Robert

Cicero Series. A lively yet fact-based account, in two parts, about Cicero, a "new man" from the provinces, and his path to Rome's highest office in the 1st century BC.

Imperium. Simon & Schuster, 2006. 305p. 074326603X.
Conspirata. Simon & Schuster, 2010. 340p. 9780743266109.

Must Read

★ **McCullough, Colleen.** *The First Man in Rome*. William Morrow, 1990. 896p. 068809368X. The political rivalry between statesmen Gaius Marius and Lucius Cornelius Sulla takes center stage during the declining years of the Roman Republic, circa 110 BC. First in the <u>Masters of Rome Series</u>.

Moran, Michelle

Moran's novels of ancient Egypt, briskly paced with plenty of historical detail, can be enjoyed by young adults as well.

📖 *Cleopatra's Daughter*. Crown, 2009. 431p. 9780307409126. The story of Kleopatra Selene and her twin brother taken to Rome after the suicide of their parents, Cleopatra and Mark Antony.

📖 *The Heretic Queen*. Crown, 2008. 383p. 9780307381750. Princess Nefertari rises from palace outcast and suspected heretic to become Pharaoh Ramses' beloved wife.

📖 *Nefertiti*. Crown, 2007. 460p. 9780307381460. The family bond and rivalry between ambitious Nefertiti and her peace-loving younger sister, Mutny.

Must Read

★ **Pressfield, Steven.** *Gates of Fire*. Doubleday, 1998. 386p. 03854 92510. The valiant but hopeless defense made by 300 Spartan soldiers against Persia at the Battle of Thermopylae in 480 BC. Thrilling writing and exemplary character development.

Quinn, Kate

Daughters of Rome. Berkley, 2011. 385p. 9780425238974. The lives, loves, and schemes of four female cousins during the Year of the Four Emperors, AD 69.

Mistress of Rome. Berkley, 2010. 469p. 9780425232477. In this lush, romantically tinged epic of first century Rome, Thea, an ambitious slave girl, captures the eye of Emperor Domitian.

Must Read

★ **Renault, Mary. _The King Must Die_**. Pantheon, 1958. 338p. History mingles with myth in this classic novel about Theseus, the future King of Athens.

📖 **Rourke, Mary. _Two Women of Galilee_**. Mira, 2006. 244p. 0778323749. A gentle story of Mary, future mother of Jesus, and her cousin Joanna, a late believer in Him.

Europe and the British Isles

Historical novels set in Europe, England, Scotland, or Ireland from the Middle Ages through the mid-20th century.

Alexander, Robert. _The Romanov Bride_. Viking, 2008. 306p. 9780670018819. The lead-up to the Bolshevik Revolution as seen by Grand Duchess Elizabeth, a member of the Romanov imperial family, and Pavel, a revolutionary peasant whose path frequently crosses hers.

Anton, Maggie

Thoroughly researched, the **Rashi's Daughters Trilogy** fictionalizes the three daughters of medieval Jewish scholar Rashi: Joheved, Miriam, and Rachel.

📖 **_Rashi's Daughters: Book 1, Joheved_**. Banot, 2005. 369p. 0976305054. In this first volume, Rashi's eldest daughter, who loves learning, chooses between her marriage and her love for the Talmud.

Bennett, Vanora. _Portrait of an Unknown Woman_. William Morrow, 2007. 417p. 9780061256516. Two of Hans Holbein's paintings of Thomas More's family reveal hidden truths. An intriguing interpretation of Tudor times seen through the eyes of More's adopted daughter, Meg Giggs.

Cameron, Michelle. _The Fruit of Her Hands_. Pocket, 2009. 436p. 9781439118221. A smoothly written novel about Shira of Ashkenaz, wife of noted rabbi Meir of Rothenburg in 13th century Europe.

Campion, Emma. _The King's Mistress_. Crown, 2010. 464p. 9780307589255. Merchant's daughter Alice Perrers, stereotyped throughout history as the grasping mistress of Edward III, is presented sympathetically.

Chadwick, Elizabeth. *The Greatest Knight.* Sourcebooks, 2009. 549p. 9781402225185. A rousing historical novel of William Marshal, a knight who served four successive kings of medieval England.

📖 **Cross, Donna Woolfolk.** *Pope Joan.* Three Rivers, 2009. 425p. 9780307452368. In 9th century Germany, a woman secretly takes her deceased brother's place at school and rises to become head of the Catholic Church. This novel about a strong woman who endures adverse circumstances is popular with book groups.

Cullen, Lynn. *The Creation of Eve.* Putnam, 2010. 400p. 978039915 6106. Sofonisba Anguissola, the first major female Renaissance portraitist, becomes embroiled in drama at the Spanish royal court.

Delaney, Frank. *Venetia Kelly's Traveling Show.* Random House, 2010. 427p. 9781400067831. In 1932, a major election year for Ireland, a teenager joins a traveling show in search of his missing father.

Delors, Catherine. *Mistress of the Revolution.* Dutton, 2008. 451p. 9780525950547. Young noblewoman Gabrielle de Montserrat makes difficult choices in order to survive the treacherous years of the French Revolution.

Dunnett, Dorothy

Complex and erudite, the six volumes of **The Chronicles of Lymond** follow an enigmatic 16th century Scottish nobleman, Francis Crawford of Lymond, throughout Europe as the political tides continue to shift.

> *The Game of Kings.* Putnam, 1961. 543–543p.
> *Queens' Play.* Putnam, 1964. 432p.
> *The Disorderly Knights.* Putnam, 1966. 503p.
> *Pawn in Frankincense.* Putnam, 1969. 486p.
> *The Ringed Castle.* Putnam, 1972. 521p.
> *Checkmate.* Putnam, 1975. 581p. 0399114343.

Eisdorfer, Erica. *The Wet Nurse's Tale.* Putnam, 2009. 259p. 97803991 55765. A lively, bawdy story of Victorian-era wet nurse Susan Rose and her determination to get back the child she was forced to give up.

Follett, Ken. *Fall of Giants.* Dutton, 2010. 985p. 9780525951650. An epic, multistranded depiction of five families from the United States, Britain, and Europe who get drawn into the global conflict later known as the World War I.

Must Read

★ **Follett, Ken.** ***The Pillars of the Earth***. NAL, 1990. 896p. 068809368X. A multigenerational epic, featuring strong storytelling and colorful characters from all walks of life, about the construction of a magnificent Gothic cathedral in 12th century England. Made into a TV miniseries in 2010.

Gael, Juliet. *Romancing Miss Bronte*. Ballantine, 2010. 432p. 9780345520043. Mixes fact with fiction in the unexpected love story between Charlotte Brontë and her father's curate, Arthur Bell Nichols.

Gortner, C. W. *The Confessions of Catherine de Medici*. Ballantine, 2010. 416p. 9780345501868. A first-person account of Catherine de Medici, from orphaned Florentine heiress to neglected queen and wife through the time she comes into her own as powerful Queen Mother of France.

Gregory, Philippa

Cousins' War Series. First-person biographical novels about ambitious, powerful royal women during the Wars of the Roses. These can be read as prequels to her *Tudor Novels*, below.

>   *The White Queen*. Touchstone, 2009. 415p. 9781416563686. Beautiful Elizabeth Woodville uses her skills in witchcraft to capture the heart of King Edward IV.
>   *The Red Queen*. Touchstone, 2010. 387p. 9781416563723. Margaret Beaufort, a plain and pious heiress, schemes to achieve her destiny as mother of the future King Henry VII.
>   *The Lady of the Rivers*. Touchstone, 2011. 443p. 9781416563709. Jacquetta of Luxembourg, the future mother of "white queen" Elizabeth Woodville, copes with her family's involvement in the Wars of the Roses.

Tudor Novels. Gregory's best-selling novels of Tudor-era women include incisive characterizations and rich depictions of court life and drama.

>   *The Boleyn Inheritance*. Touchstone, 2006. 518p. 0743272501. Crafty Jane Rochford, intelligent Anne of Cleves, and naive, flirtatious Katherine Howard share the legacy of Anne Boleyn's fall from grace.
>   *The Constant Princess*. Touchstone, 2005. 393p. 074327248X. To achieve her dream of becoming Queen of England, Catalina of Aragon claims her marriage to Henry VIII's older brother was never consummated.

The Other Queen. Touchstone, 2008. 442p. 9781416549123. Shifting loyalties during Mary Queen of Scots' imprisonment in England, from the viewpoints of Mary, the Earl of Shrewsbury, and his redoubtable and thrifty wife, Bess.

Must Read

★ 🎖 📖 **Gregory, Philippa.** ***The Other Boleyn Girl***. Scribner Paperback Fiction, 2002. 664p. 0743227441. Inspiring a movie and a royal woman craze in Historical Fiction, Gregory's breakout novel features the rivalry between Mary Boleyn and her ambitious sister Anne for Henry VIII's affections. RNA Romantic Novel of the Year.

Harper, Karen. *Mistress Shakespeare*. Putnam, 2009. 370p. 9780399155451. Basing her novel upon the puzzling existence of marriage licenses between Shakespeare and two different Annes, Harper imagines the life of spirited Anne Whateley, his true love and helpmeet in London.

Higginbotham, Susan. *The Stolen Crown*. Sourcebooks, 2010. 400p. 9781402237669. The Wars of the Roses through the eyes of Katherine Woodville, sister of the queen, and her husband the Duke of Buckingham.

Must Read

★ **Holland, Cecelia.** ***Great Maria***. Knopf, 1974. 519p. 0394485092. Maria, wife to an ambitious knight in southern Italy in the 11th century, proves that women can indeed hold power in an era that supposedly granted them little.

Kalogridis, Jeanne. *The Devil's Queen*. St. Martin's, 2009. 470p. 9780312368432. Catherine de Medici, the Italian-born queen of 16th century France, relies on her political expertise and training in the black arts. Lush and occasionally lurid.

Maitland, Karen

Company of Liars. Delacorte, 2008. 465p. 9780385341691. In this darkly compelling tale set in 1348, nine travelers band together to outrun the Black Plague. Each person hides a secret.

The Owl Killers. Delacorte, 2009. 509p. 9780385341707. Conflicts between paganism and Christianity in the tiny village of Ulwich in early 14th century England. Edgy suspense and supernatural themes.

Moran, Michelle. *Madame Tussaud*. Crown, 2011. 448p. 9780307588654. The tumultuous life story of Marie Tussaud, both before and after she became a famous wax sculptor during the French Revolution.

Mountain, Fiona. *Lady of the Butterflies*. Putnam, 2010. 544p. 9780399156366. A powerful novel about an extraordinary and misunderstood woman: Lady Eleanor Glanville, a 17th century naturalist who lived her life to the fullest.

Penman, Sharon Kay

While each novel in Penman's Plantagenet Series stands alone, they unite to form a comprehensive picture of 12th century English royalty, from the civil wars of Stephen and Matilda through the tumultuous years of Henry II and Eleanor of Aquitaine. Outstanding characterizations and historical detail.

> *When Christ and His Saints Slept*. Holt, 1995. 746p. 0805010157.
> *Time and Chance*. Putnam, 2002. 528p. 0399147853.
> *Devil's Brood*. Putnam, 2008. 734p. 9780399155260.
> *Lionheart*. Putnam, 2011. 594p. 9780399157851.

Must Read

★ **Penman, Sharon Kay. *The Sunne in Splendour*.** Holt, Rinehart, and Winston, 1982. 936p. Richard III, described by Shakespeare as a hunchbacked traitor, is restored to his proper place as a strong yet misunderstood monarch of medieval England.

Plaidy, Jean

One of royal chronicler Plaidy's best-known series, the 15-volume **Plantagenet Saga** sticks close to historical fact as it traces the English monarchy from the 12th through 15th centuries. *The Plantagenet Prelude* is the first book. Plaidy's other series include the **Norman Trilogy**, **Georgian Saga**, **Tudor Novels**, and the **Queens of England Series**, recommended for those who like their royal history dramatically yet straightforwardly told.

Scott, Susan Holloway. *Royal Harlot*. NAL, 2007. 284p. 0451221346. The notorious Barbara Villiers Palmer, whose sensuality reaped numerous rewards at court, becomes official mistress to Charles II of England.

Must Read

★ **Seton, Anya.** *Katherine*. Houghton Mifflin, 1954. 588p. The star-crossed love story between John of Gaunt, son of King Edward III in medieval England, and his children's governess, Katherine de Roet. A novel beloved by Historical Fiction as well as Romance readers.

Smith, Anne Easter. *A Rose for the Crown*. Touchstone, 2006. 649p. 0743276876. Kate Haute becomes the mistress of King Richard III and the mother of his children. Lengthy, romantic biographical fiction.

Stachniak, Eva. *The Winter Palace*. Bantam, 2012. 464p. 9780 553808124. Varvara, a Polish servant girl, becomes the spy of the woman who will become Catherine the Great and watches her crafty rise to power.

Vantrease, Brenda Rickman. *The Mercy Seller*. St. Martin's, 2007. 432p. 9780312331931. Religious conflicts predominate in this novel about a female scribe with Lollard sympathies in early 15th century Prague and France.

Weir, Alison

Innocent Traitor. Ballantine, 2007. 402p. 9780345494856. Multiple perspectives from those in her circle form a well-rounded portrait of Jane Grey, the nine days' queen.

The Lady Elizabeth. Ballantine, 2008. 477p. 9780345495358. The childhood and adolescence of Elizabeth I, an impressionable young woman who overcomes many obstacles to rule as queen.

The United States

Historical novels set in America between colonial times and the mid-20th century.

📖 **Dallas, Sandra.** *Prayers for Sale*. St. Martin's, 2009. 305p. 9780312 385187. Unexpected friendship springs up between an elderly woman and a teenager in 1936 Colorado. Historical women's fiction that warms the heart as it tackles complex issues.

Grissom, Kathleen. *The Kitchen House*. Touchstone, 2010. 368p. 978143 9153666. In this wrenching debut, Lavinia, a white indentured servant on an 18th century Virginia plantation, views the injustices of slavery from both sides.

Gunning, Sally. *The Widow's War*. William Morrow, 2006. 303p. 0060791578. On Cape Cod in the late 18th century, widow Lyddie Berry refuses to give up her independence and faces the social consequences.

Hambly, Barbara. *Patriot Hearts*. Bantam, 2007. 430p. 9780553804287. Veteran novelist Hambly, who specializes in early American settings, details the intimate lives of four women close to the first four U.S. presidents: Martha Washington, Abigail Adams, Sally Hemings, and Dolley Madison.

☐ **Howe, Katherine.** *The Physick Book of Deliverance Dane*. Voice, 2009. 371p. 9781401340902. In this briskly paced multiperiod novel, a grad student from Marblehead, Massachusetts, discovers a spell book dating from the time of the Salem witch trials. Supernatural elements.

Kamensky, Jane, and Jill Lepore. *Blindspot: By a Gentleman in Exile and a Lady in Disguise*. Spiegel & Grau, 2008. 500p. 9780385526197. A playful cross between mystery and traditional historical involving a portrait painter, his female apprentice (in disguise as a man), and the death of a patriot in 1764 Boston.

🎗 ☐ **Kent, Kathleen.** *The Heretic's Daughter*. Little Brown, 2008. 332p. 9780316024488. A chilling fictional account of the Salem witch trials from the viewpoint of young Sarah Carrier, whose redoubtable mother Martha refuses to make a false confession of witchcraft and is hanged in 1692. Langum Prize.

Kolpan, Gerald. *Etta*. Ballantine, 2009. 322p. 9780345503688. Picaresque adventure in this imagined life of Etta Place, a Philadelphia debutante turned outlaw and mistress of the infamous Sundance Kid.

Lehane, Dennis. *The Given Day*. William Morrow, 2008. 704p. 9780688163181. An epic set at a pivotal but little-documented (at least in fiction) time in U.S. history: the Boston Police Strike of 1919. Features a multiethnic cast from all walks of life.

McNees, Kelly O'Connor. *The Lost Summer of Louisa May Alcott*. Putnam, 2010. 352p. 9780399156526. In an attempt to explain the inspiration for Jo in *Little Women*, McNees imagines a romance between the famed novelist and a young man in 1855 New Hampshire.

📖 **Newman, Janis Cooke.** *Mary*. MacAdam/Cage, 2006. 705p. 193156163X. Revisionist Historical Fiction about First Lady Mary Todd Lincoln, a woman not insane but overemotional and misunderstood.

📖 **O'Brien, Patricia.** *Harriet and Isabella*. Touchstone, 2008. 343p. 9781416552208. Courtroom and family drama in Gilded Age New York as Harriet Beecher Stowe and her sister, Isabella, find themselves on opposite sides of their brother Henry's scandalous adultery trial.

🏵 📖 **Oliveira, Robin.** *My Name is Mary Sutter*. Viking, 2010. 384p. 9780670021673. A finely detailed novel about a courageous woman's fight to overcome prejudice and become a surgeon during the Civil War. Michael Shaara Award.

Must Read

★ 🏵 **Shaara, Michael**. ***The Killer Angels***. ***McKay,*** 1974. 374p. 0679504664. Brutality and heroism at the 1863 Battle of Gettysburg, seen through the eyes of the real-life men who fought in it. Pulitzer Prize.

🏵 **Taylor, Nick.** *The Disagreement*. Simon & Schuster, 2008. 360p. 9781416550655. During the Civil War, John Alan Muro finds himself torn between family responsibilities and his dreams of a medical career. Michael Shaara Award.

The Middle East

Lush, exotic, and adventurous historical novels in Middle Eastern settings.

📖 **Amirrevani, Anita.** *The Blood of Flowers*. Little, Brown and Co., 2007. 376p. 9780316065764. A young woman in 17th century Iran struggles to overcome her repressive environment to become a rug designer. Sumptuous detail on art and Persian folktales.

Hickman, Katie. *The Aviary Gate*. Bloomsbury, 2008. 339p. 9781596914759. An Oxford researcher in modern Constantinople traces the story of Celia Lamprey, a 17th century Englishwoman who becomes the Ottoman Sultan's concubine. Parallel narratives.

Johnson, Jane. *The Tenth Gift*. Crown, 2008. 385p. 9780307405227. Two lush and transporting stories are linked through embroidery patterns: that of an English craft shop owner and a 17th century Cornish servant captured into slavery in Morocco.

Pasha, Kamran. *Mother of the Believers*. Atria, 2009. 527p. 9781416579915. An eye-opening look at the birth of Islam seen through the eyes of A'isha, the Prophet Muhammad's youngest and best-loved wife.

Perry, Anne. *The Sheen on the Silk*. Ballantine, 2010. 515p. 9780345500656. History and light mystery mingle as a young woman physician disguised as a eunuch tries to clear her brother's name in 13th century Byzantium, a crossroads of cultures and religions.

📖 **Russell, Mary Doria.** *Dreamers of the Day*. Random House, 2008. 255p. 9781400064717. Agnes Shanklin, a likeable spinster from Cleveland, takes a journey to Egypt and runs into members of the 1919 Cairo Peace Conference.

Asia, Africa, and the Antipodes

Not a large category; historical novels set in Asia, Africa, or Australasia, including Hawaii before statehood.

📖 **Brennert, Alan.** *Honolulu*. St. Martin's, 2009. 360p. 9780312360405. Regret, an unwanted daughter in late 19th century Korea, charts a difficult path toward independence when she travels to Oahu to become a "picture bride."

Sundaresan, Indu. *Shadow Princess*. Atria, 2010. 333p. 9781416548799. A romantic and compelling epic about the building of the Taj Mahal and the rivalry between Emperor Shah Jahan's daughters, Jahanara and Roshanara, both forbidden to marry.

Multiperiod Epics

These lengthy historical novels trace the history of a civilization or a place over an extended period of time, detailing how the political and social history of a setting shaped its people and vice versa. What this category lacks in quantity of titles, it makes up for in page count. Character development isn't always a strong point, although the setting may be considered the most important character of all. Because some multiperiod epics trace the generations of one or more families over centuries, they can be considered the ultimate family saga, though their scope is broader than most in that category.

Delaney, Frank. *Ireland*. HarperCollins, 2005. 559p. 0060563486. In the 1950s, an itinerant storyteller spins rich, folkloric tales of Ireland's long history for a young boy, Ronan, and his family. Captivated, Ronan grows up traveling the country and searching for the truth behind them.

Michener, James

Michener's entertaining novels present the meticulously researched history of the place named in the book's title, tracing it from its prehistoric past through the 20th century. Packed with history and the linked genealogies of the families depicted, his works have a strong social agenda.

> *Alaska*. Random House, 1988. 868p. 0394551540.
> *Hawaii*. Random House, 1959. 937p.
> *Texas*. Random House, 1985. 1096p. 0394541545.

Must Read

★ **Michener, James.** *Hawaii*. Random House, 1959. 937p. A many-stranded, colorful epic of America's 50th state, from its prehistoric past through its multicultural present.

Rutherfurd, Edward

The literary heir to James Michener, Rutherfurd provides entertaining, interlinked stories that span the vast history of a place. The **Dublin Saga** encompasses the history of Dublin, Ireland, and its troubled relationship with England. The dividing point between the two books is the 16th century.

> *The Princes of Ireland*. Crown, 2004. 776p. 0385502869.
> *The Rebels of Ireland*. Crown, 2006. 800p. 0385512899.
> *London*. Crown, 1997. 829p. 0517591812. England's capital city from its Roman beginnings through the present.
> *New York*. Doubleday, 2009. 862p. 9780385521383. Rutherfurd's first American-set epic. Langum Prize.

Saylor, Steven. *Roma*. St. Martin's, 2007. 555p. Hardbound, 0312328311. Follows nearly 1000 years in Rome's history through the stories of two families, covering major events from its beginnings as a minor trading post to the founding of the Roman Empire in 44 BC. *Empire* is the sequel.

Romantic Historical Novels

These novels involve readers emotionally with engaging stories that celebrate the love between two people—most typically a woman and a man. Romantic Historical Novels let readers live vicariously through the experiences of lovers from earlier periods of history. While being entertained, they can see how the political atmosphere, social factors, and everyday life of the times influence the heroes' and heroines' actions. They feature sweeping drama, vividly described settings, and a good balance between romance and historical content. Unlike Historical Romances (presented in Chapter 11), the couples in these novels may or may not have a happy ending.

Donati, Sara

The six books in the **Wilderness Series**, full of lush adventure and romance, follow the lives, loves, and fortunes of members of the Bonner family. The action sweeps from the New York frontier and Canada in the late 18th century to Louisiana and the Caribbean.

> *Into the Wilderness*. Bantam, 1998. 691p. 0553107364.
> *Dawn on a Distant Shore*. Bantam, 2000. 463p. 0553107488.
> *Lake in the Clouds*. Bantam, 2002. 613p. 0553801406.
> *Fire along the Sky*. Bantam, 2004. 624p. 0553801465.
> *Queen of Swords*. Bantam, 2006. 576p. 055380149X.
> *The Endless Forest*. Bantam, 2010. 626p. 9780553805260.

Ducharme, Diann. *The Outer Banks House*. Crown, 2010. 304p. 978030 7462237. Along the North Carolina shoreline during Reconstruction, a touching romance develops between a plantation owner's daughter and a local fisherman.

Furnivall, Kate

The interconnected novels of Furnivall's **Russian Concubine Series** include epic, cross-cultural love stories that play out against tumultuous 20th century settings, moving from St. Petersburg, Russia, in 1910 to the Bolshevik Revolution to Junchow, China, in the 1930s.

The Jewel of St. Petersburg. Berkley, 2010. 432p. 9780425234235.
The Russian Concubine. Berkley, 2007. 517p. 9780425215586.
The Girl from Junchow. Berkley, 2009. 500p. 9780425227640.

Must Read

★ **Gabaldon, Diana.** *Outlander*. Delacorte, 1991. 627p. 0385302304. Claire Randall, a former World War II combat nurse, is torn between past and present after she goes back in time to mid 18th century Scotland and falls in love with a handsome red-haired Scotsman. *An Echo in the Bone* (2009) is the latest in this six-volume series.

Haeger, Diane

The Queen's Mistake. NAL, 2009. 400p. 9780451228000. Teenaged Catherine Howard, Henry VIII's fifth wife, becomes a tragic victim of her own romantic past.

The Secret Bride. NAL, 2008. 398p. 9780451223135. Mary Tudor, the beautiful younger sister of Henry VIII, secretly weds the man she loves: the king's best friend, dashing Charles Brandon.

📖 **Hantover, Jeffrey.** *The Jewel Trader of Pegu*. William Morrow, 2008. 227p. 9780061252709. In 1598, a merchant named Abraham travels to the Burmese kingdom of Pegu, where he encounters strange customs and tender romance.

Haran, Maeve. *The Lady and the Poet*. St. Martin's, 2010. 370p. 9780312554156. A sensitively written star-crossed love story between 16th century poet John Donne and Ann More, whose parents refused permission for her to marry him.

James, Syrie. *The Lost Memoirs of Jane Austen*. Avon, 2007. 303p. 9780061341427. Imagines a gentle yet passionate midlife romance between the noted author and a gentleman she meets at a seaside resort in the early 1800s.

Koen, Karleen

The **Through a Glass Darkly Series** contains plenty of adventure and romance in wildly decadent London during the Restoration and early 18th century and, later, in prerevolutionary America. Stubborn Alice

Verney, the protagonist of *Dark Angels*, appears as the grandmother of heroine Barbara Alderley in the next two books.

> *Dark Angels*. Crown, 2006. 530p. 0307339912.
> *Now Face to Face*. Random House, 1995. 733p. 0394569296.
> *Through a Glass Darkly*. Random House, 1986. 738p. 0394553780.

Must Read

★ ♟ **Mitchell, Margaret. *Gone with the Wind*.** Macmillan, 1936. 1037p. In addition to showcasing the stormy romance between Scarlett O'Hara and Rhett Butler, Mitchell's Civil War epic is a poignant tribute to the struggles and lost glory of the South. Pulitzer Prize.

Simons, Paullina

The **Bronze Horseman Trilogy** uses World War II–era Leningrad as a backdrop and follows the troubled life of beautiful Tatiana, who falls in love with the Red Army officer her sister wants for herself. War, romance, and tragedy.

> *The Bronze Horseman*. William Morrow, 2001. 637p. 0060199261.
> *Tatiana and Alexander*. Madison Park, 2005. 559p. 158288191X.
> *The Summer Garden*. William Morrow 2011. 755p. 9780061988226.

Willig, Lauren

Regency period adventure combines with romance and the lighthearted tone of Chick Lit in the multiperiod **Pink Carnation Series**. While modern-day women investigate the elusive history of Napoleonic spies, they pursue their own romantic leads.

> *The Secret History of the Pink Carnation*. Dutton, 2004. 388p. 05295946800.
> *The Masque of the Black Tulip*. Dutton, 2005. 416p. 0525949208.
> *The Deception of the Emerald Ring*. Dutton, 2006. 400p. 0525949771.
> *The Seduction of the Crimson Rose*. Dutton, 2008. 400p. 9780525950332.
> *The Temptation of the Night Jasmine*. Dutton, 2009. 388p. 9780525950967.

The Betrayal of the Blood Lily. Dutton, 2010. 401p. 9780525951506.
The Orchid Affair. Dutton, 2011. 416p. 9780525951995.
The Garden Intrigue. Dutton, 2012. 400p. 9780525952541.

Sagas

Sagas focus on characters' domestic lives and family relationships over an extended period of time. Most Sagas follow several generations of one family or of multiple families, and because of their detailed, involved story lines, they tend to be long books. They often appear in multiple volumes, giving readers a sense of continuity as history marches on, and they emphasize social rather than political subjects. Their protagonists don't necessarily serve as instruments of change for large-scale events, but they find their lives greatly affected by the changes sweeping around them. The popularity of Sagas peaked in the 1970s and 1980s, although they still command a devoted readership, particularly among older women.

Anand, Valerie

Prolific historical novelist Anand (she also writes as Fiona Buckley) centers her **Exmoor Saga** on the daily lives, squabbles, and secrets among several families living in England's rural West Country.

> *The House of Lanyon*. Mira, 2007. 586p. 9780778325024. 15th century; the Wars of the Roses are a distant backdrop.
> *The House of Allerbrook*. MIRA, 2008. 537p. 9780778326014. This continuation takes place during Tudor times.

Cookson, Catherine

The **Tilly Trotter Saga** tells the life story of Matilda "Tilly" Trotter, a spirited young woman who survives hard times in England's County Durham in the Victorian era and, later, makes her own way on the American frontier. Full of authentic dialect and regional history.

> *Tilly*. William Morrow, 1980. 372p. 0688037151.
> *Tilly Wed*. William Morrow, 1981. 310p. 0688001882.
> *Tilly Alone*. William Morrow, 1982. 265p. 0688004555.

Delderfield, R. F.

The **Swann Family Saga** follows the descendants of Adam Swann, a British army officer, and his wife, Henrietta, as they build a transportation empire between the 1850s and World War I. The emphasis is social and economic history.

> *God Is an Englishman*. Simon & Schuster, 1970. 687p. 0671205021.
> *Theirs Was the Kingdom*. Simon & Schuster, 1971. 798p. 0671210246.
> *Give Us This Day*. Simon & Schuster, 1973. 767p. 0671216589.

Graham, Winston

The 12-volume **Poldark Saga,** a masterpiece of characterization and regional drama, is set along the bleak Cornwall coast in the late 18th and early 19th centuries.

> *The Renegade*. Doubleday, 1951. 344p. The Poldark series opener features the growing relationship between Captain Ross Poldark and his unlikely choice for wife, miner's daughter Demelza. *Ross Poldark* is an alternate title.

Must Read

★ 🎖 **Haley, Alex. *Roots***. Doubleday, 1976. 688p. 0385037872. A masterpiece of social history, this fictionalized account of the author's African ancestors begins in Gambia in the 1750s and follows their descendants as they rise up from slavery and discrimination in America. Pulitzer Prize.

Harrod-Eagles, Cynthia

The long-running **Morland Dynasty Series**, 32 volumes and counting, follows the members of one extended family, the Morlands of Yorkshire, through 500 years of English history: from the Wars of the Roses through World War I. *The Founding* is the first book.

Jakes, John

Jakes's classic **North and South Trilogy,** made into a popular TV miniseries, tells of two families, the Mains and the Hazards, on opposite sides of the U.S. Civil War.

North and South. Harcourt Brace Jovanovich, 1982. 740p. 01516 69988.

Love and War. Harcourt Brace Jovanovich, 1984. 1019p. 0151544964.

Heaven and Hell. Harcourt Brace Jovanovich, 1987. 700p. 0151310750.

Meacham, Leila. *Roses*. Grand Central, 2010. 609p. 9780446550000. In this grand Southern epic about three families from east Texas, elderly cotton magnate Mary Toliver DuMont reminisces about her long, troubled life; her romantic past; and her relationship with her land.

Morton, Kate

The Distant Hours. Atria, 2010. 562p. 9781439152782. A misdelivered letter leads Edie Burchill into uncovering a World War II–era Gothic mystery involving three eccentric sisters, their author father, a missing fiancé, and Edie's own mother. A multiperiod story.

The Forgotten Garden. Atria, 2009. 552p. 9781416550549. Spanning most of the 20th century in Australia and Cornwall, this multigenerational story delves into the origins of a little girl who arrives alone in Brisbane in 1913.

The House at Riverton. Atria, 2008. 469p. 9781416550518. An engrossing Edwardian saga with a good dose of mystery, revealed through the recollections of a now-elderly former maidservant for an aristocratic English family.

Rosen, Elizabeth Payne. *Hallam's War*. Unbridled, 2008. 473p. 9781932961492. The Hallam family of rural West Tennessee comes to terms with the reality of slavery when the Civil War breaks out. A literary saga.

Swerling, Beverly

The entertaining **City Series** traces the social and economic development of Manhattan from the 16th through late 19th centuries via the colorful Turner and Devrey families, members of which come from all walks of life. *Shadowbrook*, unlike the others, takes place in Upstate New York, Ohio, and Quebec during the French and Indian War.

City of Dreams. Simon & Schuster, 2001. 591p. 0684871726.

Shadowbrook. Simon & Schuster, 2004. 490p. 074322812X.

City of Glory. Simon & Schuster, 2006. 465p. 9780743269209.

> *City of God*. Simon & Schuster, 2008. 522p. 9781416549215.
> *City of Promise*. Simon & Schuster, 2011. 422p. 9781439136942.

Tademy, Lalita

The standalone novels in the **Cane River Series** depict African American and French Creole life and culture along Louisiana's Cane River.

> *Cane River*. Warner, 2001. 418p. 0446527327. Follows four generations of women from Tademy's ancestry from slavery through freedom, showing the complicated ties between slaves and their owners.
> *Red River*. Warner, 2007. 420p. 9780446578981. Continues Tademy's family story, beginning with the racial violence of the Colfax riots of 1873 and for the next 70 years.

Todd, Jack

Todd's **Paint Saga** is a swift-moving Western family drama with colorful characters and authentic descriptions of the landscape, from the Civil War through the 1940s.

> *Sun Going Down*. Touchstone, 2008. 467p. 9781416550488.
> *Come Again No More*. Touchstone, 2010. 368p. 9781416598497.
> *Rain Falls Like Mercy*. Touchstone, 2011. 304p. 9781416598510.

Historical Adventure

Historical Adventure novels incorporate heroic protagonists, fast-paced plots, and well-realized physical settings. Their readers become armchair travelers, learning about new, unfamiliar civilizations and ways of life as they follow the hero's journey. Many of these novels involve military action and depict the lives of soldiers and sailors from long ago. Men are the primary characters as well as the primary readers, and most of these books occur in series.

Clavell, James. *Shōgun*. Atheneum, 1975. 802p. In 1600 Japan, Elizabethan adventurer John Blackthorne encounters exotic customs, undergoes samurai training, and falls in love.

Cornwell, Bernard

🎗 *Agincourt*. Harper, 2009. 451p. 9780061578915. The pivotal battle of the Hundred Years' War, an English victory over France in AD 1415, comes alive with fierce military action and plenty of mud, blood, and gore. Reading List Award.

The **Saxon Chronicles** are seen from the viewpoint of Uhtred of Bebbanburg, a Saxon boy who comes of age as he takes the side of Alfred the Great against invading Viking warriors.

> *The Last Kingdom*. HarperCollins, 2005. 333p. 0060530510.
> *The Pale Horseman*. HarperCollins, 2006. 349p. 0060787120.
> *Lords of the North*. HarperCollins, 2007. 317p. 9780060888626.
> *Sword Song: The Battle for London*. HarperCollins, 2008. 314p. 9780060888640.
> *The Burning Land*. HarperCollins, 2009. 336p. 9780007219742.
> *Death of Kings*. HarperCollins, 2012. 336p. 9780061969652.

In Cornwell's rip-roaring **Sharpe Novels** set during the Napoleonic era, Richard Sharpe moves up the ranks in the British army as he fights evil villains around the globe on Britain's behalf. Each of the 21 books centers on a different battle or military expedition. Although *Sharpe's Tiger* (1997) is the first chronologically, they can be read in any order.

Dietrich, William

The **Ethan Gage Series**, narrated by American expatriate Gage, details his daring expeditions from Paris to the Middle East as he becomes embroiled in mysteries surrounding ancient artifacts.

> *Napoleon's Pyramids*. HarperCollins, 2007. 384p. 9780060848323.
> *The Rosetta Key*. HarperCollins, 2008. 339p. 9780061239557.
> *The Dakota Cipher*. Harper, 2009. 355p. 9780061568008.
> *The Barbary Pirates*. Harper, 2010. 328p. 9780061567964.

Forester, C. S.

The classic **Horatio Hornblower Series** includes technically accurate detail with skillful characterization as it follows the budding naval career of Horatio Hornblower during the Age of Sail.

> *Mr. Midshipman Hornblower*. Little, Brown, 1950. 310p. Kicks off the series with a 17-year-old Hornblower joining the British navy during the French Revolution.

Gemmell, David and Stella

The **Troy Series** presents a reimagined version of the traditional Trojan War myth, with Gemmell's taut writing style, fierce action, and incisive characterizations. After David Gemmell's untimely death, his wife completed the last volume of the series.

> *Troy: Lord of the Silver Bow*. Del Rey, 2005. 476p. 0345458354.
> *Troy: Shield of Thunder*. Del Rey, 2006. 490p. 0345477014.
> *Troy: Fall of Kings*. Del Rey, 2008. 447p. 9780345477033.

Guillou, Jan

In his **Crusades Trilogy**, bestselling Swedish novelist Guillou follows the travels of Swedish aristocrat Arn Magnusson on crusade to the Middle East, where he becomes a Knight Templar.

> *The Road to Jerusalem*. Harper, 2009. 399p. 9780061688539.
> *The Templar Knight*. Harper, 2010. 480p. 9780061688577.
> *Birth of the Kingdom*. Harper, 2011. 496p. 9780061688638.

Iggulden, Conn

Genghis Khan, the 13th century warrior who united the Mongol tribes, is the initial protagonist of Iggulden's action-packed **Conqueror Series**, which continues in later volumes with his descendants.

> *Genghis: Birth of an Empire*. Delacorte, 2007. 383p. 9780385339513. Alex
>   Award.
> *Genghis: Lords of the Bow*. Delacorte, 2008. 400p. 9780385339520.
> *Genghis: Bones of the Hills*. Delacorte, 2009. 405p. 9780385339537.
> *Khan: Empire of Silver*. Delacorte, 2010. 387p. 9780385339544.
> *Conqueror: A Novel of Kublai Khan*. Delacorte, 2012. 496p. 9780385343053.

The **Emperor Series** comprises four strongly plotted adventure novels about Julius Caesar, his path to power, and his military campaigns.

> *Emperor: The Gates of Rome*. Delacorte, 2003. 357p. 0385336608.
> *Emperor: The Death of Kings*. Delacorte, 2004. 469p. 0385336624.
> *Emperor: The Field of Swords*. Delacorte, 2005. 466p. 0385336632.
> *Emperor: The Gods of War*. Delacorte, 2006. 383p. 0385337671.

Lambdin, Dewey

The 17-volume (and counting) **Alan Lewrie Series** follows a young man who grows into an experienced sailor in the Royal Navy while leaving scandal in his wake when he's on land. Napoleonic adventures. *The King's Coat* (1989) begins the series.

Must Read

★ **O'Brian, Patrick. *Master and Commander*.** Lippincott, 1969. 384p. Stirring nautical adventure about Captain Jack Aubrey and his ship's surgeon, Stephen Maturin, as they fight in Britain's Napoleonic Wars. First in the 21-volume <u>Aubrey-Maturin Series</u>.

Perez-Reverte, Arturo

The **<u>Captain Alatriste Series</u>**, bestsellers in the author's native Spain, are swashbuckling adventure novels about Captain Alatriste, a legendary 17th century swordsman, and his loyal squire, Iñigo. Six titles in all.

> *Captain Alatriste*. Putnam, 2005. 253p. 039915275X. In the series debut, Diego Alatriste becomes a hired swordsman in Madrid after incurring injuries fighting in Spain's Flemish wars.

Shaara, Jeff

Shaara's fact-based **<u>World War II Trilogy</u>** mixes historical and fictional characters from both sides of the conflict in his epic story of World War II in Europe. Excellent characterization and frontline battle action.

> *The Rising Tide*. Ballantine, 2006. 536p. 034546141X.
> *The Steel Wave*. Ballantine, 2008. 493p. 9780345461421.
> *No Less Than Victory*. Ballantine, 2009. 449p. 9780345497925.

🎗 **Willocks, Tim. *The Religion*.** Farrar Straus & Giroux, 2007. 618p. 9780374248659. Mattias Tannhauser, a German soldier-of-fortune, accompanies a Maltese noblewoman back home and gets embroiled in the 1565 siege of the island. Epic storytelling, not for the squeamish. Reading List Award.

Literary Historical Novels

Literary Historical Novels use historical settings, eloquent language, and multilayered plotlines to convey contemporary themes. These character-centered works often address serious issues, and they may not have optimistic endings. Although they tend not to be quick reads, the intriguing, complex characters and involving plotlines draw readers into the story. Because they address timeless issues, these well-researched books are as likely to be called "Contemporary Fiction" as "Historical Fiction." They appeal to Mainstream Fiction readers as well as Historical Novel fans, giving them the potential to reach a wide audience. Readers interested in Literary Fiction with post-1950 settings will find additional titles in Chapter 16.

Ancient Civilizations

Literary, mythologically tinged novels set in biblical times or in ancient lands such as Greece, Rome, or Egypt.

📖 **Beutner, Katharine.** *Alcestis*. Soho, 2010. 304p. 9781569476178. Alcestis, a princess of ancient Greece who gave her life to save her husband, discovers new purpose and strength during her time in the underworld. A feminist reinterpretation of Greek mythology.

Must Read

★ 🏅 📖 **Diamant, Anita. *The Red Tent*.** St. Martin's, 1997. 321p. 0312169787. Dinah, a woman never given a voice in the Old Testament, tells her life story in this delicate yet powerful reexamination of biblical themes from a feminine viewpoint. Book Sense Book of the Year.

📖 **Elliott, Elissa.** *Eve*. Delacorte, 2009. 421p. 9780385341448. A fully human and flawed Eve alternates with her daughters in retelling the biblical story, beginning with their expulsion from the Garden of Eden.

📖 **Le Guin, Ursula K.** *Lavinia*. Harcourt, 2008. 279p. 9780151014248. In this sensitive and lyrical feminine rendering of *The Aeneid*, Lavinia, wife of Aeneas in ancient Rome, is granted a voice.

Malouf, David. *Ransom*. Pantheon, 2010. 224p. 9780307378774. This short novel poetically retells the portion of the *Iliad* dealing with Priam's ransoming of his son's body from Achilles.

Europe and the British Isles

Literary Fiction set in Europe, England, Scotland, or Ireland from the Middle Ages through the mid-20th century.

📖 **Bohjalian, Chris.** *Skeletons at the Feast*. Shaye Areheart, 2008. 372p. 9780307394958. A wealthy Prussian family desperately fights their way west out of Nazi Germany ahead of the invading Russians.

📖 **Brooks, Geraldine.** *People of the Book*. Viking, 2008. 372p. 9780670018215. Hanna Heath, a modern-day book conservator, uncovers the history of the Sarajevo Haggadah, an early illuminated Jewish text.

Must Read

★ 🏆 📖 **Byatt, A. S. *Possession*.** Random House, 1990. 555p. 03945 86239. In uncovering the secret connection (and possible romance) between two 19th century writers, two modern-day British academics draw closer to the truth and to one another. Literary fiction with parallel narratives. Booker Prize.

Must Read

★ 📖 **Chevalier, Tracy. *Girl with a Pearl Earring*.** Dutton, 1999. 233p. 052594527X. Artistic creation and social class structure are explored in Chevalier's seminal literary novel about Griet, a young maidservant in the Vermeer household in 17th century Delft.

Cowell, Stephanie. *Claude and Camille*. Crown, 2010. 338p. 978030 7463210. A literary love story about young Claude Monet and his first wife and muse Camille Doncieux.

📖 **De Rosnay, Tatiana.** *Sarah's Key*. St. Martin's, 2009. 294p. 9780312370 831. The repercussions of the Holocaust in occupied France are retold in this haunting multiperiod tale, set in 1942 and 2002.

Dunant, Sarah

Must Read

★ 📖 ***The Birth of Venus***. Random House, 2003. 397p. 1400060737. In 15th century Florence, a cloth merchant's daughter pursues her dream of becoming a painter despite social constrictions. Rich detail about women's lives at the height of the Renaissance.

📖 *In the Company of the Courtesan*. Random House, 2006. 371p. 1400063817. In 1572, courtesan Fiammetta Bianchini flees Rome for Venice, hoping to reclaim her proper place in society.

📖 *Sacred Hearts*. Random House, 2009. 415p. 9781400063826. In 1570s, Ferrara, a beautiful young noblewoman, is forced into a convent against her will.

Must Read

★ **Faber, Michel. *The Crimson Petal and the White*.** Harcourt, 2002. 838p. 015100692X. A literary epic of 19th century London, Faber's subversion of the traditional (and proper) Victorian novel takes as its heroine a sly prostitute who becomes a rich man's mistress.

Gulland, Sandra. *Mistress of the Sun*. Touchstone, 2008. 382p. 9780743298872. The touching story of Louise de la Vallière, a gentle noblewoman who became an early mistress of Louis XIV of France.

🏵 📖 **Mantel, Hilary. *Wolf Hall*.** Henry Holt and Co., 2009. 532p. 9780805080681. Thomas Cromwell rises to become Henry VIII's right-hand man when the king seeks a divorce to marry Anne Boleyn. A masterpiece of characterization, linguistic finesse, and historical recreation set at the cusp of the English Reformation. *Bring Up the Bodies* (2012) is the sequel. Booker Prize and Walter Scott Prize.

Must Read

★ 🏵 📖 **McEwan, Ian. *Atonement*.** Doubleday, 2002. 351p. 0385503954. Beginning in 1935, a girl's childhood mistake has enormous repercussions for everyone around her, especially the people whose lives she ruined. NBCC Award and ALA Notable Book.

📖 **McLain, Paula. *The Paris Wife*.** Ballantine, 2011. 320p. 9780345521309. The glamorous lives and troubled marriage of Ernest Hemingway and Hadley Richardson, his first wife, in Jazz Age Paris.

Naslund, Sena Jeter. *Abundance*. William Morrow, 2006. 545p. 978006082 5393. Marie Antoinette, the tragic Queen of France, narrates her life story in this sympathetic fictional autobiography.

🎗 📖 **Orringer, Julie.** *The Invisible Bridge*. Knopf, 2010. 597p. 9781400041169. Two Jewish Hungarian lovers get caught up in the tragic tide of history in this literary World War II epic. Reading List Award.

📖 **Shaffer, Mary Ann, and Annie Barrows.** *The Guernsey Literary and Potato Peel Pie Society*. Dial, 2008. 274p. 9780385340991. Juliet Ashton's delightful correspondence with Dawsey Adams, a Guernsey pig farmer, reveals several untold stories of World War II heroism. An epistolary novel set in 1946.

Sharratt, Mary. *Daughters of the Witching Hill*. Houghton Mifflin Harcourt, 2010. 333p. 9780547069678. Two of the accused Pendle witches in 17th century Lancashire, redoubtable matron Bess Southerns and her teenage granddaughter, Alizon Device, tell their stories.

📖 **Vreeland, Susan.** *Luncheon of the Boating Party*. Viking, 2007. 434p. 9780670038541. Renoir's creation of his masterwork (the novel's title), set along the Seine in 1880 Paris, unfolds from the viewpoint of many of his friends and models.

📖 **Waters, Sarah.** *The Little Stranger*. Riverhead, 2009. 466p. 9781594488801. Creepy drama and commentary about the changing social fabric in the post–World War II English countryside filter through this haunted house tale.

The United States

Literary Fiction set in America from colonial times through the mid-20th century.

📖 **Banks, Russell.** *The Reserve*. HarperCollins, 2008. 287p. 9780061 430251. When pilot Jordan Groves touches down on an Adirondack estate in 1936, he becomes unwittingly involved with the estate owner's spoiled and mentally unstable daughter.

📖 **Blake, Sarah.** *The Postmistress*. Amy Einhorn, 2010. 326p. 97803 99156199. In 1940, as war rages in Europe, the lives of three women— a Massachusetts postmistress, a local doctor's wife, and an American radio broadcaster in Britain—intersect in unexpected ways.

📖 **Brooks, Geraldine**

Caleb's Crossing. Viking, 2011. 306p. 9780670021048. An imaginative recreation of the life of Caleb Cheeshahteaumuck, Harvard's first Native

American graduate in the 17th century, as seen from the viewpoint of a minister's daughter.

March. Viking, 2005. 280p. 0670033359. In this literary reimagining of the father from *Little Women*, based on Louisa May Alcott's own father, Mr. March becomes an abolitionist and a chaplain to the Union army. Pulitzer Prize.

📖 **Carey, Peter.** *Parrot and Olivier in America*. Knopf, 2010. 400p. 9780307592620. Carey looks at Alexis de Tocqueville's history-making expedition to America in 1831 through a fictional lens full of wit and adventure, imagining the French philosopher as Olivier, an exiled aristocrat.

🎗 📖 **Doctorow, E. L.** *The March*. Random House, 2006. 384p. 0375506713. In this clever multivoiced novel, Sherman's devastating march through Georgia attracts a motley train of followers. Michael Shaara and NBCC Awards.

Must Read

★ 🎗 **Doctorow, E. L.** *Ragtime*. Random House, 1975. 270p. 0394469011. Intertwining the lives of characters real and fictional, Doctorow explores the exuberant spirit of early 20th century America. NBCC Award.

📖 **Ebershoff, David.** *The 19th Wife*. Random House, 2008. 514p. 9781400063970. This multiperiod tale of polygamy and faith juggles two story lines: one a modern murder mystery and the other a historical tale of Ann Eliza Young, 19th wife of Mormon prophet Brigham Young.

📖 **Ford, Jamie.** *Hotel on the Corner of Bitter and Sweet*. Ballantine, 2009. 290p. 9780345505330. Henry Lee, a Chinese American in 1980s Seattle, reminisces about his youth during World War II, when his best friend, a Japanese girl, was forced into an internment camp.

Must Read

★ 🎗 📖 **Frazier, Charles.** *Cold Mountain*. Atlantic Monthly, 1997. 356p. 0871136791. This dual-perspective literary work features a wounded deserter's flight from the Confederate battlefields back to the woman he loves in the Blue Ridge Mountains of North Carolina. National Book Award, Book Sense Book of the Year, and ALA Notable Book.

📖 **Goolrick, Robert.** *A Reliable Wife.* Algonquin, 2009. 291p. 97815 65125964. When Ralph Truitt, a wealthy businessman in 1907 rural Wisconsin, advertises for a "reliable wife," Catherine Land responds, with deadly intent. Dark literary suspense.

🎖 📖 **Gruen, Sara.** *Water for Elephants.* Algonquin, 2006. 335p. 1565124995. In this warmhearted tale, Jacob Jankowski, an elderly man in a nursing home, reminisces about his time spent as a vet for a traveling circus during the Depression. Alex Award and Book Sense Book of the Year.

Hicks, Robert

📖 *The Widow of the South.* Warner, 2005. 414p. 0446500127. Carrie McGavock (a historical character) transforms her plantation into a graveyard for Confederate soldiers who died in the Battle of Franklin, Tennessee, in 1864.

📖 *A Separate Country.* Grand Central, 2009. 424p. 9780446581646. A novel of tragedy and redemption set in 1870s New Orleans, featuring the later years of former Confederate General John Bell Hood and his wife Anna Marie.

📖 **Hill, Lawrence.** *Someone Knows My Name.* Norton, 2007. 486p. 9780393065787. In this sweeping literary epic, a young African girl, Aminata Diallo, triumphs over slavery by way of education and determination.

📖 **Horan, Nancy.** *Loving Frank.* Ballantine, 2007. 377p. 9780345494993. Mamah Borthwick Cheney flouts conventions and morals when she abandons her husband and children to run off with architect Frank Lloyd Wright in the early 20th century.

📖 **Horn, Dara.** *All Other Nights.* Norton, 2009. 363p. 9780393064926. Jacob Rappaport faces complex moral dilemmas when he's asked to spy for the Union. A unique look at Jewish spies during the Civil War.

🎖 📖 **Jones, Edward P.** *The Known World.* Amistad/HarperCollins, 2003. 400p. 0060557540. When a black slave owner dies in 1840 Virginia, the social order on the plantation is thrown into turmoil. Pulitzer Prize, NBCC Award, and ALA Notable Book.

📖 **Jordan, Hillary.** *Mudbound.* Algonquin, 2008. 320p. 9781565125698. Laura McAllan, a new farm wife on the Mississippi Delta in 1946, adjusts to rural living and the region's racial prejudices.

📖 **McBride, James.** *Song Yet Sung*. Riverhead, 2008. 359p. 9781594489723. Liz Spocott, a runaway slave in pre–Civil War Maryland, uses her precognitive dreams to help her fellow slaves escape to freedom.

Must Read

★ 🏵 📖 **Morrison, Toni.** *Beloved*. Knopf, 1987. 275p. 0394535979. Haunting literary fiction about Sethe, a former slave in post–Civil War Ohio, and the terrible choice she was forced to make regarding her infant daughter. Pulitzer Prize.

🏵 📖 **Otsuka, Julie.** *The Buddha in the Attic*. Knopf, 2011. 144p. 9780307700001. This short poetic novel follows the lives of young women brought from Japan to San Francisco to be "picture brides" in the 1920s. Langum Prize.

📖 **Perkins-Valdez, Dolen.** *Wench*. Amistad, 2010. 293p. 9780061706547. At Tawawa House, a resort in the free state of Ohio in the 1850s, four slave mistresses accompanying their white masters develop a sisterly bond.

📖 **Rash, Ron.** *Serena*. Ecco, 2008. 371p. 9780061470851. In this tale of twisted love, betrayal, and violent revenge, logging magnate George Pemberton brings his new wife Serena to the backwoods of North Carolina in 1929 and discovers her true character.

📖 **Vreeland, Susan.** *Clara and Mr. Tiffany*. Random House, 2011. 405p. 9781400068166. Clara Driscoll, head of Louis Comfort Tiffany's women's division and designer of many of his stained-glass masterpieces, desires to be recognized for her artistic talents in late 19th century New York City.

Canada, Greenland, and the Arctic

Historicals set in Northern climes. Canada is the most common setting.

📖 **Adamson, Gil.** *The Outlander*. Ecco, 2008. 389p. 9780061491252. In 1903, Mary Boulton, a young widow who killed her brutal husband, flees west across Canada, her husband's nasty brothers in pursuit. A novel of survival and suspense.

📖 **Mitchell, Shandi.** *Under This Unbroken Sky*. Harper, 2009. 346p. 9780061774027. This dark frontier tale set in the Depression-era Canadian West features a dysfunctional Ukrainian immigrant family.

📕 **Norman, Howard.** *What Is Left the Daughter*. Houghton Mifflin Harcourt, 2010. 256p. 9780618735433. Recounting his youth in World War II–era Nova Scotia, Wyatt Hillyer tells his daughter, whom he never knew, the story of a crime kept long hidden.

Latin America and the Caribbean

Literary Novels set south of the U.S. border: Mexico, Jamaica, and Haiti.

📕 **Allende, Isabel.** *Island Beneath the Sea*. Harper, 2010. 457p. 9780061988240. Allende, a lyrical and vivid storyteller, recounts the story of Zarité, a mulatto whose life intertwines with that of 18th-century Haiti.

📕 **James, Marlon.** *The Book of Night Women*. Riverhead, 2009. 417p. 9781594488573. Racial and sexual power struggles ensue on a plantation in 19th century Jamaica, where a secret society believes green-eyed Lilith holds the key to a successful slave revolt.

🎖 📕 **Kingsolver, Barbara.** *The Lacuna*. Harper, 2009. 507p. 9780060852573. Kingsolver inserts incisive political commentary into her novel about Mexican American Harrison William Shepherd, caught between two countries in the 1930s–1950s. Orange Prize.

🎖 📕 **Levy, Andrea.** *The Long Song*. Farrar, Straux & Giroux, 2010. 320p. 9780374192174. Miss July, a house slave on a 19th century Jamaican sugar plantation, narrates in lilting voice the story of her life and the Great Slave Revolt on the island. Walter Scott Prize.

The Middle East

Literary novels with Middle Eastern settings: Egypt, Israel, Palestine, and Iraq.

📕 **Diamant, Anita.** *Day After Night*. Scribner, 2009. 294p. 9780743299848. Four Jewish women refugees establish a bond of friendship while in an internment camp in post–World War II Palestine.

📕 **Pullinger, Kate.** *The Mistress of Nothing*. Touchstone, 2011. 250p. 9781439193860. Sally Naldrett, lady's maid to British noblewoman Lady Duff Gordon on her trip to Egypt in the 1860s, is caught between her employer and her desire to be an independent woman.

📕 **Shalev, Meir.** *A Pigeon and a Boy*. Schocken, 2007. 311p. 9780805242515. A romantic tale involving a homing pigeon handler during Israel's war for independence in 1948 intertwines with a modern story.

Unsworth, Barry. *Land of Marvels.* Doubleday, 2009. 287p. 9780385520072. Representatives from several European countries vie for footholds in Mesopotamia (modern-day Iraq) in 1914, foreshadowing today's imperialist tendencies in the region.

Asia, Africa, and the Antipodes

Literary novels set in distant lands such as Australia, China, India, and Japan.

Must Read

★ 📖 **Golden, Arthur.** *Memoirs of a Geisha.* Knopf, 1997. 434p. 03754 00117. Sayuri, a peasant girl from northern Japan in the early 20th century, reveals how she became a world-famous geisha, with copious detail on dance, costume, and training in other social graces.

📖 **Grenville, Kate.** *The Lieutenant.* Atlantic Monthly, 2009. 307p. 9780802119162. Daniel Rooke, a talented British astronomer, travels to New South Wales in 1788 with the military, and his friendship with a young Aboriginal girl forces him into a tough position.

📖 **Kim, Eugenia.** *The Calligrapher's Daughter.* Holt, 2009. 386p. 97808050 89127. Debut novelist Kim, inspired by her mother's life story, writes sensitively about a young Korean woman torn between family and independence in the early 20th century.

Mandanna, Sarita. *Tiger Hills.* Grand Central, 2011. 468p. 9780446564106. The love triangle between three young people in Coorg in southern India in the late 19th century changes their lives forever. A sweeping epic with wonderful historic and geographic detail.

📖 **Min, Anchee.** *Pearl of China.* Bloomsbury, 2009. 288p. 9781596916975. Min, a Chinese American novelist, imagines the life of Pearl Buck in early 20th century China, seen through the eyes of her fictional best friend, Willow.

📖 **Mitchell, David.** *The Thousand Autumns of Jacob de Zoet.* Random House, 2010. 496p. 9781400065455. Interweaving a multiplicity of styles, voices, and motifs, Mitchell sets his literary masterpiece at the crux of two civilizations, Japanese and Dutch, which meet and mingle on the Japanese trading island of Dejima in 1799.

See, Lisa

📖 *Shanghai Girls*. Random House, 2009. 314p. 9781400067114. Pearl and May Chen, two liberated, beautiful young women in 1920s Shanghai, undergo a cultural shift when they're forced to leave home and begin a new life in Los Angeles.

📖 *Snow Flower and the Secret Fan*. Random House, 2005. 258p. 1400060281. A story of the intimate long-term friendship between Lily and Snow Flower in rural 19th century China.

Alternate History

Novels of Alternate (or "alternative") History dramatize other possible outcomes for past events. Their plots hinge on one particular event, typically a military maneuver in a major battle, and examine what may have happened if the result had turned out differently. Because these books deliberately break the rules—they run counter to known history—not all Historical Fiction readers consider them to be part of the field. They appeal to philosophically minded Historical Fiction readers who enjoy puzzling through the causes and effects of major turning points in history. Most books in this relatively small category are fast paced and action oriented, due to the wartime focus.

Conroy, Robert

1942. Ballantine, 2009. 358p. 9780345506078. This swift-moving Thriller, seen from the viewpoint of fictional characters, presupposes that Hawaii was occupied by Japan following the Pearl Harbor attack in 1942.

1945. Ballantine, 2007. 432p. 9780345494795. The tide of war turns when Emperor Hirohito is prevented from surrendering following Hiroshima and Nagasaki, and the United States is forced to invade Japan.

Red Inferno: 1945. Ballantine, 2010. 353p. 9780345506061. Conroy moves to post–World War II Berlin, where Stalin's Red Army attacks American forces moving toward the city.

Fleming, Thomas J. *The Secret Trial of Robert E. Lee*. Forge, 2006. 336p. 0765313529. Confederate General Lee is tried for treason after the end of the Civil War, his treatment debated by newspaper reporters on both sides.

Gingrich, Newt, and William S. Fortschen

The Gettysburg Series, coauthored by former Speaker of the House Gingrich and historian Fortschen, imagines a Confederate victory at the Battle of Gettysburg.

> *Gettysburg*. St. Martin's, 2003. 463p. 031230935X.
> *Grant Comes East*. St. Martin's, 2004. 404p. 0312309376.
> *Never Call Retreat*. St. Martin's, 2005. 496p. 0312342985.

In the World War II Series, the duo collaborates on the subject of the Pacific War, imagining that different Japanese leadership at Pearl Harbor would have altered the course of the fighting.

> *Pearl Harbor: A Novel of December 8th*. St. Martin's, 2007. 366p. 9780312363505.
> *Days of Infamy*. St. Martin's, 2008. 369p. 9780312363512.

Turtledove, Harry. *The Man with the Iron Heart*. Del Rey, 2008. 530p. 9780345504340. What if SS leader Reinhard Heydrich had survived the assassination attempt that killed him in 1942?

TOOLS AND RESOURCES

Bibliographies and Encyclopedias

Adamson, Lynda M. *American Historical Fiction: An Annotated Guide to Novels for Adults and Young Adults*. Phoenix: Oryx, 1999. Lists over 3,300 novels with American historical settings.

Adamson, Lynda M. *World Historical Fiction: An Annotated Guide to Novels for Adults and Young Adults*. Phoenix: Oryx, 1999. Over 6,000 novels set between prehistory and the late 20th century; excludes U.S. settings.

Hooper, Brad. *Read On . . . Historical Fiction: Reading Lists for Every Taste*. Westport, CT: Libraries Unlimited, 2006. A collection of reading lists, chosen by appeal factor, subjects, and other creative themes.

Johnson, Sarah L. *Historical Fiction: A Guide to the Genre*. Westport, CT: Libraries Unlimited, 2005. A subgenre-based guide to current and popular Historical Fiction.

Johnson, Sarah L. *Historical Fiction II: A Guide to the Genre*. Westport, CT: Libraries Unlimited, 2009. A companion volume to the above, covering novels published between mid-2004 and 2008.

Awards

Historical novels have dominated literary prize committees' short lists in recent years, with Hilary Mantel's *Wolf Hall* (2009), winner of both the Booker Prize and the Walter Scott Prize, as the most prominent example.

Langum Prize. Awarded annually since 2003 for excellence in American-set historical novels. http://www.langumcharitabletrust.org

Michael Shaara Award. Annual award for excellence in Civil War fiction, sponsored by the Civil War Institute at Gettysburg College. http://www.gettysburg.edu/cwi/events/shaara/

The Reading List. Inaugurated in 2007 by the CODES of RUSA, a division of ALA, highlighting outstanding genre fiction. Historical Fiction is one of the eight categories. http://www.ala.org/rusa/awards/readinglist

Walter Scott Prize. A major new U.K. literary prize for the genre, worth £25,000, which defines Historical Fiction using Scott's original criterion: novels set at least 60 years before publication. No website.

Online Resources

The **Historical Novel Society** (www.historicalnovelsociety.org) offers book reviews, lists of forthcoming titles, interviews, articles, and author websites.

HistoricalNovels.Info (www.historicalnovels.info) is Margaret Donsbach's extensive bibliography of historical novels.

At **Reading the Past** (www.readingthepast.com), Sarah Johnson, the author of this chapter, provides news, reviews, and commentary on the Historical Fiction field.

FIVE FAN FAVORITES

- Bernard Cornwell. *The Last Kingdom*—Historical Adventure
- Kathleen Kent. *The Heretic's Daughter*—Traditional Historical Novel—United States

- Hilary Mantel. *Wolf Hall*—Literary Historical Novel—British Isles
- Lisa See. *Snow Flower and the Secret Fan*—Literary Historical Novel—Asia, Africa, and the Antipodes
- Mary Ann Shaffer and Annie Barrows. *The Guernsey Literary and Potato Peel Pie Society*—Literary Historical Novel—British Isles

Chapter 8

Mystery Fiction

Lesa Holstine

A recent analysis of book sales done by Publisher Alley showed that books in the Mystery genre account for almost 20 percent of sales. Why? What are Mysteries, and why are they so popular?

DEFINITION

A Mystery can be defined as a work of fiction in which the character is asked to solve a puzzle. Mysteries combine crime and detection, in a story in which a fictional detective tries to solve the puzzle before the reader does. There is an unstated agreement that the author will "play fair" with the reader by providing clues, not hiding them from the reader. According to Reader's Advisor Online, "The central question is 'whodunit?', and the focus of these stories is on the detective and the process he or she uses to solve the crime. The detectives in these stories are often characters who are developed over multi-title series and who vary in type from amateur to professional, while the tone can vary from Cozy to Hard-Boiled."

CHARACTERISTICS AND APPEAL

Why do Mysteries appeal to readers? Mysteries are puzzles. Readers enjoy the chance to pit themselves against the detective in the book. There is a clear structure in the books. A crime occurs, followed by an investigation, and a resolution. The author provides clues, and the reader, along with the characters, can follow the case to its conclusion. Many readers like the orderly nature of the Mystery, and the strong story, with good and bad easily determined, and justice triumphing at the end.

But, most readers of Mysteries will also say they read the books for the appeal of the characters. Publishers understand that attraction to character, and, with a few exceptions, Mysteries are written in series so that readers will return again and again to a character they find appealing. Whether readers are attracted originally to a Mystery for the historical setting and context, the foreign setting, or the procedure involved in solving a Mystery, they usually return to a series because they are interested in reading about the character.

BRIEF HISTORY

Edgar Allan Poe is usually considered the father of the Mystery, with the creation of his detective, C. Auguste Dupin, who solved crimes in three stories, beginning with "Murders in the Rue Morgue" (1841). But it was Arthur Conan Doyle who popularized the genre with his Sherlock Holmes stories, written in the late 19th century. The period between the wars, 1920–1940, marked the "Golden Age" of Mysteries, thanks to authors such as Agatha Christie, who introduced the eccentric Hercule Poirot in 1920 in *The Mysterious Affair at Styles*. Other authors who represent that era in England are Dorothy L. Sayers, Ngaio Marsh, John Dickson Carr, and Josephine Tey. In the United States, Rex Stout and Ellery Queen represent authors of that period who still remain popular. But, the 1920s also brought authors to prominence who had originally written for pulp magazines, such as *Black Mask*. Those authors represent the Hard-Boiled school, a darker style of writing. Raymond Chandler and Dashiell Hammett are two of the fathers of this school.

While Mysteries continued to be published, the next major movements occurred between 1970 and 1990. Regional Mysteries, focusing on setting as well as character, became popular, taking Mysteries out of the English villages and large American cities. Tony Hillerman's first Southwest Mystery, *The Blessing Way*, published in 1970 allowed readers to discover new and exotic settings.

One of the giant changes to the genre came about with the inclusion of women private investigators. There had been some, but in 1982, Marcia Muller's second Sharon McCone book. was released, the same year as Sue Grafton's *A is for Alibi* and *Indemnity Only* by Sara Paretsky. Now, women investigators and female authors filled a prominent place in the genre. In addition, ethnic, religious, and racial issues were represented in works by authors such as Walter Mosley, Harry Kemelman, and Howard Fast writing as E. V. Cunningham. Gay and lesbian detectives also surfaced in this period. At the same time, authors began to write about characters who specialized in a field, such as Diane Mott Davidson who wrote about a caterer and Patricia Cornwell who kicked off a trend in Forensic Mysteries that continues to this day.

In 2004, the Mystery field underwent another major shift when Barbara Peters of Poisoned Pen Bookstore held the first Thriller conference in the United States. Until then, Thrillers were considered part of the Mystery genre, but after that conference, the International Thriller Writers formed. The following year, the first ThrillerFest was held, and Thrillers broke off from the Mystery genre, making it more difficult to differentiate between Mysteries with detectives and Thrillers. In Great Britain, the two genres remain lumped together, under Crime Fiction.

CURRENT TRENDS

So, where is the Mystery field going now? In recent years, there has been an explosion in Cozy Mysteries such as Julie Hyzy's <u>White House Chef series</u> and Jane K. Cleland's <u>Josie Prescott Antiques</u> books. This niche in the Traditional Mystery subgenre is represented by genteel characters and gentle stories, where everyone and everything is nice and civilized, and the murder usually occurs off-scene with no directly observed violence. Today, crafts, cats, cooking, and other hobbies are popular in these light-hearted comfort reads.

There has also been a movement toward Mysteries set in foreign countries, or translated Mysteries. Currently, the Scandinavians are particularly popular in Thrillers and Mysteries, with such blockbuster titles as Stieg Larsson's *The Girl with the Dragon Tattoo* and Jo Nesbø's *The Snowman*. Soho Press is notable for doing an outstanding job publishing books with exotic settings such as Brazil, France, and Australia. Increasingly, American Mystery readers look beyond the borders of English-speaking countries as settings for their Mysteries. For example, Keigo Higashino's Edgar-nominated Mystery, *The Devotion of Suspect X*, is set in Japan. Rebecca Cantrell's award-winning *A Trace of Smoke* is set in 1930s Berlin.

Mystery readers are also looking to the past. Numerous Historical Mysteries are being published, representing virtually all historical periods. Today's Mysteries frequently include historical figures such as Jane Austen or Abigail Adams as the detective or a major character in the story. Barbara Hambly, under the name Barbara Hamilton, wrote three books featuring Abigail Adams, including the award-nominated *A Marked Man*. Gyles Brandeth's Mysteries feature poet and playwright Oscar Wilde. It will be interesting to see what authors break out in the next five years and what changes occur in the genre.

THEMES AND TYPES

> ### Mystery Fiction Key
>
> Traditional Mysteries
> Cozy Mysteries
> Historical Mysteries
> Procedurals
> Private Investigators
> Crime Capers
> Genreblends

Traditional Mysteries

Cozy Mysteries have become very popular in recent years, leading to confusion between the terms "Cozy Mystery," "Soft-Boiled Mystery," and "Traditional Mystery." For the purposes of this book, the terms "Cozy Mystery" and "Soft-Boiled Mystery" are interchangeable. They are Mysteries with little violence, sexual content, or abusive language. Most violence takes place offstage. Right and wrong are clearly defined. The violence is seen as a failure of society, and the community is usually a small town or a closed setting. In most cases, an amateur sleuth is the detective.

However, Cozies are a subset of the Traditional Mystery. Cozies are gentle Mysteries in which the world is seen as quite nice, except for the murder. As mentioned previously, crafts, cats, hobbies, and cooking are often subjects for Cozy Mysteries. They're lighthearted, and sometimes humorous, comfort reads.

Traditional Mysteries, on the other hand, may explore dark, sometimes disturbing themes. In discussing Traditional Mysteries, the late Enid Schantz of Rue Morgue Press said,

> In my view all cozies are traditional mysteries but by no means all traditional mysteries are cozies. A traditional mystery may feature either a professional or an amateur detective (but not, as a rule, a private detective) but is not a police procedural where the emphasis is on police work (Ed McBain). There is a minimum of violence and often a closed setting, and usually the murderer and the victim know each other. Examples of traditional mystery writers are Ngaio Marsh,

Josephine Tey, Ellery Queen, Rex Stout, etc. A cozy is a type of traditional mystery which is gentled down even further, where everyone and everything is quite nice except the murder.

Gary Warren Niebuhr, in *Make Mine a Mystery*, sees the Traditional Mystery embodying the traits of the Cozy, but including some of the violence of a Hard-Boiled Mystery. He says violence establishes the serious nature of the crime, although it's not graphically described. The goal of the detective is to find a solution to the crime, although justice may not come about as usually expected.

Historical Mysteries can be either Cozy or Traditional, but the emphasis in the stories is on the setting, the time period in which the book is set. Readers read these books not only for the puzzle and characters, but also for the appeal of the atmosphere and historical details of a particular time period. Research and accuracy as to detail are very important for readers of Historical Mysteries. These are Mysteries set in the past, emphasizing a time period of historical significance, but it's a matter of debate how far in the past the story must be set to make it a Historical Mystery. Is it 25 years? Are the 1980s now appropriate for Historical Mysteries? The website *Stop You're Killing Me!* uses the 1980s as a cutoff point. Nothing more recent is considered a historical Mystery.

With the great number of series in the Mystery genre, it would be difficult to provide annotations for all of them. Instead, this chapter focuses on the series as a body of work. For the sake of this book, Traditional Mysteries are listed first, with subsets of Cozies and Historical Mysteries.

Albert, Susan Wittig

🎖 **China Bayles Series** (1992–). Albert's series features an herbalist and former attorney in Pecan Springs, Texas. The series started with *Thyme of Death*, an Agatha and Anthony Award nominee. As of this writing, there are 21 books in the series.

Barber, Christine

🎖 **Lucy Newroe Series** (2008–2010). Barber's books feature a newspaper editor and volunteer EMT in Santa Fe, New Mexico. *The Replacement Child* (2008) was the first winner of the Tony Hillerman Award for Best Debut Mystery set in the Southwest. The second book, *The Bone Fire* (2010), was a finalist for the 2011 Hillerman Sky Award for the Mystery that best captures the landscape of the Southwest.

Bowen, Gail

🎗 **Joanne Kilbourn Series** (1990–). A political science professor in Regina, Saskatchewan, Canada, is the protagonist in this series. As of this writing, there are 12 titles in the series, including the Arthur Ellis Award Winner for Best Novel, *A Colder Kind of Death* (1994).

Bradley, Alan

🎗 **Flavia de Luce Series** (2009–). In the 1950s, in the village of Bishop's Lacey, England, an 11-year-old prodigy from an eccentric family takes up sleuthing. She is also an aspiring chemist with a fondness for poisons. The series is planned for six books. The debut title, *The Sweetness at the Bottom of the Pie* (2009), won numerous awards: Agatha and Arthur Ellis Award Winner for Best First Novel, Dilys Award Winner, Anthony Award Finalist for Best Mystery, and Barry and Macavity Award Finalist for Best First Novel.

Coel, Margaret

🎗 **Wind River Reservation Series** (1995–). Set on the reservation in Wyoming, this series features Father John O'Malley, a Jesuit missionary, and Vicky Holden, an Arapaho attorney. The 15 books, as a body of work, deal with Native American issues of progress versus tradition, and have garnered awards for novels set in the American West. *The Spider's Web* (2010) was the winner of the 2011 Hillerman Sky Award.

Davidson, Hilary

🎗 **Lily Moore Series** (2010–). Two books, *The Damage Done* (2010) and *The Next One to Fall* (2012) introduce Lily Moore, a travel writer haunted by the destructive relationships in her family, including alcoholism, addiction, and manipulation. *The Damage Done* won the Anthony Award for Best First Novel and was an Arthur Ellis and Macavity nominee.

Grabenstein, Chris

🎗 **John Ceepak Series** (2005–). John Ceepak, a veteran of the Iraq war and a police officer, and his sidekick, Danny Boyle, work in the resort town of Sea Haven, New Jersey. There are seven books in the series, marked by the strength of the Ceepak/Boyle relationship and the clever use of dialogue and humor. *Tilt-a-Whirl* (2005) won the Anthony Award for Best First Novel.

Hirahara, Naomi

🎗 **Mas Arai Series** (2004–2010). A Japanese American Hiroshima survivor working as a gardener is also an amateur sleuth in Los Angeles. There are four books in the series rich with details about the Japanese American experience and community in Los Angeles. *Snakeskin Shamisen* (2006) was the Edgar Award Winner for Best Paperback.

Must Read

★ 🎗 🎬 **Johnson, Craig, Walt Longmire Series** (2004–). The eight books feature the world-weary sheriff of Absaroka County, Wyoming. The rugged Western setting, the wit, and a cast including a tough female deputy, a Native American sidekick, and a dog add to the appeal. A television series, *Longmire*, premiered on A&E TV in 2012. The debut novel, *The Cold Dish* (2004), was the winner of Le Grand Prix des Litteratures Policieres in France and a Dilys Award Finalist.

Malliet, G. M.

🎗 **Arthur St. Just Series** (2008–2010). Detective Chief Inspector Arthur St. Just of the Cambridgeshire Constabulary, England, and Sergeant Finn are featured in a three-volume series representative of the Traditional English country house Mystery. *Death of a Cozy Writer* (2008) was the Agatha Award Winner for Best First Novel and an Anthony and Macavity Award nominee for Best First Novel.

Must Read

★ 🎗 **Penny, Louise, Armand Gamache Series** (2005–). With seven books, this series has won numerous awards and nominations for the Traditional Mysteries that feature Gamache, Chief Inspector of the Sûreté du Québec. Most of the books are set in the idyllic village of Three Pines in southern Quebec, bringing back recurring characters, lost souls who found their way to the charming town. Once a murder occurs, they find themselves answering to the observant, fatherly Gamache and his team. Every book in the series has been an award winner or nominee. *Bury Your Dead* (2010), the sixth book, a haunting story featuring an introspective Gamache suffering from past decisions, won the Agatha, Anthony, Arthur Ellis, Macavity, and Nero Awards for Best Novel. It was also the Dilys Award Winner, given annually by the Independent Mystery Booksellers Association to the Mystery that the member booksellers most enjoyed selling, and a Barry Award finalist.

Must Read

★ 🎗 **Spencer-Fleming, Julia, <u>Clare Fergusson/Russ Van Alystyne Series</u>** (2002–). The seven-volume series featuring Clare Fergusson, an Episcopal priest and former military helicopter pilot, and Russ Van Alstyne, chief of police in Millers Kill, New York, received numerous awards and nominations. The popularity is due to the relationship between the two lead characters, as well as Clare's struggle between her religion and her personal beliefs. The debut novel, *In the Bleak Midwinter* (2002), was the winner of the St. Martin's Malice Domestic Award, and then went on to garner Agatha, Anthony, Barry, and Macavity Awards for Best Novel, as well as a Dilys Award and a nomination for the Nero Award.

Cozy Mysteries

As stated earlier, Cozies are gentle Mysteries in which the world is seen as quite nice, except for the murder. As mentioned previously, crafts, cats, hobbies, and cooking are often subjects for Cozy Mysteries. They're lighthearted, and sometimes humorous, comfort reads.

Aames, Avery

🎗 <u>**Cheese Shop Series**</u> (2010–). Charlotte Bessette is the proprietor of Fromagerie Bessette in the three Mysteries set in fictional Providence, Ohio. The small town in Amish country is home to interesting characters such as Charlotte's twin nieces and her French grandmother who is the mayor. *The Long Quiche Goodbye* (2010) won the Agatha Award for Best First Novel.

Must Read

★ 🎗 **Andrews, Donna, <u>Meg Langslow Series</u>** (1999–). These 14 books are some of the most popular representatives of the Cozy subgenre, receiving numerous awards. The series features Meg Langslow, a decorative blacksmith in a southern town and the only levelheaded family member, along with her eccentric relatives. The first book, *Murder with Peacocks* (1999), was the Agatha, Anthony, and Barry Awards Winner for Best Novel and a nominee for Macavity and Dilys Awards.

Cleland, Jane K.

Josie Prescott Antiques Mystery Series (2006–). Following the trend of protagonists with unusual jobs, the seven books in this series feature an antiques dealer who owns an auction house in a small town in coastal New Hampshire. *Consigned to Death* (2006) was nominated for the Agatha and Macavity Awards for Best First Novel.

Must Read

★ 🎗 **Davidson, Diane Mott, Goldy Schulz Culinary Mysteries** (1987–). If anyone kicked off the popularity of cooking Cozies, it was Davidson with her 16-book series that includes recipes. Goldy Korman, later Goldy Schulz, is a mom and caterer in Aspen Meadow, Colorado. The first book, *Catering to Nobody,* was an Agatha, Anthony, and Macavity nominee for Best First Novel.

Duncan, Elizabeth J.

🎗 **Penny Brannigan Series** (2009–). Cozy Mysteries can take place in any small town. Duncan's three books feature a mature manicurist and expatriate Canadian living in Llanelen, Wales. *The Cold Light of Mourning* (2009) was the winner of the Minotaur Books/Malice Domestic Best First Traditional Competition and nominee for Agatha and Arthur Ellis Awards for Best First Novel.

Must Read

★ 🎗 **Hart, Carolyn, Death on Demand Series** (1987–). This 22-volume series has garnered numerous awards for the books that feature Annie Laurance, a Mystery bookstore owner, and Max Darling, an investigator in

Broward's Rock, South Carolina. Bookstores are another popular subject for Cozy series. Although the first book in the series, *Death on Demand* (1987), was nominated for awards, the third book, *Something Wicked* (1988), was the first in the series to win. It was the Agatha Award Winner for Best Novel and Anthony Award Winner for Best Paperback.

_____

Hyzy, Julie

🎗 **White House Chef Series** (2008–). There are five books in this award-winning series with its unusual setting, the White House, but they still have that closed setting crucial to so many Cozy Mysteries. Titles with puns and Mysteries with humor and recipes are popular in the Cozy subgenre. The first book, *State of the Onion* (2008), introduced Assistant Chef Olivia Paras, who vies for the position of White House Chef. She accidentally becomes involved in an investigation when she stops an intruder on the lawn with a frying pan. It went on to win Anthony and Barry Awards for Best Paperback.

Lakin, Rita

🎗 **Gladdy Gold Series** (2005–). The seven books in this series show amateur sleuths can be any age as exemplified by 75-year-old Gladdy Gold and her gang of eccentric retirees in Fort Lauderdale, Florida. *Getting Old Is a Disaster* (2008) was the Lefty Award Winner for Most Humorous Mystery.

Viets, Elaine

🎗 **Dead-End Job Mystery Series** (2003–). Helen Hawthorne, a woman on the run from her ex-husband and the courts, takes a series of dead-end jobs in Fort Lauderdale, Florida. There are 10 books in this best-selling series that features eccentric characters and offbeat murders. *Murder with Reservations* (2007), in which Helen works as a hotel maid, won the Lefty Award and was nominated for the Agatha Award for Best Novel.

Historical Mysteries

As stated earlier, Historical Mysteries are read not only for the puzzle and characters, but also for the appeal of the atmosphere and historical details of a particular time period.

Must Read

★ ⚑ **Bowen, Rhys, <u>Molly Murphy Series</u>** (2001–). Setting—1900s, New York City. The 11 books in this series feature an Irish immigrant in early 20th century New York who wants to be a private investigator. Introduced in *Murphy's Law* (2001), Molly was forced to flee Ireland when she accidentally killed a man, and she ends up in New York. The books have won Agatha, Anthony, and Macavity Awards for Best Historical Novel, as well as nominations for Bruce Alexander Historical Mystery and Mary Higgins Clark Awards.

⚑ <u>**Royal Spyness Mystery Series**</u> (2007–). Setting—1930s, England. These five books feature Lady Georgiana Rannoch (Georgie), a penniless 20-something member of the extended royal family in 1930s England. In each book, the young woman, 34th in line to the throne, takes on unusual assignments from the Queen, such as recovering a stolen snuffbox. *A Royal Pain* (2008), in which Georgie hosts a Bavarian princess who shoplifts, won the Macavity Award for Best Historical Novel. Series books have been nominated for Agatha and Bruce Alexander Historical Mystery Awards.

⚑ **Cantrell, Rebecca**

<u>**Hannah Vogel Series**</u> (2009–). Setting—1930s, Berlin, Germany. A crime reporter in 1930s Berlin, Germany, takes center stage in this atmospheric series of three books with complex characters and intricate plots. The debut Mystery, *A Trace of Smoke* (2009), was the winner of the Bruce Alexander and Macavity Awards for Best Historical Novel, and was nominated for the Barry Award. The other books in the series were also Bruce Alexander Historical Award nominees.

Cleverly, Barbara

⚑ <u>**Joe Sandilands Series**</u> (2001–). Setting—1920s, India, France, and London. A Scotland Yard detective is assigned first to India, and then returns to post–World War I Europe in a nine-book series that captures the atmosphere of India and a declining British Empire moving into the Jazz Age. The third book, *The Damascened Blade* (2003), won the Historical Dagger Award, and later books have been award nominees.

Franklin, Ariana

Mistress of the Art of Death Series (2007–2010). Setting—12th-century England. Four volumes feature an Italian medical doctor in 12th-century England, Adelia, a "mistress of the art of death." The books combine atmosphere and history with a strong female heroine in an unusual role for the times, medical examiner. The debut novel, *Mistress of the Art of Death* (2007), was the winner of the Historical Dagger Award and the Macavity Award for Best Historical Novel. Franklin died in 2011.

Goodwin, Jason

Yashim Series (2006–). Setting—1830s, Istanbul, Turkey. Four volumes in historian Goodwin's series feature Yashim Togabu, a eunuch for an Ottoman sultan in 1830s Istanbul, Turkey, in the waning years of the Ottoman Empire. The exotic, sinister atmosphere helped make the first book, *The Janissary Tree* (2006), the Edgar Award Winner for Best Mystery Novel, and was nominated for the Historical Dagger and Macavity Awards for Best Novel.

Kerr, Philip

Bernie Gunther Series (1989–). Setting—1930s and 1940s, Berlin, Germany, and elsewhere. Gunther, a German private eye, hates the Nazis. This eight-volume series begins in Berlin, Germany, in 1936. Like Rebecca Cantrell's books, the appeal is the noir atmosphere and history of that period of German history. *If the Dead Rise Not*, the sixth book, filled in Gunther's backstory, telling of his relationship with an American reporter in 1934. It went on to win the Historical Dagger Award and was nominated for the Barry Award for Best British Crime Novel.

Perry, Anne

Charlotte and Thomas Pitt Series (1979–). Setting—19th-century Victorian England. This series features a police inspector and his wife, who married beneath her class. This is one of Perry's two popular, long-running series set in Victorian England; books that appeal for characters, social consciousness, and atmosphere. Several have been nominated for awards, including *Buckingham Palace Gardens* (2008), which takes Pitt to the palace when the body of a prostitute is found after a stag party presided over by the Prince of Wales. There are 27 titles in this series.

🎗 **William Monk Series** (1990–). Setting—19th-century Victorian England. This series, comprised of 17 books, is known for the amnesiac police inspector who becomes a private detective. The first book, *The Face of a Stranger* (1990), introduces Monk as he relearns who he is after waking up in a London hospital. It was an Agatha and Macavity nominee for Best Novel.

Pintoff, Stefanie

🎗 **Simon Ziele Series** (2009–). Setting—Early 1900s, New York. Three books—featuring Simon Ziele, a former New York City police detective, now in Dobson, Westchester County, New York—appeal not only for the historical detail, but also for a character interested in the scientific possibilities for crime-solving in the early 20th century. The debut Mystery, *In the Shadow of Gotham* (2009), was the winner of the Minotaur/MWA Best First Crime Novel Award, Edgar Award Winner for Best First Novel, and nominee for Agatha, Anthony, and Macavity Awards.

Sansom, C. J.

🎗 **Matthew Shardlake Series** (2003–2010). Setting—16th-century England. These books, rich in historical detail of Tudor England, find hunchbacked lawyer Matthew Shardlake immersed in the politics and culture of mid-16th-century England. All five books in the series were nominated for Historical Dagger Awards. *Dark Fire* (2004), with a plot involving Thomas Cromwell, Henry VIII's vicar general, and alchemy, won that award.

Must Read

★ 🎗 **Stanley, Kelli, Miranda Corbie Series** (2010–). Setting—1940s San Francisco. Two books feature Miranda Corbie, a Spanish Civil War nurse and ex-escort. Now, she's a private investigator in 1940s San Francisco, a corrupt, gritty city. She's a woman, damaged by her past, trying to make it in a man's world. The stories are appealing due to the atmosphere and accuracy of the period detail, as well as the character of Miranda. *City of Dragons* (2010) won the Macavity Award for Best Historical Novel and was a nominee for the Bruce Alexander Award and the Shamus Award for Best First P.I. Novel.

Westerson, Jeri

🎗 <u>**Crispin Guest Mysteries**</u> (2008–). Setting—Late-14th-century England. Westerson's four books are called "Medieval Noir," combining medieval historical details with a dark, noir atmosphere. Guest is a disgraced knight reduced to living by his wits on the "mean streets" of 1384 London, England. *Veil of Lies* (2008) introduces the former nobleman who uses his powers of deduction to earn a living as a "tracker," a medieval detective. All four books have been nominees for Macavity and Bruce Alexander Awards for Best Historical Novel.

Must Read

★ 🎗 **Winspear, Jacqueline, <u>Maisie Dobbs Series</u>** (2003–). Setting—1930s, England. The nine titles in this series have received numerous awards and nominations for the character and atmosphere created in those novels of a female nurse during World War I who becomes a psychologist and private investigator in England following the war. The stories are rich in detail of the postwar years in England. The first book, *Maisie Dobbs* (2003), was the Agatha and Macavity Winner for Best First Novel, as well as a nominee for the Anthony, Barry, Edgar, and Dilys Awards. Other books in the series have won or been nominated for numerous awards as well.

Procedurals

Gary Warren Niebuhr, in *Make Mine a Mystery* (2003), referred to this category as "The Public Detectives." As he said, this category is the most realistic Mystery category, covering the police and other professionals whose work allies them with the police, such as investigative journalists, park rangers, and game wardens. Many of the foreign Mysteries gaining popularity also fall under this category. Readers who enjoy Procedurals may appreciate the characters, but they may also read for realism and setting. Because this category covers the police and other professionals, it's a large category.

Ault, Sandi

🎗 <u>**Wild Series**</u> (2007–2010). Meet Jamaica Wild, a resource-protection agent for the Bureau of Land Management, her wolf, and her Tanoah Pueblo medicine teacher in northern New Mexico. The four books in this series are rich in details of Pueblo culture and the wilderness Wild patrols. *Wild Indigo* (2007), the first book, was a Mary Higgins Clark Award winner.

Barr, Nevada

♟ <u>Anna Pigeon Series</u> (1993–). The 17 books in this series focus on Pigeon, a park ranger at various national parks in the United States. Pigeon is a troubled character, a work-oriented loner who battled alcohol dependence. Readers return to this series not only for the character of Anna, but also for the vivid descriptions of the settings. *Track of the Cat* (1993), the atmospheric debut novel, won the Agatha and Anthony Awards for Best First Novel and was a Macavity Award nominee.

Blunt, Giles

♟ <u>John Cardinal Series</u> (2001–). Four atmospheric Police Procedurals follow detective Cardinal and his partner in Algonquin Bay, Ontario, Canada. This series is known for its complex characters and plots. A fifth book in the series, *Crime Machine*, was published in Canada in 2010, with a sixth due for publication. The four U.S. publications were all nominees for awards. *Forty Words for Sorrow* (2001), the debut novel, won the Silver Dagger Award and was nominated for the Arthur Ellis Award for Best Novel.

Box, C. J.

♟ <u>Joe Pickett Series</u> (2001–). Pickett, a game warden in the Bighorn Mountains of Wyoming, is the protagonist in these 12 books. Pickett is an unremarkable hero, an honest man known for his commitment to family and justice. Readers return to the books to read about Pickett and his dangerous job in the rough Wyoming setting. The debut, *Open Season* (2001), was an Anthony and Barry Award winner for Best First Novel and a nominee for Edgar and Macavity Awards for Best First Novel.

Must Read

★ ♟ **Burke, James Lee, <u>Dave Robicheaux Series</u>** (1987–). Although Burke, the winner of the Grand Master Award from Mystery Writers of America, has written other books and even won awards for them, he is beloved for the 19 books in this series, which feature the deputy sheriff in New Iberia, Louisiana. The books are known for the richness of the writing, the characters, and the Louisiana setting. *The Tin Roof Blowdown* (2007), the 16th book in the series, may not have won awards, but many consider it Burke's best book, an eloquent story of post-Katrina New Orleans in which Robicheaux' search for missing people allows him to vent his frustration. It was a nominee for the Gold Dagger Award and Anthony Award for Best Mystery Novel.

Burke, Jan

♟ Irene Kelly Series (1993–). A tough, resilient investigative reporter in Southern California plays the star role in this 11-volume series. Eight of the books have been award winners or nominees, including the latest, *Disturbance* (2011), in which Irene once more faces the serial killer who traumatized her in the Edgar Award–winning *Bones* (1999).

Cleeves, Ann

♟ Shetland Islands Quartet (2006–2010). Although she's written a number of books, it's this four-volume quartet that has brought her recognition. The atmospheric series features Jimmy Perez, a police detective inspector in the isolated Shetland Islands, north of Scotland. The Mysteries are popular due to the dark atmosphere, the closed communities, and Perez, a loner with a unique method of investigation. *Raven Black* (2006), the first in this series, illustrates Perez' skill in uncovering the secrets and lies of a small community. It was a Gold Dagger Award Winner.

Must Read

★ ♟ **Connelly, Michael, Harry Bosch Mysteries** (1992–). Connelly exemplifies today's Police Procedurals with these 17 titles, although he has won awards for his series featuring lawyer Mickey Haller as well. Bosch was a homicide detective in Los Angeles for 28 years before retiring in book nine to become a private investigator. The books are character-driven procedurals featuring a loner who works within a police department, but refuses to play by the rules. In 2008, Connelly brought his two popular characters, Bosch and Mickey Haller, together in the Anthony Award–winning novel, *The Brass Verdict*.

Cotterill, Colin

🔖 <u>Dr. Siri Investigation Series</u> (2004–). These eight volumes feature an unusual setting, Laos in the 1970s, and an unusual protagonist, Dr. Siri Paiboun, the 70-something "reluctant national coroner, confused psychic, and disheartened communist." These books appeal for setting and the witty character of Dr. Siri. *Thirty-Three Teeth* (2005), the second in the series, won the Dilys Award.

Must Read

★ 🔖 **Crombie, Deborah, <u>Duncan Kincaid/Gemma James Series</u>** (1993–). Kincaid is a Scotland Yard superintendent and James is a sergeant (later detective inspector) in these excellent examples of Police Procedurals. The books are complex stories with protagonists who are professionally and personally connected. These 14 titles have frequently been nominated for awards. In *Where Memories Lie* (2008), the Macavity Award Winner for Best Novel, the two leads work together on a cold case with links to Nazi Germany.

Disher, Garry

🔖 <u>Inspector Hal Challis and Sergeant Ellen Destry Investigation Series</u> (1999–2009). Disher takes Police Procedurals to Australia, as Challis and Destry work on the Peninsula, southeast of Melbourne. These five volumes are excellent examples of procedurals with strong character development and an interesting setting. *Chain of Evidence* (2007), the fourth book, won the Ned Kelly Award for Best Novel, given for excellence in Australian crime-writing.

Fairstein, Linda

🔖 <u>Alex (Alexandra) Cooper Series</u> (1996–). Fairstein uses her expertise as a sex crimes prosecutor to bring together Cooper, the sex crimes prosecutor for Manhattan, with police investigations involving Cooper's friend, homicide detective Mike Chapman, and fascinating details about the history and city of New York. Several of the 14 titles have been Macavity Award nominees for Best Novel. *The Deadhouse* (2001), involving an abandoned hospital on Roosevelt Island where smallpox victims went to die in the 19th century, was the Nero Award Winner.

Fradkin, Barbara

🏵 **Michael Green Series** (2000–2010). Green works as a police inspector in Ottawa, Ontario, Canada. These eight titles appeal for the day-to-day workings of a police investigation and the character of Green. He is an impetuous man whose passion for justice often interferes with family, friends, and police protocol. These books are complex psychological stories. *Honour Among Men* (2006), the fifth book, won the Arthur Ellis Award for Best Novel.

French, Tana

🏵 **The Dublin Murder Squad** (2007–). French's four books feature various members of the squad with emphasis on different police detectives in each of the four books. These Mysteries are known for the characters and the sense of place, Dublin, Ireland, as well as the psychological insight and police procedures. The debut novel, *In the Woods* (2007), won the Edgar, Barry, Macavity, and Anthony Awards for Best First Novel.

Hill, Reginald

🏵 **Dalziel/Pascoe Series** (1970–2009). Hill won the Diamond Dagger Award in 1995 for his procedurals featuring a pair of police inspectors, Superintendent Andrew Dalziel and Sergeant Peter Pascoe, in Yorkshire, England. The 25 volume series was a frequent award nominee, with stories marked by the contrast between Fat Andy, a coarse but shrewd policeman, and Pascoe, a much more liberal character. *On Beulah Height* (1998) won the Barry Award for Best Novel. The last Dalziel/Pascoe Mystery, *Midnight Fugue* (2009), marked by the same suspense and humor as previous works, was a finalist for the Barry Award. Hill died in 2012.

Indridason, Arnaldur

🏵 **Reykjavik Murder Mysteries** (2004–). These books follow Erlendur Sveinsson, a detective inspector, and his colleagues in Reykjavik, Iceland. These Mysteries appeal because of the Icelandic setting, the dark stories, and the tortured character of Erlendur. Six of Indridason's Mysteries have been translated into English, including *Silence of the Grave* (2005), winner of the Gold Dagger Award, and *The Draining Lake* (2007), a Barry Award winner.

MacBride, Stuart

🏵 **Logan McRae Mysteries** (2005–). McRae, a detective sergeant in Aberdeen, Scotland, stars in this gritty seven-book series that appeals for its noirish atmosphere, the characters, and gallows humor. *Cold Granite* (2005), the debut Mystery, was the Barry Award Winner for Best First Novel.

Maron, Margaret

Deborah Knott Series (1992–). This popular series features a district judge in North Carolina. The books' greatest appeal is in the characters, particularly Knott's large and extended family. The rural North Carolina setting and lifestyle is vividly captured in these stories. The 17 books have garnered frequent awards and nominations, with *Bootlegger's Daughter* (1992) winning the Agatha, Edgar, Anthony, and Macavity Awards for Best Mystery Novel.

Parks, Brad

Carter Ross Series (2009–). Three books feature Carter Ross, a compassionate investigative reporter in Newark, New Jersey. The stories are complex, tragic Mysteries marked by humor, with a protagonist skilled at his job, but hopeless in personal relationships. The newsroom and the streets and politics of Newark come to life in this series that began with *Faces of the Gone* (2009), winner of the Shamus Award for Best First Novel and the Nero Award.

Qiu Xiaolong

Inspector Chen Series (2000–). Seven books feature Chen Cao, an inspector in the Shanghai Police Department, China. The exotic setting of China and the character of Chen himself, a poet and translator assigned to the Shanghai Police Department for a "productive" job, contribute to the series' appeal. The first book, *Death of a Red Heroine* (2000), showing Chen caught between the past and the progressive present, was the winner of the Anthony Award for Best First Novel and a nominee for the Barry and Edgar Awards.

Robinson, Peter

Alan Banks Mysteries (1987–). The 19 books in this series appeal as procedurals, but the greatest draw is the character of Banks, Eastvale detective chief inspector in Yorkshire, England. This charming man's love of music is evident in the books. The stories entwine the personal and professional life of this imperfect man with personal demons. Fourteen of the books have won or been nominated for awards, including *Cold Is the Grave* (2000), winner of the Arthur Ellis Award for Best Novel.

Ryan, Hank Phillippi

🎗 **Charlotte McNally Series** (2007–2010). These four books are narrated by Charlotte "Charlie" McNally, a 40-something TV investigative reporter in Boston, Massachusetts. The books feature a strong dose of realism (the author is a TV investigative reporter) and fascinating characters. In each of the Mysteries, Charlie researches a big story, beginning with *Prime Time* (2007), winner of the Agatha Award for Best First Novel.

Vargas, Fred

🎗 **Commissaire Adamsberg Mysteries** (1990–). Vargas' Mysteries feature Jean-Baptiste Adamsberg, commissioner of police or chief inspector, in Paris, France. Adamsberg, a sleuth who relies on intuition and has a reputation for solving big cases, is a compelling character, and with Paris as the setting, this is a winner. Six of Vargas' Mysteries have been translated into English, including *The Chalk Circle Man* (2009), winner of the International Dagger Award and the book that introduced Adamsberg.

Private Investigators

Private investigators, whether paid or unpaid, offer the reader the "lone wolf," the detective dedicated to the client's cause. Raymond Chandler's Philip Marlowe, the forerunner of today's fictional private detectives, was the embodiment of the detective's code—to find the truth, no matter the cost. The modern Detective Novel appeals for the characters of the detectives themselves, the setting, which is often an important element of the story, and, of course, the Mystery, with its search for answers. Often, that Mystery deals with relevant topics in the news at the time of the book's writing. These themes, along with a tone that tends to be darker than in the other subgenres, make the Private Detective Novels the Hard-Boiled books of the Mystery genre.

Bruen, Ken

🎗 **Jack Taylor Series** (2001–). After Taylor is kicked out of Ireland's Garda Siochna police force for drinking, he becomes a "finder." Read these nine books for Taylor's tormented character and the setting of Galway, Ireland, as well as the dark, gritty atmosphere. The fifth book, *Priest* (2006), in which Taylor has just been released from the loony bin, won the Barry Award for Best British Crime Novel.

Chercover, Sean

¶ Roy Dudgeon Series (2007–2008). Disillusioned newspaper reporter Ray Dudgeon has turned private investigator in Chicago, Illinois. The books appeal for the flawed, realistic characters, the insightful commentary, and the gritty atmosphere. Chercover, himself a private investigator, has written two award-nominated books in this series. The first, *Big City, Bad Blood* (2007), was the winner of the Shamus Award for Best First Novel and a nominee for Anthony, Arthur Ellis, and Barry Awards.

Coleman, Reed Farrell

¶ Moe Prager Series (2002–). Moe (Moses) Prager is an ex-cop turned private investigator in New York City in the 1980s. The books have a dark atmosphere and a likable detective. Although he's written other series, it's these seven novels that are award nominees and winners. The third book in the series, *The James Deans* (2005), was inspired by the real-life Gary Condit/Chandra Levy case. It was the winner of Anthony, Barry, and Shamus Awards for Best Paperback and an Edgar and Macavity Award nominee.

Connolly, John

¶ Charlie Parker Mysteries (1999–). These 10 novels feature a former New York homicide cop who becomes a private detective after leaving the force when his wife and daughter are murdered. Parker's cases take him throughout the country. Readers enjoy the wisecracking, tormented Parker, as well as the dark, often chilling, atmosphere. *The White Road* (2003), the fourth book in the series, won the Barry Award for Best British Crime Novel for the story of Parker's investigation of a racially charged case.

Crais, Robert

¶ Elvis Cole and Joe Pike Series (1987–). They're private eyes in Los Angeles. The books are Hard-Boiled Detective Novels that appeal for the fast pace, dialogue, and, most important, the characters. Crais called them "Two underdogs who have turned themselves into heroes." Elvis Cole is the sensitive, wisecracking one, while Pike is the strong, violent bad boy. Crais has won numerous awards and nominations for the 15 books in this series, including a Barry Award for Best Thriller, along with an Anthony Award nomination for *The Watchman* (2007).

Fate, Robert

♟ **Baby Shark Series** (2006–2009). Kristin Van Dijk, a pool hustler turned private investigator in West Texas in the 1950s, takes center stage in these four books that engage readers with compelling characters, particularly Baby Shark, and the fast pace. The first book, *Baby Shark* (2006), introduced Kristin, a young woman who learned self-defense skills in order to take on the men who attacked her and left her for dead. The book was an Anthony Award nominee, as was the sequel, *Baby Shark's Beaumont Blues* (2007).

Krueger, William Kent

♟ **Cork O'Connor Series** (1998–). These 11 books feature a man who is three-quarters Irish and one-quarter Ojibwe, the charismatic ex-sheriff turned private eye in Aurora, Minnesota. The books are known for the portrayal of small-town life, the vivid description of Minnesota's lake country, and the exploration of Cork O'Connor's character. O'Connor is an honest man committed to keeping his small town and his family safe. *Thunder Bay* (2007), a suspenseful novel that explored family issues, was a Dilys Award Winner and Anthony Award nominee.

Must Read

★ 🎞 **Lehane, Dennis, Kenzie/Gennaro Series** (1994–2010). The six books in the Patrick Kenzie and Angela Gennaro series are set in Dorchester, Massachusetts, where the team of private detectives deals with ugly cases in a blue-collar town. The relationship between the two detectives, the gritty plots, and the setting appeal to readers. All six books, beginning with *A Drink Before the War* (1994), were award winners or nominees. It appeared that the series had ended in 1999 after five books. Lehane moved on to standalones, such as *Mystic River* and *Shutter Island*. Then, in *Moonlight Mile* (2010), the now-married pair returned in a story that traced its origins to the disappearance of a young girl in *Gone, Baby, Gone* (1998). Twelve years later, Patrick Kenzie still has to deal with a complex case that tests his ethics. The book was a Barry and Dilys Award nominee. Several of Lehane's books have been made into movies.

Lippman, Laura

🎗 Tess Monaghan Series (1997–). Monaghan is a journalist turned private investigator in Baltimore, Maryland. The books appeal for the character of Tess, the "accidental private investigator," the unorthodox friends, as well as the urban setting of Baltimore, almost a character in itself in the books. Lippman has gone on to receive acclaim for standalones as well, but it was as the author of these 11 books that she made her reputation. *No Good Deeds* (2006), the ninth book, in which Tess protects a homeless teen who witnessed a murder, was the most recent award winner, winning the Anthony Award for Best Mystery Novel.

Mosley, Walter

🎗 Easy Rawlins Series (1990–2007). Rawlins is a black World War II veteran, unlicensed private investigator, and a real-estate investor. The 11 books appeal for the unusual role for a black man at that time, a sleuth in 1940s Los Angeles. *Devil in a Blue Dress* (1990) launched the series by taking readers into an Los Angeles not seen in previous novels, the streets and hidden places of South Central Los Angeles. The book was the winner of the New Blood Dagger and Shamus Awards and an Edgar Award nominee.

Must Read

★ 🎗 **Muller, Marcia, Sharon McCone Series** (1977–). McCone is a legal investigator and private eye in San Francisco in one of the first American Mystery series to feature a female protagonist. Even after 30 books in the series, Muller continues to receive award nominations for these books with their strong characterizations. Muller was awarded the Eye Lifetime Achievement Award and the Grand Master Award from Mystery Writers of America on the strength of this series and for Muller's contribution to the private eye subgenre.

Must Read

★ 🎗 **Parker, Robert B., Spenser Series** (1973–2011). Over the years, Spenser, the Boston private investigator, has come to represent the quintessential private eye, with his sidekick, Hawk, and his code of conduct.

Spenser was a character who influenced many of the other writers of private eye fiction, such as Robert Crais and Dennis Lehane. Readers returned to read about Spenser, the romantic, the character who was a gourmet cook, a boxer, a man who couldn't accept failure, and a hired gun who could recite poetry. He was a loyal friend who inspired loyalty from women, cops, and other hired guns. Spenser, his relationships, and his witty use of language appealed to readers. Although he wrote many other books and other series, Parker's Grand Master and Eye Achievement Awards were undoubtedly based on the 40 books in this series. Parker died in 2011, and his widow asked author Ace Atkins to continue the series.

Richards, Linda L.

🎗 **Kitty Pangborn Series** (2008–2009). These two books exemplify the Noir novel, with the dark atmosphere, Depression-era setting, and the street-smart, hard-drinking detective with the savvy secretary. Kitty Pangborn is secretary to private eye Dexter J. Theroux in 1930s Los Angeles, assisting with some of the investigative work. The second book, *Death Was in the Picture* (2009), contrasts Kitty's lifestyle as a society girl forced to work after her father's suicide left her with no money, with the parties and Hollywood lifestyle. The book won the Panik Award for Best Los Angeles Noir.

Crime Capers

Caper Stories are marked by humor. This subgenre usually involves one or more crimes, with an emphasis on theft, swindles or kidnappings, and something goes wrong. The focus in these stories is usually on the perpetrators of the caper, the criminals. Humor, adventure, and clever characters are components of Capers. Donald Westlake's Dortmunder novels, featuring John Archibald Dortmunder and his gang of inept thieves, are prime examples. The other master of this subgenre, Elmore Leonard, often features petty crooks, ex-cons, and "entrepreneurs" in his novels. Unlike other subgenres, Capers are often standalone novels. If the book was a standalone, it is annotated here.

Berney, Lou. *Gutshot Straight*. William Morrow, 2010. 304p. 9780061766046. Charles "Shake" Bouchon intended to go straight when released from prison, but the head of Los Angeles's Armenian mob asks him to run one errand: drive a car to Las Vegas and leave it with a strip club owner. But, the "package" in the car is a stripper named Gina, and everything goes wrong when Shake refuses to turn her over. On the run from the Armenian mob and the strip club owner's employees, with a stolen briefcase in hand, Shake can't even trust Gina. The outrageous, larger-than-life characters, including charming thieves, and a fast-paced plot in which nothing goes right for the protagonist make this an appealing caper.

Must Read

★ ■ **Coonts, Deborah, Lucky O'Toole Novels** (2010–). Lucky is head of customer relations for the mega-casino Babylon Hotel, "the most over-the-top mega casino/resort on the Las Vegas strip." As head troubleshooter, it's her job to keep the wrong type of publicity away from the Babylon. They don't want customers to know about the body that fell from their helicopter, or the local attorney locked out of his room while he was nude. The three books highlight Vegas, everything from the Adult Industry's annual banquet to female impersonators and whorehouses, with all its outrageous behavior. *Wanna Get Lucky?* (2010) introduced Lucky, a sarcastic, strong woman with a big heart and a need to be loved. All three books are fast paced, sexy Capers featuring outlandish characters. Las Vegas itself has a starring role in this humorous series.

Must Read

★ ♟ ■ **Evanovich, Janet, Stephanie Plum Novels** (1994–). An inept Trenton, New Jersey, bounty hunter, her family, friends, and romantic interests form the core of this 18-book series, with the addition of four "between the numbers" holiday books. These definitely fall into the Capers category, with unusual characters, exploding cars, sexual tension, funny dialogue, and ridiculous situations. *One for the Money* (1994) launched the series. It won the New Blood Dagger and Dilys Awards. It was a nominee for Agatha, Last Laugh Dagger, Edgar, Anthony, Macavity, and Shamus Awards. In 2012, it was made into a movie.

8

Kozak, Harley Jane

♟ **Wollie Shelley Series** (2004–2009). These four books feature a greeting-card artist and serial dater in Los Angeles. Wacky characters and screwball comedy plots have contributed to the success of the series. In the debut, *Dating Dead Men* (2004), Wollie accepts a job doing research for a radio personality, dating 40 men in 60 days, while handling a few odd murder scenarios. The book won Agatha, Anthony, and Macavity Awards for Best First Novel.

Must Read

★ 🎙 **Littlefield, Sophie, <u>Stella Hardesty Series</u>** (2009–). A 50-year-old woman who was a victim of domestic violence, Stella now runs a sewing machine repair shop in a small town in Missouri, while helping other abused women. These four books are appealing because of their humor, but, most of all, because of the character of Stella. She is outspoken, has a foul mouth, and her methods of dealing with abusive men involves weapons and other instruments of torture. She's smitten with the local sheriff, Goat Jones, but that won't stop her from a life of crime. She's a hard-nosed woman with a heart of gold, who will do anything for abused women and innocent children. It's that determination to help others that lands her in hot water, as in the debut novel, *A Bad Day for Sorry* (2009), when a friend's ex kidnaps her little boy, and Stella sets out to retrieve him. That book went on to win the Anthony for Best First Novel and was a Barry, Edgar, and Macavity Award nominee.

Genreblends

J. D. Robb (Nora Roberts) has been combining genres since the mid-1990s in her Eve Dallas <u>In Death</u> series, featuring a police officer in futuristic New York City, with the addition of a great deal of sex. But, in recent years, genreblending has exploded as Mystery writers added vampires, ghosts, cowboys, and wizards, and even classic literature (Jane Austen) to the Mystery genre, adding additional audiences who might not have read a Mystery. For some, the appeal is still in the mystery element, but the supernatural has become very popular. Even in these books, though, the emphasis is still on character and plot.

Must Read

🎬 **Butcher, Jim, <u>The Dresden Files</u>** (2000–). These 15 books feature Harry Dresden, the only wizard listed in the Chicago yellow pages. Earlier titles in the series emphasized crime fighting and the mystery, although the villains may have been from other worlds. Emphasis in more recent releases is on the magic and fights between wizards, vampires, and other creatures. The returning characters including Harry, police detective Karin Murphy, Harry's half-brother who is a vampire, and Bob, the talking skull, are a primary appeal to this series. *Storm Front* (2000) introduced Harry, Murphy, and Bob, but the ongoing addition of intriguing characters contributed to the richness of this series, based in Chicago, but with adventures in the dangerous Faerie realms. Harry and his companions are in constant danger, with ongoing wars with vampires and other supernatural creatures. Harry's backstory, his dire predicaments, and his wry humor only add to this series' popularity. In 2010, Butcher added a major twist when he appeared to kill Harry in *Changes.* In 2007, the books were made into a TV miniseries, *The Dresden Files.*

Must Read

★ 🎬 🎞 **Harris, Charlaine, Sookie Stackhouse Series** (2001–). These wildly popular bestsellers were made into an HBO TV series, *True Blood.* The 13 books feature Sookie Stackhouse, a cocktail waitress and telepath, along with vampires, werewolves, and various romantic interests in small-town Louisiana. The combination of the supernatural and mystery make for great reader appeal. *Dead until Dark* (2001), the debut novel, was the Anthony Award Winner for Best Paperback and an Agatha and Dilys Award nominee.

Hockensmith, Steve

🎬 **Holmes on the Range Series** (2006–). Brothers and cowboys in 1890s Montana, Otto "Big Red" and Gustav "Old Red" Amlingmeyer became interested in being detectives after they read a Sherlock Holmes story. Hockensmith combines Westerns and Mystery in these five books. This series appeals for the colorful characters, beginning with Sherlock Holmes wannabe, Gustav, and his Watson, Otto. These lighthearted Mysteries are marked by slapstick, nonstop action and Hockensmith's frequent tributes to the Great Detective. *Holmes on the Range* (2006), the first book, was nominated for numerous awards.

Must Read

★ **Robb, J.D., In Death Series.** (1995–). Eve Dallas, a homicide lieutenant in futuristic New York City, stars in the 43 books and novellas that make up a series that combines a future world, sex, and a Police Procedural. If that isn't enough to attract readers, the characters of Eve Dallas and her wealthy businessman husband, Roark, are. In *Celebrity in Death* (2012), Eve's successful cases have even been made into a movie, but that doesn't mean she can forget her role as a cop when an actress ends up dead. Suspense, glamour, violence, and steamy romance combine in Robb's best-selling series.

TOOLS AND RESOURCES

Bibliography

Herald, Diana Tixier. *Genreflecting: A Guide to Popular Reading Interests*, edited by Wayne A. Wiegand. 6th ed. Westport, CT: Libraries Unlimited, 2006.

Niebuhr, Gary Warren. *Make Mine a Mystery: A Reader's Guide to Mystery and Detective Fiction*. Westport, CT: Libraries Unlimited, 2003.

Steinbrunner, Chris, and Otto Penzler, eds. *Encyclopedia of Mystery and Detection*. New York: McGraw-Hill Book Company, 1976.

Online Resources

There is a wealth of material online pertaining to Mysteries. You can find information about the genre or any subgenre you find interesting. Librarians, booksellers, and readers may find the following sites particularly useful:

The Bloodstained Bookshelf (http://www.mirlacca.com/Bookshelf.html) is a monthly list of recent and forthcoming print Mysteries published in the United States.

Cozy Mystery List (http://www.Cozy-mystery.com) is a guide to Cozy Mystery books and DVDs.

DorothyL (http://www.dorothyl.com) provides the subscription information and a discussion list for Mystery lovers and authors.

The Readers' Advisor Online Blog (http://www.readersadvisoronline .com/blog) provides news and weekly updates for readers' advisors and others working with readers.

Stop, You're Killing Me! (http://www.stopyourekillingme.com) is a "resource for lovers of mystery, crime, thriller, spy, and suspense books." It lists over 3,800 authors with chronological lists of their books, both series and non-series. There is also a geographical index and other special indexes.

What's Next Database (http://ww2.kdl.org/libcat/whatsnext.asp) is the KDL What's Next: Books in Series database, developed and maintained by the Kent District Library (Kent County, Michigan). Find books in series by author, series or titles.

FIVE FAN FAVORITES

- Rhys Bowen. *A Royal Pain*—Historical Mysteries
- Michael Connelly. *The Brass Verdict*—Procedural
- Julie Hyzy. *State of the Onion*—Cozy Mysteries
- Dennis Lehane. *Moonlight Mile*—Private Investigator
- Louise Penny. *Bury Your Dead*—Traditional Mysteries

Chapter 9

Thrillers

Andrew Smith

In the first quarter of 2012, when the editors were preparing this edition of *Genreflecting*, Thrillers of all kinds dominated the *New York Times* hardcover bestseller lists. Nearly one-third of the books were by familiar names like Patterson, Grisham, Cussler, and Clancy. Looking at those figures (and at the simultaneous popularity of nonfiction books that offer Thriller elements), it is easy to see that readers plainly want the charge that Thrillers gives them.

DEFINITION

What is a Thriller? In the introduction to *Thrillers: 100 Must Reads*, David Hewson (author of the Nic Costa police detective series) says that the goal of Thrillers is " . . . to provide the sudden rush of emotions: the excitement, suspense, apprehension, and exhilaration that drive the narrative." From a reader's perspective, it means that any story that jacks up the pulse or shortens the breath can have the tag "Thriller" without fear of contradiction.

CHARACTERISTICS AND APPEAL

The chief appeal of what Joyce Saricks calls "Adrenaline Fiction" is a sense that the reader can vicariously experience danger or moral quandaries, or call on physical courage and prowess. That sense also makes series characters attractive, because their values and abilities are well established in the reader's mind even before opening the next title in a series. Creating that vicarious sense may depend on fairly two-dimensional characters in explosively episodic brief chapters. It may just as easily involve building suspense as a well-developed character is forced out of a normal life into a dark world of violence and betrayal.

Thrillers are about power—who doesn't have it, who's misusing it, and what it will cost to restore some kind of balance to the world. Ordinary characters rely on rules and institutions to keep chaos at bay, while those who don't care about the consequences manipulate them for their own ends. Thriller protagonists often are forced across the boundaries of civilized behavior, and that comes with a cost for most characters. Some—Lee Child's Jack Reacher and superspy James Bond come to mind—may not have qualms about killing, but their implicit moral code allows the reader to enjoy the mayhem. More innocent characters make readers empathize with their loss of illusions and wonder how they might feel in that same situation.

Thriller writers have the world at their fingertips, so place is important to readers. That sense of place can range from the layout of an assassin's nest to an isolated border crossing into a hostile country. Authors strive to describe those places in relevant detail and to use those details in creating a logical framework for the character to move through. Authors also have a universe of settings to choose from, which allows them to select characters from diverse backgrounds, but authors have to master details to keep the story feeling real. Readers can expect to close the book having learned a Russian phrase or two, a forensic procedure, or the capabilities of a cutting-edge missile defense system.

The border between Thrillers and Mysteries is as wispy as a San Francisco fog bank. There is always a puzzle at the heart of a Thriller, but readers and characters may have no idea as to its scale. Simple actions, like a break-in to the wrong house, might expose enormous conspiracies; in a different story, chases and killings might result when a missed phone call triggers mistrust. Mysteries, as Lesa Holstine defines them in Chapter 8, rely on an implied contract between reader and writer, where all the pieces are visible. Thriller writers have no such constraints. In fact, withholding the last piece until the crucial moment can be the triumphant moment of the roller coaster ride the reader has experienced to that point. When reviewers and publishers praise "plotting," what they are describing is the delight the reader feels in skilled misdirection. There may be uncertainty within the fog bank, but readers know which neighborhood they are in when they emerge from it.

Pacing is essential in the Thriller. They usually begin with a devastating event that jars the protagonists into a murky situation and starts them on the quest to find the roots of the incident. As the plot develops, more, though smaller, events keep both the protagonist and the reader continuing through the story. The speed of the plot may be interrupted by shifts in the point of view from the main character to his opponents, shifts which illuminate the depths of the danger the protagonist faces. As plot threads begin to tighten, confrontations between the hero and the antagonist (or his henchmen) become more frequent, until the two battle face-to-face.

BRIEF HISTORY

The 19th century saw the birth of the Thriller, from *The Last of the Mohicans* to *Twenty Thousand Leagues under the Sea*. At the same time those acclaimed classics were making a fortune, dime Westerns—hurriedly written, shoddily published, and quickly forgotten—divided the world into villainous black hats and noble white hats, enthralling readers looking for nonstop excitement. In the first quarter of the 20th century, the chasm between "respectable" adventure stories (usually Mysteries) and the seedier pulp novels deepened. But with the arrival of Raymond Chandler and Dashiell Hammett, critics and readers realized that the definition of a well-written story could include heroes handy with guns and aiming for retribution through their own moral codes.

Thrillers have always reflected the fears and hopes of the larger society. The period after World War II was the cradle of the genre, when men—and Thrillers were usually marketed toward men—seemed to place more trust in firepower and quick thinking than in the slower course of justice. Espionage and military stories recalled the heroism and clear-cut causes of the war while offering escape from the pall of the Cold War. Science, with its vision of the future sometimes obscured by a mushroom cloud, was not always the domain of the rational intellect, while the study of mental health opened windows into souls darker and more exciting than the faces they presented to the world.

Events through the turbulent last quarter of the 20th century exposed the fragility of social institutions and the fallibility of those entrusted with the responsibility of protecting good citizens. Corruption, from the precinct house to the White House, was in newspaper headlines, and Thrillers catalogued those failures. But they also offered the hopeful view that corruption could be uncovered and defeated, and the fabric of society stitched back together. And at the opening of the 21st century, we discovered that we are vulnerable in many ways but that individual people working together could also become heroes.

CURRENT TRENDS

Thriller writers are continually looking for new settings and scenarios to stimulate their readers, and readers look for authors who meet their particular reading tastes. Within the wide world of Thriller Fiction, here are some standout trends that are on a real growth curve.

Apocalyptic Thrillers

The end of the world—or more appropriately, people struggling to survive the end of the world—offers a rich vein for writers to explore. Natural, supernatural, or man-made apocalyptic scenarios cut right to the heart of what it means to let your worst instincts take over and still walk away with some measure of humanity. These aren't philosophical musings; after all, at their hearts, Thrillers are about ending with a bang, not a whimper.

Christian Thrillers

While novels with Christian themes have been a staple on bookshelves for many years, they usually dealt with more personal issues and an awareness of the possibilities of salvation. In past years, authors such as Tim LaHaye and Frank Peretti began writing story lines that forced characters to call on their faith to confront evil. Other writers have recently expanded into darker elements that echo mainstream Thrillers but maintain a distinct Christian voice.

Thrilling Women

From its earliest days, Thriller Fiction was the exclusive domain of male authors. Marcia Muller and Sara Paretsky changed that when they kicked in the door with their hard-hitting Mysteries. Women like Catherine Coulter, Nora Roberts, and Iris Johansen, who had honed their chops on Romance and Romantic Suspense, began taking over bookshelves with stories that proved women could write quality Thrillers. Publishers paid attention, producing titles that might formerly have been tagged with an undeserved reputation as "women's Romance books," and both critics and readers have recognized the strength of their storytelling and character creation.

THEMES AND TYPES

Key to Thrillers

Adventure
Conspiracy
Espionage
Religious

(Continued)

Crime
Cyber
Financial
Forensic
Law Enforcement
Legal
Medical
Military
Political
Psychological Suspense
Religious
Vigilante

1

2

3

4

Adventure Thrillers

There's nothing quite like that Saturday matinee feeling you get when a two-fisted man surmounts incredible odds to rescue the brave woman and thwart the villain's nefarious plans—that's what Adventure Thrillers are all about. Readers love these plot-driven stories that rocket along to explosive climaxes, and aren't too concerned if the details don't quite fit and the characters are a tad two-dimensional. When the world is black-and-white and it's easy to know that the good guys are on the side of Truth and Right, readers can relax and let the action carry them through.

5

6

Adams, Will

Daniel Wilcox Series. Wilcox, an enthusiastic archaeologist, has a knack for showing up in the right places at the right times and is smart enough to know it. Adams knows his history and knows how to use his heroic characters (and their not-quite-so-villainous counterparts) to drive fast-moving plots.

7

The Alexander Cipher. Grand Central, 2009, 336p. 9780446404709.
The Exodus Quest. Grand Central, 2010, 336p. 9780007250882.

8

Arruda, Suzanne

Jade del Cameron Series. An ambulance driver in World War I, del Cameron had experiences that made returning to civilian life impossible. She's tough, fierce, a deadly shot, and a determined detective. The African setting

9

is a big appeal in these stories, giving del Cameron lots of exotic locales to roam.

> *Mark of the Lion*. New American Library, 2006, 352p. 9780451219589.
> *Stalking Ivory*. New American Library, 2007, 352p. 9780451221681.
> *The Serpent's Daughter*. Obsidian, 2007, 352p. 9780451224651.
> *The Leopard's Prey*. Obsidian, 2009, 384p. 9780451227614.
> *Treasure of the Golden Cheetah*. Obsidian, 2009, 368p. 9780451229434.
> *The Crocodile's Last Embrace*. New American Library, 2010, 384p. 9780451231178.

Bell, Ted

__Alexander Hawke Series__. Alex Hawke could be anyone's model of a larger-than-life character. The wealthy Royal Navy veteran and charismatic friend of the powerful is a perfect match for the Adventure Thrillers Bell creates. *Hawke* (2003) is first in the series.

> *Spy*. Atria, 2006, 432p. 9780743277242.
> *Tsar*. Atria, 2008, 248p. 9781416550433.
> *Warlord*. William Morrow, 2010, 544p. 9780061859311.
> *Phantom*. William Morrow 2012; 496p. 9780061859304.

Essential Author

★ **Cussler, Clive, __Dirk Pitt Series__, *Trojan Odyssey***. Putnam, 2003, 496p. 9780425199329. In the 17th of the 21-book series, Pitt must save guests from an underwater luxury hotel imperiled by a superhurricane. At the same time, Pitt's newly discovered adult children are trapped undersea with an ancient and impossible relic. Like his NUMA Files Series and the Oregon Files Series, these thrilling sea stories include lots of techie systems and weaponry, deadly battles, and incredible escapes. The chief appeals to his legions of readers.

Dietrich, William

__Ethan Gage Adventures Series__. Like a 19th century Forrest Gump, Ethan Gage meets the luminaries of his time and participates in great history-making events. He would rather spend time in comfort, preferably with a lady, than in feats of derring-do, but his ingenuity and his courage make him an ideal agent for those in power.

Napoleon's Pyramids. HarperCollins, 2007, 384p. 9780062191489.
The Rosetta Key. HarperCollins, 2008, 352p. 9780062191571.
The Dakota Cipher. HarperCollins, 2009, 368p. 9780061568084.
The Barbary Pirates. HarperCollins, 2010, 320p. 9780062191410.
The Emerald Storm. HarperCollins, 2012, 368p. 9780061989209.

McDermott, Andy

<u>**Nina Wilde and Eddie Chase Series**</u>. Together with her bodyguard Eddie Chase, archaeologist Wilde is following in her parents' footsteps, exploring historical and mythological places around the world. Their names—Wilde Chase—give a sense of what to expect in these high action yarns.

The Hunt for Atlantis. Bantam, 2009, 512p. 9780553592856.
The Tomb of Hercules. Bantam, 2009, 483p. 9780553592948.
The Secret of Excalibur. Bantam, 2010, 500p. 9780553592955.
The Covenant of Genesis. Bantam, 2010, 512p. 9780553592962.
The Pyramid of Doom. Bantam, 2010, 512p. 9780553593631.
The Sacred Vault. Bantam, 2011, 500p. 9780553593648.
Empire of Gold. Bantam, 2011, 522p. 9780553593655.

Reilly, Matthew

<u>**Jack West Jr. Series**</u>. These death-defying, entirely implausible adventures target the adrenal glands for that old-fashioned comic-bookstore feel. West and his international team of intellectual commandoes face off against the world's bad guys. For the most fun, readers must start at the beginning.

Seven Deadly Wonders. Simon & Schuster, 2005, 400p. 9781416505068.
The Six Deadly Stones. Simon & Schuster, 2007, 352p. 9781416505075.
The Five Greatest Warriors. Simon & Schuster, 2010, 400p. 97814
16577584.

Rollins, James

Altar of Eden. William Morrow, 2009, 448p. 9780061231438. A veterinarian and a Border Patrol agent search the Louisiana bayous for a genetically enhanced animal while evading its creator.

<u>**SIGMA Force Series**</u>. Highly trained Special Forces veterans skilled in various branches of science search the world for useful or threatening technology. Rollins limits the downtime between action scenes, so these stories move like rocket sleds.

Black Order. William Morrow, 2006, 448p. 9780062017895.
The Judas Strain. William Morrow, 2007, 516p. 9780062017925.
🎗 *The Doomsday Key*. William Morrow, 2009, 448p. 9780061231414—
    Library Journal's Best Thriller of 2009.
🎗 *The Devil Colony*. William Morrow, 2011, 448p. 9780061785658—
    Library Journal's Best Thriller of 2011.
Bloodline. William Morrow, 2011, 448p. 9780061784798.

Tonkin, Peter

Richard Mariner Series. Dauntless British sea captain Mariner and his terrific wife Robin helm enormous vessels all over the world. These 25 books are rousing old-fashioned sea stories perfect for readers who find Patrick O'Brian too slow but still want salt air in their lungs. *Cape Farewell* (2006) is a good place for readers new to the series to begin.

High Wind in Java. Severn House, 2007, 217p. 9780727865595.
Benin Light. Severn House, 2008, 215p. 9780727866721.
River of Ghosts. Severn House, 2009, 218p. 9781847511287.
Volcano Roads. Severn House, 2010, 215p. 9780727868282.
The Prison Ship. Severn House, 2010, 256p. 9781847512345.
The Red River. Severn House, 2011, 224p. 9781847512970.
Ice Station. Severn House, 2011, 218p. 9781847513564.
The Dark Heart. Severn House, 2012, 208p. 9780727881656.

Conspiracy Thrillers

THEY are out there, and readers know it. THEY control government, the media, and the churches; and THEY are determined to keep their secrets. Only one person, with a little help from his friends, can expose the truth about their agenda. That is the formula for the successful Conspiracy Thriller, and it has proven effective for two generations.

Conspiracy Thrillers can be loosely divided into two subsets: the Espionage Thriller, which has been a staple since the end of World War II, and the Religious Conspiracy Thriller, which was kick-started by Dan Brown's 2003 Thriller *The Da Vinci Code*. Earlier writers of this style suddenly saw a resurgence of interest as readers demanded more, and when those few titles didn't sate their appetite, publishers began pursuing others to create new titles and series.

Espionage Thrillers

Spies are the ultimate loners. Armed only with cunning and charm (and maybe a pistol or interesting gadgets), they infiltrate their enemies' strongholds on the orders of their masters. Readers expect details about tradecraft—the arts of tailing targets, forgery and deceit, and a complex endgame that resolves the threat.

Abbott, Jeff

Sam Capra Series. Capra's pregnant wife betrayed him and killed their CIA colleagues. Tracking her and their infant child, he must also evade CIA assassins and do the bidding of a mysterious group that claims to have his family. Abbott writes fast-moving scenes that take the reader into the pits of torture and evil, while capturing the anguish of a conflicted man.

> *Adrenaline*. Grand Central, 2012, 416p. 9780446575171.
> *The Last Minute*. Grand Central, 2012, 448p. 9780446575201.

Battles, Brett

Jonathan Quinn Series. Quinn specializes in "cleaning" crime sites or intelligence operations to prevent discovery or mislead investigators, but he is no superspy hero. Along with his girlfriend and his apprentice cleaner, Quinn makes his way through a world that calls for trust, but where no one can be trusted.

> *The Cleaner*. Delacorte, 2007, 368p. 9780440244387.
> 🎗 *The Deceived*. Delacorte, 2008, 358p. 9780440243717—Barry Award for Best Thriller.
> *Shadow of Betrayal*. Delacorte, 2009, 419p. 9780440243724.
> *The Silenced*. Dell, 2011, 432p. 9780440245674.

Berenson, Alex

John Wells Series. Wells is assigned to infiltrate al-Qaeda, but his experiences lead him to a genuine crisis of faith. His failure to prevent the 9/11 attacks or to kill Osama bin Laden makes him the object of ongoing suspicion of some in the CIA. Berenson sets up explosive plots that allow the globe-trotting Wells to save the world at the last moment.

> 🎗 *The Faithful Spy*. Random House, 2006, 352p. 9780515144345—2007 Edgar Award for Best First Novel.
> *The Ghost War*. Putnam, 2008, 352p. 9780515145823.
> *The Silent Man*. Putnam, 2009, 432p. 9780515147537.

9

The Midnight House. Putnam, 2010, 400p. 9780515148954.
The Secret Soldier. Putnam, 2011, 401p. 9780515150346.
The Shadow Patrol. Putnam, 2010, 400p. 9780399158292.

Eisler, Barry

Ben Treven Series. A plausibly deniable agent in the netherworld of terrorist hunting, Treven is a ruthless killer able to strike swiftly and disappear. He's also easily manipulated in his world of double- and triple-crosses, but conspirators had better beware if he finds he's been used.

Fault Line. Ballantine, 2009, 256p. 9780345505095.
Inside Out. Ballantine, 2010, 256p. 9780345505118.

John Rain Series. Rain, half-Japanese, half-American, and all-lethal, is an assassin with dozens of ways to kill and make it look natural, but no sense of how to live. As his story develops, he comes to gather a kind of fellowship of like-minded souls (including Ben Treven) that will become important to future books. *Rain Fall* (2002) alternates moodiness with furious action while establishing Rain's character.

The Last Assassin. Putnam, 2006, 352p. 9780451412409.
Requiem for an Assassin. Putnam, 2007, 368p. 9780451412577.
The Detachment. Thomas & Mercer, 2011, 324p. 9781612181554.

Fleming, Ian

007: Carte Blanche. Jeffery Deaver; Simon & Schuster, 2011, 448p. 978145 1629354. Deaver's entry in the James Bond canon brings the British secret agent into the 21st century, complete with service in Afghanistan and his own iQPhone.

Devil May Care. Sebastian Faulks writing as Ian Fleming; Doubleday, 2008, 304p. 9780307387875. Still recovering from injuries he received in *The Man with the Golden Gun*, Bond is put on the trail of a manufacturer who plans to use the newfound freedom of the 1960s to engineer England's destruction.

Flynn, Vince

Mitch Rapp Series. Veteran agent Rapp is the man to go to when the prospect of terrorism rears its head. Both D.C. politics and Islamic plotting might be responsible for mayhem and murder, but Mitch Rapp always has a swift response. Filled with set-piece action scenes, these are fast and furious reads without much complication. New readers will want to check out *Memorial Day* (2004), the fourth in the series.

> *Act of Treason*. Atria, 2006, 432p. 9781416542261.
> *Protect and Defend*. Simon & Schuster, 2007, 416p. 9781416505037.
> *Extreme Measures*. Atria, 2006, 432p. 9781416505044.
> *Pursuit of Honor*. Pocket Books, 2009, 432p. 9781416595175.
> *American Assassin*. Atria, 2010, 435p. 9781416595199.
> *Kill Shot*. Atria, 2011, 448p. 9781416595205.

Grant, Andrew

David Trevellyan Series. British Naval Intelligence officer Trevellyan believes that a straight line is the shortest distance for a bullet, and he's happy to be the bullet. Alternating his current day activities (and the first two novels take place over the course of about 48 hours) with the details of his training, we learn how he acquired the mind-set and skills he demonstrates when he swings into action.

> *Even*. Minotaur, 209, 352p. 9780312358488.
> *Die Twice*. Minotaur, 2010, 352p. 9780312537944.

Hagberg, David

Blowout. Doherty, 2012, 448p. 9780765365873. A plan to create a cellular organism to consume coal and produce clean methane is endangered by a conspiracy among oil producers, a wealthy investor, and a homegrown right-wing terrorist.

Burned. Forge, 2007, 336p. 9780765357519. An American couple travels to Russia to work out the sticky details of a business deal, but their partners shoot David in the head and kidnap Patti for a $20-million ransom.

Kirk McGarvey Series. Unorthodox superspy McGarvey has been on the front lines of espionage from the Cold War to the War on Terror. These are well-researched and informative stories with a complex, heroic character. *Soldier of God* (2005) is the 10th book in the 16-book series and a great place for readers to begin.

> *Dance with the Dragon*. Forge, 2007, 384p. 9780765347343.
> *The Expediter*. Forge, 2009, 400p. 9780765349804.

The Cabal. Forge, 2010, 400p. 9780765359872.
Abyss. Tor, 2011, 496p. 9780765363732.
Castro's Daughter. Forge, 2012, 400p. 9780765320216.

Ignatius, David

Bloodmoney. Norton, 2011, 368p. 9780393341799. Sophie Marx discovers that the CIA unit she's working for has become corrupt. Her boss is manipulating financial markets, while a vengeful man penetrates security and kills four of her colleagues.

Body of Lies. Norton, 2007, 320p. 9780393334296. Roger Ferris goes deep undercover to find the architect of a series of European car bombs. With the assistance of Jordan's head of intelligence, he penetrates a network to create divisions, but may be a tool in a larger game.

The Increment. Norton, 2009, 400p. 9780393338317. An Iranian nuclear scientist tries to warn the CIA about the success of their program but wants out of the country. A senior agent goes into Iran but finds agendas with different goals.

Preston, Douglas, and Lincoln Childs

Gideon Crew Series. Preston and Childs open a new series with Gideon Crew, an accomplished man using his remaining life span trying to prevent nuclear crimes. Like their other work, these stories are rich with detail and move very swiftly from start to finish.

> *Gideon's Sword*. Grand Central, 2011, 480p. 9780446564311.
> *Gideon's Corpse*. Grand Central, 2012, 480p. 9780446564373.

Reich, Christopher

Jonathan Ransom Series. The confused and frightened Ransom battles with espionage and police forces who think his secret agent wife has sold out. Ransom is out of his depth, but he holds on to the hope that his wife is the woman he knew, not the terrorist she's accused of being.

> *Rules of Deception*. Doubleday, 2008, 320p. 9780307387820.
> *Rules of Vengeance*. Doubleday, 2009, 432p. 9780307387837.
> *Rules of Betrayal*. Doubleday, 2010, 368p. 9780307473813.

Essential Author

★ ♟ **Silva, Daniel, <u>Gabriel Allon Series</u>, *Prince of Fire*.** Putnam, 2005, 416p. 9780451215734. Allon's life as an art restorer is blown when his record of espionage and assassination is released. To control the damage, he rejoins the endless cycle of Middle East retribution. Silva writes tightly plotted stories that have little downtime and that hinge on the courage of Allon and his team. *The Kill Artist* (1991) was first in the 12-book series; *The Messenger* (2006) won the Barry Award.

Thor, Brad

<u>**Scot Harvath Series**</u>. Double supersecret agent Harvath is a genuine American hero, even if his work includes torture. His travels take him all over the world, usually to trouble spots that haven't quite hit the public eye. Start with *The Lions of Lucerne* (2002).

> *Takedown*. Atria, 2006, 416p. 9781451636154.
> *The First Commandment*. Atria, 2007, 404p. 9781451635669.
> *The Last Patriot*. Atria, 2008, 404p. 9781416543848.
> *The Apostle*. Pocket Books, 2009, 400p. 9781416586586.
> *Foreign Influence*. Atria, 2010, 368p. 9781416586609.
> *Full Black*. Atria, 2011, 368p. 9781451675245.

Religious Conspiracy Thrillers

Readers who followed the puzzle-driven *Da Vinci Code* look for stories that highlight some little-known aspect of theological history brought into the modern world. The stories hearken back to a past when religion (usually Christianity) was purer and before secret societies protected by fanatics shaped the Church to their own ends. The protagonists are not religious, or even spiritual, but they are familiar with religious traditions, and may even experience a spark of awakening in these fast-moving stories.

Becker, James

<u>**Chris Bronson Series**</u>. British detective Bronson stumbles into biblical Mysteries in the course of his official murder inquiries. Fortunately, his ex-wife is a British Museum conservator who can help him, and the friendly byplay between them is a relief to the high-speed chase scenes through the modern Middle East.

9

The First Apostle. Signet, 2009, 341p. 9780451226709.
The Moses Stone. Onyx, 2010, 480p. 9780451412874.
The Messiah Secret. Onyx, 2010, 480p. 9780451412980.
The Nosferatu Scroll. Bantam, 2011, 450p. 9780451236197.
Echo of the Reich. Signet, 2012, 480p. 9780451238290.

Berry, Steve

Cotton Malone Series. Copenhagen bookseller Malone is a retired spy, has a billionaire sponsor, and lots of beautiful women are ready to help him solve little-known historical conspiracies. Berry's complex page-turners offer dangerous brotherhoods and ingenious puzzles to engage the reader's curiosity along with their excitement.

The Templar Legacy. Ballantine, 2006, 496p. 9780345504418.
The Alexandria Link. Ballantine, 2007, 496p. 9780345485762.
The Venetian Betrayal. Ballantine, 2007, 464p. 9780345485786.
🎗 *The Charlemagne Pursuit.* Ballantine, 2008, 384p. 9780345485809 —
    Library Journal's Best Thriller of 2008.
The Paris Vendetta. Ballantine, 2009, 352p. 9780345505484.
The Emperor's Tomb. Ballantine, 2010, 480p. 9780345505507.
The Jefferson Key. Ballantine, 2011, 480p. 9780345505521.
The Columbus Affair. Ballantine, 2011, 426p. 9780345526519.

Brokaw, Charles

Thomas Lourds Series. These action-driven novels center on a brilliant and handsome translator of ancient languages. Accompanied by sexy women, Lourds coolly survives quick-moving chases and gunfights to solve these puzzles.

The Atlantis Code. Forge, 2009, 432p. 9780765354358.
The Lucifer Code. St Martin's, 2010, 368p. 9780765360694.
The Temple Mount Code. Forge, 2011, 352p. 9780765328717.

Christopher, Paul

Finn Ryan Series. A refreshing view in a genre dominated by male heroes, Ryan is an intrepid woman who travels to far-flung parts of the world and crosses paths with villains. Graphic descriptions of both sex and violence keep the pages turning, which is probably best, since neither characters nor history is fleshed out.

Michaelangelo's Notebook. New American Library, 2005, 358p. 9780451411860.
The Lucifer Gospel. Onyx, 2006, 357p. 9780451412232.
Rembrandt's Ghost. Signet, 2007, 355p. 9780451221759.
The Aztec Heresy. Signet, 2008, 346p. 9780451224521.

Templars Series. As former Army Ranger and West Point instructor John Holliday finds, the Knights Templar held power both longer and in a greater empire than ever known before. Along with his niece and an Israeli archaeologist, he must defend himself from governments, spies, and sinister brotherhoods bent on preserving their secrets.

The Sword of the Templars. Signet, 2009, 336p. 9780451227409.
The Templar Cross. Signet, 2010, 391p. 9780451228857.
The Templar Throne. Signet, 2010, 400p. 9780451230683.
The Templar Conspiracy. Signet, 2011, 400p. 9780451231901.
The Templar Legion. Signet, 2011, 386p. 9780451233585.
Red Templar. Penguin, 2012, 400p. 9780451236302.
Valley of the Templars. Penguin, 2012, 400p. 9780451237156.

Essential Author

★ **Khoury, Raymond, Sean Reilly and Tess Chaykin Series**, *The Last Templar*. Dutton, 2006, 416p. 9780451219954. Archaeologist Chaykin and FBI agent Reilly search for a code-breaking device stolen from a collection of Vatican treasures.

Crime Thrillers

Crime Thrillers turn the idea of an ordered, predictable world on its head by taking the viewpoint of men and women who live to break the law. Are they the good guys? Other criminals, including bad cops, are the usual antagonists, so readers expect deception, betrayal, and a violent resolution to the story.

Atkins, Ace

Devil's Garden. Putnam, 2009, 368p. 9780425232668. Dashiell Hammett investigates murder accusations against comedian Fatty Arbuckle.

Infamous. Putnam, 2010, 416p. 9780425239018. A kidnapping by Machine Gun Kelly starts a criminal race to steal the ransom.

White Shadow. Putnam, 2006, 384p. 9780425230541. The death of a Miami mob boss reveals the city's secrets.

Wicked City. Putnam, 2008, 352p. 9780425227077. An ordinary man becomes the leader of citizens determined to take their town back from the Mob.

Collins, Max Allen

Quarry Series. Assassin-for-hire Quarry is a stone killer paid very well by his intermediary, The Broker. First introduced in 1985, Collins brought back an older, though no less lethal, Quarry in 2006, then went back to earlier points in his history.

The Last Quarry. Countryman Press, 2006, 256p. 9780857683700.
The First Quarry. Hard Case Crime, 2008, 256p. 9780857683649.
Quarry in the Middle. Hard Case Crime, 2009, 206p. 9780857683526.
Quarry's Ex. Leisure Books, 2010, 208p. 9780857682864.

Hunt, James Patrick

Bridger Series. Dan Bridger is a mechanic by day, a professional thief by night, and a vengeful man when double-crossed. Hunt conveys the stories with terse dialogue, a good feel for place, and a character that is tougher than he appears but who still has a tender spot.

Bridger. Five Star, 2010, 240p. 9781594148613.
Police and Thieves. Five Star, 2011, 240p. 9781432825072.

Lindsay, Jeff

Dexter Series. One of the oddest Crime Thriller series follows the career of a serial killer of serial killers. Using first-person narration, Lindsay immerses readers in Dexter Morgan's mind, following the details of his searches for "playmates" through Miami's Wild West of ordinary homicide. Dexter analyzes emotions he can't feel, which makes these stories occasionally funny. *Darkly Dreaming Dexter* (2004) is an essential introduction to the entire cast of people around Dexter.

Dexter in the Dark. Doubleday, 2007, 368p. 9780307276735.
Dexter by Design. Doubleday, 2009, 368p. 9780307276742.
Dexter is Delicious. Doubleday, 2010, 320p. 9780307474926.
Double Dexter. Doubleday, 2011, 320p. 9780385532372.

Perry, Thomas

Fidelity. Harcourt, 2008, 368p. 9781593155940. The widow and the assassin of a private investigator search for answers—Emily because she wants to know why her husband left her broke, and Jerry because he wants to blackmail the client who hired him. Then the client joins in.

Nightlife. Random House, 2006, 384p. 9780345496003. Detective Catherine Hobbes is searching for a killer. She doesn't know that Tanya Starling is adopting different identities and committing murder under each of them.

Silence. Harcourt, 2007, 448p. 9781593155230. Retired detective Jack Till must search for Wendy Harper, the woman he taught to disappear, to prove that she wasn't murdered. But a husband-and-wife hit team is just waiting for her to show up.

Strip. Houghton Mifflin Harcourt, 2010, 432p. 9780151015221. Joe Carver arrives in Los Angeles just as a thief rips off a strip club. The owner's henchmen come after Carver, while the original thief decides on a repeat attempt, and a foolhardy cop thinks the money might solve some of his problems.

Piccirilli, Tom

The Cold Spot. Bantam, 2008, 303p. 9780553590845. Chase has escaped the life his grandfather trained him in—getaway driver. Now living with Lila, the Mississippi deputy who reformed him, he wants nothing more than to forget his upbringing.

🏵 *The Coldest Mile*. Bantam, 2009, 335p. 9780553590852. When Lila is murdered, Chase vows revenge. Taking up his old profession, he intends to rip off his employers. With the money, he can search for his grandfather, but finding him may be the last thing he does. It won the International Thriller Writers Award for Best Paperback Original.

The Dead Letters. Bantam, 2006, 363p. 9780553384079. Eddie Whitt's daughter was murdered by a serial killer named Killjoy. Eddie has since devoted his life to hunting Killjoy, but may have crossed his own line into insanity.

Every Shallow Cut. ChiZine, 2011, 175p. 9781926851105. A nameless narrator sets off across the country to find his brother, accompanied by his bulldog, his self-recriminations, and a gun.

The Fever Kill. Creeping Hemlock Press, 2008, 184p. 9780976921745. Returning to his hometown in the wake of his father's death, Crease stirs up old trouble to add to his woes. Crease is an undercover cop, but his identity was blown and he's running from his murderous target.

Headstone City. Bantam, 2006, 336p. 9780553587210. "Dane" Danetello, newly released from prison, is back driving cabs around Brooklyn with spirits of the dead riding along with him. He's also being hunted by the Mob and his old partner.

🎗 *The Midnight Road*. Bantam, 2007, 317p. 9780553384086. After Flynn crashes into a frozen lake and dies for nearly half an hour, people around him start dying at the hand of a mysterious killer. It won the International Thriller Writers Award for Best Paperback Original.

Shadow Season. Bantam, 2009, 304p. 9780553592474. Ex-cop Finn now teaches at a private girls school. The school is nearly deserted for the Christmas holidays when a pair of murderers starts a killing spree, leaving Finn to protect the remnant.

Sakey, Marcus

The Amateurs. Dutton, 2009, 368p. 9780525951261. Four friends decide to pull off a heist. The setup goes wrong and suddenly the quartet has to navigate between suspicious cops, a vengeful gang, and the realization that they weren't as close as they'd thought.

At the City's Edge. Minotaur, 2008, 320p. 9780312943738. Jason Palmer returns from Baghdad to bloodshed on the streets of Chicago. After his brother is murdered, Jason veers between wanting to unleash revenge and caring for his nephew.

Good People. Dutton, 2008, 336p. 9780451412744. Anna and Tom Reed discover that money has a price when they stumble on a $400,000 stash in their tenant's apartment. People on both ends of a blown drug deal want it back.

The Two Deaths of Daniel Hayes. Dutton, 2011, 400p. 9780525952114. A man stumbles from the Atlantic Ocean with no idea who he is. As he slowly recovers his memory, he realizes that he must face up to something that happened to him in California.

Essential Author

★ **Stark, Richard, <u>Parker Series</u>, *Firebreak*.** Mysterious Press, 2001, 297p. 9780226770659. Parker joins a plan to steal an art collection worth a fortune from a dot-com millionaire's illegal stash. Stark starts the action right away and builds to high-octane climaxes in this classic series.

Swierczynski, Duane

The Blonde. St. Martin's, 2006, 256p. 9780312374594. Harmless flirtation in an airport bar turns deadly when a young woman shanghais Jack Eisley and forces him to stay within 10 feet of her at all times.

🎖 *Expiration Date*. Minotaur, 2010, 224p. 9780312363406. Mickey Wade suddenly finds himself able to move between the 1970s and the present. He hopes he can use that ability to locate and stop the kid who killed his father. It won the Anthony Award for Best Paperback Original.

Severance Package. St. Martin's, 2008, 272p. 9780312343804. Jamie De-Broux gets caught in a war between two intelligence agencies, one of which is camouflaged by the finance company where he works.

Vachss, Andrew

__Burke Series__. Over the course of 18 novels (starting with *Flood* in 1998), Burke has mercilessly eliminated predators who profit from sexual abuse of the young. Aided by a virtually invisible army of street people, Burke tries to rescue these children, but he isn't always successful.

> *Mask Market*. Pantheon, 2006, 241p. 9780307454812.
> *Terminal*. Pantheon, 2007, 256p. 9780307387059.
> *Another Life*. Pantheon, 2008, 288p. 9780307390394.

Haiku. Pantheon, 2009, 224p. 9780307475282. A group of homeless men has to execute a plan to save one member's extensive collection of Mysteries from a doomed building.

The Weight. Pantheon, 2010, 288p. 9780307741318. After five years in prison on a phony charge, "Sugar" Caine is on the streets looking for the payoff for his last crime.

That's How I Roll. Pantheon, 2011, 224p. 9780307379948. Multiple murderer Esau Till is writing his autobiography from Death Row as protection for his easily misled brother.

Blackjack. Vintage Books, 2012, 176p. 9780307949578. A touch of horror joins Vachss' crime writing as killer-for-hire Cross and his band of accomplices track a killer who, among other things, takes his victims' spines.

Cyber and Technothrillers

Computers rule our world, and the people who operate them rule the computers. Sure, we know how to e-mail, but do we know how to hack? Do we know how to protect our loved ones from people bent on manipulating our data? With technology revolutionizing society seemingly every month, it isn't hard to use the cyberworld to make readers want to pull the plug on their Internet connection.

Technothrillers employ the same kinds of cutting-edge technology and theory, venturing into the realms of physics, biology, astronomy, and space travel. These Technothrillers don't focus on military hardware, instead concentrating on the dangers that probing deep secrets without wisdom can create. Readers expect information detailed enough to follow the plot, but not so detailed as to bog it down.

Child, Lincoln

Much as he does with Douglas Preston in the **Special Agent Pendergast Series** (found in the Horror chapter), Child writes stories of explorations that release danger into the world. They rely on strong personalities, remote locations, and secrets best left buried.

> *Deep Storm*. Doubleday, 2006, 384p. 9781400095476.
> *Terminal Freeze*. Doubleday, 2009, 336p. 9781400095483.
> *The Third Gate*. Doubleday, 2012, 368p. 9780385531382.

Essential Author

★ **Crichton, Michael, *Prey***. HarperCollins, 2002, 367p. 9780061703089. A groundbreaking technology escapes from a desert lab and begins hunting its human creators. Crichton creates interludes between dangerous episodes to have his characters explain the science, but does it in a way that maintains the rising tempo of the plot.

Suarez, Daniel

Information technology consultant Suarez has an inside track in writing his **Cyber Thrillers**, writing cautionary tales about our overreliance on new technology.

> *Daemon*. Dutton, 2009, 432p. 9780451228734.
> *Freedom*. Dutton, 2010, 400p. 9780451231895.

Tracy, P. J.

Monkeewrench Series. Home to a crew of eccentric, sometimes scary computer geniuses, Monkeewrench software helps police hunt serial killers with cutting-edge programs. These are not entirely grim stories—moments of affection and humor lighten the stories but make the danger more personal to the reader. Start with *Monkeewrench* (2003), first in the series and the 2004 Anthony Award winner for Best First Novel.

🎗 *Snow Blind.* Putnam, 2006, 320p. 9780451412362—2006 *Romantic Times* Reviewers' Choice Award for Best Mystery and Suspense Novel.
Shoot to Thrill. Penguin, 2010, 320p. 9780451413055.

Financial Thrillers

Most people don't comprehend many financial transactions beyond the level of balancing their checkbooks. However, it isn't hard to understand the attraction of Financial Thrillers when you look in the newspaper and see financial crimes played out in the headlines. Readers want stories with industry insiders exploiting loopholes or complex financial transactions with unimaginable amounts of money at stake.

Finder, Joseph

🎗 *Killer Instinct.* St. Martin's, 2006, 416p. 9780312347499. Jason Steadman's career takes off when he hires ex-Special Forces soldier Kurt Semko to play on his company softball team. Bad things start happening to his rivals, but Kurt's help could be a double-edged sword. It won the 2007 Thriller Award for Best Novel.

Nick Heller Series. Nick Heller handles corporate intelligence, using his special military experience. He is an old-fashioned guy with a strong sense of honor and justice, willing to put himself into danger to help those who earn his loyalty.

> *Vanished.* St. Martin's, 2009, 400p. 9780312946517.
> *Buried Secrets.* St. Martin's, 2011, 400p. 9781250000361.

🎗 *Power Play.* St. Martin's, 2007, 384p. 9780312347505. A corporate retreat is already going wrong for Jake Landry, the lowest man on the totem pole. Then a group of armed men break into the isolated resort, and it's up to Jake to rescue his coworkers. It won *Library Journal*'s Best Thriller of 2007.

Essential Author

★ **Frey, Stephen, Christian Gillette Series, *The Chairman***. Ballantine, 2005, 320p. 9780345457615. Gillette is tapped as the new head of Everest Capital in this first of a five-book series, and that makes him the target of assaults on his life and reputation. Frey finds personal drama in the powerful and rarified world of private equity funds.

Vonnegut, Norb

The Gods of Greenwich. Minotaur, 2011, 336p. 9781250000354. Jimmy Cusack loses his hedge fund and takes an undesirable job to cover his huge debts. He learns that the head guy is making bets that will cause a meltdown when, not if, they're discovered.

Top Producer. Minotaur, 2009, 352p. 9780312388300. Investment adviser Grove O'Rourke witnesses the very public murder of his friend and mentor. While helping the man's widow sort out his affairs, he comes across evidence of fraud.

The Trust. Minotaur, 2012, 336p. 9781250003898. Grove O'Rourke temporarily manages a philanthropic organization and must investigate evidence that one of their funds is running a huge porn operation. He also discovers why his predecessor died.

Forensic Thrillers

The science of forensic detection goes all the way back to Edgar Allan Poe and "The Murders in the Rue Morgue." In Mysteries, forensic science plays a supporting role, feeding information to the professional investigator; in Forensic Thrillers, the specialists become the primary searchers, getting more involved than they should. The chief appeal to fans of the Forensic Thriller is the elaborate detail about state-of-the-art detection methods. Chemical, biological, ballistic, and fingerprint analysis are familiar to most readers, so writers have expanded into other areas where forensic specialists operate—postmortem reconstruction, psychological inquiry, and even financial scrutiny.

Bass, Jefferson

<u>Body Farm Series</u>. Dr. Bill Brockton is the founder of the legendary Body Farm and a consultant on special cases. His personal life is a mess as well; after losing his wife before the series begins, he becomes unhappily involved with different women. These stories have gruesome levels of detail, so readers should be warned.

> *Carved in Bone*. William Morrow, 2006, 352p. 9780060759827.
> *Flesh and Bone*. William Morrow, 2007, 368p. 9780060759841.
> *The Devil's Bones*. William Morrow, 2008, 352p. 9780060759902.
> *Bones of Betrayal*. William Morrow, 2009, 368p. 9780061284755.
> *The Bone Thief*. William Morrow, 2010, 344p. 9780061284779.

The Bone Yard. William Morrow, 2011, 352p. 9780061807046.
The Inquisitor's Key. William Morrow, 2012, 352p. 9780061806797.

Beckett, Simon

David Hunter Series. British forensic anthropologist David Hunter retreated to a small medical practice in the country, but is drawn back into the world of forensics against his will. Hunter is morose and distant, a loner who is happiest doing his investigative work and handing off the results, but his cases demand more commitment from him—especially when they imperil his life.

The Chemistry of Death. Delacorte, 2006, 320p. 9780440335955.
Written in Bone. Delacorte, 2007, 336p. 9780440335962.
Whispers of the Dead. Delacorte, 2009, 400p. 9780440335979.
The Calling of the Grave. Bantam, 2011, 336p. 9780593063453.

Black, Lisa

Theresa MacLean Series. MacLean, a forensic investigator with the Cleveland Police Department, is trying to resolve her personal issues even as she handles difficult cases. Black not only offers plenty of detail about the difficulty of crime scene investigation, but also delves into the politics that make MacLean's work even harder.

Takeover. William Morrow, 2008, 352p. 9780061544477.
Evidence of Murder. William Morrow, 2009, 352p. 9780061544507.
Trail of Blood. William Morrow, 2010, 352p. 9780061989360.
Defensive Wounds. William Morrow, 2011, 352p. 9780061989421.

Deaver, Jeffery

Kathryn Dance Series. Kathryn Dance works for the California State Board of Investigation as an interrogator who analyzes body movement for clues. She was introduced in the 2006 Lincoln Rhyme novel *The Cold Moon*, with a return appearance in *The Burning Wire*, but is the central character in the series' other books.

The Sleeping Doll. Simon & Schuster, 2007, 448p. 9780743491587.
Roadside Crosses. Simon & Schuster, 2009, 416p. 9781416550006.
XO. Simon & Schuster, 2012, 448p. 9781439156377.

Essential Read

★ **Lincoln Rhyme Series, *The Vanished Man***. Simon & Schuster, 2003, 432p. 9780743437813. Quadriplegic Rhyme was the preeminent criminologist in New York City before the accident that left him crippled. When the NYPD is baffled by a series of crimes emulating famous stage illusions, he sends his on-scene investigator and girlfriend Amanda Sachs to the scenes as his eyes and ears. Deaver alternates points-of-view between investigators and murderers, giving explicit details of these crimes.

Gardiner, Meg

<u>Jo Beckett Series</u>. Beckett is a consulting forensic psychiatrist to the San Francisco Police Department. When investigators need to understand the mental state of a dead person to distinguish between murder and suicide, or to find a motive, they call on her. That puts her directly into the path of danger.

> *The Dirty Secrets Club*. Dutton, 2008, 304p. 9780451227171.
> *The Memory Collector*. Dutton, 2009, 368p. 9780451230263.
> *Liar's Lullaby*. Dutton, 2010, 368p. 9780451233875.
> *The Nightmare Thief*. Penguin, 2011, 368p. 9780451235961.

Gerritsen, Tess

<u>Rizzoli and Isles Series</u>. While Boston detective Jane Rizzoli and medical examiner Maura Isles work together professionally, they also have personal interactions that aren't very smooth. The solo Rizzoli stories begin with *The Surgeon* (2001), but Isles wasn't introduced until *The Sinner* (2003). Like most series involving medical examiners and homicide detectives, expect lots of ghastly details in these nine books.

> *The Mephisto Club*. Ballantine, 2006, 368p. 9780345477002.
> *The Keepsake*. Ballantine, 2008, 368p. 9780345497635.
> *Ice Cold*. Ballantine, 2010, 368p. 9780345515490.
> *The Silent Girl*. Ballantine, 2010, 368p. 9780345515513.

Essential Authors

★ **Johansen, Iris, <u>Eve Duncan Series</u>, *Blind Alley*.** Bantam, 2004, 352p. 9780553586503. Eve Duncan recreates faces from grisly remains to identify missing children. It is the forensic sculptor's way of paying tribute to her daughter

Bonnie, who disappeared at the age of seven in series intro *The Face of Deception* (1998). In this story, fifth in the series, Eve helps search for a serial killer targeting women who bear a resemblance to the statue of a woman killed in the eruption of Mount Vesuvius.

─────────

─────────

Must Read

★ **Reichs, Kathy, <u>Temperance Brennan Series</u>,** *Fatal Voyage*. Scribner, 2001, 363p. 9780671028374. Temperance "Tempe" Brennan divides her time between North Carolina, where she teaches forensic anthropology, and Canada's Quebec Province, where she works as a pathologist. Fourth in the Brennan series, Fatal Voyage follows Tempe's work on a plane crash that yields a body part that can't be matched to any of the dead passengers. Deja Dead (1997) kicks off the 14-volume series.

─────────

Law Enforcement Thrillers

Distinguishing between Mysteries with professional law enforcement characters and Law Enforcement Thrillers is tricky, and is probably the one place where hardcore fans of either genre are most likely to be forgiving. Some key differences that point to the Thrillers—even in a dangerous job, the main character faces increased risk as a result of the investigation. The character does not have an entire organization to rely on, so the danger becomes personal. Police procedure takes a backseat to unorthodox methods and instinct, so the end focus is not necessarily on an arrest, but stopping the villain permanently.

Atkins, Ace

<u>Quinn Colson Series</u>. Colson, an Army Ranger, returns to his small Mississippi town to find that the evils of the 21st century have hit it hard. His right-or-wrong view of the world can blind him to subtlety, but he is able to make the transition from lone crime fighter to elected sheriff.

The Ranger. Putnam, 2011, 352p. 9780425247495.
The Lost Ones. Putnam, 2012, 352p. 9780399158766.

9

Deaver, Jeffery

🎗 *The Bodies Left Behind*. Simon & Schuster, 2008, 288p. 9781416595625. Deputy Brynn MacKenzie finds a young woman who witnessed a double murder, and the two must help each other survive. It won the 2009 Thriller Award for Best Novel.

Edge. Simon & Schuster, 2010, 368p. 9781439156360. Protecting a D.C. cop, Corte outwits a no-holds-barred pursuer who considers the contest personal.

Essential Author

★ **DeMille, Nelson, <u>John Corey Series</u>, *Night Fall***. Warner, 2004, 496p. 9780446177924. Corey, a former New York City detective, is detailed to a terrorism task force, where he disobeys orders and investigates the real-life crash of TWA Flight 800.

Parker, T. Jefferson

<u>Charlie Hood Series</u>. Three-time Edgar Award winner Parker concocts high-speed stories set around the badlands of the Mexican border, where the drug and weapons trade flows through his backyard. Readers need to start with the first of the five books in the series, *LA Outlaws* (2008).

> *LA Outlaws*. Dutton, 2008, 384p. 9780451226112.
> *The Renegades*. Dutton, 2009, 416p. 9780451227546.
> *Iron River*. Dutton, 2010, 384p. 9780451232427.
> *The Border Lords*. Dutton, 2011, 384p. 9780525952008.
> *The Jaguar*. Dutton, 2011, 368p. 9780525952572.

Zuiker, Anthony

<u>Level 26 Trilogy</u>. Along with Duane Swierczynski (see Crime Thrillers), Zuiker created Level 26, a secret group of investigators working to bring the worst serial killers in the world to ground. The series offers links to optional Web video enhancements.

> *Dark Origins*. Dutton, 2009, 384p. 9780451232380.
> *Dark Prophecy*. Dutton, 2010, 400p. 9780525951858.
> *Dark Revelations*. Dutton, 2010, 400p. 9780525951971.

Legal Thrillers

Fascination with the American justice system—from police to courtrooms—offers bountiful options for Thriller writers. Readers want to see courtroom scenes, with strategic and tactical maneuvering that creates or undermines the case at hand. They expect a fairly visible divide between prosecution and defense, with judges often appearing as ineffectual or biased referees. And they expect a clear delineation of the stakes of the case—what it is about, how it will unfold, and what the consequences are for both sides.

Bell, James Scott

Ty Buchanan Series. Buchanan walks away from a high-powered career when his fiancée is killed and takes a job helping poor clients. While not overtly Christian, Bell uses Ty's life to demonstrate biblical living.

Try Dying. Center Street, 2007, 280p. 9781599951980.
Try Darkness. Center Street, 2008, 304p. 9781599952437.
Try Fear. Center Street, 2009, 304p. 9781599956862.

Caldwell, Laura

Izzy MacNeil Series. Attorney Caldwell blends her Chick Lit and Romantic Suspense experience into a charming series of Legal Thrillers. Fiery redhead MacNeil works in Chicago as an entertainment lawyer, but the men in her life have a penchant for big-time trouble that requires her help.

Red Hot Lies. Mira, 2009, 420p. 9780778326502.
Red Blooded Murder. Mira, 2009, 420p. 9780778326588.
Red, White and Dead. Mira, 2009, 420p. 9780778326663.
Claim of Innocence. Mira, 2011, 400p. 9780778329329.
A Question of Trust. Mira, 2011, 400p. 9780778313212.

Dugoni, Robert

David Sloane Series. David Sloane was legendary in his defense of corporations sued in wrongful death court cases. An unbroken string of victories didn't bring him any happiness, so he changed his life and became the attorney of last resort for plaintiffs with complex, even impossible, cases. There are five books in the series.

The Jury Master. Warner, 2006, 448p. 9780446617079.
Wrongful Death. Touchstone, 2009, 384p. 9781416592976.
Bodily Harm. Touchstone, 2010, 384p. 9781416592983.
🏅 *Murder One*. Touchstone, 2011, 384p. 9781451606706—*Library Jour-nal*'s Top Thrillers of 2011
The Conviction. Touchstone, 2012, 384p. 9781451606720.

Essential Author

🏅 **Fairstein, Linda, Alexandra Cooper Series, *The Deadhouse*.** Scribner, 2001, 414p. 9780671019549. When an abused wife is murdered, Cooper investigates, although the list of suspects grows to include the woman's coworkers, drug traffickers, and treasure hunters. It won the 2001 Nero Award for literary excellence in the Mystery genre.

Grippando, James

Jack Swytek Series. The multiethnic city of Miami gives Grippando space to combine Legal, Political, and International Thrillers. Swytek is a confrontational criminal defense lawyer willing to buck authority just for the heck of it. There are nine books in the series, starting with *The Pardon* in 1994.

Got the Look. HarperCollins, 2006, 400p. 9780060565688.
When Darkness Falls. HarperCollins, 2006, 336p. 9780062087942.
Last Call. HarperCollins, 2008, 304p. 9780062088048.
Born to Run. HarperCollins, 2008, 336p. 9780061556159.
Afraid of the Dark. HarperCollins, 2011, 416p. 9780061840296.
Need You Now. HarperCollins, 2012, 368p. 9780061840302. Junior investment banker Patrick Lloyd investigates the disappearance of billions of dollars in a Ponzi scheme.

Margolin, Phillip

Amanda Jaffe Series. Jaffe is a brilliant attorney with excellent instincts and the courage to stand her ground in tough situations. Because she frequently represents murderers, she confronts violence on a regular basis. The four books featuring Jaffe start with the grisly, twisty novel *Wild Justice* (2000).

Ties That Bind. HarperCollins, 2003, 352p. 9780060083250.
Proof Positive. HarperCollins, 2006, 320p. 9780060735067.
Fugitive. HarperCollins, 2009, 352p. 9780061236242.

Dana Cutler and Brad Miller Series. Private detective Cutler and attorney Miller cross into political minefields when seemingly ordinary cases bring them into the world of the high and mighty.

> *Executive Privilege*. HarperCollins, 2008, 368p. 9780061236228.
> *Supreme Justice*. HarperCollins, 2010, 352p. 9780061926525.
> *Capitol Murder*. HarperCollins, 2012, 342p. 9780062069887.

Martini, Steve

Paul Madriani Series

The Attorney. Putnam, 2000, 429p. 9780515130041. Madriani helps a lottery winner whose ex-con daughter tries to blackmail him. Madriani is a career defense attorney with impeccable procedure and a flair for courtroom dramatics. Although he gets involved with drama and investigations, the focus of the 12 books in the series (starting with *Undue Influence*, 1993) is definitely in the courtroom.

Scottoline, Lisa

Rosato and Associates Series

Rosato and Associates Series. Scottoline's 13-volume series started with *Everywhere That Mary Went* (1993). The all-woman Philadelphia law firm offers plenty of courtroom time with different associates. Scottoline also has a deft touch with humor. She won the Edgar Award in 1995 for *Final Appeal*.

> *Lady Killer*. HarperCollins, 2008, 355p. 9780060833213.
> *Think Twice*. St. Martin's, 2010, 374p. 9780312380762.

Dirty Blonde. HarperCollins, 2006, 368p. 9780060742911. Federal judge Cate Fante has a double life that comes to light in the wake of a sensational civil trial. When both the plaintiff and defendant wind up dead, Fante's life threatens to become the subject of a dramatic TV series.

Daddy's Girl. HarperCollins, 2007, 336p. 9780060833152. After agreeing to teach a class at a local prison, law professor Natalie Greco is caught up in a riot. The final words of a dying guard drag her in a deadly conspiracy that yanks her out of her drab life.

Look Again. St. Martin's, 2009, 352p. 9780312380731. Adoptive mother Kate Gleeson learns that her son may have been kidnapped as an infant. While tracing the story, the reporter uncovers evidence that Will's case is not unique. Meanwhile, someone trying to hush up the case is getting closer to her.

Save Me. St. Martin's, 2011, 384p. 9780312380793. Rose McKenna saves two girls when their school is torn apart by an explosion. Instead of being treated as a hero, she is vilified. She also second-guesses herself, because her child was not the first one she tried to rescue.

Come Home. St. Martin's, 2012, 384p. 9780312380823. When her devious ex-husband dies in an apparent suicide, Dr. Jill Farrow agrees to help her stepdaughter Abby look into it. Her investigation alienates her fiancé and her own daughter.

Singer, Randy

By Reason of Insanity. Tyndale House, 2008, 350p. 9781414315478. Catherine O'Rourke is charged with murder when details from her vivid dreams match a series of crimes.

False Witness. Waterbrook Press, 2007, 352p. 9781414335698. Three law students find themselves working for a couple with a mysterious background.

Fatal Convictions. Tyndale House, 2010, 392p. 9781414333205. An imam is accused of murdering a convert to Christianity, and no reputable lawyer in town will touch his case.

The Justice Game. Tyndale House, 2009, 400p. 9781414316345. When a woman is shot, her husband sues the company who illegally sold the gun to the killer.

The Last Plea Bargain. Tyndale House, 2012, 400p. 9781414333212. Prosecutor Jamie Brock's trust in the court system is tested by the impending execution of a possibly innocent man and a backlog that may set guilty people free.

Teller, Joseph

Jaywalker Series. Harrison J. Walker frequently serves as a public defender in New York City's court system, where he alienates judges with his personal and professional behavior.

🎗 *The Tenth Case*. Mira, 2008, 384p. 9780778326052—Winner of the 2009 Nero Award for literary excellence in the Mystery genre.
Bronx Justice. Mira, 2009, 384p. 9780778326359.

Depraved Indifference. Mira, 2009, 375p. 9780778326915.
Overkill. Mira, 2010, 359p. 9780778327769.
Guilty as Sin. Mira, 2011, 318p. 9780778312338.

Essential Author

★ 🎖 **Turow, Scott, *Reversible Errors***. Farrar, Straus and Giroux, 2002, 448p. 9780446584166. Weeks before an inmate is executed, another man confesses to the crime and suddenly an open-and-shut case becomes murky. Turow's stories based in the fictional Kindle County examine the intersection of law and society, but are no less exciting for their thoughtful approaches. He is widely credited with inventing the Legal Thriller with his 1987 title *Presumed Innocent*. *Reversible Errors* was a 2002 *New York Times* Notable Book.

Medical Thrillers

In a society where doctors are held in awe and hospitals are the new cathedrals, some writers like to imagine the snakes on the caduceus as poisonous vipers. Readers expect settings that revolve around medicine—hospitals, individual practices, drug labs, and medical schools especially—and exotic symptoms that challenge even the most dedicated physician. There are plenty of villains to choose from: doctors themselves, administrators, health insurance companies, drug manufacturers, etc.—anyone who can unilaterally make life-or-death decisions over ordinary people.

Essential Author

★ **Cook, Robin, *Shock***. Putnam, 2001, 370p. 9780425182864. Two young women investigate the fertility clinic where they donated their eggs and find a nest of lies. Cook writes about the frontiers of medicine with enough detail to engage the reader, but without bogging down the narrative. His fast-starting plots build to high-tension endings that hang on unusual plot twists and lots of violence.

Kalla, Daniel

Blood Lies. Forge, 2007, 320p. 9780765357922. Seattle doctor Ben Dafoe's fiancée has just been murdered, and his unusual blood type is on the scene. He goes underground in Canada to identify the real killer before the cops pin the murder on him.

The Far Side of the Sky. HarperCollins, 2011, 448p. 9780765332332. During World War II, surgeon Franz Adler works in a Shanghai refugee hospital where he must struggle against the Japanese occupation and his complicated love for a Eurasian nurse.

Of Flesh and Blood. Forge, 2010, 448p. 9780765361028. An intergenerational feud between two families threatens the work being done at a prestigious hospital and research facility, even as an epidemic affects the patients.

Pandemic. Tor, 2005, 407p. 9780765350848. Traveling to China to investigate a superflu that kills 25 percent of those infected, Dr. Noah Haldane finds that international travel is being used to spread the disease.

Resistance. Tor, 2006, 391p. 9780765354396. As an antibiotic-immune infectious disease spreads through U.S. and Canadian medical facilities, two experts join forces when they discover that the disease has been deliberately spread.

Palmer, Michael

The Fifth Vial. St. Martin's, 2007, 384p. 9780312937744. Three separate stories converge as a worldwide traffic in human organs comes to light.

The First Patient. St. Martin's, 2008, 384p. 9780312937751. Gabe Singleton becomes the President's personal physician, where he discovers that the President is going insane. Ethics and politics may prevent him from doing anything.

A Heartbeat Away. St. Martin's, 2011, 384p. 9780312587512. The U.S. government is shut down when a terror group looses a highly contagious virus during the State of the Union address.

The Last Surgeon. St. Martin's, 2010, 384p. 9780312587505. Mysterious deaths bring nurse Jillian Coates, Dr. Nick Garrity, and psycho killer Franz Koller together. When Koller finishes his mission, Coates and Garrity will become loose ends.

Oath of Office. St. Martin's, 2012, 384p. 9780312587536. When a doctor shoots up his practice and kills himself, his peer counselor tries to find out why and discovers a major threat.

The Second Opinion. St. Martin's, 2009, 384p. 9780312937768. Finding a way to communicate with her comatose father, Dr. Thea Sperelakis unravels the medical fraud she believes he uncovered, even as her family pushes to withdraw life support.

Military Technothrillers

It's a dangerous world out there, and only courageous men and women armed with cool gadgetry can protect us from it. Expect to read lots of information about military hardware and boots on the ground in geopolitical hotspots. Top Military Technothriller authors try to depict bravery, intelligence, camaraderie, and fighting skills that don't expire with the headlines, which can make older series entries just as entertaining to new readers.

Bond, Larry

<u>Red Dragon Rising Series</u>. With drought and famine killing their people, the Chinese Army launches an invasion of Vietnam, while the United States wants to counter them without starting World War III. (The series is projected to last through four books.

> *Shadows of War*. Forge, 2009, 416p. 9780765321374.
> *Edge of War*. Forge, 2010, 384p. 9780765360991.
> *Shock of War*. Forge, 2012, 368p. 9780765321398.

<u>Jerry Mitchell Series</u>. A carrier-trained pilot, Jerry Mitchell was seriously injured in a plane crash. Reassigned to submarine duty, he encounters danger and tense underwater confrontations. There are three books in the series.

> *Dangerous Ground*. Forge, 2005, 336p. 9780765347008.
> *Cold Choices*. Forge, 2009, 480p. 9780765358462.
> *Exit Plan*. Forge, 2012, 432p. 9780765331465.

Brown, Dale

<u>Patrick McLanahan Series</u>. Pilot McLanahan makes sanctioned and solo attacks on America's enemies, amid domestic battles against corruption and incompetence. Even with the latest technology, his old-fashioned flying skills are still essential. There are 17 titles, beginning with *Flight of the Old Dog* (1987).

> *Strike Force*. William Morrow, 2007, 432p. 9780061173691.
> *Shadow Command*. William Morrow, 2008, 355p. 9780061173721.
> *Rogue Forces*. HarperCollins, 2009, 432p. 9780061560880.
> *Executive Intent*. William Morrow, 2010, 432p. 9780061560903.
> *A Time for Patriots*. William Morrow, 2011, 376p. 9780061990007.

Essential Author

★ **Clancy, Tom, <u>Jack Ryan Series</u>, *The Bear and the Dragon*.** Putnam, 2000, 1028p. 9780425180969. President Jack Ryan directs U.S. military and intelligence forces as a series of assassinations leads to a Chinese invasion of Russia. Clancy single-handedly invented the Military Technothriller genre with his 1984 surprise hit, *The Hunt for Red October*. His lengthy stories, usually centered on Jack Ryan's career, feature detailed descriptions of geopolitical maneuvering, military technology, and intelligence operations on a global scale.

Coughlin, Jack

<u>Sniper Series</u>. Top Marine Corps sniper Kyle Swanson operates only under the President's direction, since he's supposed to be dead. He and his team still have to cope with messy personal relationships and doubts about their work.

> *Kill Zone*. St. Martin's, 2007, 352p. 9780312945671.
> *Dead Shot*. St. Martin's, 2009, 320p. 9780312359485.
> *Clean Kill*. St. Martin's, 2010, 336p. 9780312358075.
> *An Act of Treason*. St. Martin's, 2011, 304p. 9780312572655.
> *Running the Maze*. St. Martin's, 2012, 304p. 9781250016393.

Huston, James W.

Falcon Seven. St. Martin's Press, 2010, 320p. 9780312544133. Two American aviators are tried as war criminals after accidentally bombing a Pakistani hospital.
Marine One. St. Martin's, 2009, 323p. 9780312381738. Mike Nolan must defend the manufacturer of the President's helicopter after it crashes. The white-hot glare of publicity masks a shadowy world that hints at a deeper conspiracy.

Political Thrillers

Everyone knows that politicians are corrupt and the worse they are the better readers like it. Look for stories of wide-eyed innocents discovering the sausage factory, worldly politicos facing corruption even they can't stomach, or intrepid reporters following clues where they will. Readers like details of backroom finagling that tampers with elections, smears the righteous, and damages confidence in democracy.

Essential Author

★ **Baldacci, David, <u>Camel Club Series</u>, *The Camel Club***. Warner, 2005, 448p. 9780446615624. In the first of his five books in the series, four eccentric conspiracy theorists witness the murder of a Secret Service agent and land in the middle of a larger conspiracy than they ever imagined.

Lawson, Michael

Joe DeMarco Series. Joe DeMarco is the guy who collects illegal cash and does under-the-table favors for Speaker of the House Mahoney, but all in good causes. Lawson knows behind-the-scenes Washington, but even the bureaucratic infighting pales in comparison to the plots the sarcastic and self-deprecating DeMarco uncovers.

> *The Inside Ring*. Doubleday, 2005, 272p. 9780802145598.
> *The Second Perimeter*. Doubleday, 2006, 336p. 9780802145604.
> *House Rules*. Atlantic Monthly, 2008, 336p. 9780802144195.
> 🎗 *House Secrets*. Atlantic Monthly, 2009, 384p. 9780802144805—
>   *Library Journal*'s Best Thriller of 2009.
> *House Justice*. Atlantic Monthly, 2010, 384p. 9780802145352.
> *House Divided*. Atlantic Monthly, 2011, 345p. 9780802119780.
> *House Blood*. Atlantic Monthly, 2012, 416p. 0802119940.

Meltzer, Brad

🎗 *The Book of Fate*. Warner, 2006, 528p. 9781455508167. Wes Holloway crosses paths with a shadowy faction that has operated since the country's founding. He must also solve a code created by Thomas Jefferson. It won *Library Journal*'s Best Thriller of 2006.

The Book of Lies. Grand Central, 2008, 368p. 9781455508174. The weapon used to kill the father of Superman's creator is also a link in the chain that stretches all the way back to the world's first murder—Cain slaying Abel.

The Inner Circle. Grand Central, 2011, 400p. 9780446616157. Showing off to a friend, archivist Beecher White finds a codebook used by George Washington to communicate with a spy ring, but it may not be a historical curiosity.

Psychological Suspense

Abrahams, Peter

Delusion. William Morrow, 2008, 304p. 9780061138003. Nell Jareau learns that a man she sent to prison for murder is going to be released because her testimony was flawed. At the same time, the innocent man struggles to reenter an unfamiliar world.

End of Story. William Morrow, 2006, 352p. 9780061130342. Aspiring writer Ivy Seidel takes a job teaching maximum security prisoners.

She meets an inmate more talented than she and begins investigating the circumstances of his crime.

Nerve Damage. William Morrow, 2007, 288p. 9780061137983. Artist Roy Valois discover an error about his long-dead wife and comes up against a tangle of lies that makes him question their marriage.

DeMille, Nelson

The Gate House. Grand Central, 2008, 688p. 9780446618823. John Sutter, first seen in 1990's *The Gold Coast*, survived his attempt to defend mobster Frank Bellarosa, but Frank didn't. Now Bellarosa's son Anthony is out for revenge and Sutter's family is his first stop.

Doetsch, Richard

🎗 *The 13th Hour*. Atria, 2009, 304p. 9781439147948. Nick Quinn is given a precious gift—the chance to go back in time to find out if he really did kill his wife earlier that day. Telling the tale in reverse adds real impact to a scary story. It won *Library Journal*'s Thriller of the Year for 2009.

🎗 *Half Past Dawn*. Atria, 2011, 352p. 9781439183977. Waking up with no memory of the previous night, Jack Keeler finds wounds and a tattoo on his body, his wife missing, and both declared dead. Keeler has to decipher the tattoo and confront a killer before he loses his wife for good. It won *Library Journal*'s Best Thriller of 2011.

Harris, Robert

The Fear Index. Doubleday, 2012, 304p. 9780307957931. A scientist recovering from a mental breakdown develops a method of predicting financial markets, but its success, and the sense that someone is watching him, frightens him.

🎗 *The Ghost*. Simon & Schuster, 2007, 352p. 9781416551829. An unnamed ghostwriter is hired to help a former British Prime Minister write his memoirs, but gets more involved than he'd like. It won the 2008 International Thriller Writers Award for Best Novel.

Hart, John

🎗 *Down River*. St. Martin's, 2007, 352p. 9781250024398. Popular opinion in his small hometown has it that Adam Chase was freed despite committing murder. Five years later, Chase returns to a deeply divided town after hearing from an old friend, and violence seems to have returned with him. It won the Edgar Award for Best Novel.

Iron House. St. Martin's, 2011, 352p. 9780312380342. Michael wants to escape his life as a Mob enforcer to live with the woman he loves. Now he must rescue her and his brother before another mobster destroys everything in his life.

The King of Lies. St. Martin's, 2006, 320p. 9781250024404. Small town lawyer Work Pickens is juggling a mistress, a suicidal sister, a pushy wife, and a missing father. When his father turns up dead, the list of suspects shows how many people hated him, including Pickens himself.

🕯 *The Last Child*. Minotaur, 2009, 384p. 9780312642365. A 13-year-old boy searches for his twin sister, who vanished a year before. Along with a detective who can't let go of the case, Johnny's search takes on new urgency when another girl disappears. It won the Edgar Award for Best Novel.

Iles, Greg

Penn Cage Series. First seen in *The Quiet Game* (1999), Penn Cage is a former Texas prosecutor who returns to his Natchez roots. And although he gave up practicing law to become a novelist, Cage still returns to the bar when the people he cares about need him.

> *Turning Angel*. Scribner, 2005, 512p. 9780743454162.
> *The Devil's Punchbowl*. Simon & Schuster, 2009, 480p. 9781416552-4557.
> *Bone Tree*. Scribner, 2012, 504p. 9781439140291. The first part of a longer novel titled *Unwritten Laws*, its publication has been delayed by Iles' injuries in a major car accident.

Third Degree. Scribner, 2007, 528p. 9781416524540. Warren Shields takes his wife hostage while ransacking their home searching for the identity of her lover. The complexity of their marriage is revealed in the course of one day as both Laurel and Warren's secrets come to light.

True Evil. Scribner, 2006, 512p. 9781416524533. Dr. Chris Shepard is asked by an FBI agent to help her investigate a divorce attorney. His clients' spouses have a high mortality rate, and Shepard's wife had an appointment to see the man.

Hurwitz, Gregg

🎗 *The Crime Writer*. Viking, 2007, 320p. 9780143113447. Crime novelist Drew Danner is in the middle of his own mystery—why he regained consciousness to find himself charged with the murder of his ex-fiancée. It won *Library Journal*'s Best Thriller of 2007.

The Survivor. St. Martin's, 2012, 416p. 9780312625511. Distraught, Nate Overbay is preparing to jump off a bank building, but interrupts a robbery. The thieves' boss threatens his estranged family unless Nick finishes the job.

They're Watching. St. Martin's, 2010, 368p. 9780312544171. English teacher Patrick Davis is manipulated into carrying out a weird assortment of good and bad deeds as someone pushes him toward a confrontation he does not want.

Trust No One. St. Martin's, 2009, 352p. 9780312389567. Nick Horrigan finds himself reopening the 17-year-old case surrounding his stepfather's death, which may affect a coming election.

🎗 *You're Next*. St. Martin's, 2011, 416p. 9780312534912. Mike Wingate doesn't understand why two lowlifes have started harassing him and how he's been labeled a terrorist. It won *Library Journal*'s Best Thriller of 2011.

Patterson, Richard North

The Devil's Light. Scribner, 2011, 352p. 9781451616811. An al-Qaeda terrorist steals a nuclear device, which he plans to detonate in Israel. Disgraced CIA agent Brooke Chandler must find the device and stop the coming disaster.

Eclipse. Holt, 2009, 384p. 9780312946388. American attorney Damon Pierce travels to a West African country to represent a political prisoner in a show trial mounted by the military dictatorship.

Exile. Holt, 2007, 576p. 9780312938543. Attorney David Wolfe is asked to defend a former lover against terrorism charges. Wolfe's search for the truth leads him into the tangled world of Israeli and Palestinian politics.

Fall from Grace. Scribner, 2012, 352p. 9781451617054. Adam Blaine sorts through the suspects when his demanding father plunges to his death, and Blaine must execute his will.

In the Name of Honor. Holt, 2010, 384p. 9780312946401. Military attorney Paul Terry is given the impossible task of defending a soldier accused of murder. The lives of the killer and the victim were intertwined by their love of the same woman and by their traumatic service in Iraq.

The Race. Holt, 2007, 352p. 9780312945176. Corey Grace gets into a vicious primary fight for the Presidential nomination, but his past threatens to undo his plans and his principles are tested by his opponents' methods.

The Spire. Holt, 2009, 384p. 9780312946395. Mark Darrow becomes president of his troubled alma mater. Years before, a friend was convicted of a campus murder; now Darrow believes the person really responsible is coming after him.

Essential Author

★ **Pelecanos, George,** ***The Night Gardener***. Little, Brown and Co., 2006, 384p. 9780316056502. Detective Gus Ramone goes outside the Washington D.C. police department to solve the murder of a local teen. As in his other 17 novels, Pelecanos paints his bleak, violent images on the canvas of Washington, using pop culture to establish time frames ranging from the 1950s to the present day.

Staub, Wendy Corsi

Dead Before Dark. Zebra Books, 2009, 473p. 9781420101324. A serial killer dubbed "The Night Watchman" targets Lucinda Sloane, a psychic detective.

Don't Scream. Zebra Books, 2007, 448p. 9780821779729. Four women are going to die on their birthdays, in retribution for a crime they committed years before.

Dying Breath. Zebra Books, 2008, 416p. 9781420101317. Cam Hastings has visions of kidnappings and murders, including that of her daughter, and tries to outwit the murderer.

The Final Victim. Kensington, 2006, 475p. 9780821779712. Family secrets turn to murder when the Remington family returns to their isolated ancestral home for the reading of a will.

Live to Tell Series. The aftereffects of a kidnapping echo through the lives of three families over the course of 30 years, even as the possibility arises that the kidnapper threatens them again. Start with *Live to Tell*.

Live to Tell. Avon Books, 2010, 390p. 9780061895067.
Scared to Death. Avon Books, 2010, 416p. 9780061895074.
Hell to Pay. Avon Books, 2011, 416p. 9780061895081.

White, Kate

Hush. Harper, 2010, 341p. 9780061576652. Lake Warren has her first post-divorce job, marketing a fertility clinic. Trying to protect her reputation, she covers up her one-nighter with a coworker who was later murdered.

The Sixes. Harper, 2011, 376p. 9780062088703. Disgraced writer Phoebe Hall moves to a small college town to teach, but when a secret campus society is accused of killing a student, Hall searches for the murderer.

Religious Thrillers

Religious Thrillers are generally aimed at the conservative evangelical audience, readers who believe that heroes should rely on God's assistance, not their own wiles. They can also be broken down into two categories: Inspired Religious Thrillers feature characters who find or turn to God when in despair and Spiritual Warfare Religious Thrillers cast The Enemy as the antagonist. The Enemy may present itself as an undisguised physical presence, temptation, or as other people doing The Enemy's bidding. The Enemy can only be defeated when born-again Christians claim their strength through God.

Early Religious Thrillers had no sex, very little violence, and no bad language. As the genre has evolved and writers have taken on different scenarios, those elements, especially violence, have begun to crop up. Still, the actual violence is either offstage or is depicted without graphic language. It is the tension of the situation that provides the thrills.

Essential Author

★ **Dekker, Ted, Paradise Series, Showdown**. WestBow Press, 2006, 366p. 9781595546135. A small mountain town falls under the spell of a charismatic preacher named Marsuvees Black, while not far away an experiment in the nature of good and evil forms the lives of a group of children. Dekker's allegorical books offer redemption and hope in their story arc, and his skill with plotting also attracts mainstream readers to his Thrillers.

James, Steven

Patrick Bowers Series

> *The Queen*. Fleming H. Revell, 2011, 517p. 9780800719203. FBI agent Patrick Bowers finds a connection between old and new conflicts while investigating a double homicide and encountering an old nemesis. James is a two-time winner of the Christy Award for Suspense writing.

Blackstock, Terri

Double Minds. Zondervan, 2009, 336p. 9780310250630. Christian songwriter Parker James is on the verge of her breakthrough. When a coworker is murdered, the dark side of the Christian music business is revealed.

Intervention Series. The Covington family struggles with drug addictions that surround and threaten them. Battling their personal demons, wounded by the fallout from other users, and threatened by past events, Emily, Lance, and their mother Barbara turn to God to see them through.

> *Intervention*. Zondervan, 2009, 352p. 9780310250654.
> *Vicious Cycle*. Zondervan, 2011, 336p. 9780310250678.
> *Downfall*. Zondervan, 2012, 352p. 9781594154232.

Predator. Zondervan, 2010, 334p. 9780310250661. A 14-year-old girl is killed by an online stalker using a popular social media site. In the wake of her murder, her sister, devastated by her death, sets a trap for the killer with the help of the site's founder.

Restoration Series. All electronics in the world go silent for some unknown reason. The Branning family's newfound faith is tested as they try to get their neighbors to work together, and a serial killer crops up in their now isolated community.

> *Last Light*. Zondervan, 2005, 384p. 9780310257677.
> *Night Light*. Zondervan, 2006, 368p. 9780310257684.
> *True Light*. Zondervan, 2007, 384p. 9781594152160.
> *Dawn's Light*. Zondervan, 2008, 416p. 9780310257707.

Bunn, T. Davis

Book of Dreams. Howard Books, 2011, 256p. 9781416556701. Psychiatrist Elena Burroughs takes on a mysterious patient suffering identical nightmares each night. With the help of an ancient book, Elena is able to identify the danger the dream foretells.

🏃 *Lion of Babylon*. Bethany House, 2011, 378p. 9780764209055. Former intelligence agent Marc Royce is sent into Iraq, where he finds the people searching for spiritual meaning amid the post-occupation chaos. It won *Library Journal*'s Best Christian Fiction of 2011.

Imposter. WestBow Press, 2006, 300p. 9781595542267. Loner FBI agent Matt Kelly begins to think his mother's death may be related to his father's run for political office.

Storm Syrell Series. An antiques dealer with a tidy life is thrown into chaos when her grandfather dies and leaves her several mysterious objects. Treasurer hunter Harry Bennett accompanies Syrell as she decodes clues to find miraculous artifacts that may have deep implications on her own spiritual life.

> *Gold of Kings*. Howard Books, 2009, 342p. 9781416556329.
> *The Black Madonna*. Howard Books, 2010, 336p. 9781416556336.

Cavanaugh, Jack

Kingdom Wars Series. Part-angel Grant Austin seeks ways to prevent fallen angels from carrying out their evil plans. Despite his imperfections, he serves as an ambassador between Heaven and Earth, but still grapples with his need to rely on God.

> *A Hideous Beauty*. Howard Books, 2007, 368p. 9781416543404.
> *Tartarus*. Howard Fiction, 2008, 320p. 9781416543879.

Eason, Lynette

Deadly Reunions Series

> *When the Smoke Clears*. Revell, 2012, 352p. 9780800720070. Smokejumper Alexia Allen is on mandatory leave when family secrets, murder, arson, a high school reunion, and a handsome detective disrupt her plans.

Women of Justice Series

> *Too Close to Home*. Revell, 2010, 332p. 9780800733698. Special Agent Samantha Cash is a computer expert assigned to work with police chief Connor Wolfe. They hunt a serial killer targeting teen girls, including Wolfe's daughter.

Don't Look Back. Revell, 2010, 368p. 9780800733704. Twelve years after a traumatic experience, Jamie Cash (Samantha's sister) is ready to trust again, but the man who brutalized her returns to finish what he started.

A Killer among Us. Revell, 2011, 345p. 9780800733711. Hostage negotiator Kit Kenyon and homicide detective Noah Lambert are brought together to search for a serial killer who is also hunting them.

Rosenberg, Joel C.

Jon Bennett and Erin McCoy Series. Bennett, a Wall Street financial genius, and his bodyguard/love interest McCoy struggle to keep the Middle East from deteriorating further, but it seems that biblical prophecies may be thwarting their best efforts.

The Last Jihad. Forge, 2003, 304p. 9780765346438.
The Last Days. Forge, 2003, 336p. 9780765348203.
The Ezekiel Option. Tyndale House, 2005, 413p. 9781414303444.
The Copper Scroll. Tyndale House, 2006, 229p. 9781414303475.
Dead Heat. Tyndale House, 2008, 416p. 9781414311623.

Twelfth Imam Series. CIA officer David Shirazi takes on the Iranian nuclear program amidst rumors that the "Muslim Messiah" has come and is planning to provoke an all-out war.

The Twelfth Imam. Tyndale House, 2010, 490p. 9781414311647.
The Tehran Initiative. Tyndale House, 2010, 490p. 9781414319353.

Vigilante

Vigilantes have but one focus—to punish injustice. Because these avengers operate outside the law, they have a code of their own, usually along the lines of "an eye for an eye" but sometimes more extreme. While they are loners, most of these heroes have useful networks on both sides of the legal line, usually others who privately share the hero's values but can't use his methods. Fans of these "white knight" Thrillers expect to see lots of violent shortcuts taken to exact revenge from those whom the law cannot touch. While these heroes might have a law enforcement or investigative background, they are usually gifted at stirring up trouble to achieve their brand of justice.

Bazell, Josh

Peter Brown Series. Former hit man Brown became a dedicated physician while in the Witness Protection Program. After being spotted by an ex-colleague, he's back on the run. Fast-moving, violent, and occasionally over-the-top scenes are laced with black humor that offers relief before diving back into the battle.

> *Beat the Reaper*. Little, Brown, 2009, 320p. 9780316032216.
> *Wild Thing*. Reagan Arthur, 2012, 240p. 9780316032193.

Essential Author

★ ⚑ **Child, Lee, Jack Reacher Series, *One Shot***. Delacorte, 2005, 384p. 9780440246077. A former soldier arrested for murdering five civilians will only talk to ex-military policeman Reacher. Reacher wants the man dead for a past crime, but as he digs deeper, he discovers that the evidence is too perfect. It was one of *Library Journal*'s Best Thrillers of 2005. Child has created the perfect vigilante—a mountain of a man with a keen mind and zero regrets for the violence he unleashes on bad guys as he drifts across the United States. The 17-book series began with *The Killing Floor* in 1997.

Collins, Max Allen

J. C. Harrow Series. The host of reality TV show *Crime Seen!*, former sheriff Harrow uses the venue to track down criminals but stays focused on vengeance for his own murdered family. A tragically heroic figure, Harrow is threatened by the killers he's chasing.

> *You Can't Stop Me*. Pinnacle, 2010, 368p. 9780786021345.
> *No One Will Hear You*. Pinnacle, 2011, 320p. 9780786021352.

Mike Hammer Series. Collins' seamless transition into Mickey Spillane's New York still sees the quick-drawing quick-fisted private investigator getting in the gutter with bad guys (and dames). While not subtle in any sense, they offer plenty of the guns, girls, and guts that kept Hammer going for 50 years.

> *The Goliath Bone*. Harcourt, 2008, 288p. 9781593155971.
> *The Big Bang*. Harcourt, 2010, 256p. 9780547521701.
> *Kiss Her Goodbye*. Harcourt, 2011, 288p. 9780547541204.
> *Lady, Go Die*. Titan, 2012, 272p. 9780857684653.
> *The Consummata*. Hardcase Crime, 2011, 256p. 9780857682888. A non-series entry that follows up on a character from 1967's *The Delta Factor*.

Nathan Heller Series. Nate Heller, former Chicago cop and Marine veteran of Guadalcanal, solves actual mysteries from the 1940s through the 1960s. Plenty of people want those puzzles left in the box, so Heller's life is in danger everywhere he goes. AmazonEncore rereleased the 1984 Shamus Award winner *True Detective* in 2011.

> *Bye Bye Baby*. Forge, 2011, 352p. 9780765361462.
> *Target Lancer*. Forge, 2012, 318p. 9780765321800.

Ghelfi, Brent

Volk Series. Alex Volkovoy is a feared man in Russia's new gangster economy, a profitable and effective mask for his work helping to steer Russia through the post-Soviet chaos. Readers can expect graphic violence and sex, but there is a surprising trace of redemption to the anarchy he creates.

> *Volk's Game*. Holt, 2007, 304p. 9780312427849.
> *Volk's Shadow*. Holt, 2008, 320p. 9780805082555.
> *The Venona Cable*. Holt, 2009, 317p. 9780805088946.
> *The Burning Lake*. Poisoned Pen Press, 2011, 250p. 9781590589274.

Hall, James W.

Thorn Series. Thorn takes life one day at a time in the solitude of his isolated Florida home. Still, the outside world insists on intruding, sometimes violently, and Thorn responds in kind. *Under Cover of Daylight* (2001) was the first of the 12 books, but Hall won the 2003 Shamus Award for *Blackwater Sound*, a good place to enter Thorn's world.

> *Magic City*. Minotaur, 2006, 352p. 9780312947477.
> *Hell's Bay*. Minotaur, 2008, 320p. 9780312944179.
> *Silencer*. St. Martin's, 2010, 276p. 9780312543792.
> *Dead Last*. Minotaur, 2011, 304p. 9780312607326.

Hallinan, Tim

Poke Rafferty Series. American expatriate and freelance writer Rafferty has a penchant for attracting trouble in the exotic world of Thailand. Hallinan steeps the reader in the sights and sounds of Bangkok, from the sex tourists to the daily lives of ordinary people, while crafting dark and deceptive Thrillers.

A Nail Through the Heart. William Morrow, 2007, 336p. 9780061257223.
The Fourth Watcher. William Morrow, 2008, 304p. 9780061257261.
Breathing Water. William Morrow, 2009, 346p. 9780061672255.
The Queen of Patpong. William Morrow, 2010, 304p. 9780061672279.
The Fear Artist. Soho Crime, 2012, 350p. 9781616951122.

Hunter, Stephen

Bob Lee Swagger Series. Swagger (or Bob the Nailer, as he is known) is a master sniper reluctant to leave the home and family he struggled to create, but is still drawn into missions that require his special brand of honor and skill. Hunter gives lots of technical details about guns and ammo, but that doesn't slow the narrative. The seven-book series started with *Point of Impact* in 1993.

The 47th Samurai. Simon & Schuster, 2007, 480p. 9780743458009.
Night of Thunder. Simon & Schuster, 2008, 304p. 9781416565147.
I, Sniper. Simon & Schuster, 2009, 400p. 9781416565178.
Dead Zero. Simon & Schuster, 2010, 384p. 9781439138663.

Earl Swagger Series. Bob Lee's father, a World War II Congressional Medal of Honor winner, faces institutional corruption as an Arkansas State Trooper.

Hot Springs. Simon & Schuster, 2000, 478p. 9781451627237.
Pale Horse Coming. Simon & Schuster, 2001, 491p. 9780671035464.
Havana. Simon & Schuster, 2003, 480p. 9781451627244.

Ray Cruz Series. Cruz, known as "The Cruise Missile," is the top-notch Marine sniper introduced in *Dead Zero*, the seventh Bob Lee story. Like all Hunter's heroes, he is an uncomplicated man who is most at home with a mission to accomplish. He's also Bob Lee's son, born in Vietnam and lost, along with his mother, during the Tet Offensive.

Dead Zero. Simon & Schuster, 2010, 384p. 9781439138663.
Soft Target. Simon & Schuster, 2011, 384p. 9781451675344.

Rucka, Greg

Atticus Kodiak Series. Kodiak is a professional bodyguard, trained in the U.S. Army's Executive Protection Service. Rucka engages readers with details of the methods and equipment pro bodyguards use. There are seven books in the series, but readers can start with *Critical Space* (2001), in which Kodiak is hired to protect an assassin who has already tried to kill him.

> *Patriot Acts*. Bantam, 2007, 352p. 9780553588996.
> *Walking Dead*. Bantam, 2009, 308p. 9780553589009.

Jad Bell Series

> *Alpha*. Mulholland Books, 2012, 320p. 9780316182287. Delta Force veteran Bell goes undercover as a security director at a major theme park. He must play hide-and-seek to free hostages when terrorists attack the park.

Queen and Country Series. Tara Chace is Her Majesty's top assassin. Chace often finds herself thrown back on her own resources, where she feels truly alive. The series starts with *A Gentleman's Game* (2004), and is based on a set of award-winning graphic novels.

> *Private Wars*. Bantam, 2005, 368p. 9780553584936.
> *The Last Run*. Bantam, 2010, 272p. 9780553589016.

Stevens, Taylor

Vanessa Michael Monroe Series. Abandoned by her missionary parents in Africa when she was only 15, Monroe now works as an "informationist," gathering business intelligence by blending into unfamiliar cultures. Usually a loner, she sometimes works with security consultant Miles Bradford.

> *The Informationist*. Crown, 2011, 304p. 9780307717108.
> *The Innocent*. Crown, 2011, 336p. 9780307717139.

Swierczynski, Duane

Charlie Hardie Series. Hardie house-sits for wealthy clients, drinking and trying to forget the family he's no longer allowed to see. An accidental encounter drags him into a long-lived and powerful conspiracy, and he looks for leverage to turn the tables. Since this is a trilogy centered on Hardie's battle, it is essential to start with *Fun & Games* and plan to read all three back-to-back.

> *Fun & Games*. Mulholland Books, 2011, 256p. 9780316133289.
> *Hell & Gone*. Mulholland Books, 2011, 256p. 9780316133296.
> *Point & Shoot*. Mulholland Books, 2012, 256p. 9780316133302.

9

White, Randy Wayne

__Doc Ford Series__. Ford is a mild-mannered marine biologist on Sanibel Island, Florida. He also has a license to kill from his Special Forces days, and is often blackmailed into using it. White's series is rich in both depictions of underwater settings and violent action. The 18 books in the series start with *Sanibel Flats* (1990), but *Tampa Burn* (2004) brings Doc's past to light.

> *Dark Light*. Putnam, 2006, 352p. 9780425214442.
> *Hunter's Moon*. Putnam, 2007, 352p. 9780425220375.
> *Black Widow*. Putnam, 2008, 352p. 9780425226704.
> *Dead Silence*. Putnam, 2009, 352p. 9780425233306.
> *Deep Shadow*. Putnam, 2010, 368p. 9780425240090.
> *Night Vision*. Putnam, 2010, 368p. 9780399157059.
> *Chasing Midnight*. Putnam, 2012, 336p. 9780399158315.

TOOLS AND RESOURCES

Herald, Diana Tixier. *Genreflecting: A Guide to Popular Reading Interests*, edited by Wayne A. Wiegand. 6th ed. Westport, CT: Libraries Unlimited, 2006.
Morrell, David, and Hank Wagner. *Thrillers: 100 Must Reads*. Longboat Key, FL: Oceanview Publications, 2010—A publication of the International Thriller Writers.
Mystery Scene Magazine, New York. http://www.mysteryscenemag.com/
Niebuhr, Gary Warren. *Make Mine a Mystery: A Reader's Guide to Mystery and Detective Fiction*. Westport, CT: Libraries Unlimited, 2003.

FIVE FAN FAVORITES

- Lee Child. *One Shot*—Vigilante
- Daniel Silva. *Prince of Fire*—Conspiracy/Espionage
- Brad Meltzer. *The Book of Fate*—Political
- Jeffry P. Lindsay. *Darkly Dreaming Dexter*—Crime
- Joel C. Rosenberg. *The Twelfth Imam*—Christian

Chapter 10

Westerns

Diana Tixier Herald

Western literature is of the spirit, our spirit, the spirit of America. Western literature is the motivation of people to succeed in lands greater than themselves. The Western is full of souls filled with concern, fear, joy and desire. In a phrase, it is the literature of America's soul.

—*Cotton Smith (November 20, 2006, Western Writers of America news release)*

For decades, it has been widely held that Westerns were a dying genre; but, year after year, they survive. Of course, the Western genre is not large. It is not flashy or popular, but it keeps being published, sold, and read. Old readers may die off, but, each year, some intrepid readers find their way to the genre and make it their own. Like all genres, Westerns are seeing more genreblending and connections to other genres.

Spur award winner, Win Blevins, talks about the new Westerns on his website:

We are seeing, being created right now a new western for a new, young, hip audience. . . . Its heroes aren't cowboys and soldiers, but Indians, mountain men, women, blacks, Hispanics, Mormons, and all the other westerners who were shoved aside in the first myth. It's more complex, more interesting, more fully human than the old myth. It deals less with taming the country and more with living with it.

—*Win Blevins*

Traditional Westerns have become a niche category. They are not booming with the big publishers; however, Forge, an imprint of Tom Doherty and Associates (now part of Macmillan), continues to regularly publish Westerns of all kinds. The shift in publishing from major publishers becomes evident when perusing recent award winners and their publishers. The Spur Award for Best First Novel category has seen winners and finalists from small, independent publishers and self-publishers, and in e-book and POD (print on demand) formats in recent years.

Women, especially through efforts of groups like Women Writing the West and the Willa Awards, are also making inroads into the genre; more and more Westerns are now being published by women. The popularity of Western Romances is also bringing Romance writers, who are usually female, into the ranks of Western writers.

In general, Western readers are not moved by trendiness; so Western publishing is heavy with reprints of beloved classics. Authors who were popular scores of years ago remain popular today. Currently, there are no authors who dominate the genre as Zane Grey, Louis L'Amour, and Elmer Kelton did in the past; but there are enough authors writing to provide the reader with a rich diversity of tales and keep them happy as they mix the old with the new.

Westerns have always been closely tied to other media, from silent movies to TV, and now 3-D movies. It seems there is no way to talk about them without mentioning these nonprint mediums. John Mort's *Read the High Country: A Guide to Western Books and Films* (Libraries Unlimited, 2006) covers both thoroughly.

DEFINITION

> The West represents a way of thinking, a sense of adventure, a willingness to cross into a new frontier.
>
> —*Women Writing the West*

At its core, the Western is an adventure novel. On the surface it may appear simple, often using straightforward prose and simple dialogue to convey the lack of pretence necessary for life on a frontier, but this quality emphasizes the nature of the characters and the settings in which they operate. Westerns are about the core values and behaviors of the protagonists without lots of external trappings. Issues of right and wrong, good and bad are explored. Survival often drives the characters. It can mean surviving hardship, starvation, hostile attacks, disease, accident, or isolation. It can mean economic survival—saving the homestead from foreclosure, keeping the range open for cattle, protecting the mining claim. Sometimes it means the survival of a way of life.

Westerns almost always feature characters who have a "frontier mindset." These characters are not comfortable with the status quo. They have to make their own way in the world. They are willing to head into the unknown, take risks, and live according to their own beliefs.

CHARACTERISTICS AND APPEAL

10

The appeal of the Western is the combination of independent, resourceful characters, a setting remote from the amenities of urban life, and a concrete plot where the reader knows that there will be a resolution to everything happening. Some readers read Westerns for all those appeal factors, but some readers read for the specific factors that appeal to them.

11

BRIEF HISTORY

In her essay on the "History and Evolution" of Westerns in the 6th edition of *Genreflecting* (Libraries Unlimited, 2006), Connie Van Fleet states that "most scholars identify *The Last of the Mohicans* (1826) or *The Prairie* (1827) by James Fenimore Cooper as the first Western novel." John Mort in *Read the High Country* (Libraries Unlimited, 2006) details the elements in Cooper's work that influenced the genre. Other influences on the Western novel came from dime novels of the late 19th century, Mark Twain's 1872 travel book, *Roughing It*, and short stories by Bret Harte and Stephen Crane. Both acknowledge Owen Wister's *The Virginian* (1902) as the first actual Western novel that shaped the genre.

12

13

Westerns really took off in popularity with Zane Grey writing prolifically in the early 20th century. According to Frank Gruber via John Mort, Westerns hit their peak of popularity in 1958 with roughly a third of television shows and a third of paperbacks sold being Westerns. Publishing of Louis L'Amour's novels began in the 1950s, and he became one of the bestselling writers of all time with more than 300 million of his books being sold by the end of the century (Louis L'Amour Official Website). The 1990s were a low point for the publication of Westerns, but the genre has been slowly rebuilding although many of the Westerns being published now are called Historical novels or Mainstream novels.

14

15

Advising the Reader

16

As in all readers' advisory, it is crucial to listen to the reader and be sensitive to what he or she wants. With Westerns, it is important to know if the reader wants traditional Westerns only or is willing to try something a little different. Some Western readers are attracted to the genre because many of the titles have sharply delineated stories of morals and they enjoy reading about upstanding individuals of good character. Other readers want to read only Westerns set in the historic western United States that could be defined as the area west of the Mississippi River and set in the 19th century. Some readers are simply drawn to the adventurous and independent streak in these characters, and so may also enjoy many of the genreblends.

17

18

It is essential to talk with readers to identify what it is they like about Westerns. Informal, in the stacks interviews with Western readers indicate they want traditional Westerns but some, particularly voracious readers who are afraid of running out of Westerns, are interested in venturing into Science Fiction, Fantasy, or Romance novels that have strong Western appeal.

CURRENT TRENDS

Genreblending has become prevalent in all genres, and it is perhaps through genreblending that Westerns will survive and even thrive in the future.

While Westerns have their roots in the history of the American West, the essence of the genre lies in the ruggedly individualistic characters that people a frontier setting. This has extended appeal to readers who find similar characters in the one-season Science Fiction television show *Firefly*, which has achieved cult like status years after being canceled. The combination of Science Fiction/ Fantasy and Western ambiance also appears in the Science Fantasy novel *Alloy of Law* by master fantasist Brandon Sanderson. Westerns set in a West that never was are drawing readers to Steampunk titles, such as Cherie Priest's series, The Clockwork Century, that started with *Boneshaker* and Emma Bull's *Territory*, which added magic to the shoot-out at the OK Corral in the Weird West.

Romance continues to feature the West in both historical and contemporary settings. Many Westerns published within the Romance genre are true to the traditions and tropes of the Western genre along with providing a happily ever after love story. Unfortunately, the popularity of the setting has led some Romance authors into writing Cowboy Romances that have none of the defining features of a Western, so we need to be selective when suggesting Western Romance titles.

Some Romance readers who are drawn to Western settings and characters enjoy the adventure aspects and story; and now with relationships playing a bigger role in Historical novels of the West or Westerns, they are finding novels that appeal to them in the Western genre.

While Westerns are not widely published for the teen market, there are a few every year that will appeal to adult readers of Westerns. The popularity of Young Adult novels with bestsellers in other genres such as *The Hunger Games* and *Twilight* has removed the stigma some adults felt about reading YA.

During the heyday of Westerns, novels featuring women and people of color were few and far between. Now they are making up a larger proportion of the Westerns published each year, and they are winning awards. The 2011 Spur Award for Best Western Long Novel was *Last Train from Cuernavaca* by Lucia Clair Robson, set in Mexico during the Revolution and featuring a Mexican female protagonist and the 2012 Spur Award for Best Western Short

Novel was *Legacy of a Lawman* by Johnny D. Boggs based on Marshal Bass Reeves, an African American.

Because this book only provides benchmark titles and recent titles, advisors looking for more detailed information about the genre are encouraged to consult Mort's *Read the High Country* and earlier editions of *Genreflecting*, both invaluable in finding titles for their readers.

NOTES

Blevins, Win. http://www.winblevins.com/whoisthisguy.html

Herald, Diana Tixier. *Genreflecting: A Guide to Popular Reading Interests*, edited by Wayne A. Wiegand. 6th ed. Westport, CT: Libraries Unlimited, 2006. Also see earlier editions.

Louis L'Amour Official Website. http://www.louislamour.com/community/stamp.htm

Mort, John. *Read the High Country: A Guide to Western Books and Films*. Westport, CT: Libraries Unlimited, 2006.

Western Writers of America. http://www.westernwriters.org

Women Writing the West. http://www.womenwritingthewest.org

THEMES AND TYPES

Key to Westerns

Traditional Westerns
    Bad Men and Good
    Cowboys
    Lawmen
    Singular Women
    Wagons West
Native Americans
Rooted in Reality
Literary Westerns
The New West

(Continued)

> Genreblends
>> The Weird West
>> Westerns with a Touch of Fantasy
>> Romantic Westerns
>> Mysterious Westerns

Traditional Westerns

These stories, set in the American West in the last half of the 19th century or the early years of the 20th century, feature the traditional themes of good men versus bad, ranching, mining, and much more. In the earliest editions of *Genreflecting*, this type made up the bulk of published Westerns; and while not many of this type are now being published, they still make up the majority of public library Western collections and are still read by fans of the genre. When Westerns were a large publishing category, there were many traditional Westerns that were rather formulaic, but the small number of titles published recently seems to have honed the genre with unique and well-crafted Westerns becoming prevalent.

Bad Men and Good

The color of a man's hat doesn't necessarily define which side he is on and sometimes those who appear bad have a core of good.

🎗 **Averill, Thomas Fox.** *Rode*. University of New Mexico Press, 2011. 206p. 9780826350299. Framed for a murder, Robert Johnson lights out for the West on a spectacular stallion, fleeing a bounty hunter, facing peril, and doing what he can to clear his name and returns to Tennessee and Jo Benson, the woman he loves. Inspired by the ballad, "The Tennessee Stud," Western Heritage Award winner.

Buchanan, Carol. *Gold Under Ice*. Missouri Breaks Press, 2010. 407p. 9780982782217. In 1864, with the Civil War and the conflict between gold and greenbacks raging, Daniel Star, a vigilante and lawyer, who is trying to make back his family's fortunes in Montana territory, rescues a man who had been sent to summon him back to New York. It is a sequel to the Spur Award winning *God's Thunderbolt: The Vigilantes of Montana*.

deWitt, Patrick. *The Sisters Brothers*. Ecco, 2011. 328p. 9780062041265. This sometimes humorous, sometimes violent picaresque story set in the California gold rush features two killers for hire, brothers: Charlie Sisters, the mean one, and Eli Sisters, the fat one.

♣ **McCoy, Max.** *Damnation Road*. Pinnacle, 2010. 272p. 9780786021 215. When Jacob Gamble, an aging outlaw, attempts to rob a train, he discovers a now dead thief beat him to the safe and he is named a hero. This turn of events does not help his financial status but a perilous quest for a lost treasure might, if he survives. Spur Award winner.

McGarrity, Michael. *Hard Country*. Penguin, 2012. 624p. 9780525952466. After the deaths of his wife and brother, John Kerney leaves his infant son behind and starts over in New Mexico starting a saga that spans events in one family's southwestern history from 1875 to 1918.

Must Read

★ **Schaefer, Jack. *Shane*.** Bantam, 1949. 119p. 9780553271102. Shane, an honorable gunfighter, hires on with a Wyoming family and becomes involved with the conflict between homesteaders and a cattle baron.

Cowboys

The ranching life is never easy, and the cowboys and ranchers face all kinds of conflicts from range wars to shoot-outs.

♣ **Boggs, Johnny.** *Hard Winter*. Five Star, 2009. 232p. 9781594148033. Jim Hawkins tells his grandson of the wildlife he lived as a teenaged cowboy after running away from Indiana. Making friends in Texas, he ends up in Montana working on a big cattle operation as a range war threatens to erupt, but the hardest thing he faces is a deadly winter. Spur Award winner.

Vories, Eugene C. *Piñon Mesa*. Vories Family Publishers, 2005. 317p. 9780971398337. Betrayed by his wife, his cousin, and the uncle who raised him, Alan Stuart is determined to make a go of ranching on Piñon Mesa even if it means going against everything he believed in as a cattleman and bringing in sheep.

Must Read

★ 🎬 **Wister, Owen. *The Virginian*.** Macmillan, 1902. 301p. 9780 394574745. A Wyoming ranch foreman faces difficult choices, a shoot-out with an enemy, and finds love with a good woman

---

Lawmen

Raw frontiers attract the lawless, but there are always those to attempt to make order out of chaos and civilize it.

🎖 **Boggs, Johnny D.** *West Texas Kill*. Thorndike Large Print, 2011. 441p. 9781410437884. Texas Ranger Sergeant Dave Chance turns a murderer loose to help him take down a greedy Ranger Captain who has gone rogue and traumatized the very people he was supposed to protect. Spur Award winner.

Parker, Robert

🎬 **Virgil Cole and Everett Hitch Series**. Virgil Cole and Everett Hitch take on dangerous enemies as they bring order to the West facing down murderous ranchers, hired guns, and greedy mine owners.

> *Appaloosa*. Putnam, 2005. 276p. 9780399152771.
> *Resolution*. Putnam, 2008. 292p. 9780425227992.
> *Brimstone*. Putnam, 2009. 293p. 9780399155710.
> *Blue-Eyed Devil*. Putnam, 2010. 288p. 9780399156489. In the fourth and last entry in the series (Parker died in 2010), Cole and Hitch go up against Apaches and the corrupt chief of police who has taken over the town.

Richards, Dusty

Herschel Baker Series. Herschel Baker, a rancher, steps up when injustice is being done and ends up becoming the sheriff of Yellowstone County, Montana, in this series that brings in Herschel's various relatives.

> 🎖 *The Horse Creek Incident*. Jove, 2006. 295p. 9780515142174—Spur Award
> *Montana Revenge*. Berkley, 2007. 284p. 9780425217580.
> 🎖 *The Sundown Chaser*. Berkley, 2009. 278p. 9780425226964.—Western Heritage Award
> *Wulf's Tracks*. Berkley, 2010. 282p. 9780425233337. Wulf flees his abusive stepfather and goes to his cousin Herschel who deputizes him.

Singular Women

Once a rarity in Westerns, strong independent women have gained a foothold in the genre in recent years, with their stories looking much different than the stories from the heyday of Westerns when they served more as props than protagonists.

Gloss, Molly. *Hearts of Horses*. Houghton Mifflin, 2007. 289p. 978 0618799909. Martha Lessen, an independent 19-year-old, travels around breaking horses, while the men are off fighting World War I, and ends up staying the winter with a farming couple in Shelby, Oregon.

10

Must Read

★ 🎬 **Portis, Charles.** *True Grit*. Simon & Schuster, 1968. 235p. 9781590204597. Fourteen-year-old Mattie Ross joins forces with a marshal and a Texas Ranger to find the outlaw who killed her father.

11

12

🎗 **Robson, Lucia St. Clair.** *Last Train from Cuernavaca*. Forge, 2010. 349p. 9780765313355. The Mexican Revolution changes the lives of two women in 1913, one a British ex-pat who owns a hotel and the other a teenaged girl who disguises herself and joins the Zapatistas. Spur Award winner.

13

Wagons West

The way west was filled with danger from accidents, disease, and violence and often families were involved imbuing these stories with relationship as well as survival issues.

14

Blevins, Win

15

<u>Rendezvous Series</u>. After Sam Morgan left his childhood home in Pennsylvania in 1822, he became one of the first white men to cross the Rockies, becoming a mountain man, trapping, falling in love, marrying a Crow Indian girl, searching for a river route from the Great Salt Lake to California, rescuing an Indian captive, and experiencing a multitude of adventures and relationships.

16

🎗 *So Wild a Dream*. Forge, 2003. 400p. 9780765344816—Spur Award
Beauty for Ashes. Forge, 2004. 384p. 9780765305749.
Dancing with the Golden Bear. Forge, 2005. 380p. 9780765305756.
Heaven Is a Long Way Off. Forge, 2006. 304p. 9780765305763.
A Long and Winding Road. Forge, 2007. 352p. 9780765305770.
Dreams beneath Your Feet. Forge, 2008. 316p. 9780765305787. With the demise of the fur trade in 1840, Sam Morgan is persuaded to move to coastal California with his daughter, where he plans to trade

17

18

for horses. Along the Oregon Trail, their party discovers a psychopath has been terrorizing Indian villages.

🎗 **YA** **McKernan, Victoria.** *The Devil's Paintbox.* Alfred A. Knopf, 2009. 359p. 9780375837500. Fifteen-year-old Aiden Lynch and his thirteen-year-old sister Maddy, Kansas orphans, leave their drought stricken farm in Kansas and face disaster, disease, and heartbreak when they join a wagon train headed for Seattle. Spur Award winner.

Native Americans

The recent trend in novels featuring Native American protagonists has been heavy on fantasy and the mystical beliefs of indigenous societies.

Fox, Caleb

Ancient Cherokee Series. Fox, a pseudonym of award-winning Western author Win Blevins, utilizes mythology in these colorful, fantastical tales of early ancestors of the Cherokee.

> *Zadayi Red.* Tor, 2009. 352p. 9780765319920. A seer of the Galayi people sets her adopted son Dahzi on a path that will take him through different worlds as he tries to save the important talisman, the Eagle Feather Cape that is essential for the survival of the Galayi.
> *Shadows in the Cave.* Tor, 2010. 320p. 9780765319937. A shape-shifter must defy his father for the protection of the tribe.

Gear, W. Michael, and Kathleen O'Neal Gear

The First North Americans Series. This series has also been called North America's Forgotten Past Series. Written by a couple of archaeologists, each well-researched standalone volume deals with Native communities on the cusp of change.

> *People of the Wolf.* Forge, 1990. 435p. 9780812507379.
> *People of the Fire.* Forge, 1991. 467p. 9780812507393.
> *People of the Earth.* Forge, 1992. 587p. 9780812507423.
> *People of the River.* Forge, 1992. 400p. 9780312852351.
> *People of the Sea.* Forge, 1993. 425p. 9780312931223.
> *People of the Lakes.* Forge, 1994. 608p. 9780312857226.
> *People of the Lightning.* Forge, 1995. 414p. 9780312858520.
> *People of the Silence.* Forge, 1996. 493p. 9780312858537.
> *People of the Mist.* Forge, 1997. 432p. 9780312858544.

People of the Masks. Forge, 1998. 416p. 9780312858575.
People of the Owl. Forge, 2003. 560p. 9780312877415.
🦌 *People of the Raven.* Forge, 2004. 494p. 9780765308559—Spur Award
People of the Moon. Forge, 2005. 528p. 9780765308566.
People of the Nightland. Forge, 2007. 477p. 9780765314406.
People of the Weeping Eye. Forge, 2008. 432p. 9780765314383.
People of the Thunder. Forge, 2009. 383p. 9780765314390.
People of the Longhouse. Forge, 2010. 304p. 9780765320162. The 17th novel in the series is also the first in a subseries dealing with the Iroquois. Early in the 15th century, Odeon and Tutelo, young Iroquois siblings, are kidnapped into sexual slavery when their village is taken by warriors or the Mountain People.
The Dawn Country. Forge, 2011. 304p. 9780765320179.
The Broken Land. Forge, 2012. 368p. 9780765326942.

Simmons, Dan

Black Hills. Little, Brown and Co., 2010. 487p. 9780316006989. When 10-year-old Sioux warrior Paha Sapa counts coup on George Armstrong Custer, the general's ghost moves in. His story and that of the West twine together for the next six decades.

Rooted in Reality

The Westerns in this section feature stories that include actual historical events and characters. Many of them are award winners and feature meticulous research. Some earlier editions of *Genreflecting* included a "Celebrity Western" category, but now, even though many of the real-life characters have familiar names, more writers are telling the stories of lesser known Western characters. *Doc* by Mary Doria Russell, found in the "Literary Westerns" section, also fits this category.

🌺 Agonito, Rosemary, and Joseph Agonito. *Buffalo Calf Road Woman: The Story of a Warrior of the Little Bighorn.* The Globe Pequot Press/Two Dot Books, 2006. 242p. 0762738170. Buffalo Calf Woman saved her brother's life in the battle the Cheyenne call "The Battle Where the Girl Saved Her Brother." She then went on to fight in the Battle of Little Big Horn. This is the story of a heroic woman against the backdrop of the end of the era when the Cheyenne were free on the northern plains. Western Heritage Award winner.

🌺 Boggs, Johnny. *Legacy of a Lawman.* Five Star, 2011. 226p. 97815 94149405. Bass Reeves, the legendary African American deputy marshal, who became famous for his long career in Indian Territory, is the protagonist in this novel that pits him against a villain who may be the death of him. It won the Spur Award.

♠ **Burton, Gabrielle.** *Impatient with Desire*. Hyperion, 2009. 256p. 97814 01341015. Tamsen Donner tells her story in letters and her journal from her early years, courtship and marriage to George Donner through the westward journey that strands them in the Sierras where the party resorts to cannibalism. Western Heritage Award winner.

Must Read

★ **Cather, Willa.** ***Death Comes for the Archbishop***. Knopf, 1926. 299p. 0679728899 (1990 Vintage Books edition). Based on the real-life first Archbishop of Santa Fe-Jean Lamy, Jean Latour is sent by the Catholic Church to Santa Fe in the 1940s as its first bishop when New Mexico becomes a territory of the United States.

♠ **Eickhoff, Randy Lee.** *And Not to Yield: A Novel of the Life and Times of Wild Bill Hickok*. Forge, 2004. 430p. 9780812567762. This biographical novel follows the life of James Butler Hickok, from his childhood in Illinois— through a brief stint homesteading in Kansas, serving in the Union Army, fighting Indians, and many other occupations—to became a legend in his own time known as "Wild Bill Hickok." Western Heritage Award winner.

Estleman, Loren D. *Roy & Lillie: A Love Story*. Forge, 2010. 270p, 9780765322289. A fictionalized dual biography in letters of Judge Roy Bean, frontier justice of the peace/bad boy, and Lillie Langtree, British beauty and actress.

📖 **Giles, Paulette.** *The Color of Lightning*. HarperCollins, 2009. 349p. 9781554683178. Based on the story of Britt Johnson, a former slave living in West Texas, who was away from home during the Elm Creek raid of 1864 in which Native Americans killed part of his family and captured others. Alan C. Huffines' *Killed By Indians, 1871* also deals with Britt Johnson's tale.

♠ 🎞 **Geoffrion, Alan.** *Broken Trail*. Fulcrum Press, 2006. 388p. 9781 555916053. When a rancher and his nephew are herding several hundred horses to Wyoming for sale to the British Army for use in the Boer War, they encounter five enslaved Chinese girls who are being transported to a mining camp to be forced into prostitution. Western Heritage Award winner.

Huffines, Alan C. *Killed by Indians, 1871*. Texas Wesleyan University Press, 2010. 208p. 9780983152200. A western hero, Britt Johnson, a slave in West Texas, worked relentlessly to reclaim his family and others who had escaped death and been captured by Indians in the Elm Creek raid of 1864, and became a Texas legend. *The Color of Lightning* by Paulette Giles also deals with the story of Britt Johnson.

Myers, Cindi. ***The Woman Who Loved Jesse James***. Bell Bridge Books, 2012. 242p. 9781611940824. Zee Mimms, a minister's daughter, and her cousin Jesse James' story is told through their nine-year courtship, birth of four children, loss of two, lives using aliases, up to the slaying of Jesse. Attractive narcissists, Zee and Jesse only care about doing and getting what they want.

🎗 📖 **Wheeler, Richard.** ***Snowbound***. Forge, 2010. 302p. 978 0765316622. This biographical novel about John Charles Fremont focuses on the adventure and survival issues of his fourth expedition, the deadly expedition that took him into Colorado as he surveyed a railroad route along the 38th parallel. Spur Award winner.

YA **Wilson, John.** ***Ghost Moon***. Orca, 2011. 172p. 9781554698790. Set in New Mexico during the Lincoln County War, this brief and spare story conveys a realistic look at life in 1878 New Mexico, Billy the Kid, the Regulators, the U.S. Army, the Apache, and events that happened then. While it is the middle volume in a trilogy, it stands alone just fine. This is a sequel to *Written in Blood*.

Literary Westerns

Literary Westerns emphasize language, characterization, and setting, with adventuresome plots taking a backseat. The Western Literature Association (http://www.usu.edu/westlit/reading-suggestions/) lists contemporary fiction of the American West from 1990 to 2000, which features several titles with great appeal for readers of this category.

🎗 📖 **Askew, Rilla.** ***Harpsong***. University of Oklahoma Press, 2007. 243p. 9780806138237. In Depression era Oklahoma, 14-year-old Sharon Thompson marries harmonica player Harlan Singer and they hit the road, riding the rails through America's heartland but always returning to Oklahoma. Western Heritage and Willa Award winner.

Must Read

★ 🎞 **Clark, Walter Van Tilburg.** ***The Ox-Bow Incident***. Random House, 1940. 240p. 9780812972580. Two cowboys become the focus of Mob violence in the small town of Bridger's Falls.

📖 🎗 **Harrigan, Stephen.** *Remember Ben Clayton*. Knopf, 2011. 353p. 9780307265814. A tragic family history involving Indian captivity, a massacre, and dark secrets come to light when a wealthy West Texas rancher hires a sculptor to create a memorial for his son, killed in World War I.

Must Read

★ 🏇 🎬 **McCarthy, Cormac. *All the Pretty Horses*.** Knopf, 1992. 301p. 9780394574745. Teenaged cowboy John Grady Cole drifts into Mexico where he finds trouble and love. National Book Award and Western Heritage Award winner.

🏇 **Olmstead, Robert. *Far Bright Star*.** Algonquin Books, 2009. 207p. 9781 565125926. As America prepares to enter World War I, cavalryman Napoleon Childs takes a band of misfits destined to be cavalrymen into the Mexican desert hunting for Pancho Villa and encounters hardship, death, and destruction. Spur Award winner.

★ **Russell, Mary Doria. *Doc*.** Random House, 2011. 394p. 9780679604 396. A year in the life of southern gentleman John Henry "Doc" Holliday who lands in Dodge City, Kansas, after tuberculosis forces him to leave his dental practice in Georgia. While there, he meets the three Earp brothers, Bat Masterson, "Big Nose Kate," and other legends of the wild West.

Sojourner, Mary. *Going through Ghosts*. University of Nevada Press, 2010. 264p. 9780874178098. A down-and-out cocktail waitress in a desolate Nevada casino befriends a young Native woman who is murdered. She embarks on a journey of discovery with the help of a healer and the ghost of the murdered woman.

The New West

The West is a state of mind not always tied to a specific time period. Titles in this section deal with the post-horse era but still focus on the concerns that have always been prevalent in the West: use of resources, minding one's own business, standing up for what is right, and peopled by rugged individuals who put their values above comfort. Readers may also enjoy the contemporary novels in the "Mysterious Westerns" section of this chapter.

Blew, Mary Clearman. *Jackalope Dreams*. University of Nebraska Press, 2008. 390p. 9780803215887. The resiliency of a Western woman is showcased in this story of Montana middle-school teacher Corey Henry, who, when nearing 60 is fired from her job, loses her dad to suicide and is sued for assault on a student.

Dallas, Sandra

Tallgrass. St. Martin's, 2007. 305p. 9780312360191. A 13-year-old girl tries to make sense of life in the 1940s living next to a Japanese internment camp on Colorado's high plains.

Whiter Than Snow. St. Martin's, 2011. 320p. 9780312663162. A Colorado mining community faces tragedy in the 1920s when an avalanche buries nine children.

🎗 **Flynn, Robert.** *Echoes of Glory*. Texas Christian University Press, 2009. 215p. 9780875653891. When the sheriff of fictional Texas County decides to step down during the Reagan years, the town's legends are imperiled by some ugly truths about heroes of the Korean War. Spur Award winner.

Henry, Joe. *Lime Creek*. Random House, 2011. 142p. 9781400069415. In lyrical prose, the 20th century story of a ranching family begins when Spencer Davis brings a wife back to Wyoming from Massachusetts, and in eight connected stories, kids, war, and high school sports illuminate the life of this family.

Genreblends

Genreblending has become a norm rather that an exception. Types that were at one time considered to be eccentric variations are now commonplace. Fans of Westerns and general readers can now enjoy Westerns combined with mystery, romance, fantasy, science fiction, and paranormal.

The Weird West

The Weird West includes stories that take place in a West rich in magic, the paranormal, or strange science. The precursor of this subgenre could be thought of as the TV show and later the movie *The Wild Wild West*. A more contemporary movie that exemplifies this subgenre is *Cowboys and Aliens*. The trend has been showcased in the anthology *Westward Weird* (DAW, 2012. 311p. 9780756407186).

YA **McQuerry, Maureen Doyle.** *The Peculiars*. Amulet, 2012. 359p. 9781419701788. As Lena sets off to find her father beyond the borders of 19th-century civilization, she becomes the victim of a train robber. While trying to earn back the money needed for a guide, she spies for the handsome sheriff eventually bringing on disaster in this combination of steampunk and the wild West.

Priest, Cherie. *Boneshaker*. Tor, 2009. 416p. 9780765318411. In 1880, while the Civil War churns on, Briar, the daughter of an infamous lawman, ventures into blight-poisoned and zombie-infested Seattle searching for her teen-aged son.

Sanderson, Brandon. *The Alloy of Law*. Tor, 2011. 332p. 9780765330420. Waxillium Ladrium has left the Roughs and his career as a frontier lawman behind to return to the city following the death of his sister and uncle, but has to take up his guns and magical abilities again to stop the Vanishers, a gang that has been robbing trains in a way that has all mystified.

Westerns with a Touch of Fantasy

With the current popularity of and interest in fantasy and the paranormal, it is not surprising that elements from those genres are showing up more frequently in Westerns. The books in this section are set in the historic West with magic playing a role, but not necessarily being the focus.

Bull, Emma. *Territory*. Tor, 2007. 318p. 9780312857356. As Mildred, a young-widowed typesetter, becomes enmeshed in the politics and day-to-day life of Tombstone, she helps the mysterious Jesse Fox delve into a ritual murder finding that dark magic is running rampant in the days leading up to the shoot-out at the OK Corral.

YA Holt, Kimberly Willis. *The Water Seeker*. Henry Holt, 2009. 309p. 9780805080209. Amos is the son of a mountain man who rarely pops into his life. His mother died when he was born and he lives with several different people in many different places as he grows up under the watchful eye of his dead mother.

YA Mitchell, Saundra. *The Springsweet*. Harcourt, 2012. 278p. 978054760 8426. Disgraced in Baltimore, Zora goes to the Oklahoma Territory to stay with her young-widowed aunt, experiences the hardships of living in a "soddie" while trying to prove up her Aunt's claim, and discovers a talent for dowsing.

Romantic Westerns

The stereotypical Western reader wouldn't touch Romance with a 10-foot pole, but Western readers come in a variety of flavors. Several Romance authors and readers have taken Westerns to heart. The character of Western heroes, the strong independence, strength of will, and dedication to standing up for what they think is right, all translate well into romance; so it is no wonder that Romances with a strong Western flavor are attractive to readers of Westerns. At the PLA conference in Philadelphia in 2012, two different sessions on genres addressed the fact that Western Romances, both historical and contemporary, were trending with Romance readers. Strangely enough, in Romance Westerns, some books in the same series may be historical and others contemporary.

Johnson, Joan. *The Texas Bride*. Random House, 2012. 384p. 9780345527448. An orphan signs on as a mail-order bride but is secretly bringing her two younger brothers along when she travels to marry struggling rancher Jake Creed, who has a two-year-old daughter he failed to mention.

Miller, Linda Lael

Stone Creek Series. Set in Stone Creek, Arizona, the novels published by Harlequin are set in the early 1900s and the ones published by Silhouette have contemporary settings, but they all deal with the independent, frontier minded folk of this little town.

> *The Man from Stone Creek*. Harlequin, 2006. 331p. 9780373771158. Sam O'Ballivan, a Ranger, goes undercover as a school master in Haven, Arizona, a town that is run by a ruthless family who may be involved in the train robberies he is investigating.
> *A Stone Creek Christmas*. Silhouette, 2007. 217p. 9780373249398.
> *A Wanted Man*. Harlequin, 2007. 347p. 9780373772360.
> *The Rustler*. Harlequin, 2008. 379p. 9780373773305.
> *The Bridegroom*. Harlequin, 2009. 346p. 9780373773886.
> *At Home in Stone Creek*. Silhouette, 2009. 217p. 9780373654871. The sixth title in this series is a contemporary featuring Ashley O'Ballivan who finds her herself and her heart in danger when a security expert working with the DEA comes to her bed-and-breakfast inn to recuperate.

McKettrick Series. The series starts with *High Country Bride* (2002) in which a ranch owner decrees that the first of his three sons to marry and produce a grandson will inherit the ranch, so the eldest brother, Rafe, sends for a mail-order bride.

> *High Country Bride*. Pocket, 2002. 435p. 9780743422734.
> *Shotgun Bride*. Pocket, 2003. 432p. 9780743422741.
> *Secondhand Bride*. Pocket, 2004. 433p. 9780743422758.
> *McKettrick's Choice*. HQN, 2005. 345p. 9780373770298.
> *Sierra's Homecoming*. Silhouette, 2006. 248p. 9780373247950.
> *McKettrick's Luck*. HQN, 2007. 378p. 9780373771851.
> *McKettrick's Pride*. HQN, 2007. 376p. 9780373771905.

McKettrick's Heart. HQN, 2007. 315p. 9780373771943.
The McKettrick Way. HQN, 2007. 248p. 9780373248674.
A McKettrick Christmas. HQN, 2008. 280p. 9780373773022.
McKettricks of Texas: Tate. HQN, 2010. 360p. 9780373774364.
McKettricks of Texas: Garrett. HQN, 2010. 376p. 9780373774418.
McKettricks of Texas: Austin. HQN, 2010. 378p. 9780373774463.
The Lawman's Christmas. HQN, 2011. 256p. 9780373776146. Early in the
    20th century, the new marshal of Blue River, Texas, enters into a mar-
    riage of convenience with the late marshal's widow.

Mysterious Westerns

Westerns have always combined well with Mysteries and continue to be
popular with fans. Some of the subgenres described by Betty Rosenberg in earlier editions of *Genreflecting*, such as "Bad Men and Good" and the "Law and
Lawmen," made a natural marriage of Mystery and Western. The contemporary West is a popular setting for Mysteries often including Native American
communities, perhaps as a result of the longtime popularity of Tony Hillerman's novels set in the Four Corners.

Ault, Sandi

Jamaica Wild Series. Stationed in northern New Mexico, Bureau of Land
Management Resource Protection Agent Jamaica Wild, accompanied by her
wolf companion, solves mysteries blending outdoor adventure, Native culture, spirituality, and preservation of natural ecosystems.

Wild Indigo. Berkley, 2006. 320p. 9780425213698.
Wild Inferno. Berkley, 2008. 304p. 9780425219225.
Wild Sorrow. Berkley, 2009. 304p. 9780425225837.
Wild Penance. Berkely, 2010. 297p. 9780425232323. The fourth entry in the
    series takes Jamaica into the world of Los Penitentes after she sees a
    crucified victim thrown from the Rio Grande Gorge bridge.

Box, C. J.

Joe Pickett Series. Family man, Joe Pickett, a game warden in rural Wyoming,
has run-ins with a variety of miscreants in the wilderness.

Open Season. Putnam, 2001. 293p. 9780425185469.
Savage Run. Putnam, 2002. 272p. 9780399148873.
Winterkill. Putnam, 2003. 352p. 9780425195956.
Trophy Hunt. Putnam, 2004. 352p. 9780425202937.

Out of Range. Putnam, 2005. 320p. 9780425209455.
In Plain Sight. Putnam, 2006. 224p. 9780709082316.
Free Fire. Putnam, 2007. 368p. 9780399154270.
Blood Trail. Putnam, 2008. 320p. 9780399154881.
Below Zero. Putnam, 2009. 352p. 9780399155758.
Nowhere to Run. Putnam, 2010. 368p. 9780399156458.
Cold Wind. Putnam, 2011. 400p. 9780399157356.
Force of Nature. Putnam, 2012. 385p. 9780399158261. Joe is trying to save his friend Nate from an enemy who is out to eliminate witnesses to a long-ago crime, but it has put the lives of the Pickett family in jeopardy.

Burke, James Lee

Hack Holland Series. Hackberry Holland, a Korean War veteran and a former POW, was first seen in the 1971 novel *Lay Down My Sword and Shield*, in which he was running for Congress. He reappeared in 2009, done with being a lawyer, politician, and drunk, in *Rain Gods*, as sheriff in a Texas border town.

Lay Down My Sword and Shield. Countryman Press, 1971. 266p. 9780881501506
Rain Gods. Simon & Schuster, 2009. 434p. 9781439128244.
Feast Day of Fools. Simon & Schuster, 2011. 9781451643114. The septuagenarian sheriff and his deputy Pam Tibbs deal with a Mexican crime lord, a mysterious Chinese woman who helps illegal immigrants, and Hackberry's nemesis, serial killer Preacher Jack Collins.

Must Read
★ **Hillerman, Tony, Joe Leaphorn/Jim Chee Mysteries**. Between 1970 and 2006, 18 mysteries were published that featured Navajo Tribal Police officers and opened up a window into Native life in the Four Corners area.

Hockensmith, Steve

Holmes on the Range Series. In 1893, Otto "Big Red" and Gustav "Old Red" Amlingmeyer, cowboy brothers and fans of the Sherlock Holmes stories, start their own sleuthing adventures as they travel the West from Montana to San Francisco and Texas in this humorous series.

Holmes on the Range. St. Martin's, 2007. 304p. 9780312358044.
On the Wrong Track. St. Martin's, 2007. 336p. 9780312347819.
The Black Dove. St. Martin's, 2008. 304p. 9780312347826.
The Crack in the Lens. St. Martin's, 2009. 320p. 9780312379421.
World's Greatest Sleuth! St. Martin's, 2011. 336p. 9780312379438. The
    fifth novel in the series takes the brothers to Chicago to participate
    in a Sherlockian competition, but stumble onto a cheesy murder
    case.

Johnson, Craig

Walt Longmire Series. Walt Longmire, the recently widowed, nearing
retirement, sheriff of Absaroka County, Wyoming, in this multiaward winning
series is known for his intensity, cultural sensitivity, and devotion to Western justice. In 2012, A&E started filming *Longmire*, a television based on the
series.

The Cold Dish. Penguin, 2004. 400p. 9780143036425.
Death without Company. Penguin, 2006. 320p. 9780143038382.
Kindness Goes Unpunished. Viking, 2007. 304p. 9780670031573.
🎗 *Another Man's Moccasins*. Viking, 2007. 304p. 9780670018611—
    Spur Award
The Dark Horse. Viking, 2009. 318p. 9780670020874.
Junkyard Dogs. Viking, 2010. 320p. 9780670021826.
Hell Is Empty. Viking, 2011. 320p. 9780670022779. In this seventh Long-
    mire novel, Walt ventures alone into the wilderness in the face of a
    threatening blizzard on the trail of three escaped murders, one con-
    victed of killing Virgil While Buffalo's grandson.
As the Crow Flies. Viking, 2012. 320p. 9780670023516.

🎗 Mims, Meg

Double Crossing. Astraea Press, 2011. 257p. 9781936852482. Following the
    murder of her father, Lily Granville leaves Chicago in 1869 on the newly
    opened transcontinental railroad to find her father's killer and the missing
    deed to California gold mine. Spur Award winner.

Thurlo, Aimée, and David Thurlo

Ella Clah Series. Navajo Tribal Police special investigator and former FBI
agent, Ella Clah works in both the white and Navajo worlds and deals with
the conflicts that arise between the traditionalist and modernist factions on the
reservation.

Blackening Song. Forge, 1995. 384p. 9780765302564.
Death Walker. Forge, 1996. 384p. 9780765306517.
Bad Medicine. Forge, 1997. 352p. 9780765311375.
Enemy Way. Forge, 1999. 352p. 9780312855208.
Shooting Chant. Forge, 2000. 352p. 9780812568684.
Red Mesa. Forge, 2001. 384p. 9780812568691.
Changing Woman. Forge, 2002. 384p. 9780812568707.
Tracking Bear. Forge, 2003. 384p. 9780765343963.
Wind Spirit. Forge, 2004. 320p. 9780765343970.
White Thunder. Forge, 2005. 256p. 9780765311740.
Mourning Dove. Forge, 2006. 336p. 9780765350350.
Turquoise Girl. Forge, 2007. 304p. 9780765317155.
Coyote's Wife. Forge, 2008. 352p. 9780765317162.
Earthway. Forge, 2009. 336p. 9780765317179.
Neverending Snake. Forge, 2010. 384p. 9780765324504.
Black Thunder. Forge, 2011. 320p. 9780765324511. Ella Clah investigates a serial killer whose victims have little in common except for being killed in the same week in different years.

RESOURCES

Readers' Advisory Guides

Herald, Diana Tixier. *Genreflecting: A Guide to Popular Reading Interests*, edited by Wayne A. Wiegand. 6th ed. Westport, CT: Libraries Unlimited, 2006. Also see earlier editions.

Mort, John. *Read the High Country: A Guide to Western Books and Films*. Westport, CT: Libraries Unlimited, 2006.

Roundup Magazine. http://www.westernwriters.org/roundup.html. A good source of reviews.

Awards

Owen Wister Award. A lifetime achievement award by the Western writers of America. http://www.westernwriters.org/owen_wister_award_history.htm

Spur Award. Awarded annually by the Western Writers of America in several categories including Best Western Short Novel, Best Western Long Novel, Best Original Mass Market Paperback, and Best First Novel. http://www.westernwriters.org/spur_award_history.htm

Willa Award. Awarded annually by Women Writing the West. Categories include Contempory, Historical, and Original Softcover. http://www .womenwritingthewest.org/willaCurrentFinalists.html

Western Heritage Award. Also called "National Cowboy & Western Heritage Museum Western Heritage Award" was established to honor and encourage the legacy of those whose works in literature, music, film, and television reflect the significant stories of the American West. http://www.nationalcowboymuseum.org

Organizations

Western Writers of America. http://www.westernwriters.org

Women Writing the West. http://www.womenwritingthewest.org/

FIVE FAN FAVORITES

- Win Blevins. <u>Rendezvous Series</u>—Traditional—Wagons West

- Eugene C. Vories. *Piñon Mesa*—Traditional—Cowboys

- Mary Doria Russell. *Doc*—Literary Westerns

- Cherie Priest. *Boneshaker*—Genreblends—Weird West

- James Lee Burke. <u>Hack Holland Series</u>—Genreblends—Western Mysteries

---

Chapter 11

Romance Fiction

Shelley Mosley and John Charles

In 2011, Romance fiction accounted for 1.368 billion dollars in book sales (Romance Writers of America). With 13.4 percent of the book market, Romance Fiction continues to outsell every other fiction genre, including Mystery and Suspense novels, Science Fiction and Fantasy books, and even Literary Fiction (you know, those books Oprah reads). Yet in many public libraries, Romance Fiction is frequently misunderstood, if not completely ignored by library staff. But developing a great Romance collection and working with readers is really quite easy once you get rid of any preconceived notions you might have about Romance Fiction . . . and Romance readers.

DEFINITION

The first step in becoming a better Romance readers' advisor is to understand the genre itself. In order for a book to be considered a Romance novel, it must have two things: the main focus of the story must be on the romantic relationship between the book's two protagonists, and the book must have a happily optimistic, emotionally satisfying ending. These are the only two elements a book must have to fit within the Romance genre. As you can tell, this not only gives Romance authors a great deal of latitude when it comes to writing their books, but it is also one reason why the Romance genre has such an incredible range of story types from which to choose.

CHARACTERISTICS AND APPEAL

There are many reasons for the popularity of Romance Fiction with readers. The first is the genre's built-in guarantee of a happy ending. Romance readers know that no matter what problems, struggles, issues, etc., the hero and heroine in a love story encounter, by the end of the book, things are going to turn out okay. It is very important not to underestimate the power of a Happily Ever After ending (or HEA, as we say in the genre) for readers. This doesn't mean that every Romance novel ends with the protagonists marching down the aisle while Mendelssohn's "Wedding March" plays in the background, but it does mean that by the end of a Romance, readers believe that things look good for the couple's future together.

Romance novels are emotion-driven stories. Romance readers want an emotional connection with the characters in a Romance Novel, and Romance writers deliver this. The intense emotional power of Romance Fiction is often criticized by those who don't understand the genre, but for Romance readers, nothing beats the rush of falling in love again.

There is an incredible range of reading opportunities available within the Romance genre. Romances can be sweet and charming or dark and intense. A Romance Novel can be set in the distant past or the far-flung future. Romance Novels can be set in small-town America, the glittering capitals of Europe, or even on a distant planet. This diversity of choice is another appeal element for many Romance readers.

One common misperception about Romance Fiction is that "these books" are all light, inconsequential reads that have nothing to do with the "real world." First and most importantly, there is nothing wrong with reading to escape the everyday stresses and strains of the "real world." What reader wouldn't like to take a temporary vacation from the day-to-day demands of work and home by romantically sparring with a duke in Eloisa James' *The Duke is Mine* (2012) or searching for a long-lost treasure with a cynical Foreign Legionnaire reject in Connie Brockway's *The Other Guy's Bride* (2011) or using unique powers to battle evil, as does the hero in Christina Dodd's *Scent of Darkness* (2007).

While these Romances (and many others) imaginatively sweep readers away into different times and places, there are an equal number of Romances that have incorporated "real" issues into their plots, including Judith Arnold's *Barefoot in the Grass* (1996, breast cancer), Emilie Richards' *Endless Chain* (2005, the sanctuary movement), Lisa Kleypas' *Blue Eyed Devil* (2008, spousal abuse), and both Sandra Kitt's *The Color of Love* (1995) and Geri Krotow's *What Family Means* (2009, interracial Romance). From light and frothy love stories to emotionally intense Romances that tackle real issues with compassion and conviction, the Romance genre has it all.

BRIEF HISTORY

Romance has been a key ingredient in stories—both written and oral— since the dawn of time. From Solomon and Sheba to Anthony and Cleopatra, people in ancient times loved a good couple, but it took a while for writers to get the "happily ever after" part of the Romance equation into print. By the 18th century, when *Pamela; or, Virtue Rewarded* (1740) by Samuel Richardson debuted, the Romance Novel as we know it today had finally arrived on the literary scene. A Cinderella tale of a lowly servant who eventually marries her boss, *Pamela* is considered by many critics to be not only the first novel written in English, but also the first written Romance Novel.

The 19th century ushered in two great Romance writers: Jane Austen and Charlotte Bronte. Austen wrote six witty and unforgettable tales of love and Romance, including her classic *Pride and Prejudice* (1813), and her books became the inspiration for the Regency Romance subgenre of Romance Fiction. Bronte's evocative and atmospheric *Jane Eyre* (1847) took the genre into a slightly darker direction, and her tale of an orphan governess who ultimately wins the love of her employer became the inspiration for many Gothic Romances written in the 20th century.

In the 20th century, Romance Fiction continued to find favor with readers as the genre expanded in new directions. In 1919, E. M. Hull's *The Sheik* was published. Not only did Hull's book inspire a classic silent movie with Rudolph Valentino, but also its sexy, arrogant, domineering hero became the model for every über-alpha hero that has since followed. Georgette Heyer, considered to be the "Godmother of the Regency Romance," wrote her first Romance, *The Black Moth*, which was published in 1921. Heyer's first Regency Romance was followed by more than two-dozen other Romances that set the bar for all Regencies that followed.

In 1938, *Rebecca* by Daphne Du Maurier was published. While a few critics might quibble about its place in the Romance genre, Du Maurier's timeless tale of a heroine struggling to determine if she married a murderer became the literary model for a host of Romantic Suspense and Gothic writers who would follow in Du Maurier's footsteps. Mary Stewart carried on the contemporary Romantic Suspense torch with the publication of her first book, *Madame Will You Talk*, in 1955, while Victoria Holt launched the boom in Gothic Romances in the 1960s with *Mistress of Mellyn*, published in 1960.

A new brand of Historical Romances took the market by storm in the 1970s with the publication of Kathleen Woodiwiss' *The Flame and the Flower* (1972) and Rosemary Rogers' *Sweet, Savage Love* (1974). Both novels not only served up sweeping love stories set in the past, but also plenty of sexy, steamy love scenes. Contemporary Romances had their turn at the top of the market in the 1980s and 1990s as Harlequin expanded its lines of series Romances, and Bantam and Kensington launched their own Contemporary lines, introducing readers to such authors as Nora Roberts, Sandra Brown, and Jennifer Crusie.

As the world turned the page on the 20th century and entered into the 21st century, vampires, werewolves, and warlocks took over the Romance genre. Christine Feehan's first "Dark" book, *Dark Prince*, was published in 1999; Sherrilyn Kenyon introduced her world of Dark-Hunters with *Night Pleasures* in 2002; and J. R. Ward's *Dark Lover* hit the market in 2005. Suddenly, Paranormal Romances became the hottest ticket in Romance Fiction.

While the Romance genre continues to expand into new areas (Steampunk anyone?) and subgenres mingle and mix to create new hybrids of Romances, one thing remains consistent—readers will always find time for a good love story.

CURRENT TRENDS

Just as in the world of fashion, trends come and go in Romance Fiction, but one trend that seems to have the real staying power is that of "connected" Romances. Readers love series because they not only deliver a new and different story with each book, but also because every book is also set in a familiar landscape for the reader.

Romance Fiction doesn't do series in quite the same way as other genres (primarily because by the very definition of a Romance, the story must end with a happily ever after for the protagonists), but what Romance writers have come up with is the idea of connected or linked novels. Some Romance writers choose to create a "series" around a group of individuals who work together, such as Suzanne Brockmann's Navy S.E.A.L. Team Ten Series. Other writers link their books through a family connection, such as Stephanie Laurens' Cynster historical Romances. Still other authors choose to connect their books by giving them a common geographic setting, such as Robyn Carr's Virgin River books. However they do it, connected books continue to remain popular with Romance readers.

Comedy is also back in fashion with Romance readers. Perhaps, it's an antidote to the dreary and depressing state of the world, but more and more Romance writers are incorporating humor—both subtle and slapstick—into their story lines. While some writers, such as Jennifer Crusie and Julia Quinn, have always been known for their comic literary touch, new writers, including Kieran Kramer and Kristan Higgins, are also adding a generous soupçon of wit and whimsy to their love stories.

Inspirational Romance is also hot (well, not "hot" in a romantic sense) with readers, and the market for faith-based love stories continues to increase in popularity. Romance publishing juggernaut Harlequin launched its own inspirational line, Steeple Hill, 15 years ago by offering readers 3 titles per month. The Steeple Hill line of Inspirational Romances now includes more than a dozen titles published each month in a variety of Romance subgenres. Many Romance readers who may have never tried an Inspirational Novel in the past are discovering that these Romances offer a sweetly satisfying love story without all the sensual steam found in other Romances.

Cowboys are also making a comeback in the world of Romance. Decades ago, the Western Romance was a staple of the Historical market, but reader demand declined over the years, and many Western authors switched to other time periods and settings or completely new subgenres. Now a whole new posse of authors including Kaki Warner, Carolyn Brown, and Katie Lane are riding into the Romance corral to join long-standing authors such as Linda Lael Miller, who has been writing about Romance in the West for more than two decades.

Working with Romance Readers

Every fiction genre has its own particular issue that must be factored into the readers' advisory interview. With the Romance genre, it is sex. There is a wide range of sensuality within the Romance genre, and Romances range from light and charming to sexy and steamy in tone. The minute a reader begins talking about their favorite Romances, they are giving us clues as to what kind of a Romance they want to read. If the reader uses words like "sweet" or "gentle," or mentions that their favorite authors are Debbie Macomber or Beverly Lewis, they probably want a less sexy Romance than a reader who states they loved everything Bertrice Small or Susan Johnson has written or that they enjoy "hot" love stories.

Some readers will enjoy any and all love stories, while other readers only want books from within a certain subgenre of Romances. In addition, many Romance authors—including Christina Dodd, Julie Garwood, and Lisa Kleypas—now write in several different subgenres. Does the reader want everything by Lisa Kleypas or just her Historical Romances? This is another important point to discuss with the reader while you are helping them find a new Romance to try.

THEMES AND TYPES

Key to Romance

Contemporary Romance
Romantic Suspense
Historical Romance

(Continued)

Regency Romance
Paranormal Romance
Inspirational Romance

Every Romance Novel has those two main elements we talked about earlier: a story that focuses on the romantic relationship between the hero and heroine, and a happily optimistic, emotionally satisfying ending. Once a book has these two components, it can be set in a variety of locations, a range of different time periods, and have any number of different plots and still be considered a Romance. These different settings and plot characteristics create the different subgenres within Romance Fiction.

Contemporary Romance

By its very definition, a Contemporary Romance is set in the present day, but the book itself can take place anywhere in the world, from a small town in America to a glamorous foreign locale. Contemporary Romances can be humorous and sexy, such as *Bet Me* (2004) by Jennifer Crusie or *It Had to Be You* (1994) by Susan Elizabeth Phillips, or emotionally intense and compelling, such as *This Time Forever* (1992) by Kathleen Eagle. Contemporary Romances are the largest subgenre of Romance Fiction because so many series Romances are Contemporary Romances too. Series Romances (sometimes referred to as Category Romances) are Romance lines in which the stories conform to a specific pattern set by a publisher such as Harlequin. Series Romances are usually numbered and the publisher provides guidelines in terms of the length of the story, sensuality level, etc. Harlequin is currently the leading publisher of Series Romance Fiction in the world.

Anderson, Catherine. *Phantom Waltz*. Signet, 2007. 432p. 9780451220684.
   Bethany Coulter, confined to a wheelchair, is broken in body and soul, but rancher Ryan McKendrick is determined that she'll learn to love him. (Second book in the <u>Coulter Family Series</u>.)

Bevarly, Elizabeth. *Fast and Loose*. Berkley, 2008. 304p. 9780425220856.
   Celebrity thoroughbred trainer Cole Early needs a place to stay during the Kentucky Derby, and for the right price, artist Lulu Flannery might be willing to rent out her bungalow. (First book in the <u>Kentucky Derby Trilogy</u>.)

Must Read

♥ ★Crusie, Jennifer. *Bet Me*. St. Martin's, 2004. 448p. 9780312303464. When Minerva Dobbs overhears her exboyfriend betting Calvin Morrisey that he can't bed Min in a month, Min decides to turn the tables on them both by flirting with Cal and then dumping him. It won a RITA Award.

Gibson, Rachel. *Any Man of Mine*. Avon, 2011. 373p. 9780061579110. Two years after they impulsively got married in Las Vegas, hockey star Sam LeClaire turns up in Seattle hoping he can just pick up where things left off with his wife Autumn Haven.

Greene, Jennifer. *Blame It on Cupid*. Mira, 2009. 384p. 9780778303565. Merry's best friend dies, and Merry inherits her daughter, 11-year-old Charlene. But Merry knows partying, not parenting, and the only person she can turn to for advice is her neighbor Jack MacKinnon, a single dad.

♥ Higgins, Kristin. *Too Good to Be True*. HQN, 2009. 379p. 9780373775156. After her ex-fiancé starts dating her younger sister, Grace Emerson invents a new man for herself only to discover her fictional boyfriend is starting to sound a lot like her new neighbor Callahan O'Shea. It won the RITA Award.

Kitt, Sandra. *Adam and Eva*. Silhouette, 2006. 256p. 9780373285570. Eva Duncan goes to the Virgin Islands for six weeks looking for rest and relaxation, but finds instead newly divorced dad, Adam Maxwell, and his 10-year-old daughter, Diane.

Linz, Cathie. *Mad, Bad, and Blonde*. Berkley, 2010. 300p. 9780425233405. When librarian Faith West is stood up at the altar, she decides to take her Mediterranean honeymoon by herself. Then she meets dreamy Caine Hunter, the ideal man in every way . . . except he's a spy for her father's business competitor.

Mallery, Susan. *Tempting*. HQN, 2007. 384p. 9780373772100. Dani Buchanan's search for her biological father leads her to Senator Mark Canfield, a candidate for U.S. President. But Mark's adopted son, Alex, the senator's devoted, right-hand man, has his suspicions about this spunky woman who claims to be his father's daughter. (Third book in The Buchanans Series.)

Must Read

★ **Phillips, Susan Elizabeth.** *Nobody's Baby but Mine*. Avon, 1997. 384p. 9780380782345. Genius Jane Darling, physics professor, wishes for a baby, but wants to make sure her child will have "normal" intelligence and not be the social pariah she was. What better way to assure this than to mate with a "dumb jock?" Star quarterback Cal Bonner seems to fit the bill, but unbeknownst to Jane, underneath that helmet is an amazing brain. (Third book in the Chicago Stars Series.) Conventional publishing wisdom dictated that sports figures couldn't sell Romances, but Susan Elizabeth Phillips proved this wrong by not only creating football heroes to die for in her Chicago Stars Series, but also an irresistible golf player as well in *Lady Be Good!*

Ray, Francis. *It Had to Be You*. St. Martin's, 2010. 304p. 9780312365073. Classical violinist Laurel Raineau needs a record producer, and Zachary Alright Wilder wants it to be him. He just doesn't know how to get Laurel to trust him when he's built his business on hip-hop and rap. (Fourth book in the Grayson Friends Series.)

Ridgway, Christie. *Crush on You*. Berkley Sensation, 2010. 304p. 9780425235133. Alessandra Baci has a new challenge—to save her family's Napa Valley vineyard. But Alessandra's plans to fix up a historical cottage as a wedding chapel and market their wine as wedding wine requires a bit of help from her new neighbor, Penn Bennett. (First book in the Three Kisses Trilogy.)

Roberts, Nora. *Happy Ever After*. Berkley, 2010. 368p. 9780425236758. Now that her business partners and best friends have found true love, wedding planner Parker "Legs" Brown is the only unattached member of the group. Then her brother's friend, hunky mechanic, former stuntman Malcolm Kavanaugh unexpectedly kisses her after he fixes her tire. (Fourth book in the Bride Quartet.) Nora is known as the "Queen of Romance" for a reason: her last 25 titles have hit number one on the *New York Times* bestseller lists and she recently published her 200th Romance novel (*The Witness*) in 2012.

♟ **Shalvis, Jill.** *Simply Irresistible*. Warner Forever, 2010. 336p. 9780446571616. Maddie Moore is surprised to discover Jax Cullen, the contractor she has hired to renovate her hotel, is the same man she ran off the road on the way into Lucky Harbor. (First book in the Lucky Harbor Series.) It won the RITA Award.

Thompson, Vicki Lewis. *Talk Nerdy to Me.* St. Martin's, 2006. 368p. 9780312939076. Charlie Shepherd finds out that his neighbor, fashion model Eve Dupree, is as brainy as she is beautiful.

Wiggs, Susan. *Table for Five.* Mira, 2005. 400p. 9780778313823. When their parents are killed, Lily Robinson inherits the three Hollway children. The father's half-brother, ex-golfer Sean Maguire, just about ready to start a comeback tour, is named as guardian in an old will, and since neither he nor Lily will give up guardianship, they're forced to form a family. Wiggs got her start writing historical Romances, but she has since switched things up by writing both contemporary Romances and women's fiction novels.

Romantic Suspense

In the Romantic Suspense and Gothic subgenre, writers blend elements from the Romance genre with those from the Mystery/Suspense subgenres into one compelling story line. While the amount of Suspense versus Romance can vary from book to book, the ideal blend is a 50/50 split between the genres, such as that found in Daphne du Maurier's classic *ebecca* (1938). Both Romantic Suspense novels and Gothic novels focus on fusing danger and desire into one plot, with the main difference between the two being time period and setting. Romantic Suspense novels almost always take place in the present day and can be set anywhere in the world. The incomparable Mary Stewart is an excellent example of this, having used Greece as a setting in *My Brother Michael* (1959), France in *Madam, Will You Talk?* (1954), England in *The Ivy Tree* (1961), and Austria in *Airs above the Ground* (1965). Gothic Romances are usually set in the past (most frequently the late 19th century) and take place in an isolated location such as a castle or remote estate. Victoria Holt, called the "Queen of the Gothics," was known for this, having used such settings in many of her novels including *Mistress of Mellyn* (1960), *Bride of Pendorric* (1963), and *The Shivering Sands* (1969), all quintessential examples of the classic Gothic Romance.

Adair, Cherry. *White Heat.* Ballantine Books, 2007. 336p. 9780345476449. Art restoration expert Emily Greene finds herself reunited with her old lover Max Aries, when Max's father, Daniel, is found dead. (Second book in the Black Rose Trilogy.)

Brennan, Allison. *If I Should Die*. Ballantine Books, 2011. 512p. 97803455 20418. While chasing an arsonist, lovers' private investigator Sean Rogan and would-be FBI agent Lucy Kincaid find a corpse in an old mine shaft, but when they return, it has disappeared. Now someone's trying to kill them too. (Third book in the Lucy Kincaid and Sean Rogan Series.)

Brockmann, Suzanne. *Hot Pursuit*. Ballantine Books, 2009. 403p. 978034550 1578. Alyssa Locke's latest assignment protecting an old friend running for public office puts her back in the path of a very determined serial killer known as the "Dentist." (15th book in the Troubleshooter Series.)

Brown, Sandra. *Lethal*. Grand Central Publishing, 2011. 472p. 9781455501472. In order to clear his name of murder, Lee Coburn will stop at nothing to locate a valuable object owned by Honor Gillette's late husband.

Garwood, Julie. *The Ideal Man*. E. P. Dutton, 2011. 336p. 9780525952251. Dr. Ellie Sullivan saved FBI agent Max Daniels' life in the operating room, and now it's his turn to save her when Ellie becomes the target of the couple who shot Max.

🎗 **Gerard, Cindy.** *Take No Prisoners*. Pocket Star, 2008. 384p. 9781416566748. Abbie Hughes, a blackjack dealer in Las Vegas, finds herself a player in Sam Lang's revenge against the smuggler who killed his sister. (Second book in the Black Ops Series.) It won a RITA Award.

Griffin, Laura. *One Last Breath*. Pocket, 2007. 464p. 9781416537373. Private investigator Marco Juarez has his own reasons for helping part-time journalist Feenie Malone investigate the connection between her ex-husband and criminal Rico Martinez.

Howard, Linda. *Ice*. Ballantine Books, 2009. 198p. 9780345517197. Things have always been a bit frosty between Gabriel McQueen and Lolly Helton until the two find themselves caught in an ice storm with a very determined killer on their trail.

Jackson, Lisa. *Devious*. Kensington, 2011. 432p. 9780758225658. The same day Val Houston learns that her sister has been strangled, Val's estranged husband, Slade, suddenly turns up in New Orleans. Coincidence?

Must Read

★ **Krentz, Jayne Ann.** *Sizzle and Burn*. Putnam, 2008. 359p. 9780399154454. Private investigator Zack Jones wants Raine Tallentyre to use her ability to "hear voices" to help him find a missing scientist. Krentz is known for infusing her Romantic Suspense novels with both a dash of wit and a soupçon of the paranormal.

Lowell, Elizabeth. *Death Echo*. William Morrow and Company, 2010. 400p. 9780061629754. Former CIA agent and current St. Kilda consulting operative Emma Cross needs transit captain MacKenzie Durand's help tracking a missing yacht that might be tied into a terrorist plot.

Neggers, Carla. *The Widow*. Mira, 2006. 352p. 9780778323037. Boston homicide detective Abigail Browning travels to Maine to find the answers to her husband's death seven years earlier.

Robards, Karen. *Justice*. Gallery, 2011. 384p. 9781439183700. Attorney Jessica Ford has taken on a new name and identity after witnessing the murder of the First Lady, but Secret Service agent Mark Ryan still thinks Jessica is in danger.

Must Read

★ **Roberts, Nora. *Northern Lights***. Putnam, 2004. 672p. 97803 99152054. After her missing father's body is discovered in an ice cave, Lunacy, Alaska's new police chief Nate Burke tries to keep Meg Galloway safe from a killer, who is willing to kill again to keep old secrets safely buried. Roberts is a three-time winner of a RITA for her perfectly balanced Romantic Suspense novels.

Rose, Karen. *You Belong to Me*. Signet, 2011. 512p. 9780451233578. Baltimore medical examiner Lucy Trask needs Detective J. D. Fitzpatrick's help if she wants to avoid becoming a driven serial killer's next victim.

Historical Romance

Historical Romances mix Historical Fiction and Romance into one captivating story, and from the publication of Kathleen Woodiwiss's *The Flame and the Flower* in 1972 through the 1980s, which saw the publication of several of Judith McNaught's unforgettable novels including *Whitney My Love* (1986), to the present day, Historical Romances have remained a popular subgenre with readers. For the purposes of this book, in order for a book to be considered a Historical Romance, it must have been set at least 50 years ago, which means the general cutoff date for Historical Romances was World War II. Historical Romances have been set in a wide range of past times, but there are a few eras that are especially popular with readers, including the Middle Ages (c. 11th–15th centuries), the Regency period (c. 1811–1820), and the Victorian era (1830s–1890s). Romances set in post–Civil War American, especially those taking place in the West, are another popular setting with readers. The amount of historical detail that an author incorporates into their Romance can vary, with some writers such as Madeleine Hunter and Kaki Warner opting for a strong sense of history and period details in their books, while other authors such as Johanna Lindsey and Julia Quinn choosing to use a lighter touch with history in their Romances.

Alexander, Victoria. *The Perfect Mistress*. Zebra, 2011. 400p. 9781420117059. Harrison Landingham will try anything—including seduction—to keep Julia Winterset from publishing her grandmother's scandalous memoirs.

Boyle, Elizabeth. *Confessions of a Little Black Gown*. Avon, 2009. 380p. 9780061373237. When Thalia Langley loses her luggage and ends up with another woman's black dress, she finds herself caught up in a dangerous game of espionage with Lord Larken. (Fourth book in the Bachelor Chronicles Series.)

Brockway, Connie. *The Golden Season*. Onyx Books, 2010. 388p. 9780451412836. Lydia Eastlake has one season to find a wealthy husband, and she immediately sets her sights on sexy Captain Ned Lockton.

Carlyle, Liz. *Tempted All Night*. Pocket Books, 2009. 438p. 9781416593133. Spinsterish Phaedra Northampton and rakish Tristan Talbot team up to find the killer of a mysterious Russian.

🎗 **Chase, Loretta.** *Silk Is for Seduction*. Avon, 2011. 371 p. 9780061632686. Marcelline Noirot needs more money if she wants to keep her dressmaking shop in business, which means finding a way to convince the Duke of Clevedon (and his ill-dressed new fiancée) to become her latest customers. It was named to the RUSA Reading List of 2012.

Dodd, Christina. *In Bed with the Duke*. Signet, 2010. 400p. 97890451229335. Michael Durant's plans to reclaim the throne of Morcadia take an unexpected turn when he encounters Emma Chegwidden lost in the forest.

Enoch, Suzanne. *Taming an Impossible Rogue*. St. Martin's, 2012. 384p. 9780312534523. Impoverished Keating Blackwood accepts his cousin's offer to pay him 10,000 pounds if he brings back Fenton's runaway bride, Lady Camille Pryce, but once Keating finds Camille, he wants to keep her for himself.

Hoyt, Elizabeth. *The Raven Prince*. Warner, 2006. 384p. 9780446618472. Penniless widow Anna Wren needs a job—any job—and that means she is willing to consider becoming the cranky Earl of Swartingham latest secretary. (First book in the Princes Trilogy.)

Hunter, Madeline. ***Ravishing in Red***. Jove, 2010. 360p. 9780515147544. Audrianna Kelmsleigh will have to find a way to work with Sebastian Sommerhays if she wants to clear her father's reputation as a traitor. (First book in the Rarest Blooms Quartet.)

James, Eloisa. ***A Kiss at Midnight***. Avon, 2010. 380p. 9780061626845. When Prince Gabriel meets Kate at a ball, he is instantly smitten, but Kate thinks the Prince is anything but charming.

Jeffries, Sabrina. ***The Truth about Lord Stoneville***. Pocket, 2010. 380p. 9781439167519. When his grandmother threatens to cut his inheritance unless he gets married, Oliver Sharpe decides to find the most unsuitable fiancée he can: Maria Butterfield. (First book in the Hellions of Halstead Hall Quintet.)

Jenkins, Beverly. ***Night Hawk***. Avon, 2011. 384p. 9780062032645. Ian Vance, known as Night Hawk, a tough bounty hunter, finds himself in love with Maggie Freeman, who is trying to escape a band of vigilantes who want her to hang for a crime she didn't do.

Must Read

★ **Kinsale, Laura.** ***Flowers from the Storm***. Avon, 1992, 560p. 9780380761326. After a stroke costs him the power of speech, Christian, Duke of Jervaulx, is placed in an asylum, where he meets the one person who believes he will speak again: quiet Quaker Maddy Timms. Kinsale is known for her intense, richly emotional Historical Romances.

Kleypas, Lisa. ***Married by Morning***. St. Martin's, 2010. 400p. 9780312605384. The last person Leo Hathaway would ever consider marrying is sharp-tongued Catherine Marks until Leo discovers he has one year to find a wife and produce an heir or he will lose the family estate. (Fourth book in the Hathaway Series.)

Krahn, Betina. ***The Book of True Desires***. Jove, 2006. 352p. 9780515141702. Cordelia Blackburn needs money for her expedition to find three Mayan stone carvings and the "Gift of the Jaguar." Her grandfather is willing to fund her search—if his haughty butler, Hartford Goodnight, accompanies her. It won the RITA Award.

Kramer, Kieran. ***When Harry Met Molly***. St. Martin's, 2010. 432p. 9780312611644. When his mistress abandons him for another man, Harry

Traemore persuades Molly Fairbanks to impersonate her in order to win a bet. (First book in the Impossible Bachelors Quartet.)

Laurens, Stephanie. *The Capture of the Earl of Glencrae*. Avon, 2012. 496p. 9780062068620. It's love at first sight when Angelica Cynster first sees the eighth Earl of Glencrae, and then he kidnaps her. (Third book in the Cynster Sisters Trilogy.)

Lindsey, Johanna. *When Passion Rules*. Gallery, 2011. 400p. 9781451628371. Alana Farmer has no idea she is really the Princess of Lubinia until Christopher Becker, the captain of the palace guards, arrests her for treason.

MacLean, Sarah. *Nine Rules to Break When Romancing a Rake*. Avon, 2010. 432p. 9780061852053. Before she becomes a permanent part of the sisterhood of spinsters, Calpurnia Hartwell comes up with a list of nine things she has always wanted to do. (First book in the Love by the Numbers Trilogy.)

Medeiros. Teresa. *The Pleasure of Your Kiss*. Pocket, 2011. 506p. 9781439157893. When Ashton Burke agreed to rescue his older brother's fiancée, Clarinda Cardew, from a sultan's harem, he never expected to fall in love with her himself.

Miller, Linda Lael. *The Rustler*. HQN, 2008. 336p. 9780373773305. Reformed rustler Wyatt Yarbro finds out the woman of his dreams, Sarah Tamlin, who has some secrets of her own. (Third book in the Stone Creek Series.)

Must Read

★ **Putney, Mary Jo.** *The Rake*. Topaz, 1998. 352p. 9780451406866. Wastrel and drunkard Reginald Davenport discovers the steward who has kept his estate running and out of bankruptcy is a woman: Alys Weston

---

Quick, Amanda. *Crystal Gardens*. Putnam, 2012. 338 p. 9780399159084. Evangeline Ames plans for a quiet rest in the country take an unexpected turn when she discovers someone wants to kill her.

Quinn, Julia. *Just Like Heaven*. Avon, 2011. 325p. 9780061491900. Marcus Holyrod promised his best friend Danile Smythe-Smith he would not let Daniel's sister Honoria marry an idiot, which means Marcus may have to propose to her himself. (First book in the Smythe-Smith Quartet.)

Thomas, Jodi. *Wild Texas Rose*. Berkley, 2012. 380p. 9780425250372. Rose McMurray has turned down three marriage proposals, but a Texas Ranger thinks he can break the trend. (Sixth book in the <u>Whispering Mountain Series</u>.)

🎗 **Warner, Kaki.** *Pieces of Sky*. Berkley, 2010. 432p. 9780425232149. When the stagecoach in which she is traveling crashes, refined Englishwoman Jessica Thornton is forced to take refuge with rough-around-the-edges rancher Brady Wilkins. (First book in the <u>Blood Rose Trilogy</u>.) It won a RITA Award.

Regency Romance

When Romance readers talk about "Regency" Romances, they are really referring to the traditional Regency Romance. While these Romances are set in the same time period as a Historical Regency Romance, there are some differences between the two. Traditional Regency Romances are almost always shorter in word count and they are always sweeter (less sexy) in tone than a Regency historical. The focus in most Regency Romances is on the upper-class British society (known as the ton), the story often features lots of witty dialogue between the hero and heroine, and Regency readers are consumed with historical accuracy in their Romances. When both Signet and Zebra cut their traditional Regency lines in the mid-2000s, Regency readers were faced with a dearth of new titles from which to choose. Fortunately, older Regency titles continue to be re-released (both in print and electronically), which means this small (but important) group of Romance readers will always have a love story that suits their literary needs.

Must Read

★ **Balogh, Mary.** *The Plumed Bonnet*. Signet, 1996. 224p. 97804 51190512. Much to the Duke of Brightwater's surprise, everything Stephanie Grey told him about being robbed turns out to be true, which leaves him no choice but to offer to marry her. Balogh got her start writing traditional Regencies before moving onto longer, sexier Regency Historical Romances.

Beverley, Jo. *Deirdre and Don Juan*. Avon, 1993. 217p. 9780380772810. The Earl of Everdon is looking for a plain woman to marry, but much to his surprise, Deirdre Stowe isn't exactly thrilled with his blunt proposal.

Farr, Diane. *Fair Game*. Signet, 1999. 224p. 9780451198463. After Clarissa's mother barters her off to Viscount Kilverton she has to find a way to convince him she is nothing like her infamous mother.

Must Read

★ **Heyer, Georgette.** *Sylvester or The Wicked Uncle*. Sourcebooks Casablanca, 1972. 400p. 9781402238802. Sylvester, Duke of Salford, is all set to propose to the eminently respectable Phoebe Marlow until he discovers she is the author of an anonymous novel in which he is featured as the villain! Heyer set the standard for the traditional Regency Romance novel, and even today her books are cherished by Romance readers.

Jensen, Emma. *Best Laid Schemes*. Fawcett, 1998. 197p. 9780449002346. When Tarquin Rome begins searching for a suitable woman to marry, he never thought clumsy Sibyl Cameron would make the final cut.

Kelly, Carla. *The Wedding Journey*. Signet, 2002. 240p. 9780451206954. Captain Jesse Randall proposes to Nell Mason on the battlefields of Spain, but will their marriage survive the long journey back to England?

Kerstan, Lynn. *Celia's Grand Passion*. Fawcett Books, 1998. 214p. 9780449001837. Celia Greer vows she will be the one to finally melt Lord Kendal's cold heart.

McCabe, Amanda. *Scandal in Venice*. Signet, 2001. 217p. 9780451202864. Elizabeth Everdean's plans on reinventing herself in Venice are threatened by the unexpected arrival of Nicholas Hollingworth.

🎗 **Metzger, Barbara.** *A Debt to Delia*. Signet, 2002. 224p. 9780451205865. In order to repay a battlefield debt of honor, Major Tyverne St. Ives tries to convince Delia Croft to marry him. It won the RITA Award.

Nash, Sophia. *Lord Will and Her Grace*. Signet, 2005. 224p. 9780451214737. Can Will Barclay help Sophie Somerset find a suitable man before she can teach him how to attract an appropriate lady?

Richardson, Evelyn. *My Wayward Lady*. Signet, 1997. 224p. 9780451192059. Lord Adrian Chalfont is all set to marry the highly suitable but extremely boring Alicia De Villiers until he runs into Lady Harriet Fareham at the scandalous Mrs. Lovington's Temple of Venus.

Scott, Regina. *Utterly Devoted*. Kensington, 2002. 220p. 97800821772829. Jareth Darby must apologize to every woman he has ever romantically wronged, but Eloisa Watkin refuses to believe a rake can change his spots so easily!

Paranormal Romances

Paranormal Romances are currently the hottest of all the Romance subgenres with readers, but this was not always the case. While a few Paranormal Romances such as Jude Deveraux's *A Knight in Shining Armor* (1989), Diana Gabaldon's *Outlander* (1991), and Jayne Ann Krentz's *Shield's Lady* (1989, written as Amanda Glass) earned spots on readers' list of all time favorite Romances, this subgenre really didn't really go supernova with readers until the late 1990s and early 2000s when Christine Feehan and Sherrilyn Kenyon began writing in this subgenre. The Paranormal subgenre includes Fantasy Romances, which blend elements from the Fantasy genre with Romance; Futuristic Romances, which combine elements from Science Fiction with a Romance; and Paranormal Romances, in which supernatural or horror elements are merged into a love story. One reason for the current popularity of Paranormal Romances is the heroes, since writers in the Paranormal subgenre can create the kind of über-alpha, edgy-alpha heroes many readers love. Not all Paranormal Romances, however, are dark and edgy in tone. Paranormal Romances range from the light and humorous, such as Angie Fox's <u>Demon Slayer Series</u>, to the more intense and sexy, such as the <u>Midnight Breed</u> books written by Lara Adrian.

Abé, Shana. *The Smoke Thief.* Bantam, 2006. 352p. 9780553588040. Clarissa Rue Hawthorne, half-mortal, half-dra'kon (a shape-shifter who can turn into a dragon), has fled Darkfrith without permission and has become a jewel thief. Now Christoff, their leader, has come to take her back. (First book in the <u>Dra'kon Series</u>.)

Adrian, Lara. *Kiss of Midnight.* Dell, 2007. 432p. 9780553589375. The murder Gabrielle Maxwell witnesses is done by vampires. Lucan Thorne, a vampire Breed warrior, protects his clan from humans and Rogues, but now he has to watch over Gabrielle. (First book in the <u>Midnight Breed Series</u>.)

Bretton, Barbara. *Casting Spells.* Berkley, 2008. 320p. 9780425223642. Yarn shop owner Chloe Hobbs, who is half-sorceress, lives in Sugar Maple with her otherworldly matchmaker friends, but a human detective, Luke MacKenzie, is the one who catches her eye. (First book in the <u>Sugar Maple Series</u>.)

Castle, Jayne. *Silver Master.* Jove, 2007. 320p. 9780515143553. Matchmaker and para-resonator Celinda Ingram falls for security specialist Davis Oakes when he hunts for the "toy" she got her pet dust bunny, a potent relic sought by others. (Fourth book in the Ghost Hunters Series.)

🎗 **Cole, Kresley.** *A Hunger Like No Other*. Pocket Star, 2006. 384p. 9781 416509875. After 150 years of torture at the hands of the vampires, Lachlain, king of the Lycans, scents his mate. Unfortunately, she's half-vampire. (First book in the Immortals after Dark Series.) It won a RITA Award.

Feehan, Christine. *Dark Curse*. Berkley, 2008. 464p. 9780515146998. Carpathian Nicolas De La Cruz falls in love with Lara Calladine, a mixed-blood dragon-seeker, human, and mage. (19th book in the Dark Series.)

Fox, Angie. *The Accidental Demon Slayer*. Love Spell, 2008. 320p. 9781463558307. Lizzie Brown had no idea she was a demon slayer until her tattooed, motorcyle-riding grandmother shows up for the first time in Lizzie's life. Now a bunch of demons want to kill Lizzie, and only Dimitri, Lizzie's handsome shape-shifting griffin protector, is saving her sanity . . . and her life. (First book in Accidental Demon Slayer Series.)

Must Read

★ **Gabaldon, Diana.** *Outlander*. Delacorte Press, 1991. 688p. 9780440423201. It's a Romance! It's a Time Travel! It's Historical Fiction! It's all of the above! Gabaldon's tale of Clare and her Highlander, Jamie, whose love reaches across time and space, is just plain awesome. Gabaldon's Outlander Series has become a cult favorite. (First book in the Outlander Series.)

Must Read

★ **Kenyon, Sherrilyn.** *Acheron*. St. Martin's, 2008. 728p. 9780312949419. After a painful relationship with the goddess Artemis, Acheron, son of destroyer-goddesss Apollymi, finds love with a human. (12th book in the Dark-Hunter Series.)

Krinard, Susan. *Chasing Midnight*. HQN, 2007. 384p. 9780373772186. Allegra Chance is more than a Jazz Age flapper—she's a vampire who falls for Griffin Durant, a werewolf, one of the vampires' most hated enemies.

Kurland, Lynn. *One Magic Moment*. Jove, 2011. 384p. 9780515149517. When Medieval scholar Tess Alexander meets mechanic John de Piaget, she is surprised at how much he resembles a man born 800 years earlier.

Liu, Marjorie M. *Darkness Calls*. ACE, 2009. 303p. 9780441017300. Female warrior Maxine Kiss has fallen for Grant, a former priest who runs a homeless shelter. Because Grant is a Lightbringer, the Avatars want to kill him, and Maxine too, for protecting him. (Second book in the Hunter Kiss Series.)

MacAlister, Katie. *Steamed*. Signet. 2010. 352p. 9780451229311. Airship Captain Octavia Pye is astonished to find an unconscious man and woman onboard. She figures they're either spies or pirates, but they're really Dr. Jack Fletcher and his sister, thrown into her steam technology universe after a lab explosion.

Moning, Karen Marie. *Spell of the Highlander*. Dell, 2006. 416p. 9780440240976. Archaeology student Jessi St. James frees a Highlander trapped in time. (Seventh book in the Highlander Series.)

Rowe, Stephanie. *Date Me, Baby, One More Time*. Warner Books, 2006. 336p. 9780446617666. Because of the Curse, it's time for Derek LaValle and his twin brother to die. The only way to break the Curse is to behead the Guardian and steal the Goblet of Eternal Youth, but unfortunately, Derek is in love with Justine Bennett, the Guardian. (First book in the Immortally Sexy Series.)

Sands, Lynsay. *The Accidental Vampire*. Avon, 2008. 384p. 9780061229688. Vampire Elvi's old human friends worry about her being alone, so they run an ad for a male vampire companion for her. When vampire Victor Argeneau investigates this for the Council, he's stunned to discover she's his life mate. (Seventh book in the Argeneau Series.)

Showalter, Gena. *Enslave Me Sweetly*. Pocket Books, 2006. 304p. 9780743497503. After failing to eliminate her target, alien assassin Eden Black is assigned a new partner—human agent Lucius Adaire. (Second book in Alien Huntress Series.)

Singh, Nalini. *Angel's Blood*. Berkley Sensation, 2009. 9780425226926. When a vampire goes rogue, the angels hire Elena Deveraux to bring them back. Now Raphael hires her to track a fellow archangel, but Elena isn't sure whether he's going to kiss her or kill her first. (First book of the Guild Hunter Series.)

Sparks, Kerrelyn. *Be Still My Vampire Heart*. Avon, 2007. 384p. 9780061118449. As far as Emma Wallace, a member of the CIA's Stake-Out team, is concerned, the only good vampire is a dead vampire, which means Emma must kill Angus MacKay, a Scottish warrior and owner of a security company sent to stop her. (Third book in the Love at Stake Series.)

Ward, J. R. *Dark Lover*. Signet, 2005. 416p. 9780451235954. The only one who can help Beth Randal survive her "transition" from human to vampire is vampire warrior Wrath. (First book in the <u>Black Dagger Brotherhood Series</u>). Ward puts her own distinctive stamp on the vampire Romance with her Black Dagger Brotherhood books, and the resulting Romances are dark, edgy, and scorchingly sexy.

Inspirational Romance

Faith and religion play an important part in one or more of the protagonists' lives in these love stories. Inspirational Romances are almost always sweet (less sexy) in tone, and titles from this subgenre can be excellent suggestions for readers who want a "gentle" Romance. The best authors writing in this subgenre can deliver a faith-based message without resorting to didacticism and dogmatic preaching.

Alexander, Tamara. *Rekindled*. Bethany House, 2006. 298p. 9780764201080. Badly burned and left for dead, it's a while before Larson Jennings returns home. His pregnant wife, Kathryn, has been trying unsuccessfully to run their Colorado Territory ranch alone. Now it's time to put the pieces back together. (First book in the <u>Fountain Creek Chronicles</u>.)

Austin, Lynn. *While We're Far Apart*. Bethany House, 2010. 416p. 9780764204975. In a Brooklyn apartment during World War II, Eddie Shaffer's wife has died, and Penny Goodrich offers to take care of his children because she's always loved Eddie and hopes he'll learn to love her too.

Must Read

★ **Gist, Deanne.** *A Bride in the Bargain*. Bethany House, 2009. 368p. 9780764204074. Joe Denton needs to get married again, or he'll lose his land. Now Joe must convince Anna Mercer, who came to Seattle to be a cook, to say yes to his proposal.

Hake, Cathy Marie. *Forevermore*. Bethany House, 2008. 352p. 9780764203183. Widower Jakob Stauffer is perplexed by free-spirited cook Hope Ladley and her mixed-up sayings. But his daughter and his sister adore Hope, and he can't deny the light she's brought into his life.

Hannon, Irene. *Deadly Pursuit*. Fleming, 2011. 325p. 9780800734572. Dating St. Louis police detective Mitch Morgan proves to be a godsend for Alison Taylor when she starts receiving anonymous phone calls. (Second book in the <u>Guardians of Justice Series</u>.)

Harris, Yvonne. *The Vigilante's Bride*. Bethany House, 2010. 297p. 9780764208041. Luke Sullivan wants the money Bart Axel has stolen from him, but when Luke stops Axel's stagecoach to get the money, he sees Axel's mail-order bride and takes her, too.

Hauck, Rachel. *Diva Nashvegas*. Thomas Nelson, 2007. 320p. 9781595541918. Country music superstar Aubrey James comes face-to-face with her well-hidden past when a member of the band sells her story to the tabloids.

Klassen, Julie. *The Maid of Fairbourne Hall*. Bethany House, 2011. 400p. 9780764207099. While waiting out her inheritance, Margaret Macy accepts a job as the new maid at Fairbourne Hall.

Landis, Jill Marie. *Heart of Stone*. Zondervan, 2010. 320p. 9780310328728. Reverend Brand McCormick loves Laura Foster, who is not the respectable widow she appears to be. (First book in the Irish Angels Series.)

Must Read

★ **Lewis, Beverly. *The Postcard*.** Bethany House, 1999. 288p. 0764203401. Philip Bradley, a jaded journalist doing a report on the Amish, discovers a postcard written in Pennsylvania Dutch. While unraveling its mystery, Philip finds unexpected Romance with widow Rachel Yoder. Lewis' 1997 novel, *The Shunning*, made Amish Romances popular. (First book in the Amish Country Crossroads.)

Mills, DiAnn. *A Woman Called Sage*. Zondervan, 2010. 304p. 9780310293293. After a gunman kills Sage Morrow's husband, she becomes a bounty hunter, but when she partners with Marshal Parker Timmons to look for two missing boys, a minister starts ugly rumors about her and Parker.

Pattillo, Beth. *Earth to Betsy*. WaterBrook Press, 2006. 304p. 9781400071791. When Rev. Betsy Blessing gets a promotion and a fiancé, she discovers you have to be careful what you pray for. (Second book in the Rev. Betsy Blessing Series.)

Raney, Deborah. *Remember to Forget*. Howard Books, 2007. 368p. 9781582296432. Hiding from an abusive boyfriend, Maggie Anderson meets widower Trevor Ashlock. (First book in the Clayburn Novels Series.)

Smith, Jill Eileen. *Bathsheba*. Revell, 2011. 346p. 9780800733223. This is the retelling of the story of David and Bathsheba. It's good to be king. (Third book in the <u>Wives of King David Series</u>.)

Snelling, Lauraine. *On Hummingbird Wings*. Faithwords, 2011. 352p. 9780446582117. When Gillian Ornsby returns home to take care of her mother Dorothy, she finds herself relying on next-door neighbor Adam for some much needed help with her mother's neglected garden.

Warren, Susan May. *Finding Stephanie*. Tyndale, 2008. 384p. 9781414310190. Everyone is against Stefanie Noble taking in three runaways, especially Lincoln Cash. (Third book in the <u>Noble Legacy Series</u>.)

Wingate, Lisa. *Blue Moon Bay*. Bethany House, 2012. 352p. 9780764208225. With her future as an architect in the balance, Heather Hampton tries to convince her family—and banker Blaine Underhill—to sell the ancestral home to make way for an industrial plant, her first major project.

RESOURCES

Awards

The Reading List. Created by Collection Development and Evaluation Section (CODES) of the Reference and User Services Association (RUSA) within American Library Association (ALA), the best books in eight categories, including Romance Fiction, are selected by a committee of CODES members.

The RITA. Given out annually by the Romance Writers of America (RWA) to published Romances in 12 different categories. RITA finalists are chosen by published Romance writers (and members of RWA) with the winners announced at RWA's annual conference in the summer. RWA also sponsors a Golden Heart contest for unpublished Romance novels in 10 different categories.

Print Resources

Bouricius, Ann. *The Romance Readers' Advisory: The Librarian's Guide to Love in the Stacks*. American Library Association, 2000. Practical advice on working with Romance readers and developing a Romance Fiction collection.

Charles, John, and Shelley Mosley. *Romance Today: An A to Z Guide to Contemporary American Romance Writers*. Greenwood, 2007. Bio-critical essays on more than 100 American Romance writers.

Krentz, Jayne Ann, ed. *Dangerous Men and Adventurous Women: Romance Writers on the Appeal of the Romance*. University of Pennsylvania Press, 1992. A number of award-winning and best-selling Romance writers talk about why writers and readers love Romance.

Mussell, Kay, and Johanna Tunon. *North American Romance Writers*. Scarecrow, 1999. More Romance writers talking about the appeal of the genre and why they write Romances.

Ramsdell, Kristin. *Romance Fiction: A Guide to the Genre*. Libraries Unlimited, 2012. A solid introduction to Romance writers, Romance readers' advisory work, and Romance Fiction collection development.

Vasudevan, Aruna, and Lesley Henderson, eds. *Twentieth-Century Romance and Historical Writers*. 3rd ed. St. James Press, 1997. Bio-critical essays on popular Romance and historical fiction novelists.

Online Resources

Romance Writers of America. www.rwa.org. This is a national association for aspiring and published Romance writers. Includes lists of best-selling authors and award-winners, current releases, RITA Award winners, links to local chapters, and special section for librarians and booksellers.

Romance Readers Anonymous Listserv (RRA-L). http://groups .yahoo.com. This Listserv is one of the longest running forums on Romance Fiction for both readers and authors of the genre.

RomanceScholar. http://mailman.depaul.edu/mailman/listinfo/Romancescholar. This is an academic Listserv for scholars and teachers of Romance Fiction.

RT Bookreviews. www.rtbookreviews.com. This site includes almost comprehensive review coverage of Romance titles, author profiles and interviews, and lists of Romances by subgenre.

FIVE FAN FAVORITES

- Deanne Gist. *A Bride in the Bargain* — Inspirational
- Kresley Cole. *A Hunger Like No Other* — Paranormal
- Laura Griffin. *One Last Breath* — Romantic Suspense
- Elizabeth Hoyt. *The Raven Prince* — Historical
- Kristan Higgins. *Too Good to Be True* — Contemporary

10

11

12

13

14

15

16

17

18

Chapter 12

Women's Fiction

Rebecca Vnuk

Women's Fiction—this subset of General Fiction can be hard to define and, in fact, has not traditionally been seen as a separate genre—is more of a reading interest, if anything. Steady gains in popularity, however, mean that readers demand more and librarians must know what those readers are looking for when they want Women's Fiction.

DEFINITION

The two big questions that come up when discussing books in the category of Women's Lives and Relationships (also known as Women's Fiction) are "What is it that classifies a book as Women's Fiction?" and "Is Women's Fiction actually a genre?" There are no easy answers. It's almost a case of "you know it when you read it," but that's awfully subjective. The trouble is these stories can follow any number of formats and have any kind of tone—they can be romantic or suspenseful (or both!), or they can be humorous or tragically sad. In a way, Women's Fiction is really a subset of General or Mainstream Fiction.

When asked to define Women's Fiction, my answer is always this: The common thread is that the central character (or characters) is a woman (or are women), and the main thrust of the story is something happening in the life of that woman (e.g., apart from the overarching themes of romance or mystery). These novels explore the lives of female protagonists, with a focus on their relationships with family, friends, and lovers. Emotions and relationships are keys across the board.

Another interesting question that often comes up is, "Does a Women's Fiction author have to be a woman?". My personal opinion is, yes. I have yet to read a Women's Fiction novel written by a man. Chris Bohjalian is often brought up to me as an example of a man who writes novels that could possibly be classified as Women's Fiction, and my reply is that while he does use women protagonists, his books identify much more with Literary Fiction (or just General Fiction) than they do Women's Fiction. They don't have that nuance that gets into the character's head about what's going on in her life and they don't delve into her relationships and her emotions.

How Is Women's Fiction Different from Romance?

Women's Fiction shares attributes with a number of genres (e.g., Historical, Mainstream, or Literary), but the hardest genre to differentiate Women's Fiction from is Romance. After all, both genres feature female characters and emphasize relationships. So, how do the two differ? After all, the characters do fall in love in a large percentage of Women's Fiction novels. Boyfriends, husbands, and lovers show up as main characters, so how can you tell?

- Romance is focused on a love/sexual relationship; Women's Fiction can incorporate love and sex but the focus is on other aspects of the character's relationships (i.e., family, friends, work life).

- Romance tends to have a happy ending; this is not guaranteed in Women's Fiction.

- In Romance, the happy ending usually means that the love relationship is a success; in Women's Fiction, not necessarily.

- Romance successfully follows a "formula"; Women's Fiction can take any story structure it wants.

- Lovers are main characters on par with the main female character in a Romance; Women's Fiction relegates them to secondary characters.

In short, while Women's Fiction often incorporates elements of Romance, there is more to the story than the love interest or sexual relationship. There are many Women's Fiction titles that do not have any romantic piece at all—the stories are about women and their families, women and their friends (and enemies), women in the home and in the workforce, and women discovering what they want their lives to be about.

CHARACTERISTICS AND APPEAL

The two main categories of appeal for this genre are *characters* and *story*, which tend to be intertwined. Readers enjoy Women's Fiction because they can identify with a character. A large part of the appeal of these books is a sense of recognition—feeling as though you are that character, you know that character, or you recognize what that character is going through. Readers want to see themselves or the people they know on the pages of these books (if not that, then a character leading the life they'd like to have!). Characters in Women's Fiction are realistically drawn, even when they are over-the-top glamorous, overdramatic, or humorous, they still tend to be recognizable as real people.

Because the story line of the books focuses on relationships, characters are of the utmost importance in these novels. Everything else is a variable. Pacing varies widely from book to book, as do language and setting. In general, the books have a contemporary setting. That's not to say that many Historical novels cannot also have Women's Fiction elements, but a historical setting generally means a book would be categorized as Historical Fiction. Dialogue tends to be natural, realistic, and paced to fit the plot.

BRIEF HISTORY

Early feminist writers and 19th-century writers of "domestic" fiction can be credited with the creation of this genre. One could say that among the original Women's Fiction authors you can count Jane Austen, The Brontes, and Louisa May Alcott. These authors wrote about what was happening in the lives of women in their times; and even today, Women's Fiction tends to mirror the trends and issues of the period it was written in (unless it is specifically historical in nature). In 1936, Margaret Mitchell published *Gone with the Wind*. While some fans, particularly of the film version, would call it a Romance, it is firmly in Women's Fiction territory as it explores Scarlett's life in wartime, her emotions over not only the men in her life but also her family and homestead, and the unflinching look it takes at a woman's place in a country in crisis.

In the mid-20th century, Women's Fiction began to change with the times and evolved from meek domestic stories to full-on domestic dramas. Grace Metalious's *Peyton Place* was published to much controversy in 1956; and the salaciousness of Jacqueline Susann's *Valley of the Dolls* was a hit in 1966. Feminism came to the forefront in the 1970s, with Marilyn French's *The Women's Room*, Erica Jong's *Fear of Flying*, and Judy Blume's *Wifey* as prime examples. The "me decade" of the 1980s is perfectly mirrored in the tales of glitz and glamour penned by Jackie Collins and Judith Krantz.

The late 1990s through the mid-2000s saw the meteoric rise of Chick Lit novels, launched by Helen Fielding and her neurotic Bridget Jones, spurred on by the success of pop culture icons like *Sex and the City*. These books focus on single, 20- or 30-something female protagonists usually trying to find their way in life, in the big city, or in a new fabulous career. The stories are humorous and generally lighthearted. Chick Lit in its original form has been on the wane in recent years, but has not gone away entirely. Instead, it's grown up a bit. The focus now tends to be on slightly more serious life issues instead of shoes. As yesterday's Chick Lit fans have matured and diversified their interests, there has also been quite a branching out from the "single-in-the-city" books into subgenres such as Mommy Lit, Hen Lit, and Widow Lit. It's really come down to a smooth blurring of the edges—it's often harder these days to pigeonhole something as Chick Lit instead of simply Women's Fiction.

Benchmark Authors

1. Elizabeth Berg
2. Maeve Binchy
3. Barbara Taylor Bradford
4. Sandra Brown (also writes Romance)
5. Barbara Delinsky
6. Sue Miller
7. Jodi Picoult
8. Nora Roberts (also writes Romance)
9. Danielle Steel
10. Jennifer Weiner

CURRENT TRENDS

As mentioned, currently, one of the dominant subgenres in Women's Fiction is what I like to call "Chick Lit Grows Up." In the inevitable progression of the Chick Lit of the 1990s and early 2000s, publishers have now largely moved away from "single in the city" books to those about young brides, young mothers, young divorcees, and even young widows. These are still lighthearted and fun stories, but not focusing on dating, fashion, or the workplace. Marian Keyes, Jennifer Weiner, and Jane Green are all excellent examples of authors who have moved away from the typical Chick Lit story line into more mature, introspective stories while retaining their senses of humor and excellent character development.

On the flip side, there is the current crop of Issue-Driven novels. These titles are darker, dealing with family problems and issues—more "hot topic," Oprah-esque tales. (It's interesting to note that Issue-Driven novels continue to increase in popularity, even without the assistance of Oprah's book club.) These are heavy books about heavy issues. Jodi Picoult is the reigning queen of Issue-Driven fiction, with Barbara Delinsky as her somewhat lighter lady-in-waiting. Typical family problems pale in comparison after reading these books, which is what a large part of the appeal is for this trend.

Ensemble Fiction is also gaining new ground—there has been an explosion of Women's fiction books with large casts of characters—novels featuring craft circles, book clubs, reuniting college friends, sisters, and coworkers. Again, this speaks to the appeal of women wanting to read about characters that are like themselves, or who they would like to be—readers can easily find a character within the group that they can identify with, or they can see their friends in. Related to this is the rise of books featuring crafting topics—knitting circles, quilters, scrapbookers, you name it. These dovetail with the Ensemble Fiction, in that they feature a large cast of characters and they mirror the times.

Humor is another recent trend. It's always been a hallmark of Chick Lit, but humor in Women's Fiction seems to be outpacing the more serious stuff these days. This is partially because it's as fluid as Women's Fiction itself—it covers all kinds of story lines, and even crosses generations. Authors like Meg Cabot, Mary Kay Andrews, and Sophie Kinsella are well known for their comic timing, witty dialogue, and fast-paced fun novels.

THEMES AND TYPES

Key to Women's Fiction Genre

General Women's Fiction
Romantic
Chick Lit
Mommy Lit
Women of a Certain Age
Issue-Driven
Humorous
Gentle
Family Sagas
Family Fiction

The following are some general categories of the types of stories the Women's Fiction authors in this book are known for. In addition to getting a quick sense of that sort of books that a given writer publishes, you can also use these lists to find other writers that you might enjoy (i.e., if you enjoy Chick Lit, you'll see who is known for that type of book). Keep in mind that not all of the authors listed fit into a given category, nor are any of the authors limited to the categories mentioned.

General Women's Fiction

Baker, Ellen. *Keeping the House*. Random House, 2007. 544p. 1400066352. Baker does double duty, telling the story of a family from 1896 through the end of World War I, and the parallel story of a woman named Dolly bucking convention in the 1950s.

Must Read

★ Berg, Elizabeth. *The Last Time I Saw You*. Random House, 2010. 256p. 9781400068647. Five classmates contemplate attending their 40th high school reunion, each with their own agenda.

Briscoe, Connie. *P. G. County*. Doubleday, 2002. 336p. 0385501617. This soapy novel follows the denizens of one of the country's most affluent African American neighborhoods, Prince George's County, Maryland.

De Los Santos, Marisa. *Belong to Me*. William Morrow, 2008. 400p. 0061240273. Familial bonds and friendships are tested in this novel of ulterior motives, secrets, and family.

Hannah, Kristin. *Firefly Lane*. St. Martin's, 2008. 496p. 9780312364083. Childhood best friends find their bond tested when they grow up. Kate and Tully are as different as can be, but manage to remain close and keep each other's secrets until ambition finally drives them apart.

Jackson, Joshilyn. *Gods in Alabama*. Warner, 2005. 288p. 0446524190. How's this for a premise: When Arlene runs away from home, she makes three promises to God—she will stop sleeping around, she will never tell another lie, and she will never return to Alabama. All He has to do in return is keep the body hidden.

Keyes, Marian. *Lucy Sullivan Is Getting Married*. Avon, 2002. 624p. 9780060090371. Or is she? A fortune-teller predicts Lucy will be married within a year, but with no romantic prospects in her life, Lucy is pretty skeptical.

Kinsella, Sophie. *Remember Me?* Dial, 2008. 384p. 9780385338721. After a nasty bump to the head, Lexi wakes up in a hospital room, unable to remember the past three years of her life.

Lansens, Lori. *The Wife's Tale.* Little, Brown and Co., 2010. 368p. 9780316069311. When her husband disappears, an overweight housebound woman travels from Canada to California to find him, finding herself along the way as well.

Michaels, Fern. *The Marriage Game.* Pocket, 2007. 290p. 9780743477451. Samantha Rainford gets home from her honeymoon to discover she's already been served with divorce papers. But if that's not bad enough, she also finds out there are three other Mrs. Rainfords out there.

Must Read

★ **Packer, Ann.** *The Dive from Clausen's Pier.* Knopf, 2002. 369p. 03754 12824. In this absorbing story with wonderful characters, a young woman leaves her fiancé despite his having been injured in an accident, in order to discover what she really wants from life.

Radish, Kris. *Annie Freeman's Fabulous Traveling Funeral.* Bantam, 2006. 352p. 0553382640. When Annie dies of ovarian cancer, she leaves instructions to gather her four best friends from across the country for a road trip, to scatter her ashes in meaningful places.

Must Read

★ **Scotch, Allison Winn.** *Time of My Life: A Novel.* Crown, 2008. 288p. 0307408574. After learning that her postcollege boyfriend is engaged, Jillian wishes she could go back and see what might have been. And then she wakes up—seven years in the past.

Shaffer, Louise. *Looking for a Love Story.* Ballantine, 2010. 320p. 9780345502100. Francesca, a writer, is hired to ghostwrite the memoirs of a husband and wife vaudeville team, and uncovers her own love life and family history.

Smolinksi, Jill. *The Next Thing on My List.* Shaye Areheart, 2006. 304p. 9780307351241. After her hitchhiking passenger is killed in an accident, a woman discovers the girl's "20 Things to Do by My 25th Birthday" list and decides to follow it.

Trigiani, Adriana. *Big Stone Gap*. Random House, 2000. 272p. 0375504036. Trigiani perfectly captures a snapshot of life in a small Appalachian town with the story of Ave Maria Mulligan and her friends, as Ave Maria delves into secrets from her family's past.

Must Reads

★ **Weiner, Jennifer.** *Little Earthquakes*. Atria, 2004. 432p. 0743470095. Four unlikely friends bond over motherhood in this realistic look at raising a baby while still dealing with the rest of their lives.

★ **Wells, Rebecca.** *Divine Secrets of the Ya-Ya Sisterhood*. Harper, 1996. 368p. 0060173289. Follows the wild adventures of four childhood best friends who grow up to be amazing, if a touch crazy, women.

Wolitzer, Meg. *The Ten-Year Nap*. Riverhead, 2008. 320p. 9781594489785. Get a glimpse into the lives of different mothers who gave up their careers to have children. All are conflicted and influenced by outside pressures from family and friends.

Romantic

Romantic Women's Fiction features a love story, but unlike a traditional romance, does not have to have a happy ending, nor is the romance element the main plot point. Other relationships and the main character herself are more important than the love story. Well-known authors who write romantic-themed Women's Fiction include Sandra Brown, Meg Cabot, Claire Cook, Barbara Delinsky, Katie Fforde, Kristin Hannah, Nora Roberts, and Danielle Steel.

Must Read

★ **Ahern, Cecelia.** *P. S. I Love You*. Hyperion, 2004. 375p. 1401300901. Holly discovers a year's worth of letters that her late-husband Gerry left for her to read after his untimely death.

Evans, Harriet. *Love Always*. Gallery Books, 2011. 480p. 9781451639629. When Natasha returns to Cornwall for her grandmother's funeral, she discovers the diary of her aunt Cecily, who died when she was just a teenager. Within the diary's pages, Natasha finds a tale of forbidden love and heartbreak.

Fforde, Katie. *Love Letters*. St. Martin's, 2011. 400p. 9780312674533. Laura takes a job with a literary agent booking authors for signings and festivals. When she meets handsome and reclusive author Dermot, she falls head over heels and is willing to do anything to have him attend one of her events.

Jio, Sarah. *The Violets of March*. Penguin, 2011. 304p. 9780452297036. After a heartbreaking divorce, Emily visits her elderly aunt and comes across a diary from the 1940s. She becomes drawn into the details of a mysterious stranger's life, while grappling with her feelings for an ex-boyfriend as well as a new man on the scene.

Chick Lit

Writing breezy and often humorous novels, the following authors are known for Chick Lit: Cecelia Ahern, Meg Cabot, Helen Fielding, Jane Green, Marian Keyes, Sophie Kinsella, Sarah Mlynowski, Jennifer Weiner, and Laura Zigman.

Green, Jane. *Jemima J*. Broadway, 2000. 384p. 9780767905183. Desperate to gain the confidence to get to know her cute workmate, overweight Jemima starts off with Internet dating, figuring she can gain some social skills while hiding behind an online persona.

Harbison, Beth. *Thin, Rich, Pretty*. St. Martin's, 2010. 352p. 9780312381981. Three summer camp rivals meet up 20 years later, where secrets from camp come to the surface, making them realize it's time to grow up,

Kargman, Jill. *Arm Candy*. Dutton, 2010. 336p. 9780525951599. On the brink of a supermodel's 40th birthday, she catches her longtime lover in bed with another woman. She's always been able to turn a blind eye to it in the past, but at this point in her life, it's too much.

Must Reads

★ **Ross, Jennifer.** *The Icing on the Cupcake*. Ballantine, 2010. 320p. 9780345492968. When a spoiled young woman runs off to New York City after being dumped, she decides to use her baking skills to open a cupcake bakery all on her own.

★ **Wolff, Isabel.** *A Vintage Affair*. Bantam, 2010. 368p. 9780553807 837. Vintage clothing lover Phoebe opens her own resale boutique in London, and deals with her crazy love life and even crazier family.

Mommy Lit

After the single girls got their moment in the spotlight with the rise of Chick Lit, publishers inevitably started turning out humorous looks at motherhood.

Bilston, Sarah

Bed Rest. Avon, 2007. 240p. 9780060889951.
Sleepless Nights. Harper, 2009. 304p. 9780060889944.

In *Bed Rest*, lawyer Quinn flounders when all of a sudden she is put on bed rest for the last three months of her pregnancy. Followed up by *Sleepless Nights*, where we find Quinn totally thrown off her game by a new baby, not to mention her husband's impending layoff.

Must Read

★ **Center, Katherine. *The Bright Side of Disaster*.** Ballantine, 2007. 249p. 9781400066377. In this humorous novel, a young woman's boyfriend has a panic attack and leaves her the day before she gives birth. Luckily, her mother and her friends are there to help out.

Gaskell, Whitney. *Mommy Tracked*. Bantam, 2007. 384p. 9780553589696. A newly divorced restaurant critic and single mother joins a support group for mothers.

Scheibe, Amy. *What Do You Do All Day?* St. Martins, 2005. 320p. 9780312343033. A former antiques expert for Christies now spends her days raising a five-year-old and a newborn. Think *Sex and the City* crossed with *Parents* magazine.

Wilde, Samantha. *This Little Mommy Stayed Home*. Bantam, 2009. 400p. 9780385342667. A new mother juggles baby stress, an overworked husband, and her dysfunctional parents.

Williams, Polly. *The Yummy Mummy*. Hyperion, 2007. 384p. 1401302319. A new mom feels lost without her high-powered PR job at a prestigious British firm, yet she's not sure where she fits in now with a six-month-old in tow.

Zigman, Laura. *Piece of Work*. Warner, 2006. 304p. 044657838X. A warm and wry look at the struggle between raising a family and having a career.

Women of a Certain Age

A natural progression from Chick Lit, there is also a subset of novels that are just as breezy and fun but feature more mature characters and life situations.

Buchan, Elizabeth. *Revenge of the Middle-Aged Woman*. Viking, 2003. 368p. 0670032069. As she picks up the pieces after her husband of 25 years leaves her, Rose realizes that living well is the best revenge.

Dawson, Maddie. *The Stuff That Never Happened: A Novel*. Crown, 2010. 336p. 9780307393678. After almost 30 years of marriage, a woman realizes she still pines for the man she had an affair with shortly after the wedding.

Gaffney, Patricia. *Mad Dash*. Crown, 2007. 355p. 9780307382115. Faced with empty nest syndrome, free-spirited Dash has just about had it with her fastidious husband and contemplates divorce after 20 years of marriage.

Ironside, Virginia. *No! I Don't Want to Join a Book Club: Diary of a Sixtieth Year*. Viking, 2007. 240p. 9780670038183. About to turn 60, Marie looks forward to relaxing and being comfortable, unlike some of her friends, who want to take up hang gliding or go on African safaris.

King, Cassandra. *Same Sweet Girls*. Hyperion, 2005. 416p. 1401300383. Six college friends who have met up twice a year for 30 years are preparing for a trip to Alabama when one of them becomes terminally ill, testing the strength of their bond.

Issue-Driven

Often featuring ripped-from-the-headlines stories, these novels tend to be fast-paced and emotional. Other novels with similar appeal, while not quite as dramatic, showcase characters dealing with death, divorce, and other family problems. Authors known for Issue-Driven Fiction include Barbara Delinsky, Joy Fielding, Sue Miller, Jacquelyn Mitchard, Jodi Picoult, and Anita Shreve.

Must Read

★ 📖 **Delinsky, Barbara.** *Family Tree*. Doubleday, 2006. 368p. 9780385518659. When a Caucasian couple's first baby has distinctly African American coloring and features, suspicions and accusations abound. An engrossing look at issues of race, family, and trust.

Endicott, Marina. *Good to a Fault*. Harper, 2010. 384p. 9780061825897. A woman finds herself taking care of an entire family when she discovers their mother is dying of cancer.

Must Read

★ **Giffin, Emily.** *Heart of the Matter*. St. Martin's, 2010. 384p. 978031255 4163. A woman's cushy life is about to be turned upside down when she discovers her husband has been contemplating an affair with the mother of one of his patients.

Griffin, Bettye. *Nothing but Trouble*. Kensington, 2006. 304p. 9780758207395. Three best friends find their relationships tested when one of their sisters enters the picture and starts causing trouble among the women and their men.

Hannah, Kristin. *Home Front*. St. Martin's, 2012. 400p. 9780312577209. Jolene, a National Guard pilot, fears her marriage to Michael is falling apart. Then an unexpected deployment sends Jolene to Iraq and leaves Michael at home, unaccustomed to being a single parent to their two little girls.

📖 **Hegland, Jean.** *Windfalls*. Atria, 2004. 352p. 9780743470070. This powerful look at motherhood and poverty follows the parallel lives of two very different women, Anna and Cerise.

📖 **Kline, Christina Baker.** *Bird in Hand*. William Morrow, 2009. 288p. 9780688177249. When Allison is involved in a car crash that kills a young child, she discovers she cannot count on her husband to support her emotionally. Mainly because he's been having an affair with her best friend.

McDonough, Yona Zeldis. *In Dahlia's Wake*. Doubleday, 2005. 293p. 0385503628. Naomi and Rick are a Brooklyn couple struggling in the aftermath of their young daughter's death.

Must Read

★ **Moriarty, Laura.** *The Rest of Her Life*. Hyperion, 2007. 320p. 978140 1302719. The smartly woven tale of a mother trying to connect to her teenage children after her daughter causes a fatal car accident.

Picoult, Jodi. *Handle with Care*. Atria, 2009. 496p. 9780743296410. When her daughter, born with a bone disease, needs money for her long-term care, a woman must decide if she should sue the doctor, who happens to be her best friend.

Quindlen, Anna. *Every Last One*. Random House, 2010. 299p. 9781400065745. A mother is trying to deal with her three teenage children when fatal tragedy strikes the family.

Racculia, Kate. *This Must Be the Place*. Henry Holt, 2010. 368p. 9780805092301. When a woman dies unexpectedly, her husband realizes she lived a secret life before their marriage.

Rice, Luanne. *Perfect Summer*. Bantam, 2003. 464p. 0553584049. Bay's seemingly perfect life is shattered when her husband goes missing and shortly after, the FBI shows up to tell her that he is under investigation for embezzlement.

Stewart, Leah. *Husband and Wife*. Harper, 2010. 352p. 9780061774508. A woman struggles to find her place as a writer and a young mother in the aftermath of her husband's infidelity.

Trollope, Joanna. *Friday Nights*. Bloomsbury, 2008. 336p. 9781596914070. A retired woman starts a neighborhood tradition when she invites two single young moms to her house for coffee one evening.

Must Read

★ Winston, Lolly. *Happiness Sold Separately*. Grand Central, 2006. 304p. 0446533068. Elinor and Ted's once-perfect marriage is rocked by infertility. An engrossing look inside a modern marriage, with a surprising ending.

Humorous

Humorous Women's Fiction features sassy characters, snappy dialogue, wacky plot points, and contemporary settings and issues. Good choices for humorous authors include Mary Kay Andrews, Meg Cabot, Fannie Flagg, Jane Heller, Sophie Kinsella, Lorna Landvik, and Haywood Smith.

Must Read

★ Andrews, Mary Kay. *Deep Dish*. Harper, 2008. 384p. 978006083 7365. Sparks fly as does the hilarity when a male and a female chef battle it out for their chance at TV stardom, while dealing with their own families and personal issues. Just enough romance to round the story out.

Bosnak, Karyn. *20 Times a Lady*. Harper, 2006. 352p. 9780060828356. Going into overdrive on a quest for true love, Delilah tracks down her previous 19 boyfriends, convinced that she has to make it work with one of them.

Must Read

★ **Cabot, Meg.** *Boy Meets Girl*. Avon, 2004. 387p. 0060085452. Told as a series of e-mails, memos, and voice mails, this format works as a fast read that's a lot of fun.

Cabot, Meg

<u>Queen of Babble Series</u>. A young woman finds herself in hilarious situations at work and in love because she just can't keep her big mouth shut.

> *Queen of Babble: A Novel*. William Morrow, 2006. 320p. 9780060851989.
> *Queen of Babble in the Big City*. Avon, 2008. 320p. 9780060852016.
> *Queen of Babble Gets Hitched*. Avon, 2009. 336p. 9780060852030.

Kinsella, Sophie

<u>Shopaholic Series</u>. A consummate shopper finds herself in big trouble when her spending gets out of hand. The series follows her from her single days to marriage and a baby.

> *Confessions of a Shopaholic*. Dial, 2001. 320p. 9780385335485.
> *Shopaholic Takes Manhattan*. Dell, 2002. 336p. 9780385335881.
> *Shopaholic Ties the Knot*. Dial, 2003. 336p. 9780385336178.
> *Shopaholic and Sister*. Dial, 2004. 368p. 9780385338097.
> *Shopaholic and Baby*. Dial, 2007. 368p. 9780385338707.
> *Mini Shopaholic*. Dial, 2010. 432p. 9780385342049.

Riley, Jess. *Driving Sideways*. Ballantine, 2008. 342p. 0345501101. In this laugh-out-loud road trip novel, Leigh, a young woman recovering from kidney disease, travels across the country with her best friend in order to visit the family of her organ donor.

Gentle

Here is where you will find stories of families, communities, and enduring friendships. The pace is light and leisurely. Good authors in this category include Maeve Binchy, Jennifer Chiaverini, Fannie Flagg, Lynne Hinton, Ann B. Ross, and Marcia Willett.

Must Read

★ **Binchy, Maeve. *Whitethorn Woods*.** Knopf, 2007. 352p. 9780307265 781. The residents of tiny Irish village Rossmore band together when a planned highway threatens to cut through their beloved Whitethorn Woods. With stories spanning generations, Binchy shows some of her best character work and gets the intimacies of small-town life just right.

Jacobs, Kate. *The Friday Night Knitting Club*. Putnam, 2006. 352p. 9780399154096. Georgia runs a Manhattan yarn shop and begins a Friday-night knitting club, where she becomes friends with the diverse group of women who join up.

Monroe, Mary Alice. *The Butterfly's Daughter*. Gallery, 2011. 400p. 1439170614. Luz has been raised by her grandmother Abuela, whose last wish is to take a trip to her home village in Mexico. When Abuela passes away before they can go, Luz forges ahead, taking Abuela's ashes on the trip. Along the way, she meets a cast of extraordinary women.

Wiggs, Susan. *The Goodbye Quilt*. Mira, 2011. 201p. 9780778329961. Linda and her daughter, Molly, take a cross-country trip to Molly's new college. Along the way, Linda works on a quilt filled with fabric scraps representing many memories, leading both mother and daughter to remember the past and look forward to the future.

Family Sagas

Quite popular throughout the 1970s and 1980s, the number of Sagas written today is on the wane, but readers still enjoy these lengthy, multi-generational stories that also have romantic and historical elements. Authors who became famous for their sagas include Barbara Taylor Bradford, Elizabeth Cadell, Catherine Cookson, Rosamund Pilcher, and Belva Plain. Readers who enjoy sagas may also like the "glitz and glamour" novels that were popular in the 1980s, by such authors as Jackie Collins, Olivia Goldsmith, and Judith Krantz.

Must Read

★ **Bradford, Barbara Taylor. *Just Rewards*.** St. Martin's, 2006. 496p.0312307063. In the ultimate rags-to-riches Saga, the <u>Harte Family Series</u> begins with *A Woman of Substance* (1979), in which Emma Harte rises from poverty to run the world's most famous department store. The final entry in the six-book series, *Just Rewards* (2006), finds Emma's great-granddaughters confronting relationships, rivalries, and the intricacies of the family business.

Cookson, Catherine. *Kate Hannigan's Girl*. Simon & Schuster, 2001. 288p. 0743212525. Cookson mixes romance, class struggle, and history in her lush and well-written Sagas. Her first, *Kate Hannigan* (1950), is the story of a shunned single trying to rise above poverty at the turn of the 20th century. Her final novel, published 50 years later, follows Kate's daughter, Annie, who has spent her life struggling with the stigma of illegitimacy.

Donnelly, Jennifer

The Tea Rose. Thomas Dunne, 2003. 560p. 9780312288358.
The Winter Rose. Hyperion, 2008. 720p. 9781401301033.

In *The Tea Rose*, a young woman rises above her situation to run a world-renowned tea company in Victorian-era London. The follow-up *The Winter Rose* finds an equally ambitious young woman determined to become a doctor.

Must Read

★ **Meacham, Lila.** *Roses*. Grand Central, 2010. 609p. 0446550000. When her brother defects after World War I, Mary Toliver inherits her family's Texas cotton plantation at a tender age and is determined to never let the neighboring Warwick family get any of her land—even though the Warwick heir could be the love of her life.

Family Fiction

Because Women's Fiction is so centered on relationships, family is naturally a common theme. They can be gentle, serious, or a dysfunction-palooza.

Bouret, Amy. *Mothers and Other Liars*. St. Martin's, 2010. 320p. 9780312 586584. When she realizes her adopted daughter's parents are looking for her, a woman must come to terms with the past.

Must Read

★ **Cook, Claire. *Summer Blowout*.** Hyperion, 2008. 256p. 1401322417. Bella works at her father's chain of beauty salons as a makeup artist. Problem is, so does the rest of her large extended family, including ex-wives, stepmothers, and half-siblings.

Goudge, Eileen. *Once in a Blue Moon*. Vanguard, 2009. 336p. 97815931 55346. Sisters given up for foster care are reunited as adults, having grown up in very different circumstances.

Green, Jane. *Another Piece of My Heart*. St. Martin's, 2012. 352p. 9780312591823. Andi has finally found the perfect man—Ethan, a single dad with two daughters. But Ethan's oldest, rebellious teen Emily, is determined to make Andi's life miserable.

Hilderbrand, Elin. *The Island*. Little, Brown and Co., 2010. 416p. 9780316043878. Two generations of women come together off the coast of Nantucket as they spend the summer in the family beach cottage.

Noble, Elizabeth. *Things I Want My Daughters to Know*. William Morrow, 2008. 384p. 9780061122194. Four sisters deal with the death of their beloved mother in this tearjerker. Lisa, the eldest, needs to learn she is not always in charge, Jennifer struggles with a doomed marriage, Amanda learns a family secret, and teenaged Hannah realizes it's time to grow up.

Must Read

★ **Riggle, Kristina. *Real Life and Liars*.** Avon, 2009. 352p. 9780061706 288. When a woman decides to decline breast cancer treatment, her dysfunctional but loving family gathers to try and change her mind.

Smith, Haywood. *Ladies of the Lake*. St. Martins, 2009. 384p. 9780312316952. Four middle-aged sisters are required by their grandmother's will to spend a summer together at the family vacation house.

Weiner, Jennifer. *Then Came You*. Atria, 2011. 338p. 9781451617726. Creating a family of sorts, an egg donor, a surrogate, and the infertile woman who hires them all get to tell their side of the story. Another character enters the picture in an interesting twist—the grown daughter of the soon-to-be dad gets to tell her story as well.

RESOURCES

Websites

Candy Covered Books. http://www.candycoveredbooks.com/. This site gathers reviews of Chick Lit and Women's Fiction titles.

Chick Lit Books. http://chicklitbooks.com/. This site provides reviews, author interviews, rankings, and articles about Chick Lit titles.

Chick Lit Is Not Dead. http://chicklitisnotdead.com/. This blog is written by two authors who love the genre, featuring author interviews and book news.

Chick Lit Plus. http://chicklitplus.com/. This site provided book reviews and author information for best-selling and lesser-known Chick Lit authors.

Lip Gloss and Literature. http://lipglossandliterature.blogspot.com/. Reviews and author interviews of both big-name books and up-and-comers are listed in here.

Novelicious. http://www.novelicious.com/. This U.K.-based site covers a variety of styles of Romance and Women's Fiction.

The Women's Fiction Chapter of the Romance Writers of America. http://www.rwa-wf.com/. An excellent definition of Women's Fiction can be found here, as well as other interesting resources on the genre.

Women's Fiction Writers. http://womensfictionwriters.wordpress.com/. Interviews and guest posts featuring women's fiction author can be found here, as well as writing tips for up-and-coming authors.

Books

Herald, Diana Tixier. *Genreflecting: A Guide to Popular Reading Interests, 6th Edition*. Libraries Unlimited, 2006. Contains a chapter on Women's Fiction.

Hill, Nancy Milone. *Reading Women: A Book Club Guide for Women's Fiction*. Libraries Unlimited, 2012. Gathers and provides information on over 100 Women's Fiction titles published in the last 10 years and offers brief summaries of an additional 50 titles.

Moyer, Jessica E., and Kaite Mediatore Stover, eds. *The Readers' Advisory Handbook*. ALA Editions, 2010. Provides excellent readers' advisory advice on a varied number of topics.

Ramsdell, Kristin. *Romance Fiction: A Guide to the Genre, 2nd Edition*. Libraries Unlimited, 2012. Discusses major categories of Romance/Women's Fiction and offers tips for readers' advisory and collection development.

Saricks, Joyce G. *The Reader's Advisory Guide to Genre Fiction, 2nd Edition*. ALA Editions, 2009. Includes an excellent chapter on "Women's Lives and Relationships."

Sheehan, Sarah E. *Romance Authors: A Research Guide*. Libraries Unlimited, 2010. Provides biographical and bibliographical information on over 50 Romance authors.

Vasudevan, Aruna, ed. *Twentieth-Century Romance and Historical Writers, 3rd Edition*. St. James Press,1994. Profiles more than 500 authors who have made significant contributions to Romance and Historical writing.

Vnuk, Rebecca. *Read On . . . Women's Fiction: Reading Lists for Every Taste*. Libraries Unlimited, 2009. Annotated book lists of hundreds of Contemporary Women's Fiction titles categorized according to five appeal characteristics.

Vnuk, Rebecca. *Women's Fiction Authors: A Research Guide*. Libraries Unlimited, 2009. Provides biographical and bibliographical information on over 75 contemporary Women's Fiction authors.

Zellers, Jessica. *Women's Nonfiction: A Guide to Reading Interests*. Libraries Unlimited, 2009. Guide to over 600 Nonfiction titles by and about women.

FIVE FAN FAVORITES

- Elizabeth Ahern. *P. S. I Love You*—Romantic

- Elizabeth Berg. *The Last Time I Saw You*—General Women's Fiction

- Jane Green. *Another Piece of My Heart*—Family Fiction

- Jodi Picoult. *Handle with Care*—Issue-Driven

- Jennifer Weiner. *Then Came You*—Family Fiction

10

11

12

13

14

15

16

17

18

Chapter 13

Fantasy

Lynn Wiandt and Diana Tixier Herald

In the new millennium, many readers have come to know the Fantasy genre through J. K. Rowling's blockbuster <u>Harry Potter Series</u>; but Fantasy, both historically and in the present, is much more than that. For many readers, Fantasy's popularity didn't stop with Harry Potter—it had only started. Such authors as George R. R. Martin, Patrick Rothfuss, and Brandon Sanderson have stormed onto the bestseller lists with titles like *The Name of the Wind* (2007), *The Wise Man's Fear* (2011), *A Dance with Dragons* (2011), and *Alloy of Law* (2011), creating huge followings among readers of all ages. But what exactly is Fantasy?

DEFINITION

In Fantasy stories, magic plays a central role. It is the element of magic that sets the Fantasy novel apart from its Science Fiction cousin and brings us to a simple definition of the genre. For the purpose of this book, a Fantasy story is, by definition, a story built upon a foundation of magic. It must contain, to a lesser or greater degree, elements of magic. Some Science Fiction novels, notably the Pern stories by Anne McCaffrey and her son Todd, have many of the trappings of Fantasy—bards, dragons, and a feudal society with limited technology—but, at the heart, they are Science Fiction. There is a scientific basis for everything that transpires in the stories. There is no magic, and so it is not a Fantasy series.

Magic is as much a force in the world of a Fantasy book as gravity is in our own, and, used deftly and sensitively, this magical component adds texture and nuance to the struggles and triumphs of the characters. In the finest examples of the Fantasy genre, magic does not exist in the story just as a pretty prop but is instead crucial to advancement of the plot, the growth of the characters, and the very story itself. At its best, magic is fully integrated into the DNA of the story and without it, the story itself would collapse.

How does Fantasy differ from other genres?

Of course, elements of the fantastic appear in many novels, which are not necessarily considered Fantasy. Specifically, readers often confuse Fantasy with Science Fiction, Horror, and Paranormal Romance. These genres, like Fantasy, fit under the umbrella of "Speculative Fiction"—fiction that takes place in worlds unlike our own, even those that might seem the same at first glance.

Both Science Fiction and Fantasy often feature exotic worlds and unearthly creatures. A book in either genre might have a dragon breathing fire on the cover, but the Science Fiction dragon is just a bio-engineered puppet summoned forth from a test tube. The Fantasy dragon has magic, not chemistry, running through its veins. Indeed, a famous quote by the Science Fiction writer and visionary Arthur C. Clarke puts it beautifully, "Any sufficiently advanced technology is indistinguishable from magic." Nevertheless, technology advanced past the point of common understanding is still not magic, and any story based around it would fall into the Science Fiction genre—no matter how magical the science might appear to the eyes of the characters living the story.

Horror sometimes overlaps with Fantasy, and here the distinction between the two can be more difficult to draw. Examples of the Horror genre may contain fantastical creatures and will certainly contain supernatural elements and a strong case can be made that Horror is merely a subset of the Fantasy genre, the darkest of Dark Fantasy. Some novels that are considered Horror (e.g., Stephen King's *It*, 1986) have even won awards specific to the Fantasy genre.

In its turn, Fantasy may contain frightening situations, characters, and creatures that make the hair on the back of the reader's neck stand at attention. Tolkien's Shelob, a spider of hideously gigantic proportions and appetites, could give the creature in a Stephen King novel tips on scaring children. George R. R. Martin's immense Fantasy series <u>The Song of Ice and Fire</u> contains monsters that would be perfectly at home between the pages of a Horror novel. Though Martin uses these frightening creatures to great effect, his main focus in the saga is not to primarily inspire fear and terror. His dread creatures are terrifying, but they are only a part of the greater fantasy whole. When frightening elements lurch into a Fantasy story, they will, if well drawn, provoke fear but that is not the main focus of the endeavor. They are not the whole point of the work, just one element of it. So, while the magic haunting a Horror novel is potent indeed, drawn from a dark vein, unlike the dark magic found in some Fantasy, the Horror genre employs its dark magic specifically to invoke terror. As a story would not be a Fantasy without magic, without terror, the work would not be a Horror story. For our purposes, we consider the genres separately.

Another subgenre that is often difficult to differentiate from Fantasy is the subgenre of Romantic Fiction known as Paranormal Romance. Romances that contain any kind of magical, science fiction, horror, or supernatural element are generally grouped into this category—including stories heavily influenced or solidly centered in Fantasy will often still be shelved with the Romances if the relationship between the hero and heroine is the main focus of the story. Although this separation of Paranormal Romance may seem artificial, it is partially driven by the Romance houses publishing the books as well as for the convenience of the browsing reader. It is true that there are many books shelved in the Fantasy section that also contain elements of romance, but if the Romance is the primary driving force behind the plot then, for the sake of convenience, the book will most often be shelved with other books that have romance as the core of the story.

CHARACTERISTICS AND APPEAL

What draws readers to Fantasy is the call of the imagination. Fantasy fans love to explore the possibilities of what might happen in worlds unlike our own with creatures unlike ourselves. The so-called "world building" of the genre draws readers as well, with fantastic settings often described in great detail and evolving over multiple series volumes.

Themes of transformation, whether they be a coming-of age tale or the everyman's journey to heroism, are common in the Fantasy genre. Watching an ordinary person persevere and triumph in extreme circumstances, discovering latent or new talents as they do so—whether because of or in spite of the magic infusing the story's world—is thrilling and keeps the reader turning page after page of book after book. The peculiar alchemy of the journey that works its own magic on the character of our heroes and transforms weak into strong, cowardly into brave, the immature into the adult.

These are also stories where good and evil are clearly delineated, and the resulting plots offer readers the satisfaction of a story where good forces overcome evil.

There are so many different kinds of Fantasy books—from the silly, pun-loving books of Piers Anthony to the stylized High Fantasy of Tolkien to the gritty Fantasy Noir of Jim Butcher's magical detective Harry Dresden and the intensely erotic Romantic Fantasies of Laurell K. Hamilton—that there truly is something to catch the fancy and imagination of any reader—at least any reader who doesn't mind rubbing shoulders with hobbits, elves, and miller's sons who are often rather more than they seem.

BRIEF HISTORY

Humans have always used the power of story to entertain and inform each other. Tales that may have once had a basis in actual history are transformed by generations of telling and pass into the realm of myth, legend, and tall tale. Many stories so familiar to us today—Cinderella, Snow White, and Hansel and Gretel among them—had their genesis around ancient firesides, and today many regional versions can be found. In *Cinderella* (1992), Judy Sierra's excellent survey of the tale, the author examines Cinderella type stories from all over the world, having picked them from hundreds of possible variants.

But the modern Fantasy came along more recently. In the 1930s and 1940s, J.R.R. Tolkien, considered by many to be the true father of the Fantasy genre, created books that have seeped into the consciousness of even nonfantasy readers. *The Hobbit* (1937) and the <u>Lord of the Rings Trilogy</u> are as popular today as when they were published.

CURRENT TRENDS

More than a decade after Harry Potter arrived on the scene, Fantasy is hotter than ever and its popularity shows no signs of waning. Readers young and not so young devoured J. K. Rowling's sprawling epic—on the page and on the screen—and then went looking for more. No longer relegated to cheap mass-market paperbacks, Fantasy hardbacks regularly hit the bestseller lists. A hot Fantasy book can help out a bookstore's bottom line, and many a bookseller hated to see Rowling's saga finally come to an end, if not because they were readers themselves then because they wouldn't have the sales of the next one to look forward to. Fortunately, now more than ever, writers and publishers are eager to fill the void left behind by the exit of Mr. Potter. Fantasy publishing today has taken on a breathtaking depth and breadth, running the gamut from traditional multibook High-Fantasy Sagas with dozens of characters to Cozy Fantasy Mysteries and to the very popular Urban Fantasy and the hot Erotic Fantasy subgenres.

If you are already a fan of Fantasy Fiction, this chapter will strike familiar chords as you recognize the themes, subjects, and denizens who populate Fantasy. It will also hopefully lead you to discover new authors and stories. If you are new to the genre, or drawn to this chapter because you wish to understand the popular appeal of magic-infused fiction, or simply because you want to educate yourself on current trends as well as become conversant and comfortable with some of the enduring classics of the genre, we hope that you will also find a story that can serve as a bridge, and that you too, like so many other readers, can become lost in the magic and mystery of the genre.

NOTE

Sierra Judy. *Cinderella.* Phoenix, AZ: Oryx Press, 1992.

THEMES AND TYPES

Key to Fantasy

Legends, Myths, and Fairy Tales
Epic Fantasy
Alternate and Parallel Worlds
Urban Fantasy
Humor and Satire
Magic
Mythic Reality
World of Faerie
Genreblending
    Fantasy Mysteries
    Western Fantasy
    Romantic Fantasy
Anthologies and Collections

Legends, Myths, and Fairytales

Much like the writers of Thrillers and Mysteries use the local police blotter for inspiration, Fantasy writers often use myths, legends, and fairy tales as source material for original tales. Here are some of the best since our last edition. There is always something in the stories that brings back snippets of memories of stories heard, images seen, or just a feeling, in a good way, that you've been here before, once upon a time.

Brom. *The Child Thief.* Eos, 2009. 480p. 9780061671333. A Dark Fantasy imagining of Peter Pan that begins in sixth century Britain and follows him to contemporary New York.

🎗 **Bernheimer, Kate, ed.** *My Mother She Killed Me, My Father He Ate Me: Forty New Fairytales.* Penguin, 2008. 608p. 9780143117841. In this massive anthology, an eclectic crew of writers such as Neil Gaiman, John Updike, Scott Cunningham, Francesca Lia Block, and Joyce Carol Oates weave new tales inspired by the classic and familiar. It won the 2011 World Fantasy Award for Best Collection.

YA **Cross, Gillian.** *Kill Me Softly.* Egmont, 2012. 336p. 9781606843239. Raised by two fairy godmothers, Mira is desperate to find out more about her parents who had died when she was an infant. So she goes to the city where she meets a pair of brothers in a casino resort who have diametrically opposed reactions to her. The tale puts several fairy tales into a contemporary context with characters who are archetypes of Bluebeard, Sleeping Beauty, and more.

Datlow, Ellen, and Windling, Terri, eds. *The Coyote Road: Trickster Tales*. Viking, 2007. 384p. 9780670061945. Twenty-six tales that draw inspiration from Trickster tales from around the world. Authors include Jane Yolen, Michael Cadnum, Theodora Goss, and Midori Snyder.

YA **Dixon, Heather.** *Entwined.* Greenwillow, 2011. 472p. 9780062001030. This enchanting reimagining of the 12 dancing princesses is told from the viewpoint of Azalea—the eldest of 12 sisters—all named for flowers, and takes place when their mother dies and the castle goes into mourning for a year, which means no dancing.

Flinn, Alex

YA The Kendra Chronicles. Kendra, an immortal witch who has lived for a very long time, curses some miscreants and works magic for some who need it.

> *Beastly*. HarperTeen, 2007. 304p. 9780060874162. A contemporary version of Beauty and the Beast set in New York.
> *Bewitching*. HarperTeen, 2012. 336p. 9780062024152. Some of Kendra's backstory is revealed while she takes the role of a fairy godmother for a contemporary Cinderella.

Gaiman, Neil

Must Read

🎗 *American Gods: The Tenth Anniversary Edition:* A Novel. William Morrow, 2011. 560p. 9780062059888. First published in 2002, American Gods topped the bestseller lists and went on to win almost every award it was eligible for, including the 2002 Hugo and World Fantasy Awards among many others.

For its 10th anniversary, the author expanded the work to include his preferred text.

———

♟ *Anansi Boys*. William Morrow, 2005. 352p. 9780060515188. Set in the same world as *American Gods*, *Anansi Boys* follows the misadventures of Charlie Nancy—dubbed Fat Charlie by his father—an ordinary bloke who discovers that his father was the trickster god Anansi. Winner of the 2006 Locus, Mythopoeic, British Fantasy, and Alex Awards.

♟ **Goldstein, Lisa.** *The Uncertain Places.* Tachyon, 2011. 240p. 9781616960148. Will Taylor, a student at Berkeley in the early 1970s, is drawn into the lives of the three Feierabend sisters who are still dealing with the results of a deal made by an ancestor with the fae in a long ago time. Winner of the Mythopoeic Award.

Graham, Jo. *Black Ships.* Orbit, 2008. 397p. 9780316068000. Gull's mother was raped and taken as a slave after the fall of Troy. Crippled in an accident, Gull is sent to live with the oracle Pythia as an apprentice and eventually takes her place and her name. She leaves with a shipload of Trojan refugees lead by Aeneas to become their Sybil.

♟ **Lanagan, Margo.** *Tender Morsels*. Knopf, 2008. 436p. 9780375848117. Violent and explicit, inspired by "Snow White and Rose Red," this tale of Liga and her two daughters has been praised for the beauty of Lanagan's writing. World Fantasy Award winner.

♟ **Le Guin, Ursula K.** *Lavinia*. HMH, 2008. 288p. 9780151014248. Lavinia, a princess by birth and a pawn by destiny, takes the course of her life into her own hands in this richly imagined retelling of the Aeneid. Locus Award winner.

♟ **Lord, Karen.** *Redemption in Indigo: A Novel.* Small Beer, 2010. 224p. 9781931520669. This contemporary folk tale set in the Caribbean includes a spider trickster, djombies, and a young woman who acquires a magical Chaos Stick after leaving her good-for-nothing husband. Mythopoeic Award winner.

Maguire, Gregory

Wicked Years. Maguire has taken characters from Baum's *The Wonderful Wizard of Oz* (1900) and tells their story from a different point of view starting with Elphaba, the misunderstood Wicked Witch of the West. *Wicked* was made into a blockbuster Broadway musical. A movie is in the works.

▣ *Wicked: The Life and Times of the Wicked Witch of the West.* Harper-Collins, 1995. 406p. 9780060548940.
Son of a Witch. HarperCollins, 2005. 337p. 9780060747220.
A Lion among Men. William Morrow, 2008. 309p. 9780060548926.
Out of Oz. William Morrow, 2011. 568 p. 9780060548940.

YA **Marillier, Juliet.** *Wildwood Dancing.* Knopf, 2007. 407p. 9780375833649. Marillier combines fairy tales ("The Dancing Princesses" and "The Frog Prince"), vampires, and legends of the fae in a story set in medieval Transylvania.

Meyer, Marissa

YA **Lunar Chronicles**. This Science Fantasy series is set in a world where people who live on the Moon have extraordinary powers, particularly the ability to use their glamour to manipulate the people of Earth while a deadly plague rages.

> *Cinder.* Feiwell & Friends, 2012. 387. 9780312641894. Cinder, a cyborg who works as a mechanic in New Beijing, catches the attention of Prince Kai who invites her to the ball, but not only does Cinder have to deal with a wicked stepmother, the Moon's queen, but also seems out to get her.
>
> *Scarlet.* Feiwell & Friends, 2013. 464p. 9780312642969. The adventures of Cinder continue as she escapes from prison with a vain publicity hound. Meanwhile, far away in France, Scarlet, who wears a red hoodie, delivers produce from her grandmother's farm to restaurants while worrying over Grand-mére's disappearance. She meets handsome Wolf, a prize fighter.

♟ **Petrushevskaya, Ludmilla (Keith Gessen and Anna Summers, translators).** *There Once Lived a Woman Who Tried to Kill Her Neighbor's Baby: Scary Fairy Tales.* Penguin, 2009. 224p. 9780143114666. A retrospective collection of the Russian author's 30 years of writing, these new fairy tales are dark, intense and take the reader in surprising directions. It won the 2010 World Fantasy Award for a Collection.

Valente, Catherynne M.

Deathless. Tor, 2011. 352. 9780765326300.

♟ **The Orphan's Tale**. Mythopoeic Award winner.

> *In the Night Garden.* Spectra, 2006. 483p. 9780553384031.
> *In the Cities of Coin and Spice.* Spectra, 2006. 516p. 9780553384048.

🔖 **Wilkins, Kim.** *The Veil of Gold*. Tor, 2008. 496p. 9780765320063. When an enchanted golden bear is found in the walls of a St. Petersburg bathhouse, historians Daniel and Em set out to find its history. When Daniel goes missing, Rosa, who has second sight, sets out to find him and instead finds a wizard and more problems. RUSA Reading List Award winner.

Epic Fantasy

Epic or High Fantasy is the subgenre that many people associate most closely with Fantasy. Taking place in fully realized, complexly drawn alternate worlds that are either wholly created by the author or that use a historical period in our own world as a jumping off point, Epic Fantasy draws the reader in with vivid details and so many characters that some books offer a list so the reader can keep them straight. These stories are Fantasy writ on a large scale often drawn out over many volumes. Tolkien's <u>Lord of the Rings Series</u> and George R. R. Martin's <u>Song of Ice and Fire Series</u> are two classic examples of this subgenre. The sheer length of the works allow for finely shaded character development and many complex, interweaving subplots.

Abercrombie, Joe

<u>The First Law</u>. The stories of barbarian Logen Ninefingers, nobleman Captain Jezal dan Luthar, torturer Inquisitor Glokta, and the wizard Bayaz, as they try to survive battles and in the embattled Union, are told with dark cynicism.

> *The Blade Itself*. Pyr, 2007. 531p. 9781591025948.
> *Before They Are Hanged*. Pyr, 2008. 543p. 9781591026419.
> *Last Argument of Kings*. Pyr, 2008. 639p. 9781591026907.

Abraham, Daniel

<u>The Long Price Quartet</u>. In a world of city-states, poets control magic. Machiavellian politics leads to a war and the possibility of ending the world.

> *A Shadow in Summer*. Tor, 2006. 336p. 9780765313409.
> *A Betrayal in Winter*. Tor, 2007. 320p. 9780765313416.
> *An Autumn War*. Tor, 2008. 366p. 9780765313423.
> *The Price of Spring*. Tor, 2009. 352p. 9780765313430.

<u>The Dagger and the Coin Series</u>. Told from multiple points of view, this tale of conflicts involves finance and war.

The Dragon's Path. Orbit, 2011. 592p. 9780316080682. Aging caravan guard Captain Marcus Wester wants nothing more than to keep a low profile and his men alive another day, but instead finds himself embroiled in a civil war guarding a treasure that all sides would kill to attain.

The King's Blood. Orbit, 2012. 489p. 9781841498898.

Baker, Kage. *The House of the Stag*. Tor, 2008. 350p. 9780765317452. Gard had been adopted by the simple, peaceful Yendri, and when they were attacked and enslaved by the Riders, he was the only one who fought back.

Bakker, R. Scott

The Second Apocalypse Series consists of two trilogies that began with The Prince of Nothing Trilogy and continued in The Aspect-Emperor Trilogy.

The Prince of Nothing Trilogy. Graphic, sometimes brutal, always challenging, the story is set in Eärwa, a land divided by a holy war where priest-sorcerers and philosophers battle for supremacy. Though not for all tastes, Bakker manages to rise above the clichés of the Fantasy genre and make it his own.

> *The Darkness that Comes Before*. Overlook, 2004. 608p. 9781585675593.
> *The Warrior Prophet*. Overlook, 2005. 607p. 9781585675609.
> *The Thousandfold Thought*. Overlook, 2006. 510p. 9781585677054.

The Aspect-Emperor Trilogy. Bakker's sprawling and complicated saga continues 20 years after the events in the first trilogy with Kellhus leading a second war against the Consult and their No-God.

> *The Judging Eye*. Overlook, 2009. 437p. 9781590201695.
> *The White-Luck Warrior*. Overlook, 2011. 591p. 9781590204641.
> *The Unholy Consult*. (forthcoming 2013).

Berg, Carol

🏵 **Lighthouse Duet**. Because of their magic, purebloods live strictly circumscribed lives in Navaronne, but Valen, a mapmaker who is a likable rogue, rebels, runs away, and becomes enchantment addicted. Finding sanctuary in a monastery after being abandoned by his companion, Valen discovers that using the magic he was running away from may be the only way to save a war-torn Navaronne. Mythopoeic Award winner.

> *Flesh and Spirit*. Roc, 2007. 408p. 9780451460882.
> *Breath and Bone*. Roc, 2008. 449p. 9780451461865.

Erikson, Steven

Malazan Book of the Fallen. This sprawling epic started in 1999 with *Gardens of the Moon*. The series has a huge cast of characters and three primary story arcs. The Malazan Empire fights to rule the remaining independent city-states; while on the subcontinent, the natives are rising against the Empire, and on another continent, the Empire of Lether wars with the united tribes.

> #6 *The Bonehunters*. Tor, 2007. 800p. 9780765310064.
> #7 *Reaper's Gale*. Tor, 2008. 832p. 9780765310071.
> #8 *Toll the Hounds*. Tor, 2008. 832 p. 9780765310088.
> #9 *Dust of Dreams*. Tor, 2010. 816p. 9780765316554.
> #10 *The Crippled God*. Bantam, 2011. 913p. 9780765310101.

Fox, Daniel

Moshui, the Books of Stone and Water. Set in a world like feudal China, a young emperor flees to an island, a miner is transformed by a piece of jade, and a dragon bound by magical chains is unleashed.

> *Dragon in Chains*. Del Rey, 2009. 399p. 9780345503053.
> *Jade Man's Skin*. Del Rey, 2010. 432p. 9780345503046.
> *Hidden Cities*. Del Rey, 2011. 480p. 9780345503039.

Hobb, Robin

The Rain Wild Chronicles. In the fourth subseries of the larger Realms of the Elderlings Series following Farseer Trilogy, Live Ship Traders, and Tawny Man, a band of humans and dragons take a perilous journey along a toxic river in search of a legendary dragon homeland.

> *Dragon Keeper*. Eos, 2010. 474p. 9780061561627.
> *Dragon Haven*. Eos, 2010. 508p. 9780061931413.
> *City of Dragons*. HarperCollins, 2012. 425p. 9780007273805.
> *Blood of Dragons*. HarperCollins. 2013 (forthcoming). 9780062116857.

Jordan, Robert

The Wheel of Time. One of the bestselling fantasy epics of all time started with *The Eye of the World* in 1990. Fans of this intricate, detailed epic will tell you there is no short way to describe it. It has spawned an enormous fandom with a presence at SFF conferences and online. Tor.com has run a reread of the series doing a recap and commentary on all the books (http://www.tor.com/features/series/wot-reread). It started in January 2009 and will be done with the first 13 volumes about the time the 14th and final volume is slated for release.

> #11 *Knife of Dreams.* Tor, 2005. 784p. 9780312873073.

Jordan, Robert, and Brandon Sanderson

Following Robert Jordan's death in 2007, his widow and editor, Harriet McDougal selected Sanderson to complete *A Memory of Light*, the final book in **The Wheel of Time**. The story outlined and started by Jordan turned into three volumes finished by Sanderson.

> #12 *The Gathering Storm*. Tor, 2009. 1071p. 9780765341532.
> #13 *Towers of Midnight*. Tor, 2010, 864p. 9780765325945.
> #14 *A Memory of Light*. Tor, 2013. 864p. 9780765325952.

🎗 **Kay, Guy Gavriel.** *Under Heaven*. Penguin, 2010. 592p. 9780451463302. Shen Tai, a young soldier in the Tang Dynasty, spends two years burying the dead from a battle to honor his dead father until his enemy honors him with 250 horses to take to his emperor. This is the story of his perilous journey to court. RUSA Reading List Award winner.

Kushner, Ellen

Swords of Riverside. Kushner's writing invites comparisons to Jane Austen and Georgette Heyer with rapier sharp wit and observations of society. Her series, set in Riverside, a section of an unnamed capitol city where sword-wielders congregate, has been called Mannerpunk.

> *Swordspoint: A Melodrama of Manners*. HarperCollins, 1987. 350p. 9780048233523. Accustomed to performing duels to the death for the entertainment of nobles, swordsman Richard St. Vier is drawn into the intrigue of multiple conspiracies as nobles plot against each other using him as a pawn in their deadly political games.
> *The Fall of the Kings* (**with Delia Sherman**). Bantam, 2002. 496p. 9780553381849.
> 🎗 *The Privilege of the Sword*. Spectra, 2006. 400p. 9780553382686. Young Katherine finds herself plunged into plots and politics when her uncle calls upon her to master the deadly art of the sword. Multifaceted characters match wits and swords in the glittering, mannered world of a nameless city. This long awaited entry in the Swords of Riverside Series is a fitting successor to its brilliant forebears. Kushner simply

writes some of the best-written Fantasy today. Locus Award winner.

Lynch, Scott

The Gentleman Bastard Sequence. Thief, con-artist, and adventurer Locke Lamora is the head of a band of daring rouges who live for the next heist in this rollicking caper novel set in a far off world. Science Fiction, but with all the trappings of Fantasy, the Gentleman Bastard Sequence blurs the line between the two genres.

> *The Lies of Locke Lamora*. Spectra, 2006. 512p. 9780553804676.
> *Red Seas under Red Skies*. Spectra, 2007. 576p. 9780553804683.
> *The Republic of Thieves*. (forthcoming 2013).

Must Read

🕯 **Martin, George R. R. *A Song of Ice and Fire.*** This great, sprawling, brutal epic—told from dozens of points of view and spanning two continents, Westeros and Essos—deals with intricacies of lethal politics in a world where even the seasons won't follow established rules. The first novel in the series, A Game of Thrones, has become known even to non-Fantasy fans and non-readers through the HBO series of the same name. Two titles have been published since the last edition of *Genreflecting* and two more volumes are planned.

> **#4 A Feast for Crows**. Bantam, 2005. 753p. 9780553801507.
> **#5 A Dance with Dragons**. Bantam, 2011. 1016p. 9780553801477.

Monette, Sarah

The Doctrine of Labyrinths. Felix Harrowgate, a once distinguished wizard, is insane, and Mildmay the Fox, a thief and assassin, are brought together by a wizard hunting for Felix who finds Mildmay.

> *Mélusine*. Ace, 2005. 421p. 9780441012862.
> *The Virtu*. Ace, 2006. 448p. 9780441014040.
> *The Mirador*. Ace, 2007. 432p. 9780441015009.
> *Corambis*. Ace, 2009. 421p. 9780441015962.

Newton, Mark Charan

Legends of the Red Sun. Newton described this series as, "A Fantasy series grounded in the epic tradition, though with Science Fictional and Crime plots, a firm embrace of all things Weird, and respecting modern politics."

Nights of Villjamur. Tor, 2009. 451p. 9780230712584.
City of Ruin. Tor, 2010. 470p. 9780230712591.
Book of Transformations. Tor, 2011. 418p. 9780230750067.

Redick, Robert V. S.

Chathrand Voyages. The Chathrand, a massive 600-year-old ship, is ostensibly sent on a diplomatic mission from one empire to another, bearing a bride who is to cement the peace, but its true mission is espionage.

The Red Wolf Conspiracy. Del Rey, 2009. 450p. 9780345508836.
The Ruling Sea. Del Rey. 2010. 613p. 9780345508850.
The River of Shadows. Del Rey, 2011. 528p. 9780345523815.

Rothfuss, Patrick

The Kingkiller Chronicle. Kvothe starts out as a young musician in band of players, is orphaned and eventually makes his way into a college of magic and becomes a legend. This is an epic Fantasy that focuses on one person's life journey.

🎗 *The Name of the Wind*. DAW, 2007. 672p. 9780756404079—RUSA
    Reading List Award
The Wise Man's Fear. DAW, 2011. 994p. 9780756404734.

Sanderson, Brandon

Warbreaker. Tor, 2009, 592p. 9780765320308. This one volume, standalone Epic Fantasy is about two sisters, princesses, one of whom is to marry the God King, in a world where the dead can come back as gods and a magic system that draws on color.

The Stormlight Archive. *The Way of Kings*. Tor. 2010. 1007p. 9780765326355. Kaladin, who should have been a healer, instead goes to war in a bid to save his brother's life and survives what would appear to be insurmountable odds as he protects and cares for the men in his unit who are sent out to be killed. Shardplate and shardblades, mysterious, magical armor, and swords turn their bearers into almost invincible warriors.

Mistborn. It's a world that has experienced darkness for a millennium because a prophesied hero failed and the bad guy rules. The world is a dark one with skaa, a slave class, and an interesting magic system that uses metals.

Mistborn: The Final Empire. Tor, 2006. 541p. 9780765311788.
The Well of Ascension. Tor, 2007. 590p. 9780765316882.
The Hero of Ages. Tor, 2008. 576p. 9780765316899.
The Alloy of Law. Tor, 2011. 336p. 9780765330420. This standalone novel is set centuries after the events in the trilogy in a time that has a Western feel complete with gunslingers and train robberies.

Scholes, Ken

<u>Psalms of Isaak</u>. An ancient weapon destroys the capitol city of the Named Lands and war breaks out, followed by assassinations in this far-future postapocalyptic world where magic is not out of the ordinary.

   🎗 *Lamentation*. Tor, 2008. 368p. 9780765321275—RUSA Reading List Award
   Canticle. Tor, 2009. 384p. 9780765321282.
   Antiphon. Tor, 2010. 384p. 9780765321299.

Weeks, Brent

<u>Night Angel</u>. Azoth, guild rat, apprentices to an assassin and assumes a new identity; as Kylar Stern, his life changes—assassinations, coups, God-kings, and a friend who is a king.

   The Way of Shadows. Orbit, 2008. 645p. 9780316033671.
   Shadow's Edge. Orbit, 2008. 656p. 9780316033657.
   Beyond the Shadows. Orbit, 2008. 720p. 9780316033664.

<u>Lightbringer</u>. Gavin Guile knows he only has five years to live because he is a Prism, the most powerful man in the world, a king and a god.

   The Black Prism. Orbit, 2010. 763p. 9780316075558.
   The Blinding Knife. Orbit, 2012. 704p. 9780316079914.
   The Blood Mirror. Orbit, 2013 (forthcoming).

Alternate and Parallel Worlds

Other fully developed worlds, whether our own transformed by a difference in history or that can be traveled to from our world, are featured in this subgenre. Sometimes the alternate world is a fully fleshed-out one that has no relation to our own, but rather has its own dully developed history and rules. Alternate and parallel worlds are also found in Science Fiction.

Baker, Kage. *The Bird of the River.* Tor, 2010. 272p. 9780765322968. Set in the same world as Baker's *The Anvil of the World* and *The House of the Stag*, it tells the story of Eliss and her mixed-race brother who are orphaned when their mother drowns, become crew on a barge that traverses a long river, passing through many cities and cultures.

Brett, Peter V.

Demon Cycle. When night falls, corelings rule the earth and humans hide behind wards, old symbols that keep them safe, but over the years, humans have declined losing much of their ability to fight the corelings but a prophecy gives hope that there will be a Deliverer who will save humanity.

> *The Warded Man.* Del Rey, 2009. 416p. 9780345503800.
> *The Desert Spear.* Del Rey, 2010. 583p. 9780345503817.

🏅 🎬 **YA** **Gaiman, Neil.** *The Graveyard Book.* HarperCollins, 2008. 320p. 9780060530921. After his family is slain, Nobody "Bod" Owens is raised by the ghostly residents of a cemetery where he learns many of the ghostly skills such as fading and scarring and human skills such as reading, and finds a living friend whose family figures him for an imaginary companion. Winner of the Hugo Award, Newbery Medal, and Locus Award.

McKillip, Patricia A. *The Bards of Bone Plain.* Ace, 2010. 329. 9780441019571. Phelan Cle finds riddles inside of riddles as he works on his thesis about the legendary Bone Plain where it was once believed all poetry came from and Princess Beatrice, an archaeologist, unearths an artifact that may herald change.

Miéville, China

🏅 📖 *The City & the City.* Tor, 2009. 312p. 9781405000178. This is a strange tale of two cities occupying the same space but that exist independently by common agreement of the denizens of both. It provides a thought-provoking look at group dynamics. Winner of the Hugo, British Science Fiction Association, the Arthur C. Clarke, and the World Fantasy Awards.

🏅 *Kraken.* MacMillan, 2010. 400p. 9780333989500. When British Museum curator Billy Harrow's prize giant squid disappears, he finds himself forced to confront a cult bent on bringing on Armageddon. Winner of a Locus Award.

Newton, Mark Charan

<u>Legends of the Red Sun</u>. In this series, readers are introduced to a world entering an endless winter as its sun begins to die. It is liberally doused with elements of crime, politics, and the Weird.

> *Nights of Villjamur*. Tor, 2009. 451p. 9780230712584.
> *City of Ruin*. Tor, 2010. 470p. 9780230712591.
> *Book of Transformations*. Tor, 2011. 418p. 9780230750067.

Must Read

Novik, Naomi. <u>Temeraire</u>. In a battle with a French ship, Captain Will Laurence and his crew find that in victory they have also acquired a dragon egg. While still at sea, it hatches and instead of bonding with the man who drew the lot, it bonds with Laurence. Laurence's family had not been thrilled with his choice of a naval career, but now with a dragon, he must do his duty to the king and the country and join the Aerial Corps, no place for a gentleman. Adventures abound as the dragon, Temeraire, and Will train together to fight the war and find that Temeraire is exceptional even for a dragon. Novik's dragons are fully developed characters adding to the charm of this series.

> *His Majesty's Dragon*. Del Rey, 2006. 356p. 9780345481283.
> *Throne of Jade*. Del Rey, 2006. 398p. 9780345481290.
> *Black Powder War*. Del Rey, 2006. 365p. 9780345481306.
> *Empire of Ivory*. Del Rey, 2007. 404p. 9780345496874.
> *Victory of Eagles*. Del Rey, 2008. 352p. 9780007256754.
> *Tongues of Serpents*. Del Rey, 2010. 274p. 9780345496898.
> *Crucible of Gold*. Del Rey, 2012. 323p. 9780345522863.

🎗 **Okorafor, Nnedi.** *Who Fears Death?* Daw, 2010. 386p. 9780756406172. In postapocalyptic Africa, Onyesonwu, a daughter born of rape, is tutored by a shaman so she can end the genocide that has taken so many of her people. Winner of a World Fantasy Award.

Snyder, Maria V.

<u>Study Series</u>. Convicted of murder and sentenced to execution, Yelena jumps at the opportunity to have her sentence commuted to life as the food taster for the Commander who rules Ixia. Magic is completely forbidden, but could it be that her ability to stay alive may be due to magic?

Poison Study. Mira, 2004. 409p. 9780778324331.
Magic Study. Mira, 2006. 392p. 9780373802494.
Fire Study. Mira, 2008. 441p. 9780778325345.

Swanwick, Michael. *The Dragons of Babel*. Tor, 2008. 320p. 9780765319500. When a war-dragon from New York-like Babel crashes in Faerie, he declares himself king.

YA **Taylor, Laini.** *Daughter of Smoke and Bone*. Little, Brown and Co., 2011. 417p. 9780316134026. Karou, a blue-haired teen art student living in Prague, was raised by chimera in the Brimstone's Wishshop. She earns wishes by going through a door in the Wishshop and coming out in a different city where she collects teeth for Brimstone. Everything changes when burning handprints turn up on the doors she travels through and she fights the angel who has put them there.

Tregillis, Ian

Milkweed Triptych. In this Alternate History, Raybould Marsh starts out as a young spy who sees people with peculiar powers working for Nazis and enlists Britain's secret warlocks to stop an invasion.

Bitter Seeds. Tor, 2010. 352p. 9780765321503.
The Coldest War. Tor. 2012. 352p. 9780765321510.
Necessary Evil. Tor, 2013 (forthcoming).

Whitfield, Kit. *In Great Waters*. Del Rey, 2009. 405p. 9780345491657. In this Alternate History, European royalty, descended from a Deepsman, have intermarried creating all kinds of problems; but to stop challenges, they kill any mixed Deepsman and Landsman children that are born. Whistle is abandoned on land by his mother because he just can't live under the sea. On shore, he is secretly raised by a nobleman with ulterior motives. Renamed Henry, he and Ann, a princess of England, become involved in the intense politics of the time.

Wolfe, Gene. *Sorcerer's House*. Tor, 2010. 9780765324580. Recently released from prison, Bax, staying in a motel in the American Midwest, is informed that he has inherited a huge old house. His story, dealing with supernatural beings, is told in letters.

The Soldier Series. In the ancient world, Latro, a mercenary who speaks both Latin and Greek, wakes up every day with no memories. Keeping a journal, he records his life each day so he can read it when he awakes.

♟ *Soldier of the Mist*. Tor, 1987. 335p. 9780812558159—Locus Award

Soldier of Areté. Tor, 1989. 354p. 9780312931858.

♟ *Soldier of Sidon*. Tor, 2006. 320p. 9780765316646—World Fantasy Award

Urban Fantasy

The term "Urban Fantasy" like "Dystopia" has become a buzz word and all kinds of people are applying it to all kinds of books. In particular, lots of vampire and werewolf novels are being called Urban Fantasy. The last edition of *Genreflecting* defined Urban Fantasy as "magic and technology share a place in gritty, dangerous cities." The <u>Borderland</u>, a shared world that consists of short stories and novels by various authors, is the quintessential Urban Fantasy. Urban Fantasy uses our world and its urban problems as the starting point. The characters that populate these stories may be mundane (possessing no magic of their own) or have magic in their DNA, but the world that they travel in—either by accident or by birth—is suffused in magic and magical characters, no matter how familiar it may look to the reader at first glance. Some Urban Fantasy may have a strong romantic or even erotic element and a mystery is often involved. Stories focusing on werewolves, vampires, angels, and demons are in the Horror chapter.

Andrews, Ilona

<u>Kate Daniels</u>. Kate, a mercenary, cleans up magical messes for a living in an Atlanta that is divided by factions lining up with necromancers or shapeshifters.

Magic Bites. Ace, 2007. 260p. 9780441014897.
Magic Burns. Ace, 2008. 260p. 9780441015832.
Magic Strikes. Ace, 2009. 310p. 9780441017027.
Magic Bleeds. Ace, 2010. 367p. 9780441018529.
Magic Slays. Ace, 2011. 308p. 9780441020423.

Armstrong, Kelley

<u>Women of the Otherworld</u>. The first five books in this series that includes witches, werewolves, vampires, and demons were listed in the Horror chapter of the last edition of *Genreflecting*.

Broken. Orbit, 2006. 444p. 9781841493428.
No Humans Involved. Spectra, 2007. 368p. 9780553805086.
Personal Demon. Spectra, 2008. 371p. 9780553806618.
Living with the Dead. Spectra, 2008. 372p. 9780553806649.
Frostbitten. Spectra, 2009. 352p. 9781841497761.

YA **Black, Holly, and Ellen Kushner, eds.** *Welcome to Bordertown: New Stories and Poems of the Borderlands*. Random, 2011. 516p. 97803 75867057.The first new Borderland anthology in over a decade, the contents list reads like a Who's Who of modern Fantasy with stories by Holly Black, Ellen Kushner, Cory Doctorow, Neil Gaiman, Catherynne M. Valente, Jane Yolen, and Charles de Lint, amongst others. The authors collaborating in the <u>Borderland Series</u> explored what would happen if the long-vanished land of the elves suddenly reappeared to rub shoulders with our modern world. Bordertown is the city—once mundane, but now forever altered by its proximity to the elfin lands—that separates our world from theirs. It has become a magnet for rascals, runaways, and dreamers from both sides to the Border. Titles of all the books published in the <u>Borderland</u> world can be found at http://bordertownseries.com/series.html. "Bordertown is one of the most important places where Urban Fantasy began"—Neil Gaiman (http://bordertownseries.com).

Briggs, Patricia

<u>Mercy Thompson Series</u>. Half–Native American, Mercy can shape-shift into coyote form. She works as a VW mechanic but ends up dealing with werewolves, vampires, and other fae.

Moon Called. Ace, 2006. 304p. 9780441013814.
Blood Bound. Ace, 2007. 292p. 9780441014736.
Iron Kissed. Ace, 2008. 287p. 9780441015665.
Bone Crossed. Ace, 2009. 309p. 9780441016761.
Silver Borne. Ace, 2010. 342p. 9780441018192.
River Marked. Ace, 2011. 326p. 9780441019731.
Frost Burned. Ace, forthcoming (2013). 9780441020010.

Must Read

Butcher, Jim. <u>The Dresden Files</u>. Harry Dresden is the only wizard in the Chicago phone book. So it is no wonder that when crimes turn up that have a tang of the supernatural, he is called in. (All titles are listed here as this was not included in the last edition.) *The Dresden Files* was also a TV series.

Storm Front. Roc, 2000. 384p. 9780451457813.
Fool Moon. Roc, 2001. 352p. 9780451458124.
Grave Peril. Roc, 2001. 378p. 9780451462343.
Summer Knight. Roc, 2002. 371p. 9780451458926.
Death Masks. Roc, 2003. 378p. 9780451459404.
Blood Rites. Roc, 2004. 372p. 9780451459879.
Dead Beat. Roc, 2005. 396p. 9780451460271.
Proven Guilty. Roc, 2006. 406p. 9780451460851.
White Night. Roc, 2007. 407p. 9780451461407.
Small Favor. Roc, 2008. 432p. 9780451461896.
Turn Coat. Roc, 2009. 432p. 9780451462565.
Changes. Roc, 2010. 448p. 9780451463173.
Ghost Story. Roc, 2011. 496p. 9780451463791.
Cold Days. Roc, 2012. 515p. 9780451464408.

Adjunct to the series is **Side Jobs: Stories from the Dresden Files**. Roc, 2010. 432p. 9780451463654. A collection of 11 short stories, of them previously published, set in different times, plus some content that is exclusive to this book, including "Aftermath," a follow up to 2011's *Ghost Story* that takes place 45 minutes after the close of that book. (And that contains a spoiler.)

Clare, Cassandra

YA <u>The Mortal Instruments</u>. Set in New York, Clary Fray's life changes when she sees something she shouldn't have and discovers she can see the Shadowhunters and Downworlders.

City of Bones. Margaret K. McElderry Books, 2007. 485p. 9781416914280.
City of Ashes. Margaret K. McElderry Books, 2008. 453p. 9781416914297.
City of Glass. Margaret K. McElderry Books, 2009. 541p. 9781416914303.
City of Fallen Angels. Margaret K. McElderry Books, 2011. 424p. 9781442403543.
City of Lost Souls. Margaret K. McElderry Books, 2012. 534p. 9781442416864.

Datlow, Ellen, ed. *Naked City: Tales of Urban Fantasy.* St. Martin's, 2011. 506p. 9780312385248. This is an excellent sampler of some of the best writers of Urban Fantasy including Delia Sherman, Peter S. Beagle, Patricia Briggs, and Holly Black. Highlights include a <u>Dresden</u>

<u>Files</u> short story by Jim Butcher. Eclectic, ambitious, and grittier than many takes on Urban Fantasy.

Del Franco, Mark

<u>Connor Grey Series</u>. Druid, Connor Grey, a former Guild investigator, consults with the Boston police department on cases involving the fae.

> *Unshapely Things*. Ace, 2007. 305p. 9780441014774.
> *Unquiet Dreams*. Ace, 2008. 292p. 9780441015696.
> *Unfallen Dead*. Ace, 2009. 320p. 9780441016891.
> *Unperfect Souls*. Ace, 2010. 353p. 9780441018383.
> *Uncertain Allies*. Ace, 2011. 304p. 9780441020409.
> *Undone Deeds*. Ace, 2012. 336p. 9781937007256.

Green, Simon R.

<u>Nightside</u>. John Taylor had left the Nightside, the creepy subterranean city under London where the time is always 3 a.m., five years ago, but goes back in when his investigations take him there.

> *Something from the Nightside*. Ace. 2003. 230p. 9780441010653.
> *Agents of Light and Darkness*. Ace, 2003. 233p. 9780441011131.
> *Nightengale's Lament*. Ace, 2004. 244p. 9780441011636.
> *Hex and the City*. Ace, 2005. 246p. 9780441012619.
> *Paths Not Taken*. Ace, 2005. 262p. 9780441013197.
> *Sharper than a Serpent's Tooth*. Ace, 2006. 256p. 9780441013876.
> *Hell to Pay*. Ace, 2006. 264p. 9780441014606.
> *The Unnatural Inquirer*. Ace, 2008. 246p. 9780441015580.
> *Just Another Judgement Day*. Ace, 2009. 272p. 9780441016747.
> *The Good, the Bad, and the Uncanny*. Ace, 2010. 275p. 9780441018161.
> *A Hard Day's Knight*. Ace, 2011. 294p. 9780441019700.
> *The Bride Wore Black Leather*. Ace, 2012. 320p. 9781937007133.

Hanover, M.L.N.

(International Horror Guild Award–winning author Daniel Abraham writes Urban Fantasy under the Hanover pseudonym.)

<u>The Black Sun's Daughter</u>. When Jayné Heller's uncle dies, he leaves her much more than his vast fortune, he also leaves her with some messy loose ends to tie up with a powerful cabal of wizards—the leader of which wants her dead by any means.

> *Unclean Spirits*. Pocket, 2008. 357p. 9781416575979.
> *Darker Angels*. Pocket, 2009. 368p. 9781416576778.
> *Vicious Grace*. Pocket, 2010. 384p. 9781439176290.
> *Killing Rites*. Pocket, 2011. 384p. 9781439176344.

Harrison, Kim

The Hollows. Rachel Morgan is a bounty hunting witch in vampire infested Cincinnati.

> *Dead Witch Walking*. HarperTorch, 2004. 416p. 9780060572969.
> *The Good, the Bad, and the Undead*. HarperTorch, 2005. 453p. 9780060572976.
> *Every Which Way But Dead*. Eos, 2005. 501p. 9780060572990.
> *A Fistful of Charms*. Eos, 2006. 496p. 9780060892982.
> *For a Few Demons More*. Eos, 2007. 456p. 9780060788384.
> *The Outlaw Demon Wails*. Eos, 2008. 455p. 9780060788704.
> *White Witch, Black Curse*. Eos, 2009. 504p. 9780061138010.
> *Black Magic Sanction*. Eos, 2010. 487p. 9780061138034.
> *Pale Demon*. HarperVoyager, 2011. 439p. 9780061138065.
> *A Perfect Blood*. HarperVoyager, 2012. 438p. 9780061957895.

Price, Kalayna

Alex Craft. Being able to raise the dead to question them helps Alex in her job as a private investigator in Nekros City, particularly when she is helping the police solve a homicide. Sometimes, she teams up with Falin Andrews, a fae agent.

> *Grave Witch*. Roc, 2010. 325p. 9780451463807.
> *Grave Dance*. Roc, 2011. 371p. 9780451464095.
> *Grave Memory*. Roc, 2012. 383p. 9780451464590.

Haven. A shapeshifter who turns into a small calico cat must figure out how to survive all the perils of the city Haven, after she is turned into a vampire.

> *Once Bitten*. Belle Bridge Books, 2008. 272p. 9780980245394.
> *Twice Dead*. Belle Bridge Books, 2010. 256p. 9780984325672.

Vaughn, Carrie

<u>Kitty Norville</u>. Kitty, a late night DJ in Denver, a recently turned werewolf, begins conversing with her listeners about the possibility that vampires and werewolves may actually exist and becomes an in-demand authority on the supernatural.

> *Kitty and the Midnight Hour*. Grand Central, 2005. 259p. 9780446616416.
> *Kitty Goes to Washington*. Grand Central, 2006. 321p. 9780446616423.
> *Kitty Takes a Holiday*. Grand Central, 2007. 303p. 9780446618748.
> *Kitty and the Silver Bullet*. Grand Central, 2008. 326p. 9780446618755.
> *Kitty and the Dead Man's Hand*. Grand Central. 2009. 282p. 9780446199537.
> *Kitty Raises Hell*. Grand Central. 2009. 311p. 9780446199544.
> *Kitty's House of Horrors*. Grand Central. 2010. 292p. 9780446199551.
> *Kitty Goes to War*. Tor, 2010. 334p. 9780765365613.
> *Kitty's Big Trouble*. Tor, 2011. 307p. 9780765365651.
> *Kitty Steals the Show*. Tor, 2012. 342p. 9780765365668.

Humor and Satire

Lest you think that Fantasy is only about vast armies marching off to shoot arrows at each other, fantasy does have a lighter side.

Fforde, Jasper. *Shades of Grey*. Viking, 2009. 390p. 9780670019632. A satirical look at a society where colorblindness is rampant and status is determined by what colors a person can see.

Must Read

Jones, Diana Wynne. *The Tough Guide to Fantasyland: The Essential Guide to Fantasy Travel*. Firebird, 2006 (originally published by DAW, 1996). 256p. 9780142407226. Out of print for years, Jones has added a new map and material to this hilarious send-up of fantasy clichés.

🎬 **Pratchett, Terry**

<u>Discworld</u>. An enormous and sprawling series that consists of dozens of novels and short stories as well as companion guides including a cookbook and portfolio of the cover art, some done in collaboration with writing partners. Pratchett's <u>Discworld</u> novels are set in a fantastic flat world that moves through time and space on the back of four elephants. Very popular with young adult readers, <u>Discworld</u> novels have been adapted for film, radio, and the stage as well as being turned into Graphic Novels. <u>Discworld</u> novels have been nominated for and won many awards, including the Andre Norton Award, the British Science Fiction Award, the Locus Award,

and the 2001 Carnegie Medal. The novels issued since our last edition are listed here:

Thud! Harper, 2005. 384p. 9780060815226.
🎖 *Making Money*. Harper, 2007. 352p. 9780385611015—Locus Award
Unseen Academicals. Harper, 2009. 400p. 9780061161704.
Snuff. Harper, 2011. 416p. 9780062011848.

YA **Tiffany Aching**. This subseries of Discworld features novels published for young adults that tell the story of a young witch coming of age. It started in 2003 with *The Wee Free Men*.

#3 *Wintersmith*. Harper, 2006. 336p. 9780060890315.
🎖 #4 *I Shall Wear Midnight*. Harper, 2010. 368p. 9780061433047—Andre Norton Award

Magic

Magic most often is what makes fantasy fiction Fantasy. The books in this section focus on the magic. Often they are set in our own recognizable world, but they also can occur in other times and places.

Bennett, Robert Jackson. *The Troupe.* Orbit, 2012. 512p. 9780316187527. Sixteen-year-old George Carole decides to find the father he has never known when his vaudeville troupe performs in a nearby town. Dark and literary.

Grossman, Lev

Magician. Quentin Coldwater unexpectedly ends up at a college of magic called Brakebills in New York. He has always been obsessed with a children's Fantasy series about five siblings who go through a clock and end up in a magical land called Fillory that turns out to really exist.

The Magicians. Viking, 2009. 416p. 9780670020553.
The Magician King. Viking, 2011. 400p. 9780670022311.

Huff, Tanya

The Gale Women. The women of the Gale family are strong in magic and governed by the Aunties. Living in contemporary Canada, magically talented young women of the family take on different adventures. Males born into the family face the possibility of becoming the horned Green Man or being banished.

The Enchantment Emporium. DAW, 2009. 368p. 9780756405557. Alysha
Gale's adventures in Calgary can also be called Urban Fantasy.

The Wild Ways. DAW, 2011. 295p. 9780756406868. Charlotte, Alysha's
cousin, ends up in the Maritimes when she fills in for a Celtic band
and finds a dragon.

Morgenstern, Erin. *The Night Circus*. Doubleday, 2011. 387p. 9780385534635.
Taking place over the course of 30 years starting in 1873, rival magicians
compete using one's young daughter who has real magic, and the other
using an ordinary boy.

Mythic Reality

Stories set in our world with ordinary people who encounter magic can be
called mythic reality. They may be set in the here and now or sometime in the
past. Readers who claim to not like Fantasy often like these stories. They often
appeal to readers of "Literary" Fiction.

Kay, Guy Gavriel. *Ysabel*. Roc, 2007. 416p. 9780451461292. A contemporary teen accompanying his photographer father to France becomes
embroiled in an ages-old conflict when one of his father's assistants is pos-
sessed by Ysabel. Winner of a World Fantasy Award.

Murakami, Haruki. *Kafka on the Shore*. Knopf, 2005. 448p. 97814000
43668. Kafka is a 15-year-old boy who leaves home looking for his mother
and sister, spending time in a library, while elderly Nakata, who finds lost
cats, hitches a ride with a truck driver, to eventually come together in the
midst of a mystery. Winner of a World Fantasy Award.

Riggs, Ransom. *Miss Peregrine's Home for Peculiar Children*. Quirk,
2011. 352p. 9781594744761. Jacob has always been fascinated with the
bizarre photos his grandfather Abe had of the other children he grew
up with in Wales after fleeing the holocaust in eastern Europe. His
grandfather's dying words propel Jacob to that island where he discovers the photos were not as staged as he believed, and that time and
what we believe is real are not always the case.

Valente, Catherynne M. *Palimpsest*. Spectra, 2009. 367p. 9780553385762.
This lushly surreal novel features a sexually transmitted city, maps of it
appearing on those infected who can go to the places mapped.

Must Read

Walton, Jo. *Among Others*. Tor, 2011. 302p. 9780765321534. Set in
the late 1970s, told in diary form, Mori, a Welsh teenager who loves Science Fiction, fights with her magical mother resulting in the death of her sister and goes to

her father who sends her to an English boarding school where she finds her own magic. Winner of a Nebula Award.

World of Faerie

Whether they are called the good neighbors, faerie, or fey, the world they inhabit, bordering ours, brings clashes and leads to relationships between them and us. These are not tiny Disneyesque fairies, they can be quite dark and scary. Many of the conventions found in the subgenre, such as time passing at a different rate or the dangers of eating anything in their world, have roots in Celtic folklore although tales of faerie can be set anywhere in our world. Often humans are compelled to become part of the conflict between the Seelie and Unseelie courts or are drawn in when a changeling is substituted for a human child.

Bear, Elizabeth.

Ink and Steel. Roc, 2008. 448p. 9780451462091. When Kit Marlowe is stabbed in the eye and wakes up in Faerie, Will Shakespeare is pulled in to serve Gloriana.

Must Read

Black, Holly. Modern Faerie Tales. Black's "modern faerie tales" are set in urban New York and New Jersey and have had a huge impact on young adult publishing.

> *Tithe*. Magaret K. McElderry Books, 2002. 331p. 9780689867040.
> 🏵 *Valiant*. Magaret K. McElderry Books, 2005. 320p. 9780689868221 — Andre Norton Award
> *Ironside*. Magaret K. McElderry Books, 2007. 323p. 9780689868207.

Dark, Juliet. *The Demon Lover*. Ballantine, 2012. 432p. 9780345510082. A professor of folklore discovers erotic mystery in the papers of one of her favorite Gothic authors that seems to be bleeding over into her own life.

Hamilton, Laurell K.

Meredith "Merry" Gentry Series. Series started in 2000 with *A Kiss of Shadows*, followed by *A Caress of Twilight*. Titles added to this

highly erotic series since the last edition of *Genreflecting* include the
following:

> #3 *Seduced by Moonlight*. Ballantine, 2004. 372p. 9780345443564.
> #4 *A Stroke of Midnight*. Ballantine, 2005. 416p. 9780345443601.
> #5 *Mistral's Kiss*. Ballantine, 2006. 212p. 9780345443588.
> #6 *A Lick of Frost*. Ballantine, 2007. 274p. 9780345495907.
> #7 *Swallowing Darkness*. Ballantine, 2008. 365p. 9780345495938.
> #8 *Divine Misdemeanors*. Ballantine, 2009. 333p. 9780345495969.

YA **Healey, Karen**. *Guardian of the Dead*. Little, Brown and Co., 2010. 333p.
9780316044301. Set in New Zealand, Maori legend, theater, a serial killer,
and a touch of Faerie combine in a unique tale set in a boarding school.

Kagawa, Julie

YA The Iron Fey series. Half-human, half-faery, Meghan Chase plays a pivotal
role in the war between the Summer and Winter Courts and a new danger.

> *The Iron King*. Harlequin Teen, 2010. 363p 9780373210084.
> *The Iron Daughter*. Harlequin Teen, 2010. 359p. 9780373210138.
> *The Iron Queen*. Harlequin Teen, 2011. 258p. 9780373210183.
> *The Iron Knight*. Harlequin Teen, 2011. 394p. 9780373210367.

Marr, Melissa

YA Wicked Lovely. Aislinn has always followed the rules her grandmother
drilled into her about not looking at faeries, not speaking to them, and most of
all not attracting their attention, but when she attracts the attention of Keenan,
the Summer King, her normal 21st-century life is going to be changed.

> *Wicked Lovely*. Harper Teen, 2007. 328p. 9780061214653.
> *Ink Exchange*. Harper Teen, 2008. 328p. 9780061214684.
> *Fragile Eternity*. Bowen Press, 2009. 400p. 9780061214721.
> *Radiant Shadows*. Harper, 2010. 340p. 9780061659225.
> *Darkest Mercy*. Harper, 2011. 327p. 9780061659256.

Moning, Karen Marie

Fever. A 21st-century woman, MacKayla Lane, finds her world turned upside down when she goes to Ireland after her sister is killed and finds the

Fae and one particular alpha who makes sex an addiction for human women.

> *Darkfever*. Delacorte, 2006. 309p. 9780385339155.
> *Bloodfever*. Delacorte, 2007. 303p. 9780385339162.
> *Faefever*. Delacorte, 2008. 327p. 9780385341639.
> *Shadowfever*. Delacorte, 2011. 594p. 9780385341677.

Stievater, Maggie

YA <u>Books of Faerie</u>

> *Lament: The Faerie Queen's Deception*. Flux, 2008. 325p. 978073 8713700. Deirdre Monaghan, a talented harpist with horrible stage fright, discovers that she and her loved ones are in danger from the Faerie Queen and that her new boyfriend may not be who he seems.
> *Ballad: A Gathering of Faerie*. Flux, 2009. 352p. 9780738714844. James becomes the target and love interest of Nuala, a fey who can bestow prodigious musical ability while sucking the life out of a musician. Meanwhile solitary fey are being murdered.

YA **Yovanoff, Brenna.** *The Replacement*. Razorbill, 2010. 304p. 978159 5143372. Mackie Doyle has been raised in the small town of Gentry, but despite his sister's constant care, he isn't thriving. He is so allergic to iron that he can't ride in a car or touch blood. When he tries to help a friend whose baby sister disappears, he is drawn into a dark and dangerous faerie underworld called Mayhem.

Genreblending

Fantasy is often blended with other genres especially Romance and Mystery.

Fantasy Mysteries

Mysteries with a Fantasy setting have been around for a long, long time, but the combination never seems to get old. Like most Mystery novels, they tend to come in series, as readers become attached to the sleuths, rather than as standalone novels. Many of the series in Urban Fantasy, including those by Jim Butcher and Mark Del Franco, are also Mysteries.

Bledsoe, Alex

<u>Eddie LaCross Series</u>. Hard-Boiled sword jockey, Eddie LaCross solves mysteries involving beautiful women, wayward royalty, political machinations, poisonings, and swashbuckling fights in a medieval-like world.

> *The Sword-Edged Blonde*. Nightshade Books, 2007. 232p. 9781597801126.
> *Burn Me Deadly*. Tor, 2009. 320p. 9780765322210.
> *Dark Jenny*. Tor, 2011. 348p. 9780765327437.
> *Wake of the Bloody Angel*. Tor, 2012. 352p. 9780765327451. When Eddie's landlady asks him to take on a cold case for her, he ends up going to sea with a pirate queen in search of a missing pirate.

Cook, Glenn

<u>Garrett, P. I.</u> A classic Noir detective series set in a world of elves, pixies, vampires, and organized crime. Ex-Marine and now private investigator in the fantasy city of TunFaire, Garrett has a love of leisure, an eye for the ladies, and a knack for finding trouble. Witty and full of flashes of humor, the series started in 1987 with *Sweet Silver Blues*.

> #11 *Whispering Nickel Idols*. Roc, 2005. 368p. 9780451459749. Cook's womanizing private investigator's life is complicated by religious fanatics, damsels with secrets, and the local Mafia.
> #12 *Cruel Zinc Melodies*. Roc, 2008. 416p. 9780451461926. Garrett gets in over his head when a bevy of gorgeous women entice him into taking on a case that is a lot more than it seems.
> #13 *Gilded Latten Bones*. Roc, 2010. 368p. 9780451463715. The latest and 13th book in the series finds Garrett retired and trying to settle into monogamous bliss with his sweetheart Tinnie Tate—until someone tries to kidnap her.

Western Fantasy

The old West or places that have the frontier feel of the old West have become a popular setting for Fantasy. The historical milieu gives a completely different feel than the medieval setting that once upon a time was the preferred setting for Fantasy. *Territory* by Emma Bull, which includes a bit of magic in the lead up to the shoot-out at the OK Corral, is listed in the Western chapter.

King, Stephen. *The Wind through the Keyhole*. Scribner, 2012. 309p. 978145 1658903. King's setting for his <u>The Dark Tower</u> may be postapocalyptic, but it has an undeniable Western feel. This story about some of Roland's early experiences as a gunslinger stands alone and does not need to be read as part of the series.

YA **Lackey, Mercedes, and Rosemary Edghill.** *Dead Reckoning.* Bloomsbury, 2012. 336p. 9781599906843. In a unique combination of Fantasy, Horror, and Steampunk, a Southern belle, disguised as a gunslinger, goes West looking for her missing brother and finds zombies.

YA **McQuerry, Maureen Doyle.** *The Peculiars.* Harry N. Abrams, 2012. 354p. 9781419701788. Lena has always been a little different possessing long hands and feet she tries to hide. She may have inherited them from her father who disappeared when she was five, and now she is out to find him even if he has gone beyond the frontier to the territory known for its nonhuman, peculiar, residents. On her journey, she faces a train robbery, dates a sheriff, and finds friendship in a library.

YA **Mitchell, Saundra.** *The Springsweet.* Harcourt, 2012. 275p. 9780545033428. After being disgraced in Baltimore, Zora is sent West to the Oklahoma Territory to stay with her young aunt who is trying to prove up a homesteading claim. The story is thoroughly Western with Zora's ability to witch water the aspect that makes it Fantasy.

Wrede, Patricia C.

YA <u>Frontier Magic</u>. A magical barrier exists between the 19th-century United States and the Western wilderness where beasts, both magical and mundane, roam. Twins Eff and Lan grow up on the frontier near the barrier, Lan is the magical 7th son of a 7th son, but Eff, as the 13th child, is expected to be unlucky.

> *The Thirteenth Child.* Scholastic, 2009. 344p. 9780545033428.
> *Across the Great Barrier.* Scholastic, 2011. 339p. 9780545033435.
> *The Far West.* Scholastic, 2012. 378p. 978054533442.

Romantic Fantasy

Romantic Fantasies fulfill all the requirements of a Romance novel, with the developing relationship of the hero and the heroine as the main focus, but play it out in a magic-infused world that falls into the Fantasy genre.

Fantasy is not new in the Romance genre, but it is superhot (in more ways than one) right now. Time Travel Romances and Gothic Romances with supernatural elements have traditionally been quite common, their popularity waxing and waning over the years; but some very popular books have kicked this subgenre into high gear again, notably the Twilight Series by Stephenie Meyer, the Terre D'Ange by Jacqueline Carey, and the Anita Blake and Mercedes Gentry series by Laurell K. Hamilton. Some of the popularity, too, is surely because readers who grew up with and fell in love with the couples in works like the Harry Potter Series wanted to see these characters as adults, as the vast trove of fan-written fiction (fanfic) available on the Internet can attest!

As with other Romances, Romantic Fantasies run the sensual gamut from the first sweet pangs of first love to the highly eroticized, complete with salty language and page-torching encounters between characters. One of the driving forces behind the e-book revolution was the ability to discreetly download steamy romances by publishers like Ellora's Cave—one of the first publishers of erotica, written especially for female readers.

Bujold, Lois McMaster

The Sharing Knife. Young Fawn Bluefield, pregnant and unwed, leaves her family farm to head to the city but en route meets a band of Lakewalkers, enigmatic sorcerer-soldiers who track and fight the life-sucking "malice." When Fawn is kidnapped by a "malice," Dag, one of the Lakewalkers, attempts to rescue her and his uncharged sharing knife becomes charged sending the two on a journey filled with the unexpected—From Reader's Advisor Online.

> *Beguilement*. Eos, 2007. 376p. 9780061139079.
> *Legacy*. Eos, 2007. 377p. 9780061139055.
> *Passage*. Eos, 2008. 437p. 9780061375330.
> *Horizon*. Eos, 2009. 453p. 9780061375361.

Jemisin, N. K.

The Inheritance Trilogy. The Arameri family has ruled the Hundred Thousand Kingdoms for 2,000 years by enslaving the very gods who made it.

> ♜ *The Hundred Thousand Kingdoms*. Orbit, 2010. 427p. 9780316043915—
> Locus Award.
> *The Broken Kingdoms*. Orbit, 2010. 384p. 9780316043960.
> *The Kingdom of Gods*. Orbit, 2011. 613p. 9781841498195.

Kennedy, Kathryne

The Elven Lords. Set in an alternate Georgian England, elven lords rule the island and have divided it into seven realms, each with a different sort of magic.

Half-elven children are tested and those no or minimal magic are used as slaves. While the elven lords fight between themselves, some of their progeny set about reclaiming England.

> *The Fire Lord's Lover*. Sourcebooks, 2010. 376p. 9781402236525.
> *The Lady of the Storm*. Sourcebooks, 2011. 406p. 9781402236532.
> *The Lord of Illusion*. Sourcebooks, 2012. 448p. 9781402236549.

Kowal, Mary Robinette

Shades of Milk and Honey. In a Regency England where members of the *ton* use "glamour," Jane Ellsworth finds she must stretch her abilities to preserve her family's honor.

> *Shades of Milk and Honey*. Tor, 2010. 304p. 9780765325563.
> *Glamour in Glass*. Tor, 2012. 336p. 9780765325570.
> *Without a Summer*. Tor, 2013 (forthcoming).

Mantchev, Lisa

YA **Théâtre Illuminata**. Beatrice Shakespeare Smith, Bertie, has grown up in a theater where every character from every play is bound by a book. Her four best friends are fairies and she has two love interests, one an air spirit and the other a dashing pirate.

> *Eyes Like Stars*. Feiwel & Friends. 2009. 352p. 9780312380960.
> *Perchance to Dream*. Feiwel & Friends, 2010. 341p. 9780312380977.
> *So Silver Bright*. Feiwel & Friends, 2011. 354p. 9780312380984.

Anthologies and Collections

Some of the most interesting Fantasy works are not full-length novels, but rather short stories or novellas. Though the market for short stories has faded since the days when most magazines had a fiction section, there has continued to be a place for shorter Fantasy works, either in publications such as *Lightspeed* and *Fantasy & Science Fiction* or through the commission of stories for numerous themed anthologies. Now, more short Fantasy Fiction than ever before is available to readers, albeit through nontraditional means. The advent of the Internet and especially the popularity of e-readers has been a boon to writers, providing an outlet for their shorter fiction. Online literary marketplaces such as amazon.com and bn.com make it easy for authors and publishers to offer shorter works to readers, either free of charge as a "taster" or for a small cost. Many writers are also making short stories set in their fantasy worlds available via their own websites—a great way to attract new readers of their work.

Anders, Lou, and Strahan, Jonathan, eds. *Swords and Dark Magic: The New Sword and Sorcery.* Harper Voyager, 2010. 544p. 0061723819. It contains 17 new tales of adventure and magic by some veteran masters as well as newcomers to the Sword and Sorcery world. It includes an original "Elric of Melniboné" short story by Fantasy Grand Master Michael Moorcock.

Beagle, Peter S., ed. *The Secret History of Fantasy.* Tachyon, 2010. 432p. 9781892391995. It contains 19 works of short fiction with 2 essays on the nature of Contemporary Fantasy and an intriguing, if decidedly snarky, introduction from the editor. Beagle has chosen an eclectic mix of authors including Gregory Maguire, Patricia A. McKillip, Francesca Lia Block, Stephen King, and Yann Martell. Susanna Clarke contributes "John Uskglass and the Cumbrian Charcoal Burner," a rare story about the Raven King, a character introduced in her exquisite *Jonathan Strange & Mr. Norrell* (Bloomsbury, 2004).

Beagle, Peter S., and Lansdale, Joe R., eds. *The Urban Fantasy Anthology.* Tachyon, 2011. 432p. 9781616960186. A thoughtfully selected group of stories representing the wide ranging Urban Fantasy subgenre, divided by Beagle and Lansdale into three sections: Mythic Fiction, Paranormal Romance, and Noir Fantasy. Each section presents an introductory essay by a master in that niche. While not as massive as some anthologies out there, the editors have scored some of the cream of the crop of Urban Fantasy writers and offer stories by Patricia Briggs, Charles de Lint, Neil Gaiman, Al Sarrantonio, Emma Bull, and more.

Brown, Charles N., and Strahan, Jonathan, eds. *The Locus Awards: Thirty Years of the Best in Science Fiction and Fantasy.* Harper, 2004. 528p. 9780060594268. A not to be missed collection of Locus Award–winning short fiction spanning 30 years of the prestigious award. It includes stories by Neil Gaiman, Gene Wolfe, Octavia Butler, Ursula K. Le Guin, and George R. R. Martin.

Dan, Jack, and Dozois, Gardner, eds. *Wizards: Magical Tales from the Masters of Modern Fantasy.* Berkley, 2007. 416p. 9780425215180. It contains 18 stories from some of the most celebrated Fantasy authors working today, including Peter S. Beagle, Neil Gaiman, and Gene Wolfe. Gaiman's "The Witch's Headstone" is of particular note since the author went on to develop it into the children's Fantasy novel *The Graveyard Book*, which won the Newbery Award in 2009.

Datlow, Ellen, ed. *Naked City: Tales of Urban Fantasy.* St. Martin's Griffin, 2011. 560p. 9780312604318. This work has an edgy setting of city life with magic. It includes stories by Jim Butcher and Naomi Novik.

Datlow, Ellen, and Windling, Terri, eds.

🏵 *Salon Fantastique: Fifteen Original Tales of Fantasy.* Running Press, 2006. 352p. 9781560258339. Contains 15 stories by Peter S. Beagle, Gavin Grant, Jeffrey Ford, and Gregory Maguire, and others. Winner of World Fantasy Award in 2007.

The Year's Best Fantasy and Horror. Published annually from 1988 through 2008, this series of massive anthologies presented the crème de la crème of the year's crop of Fantasy and Horror short works. Until 2002, Ellen Datlow and Terri Windling edited the collections. From 2002 until the series ended, Kelly Link and Gavin Grant took over for Windling.

Datlow, Ellen, Gavin Grant, and Link, Kelly, eds. *The Year's Best Fantasy and Horror 2008: 21st Annual Collection*. St. Martin's, 2008. 576p. 9780312380472. 2008 was unfortunately the last year for this outstanding annual anthology.

Dozois, Gardner, and George R. R. Martin, eds. *Songs of the Dying Earth: Stories in Honor of Jack Vance.* Tor, 2010. 672p. 9780765320865. This book contains 22 new stories inspired by Jack Vance's classic *The Dying Earth*, first published over 60 years ago. It includes stories by Dean Koontz, Neil Gaiman, Tanith Lee, Tad Williams, Robert Silverberg, and a preface by Jack Vance himself.

🏵 **Ford, Jeffrey.** *The Drowned Life*. HarperPerennial, 2008. 320p. 9780061435065. Includes the stories "The Drowned Life," "Ariadne's Mother," "The Night Whiskey," "A Few Things about Ants," "Under the Bottom of the Lake," "Present from the Past," "The Manticore Spell," "The Fat One," "The Dismantled Invention of Fate," "What's Sure to Come," "The Way He Does It," "The Scribble Mind," "The Bedroom Light," "In the House of Four Seasons," "The Dreaming Wind," and "The Golden Dragon." Winner of the World Fantasy Award for Best Collection.

🏵 **Fowler, Karen Joy.** *What I Didn't See: And Other Stories.* Small Beer Press, 2010. 256p. 9781931520683. Although she may best be known for her bestselling *The Jane Austen Book Club*, Fowler also has a deft hand with Speculative Fiction as she demonstrates in this story collection that won the 2011 World Fantasy Award for Best Collection.

Gaiman, Neil. *Fragile Things: Short Fictions and Wonders*. William Morrow, 2006. 400p. 9780060515225. In an eclectic mix of poetry and stories, Gaiman is sometimes brilliant and always interesting. The work includes "Monarch of the Glen," a short story set in the *American Gods* universe, and "Instructions," one of Gaiman's most beloved poems, which was later turned into a picture book illustrated by Charles Vess.

Gaiman, Neil, and Al Sarrantonio, eds. *Stories: All-New Tales*. William Morrow, 2010. 448p. 9780061230929. This work contains Elizabeth Hand's "The Maiden Flight of McCauley's Bellerophon," which won the 2011 World Fantasy Award for a Novella, and Joyce Carol Oates' "Fossil-Figures," which won for Short Stories.

Guran, Paula, ed. *The Year's Best Dark Fantasy & Horror, 2012 Edition*. Prime Books, 2011. 544p. 9781607013440. Filling the gap left by the demise of St. Martin's Year's Best Fantasy and Horror series, the highly regarded Guran, winner of several awards, compiles the best short fiction for fans of dark fantasy and Horror. It began in 2010.

🎗 **Kaye, Marvin.** *The Fair Folk: Six Tales of the Fey*. Ace, 2007. 448p. 9780441014811. It includes the stories "Uous" by Tanith Lee, "Grace Notes" by Megan Lindholm, "The Gypsies in the Wood" by Kim Newman, "The Kelpie" by Patricia A. McKillip, "An Embarrassment of Elves" by Craig Shaw Gardner, and "Except the Queen" by Jane Yolen and Midori Snyder. It won a 2007 World Fantasy Award.

Klages, Ellen. *Portable Childhoods: Stories*. Tachyon, 2007. 210p. 9781892391452. Contains 15 stories examining the dangers and treasures of childhood. It includes an excerpt from the author's debut novel *The Green Glass Sea*, and an introduction by Neil Gaiman.

Martin, George R. R.

Dreamsongs: Volume I. Bantam, 2007. 704p. 9780553805451.
Dreamsongs: Volume II. Bantam, 2007. 752p. 9780553806588.

Two massive volumes of Martin's shorter work spanning many genres. With commentary by the author, these are not to be missed for fans of the creator of the brilliant <u>Song of Ice and Fire Series</u>.

November, Sharyn, ed.

YA <u>Firebirds</u>. The common thread that unites the stories in the three volumes of this ongoing series is that their authors have been published under the Firebird imprint. November, Editorial Director for Firebird Books, has worked with dozens of bestselling and award-winning authors of fantasy and Science Fiction.

🏆 *Firebirds: An Anthology of Original Fantasy and Science Fiction*. Firebird, 2003. 432p. 9780142501429. Authors include Nancy Springer, Lloyd Alexander, Garth Nix, Diana Wynn Jones, and many others. World Fantasy Award winner.

Firebirds Rising: An Original Anthology of Science Fiction and Fantasy. Firebird, 2006. 544p. 9780142405499. This work includes stories by Emma Bull, Sharon Shinn, Tanith Lee, and Tamora Pierce.

Firebirds Soaring: An Anthology of Original Speculative Fiction. Firebird, 2009. 592p. 9780142405529. The third in the Firebirds Series offers 19 original stories from such authors as Jane Yolen, Adam Stemple, Nancy Farmer, and Nancy Springer.

Straub, Peter, ed.

🏆 *American Fantastic Tales: Terror and the Uncanny from Poe to the Pulp*. Library of America, 2009. 750p. 9781598530476. This is an ambitious roundup of American Horror and Dark Fantasy classic short fiction. The two volumes were awarded the World Fantasy Award in 2010.

🏆 *American Fantastic Tales: Terror and the Uncanny from the 1940s to Now*. Library of America, 2009. 750p. 9781598530483.

Van Gelder, Gordon, ed.

The Very Best of Fantasy & Science Fiction: Sixtieth Anniversary Anthology. Tachyon, 2009. 480p. 9781892391919. The impact of *F&SF* on its represented genres cannot be overstated. Dipping into 60 years of publishing, Van Gelder has assembled an extraordinary collection of stories that have now become classics. Stephen King's immense Dark Tower Series had its genesis with "The Gunslinger," first published in 1978. Daniel Keye's beautiful and tragic "Flowers for Algernon" was originally published in *F&SF* and is now taught in classrooms. It includes stories by Ray Bradbury, Neil Gaiman, Shirley Jackson, Roger Zelazny, and many others.

Wolfe, Gene

🏆 *The Best of Gene Wolfe: A Definitive Retrospective of His Finest Short Fiction*. Tor, 2009. 480p. 9780765321350. An enormous retrospective of the World Fantasy for Life Achievement Honoree and Science Fiction Hall of Fame Inductee's short stories. This collection won the 2010 Locus and World Fantasy Awards; many of the stories contained in this volume are award winners in their own right. Wolfe has been cited as being influential by many speculative writers and is considered by many critics to be one of the finest writers in any genre.

RESOURCES

Genre Guides

Burgess, Michael, and Lisa R. Bartle. *Reference Guide to Science Fiction, Fantasy, and Horror*. Libraries Unlimited, 2002.

Fichtelberg, Susan. *Encountering Enchantment: A Guide to Speculative Fiction for Teens*. Libraries Unlimited, 2007.

Herald, Diana Tixier, and Bonnie Kunzel. *Fluent in Fantasy: The Next Generation*. Libraries Unlimited, 2008.

Lynn, Ruth Nadelman. *Fantasy Literature for Children and Young Adults: A Comprehensive Guide*. Libraries Unlimited, 2005.

Stableford, Brian M. *Historical Dictionary of Fantasy Literature*. Scarecrow Press, 2005.

Stableford, Brian M. *A to Z of Fantasy Literature*. Scarecrow Press, 2009.

Stevens, Jen, and Dorothea Salo. *Fantasy Authors: A Research Guide*. Libraries Unlimited, 2008.

Encyclopedias

Clute, John, and John Grant. *Encyclopedia of Fantasy*. St. Martin's, 1997.

D'Ammassa, Don. *Encyclopedia of Fantasy and Horror Fiction*. Facts on File. 2006.

Pringle, David. *The Ultimate Encyclopedia of Fantasy*. Carlton, 2006.

Westfahl, Gary. *The Greenwood Encyclopedia of Science Fiction and Fantasy: Themes, Works, and Wonders*. Greenwood, 2005.

Conferences and Conventions

There are many conferences and conventions for fans of fantasy. They are often combined with Science Fiction as the two genres have a long history of being lumped together. The cons run a full gamut of scholarly to pop culture. One of the major draws for Fantasy readers is the chance to meet the authors and attend readings of their works, often from forthcoming books. Many communities host smaller cons and usually feature authors of interest to Fantasy readers.

Dragon*Con. http://dragoncon.org. This huge popular media convention focusing on Science Fiction and Fantasy is held annually in Atlanta. It has tracks for SF and Fantasy Literature, Robert Jordan's <u>Wheel of</u>

Time, and Tolkien's Middle Earth among dozens of other tracks. Many authors attend. Because of the huge number of attendees who go in costume, it often makes the news; however, they are few and far between in the tracks focusing on written Fantasy.

LeakyCon. http://www.leakycon.com. Started as a Harry Potter conference, it is now a pop-culture convention for fans. It is held in different cities each year.

Readercon. http://readercon.org/. The emphasis at this Massachusetts convention is written Science Fiction and Fantasy. Many authors attend.

Sirens. http://www.sirensconference.org. It is a conference on women in Fantasy literature. It is more of a scholarly conference than a fan convention appealing to writers and scholars.

World Fantasy Convention. http://www.worldfantasy.org. It awards the World Fantasy Award and emphasizes literature and art rather than media. It is held in a different city every year. 2012 is in Toronto, Canada, and the 2013 convention is planned for Brighton in the United Kingdom. Many authors, editors, scholars, and collectors attend with membership limited to 850.

World Science Fiction Convention. http://www.wsfs.org. Members of the convention vote on the Hugo Awards that are awarded at the convention. Even though Fantasy is not in the name, it is included. Many authors attend. The 2013 convention will be held in San Antonio, Texas.

Awards

Pretty much everything one needs to know about Fantasy awards can be found at the Locus Magazine's Award site, http://www.locus mag.com/SFAwards/index.html

Major awards include the following:

British Fantasy Award. http://www.britishfantasysociety.co.uk. It is awarded annually in several categories. Before 2012, the best novel award was called the August Derleth Award. In 2012, the procedure changed to award the Robert Holdstock Award for best fantasy novel and the August Derleth Award for best Horror novel.

Hugo Awards. www.wsfs.org/hugos.html. It is awarded by the World Science Fiction Society (which is made up of registrants for the World Science Fiction Convention, anyone who registers can vote). There are several categories including best short story, best novella, best novel, etc. The works considered may be Fantasy, Science Fiction, Horror, or Paranormal.

Locus Poll Awards. http://www.locusmag.com/SFAwards/Db/Locus.html. It is *Locus Magazine*'s annual readers' poll. It does have a category for best Fantasy novel as well as several other categories.

Mythopoeic Awards. http://www.mythsoc.org/awards/. It is awarded at the annual Mythcon by the Mythopoeic Society, which "is a national/international organization promoting the study, discussion, and enjoyment of fantastic and mythopoeic literature through books and periodicals, annual conferences, discussion groups, awards, and more. We are especially interested in the works of J.R.R. Tolkien, C. S. Lewis, and Charles Williams, prominent members of the informal Oxford literary circle known as the 'Inklings' (1930s–1950s)." Between 1971 and 1992, one award was given annually, since then they award one for an adult work and one for a work written for youth. Its award site is a good resource as they list all winners over the years and also all the finalists. Member of the society nominate titles, and a panel of judges select the winners.

Nebula Awards. http://www.sfwa.org/nebula-awards/. "The Nebula Awards® are voted on, and presented by, active members of Science Fiction and Fantasy Writers of America, Inc." Categories are Novel, Novella, Novelette, Short Story, Ray Bradbury Award, and Andre Norton Award.

World Fantasy Award. http://www.worldfantasy.org/awards/. This award is given for the categories of novel, novella, short story, anthology, and collection. The winners are chosen by a panel of five judges appointed by the World Fantasy Administration. Nominations are made by members of the current convention and two most recent conventions.

FIVE FAN FAVORITES

- Black, Holly, and Ellen Kushner, eds. *Welcome to Bordertown: New Stories and Poems of the Borderlands*—Urban Fantasy

- Gaiman, Neil. *American Gods*—Legends, Myths, and Fairytales

- Murakami, Haruki. *Kafka on the Shore*—Mythic Reality

- Martin, George, R. R. *A Song of Ice and Fire*—Epic Fantasy

- Novik, Naomi. <u>Temeraire</u>—Alternate and Parallel Worlds

Chapter 14

Horror

Kelly Fann

Since then, at an uncertain hour,
That agony returns;
And till my ghastly tale is told,
This heart within me burns.

—*The Rime of the Ancient Mariner*
by Samuel Taylor Coleridge

The standard response when asking an individual if they read Horror tends to be a variation of one of two: "Yes! I love it!" or "No. I do NOT read that stuff." Naturally, I fall in the former category. By day, I lead the normal life as a library director—smiling, cheerful, and helpful to everyone I meet. By night, my ears begin to change shape, my teeth elongate into fine points, and well, no. That's not true. By night, I'm still a librarian, but also a wife and a mother of two furry children. I just happen to also curl up with a good scary book every chance I get and have for as long as I can remember.

Reading Horror does not make one perverse. It does not, and should not, label a reader a psychopathic, with unusually creepy interests in gore and violence. Lovers of Horror are normal, everyday people from all walks of life, who absolutely love a good scare. And that's what it's all about with Horror: allowing readers to face their fears in a safe environment. Horror is an emotion and many people absolutely love to be scared.

DEFINITION

What is Horror? Quite simply, horror is an emotion. Webster's Collegiate Dictionary defines Horror as a "painful and intense fear, dread, or dismay." Unlike many other genres that deal with intellect, actions, and plots, Horror

Fiction is an emotional genre. Just as Romance elicits emotional responses of love, lust, and passion, Horror elicits emotional responses of fear, terror, and trepidation. As Tina Jens states in *On Writing Horror: A Handbook* (2007), Horror is not purely about the story's plot, it is about "how people react when they encounter the plot." With that in mind, the Horror genre is not only easy to define, but also easy to identify and understand: it is all about the fear. Horror writers bring our nightmares to life within the pages of their novels, providing readers an opportunity to face their fears in a safe environment.

It is important to note that this chapter deals with fictive Horror stories. The true-life horrors of the world—Nazi's persecution of gypsies, Jews, homosexuals, and handicapped; famine in Somalia; crime headlines on TV—are not explored.

CHARACTERISTICS AND APPEAL

Why do people voluntarily choose to read about things we naturally despise, are revolted by, and wish to avoid in our everyday realities? Horror is a paradox and many have tried to explain the devotion of Horror fans to the genre. There is a large body of scholarly work that delves into the complexities of a genre that deliberately seeks to upset the reader. Numerous theories seek to explain why Horror is pleasurable for readers. Sociologist and psychologists have time and again exerted their theories. Noel Carroll attributes fascination of Horror to the cognitive interest of curiosity. James B. Twitchell defends the idea that Horror isn't so much about the scare contained within as the stories serve as cautionary tales of what not to do. In laymen's terms, without overly convoluting the joys of Horror, a good number of people enjoy being scared for no other reason than relishing in the terrifying chill Horror novels produce. For theoretical insights into Horror's appeal, I suggest reading *The Philosophy of Horror: Or, Paradoxes of the Heart* by Noel Carroll (1990).

Horror stories serve as an escape for fans of the genre. Unlike real-life horrors, fictionalized stories that are chock full of terrifying thrills and chills allow readers to experience the uncertainties of the unknown, creatures found only in nightmares, and the fear of death in a safe haven with the choice to close the book, look away, and return to life's normalcy at any time. Horror shakes us up and tests our comfort levels, but it leaves us unscathed once we set the book back down. In this respect, what constitutes Horror depends very much on the individual reader. What may frighten one reader will not necessarily frighten all readers. What scares each of us is very personal; Horror IS personal.

What Happens in Horror Stories?

Horror stories often have many identifying characteristics that enhance their primary purpose of fear evocation. The physical settings in Horror stories are often in ruination and dilapidation (or will soon become that way). Settings and emotional states of characters are often dark, dreary, and gloomy. Many Horror stories employ the use of the supernatural, such as ghosts, haunted houses, possession, vampires, the occult, and zombies. The Horror genre can depict scenes of violence, gore and graphic sex with the use of strong language. I stress, however, that while Horror novels do employ these elements, each element is not present in all Horror novels. *American Psycho* (1991) by Bret Easton Ellis does not contain any supernatural elements; *The Lottery* (1948) by Shirley Jackson contains little gore, graphic violence, or sex; and *The Off Season* (2006) by Jack Ketchum contains every single one of these components. Bearing this in mind, it is important to know what readers are looking for in their next novel to read, and how much gore, violence, and sex they can handle.

As Horror novels strive to induce fear in the reader, the settings will be dark and eerie, the tone will be laced with foreboding and dread, the story's pace will be quick, and the antagonist is typically some form of monster—be it supernatural or of the human evil variety. In Thomas Harris's *Silence of the Lambs* (1988), Dr. Hannibal Lecter embodies the evil capable of lurking in our fellow man. In Cormac McCarthy's *The Road* (2006), mankind is thrown into a postapocalyptic hell on earth in which mankind succumbs to horrific methods of survival. The monsters in these two novels exhibit no supernatural aspects, but they still evoke an incredible amount of terror in the reader. Harris and McCarthy meet the only true requirement of Horror: their stories produce an emotional reaction of terror.

The one narrative element found in nearly all Horror stories is the element of suspense. Another element key to Horror stories is the process of proof and discovery. Horror stories maintain the interest of readers by offering tidbits and pieces of information about the unknown. Combine suspense and discovery to the main characteristic of surprise, and you have yourself a blueprint for a Horror novel success.

Expect the unexpected in Horror novels. The element of surprise is extremely important in Horror novels. For the reader to feel a sense of menace and for the story to garner an emotional response from the reader, surprise must take hold at some point in the story. Throughout the tale, the reader will develop a sense of foreboding, which invokes a feeling of dread. The foreboding moves the story forward as the jolts of surprise jump out to keep the reader interested. Often, the pacing of Horror novels is quite quick, which leaves the reader feeling a sense of urgency, of heart-pounding dread, and of an overwhelming need to turn the next page as quickly as possible in order to know what happens next.

Another important characteristic of Horror is the ending, as the story is never really resolved. Sure, the story has ended, but the evil, the monster, isn't quite gone yet. The evil may be beaten down, but it has not been completely defeated and continues to lurk just beneath the shadows, waiting to emerge. There is no true happy ending in Horror novels. This particular characteristic makes genreblending with Romance particularly difficult, as Romance typically ends on a happy note. Paranormal Romance (see Romance within this chapter) has emerged as a new subgenre, which includes the supernatural elements along with the dark settings and characters of Horror, and often do not end on an entirely happy note. Laurell K. Hamilton's <u>Anita Blake Vampire Hunter Series</u> is an example of a Paranormal Romance that employs Horror elements.

Genreblending

The elements found in Horror stories make Horror an easy genre to genreblend. Fantasy, Science Fiction, Mystery, and Suspense novels can easily incorporate horrific elements and vice versa. Most bookstores don't have a particular genre section for Horror stories and many libraries who shelve according to genre don't have a section dedicated to Horror. This is because Horror blends so easily into other genres. The *New York Times* bestseller list regularly lists Mainstream Fiction titles that are also considered to be Horror novels. Stephen King is regularly on the bestseller list alongside Dean Koontz, Scott Sigler, and Dan Simmons. If a reader desires to read outside his normal genre, check to see if any of his favorite stories contain touches of Horror and match his tastes to something new in the Horror genre. If a Science Fiction fan wants to move into Horror, *The Devil's Alphabet* by Daryl Gregory (2009) can help her make the shift. For the Mystery and Suspense fans, Psychological Horror can be a good fit. Clive Barker has several novels that work with the Fantasy genre. The blending ability of Horror makes it a fantastic genre to segue into new reading territory.

BRIEF HISTORY

While it is by no means the first tale to have horrific scenes and elements in the narrative (think Shakespeare), the first true Horror novel is considered to be Horace Walpole's *The Castle of Otranto* written in 1764, for it sparked a flurry of subsequent Gothic Horror novels after its publication. Gary Hoppenstand notes in *The Guide to the United States Popular Culture* (2001) that it was Walpole's Gothic formula that became "the dominant type of Horror Fiction for a number of years." Forsooth, Walpole's writing spawned Mary Shelley's *Frankenstein* (1818), Bram Stoker's *Dracula* (1897), Robert Louis Stevenson's *The Strange Case of Dr. Jekyll and Mr. Hyde* (1886), and as a flurry of poetry from Lord Byron, Samuel Taylor Coleridge, Edgar Allan Poe, and many other authors into the early 1900s.

The trend continued upward, however gradually on into the mid-1900s bringing forth some of the classic authors that continue to reign supreme in the Horror cannon: H. P. Lovecraft, Shirley Jackson, Richard Matheson, William Peter Blatty, and Ira Levin. The full-fledged explosion of Horror didn't occur until Stephen King showed up with *Carrie* in 1974.

It is no surprise that Stephen King transformed the world of Horror. Prior to his emergence in the literary scene, bookstores, libraries, and publishers lumped Horror in with Mainstream Fiction. The Horror Writer's Association notes that as King's popularity grew, however, publishers discovered the lucrative Horror market, which brought about an amazing boom to the genre in the 1980s. It sparked numerous eruptions of small publishing houses specializing in the gritty genre. With the help of the 1980s Horror flicks in the theaters, the Horror genre exploded back onto the scene. Horror's popularity continued to grow with each year; however, in *On Writing Horror* (2007), Mort Castle describes the genre's decline during the 1990s as Horror failed to evolve as a literary genre. In the last decade, however, the decline of Horror's popularity has ended and is now picking up steam once again with a huge push into Mainstream Fiction. Small publishing presses are specializing in pulp Horror tales that are gathering followers and sparking intense conversations and shaking up the fiction world.

Benchmark Titles

1. *Books of Blood* by Clive Barker. Berkley Trade, 1998. 528p. 9780425165584.

2. *The Shining* by Stephen King. Doubleday, 1977. 447p. 0743424425.

3. *Phantoms* by Dean Koontz. Berkley, 1983. 448p. 0425181103.

4. *Hell House* by Richard Matheson. Viking, 1971. 288p. 0312868855.

5. *Ghost Story* by Peter Straub. Coward, McCann & Geoghegan, 1979. 483p. 9780698109599.

6. *Necroscope* by Brian Lumley. Grafton, 1986. 511p. 9780586066652.

7. *Rosemary's Baby* by Ira Levin. Random House, 1967. 245p. 9780965723176.

8. *Summer of Night* by Dan Simmons. Putnam Adult, 1991. 555p. 978 0399135736.

CURRENT TRENDS

Zombies

Zombies have been around for decades since William Seabrook's *The Magic Island* (1929) that chronicled the use of voodoo to raise corpses from the grave for cheap labor. In the last few years, however, zombie-themed novels (and movies, video games, music, community events, and art) have been exploding onto the market with no abatement in sight. Zombies pose a blank slate for authors to expound upon creating a wide variety of Horror literature available with extremely new and inventive themes. George Mann's *The Affinity Bridge* (2008) is a zombie Steampunk novel set in an alternate 1900s London. *World War Z* (2006) chronicles a global zombie epidemic as it spreads across the globe (soon to be made into a movie). In *Cell* (2006) by Stephen King, zombies are created by cell phone pulses. *Monster Island* (2006) has a zombie holocaust. If it can be thought up, it can be incorporated with zombies into a delightfully scary tale. At this point, zombie titles are hitting the market almost daily creating a wide readership, including a fan base that would typically not consider themselves to be Horror readers.

Mashup Novels

Max Brooks has capitalized on the zombie movement with *A Zombie Survival Guide: Recorded Complete Protection from the Living Dead* (2003) and moved it into an entirely new arena with the onset of Horror mashups. Mashup novels combine Horror with everything from the classics such as *Pride and Prejudice and Zombies* (2009) and *Sense and Sensibility and Sea Monsters* (2009) to *Android Karenina* (2010) and *Abraham Lincoln: Vampire Hunter* (2010). The influence of zombies in the mashup literature is quite obvious with titles like *Alice in Zombieland* (2009) and *US Army Zombie Combat Skills* (2009). The mashups are done incredibly well; the cohesiveness of an added supernatural element to the classic work blends extremely fluidly shedding an interesting twist to classic pieces.

Graphic Novel Format

Speaking of zombies, with the prime time network pickup for The Walk-ing Dead Graphic Novel series, the interest in Graphic Novels has risen considerably. Many libraries already had <u>The Walking Dead Series</u> on their shelves, but with the creation of the new television series, circulations of the series has skyrocketed. The best part in the skyrocketing is the creation of new Graphic Novel readers, and once they got hold of this series, they wanted more. Fortunately, many other well-known authors were there to supply more titles. Joe Hill's <u>Locke & Key Series</u> and Scott Snyder and Stephen King's <u>American Vampire Series</u> brings vampires back to the evil creatures we once knew them to be. You get the tale as well as the imagery with Graphic Novels, and Horror stories have great images to portray.

Other Horror Graphic Novels include David Gallaher and Steve Ellis's <u>High Moon Series</u> where the Wild West meets werewolves, Stephen King's <u>Dark Tower Series</u>, which is a spin-off of his novels, and <u>Black Hole</u> by Charles Burns, which explores a plague transmitted by sex affecting teenagers and causing a murderous rampage to ensue. The <u>30 Days of Night Series</u> by Steve Niles details an Alaskan town that spends 30 days out of the year in complete darkness, which vampires view as the ultimate all-you-can-eat buffet situation. Garth Ennis's <u>Preacher Series</u> might be the original Horror Graphic Novel series that showcases the escapades of disillusioned preacher Jesse Custer, his girlfriend Tulip, and his vampire buddy Cassidy. The <u>Lucifer Series</u> by Mike Carey explores Lucifer Morningstar's attempts at playing God to take vengeance upon his enemies. The <u>Graphic Classic Series</u> takes on classic stories like those by H. P. Lovecraft, *Frankenstein*, and *Dracula* and recreates them in Graphic Novel format.

Vampires Back to Being Baddies

Speaking of vampires being bad again, this is another trend those in the Horror circles are happy to see return. Vampires are no longer heart throbs, hopeless romantics that attempt to overcome their burden of being bloodsuckers and life-takers. In *Blood Groove* by Alex Bledsoe (2009), vampires are set in 1970s Memphis with all sorts of sexist, racist, visceral, and violent acts. <u>The Passage</u> (2009) trilogy by Justin Cronin (book two came out in October 2012) has vampire creatures being at the very top of the food chain with incredible strength and speed, which is a perfect combination for killing off the world. There is a flurry of other titles that have hit the shelves or are hitting the shelves soon, and they have one common denominator—vampires are to be feared, not revered.

Series

Along with Justin Cronin's <u>The Passage</u> series as well as the aforementioned Graphic Novel series, numerous other authors are continuing the fright in series format. The idea of a fictional series is a trend in all genres, including Horror. It is a way for the public to find comfort and familiarity with something they can count on. Once a reader finds a book she enjoys, having an entire series to engage in is quite enticing. Joe McKinney's Dead World Series focuses on a zombie virus, while Jonathan Maberry's *Pine Deep Trilogy* (2006) explores serial killers and supernatural evils. There is a series devoted to vampire viruses (Guillermo del Toro's The Strain Trilogy, 2009) and another devoted to societal breakdowns with violent killers running rampant (David Moody's Hater series, 2010). Just like other genres, the Horror genre has a series covering any subgenre or theme you can think of.

Paranormal Romance

A trend leaning away from Horror is that of Paranormal Romance. Authors such as Laurell K. Hamilton with her Anita Blake Vampire Hunter Series and Sherrilyn Kenyon with her Dark Hunter Series have yielded their own readership beyond that of the Horror genre. Initially, authors and stories such as these would be categorized as Horror, but increasingly, they find their home in a separate genre altogether. Bookstores now have separate sections for Paranormal Romance, Urban Fantasy, or Dark Fantasy. While these stories contain supernatural and paranormal elements, their underlying intent is not to cause fear in the reader.

THEMES AND TYPES

Key to Horror Fiction

Gothic
Paranormal
Psychological
Visceral
Humor

Horror stories can run the gamut when it comes to themes, provided the theme is scary. Some of the more common themes that will be found in Horror novels are the following:

Ghosts and Haunted Houses: These tales will have spirits, specters, poltergeists, sightings of ghosts, or the house itself manifests paranormal activities.

Paranormal Monsters: Zombies, vampires, ghouls, golems, were-wolves, mutant creatures, mythic creatures, and other terrifying animals of terror wreak havoc on the living humans.

Human Monsters: Serial killers, rapists, psychopaths, and cannibals stalk us as we try to lead our normal lives.

Occultism and Possessions: Demons, Satanism, sorcery, witchcraft, witches, and warlocks attempt to reign supreme.

Apocalyptic and Postapocalyptic: The end is nigh, or it is on its way. The world is in chaos, destroyed by nukes, humankind's neglect of the planet, an alien invasion, or any other multitude of ways, and only a few survivors are left to make sense of it all.

Scientific and Biomedical: Cell phones kill with a ringtone, watch a movie and die 24 hours later, genetic engineering has created the ultimate killing machine; if it involves technology or technological advancements, chances are likely you'd be better off without them!

Gothic

Horror's roots are founded in Gothic fiction dating back as far the late 1700s; however, the subgenre continues to be alive and well. What makes a story truly Gothic is the driving force in the story: romantic terror. Gothic Horror is about the sublime invoking feelings of awe and awful dread at the same time. The settings are beautifully dark, dreary, and full of decay; love is torturous and painful; and the tale is shrouded in mystery.

Ackroyd, Peter. *The Casebook of Victor Frankenstein*. Nan A. Talese, 2009. 268p. 9780385530842. A twist on the classic *Frankenstein* tale, Victor Frankenstein manages to reanimate the corpse of Jack Keat, which Frankenstein promptly abandons. The monstrosity of Keat seeks out revenge upon his creator. The cast in this tale includes Percy and Mary Shelley, Lord Byron, and Godwin.

Clegg, Douglas. *Neverland: A Novel*. Vanguard Press. 2010. 304p. 978 1593155414. A timeless, methodical tale set on Gull Island off the coast of Georgia. A seemingly innocuous shack in the woods makes the perfect clubhouse for the kids vacationing in the old Victorian house on the island. The shadowy specter the children call "Lucy" becomes their focus of worship with all the sacrifices that must be made to false gods.

Cottam, F. G. *The House of Lost Souls*. Thomas Dunne Books, 2009. 352p. 9780312544324. In London, during the 1920s, journalist Paul Seaton managed to escape an evil being summoned by Aleister Crowley in the haunted Fischer House. Ten years later, three philosophy students are on the verge of losing their minds after a trip to Fisher House, and now Seaton feels compelled to return there and finish off the evil lurking within once and for all.

de Maupassant, Guy. *The Dark Side: Tales of Terror and the Supernatural*. Carroll & Graf, 1989. 252p. 9780786704194. A collection of short stories that delve into supernatural elements while highlighting de Maupassant's own personal mental illness struggles. Darkly terrifying tales full of morbid pessimism, this compilation of stories remain more focused on de Maupassant's ability to develop terrifying illusions and illicit fear of the unknown—horrors of the mind versus horrors in manifestation.

Must Read

★ **Hill, Susan.** *The Man in the Picture*. Overlook, 2008. 160p. 9781590 200919. A traditional Gothic tale of a vengeful spirit trapped inside a painting. Current owner of the painting, Theo Parmitter discovers a former student taking a strong interest in the painting, which depicts an 18th-century Venetian carnival. In discussing the painting's history, Parmitter divulges that Lady Hawdon believes her husband is imprisoned in the painting by the hands of a jilted lover.

🎀 **Kiernan, Caitlin R.** *The Red Tree*. Roc Trade, 2009. 400p. 0451462769. Seeking solitude from her troubled life, writer Sarah Crow moves to an isolated house in Rhode Island. Inside the walls of her new home, Sarah finds an unfinished manuscript written by someone who became obsessed with the giant red oak growing on the property. Sarah, too, becomes obsessed with the oak's dark past. This was a Shirley Jackson Award finalist.

Lepore, Jacqueline. *Descent into Dust*. William Morrow Paperbacks, 2010. 384p. 006187812X. Vampires are back to being a real threat in this rural Victorian setting. Emma discovers her cousin's child Henrietta is a prime target for evil and Emma is steadfast in her desire to save Henrietta. Local folklore and legends are intermixed with ghostly presences, vampires, and dark secrets of the Catholic Church.

🎀 **Paffenroth, Kim.** *Valley of the Dead: The Truth Behind Dante's Inferno*. Permuted Press, 2010. 258p. 9781934861318. A chronicle of Dante Alighieri's life as he travels into hell to create *The Divine Comedy* and the truth is unearthed about all he witnessed during the 17 years in exile from Italy. A Black Quill Award nominee.

Simmons, Dan

🎗 *Drood*. Black Bay Books, 2010. 800p. 9780316007030. Set in the 1860s, *Drood* is narrated by Wilkie Collins, friend of Charles Dickens. It kicks off with Dickens rushing to the aid of victims of the train accident at Staplehurst. In the process, he meets a strange phantasm named Edwin Drood who pits friend against friend in their quest for immortality. It won the Black Quill Award.

🎗 *The Terror*. Little, Brown and Company, 2007. 784p. 9780316017442. An 1840s doomed expedition in search of the Northwest Passage strands the ships *Erebus* and *Terror* in packed ice. Shipmates begin to perish from the elements followed by madness and cannibalism, along with an animal of terror lurking on the ice. It was nominated for Black Quill and Bram Stoker Awards.

🎗 **Waters, Sarah.** *The Little Stranger*. Riverhead, 2009. 480p. 9781594488801. This haunted house tale begotten in post–World War II Britain spins a Gothic masterpiece of mental illness, suicides, and supernatural happenings ranging from fires to visions and unearthly sounds. A Shirley Jackson Award finalist and a Black Quill Award nominee.

Paranormal

Paranormal Horror novels encompass all that cannot be explained by scientific reason. Monsters, demonic possessions, and supernatural stories of ghosts and haunted houses can all fall under Paranormal Horror. Formats of Paranormal Horror stories vary wildly with many tales written as Graphic Novels and short stories as well as novellas and full-length novels.

Antosca, Nick. *Midnight Picnic*. Word Riot Press, 2009. 188p. 9780977934331. Adam Dovey, the ghost of a murdered 6-year-old boy, seeks the help of 22-year-old Bram to avenge his death by killing his murderer; however, mortal revenge isn't enough for Dovey. Instead, Dovey seeks out his murderer's soul in the afterlife.

🎗 **Barlow, Toby.** *Sharp Teeth*. Harper, 2008. 320p. 0061430226. A novel written in free verse depicting the seedy underbelly of Los Angeles as the home of warring werewolf packs. A fine depiction of

Horror meets Noir, this coming-of-age story is filled with hard-hitting cultural topics, dark humor, and sad romance as the werewolf packs rule the streets with crime. It won the Alex Award.

Bell, Alden. *The Reapers Are the Angels*. Tor, 2010. 302p. 9780230748644. Zombies overrun all of society and 15-year-old Temple knows no other life. Taking refuge in a safe house, Abraham Todd attacks Temple, who in turn murders him and then must flee Moses who seeks to avenge his brother's death. Temple's life on the lam finds Maury, a slow mute for whom she vows to care.

🏆 **Bens Jr., Paul G. *Kelland*.** Casperian Books, 2009. 252p. 9781934081198. Against the evil is Kelland. For each character in this tale, Kelland appears in a different form, but he is there to force these strangers, by whatever means, out from their dark nightmares of abuse, violence, and depravity and into the light. It won the Black Quill Award.

🏆 **Brannon, Jason. *The Cage*.** KHP Publishers, 2007. 240p. 9780976791492. A zoo full of animals of terror only heard of through legend has a few family visitors. Naturally, the animals of terror are having a feast on the unsuspecting human visitors, who are desperately trying to find their way out of the cage. A Black Quill Award nominee.

Brooks, Max

🎬 *World War Z: An Oral History of the Zombie War*. Crown, 2006. 352p. 9780307346605. The first zombie case is found in China, and the zombie outbreak quickly hits the rest of the globe as world leaders attempt to suppress information. First-person accounts outline the world's struggle against the zombies.

The Zombie Survival Guide: Recorded Attacks. Three Rivers Press, 2009. 144p. 9780307405777. This Graphic Novel depicts all recorded zombie attacks since the dawn of mankind. From 60,000 BC in Central Africa to Ancient Rome to 1960s Soviet Union, each "attack" is recorded in vivid detail through fantastic artwork that tells the story all on its own.

Brown, Eric S. *Season of Rot: Five Zombie Novellas*. Permuted Press, 2009. 262p. 9781934861226. Five zombie novellas are included in Brown's compilation. "Season of Rot" has survivors trapped in a hospital and "Queen" puts the survivors at sea. "Rats" has the vile vermin attempting to overtake humans by biting the dead and reanimating their own personal minion. "Dead West" sees the end of the Civil War, but the war hasn't ended against the undead. Energy from space turns nearly all of mankind into cannibals in "The Wave."

Cronin, Justin. *The Passage*. Ballantine Books, 2010. 800p. 9780345504975. The entire (futuristic) United States has succumbed to a government project gone wrong. What was supposed to create the ultimate super-soldier ends up creating a virus that causes the infected to become vampires, but not in the traditional sense. These vampires are mutations with superhuman strength, speed, and insect-like in movements and features. Book two in the trilogy, *The Twelve*, explores the original 12 infected with the virus. *The Twelve* was released in October 2012.

Del Toro, Guillermo

🎬 **The Strain Trilogy**. A vampiric virus plagues the world and it becomes a battle between humanity and vampires.

> *The Strain*. William Morrow, 2009. 416p. 9780061558238. The first volume in the trilogy describes the virus's onset after a plane lands at JFK airport with only four survivors, the remaining passengers and crewmembers having been drained of all their blood. The survivors find their way out in public begin spreading the vampiric virus.
>
> *The Fall*. William Morrow, 2010. 320p. 9780061558221. After Manhattan, the vampiric virus spreads and vampires seek to take over the world. Dr. Eph Goodweather from the Centers for Disease Control attempts to thwart the virus's contamination, while the Master sets in motion mass extermination of humans.
>
> *The Night Eternal*. William Morrow, 2011. 384p. 9780061558269. Dr. Goodweather and her band of freedom fighters set out to rescue the doctor's son, Zack, while attempting to overthrow the Master and his kind; however, a traitor in their midst throws them into chaos.

🎗 **Dunbar, Robert**. *Martyrs and Monsters*. DarkHart Press, 2009. 276p. 9780980100433. This collection of short stories includes a variety of genres ranging from Horror tales of vampires and zombies to Science Fiction and Fantasy. It won the Black Glover Horrorhead Award and was nominated for a Black Quill and Bram Stoker Awards.

🎗 **Elliot, Will**. *The Pilo Family Circus*. PS Publishing, 2008. 312p. 9781906301972. Who is scared of clowns? Anyone who reads this novel will be. Monstrous, evil, gruesome, dangerous, and diabolical clowns are just one evil element in *The Pilo Family Circus*, and the circus members only get more terrifying as the story unfolds. It was nominated as Best Novel by the International Horror Guild.

Gallaher, David, and Steve Ellis. *High Moon*. DC/Zuda, 2009. 192p. 9781401224622. The Wild West meets werewolves in this Graphic Novel series. When Colin MacGregor arrives in Blest, Texas, he has one goal: catch a man with a high bounty. It's not long before Colin is recruited to rescue a kidnapped girl finds himself immersed in supernatural terrors full of evil-winged creatures, bullets, and ferocious teeth.

Gifune, Greg F. *Children of Chaos*. Delirium Books, 2009. 298p. 9781934546079. As teenagers, Phil, Jamie, and Martin commit an unspeakable act against a strange man covered in scars. Their lives are thrown in turmoil 30 years later when they are forced to confront the evil they unleashed as teens, an antichrist bent on acquiring demonic power.

Must Read

★ 🎞 **Hill, Joe.** *Heart-Shaped Box*. William Morrow, 2007. 384p. 97800 61147937. A rock-and-roll star makes the worst decision of his life when he succumbs to his need for all things macabre and buys a haunted suit online. Chock full of rock references, this novel gives the seedy side to rock stars' antics a new twist. It won a Black Quill Award and was a Bram Stoker Award nominee.

Hill, Joe. *Horns*. William Morrow, 2010. 384p. 9780061147951. Sometimes random things happen. Sometimes you just wake up with a pair of horns sprouting from your forehead and discover those who come near you feel compelled to admit their darkest desires. And sometimes things like this come in handy when you're trying to track down who killed the love of your life.

Kenyon, Nate. *Sparrow Rock*. Leisure, 2010. 336p. 9780843963779. A group of teenagers have been hanging out in a bomb shelter, where they just happen to be when a nuclear holocaust wipes out pretty much everything on earth. Staying inside to avoid the fallout seems logical, but that doesn't prevent other life forms from getting inside.

Kirkman, Robert

🎞 **The Walking Dead Series**. The dead have risen to feed on the living, causing society to crumble. Rick Grimes and his band of survivors attempt to live life and find a safe haven after the zombie apocalypse. An exploration of humanity when pitted against survival.

The Walking Dead, Book 1. Image Comics, 2006. 304p. 9781582406190.
The Walking Dead, Book 2. Image Comics, 2007. 304p. 9781582406985.
The Walking Dead, Book 3. Image Comics, 2008. 304p. 9781582408255.
The Walking Dead, Book 4. Image Comics, 2009. 304p. 9781607060000.
The Walking Dead, Book 5. Image Comics, 2010. 304p. 9781607061717.
The Walking Dead, Book 6. Image Comics, 2011. 304p. 9781607063278.
The Walking Dead, Book 7. Image Comics, 2012. 304p. 9781607064398.
The Walking Dead, Book 8. Image Comics, 2012. 336p. 9781607065937.

Koryta, Michael. *So Cold the River*. Little, Brown and Co., 2010. 512p. 9780316053631. Filmmaker Eric Shaw treks to a small Indiana town on an easy money assignment to film a tribute to dying millionaire Campbell Bradford. Eric drinks a bottle of Pluto cure-all water bottled in 1929, which causes him to begin hallucinating sending his reality off-kilter as the past works its way to the present.

Kyogoku, Natsuhiko. *The Summer of the Ubume*. Vertical, 2009. 320p. 9781934287255. Translated by Alexander O. Smith. Akihiko "Kyogokudo" Chuzenji is an exorcist that doesn't believe in ghosts. Instead, Kyogokudo creates a placebo effect by staging his patients' exorcisms and thus, curing them, but now Kyogokudo's beliefs are put to the test when his next patient is a woman who has been pregnant for 20 months. A compelling tale full of Japanese folklore.

🎗 **Langan, Sarah**. *The Missing*. Headline, 2007. 352p. 9780755333721. When a grade-school teacher treks her students to Bedford for a field trip, she unknowingly exposes them all to a virus that transforms them into highly intelligent, insatiable, and terrifying creatures. It won the Black Quill and Bram Stoker Awards.

🎗 **LaValle, Victor**. *Big Machine*. Spiegel & Grau, 2009. 384p. 9780385527989. An ex-heroin addict and former child cult member accepts an invitation to join the Unlikely Scholars who investigate the supernatural, a choice that soon connects his present with his dark past. It won the Shirley Jackson Award.

Lindqvist, John Ajvide

Handling the Undead. Thomas Dunne Books, 2010. 384p. 9780312605254. An oppressive heat wave, bizarre electrical issues, and headaches for everyone plague residents in Stockholm. Once the problems disappear, anyone who has died in the last two months rises from the dead. Inhabitants of Stockholm are faced with the chilling prospects of what their loved ones have become.

▟ *Let Me In [Let the Right One In]*. Thomas Dunne Books, 2007. 472p. 9780312355289. Bullied 12-year-old Oskar is enthralled with grisly murders and enamored with his new neighbor Eli, who never seems to leave the house except at night. After her arrival, a series of killings ensues and Oskar discovers Eli's secret: she's a vampire who will never age beyond her childhood years. Is their friendship strong enough to survive the secret? Adapted to film in *Let the Right One In*.

Little, John R.

🎗 *Miranda*. Bad Moon Books, 2008. 108p. 9780982154601. Michael lives his life in reverse of the rest of us. We are born, we age, we die, but Michael has died and is now living his life back to his birth. Moving in the opposite direction makes connections with others difficult, that is, until he meets Miranda who lives life in the same pattern. But Miranda isn't happy with her fate. It won a Black Quill and a Bram Stoker Awards.

🎗 *The Memory Tree*. Nocturne, 2007. 319p. 9780977656073. Sam Ellis has been inexplicitly shoved back in time to 1968. He meets his 13-year-old self and his parents and is also forced to face the monsters plaguing his home town all over again. It was a Bram Stoker Award nominee.

🎗 Maitland, Karen. *The Owl Killers*. Delacorte Press, 2009. 528p. 9780385341707. A small village in 1300s England is besieged by famine, floods, and plagues, but a group of Christian women appear unaffected drawing the ire of the Owl Masters, a group of pagan worshipers. The Owl Masters seek the help from the mysterious Owlman, a harbinger of death and destruction. It was a Shirley Jackson Award finalist.

Neville, Adam. *Apartment 16*. Pan, 2010. 449p. 9780330514965. Apartment 16 has been empty for 50 years with no one entering or exiting the apartment in that time. When night watchman Seth investigates disturbances coming from the apartment, he is plagued with hallucinations, paranoia, and feels compelled to paint creations that open a portal into the Void.

🎗 Partridge, Norman. *Dark Harvest*. Cemetery Dance Publications, 2006. 169p. 9781587671470. A Halloween Horror hunt tale in which teenage boys strive for the ultimate prize: a ticket out of town. All they have to do is find and kill the pumpkin-headed being, October Boy, but can it be done without learning their town's horrifying secret? It was a Black Quill Award nominee.

Quinn, Bradd. *Under*. CreateSpace, 2009. 242p. 9781448679881. They're lurking under the shed, under the basement, under your deck, and they're waiting for their chance to feed on the entire town. Birds and small animal bones begin appearing across various lawns throughout the town, followed by the shredded corpse of a beloved pet. While the townspeople blame hungry wildlife, Jacob Drake remembers the instances leading up to the mass murders in Gaston. And then he spies the culprit. Drake has to overcome his debilitating fear of the dark to save not only his family, but also the entire town.

Sigler, Scott. *Infected*. Crown, 2008. 352p. 0307406105. Alien contagions reign down upon the city from outer space with a few taking hold and germinating inside their human hosts causing the victims to turn into paranoid, homicidal killers. CIA agent Dew Phillips teams up with CCID agent Margaret Montoya to catch up to the crazed, homicidal victims, but finding the cause or a cure is increasingly difficult when the infected bodies deteriorate and liquefy. It is a genreblending of Science Fiction, Horror, and Thriller.

Snyder, Scott, and Stephen King

American Vampire. Vertigo, 2010. 200p. 9781401228309. Two separate stories are included in this Graphic Novel illustrated by Rafael Albuquereque. The first written by Scott Snyder details a 1920s Los Angeles in which a young woman, Pearl, seeks out revenge on the vampires who turned her into a vampire through means of torture. The second tale written by Stephen King tells the tale of the original American Vampire, Skinner Sweet, powered by the sun living in the wild, wild West.

American Vampire, Vol. 2. Vertigo, 2011. 160p. 9781401230708. Skinner Sweet and Pearl discover the vampires in Hollywood have nothing on the gang awaiting them in Las Vegas.

American Vampire, Vol. 3. Vertigo, 2012. 288p. 9781401233334. Henry has been recruited by a vampire-hunting group, the Vassals of the Morning Star, to Japan during World War II. His mission is to track down a new breed of vampires.

Straub, Peter. *A Dark Matter*. Doubleday, 2010. 352p. 9780385516389. Four misguided youth choose to participate in an occult ritual with Spencer Mallon, but something goes terribly wrong leaving a group member dead and the portal to hell wide open. Decades later, each of the four teenagers tells their own stories of that night.

Zafón, Carlos Ruiz. *The Angel's Game*. Doubleday, 2009. 544p. 9780385528702. French editor Andreas Corelli gives Barcelonan author David Martín the opportunity of a lifetime: the chance to write a novel with a real power to affect the minds of all who read it, but not without a cost. David soon discovers that the mysterious afflictions that plague him and his home are deeply rooted to the novel he has agreed to pen.

Psychological

Psychological Horror brings forth human monsters, personal demons, maniacs, murderers, and serial killers, all of whom are quite likely people that would typically be trusted by those they perpetrate. These novels can also focus on personal guilt, mental illnesses, hallucinations, and a blurring of realities. Violence is often very prevalent in Psychological Horror.

Adams, Poppy. *The Sister*. Knopf, 2008. 288p. 9780307268167. When two estranged sisters, Virginia and Vivien Stone, reunite after 50 years, a torrent of lurid secrets spew forth as told from Virginia's point of view. *The Sister* is a psychological tale of one family's sadistic secrets that finally begin to unravel.

Bennett, Robert Jackson. *Mr. Shivers*. Orbit, 2010. 336p. 9780316054683. During the Great Depression, Marcus Connelly traverses the desolate and barren heartland searching for his child's murderer. Along the way, Marcus encounters other lives that Mr. Shivers has destroyed. Joining forces, vengeance overcomes those shattered by Mr. Shivers's actions and humanity appears all but lost.

🏅 **Cain, Chelsea.** *Heartsick*. St. Martin's Minotaur, 2007. 336p. 9780641944895. Detective Archie Sheridan seeks the help of serial killer Gretchen Lowell to find the person responsible for murdering teenage girls around Portland, Oregon. Reminiscent of Thomas Harris's *The Silence of the Lambs* (1988). A Black Quill Award nominee.

🏅 **Evenson, Brian.** *Last Days*. Underland Press, 2009. 256p. 9780980226003. Detective Kline is forced to investigate a murder inside an underground religious cult, which will be the ultimate test of his survival skills. It was a Shirley Jackson Award finalist and a Black Quill Award nominee.

Fitzek, Sebastian. *Therapy*. St. Martin's Press, 2008. 292p. 9780312382001. Translated by Sally-Ann Spencer. A man's quest to find his missing daughter puts him in the hands of a schizophrenic children's author whose story may contain the answer to the missing girl's whereabouts.

Gonzalez, J. F. *Survivor*. Midnight Library, 2006. 299p. 9780975514405. A kidnap victim is about to be used as a snuff film star in which her perpetrators plan to videotape her torturous demise, unless she can find a way to survive.

🎗 **Heim, Scott.** *We Disappear*. Harper Perennial, 2008. 320p. 9780739499955. Children keep disappearing in Kansas and Donna, dying of cancer, is mesmerized by the events. She calls her son Scott home to assist her in her quest, and Scott quickly succumbs to her blurring lines of reality. It won a Black Quill Award.

Hill, Joe, and Gabriel Rodriguez

Locke & Key. In this Graphic Novel series, a New England mansion dubbed "Keyhouse" is filled with fantastic doors that have the power to transform those who cross their thresholds. Keyhouse also houses an evil being who desperately desires to have the darkest door in the mansion opened.

#1 *Welcome to Lovecraft*. IDW Publishing, 2008. 152p. 9781600102370. After their father is murdered by Sam Lesser, siblings Tyler, Kinsey, and Bode Locke move in with their mother at the family's estate, Keyhouse, setting the stage for supernatural forces to come forth.

#2 *Head Games*. IDW Publishing, 2009. 160p. 9781600104831. Lucas Caravaggio, aka Zack Wells, tries to keep his identity a secret while he stealthily searches the Keyhouse for all of the hidden keys.

#3 *Crown of Shadows*. IDW Publishing, 2010. 152p. 9781600106958. Kinsey tries to unravel the secrets of her family's past, while Dodge seeks out the key to the black door.

#4 *Keys to the Kingdom*. IDW Publishing, 2011. 160p. 9781600108860. Tyler begins to suspect Zack is the cause of his family's recent troubles, but there's not much he can do at the moment as he has to face down Dodge.

#5 *Clockworks*. IDW Publishing, 2012. 152p. 9781613772270. This volume provides all the backstory before the final volume (Omega) is released. History of the keys, Keyhouse, the black door, and much more is explored.

Howard, Jonathan L. *Johannes Cabal the Necromancer*. Doubleday, 2009. 304p. 9780385528085. Sorcerers, vampires, carnivals, necromancy, zombies, and the Devil are all found in this darkly humorous novel. Johannes Cabal needs a soul to further his occult practices, so he makes a deal with the devil to serve up 100 souls in exchange for one of his own.

🎗 **Kenyon, Nate.** *The Reach*. Leisure Books, 2008. 276p. 9780843960211. Sara is psychokinetic and has been since birth, which landed her in an institution subjected to drug-induced experiments. It was a Bram Stoker Award nominee.

🎗 **King, Stephen.** *Duma Key*. Scribner, 2008. 592p. 1416552510. The power of art is a power to be reckoned with in this Psychological, Supernatural Thriller. It won a Black Quill Award and a Bram Stoker Award.

🎗 **Lamberson, Gregory.** *Johnny Gruesome*. Medallion Press, 2008. 400p. 9781934755457. A high school partier and troublemaker is found dead in his car, submerged in Willow Creek. While initial reports point to a mere car accident, the violent acts of vengeance that immediately follow say quite otherwise, and now all of Johnny's enemies and friends are in mortal peril. It won a Black Quill Award and was a Bram Stoker Award nominee.

Marshal, Michael. *Bad Things*. William Morrow, 2009. 384p. 006143440X. A young child and an older man have died with no real investigations taking place into their murders. But John Henderson has been contacted by a woman who says she knows the truth about what happened to his son and he must expose the truth before she, too, mysteriously dies.

🎗 **Sokoloff, Alexandra.** *The Unseen*. St. Martin's Press, 2009. 336p. 9780312384708. The emotionally traumatized professor protagonist seeks out the Folger House with the help of her coworkers to recreate a 1965 experiment gone tragically awry. Is the malign presence the work of a villainous human monster or actual paranormal happenings? This is a true Paranormal Psychological Horror novel. It was a Black Quill Award nominee and a MonsterLibrarian.com Top Pick.

___

Must Read

★ 🎗 **Sutherland, Joel.** *Frozen Blood*. Lachesis Publishing, 2008. 244p. 9781897370612. Tara Stewart is a girl with a gritty past of abusive and vindictive family members, who now has to face them all over again at her father's funeral. Then the storm begins to rage. Hail, ice, and snow make Tara a prisoner in the last place she wants to be: a house full of past demons, with a family unwavering in their desire to see her ultimate destruction. It was a Black Quill Award and a Bram Stoker Award nominee.

___

🎗 **Tremblay, Paul G.** *The Little Sleep*. Holt Paperbacks, 2009. 271p. 9780805088496. Private investigator Mark Genevich suffers from narcolepsy interlaced with increasingly realistic hallucinations. One of these hallucinations results in a series of racy photographs, of whom he can no longer pinpoint, nor can he pinpoint who actually gave him the photos, and why someone wants them back so badly. It was a Bram Stoker Award nominee.

Visceral

The Visceral subgenre is a new take on the 1980s Splatterpunk genre. It is comprised of everything in excess. Gore, violence, sexual violence, and language are all amplified. Tales kick off incredibly fast with a great deal of visceral gore at the onset that never once relents. Visceral tales are in it for the horrific shock value.

Barron, Laird. *The Imago Sequence and Other Stories*. Night Shade Books, 2007. 239p. 9781597800884. Visceral horrors emerge in each of the stories contained in Barron's collection. Tales of ritualistic serial killings, out of control occult forces, and crafty cult practices that assail art collectors assault protagonists facing inevitable doom.

Columbia, Al. *Pim & Francie: The Golden Bear Days*. Fantagraphics, 2009. 240p. 9781606993040. While they may look like harmless vintage cartoon drawings, the depictions of children Pim and Francie continually find them in extremely violent, body-mangling situations.

🎗 **Ennis, Garth, and Jacen Burrows.** *Crossed*. Avatar Press, 2010. 240p. 9781592910908. With no warning, people are transformed into bloodthirsty killers who enjoy murder, torture, and graphic sexual violence and take the United States en masse. *Crossed* chronicles those unfortunate enough to have survived the onslaught. Extremely graphic depictions portrayed. It won the Black Glove Horrorhead Award for Best Comic/Graphic Novel.

Keene, Brian

Dead Sea. Leisure Books, 2007. 337p. 9780843958607. A zombie virus thrives in New York City as it spreads through rat bites. Lamar Reed and a group of survivors make it to Baltimore where they commandeer a Cost Guard ship and head out to sea. Their haven inside the ship is tested as zombies desperately try to make their way inside.

🎗 *Castaways*. Leisure Books, 2009. 285p. 9780843960891. TV show contestants are stranded on an island filled with hideous, havoc-wreaking, inhuman creatures who seek out the female contestants for breeding purposes. It was a Black Quill Award nominee.

Ketchum, Jack. *Off Season*. Leisure Books, 2006. 308p. 9780843956962. A group of six head to Dead River for a vacation, but unbeknownst to them, they are about to be hunted by a clan of wild humans who are very, very hungry.

Kilborn, Jack. *Afraid*. Grand Central Publishing, 2009. 384p. 9780446535939. The government has created a special force of psychotic, modified killers called the Red-ops that has crash landed in a small town in Wisconsin and begins doing what they have been trained to do: maim, torture, and kill in the most horrifically gruesome methods imaginable.

🎖 **Landsale, Joe R.** *Leather Maiden*. Knopf, 2008. 304p. 9780375414527. Cason Statler is on a downward spiral and in desperate need of getting a handle on his life, so he heads home to Texas in an attempt to get back on track. His new job as a columnist for the Camp Rapture Report puts him on the case of a college student's disappearance where quickly discovers a slew of kinky sex crimes that appears to involve his brother. It was a Black Quill Award nominee.

Masterton, Graham. *Death Mask*. Leisure Books, 2009. 323p. 9780843957921. An untraceable, nonexistent killer is beating people to death. An artist creates paintings that come to life. The artist and her family and detectives on the case work together to bring an end to the Red Mask's terror.

McCammon, Robert

Matthew Corbett. The series takes place in 18th-century Carolina where law clerk Matthew Corbett faces unspeakable horrors and malevolent men as he attempts to solve heinous crimes of murder.

> *The Queen of Bedlam*. Pocket, 2007. 656p. 9781416552611. A criminal mastermind dubbed "the Master" tests Corbett's true calling as an investigator.
> *Mister Slaughter*. Subterranean, 2010. 440p. 9781596062764. Heinous killer Tyranthus Slaughter manages to escape as he is being transported to prison and leaves a bloody wake in his path.

Must Read

★ 🎞 **McCarthy, Cormac.** *The Road*. Knopf, 2006. 256p. 9780307265432. In the aftermath of the apocalypse, a man and his son take to the road toward the sea with the man only concerned about one thing: the survival of his son. In their quest, they travel through a nightmarish hell witnessing horribly gruesome sights with only one another to live for.

Mellick III, Carlton. *Apeshit*. Avant Punk Books, 2008. 196p. 9781933929767. The stereotypical Horror setting involving six teenagers, an isolated cabin, and a weekend of partying who come face to face with a murderous psycho who just won't die. The story line never relents with the gritty, grisly gore.

🎗 **Otsuichi.** *Zoo*. VIZ Media, 2009. 300p. 9781421525877. Science fiction and Horror meld together to bring forth 10 Japanese Horror short stories full of death, destruction, and decay. It was a Shirley Jackson Award finalist.

Peck, Dale. *Body Surfing*. Atria Books, 2009. 432p. 9781416576129. Demons with voracious appetites for sex are taking over Upstate New York. These Mograns prey on humans by taking possession of their victims until exiting their bodies at orgasm. During their possession, the victims are capable of recovering from major physical traumas.

🎗 **Schwaeble, Hank.** *Damnable*. Jove, 2009. 400p. 9780515146912. Special operative Jake Hatcher been accused of using his interrogation talents a bit too far finds himself in jail, but is quickly broken out by a brother he never knew he had. Jake then sets out on a dark, dangerous, and visceral path to use his skills against to uncover a sex cult, murder scenes perpetrated by humans and demons alike, and a billionaire fraught with dreams of the apocalypse. It won a Bram Stoker Award.

Humor

Horror novels imbued with dark comedy have created a Horror subgenre all their own. Anything can happen, and usually does, in Humorous Horror novels. Serial killers, mutant zombies, headless ghosts who can't stop vomiting, everything imaginable is found in the pages of Comedic Horror. Great acts of violence are softened by deadpan humor in laugh-out-loud scenarios.

Brown, Ryan. *Play Dead*. Gallery, 2010. 344p. 1439171300. A high school football team from Killington, Texas, is having an incredible season, so much so that rival town Elmwood deems it necessary to send the Killington football team bus into the river. The football coach and the star quarterback are the only survivors and they seek out the help of local witch to reanimate their dead teammates. This is a coming-of-age story full of comedic high school antic interludes while intermixed with a great deal of gore.

Cook, Nickolas, and Lewis Carroll. *Alice in Zombieland*. Coscom Entertainment, 2009. 132p. 9781926712291. Alice is in a bizarre world of zombies and monsters and must find her way back home before the Dead Red Queen catches her or worse, she turns into a zombie.

■ **Grahame-Smith, Seth.** *Abraham Lincoln: Vampire Hunter*. Grand Central Publishing, 2010. 336p. 9780446563086. Slave owners have allied with vampires, and our hero Abraham Lincoln sets out to destroy the vampires, and slavery along the way.

Grahame-Smith, Seth, and Jane Austen. *Pride and Prejudice and Zombies*. Quirk Books, 2009. 320p. 9781594743351. Hertfordshire is besieged by zombies and while the Bennett family makes time for romance, their quest to fight the onslaught of zombies never wavers.

Hansen, Mykle. *HELP! A Bear Is Eating Me!* Eraserhead Press, 2008. 132p. 9781933929699. It's definitely not Marv's fault he's pinned underneath his own vehicle as he's being gnawed on by a bear.

Hockensmith, Steve. *Pride and Prejudice and Zombies: Dawn of the Dreadfuls*. Quirk Books, 2010. 287p. 9781594744549. This is a prequel to *Pride and Prejudice and Zombies* that explores the zombie infestation and explains how the Bennett sisters got to be such awesome zombie-fighting machines.

Kenemore, Scott. *Z.E.O.: A Zombie's Guide to Getting A(head) in Business*. Skyhorse Publishing, 2009. 272p. 9781602396487. Frustrated in your job? Take a few tips from zombies on how to get the most out of your workday.

Knapp, Eric D. *Cluck: A Murder Most Fowl*. BookSurge Publishing, 2007. 340p. 9781419682643. Man versus zombie chickens—the ultimate battle.

Louison, Cole, and the Department of the Army. *U.S. Army Zombie Combat Skills*. Lyons Press, 2009. 242p. 9781599219097. As a U.S. Army soldier, you need to know how to survive in combat with zombies. Special methods of first aid, survival, defense, and weapons training will prepare you for when the zombies attack.

Moore, Christopher. *Sacre Bleu*! William Morrow, 2012. 416p. 9780061779749. The book begins on the day of Vincent Van Gogh's death in Auvers, a village near Paris. Vincent Van Gogh has gone to a crossroads to paint in Auvers, a village near Paris. There, Van Gogh shot himself and then walked a mile to the home of his doctor to seek treatment. Why shoot yourself and then seek out treatment? Baker-turned-painter Lucien Lessard and painter and libertine Henri Toulouse-Lautrec seek out the answers to this riddle. During their search for answers, cameos are made by Renoir,

Manet, Monet, Whistler, Pissarro, Gaugin, and Seurat, a menacing character called the Colorman.

Winters, Ben H., and Jane Austen. *Sense and Sensibility and Sea Monsters*. Quirk Books, 2009. 344p. 9781594744426. After their father's untimely demise in a hammerhead shark's belly, the Dashwood sisters are evicted to an island chock-full of horrific sea monsters and dark secrets.

Must Read

★ **Wong, David.** *John Dies at the End*. Thomas Dunne, 2009. 384p. 9780312555139. Beer-swilling heroes battle meat monsters through time and space and video games. The soy sauce is tainted with a paranormal psychoactive that causes Wong and John to achieve a higher level of consciousness . . . or maybe hell has just descended on their town.

TOOLS AND RESOURCES

Genre Guides

Fonseca, A. J., and Pulliam, J. M. 2009. *Hooked on Horror III: A Guide to Reading Interests in Horror Fiction*. Genreflecting Advisory Series. Westport, CT: Libraries Unlimited.

Saricks, J. G. 2001. *The Readers' Advisory Guide to Genre fiction*. Chicago: American Library Association.

Spratford, B., and Clausen, T. 2004. *The Horror Readers' Advisory: The Librarian's Guide to Vampires, Killer Tomatoes, and Haunted Houses*. Chicago: American Library Association.

Wells, P. 2000. *The Horror Genre: From Beelzebub to Blair Witch*. London: Wallflower.

Bibliography

Joshi, S. T. 2007. *Icons of Horror and the Supernatural: An Encyclopedia of Our Worst Nightmares*. Westport, CT: Greenwood Press.

Molinari, M., and Kamm, J. 2001. *The Horror Movie Survival Guide.* [Be afraid . . . but be prepared: includes photos of fear, trivia of terror, body count index, feeding habits of highly effective monsters and more!]. New York: Berkley Boulevard Books.

Reference Material

Browne, R. B., and Browne, P. 2001. *The Guide to United States Popular Culture*. Bowling Green, OH: Bowling Green State University Popular Press.

Carroll, Noel. 1990. *The Philosophy of Horror: Or Paradoxes of the Heart*. New York: Routledge.

Castle, M., and Horror Writers Association. 2007. *On Writing Horror: A Handbook*. Cincinnati, OH: Writers Digest Books.

Hills, M. 2005. *The Pleasures of Horror*. New York: Continuum.

Jancovich, M. 2002. *Horror, the Film Reader*. London: Routledge.

Morgan, J. 2002. *The Biology of Horror: Gothic Literature and Film*. Carbondale: Southern Illinois University Press.

Spadoni, R. 2007. *Uncanny Bodies: The Coming of Sound Film and the Origins of the Horror Genre*. Berkeley: University of California Press.

Svehla, G., and Svehla, S. 1996. *Guilty Pleasures of the Horror Film*. Baltimore, MD: Midnight Marquee Press.

Twitchell, J. B. 1985. *Dreadful Pleasures: An Anatomy of Modern Horror*. New York: Oxford University Press.

Websites

The Horror Fiction Review—http://thehorrorfictionreview.blogspot.com/

MonsterLibrarian—http://www.monsterlibrarian.com/

RA for All: Horror—http://raforallhorror.blogspot.com/

FIVE FAN FAVORITES

- Max Brooks. *World War Z: An Oral History of the Zombie War*—Paranormal/Zombies
- Joe Hill. *Horns*—Paranormal
- Jack Ketchum. *Off Season*—Visceral
- Caitlin R. Kiernan. *The Red Tree*—Gothic
- David Wong. *John Dies at the End*—Humor

Chapter 15

Science Fiction

Maura Heaphy

Science Fiction (SF) is a genre that stirs up strong passions.

Each year, thousands—probably tens of thousands—of fans converge on hotels and conference centers across the world, dressed as Sith Lords, nubile alien maidens, and shambling zombies, to share their love of stories that are impossible. They have high standards, deep pockets, and long memories, and woe betide the author or filmmaker who lets them down. They are willing to argue deep questions into the small hours of the night: the relative qualities of an author's latest work, or the comparative merits of a remake versus an original, or ethical questions, such as whether Han Solo shot first.

What is it, exactly, that captures the imagination of otherwise sane, normal people? What is it about Science Fiction that keeps us coming back for more?

DEFINITION

In an interview conducted just two years before his death, Jules Verne was asked about his upstart young British rival, H. G. Wells. Verne replied, "I make use of physics. He invents."[1]

In two brief sentences (which probably sound even more elegant and dismissive in the original French), Verne captures the essence of the struggle for the soul of the genre called "Science Fiction." Can a story qualify as Science Fiction only if it is firmly rooted in scientific fact and sound extrapolation from real premises? "Making use of physics," or as Robert A. Heinlein put it, "legitimate—and often very tightly reasoned—speculations about the possibilities of the real world,"[2] may please the purists, but does it condemn the genre to an eternity in the wasteland of Literature—no more than dramatized puzzles, in which character and style are poor seconds to a scientific problem and its solution?

On the other hand, saying that Science Fiction is the literature of invention, the pure product of imagination, has problems of its own: without something to give the speculation backbone, Science Fiction would be, as author Terry Pratchett has put it, just "fantasy with nuts and bolts painted on."[3] Somewhere between those two extremes is the reality: that Jules Verne and H. G. Wells both had it right.

SF is the literature of the future, of technology, science, and adventure, but it is also the literature of self-discovery. For every story set in deepest space, in the farthest reaches of the future, there are Science Fiction stories that confront the challenges of the day after tomorrow, showing individuals who face the challenges of change—change in technology, biology, and our relationship with our environment. Change in our own minds, and our own hearts. Stories that ask how humankind would fare on very different worlds, but also "what if" the status quo were to change right here, right now—right before our eyes.

For every Science Fiction story that features the stereotypical chisel-jawed hero, there are stories that focus on less likely protagonists—women, children, the differently abled, and aliens. Outsiders and the marginalized have always found a voice in Science Fiction, as it asks "what if" the person you least expect is the only one with sufficient know-how and courage to save the day.

For the purposes of this book, Science Fiction is defined as the literature of "what if." Author Philip K. Dick probably puts it best: "The SF writer sees not just possibilities but wild possibilities. It's not just 'what if'—it's 'My God; what if,' in frenzy and hysteria. The Martians are always coming."[4]

CHARACTERISTICS AND APPEAL

What is the appeal of Science Fiction? The answer to this question is subtly different for every enthusiastic reader of SF, and changes subtly at different moments in each reader's life. The best SF teaches—and not just lessons about science and circuitry. The best SF provides a worthwhile simulacrum for the challenges of real life: reading stories of heroes and aliens can prepare us for times in our lives when we feel alienated, or feel called upon to be heroic, however mundane the circumstances may be. SF is a form of escapism, but one that keeps one foot firmly on the ground of real-life problems and the challenges that lie in wait for us around the corners of our busy, complicated lives. It creates worlds worth escaping to and enables us to understand how very similar they are to the reality we temporarily leave behind.

SF is undergoing a surge in popularity and reaching an ever wider audience, because, it could be argued, it is everywhere (movies, TV, and fiction) and because it is being incorporated into ever more appealing and relatable story lines. In the past few years, mainstream authors such as Margaret Atwood (*Oryx and Crake*, 2003 and *The Year of the Flood*, 2009), Cormac McCarthy (*The Road*, 2006), and Philip Roth (*The Plot Against America*, 2004) have made unapologetic use of the tropes of SF, proving what fans already knew—that SF can be used on serious themes, in works of the highest quality. Authors such as Michael Chabon, Karen Joy Fowler, and Jonathan Lethem move effortlessly between camps as critically acclaimed authors of serious SF who are also recognized for their mainstream work. Television series such as *Lost*, *Heroes*, *Fringe*, *Person of Interest*, and *Battlestar Galactica* have managed to capture, and hold on to, a broad audience— possibly because, in spite of whatever "weirdness" their SF story lines contain, the mirror that they hold up to the viewer reflects a world we know all too well. The rebooted *Star Trek* (2009), comic-book superheroes like *Thor* and *Captain America* (both 2011), and the staggering success of *The Hunger Games* (2012) have demonstrated that—done well—SF movies can garner critical acclaim and appeal to diverse audiences.

BRIEF HISTORY

The term "Science Fiction" was coined by editor and entrepreneur Hugo Gernsback in 1926, when he launched his magazine *Amazing Stories*. In fact, his preferred term was "scientifiction," by which he meant

> The Jules Verne, H. G. Wells, and Edgar Allan Poe type of story, a charming romance intermingled with scientific fact and prophetic vision.[5]

Gernsback has been mocked for that "charming romance" line—but it echoes the term that Wells himself used for his five ground-breaking novels of the 1890s and early 1900s: "scientific romances." It jars only because we modern readers tend to forget that "romance" is the proper term for a story that incorporates implausible and fantastic elements—the journey to strange lands in which the hero rides a waterspout to the Moon, finds unsuspected empires on the Sun, encounters wizards (or mad scientists), and conquers monsters (or aliens).

True to Gernsback's vision, and the vision of the pulp magazines he launched, American SF of the 1930s was brightly optimistic, adventure-oriented, and reflected a faith in science and authority that would have seemed appropriate for writers and publishers who "assumed that their main readership was made up of teenage boys."[6] Things were different in

Britain: while there was a tradition of "boy's own" adventure magazines, Speculative Fiction was considered suitable fare for adults, and consequently there was a tradition of darker and more mature works like Olaf Stapledon's *Last and First Men* (1930), Aldous Huxley's *Brave New World* (1931), H. G. Wells's *The Shape of Things to Come* (1938), C. S. Lewis's *Out of the Silent Planet* (1938), and George Orwell's *Nineteen Eighty-Four* (1948) to reflect the mindset of a country reeling from one technology-driven war and bracing itself to fight another.

By the 1940s, control of SF magazines had passed from Gernsback and the pulps to editors like John W. Campbell who encouraged a more mature style of writing and a more challenging approach to the subject, and worked with authors who were up to the challenge, such as Isaac Asimov, Arthur C. Clarke, and Robert A. Heinlein. When the World War II ended, exposing the true extent of its horrors and passing into long years of small hot wars, long cold wars, and nuclear anxiety, SF began to change into the darker and more challenging fiction of the 1950s and 1960s, culminating in the New Wave. Through the work of authors like J. G. Ballard, Alfred Bester, Philip K. Dick, and Frederik Pohl, the focus was moving from *out there* to *in here*: from the exploration of new worlds to the exploration of the human mind, and the human heart.

Since the major upheaval of the New Wave, SF has cycled back and forth between Verne's poles of physics and invention, discovering new possibilities along the way. Space Opera had the distinction of being the whipping boy of both Hard SF *and* the New Wave—scorned by one as fantasy, with little or no basis in science, and by the other for its lack of psychological depth. Then Space Opera discovered Postmodern self-awareness and a sense of humor, and had not one, but two reboots in the 1970s and the 1990s. In the 1980s, writers of Hard SF began to find narrative potential in the growing information technology revolution that, blended with (again) postmodern attitudes and the style of noir fiction, resulted in Cyberpunk. In the 1990s, the reaction to the excesses of Cyberpunk (and there are *always* excesses) was Humanist SF, a restatement of some of the ideas of the New Wave, in which the future was made more personal, and brought closer to home.

CURRENT TRENDS

At the end of the first decade of the 21st century, we don't have the antigravity boots and flying cars that we were always promised, but SF continues to surprise. The traditional themes and subgenres—Space Opera, Hard SF, and Military SF—continue to go from strength to strength, but there have been interesting developments in SF that challenge the traditions: Slipstream and the Mundane Manifesto, SF Mystery and Noir, and Steampunk.

The label "Slipstream" (or "interstitial" fiction) was first proposed by author Bruce Sterling, as a remedy to the formulaic laziness that he felt was creeping into SF. Slipstream freely uses the tropes of SF and Fantasy, but depends on neither hardware nor science for its narrative effect (although, not surprisingly in our technology-mad and science-obsessed times, it often makes interesting use of both). Popular authors writing slipstream are George Saunders, Benjamin Rosenbaum, Kelly Link, Jeffrey Ford, and Ted Chiang. A random sampling of novels often described as Slipstream are Thomas Pynchon's *Gravity's Rainbow* (1973), Karen Joy Fowler's *Sarah Canary* (1991), Carol Emshwiller's *Carmen Dog* (1988), and Lucius Shepard's *A Handbook of American Prayer* (2004). As Sterling said in 1989, Slipstream is all about *affect*: "a kind of writing which simply makes you feel very strange; the way that living in the late twentieth century makes you feel."[7]

The Mundane was a return to the basics proposed by British novelist Geoff Ryman, among others, at a 2002 Clarion SF writers' workshop. Ryman has described it as "privileging the likely over the unlikely,"[8] and says that it is a matter of SF's responsibility to the world we live in: "all these fantasies about flying off to the stars basically say we can burn through the planet and go somewhere else."[9] Like Jules Verne before them, Mundane SF asks writers to restrict themselves to believable technology and science as it exists now. (So, no Faster Than Light drives, no teleportation, and no time machines.) The contemporary spin that Mundane puts on Verne's distinction between physics and the imagination is that it drags the edge of the known to the reader's feet and dares him/her to look into the abyss without falling in.

The popularity of SF Mystery and Noir can be gauged by the fact that murder—off-world, interplanetary, and trans-species—has seeded itself throughout the genre (look at Jeffrey A. Carver's *Sunborn* [2008, Space Opera], Duane Swierczynski's *Expiration Date* [2010, Time Travel], George Mann's Newbury and Hobbes Investigation Series [Steampunk], Alastair Reynolds' *Terminal World* [2010, Hard SF], and Michael Chabon's *The Yiddish Policemen's Union* [2007, Alternate History]). The popularity of a mystery as a narrative hook can probably be explained by the same desire to see order restored, and justice done, that makes Detective Fiction, and TV programs like the various *CSI* franchises, so popular. SF has an inbuilt advantage, of course, that it can make death itself seem strange and exotic, whether it is dealing with alien ideas of crime and justice (Kristine Kathryn Rusch's Retrieval Artist Series) or futures in which even death has been transformed into something very different (such as Richard K. Morgan's Takeshi Kovacs Mysteries or Cory Doctorow's *Down and Out in the Magic Kingdom* [2003]).

Finally, Steampunk, a term coined in the late 1980s to describe Victorian alternate history SF, describes a version of our past in which certain technical and conceptual leaps enabled a world of gear-driven computers, steam-powered gadgets, and stately airships. Steampunk has a lot going for it: visually pleasing (All that brightly polished brass! Goggles and tweed!), it hearkens back to a version of very early SF that John Clute, in *The Encyclopedia of Science Fiction* (1999), dubbed the "Edisonade," stories of the "inventor hero who uses his ingenuity to extricate himself from tight spots."[10] It also has the attraction of being set in more innocent times when heroes and heroines had a clear moral compass (a plausible explanation for why it is so attractive to Young Adult writers and readers).

Perhaps, these developments suggest that Science Fiction has come full circle—or perhaps, it's just that all that passion must continually prowl the far fringes of the possible, looking for new ways to phrase that question—*what if?*

THEMES AND TYPES

The subgenres of Science Fiction aptly demonstrate the genre's breadth, agility, and vitality. Novels with themes of time travel, aliens, dystopias and utopias, and future society stand alongside of Space opera and the "New Weird." Blends with Horror, Romance, Erotica, Mystery, and other genres add more flavor to the mix. There is virtually something for every type of reader.

Key to Science Fiction

Space Opera
Hard SF
Military SF
Time Travel
Steampunk
Techno SF
Slipstream and the New Weird
Dystopias, Utopias, and Armageddon

(Continued)

Space Opera

The Encyclopedia of Science Fiction (1999) defines Space Opera as "colorful action-adventure stories of interplanetary or interstellar conflict." For a while, it was fashionable to mock these larger-than-life narratives by authors such as E. E. "Doc" Smith, Leigh Brackett, Poul Anderson (Technic History Series), and Gordon R. Dickson. However, the contemporary sensibilities of Samuel R. Delany (*Nova*, 1968), C. J. Cherryh (the Alliance-Union Universe), Colin Greenland (*Take Back Plenty*, 1990), and Iain M. Banks (the Culture) have demonstrated that there is a lot of life, and intriguing possibilities, in grand adventure among the stars.

Anderson, Kevin J.

Saga of Seven Suns. Human scientists experimenting with alien technology provoke a war with the Hydrogues, a hidden empire of elemental aliens.

> *Hidden Empire*. 2002. 423p. 9780446528627.
> *A Forest of Stars*. 2003. 464p. 9780446528719.
> *Horizon Storms*. 2004. 496p. 9780446528726.
> *Scattered Suns*. 2005. 496p. 9780446577175.
> *Of Fire and Night*. 2006. 544p. 9780446577182.
> *Metal Swarm*. 2007. 480p. 9780743275439.
> *The Ashes of Worlds*. 2008. 491p. 9780316007573.

Asher, Neal

The Polity Universe. The Polity Collective, a society of heavily augmented posthumans and the AIs who rule them, is engaged in a long-running war with the vicious alien Prador. *The Gabble: And Other Stories* (2008) brings together Asher's short fiction set in the Polity Universe.

> *Prador Moon*. 2006. 222p. 9780739476932.
> *Hilldiggers*. 2007. 474p. 9781405055000.
> *Shadow of the Scorpion*. 2008. 304p. 9781597801393.
> *The Technician*. 2010. 352p. 9780230708747.

Must Read

📖 **Asimov, Isaac.** SF's Renaissance man: in the <u>Foundation Series</u>, he imagined civilizations across the stars; in *I, Robot* (1950), 256 p. 9780553382563, he devised the "Three Laws of Robotics."

Bujold, Lois McMaster

The Barrayar Universe (The Miles Vorkosigan Series). There are over two-dozen volumes, so far, in Bujold's well-loved series that follows the adventures of the Vorkosigan clan, especially the malformed, charming, royal troublemaker Miles Vorkosigan—an unlikely hero, whose adversaries underestimate him at their peril. The most recent volumes in <u>The Barrayar Universe</u> are

> *Diplomatic Immunity*. 2002. 311p. 9780743435338.
> *Cryoburn*. 2010. 345p. 9781439133941.
> *Captain Vorpatril's Alliance*. 2012. 423p. 9781451638455.

🎖 **"Corey James S. A." (Daniel Abraham and Ty Franck).** *Leviathan Wakes*. 2011. 592p. 9780316129084. Lauded as yet another reboot of Space Opera. Ice miners making runs from the rings of Saturn to the mining stations of the Belt stumble upon a derelict ship and a dark secret. The first volume in the projected <u>Expanse Series</u>. Nominated for the 2012 Hugos for Best Novel, and winner of the 2012 RUSA Reading List Award.

Herbert, Brian, and Kevin J. Anderson

Dune Series. Frank Herbert wrote five sequels to his masterful 1965 novel *Dune*. After his death in February 1986, his son Brian—working with Kevin J. Anderson, and sometimes working with Herbert's notes and outlines—produced a series of prequels, sequels, and "interquels"—novels that complete the original sequence, or focus on the time periods between the original novels. The most recent novels in the sequence are

> *Hunters of Dune*. 2006. 524p. 9780765312921.
> *Sandworms of Dune*. 2007. 494p. 9780765312938. Based upon a 30-page outline left by Frank Herbert.
> *Paul of Dune*. 2008. 512p. 9780765312945.
> *The Winds of Dune*. 2009. 448p. 9780765322722.
> *The Sisterhood of Dune*. 2012. 496p. 9780765322739.

Must Read

★**Herbert, Frank.** *Dune*. 1965. 544p. 9780441013593. (Movie). Wild, gothic political thriller set on a desert planet—the only natural source of the hallucinogen that makes interstellar travel possible.

McDevitt, Jack

Alex Benedict Series. Almost 10,000 years in the future, when human civilization has spread through our galaxy, antiquarian entrepreneur Alex Benedict finds himself at the heart of a series of mysteries on which the fate of humankind depends.

> *A Talent for War*. 1989. 310p. 9780441795536.
> *Polaris*. 2004. 370p. 9780441012022.
> ♟ *Seeker*. 2005. 360p. 9780441013296. Winner of the 2007 Nebula Award.
> *The Devil's Eye*. 2008. 368p. 9780441016358.
> *Echo*. 2010. 371p. 9780441019243.
> *Firebird*. 2011. 375p. 9780441020737.

Reynolds, Alastair

Revelation Space. Over a vast span of time, humankind must cope with plagues, alien war and internecine conflicts, and the threat of an inorganic alien race known as the Inhibitors, which exterminates sentient races if they achieve beyond a certain level of technology. Reynolds sets all of his novels and short stories in the <u>Revelation Space Universe</u>; *The Prefect* is the fifth and latest novel in the series of the same name.

Revelation Space. 2000. 476p. 9780575068766.
Chasm City. 2001. 524p. 9780575068773.
Redemption Ark. 2002. 567p. 9780575068803.
Absolution Gap. 2003. 565p. 9780575074347.
The Prefect. 2008. 416p. 9780441015917.

Robinson, Spider, and Robert A. Heinlein

🏆 *Variable Star*. 2006. 320p. 9780765313126 Working from Heinlein's notes, Robinson tells the story of a youngster who flees to stars to escape a broken romance—and becomes a man. Robinson was awarded the 2008 Robert A. Heinlein Award.

Stirling, S. M.

📖 *In the Courts of the Crimson Kings*. 2008. 304p. 9780765314895. Affectionate pastiche of 1930s pulp SF, sequel to 2007's *The Sky People*. Mars and Venus are exactly as depicted in pulp-era SF, populated by prehistoric people and bizarre creatures.

Must Read

★ **Smith, E. E. "Doc." *The Skylark of Space*.** 1928. 200 p. 9781603128858. Interstellar adventures painted on a big canvas, with broad brushstrokes. Worth reading as an example of early, innocent Pulp SF—and as the earliest SF to set its adventures in galactic space.

Swann, S. Andrew

Apotheosis Trilogy. Following a civil war, the discovery of lost human colonies threatens the future of all humankind. Follows on from events in Swann's Hostile Takeover Trilogy.

> *Prophets*. 2009. 340p. 9780756405410.
> *Heretics*. 2010. 384p. 9780756406134.
> *Messiah*. 2011. 369p. 9780756406578.

Williams, Sean

Astropolis Trilogy. In the 43rd millennium, a murder victim re-awakens to realize that the intergalactic civilization he knew has been destroyed. He will stop at nothing to restore it.

Saturn Returns. 2007. 319p. 9780441014934.
Earth Ascendant. 2008. 286p. 9780441015856.
The Grand Conjunction. 2009. 336p. 9780441017133.

Hard SF

Hard SF stories are adventures based on the extrapolation of "Big Ideas" and real science. Or, as critic J. O. Bailey put it, in *Pilgrims of Space and Time* (1947), narratives of "an imaginary invention or discovery in the natural sciences . . . something that the author at least rationalizes as possible to science." Authors such as Sir Arthur C. Clarke, Larry Niven, Stephen Baxter, Greg Bear, and Joe Haldeman invest their work with science rigorous enough for the most demanding reader, while still conveying excitement, a "sense of wonder," and transcendence.

Bova, Ben

The Grand Tour of the Universe. Fictional treatment of 21st-century exploration of the Solar System. Passionate advocacy for the manned space program. The anthology *Tales of the Grand Tour* (2004) brought together Bova's short fiction in this series. Sixteen titles, beginning with *Mars* (1992). The most recent additions to the Grand Tour are

Mercury. 2005. 371p. 9780340823958.
Powersat. 2005. 400p. 9780765309235.
🎗 *Titan*. 2006. 502p. 9780340823965. Winner of 2007. John W. Campbell Memorial Award.
The Aftermath (The Asteroid Wars). 2007. 396p. 9780765304148.
Mars Life. 2008. 432p. 9780765317872.
Leviathans of Jupiter. 2011 480p. 9780765317889.

Must Read

★ **Clarke, (Sir) Arthur C**. A working scientist whose understanding of the concepts enabled him to write stories such as *Childhood's End* (1953), 256p. 9780345444059, and *Rendezvous with Rama* (1972), 288 p. 9780553287899, in which science takes mankind on a transcendent journey of the spirit.

Egan, Greg. *Incandescence*. 2008. 256p. 9781597801287. The Arkmakers, who live in a neutron star's accretion disk, must use physics in order to save their artificial world. Hard SF at its hardest: includes diagrams and cited sources.

Flynn, Michael

The Wreck of the River of Stars. 2003. 480p. 9780765300997. An intelligent and beautifully written novel that creates a second, high-tech Age of Sail, when spaceships with vast magnetic sails rode the solar winds across the immense ocean of space.

Spiral Arm Series. The author moves his universe of future space exploration several thousand years in the future, when humanity has spread itself through the Milky Way Galaxy. An alien artifact of immense power triggers conflict between factions at odds over the future of humankind.

> *The January Dancer*. 2008. 350p. 9780765318176.
> *Up Jim River*. 2010. 336p. 9780765322845.
> *In the Lion's Mouth*. 2012. 303p. 9780765322852.

🎗 📖 **Harrison, M. John.** *Nova Swing*. 2006. 252p. 9780553385014. Tourism to a wormhole where time and space are interchangeable is big business. But the artifacts and living algorithms pouring out of the wormhole are changing the world in unsettling ways. Sequel to *Light* (2002). Winner of 2007 Arthur C. Clarke and Philip K. Dick Awards.

Marusek, David. M*ind Over Ship*. 2009. 320p. 9780765317490. In the 22nd century, nanotech makes all things possible; AIs, robots, and contented clones do all the work. Life would be perfect, if it weren't for all the surplus people. Sequel to *Counting Heads* (2007).

🎗 **Moriarty, Chris.** *Spin Control*. 2007. 608p. 9780553586251. A clone scientist acquires a genetic weapon powerful enough to tear humanity apart. Winner of 2007 Philip K. Dick Award.

Sawyer, Robert. J. *Rollback*. 2007. 320p. 9780765311085. Failed rejuvenation therapy complicates the work of the woman who must translate a message from aliens on the brink of first contact. Sawyer's 1999 novel *Flashforward* was recently made into an excellent (and, sadly, short-lived) TV series.

Schroeder, Karl

The Virga Series. A fullerene balloon 3,000 kilometers in diameter, Virga is filled with air, water, and floating chunks of rock. The humans who settle in this vast environment must create their own fusion suns and "towns"—and gravity. Lurking beyond the walls of their incredible world, the mysterious threat known only as Artificial Nature threatens to destroy everything they have built.

> *Sun of Suns*. 2006. 318p. 9780765315434.
> *Queen of Candesce*. 2007. 332p. 9780765315441.
> *Pirate Sun*. 2008. 318p. 9780765315458.
> *The Sunless Countries*. 2009. 336p. 9780765320766.
> *Ashes of Candesce*. 2012. 384p. 9780765324924.

Wilson, Robert Charles

The Spin Series. Earth is cut off from the rest of the universe by mysterious aliens dubbed "Hypotheticals." Over the course of three novels, Wilson's characters learn what this means for humankind—and for themselves as individuals. Wilson's science is excellent; his understanding of his characters and their plight is even better.

> ♠ *Spin*. 2005. 368p. 9780765309389. Winner of 2006 Hugo Award.
> *Axis*. 2007. 303p. 9780765309396.
> *Vortex*. 2011. 331p. 9780765323422.

Military SF

Military SF is an SF subgenre of enormous popularity, increasingly distinct from Space Opera and Hard SF. Military SF authors respect the science, and usually have their own versions of larger-than-life intergalactic conflict, weird aliens, and dastardly Galactic Emperors. However, they—and their readers—are more interested in military strategy, the chain of command, and the pressure that technology puts on space-age warriors.

♠ **Buckner, M. M.** *War Surf*. 2009. 382p. 9780441013203. Those who can afford it are virtually immortal—and bored. The 23rd century version of a mid-life crisis is to "war surf"—drop into war zones in hellhole satellites orbiting the Earth and play soldier. For one warrior-tourist, it all goes horribly wrong. Winner of 2006 Philip K. Dick Award.

" Campbell, Jack" (John G. Hemry)

Lost Fleet Series. Captain "Black Jack" Geary is a lost hero who returns from the "dead" to find that he is the only hope to end an interstellar war that has killed millions. Hemry has recently started two new story lines that follow on from the end of the Syndic war.

> *Dauntless*. 2006. 293p. 9780441014187.
> *Fearless*. 2007. 295p. 9780441014767.
> *Courageous*. 2007. 299p. 9780441015672.
> *Valiant*. 2008. 284p. 9780441016198.
> *Relentless*. 2009. 320p. 9780441017089.
> *Victorious*. 2010. 352p. 9780441018697.
> *Beyond the Frontier: Dreadnaught*. 2011. 356p. 9780441020379.
> *Beyond the Frontier: Invincible*. 2012. 389p. 9781937007454.
> *The Lost Stars: Tarnished Knight*. 2012. 390p. 9781937077822.

Must Read

★ **Card, Orson Scott.** *Ender's Game*. 1985. 357p. 9780312932084. The story of Ender Wiggins' brutal training as a boy-soldier in humankind's life or death struggle against an alien threat, and its unexpected consequences, is immensely popular with young readers.

Drake, David

RCN Series (also known as the <u>Lt. Leary Series</u>). Daniel Leary is an officer in the Republic of Cinnabar Navy (RCN). Lady Adele Mundy is a librarian and a spy. Best known for <u>Hammer's Slammers</u>, these clever novels of political intrigue and battle action are Drake's SF homage to Patrick O'Brian's <u>Aubrey/ Maturin Series</u>. Nine volumes, beginning with *With the Lightnings* (1998). The most recently released are

> *When the Tide Rises*. 2008. 356p. 9781416555278.
> *In the Stormy Red Sky*. 2009. 378p. 9781416591597.
> *What Distant Deeps*. 2010. 370p. 9781439133668.
> *The Road of Danger*. 2012. 416p. 9781451638158.

Must Read

★ **Haldeman, Joe.** *The Forever War*. 1974. 264p. 9780312536633. Conscript soldiers in an interstellar war are alienated from the society they are supposed to defend. Haldeman's reimagining of his experience in Vietnam is bloody and heartbreaking.

Huff, Tanya

Valor Confederation Series. Gunnery Sergeant Torin Kerr of the Confederation Marines fights to keep both her officers and her marines alive to fight another day, as they deal with lethal missions throughout the galaxy.

> *Valor's Choice*. 2000. 409p. 9780886778965.
> *The Better Part of Valor*. 2002. 411p. 9780756400620.
> *The Heart of Valor*. 2007. 357p. 9780756404352.
> *Valor's Trial*. 2008. 368p. 9780756404796.
> *The Truth of Valor*. 2010. 329p. 9780756406202.

Moon, Elizabeth

Vatta's War. Kylara Vatta is a no-holds-barred space-faring heroine, fighting to liberate star systems from ruthless space pirates—and avenge the slaughter of her family. Moon's Familias Regnant Series also depicts future interstellar conflict and Imperial political intrigue, and strong female protagonists.

> *Trading in Danger*. 2003. 294p. 9780345447609.
> *Marque and Reprisal* (aka *Moving Target*). 2004. 324p. 9780345447586.
> *Engaging the Enemy*. 2006. 455p. 9781841493787.
> *Command Decision*. 2007. 385p. 9780345491596.
> *Victory Conditions*. 2008. 416p. 9780345491619.

Ringo, John

Posleen War Series (aka **Legacy of the Aldenata Series**). The Galactic Federation calls upon Humanity for help when they face attack by the Posleen. The soldiers who answer the call face treachery in the Galactic Federation, corruption and apathy in Earth's military. Eleven volumes to date, beginning with *A Hymn Before Battle* (2000). Most recent volumes in the series are

> *Yellow Eyes*, with Tom Kratman. 2007. 608p. 9781416521037.
> *Sister Time*, with Julie Cochrane. 2007. 439p. 9781416542322.
> *Honor of the Clan*, with Julie Cochrane. 2009. 351p. 9781416555919.
> *Eye of the Storm*. 2009. 432p. 9781439132739.
> *The Tuloriad*, with Tom Kratman. 2009. 384p. 9781439133040.

Scalzi, John

Old Man's War Universe. Military adventure series with a clever twist on the young soldier's "coming-of-age" space story: elderly humans are given a new lease on life, literally—battling aliens in the Colonial Defense Force.

> *Old Man's War*. 2004. 320p. 9780765309402.
> *The Ghost Brigades*. 2006. 317p. 9780765315021.
> *The Last Colony*. 2007. 320p. 9780765316974.
> *Zoe's Tale*. 2008. 335p. 9780765316981.

Shepherd, Joel

Cassandra Kresnov Series. A supersoldier—a completely synthetic, independently motivated creature in the likeness of a beautiful, athletic woman—flees oppression, but finds that she must fight for her adopted home, the Federation.

> *Crossover*. 2006. 602p. 9780732267995.
> *Breakaway*. 2007. 563p. 9780732275969.
> *Killswitch*. 2009. 447p. 9781591027430.

Weber, David

The Honorverse. Honor Harrington, of the Royal Manticore Navy, was inspired by classic naval adventures such as the Horatio Hornblower stories. Battles and intrigue, with occasional serious reflections by Weber's naval heroine on the true cost of war. Thirteen volumes in the primary series, beginning with *On Basilisk Station* (1993). The most recent in the series are

> *At All Costs*. 2005. 855p. 9781416509110.
> *Mission of Honor*. 2010. 600p. 9781439133613.
> *A Rising Thunder*. 2012. 458p. 9781451638066.

Time Travel

One of the most intriguing tropes of SF, Time Travel taps into deep-seated curiosity about time. Whether it is the desire to "be there" at key moments of history (Michael Moorcock's *Behold the Man* [1969]), solve long-forgotten mysteries (Connie Willis' *Doomsday Book* [1992]), or face up to long-extinct prey (Michael Swanwick's *Bones of the Earth* [2002]), SF enables the reader to see for themselves what has been—or what is to come. Time Travel stories also offer the possibility of temporal conundrums—the "I'm my own grandpa" story—and the twisted plots of individuals and organizations who use their ability to travel through time for personal advantage, to right past wrongs, or to protect the integrity of the time line (John Varley's *Millennium* [1983], David Gerrold's *The Man who Folded Himself* [1973], and Poul Anderson's *The Time Patrol* [1991]).

Baker, Kage

<u>**The Company Series**</u>. A mysterious consortium, Dr. Zeus Inc., recruits individuals from the past and turns them into semi-immortals who act as their agents over the centuries, turning a profit by saving lost art and extinct species. Nine novels, beginning with *In the Garden of Iden* (1997), follow Company operatives who are determined to get to the bottom of Dr. Zeus' darker motives. The most recent volumes in the series are

> *The Children of the Company*. 2005. 300p. 9780765314550.
> *The Machine's Child*. 2006. 351p. 9780765315519.
> *Not Less Than Gods*. 2010. 320p. 9780765318916.

📖 **Benson, Ann.** *The Physician's Tale* 2006. 528p. 9780385335058. In the 21st century, scattered bands struggle to survive the aftermath of bioterror attacks. In 14th-century Europe, the Black Death scours the land. A novel spanning two worlds, demonstrating that you don't need a time machine to be touched by the past.

Must Read

★ **Finney, Jack.** *Time and Again*. 1970. 399p. 9780684801056. Autohypnosis allows artist Si Morley to transport himself back to 1880s New York City to solve a mystery. A book that beautifully captures the bittersweet lure of the past—and finding love where you least expect it.

Haldeman, Joe. *The Accidental Time Machine*. 2007. 288p. 9780441014996. A likable underachiever builds a calibrator that functions as a time machine; he finds himself in vividly described, wryly imagined futures, involving jail time and unwelcome celebrity.

Swierczynski, Duane. *Expiration Date*. 2010. 256p. 9780312363406. When Mickey Wade takes a few aspirin for a hangover, he finds himself in 1972. He can control his visits to his past—at a desperate price. But it will be worth it if he can prevent the murder of his father.

Willis, Connie

<u>The Oxford Historians Series</u> (<u>"Fire Watch" Universe</u>). Time-traveling Oxford University historians visit rural England on the eve of the Black Death, Coventry during the reign of Queen Victoria, and London during the Blitz, for firsthand research. Adventures written with Willis' signature humor and flair ensue, as researchers are lost in time, and risk changing the course of history.

> 🎗 *Doomsday Book*. 1993. 445p. 9780553081312. Winner of the 1993 Hugo, Nebula, and Locus Awards for Best Novel.
> 🎗 *To Say Nothing of the Dog*. 1997. 434p. 9780553099959. Winner of the 1999 Hugo and Locus Awards for Best Novel.
> *Blackout*. 2010. 512p. 9780553803198.
> 🎗 *All Clear*. 2011. 641p. 9780553807677. Winner, with *Blackout*, of the 2010 Hugo, Nebula, and Locus Awards for Best Novel.

Steampunk

Steampunk marries Time Travel and Alternate History with the dark techno-chic of Cyberpunk: a thrilling combination of style and substance. Robert Bee, in the *Internet Review of Science Fiction*, proposes that the current popularity of Steampunk "is based on frustration over the loss of craftsmanship in the modern world." It's hardly surprising that, while as a society we have learned to make do with the disposable and the mass-produced, we should fall in love all over again with novels that highlight ingenuity and old-fashioned integrity, and technology that is brassbound and lovingly crafted.

Lake, Jay

📖 <u>Mainspring Universe</u>. Baroque whirl of geomancy and Victorian brass gears, in which the universe is an enormous clockwork mechanism. The mainspring of the Earth is running down, and a young clockmaker's apprentice must take the Key Perilous and rewind it before disaster ensues.

> *Mainspring*. 2007. 320p. 9780765317087.
> *Escapement*. 2008. 384p. 9780765317094.
> *Pinion*. 2010. 352p. 9780765321862.

Mann, George

<u>Newbury and Hobbes Investigations</u>. Wonderfully imagined Sherlock Holmes pastiches. Sir Maurice Newbury, a "gentleman investigator" for the

Crown, and his assistant Miss Veronica Hobbes pursue wrongdoers in an alternative version of 19th-century England of airships, clockwork automatons, and an undead Queen Victoria.

The Affinity Bridge. 2009. 416p. 9781905005895.
The Osiris Ritual. 2010. 336p. 9780765323217.
The Shattered Teacup. 2010. (free PDF e-book/audiobook download)
The Immorality Engine. 2011. 350p. 9781906727178.

Oppel, Kenneth

YA **Airborn Series**. Adventures of youngsters aspiring to be "astralnauts" in a parallel Earth of Zeppelin travel, dastardly pirates, flying rodents of unusual size, and other marvelous phenomena.

Airborn. 2004. 355p. 9780060531805.
Skybreaker. 2005. 340p. 9780002006996.
Starclimber. 2009. 400p. 9780060850579.

📖 **Palmer, Dexter.** *The Dream of Perpetual Motion.* 2010. 352p. 9780312558154. Harold Winslow is a prisoner aboard an airship. His only company is the disembodied voice of his one true love—and the cryogenically preserved body of her father, who imprisoned him. Attractive, retro-futuristic world building; loosely based on Shakespeare's *The Tempest.*

Priest, Cherie

Clockwork Century Universe. Priest's complex saga of an alternative 19th-century America features airships, pirates, zombies, lost war machines, and a Civil War that has been dragging on for over 20 years.

🏆 *Boneshaker.* 2009. 416p. 9780765318411. Winner of the 2010 Locus Award.
Clementine. 2010. 978201p. 9781596063082.
Dreadnought. 2010. 400p. 9780765325785.
Ganymede. 2011. 400p. 9780765329462.

Sedia, Ekaterina. *The Alchemy of Stone.* 2009. 304p. 9781607012153. Mattie, an emancipated automaton, must flee as her home city is rent by conflict between alchemists and the mechanics whose clanking, steaming inventions are changing society.

Westerfeld, Scott

Y A. <u>Leviathan Trilogy</u>. Alternate World War I: Europe is divided between the Clankers, who put their faith in machines, and the Darwinists, whose technology is based on the development of new species. Enhanced by intricate black-and-white illustrations.

> 🏵 *Leviathan*. 2009. 440p. 9781416971733. Winner of the 2010 Locus Award for YA novel.
> *Behemoth*. 2010. 495p. 9781416971757.
> *Goliath*. 2011. 543p. 9781416971771.

Wilson, Robert Charles. *Julian Comstock: A Story of 22nd-Century America* 2009. 416p. 9780765319715. Following various disasters, the 21st-century America has retreated from technology and urban life. A Steampunk dystopia combining complex characters, military adventure, and a beautifully realized, unnerving future.

Techno SF

Jeff Prucher, in *Brave New Words: The Oxford Dictionary of Science Fiction* (2007), describes Cyberpunk as focusing on "the effects on society and individuals of advanced computer technology, artificial intelligence and bionic implants in an increasingly global culture." Closely identified with authors such as William Gibson, Vernor Vinge, Rudy Rucker, and Bruce Sterling, the roots of Cyberpunk stretch back into SF of the 1950s and 1960s (e.g., Alfred Bester and James Tiptree Jr.)—a time when nuclear anxiety and unpopular wars had damped down readers' innocent trust of technology, and the powers that wield it. The spirit of Cyberpunk continues to inspire SF writers, who continue to find new ways that technology can get under our skin.

Edelman, David Louis

<u>Jump 225 Trilogy</u>. Humans are reliant on nanotech bio/logic; a young code programmer becomes the target of business rivals, totalitarian governments, and mysterious groups.

> *Infoquake*. 2008. 421p. 9781591024422.
> *MultiReal*. 2009. 522p. 9781591026471.
> *Geosynchron*. 2010. 508p. 9781591027928.

Egan, Greg. *Zendegi*. 2010. 278p. 9781597801744. AIs in a virtual world are so lifelike that their use verges on the enslavement of sentient entities. Set in a very vivid and illuminating near-future version of Iran.

Must Read

★ 📖 **Gibson, William.** *Neuromancer*. 1984. 271p. 9780441569595. The "cyber" of the infant Internet and virtual reality meets the "punk" of antihero bad attitude. Bleak paranoid plot, and edgy characters, wired up and "enhanced."

Rucker, Rudy. *Hylozoic*. 2009. 336p. 9780765320742. Giddy sequel to 2007's *Postsingular* chronicles the fight to keep Earth "gnarly" (i.e., complicated and impossible to replicate). Rucker is also the author of the groundbreaking <u>Ware Series</u> (beginning with *Software* [1982]), which are classics of the collision of human and cybernetic.

Sawyer, Robert J.

<u>**The WWW Trilogy**</u>. An experimental procedure that enables a blind girl to see also results in her assisting in the spontaneous emergence of Webmind, the beginnings of sentience on the World Wide Web.

> *Wake*. 2009. 368p. 9780441016792.
> *Watch*. 2010. 352p. 9780441018185.
> *Wonder*. 2011. 338p. 9780441019762.

Must Read

★ **Stephenson, Neal.** *Snow Crash*. 1992. 440p. 9780553380958. A computer virus is striking down hackers, and Hiro Protagonist—hacker, samurai swordsman, and pizza-delivery driver extraordinaire—is humankind's last hope.

🎗 **Vinge, Vernor.** *Rainbows End*. 2006. 368p. 9780312856847. Consideration of the human cost of instantaneous technology, by the author whose novella "True Names" was a forerunner of Cyberpunk and virtual reality in SF. Winner of the 2007 Hugo and Locus Awards.

Walter, Jon Williams. *This Is Not a Game*. 2009. 384p. 9780316003155. When a game designer is caught up in a web of murders and financial manipulation, she blends it into her latest creation, using the community of players to solve clues and sift through data.

🎗 **Walton, David.** *Terminal Mind*. 2008. 284p. 9780978732639. Two friends release a sophisticated virus called a "slicer" into the net, and must try to stop it before the political situation explodes. Winner of 2009 Philip K. Dick Award.

Slipstream and the New Weird

In 1989, author Bruce Sterling suggested the term "Slipstream" for this blend of SF and Mainstream storytelling that reconciles style (literary, experimental) and substance (weird, character-oriented). The New Weird takes this even further, in what *Booklist* describes as "grotesque Urban Noir and cross-genre experimentation." Like the NewWave of the 1960s, Humanist SF often explores the inner space of the human mind and the alienation of the human spirit.

📖 **Di Chario, Nick.** *Valley of Day-Glo*. 2008. 240p. 9780889954106. Surreal quest, through a pop-culture drenched, postapocalyptic landscape, by a young Native American named Broadway Danny Rose. Will appeal to fans of Kurt Vonnegut and Douglas Adams.

📖 **Fleming, Matthew.** *The Kingdom of Ohio*. 2009. 336p. 9780399155604. Mixes time travel, historical grit, and an alternate history of the American frontier in the romance of a time-traveler from the Lost Kingdom of Ohio, and the birth of the modern world.

Gregory, Daryl. *The Devil's Alphabet*. 2009. 400p. 9780345501172. Paxton Martin survives a retrovirus that mutates survivors into monstrous oddities. Although he is unscathed (or so it seems), he finds his blighted Tennessee hometown seething with secrets that threaten the future of all humankind.

📖 **Hall, Steven.** *The Raw Shark Texts: A Novel*. 2007. 448p. 9781841959115. Eric Sanderson's memory has been wiped by sharks that devour human essence, not flesh and blood. Aided by letters from his pre-memory-wipe self, Eric tries to piece his life together before his mind gets wiped again, probably for the last time.

📖 **Mitchell, David.** *Cloud Atlas*. 2004. 529p. 9780340822777. Five stories move through time, bisected and arranged around a sixth, the history of a postapocalyptic island. The stories' depth and meaning change as characters and details are seen from different perspectives.

📖 **Roberts, Adam.** *Yellow Blue Tibia*. 2009. 336p. 9780575083561. The autobiography of (fictional) Soviet SF writer Konstantin Skvorecky, who is commanded by Stalin to come up with a plausible alien-attack scenario. Thirty years later, it all begins to come true. Entertaining satire in the spirit of Philip K. Dick, it includes a robot Stalin.

Must Read

★ 📖 🎬 **Vonnegut, Kurt.** *Slaughterhouse Five*. 1969. 215p. 97804 40180296. A young soldier survives the firebombing of Dresden, and comes unstuck in time. He becomes an object of interest to aliens from the Planet Tralfamadore, "where the flying saucers come from." Vonnegut was the original blender of SF tropes with serious themes and consummate style.

📖 **Yu, Charles.** *How to Live Safely in a Science Fictional Universe*. 2010. 256p. 9780307379207. Alternately wildly funny and incredibly touching, this is the story of "Charles Yu," time travel machine repairman, and son of the inventor of the first working time machine. The fictional Yu's adventures as he searches for his father (who took advantage of his invention to vanish to times unknown) is a wonderful use of SF tropes in a serious story.

Dystopias, Utopias, and Armageddon

Heaven on Earth (or on the Sun, or the Moon . . .). Some of the earliest works that have been labeled SF are actually utopias (Plato's *Republic* [380 BC], Sir Thomas More's *Utopia* [1516], and Tommaso Campanella's *The City of the Sun* [1623]), written at a time when it was dangerous to criticize the status quo. As narrative, perfection lacks conflict, so modern utopian fiction tends to conceal dystopian worms deep in the utopian apple, or depicts an outside threat to the utopia's existence (Aldous Huxley's *Island* [1962], Marge Piercy's *Woman on the Edge of Time* [1976], Ursula K. Le Guin's *Always Coming Home* [1985], and Lois Lowry's *The Giver* [1993]).

Some of the most memorable examples of SF are dystopias: Yevgeny Zamyatin's *We* (1920), Aldous Huxley's *Brave New World* (1931), George Orwell's *Nineteen Eighty-Four* (1949), and Margaret Atwood's *The Handmaid's Tale* (1985). Contemporary dystopian tales are often set in a postapocalyptic world, following a natural or man-made disaster.

📖 **Atwood, Margaret.** *The Year of the Flood*. 2009. 448p. 9780385528771. Two women survive a virulent genetic pandemic. Simultaneous to events in *Oryx and Crake* (2003); different characters' perspectives on the genetic catastrophe are described in that novel.

Baxter, Stephen. *Ark*. 2009. 544p. 9780451463319. Sequel to *Flood* (2008), the story of the final years of dryland on Earth. As coastal regions disappear under the waves, the discovery of a life-sustaining planet, light years away, offers hope for a chosen few.

Birmingham, John. *Without Warning*. 2008. 528p. 9780345502896. A wave of energy slams into North America and obliterates all life within its shimmering borders. The consequences of a world in which the United States has disappeared—pirates and petty dictators, and an unending struggle to survive—are worked out in compelling detail.

Must Read

★ 📖 🎬 **Bradbury, Ray.** *Fahrenheit 451*. 1953. 176p. 9781451673319. Timeless dystopian allegory by the Master of "Fantasy Americana." Firemen are employed, not to put out fires, but as shock troops who burn forbidden books.

Collins, Suzanne

YA 🎬 **The Hunger Games Trilogy**. (Movie). Publishing phenomenon in which a postapocalyptic government uses teenagers as gladiators in a televised fight to the death. Over three volumes, Katniss Everdeen evolves from victim, focused on survival at any cost, to leader of a revolution. The movie adaptation, released in March 2012, opened to staggering box office and critical success.

> *The Hunger Games*. 2008. 374p. 9780439023481.
> *Catching Fire*. 2009. 400p. 9780439023498.
> *Mockingjay*. 2010. 400p. 9780439023511.

Doctorow, Cory

🎖 📖 *Down and Out in the Magic Kingdom*. 2003. 208p. 9780765304360. Want and poverty have been eliminated; death is a minor inconvenience. In the Bitchun Society, the only wealth is respect, and the world economy runs on karma credits, or "Whuffie points." Winner of the 2004 Locus Award for First Novel.

🎖 **YA** *Little Brother*. 2008. 384p. 9780765319852. Alternatively, a near future beset by obsessive surveillance, with echoes of Orwellian post-9/11 security policies. Winner of 2009 John W. Campbell Memorial and Prometheus Awards.

Must Read

★ **Hoban, Russell.** *Riddley Walker*. 1980. 254p. 9780253212344. A boy-hero discovers reasons for hope in an England blasted back to hard-scrabble primitivism after a long-ago nuclear war; the Iron Age meets Heironymous Bosch. Written in a version of English that is, like the setting, rusted and eroded and "just woar down a littl."

Must Read

★ 📖 **Miller, Walter M.** *A Canticle for Leibowitz*. 1959. 334p. 9780060892999. A novel of "nuclear anxiety" that transcends its time; weird spirituality, stunning imagery, and clear, memorable prose.

📖 **YA** Shusterman, Neal. *Unwind*. 2007. 335p. 9781416912040. Parents or guardians can have their unruly children "unwound"—every part of their bodies is harvested and donated. Three teens make a desperate escape on their way to the harvest camps.

Theroux, Marcel. *Far North*. 2009. 320p. 9780374153533. Narrator Makepeace Hatfield is the sole survivor of her Siberian settlement, devastated by global warming. Her search for other survivors leads her to slave gangs, gulags, and an ongoing battle to survive.

Alternate History and Parallel Realities

Alternate History is the ultimate "what-if": major differences result from one crucial change in the historical record. (For example, in Philip K. Dick's *The Man in the High Castle* [1962], an assassination attempt on President Franklin Delano Roosevelt was successful—and resulted in Nazi Germany and Japan winning a very different version of World War II. In Harry Harrison's <u>Eden Series</u> [*West of Eden*, 1984], the dinosaurs were not killed off by the asteroid, and evolve in tandem with mammals.) While there are Alternate Histories that make overt use of SF tropes (change wrought by clumsy time-travelers, or interfering aliens), the usual unspoken assumption is "just because." Or, the novel's world exists as just one of the countless alternate realities hypothesized by quantum physics. Some SF takes the possibilities of the parallel realities to interesting extremes, as characters trip from one reality to another, interacting with the locals and interfering in the course of events.

📖 **Aldiss, Brian W. *HARM*.** 2007. 225p. 9780345496713. A Grand Master of SF takes on the global War on Terror. Author Paul Fadhil Abbas Ali is arrested when his novel offends the repressive British regime. Tortured, he takes refuge in fantasies of an alternative reality.

Anderson, Taylor

Destroyermen Series. An entertaining example of the "dimensional rift" story. In 1942, the USS *Walker*, a destroyer of the U.S. Asiatic Fleet, flees a Japanese cruiser. Both vessels and their crews are transported to an alternate world where humans never evolved. Former enemies form an alliance with the locals to take on the local bad boys—the vicious, predatory Grik. *Destroyermen: Unknown Seas* (2011) and *Destroyermen: Fire on the Water* (2012) are omnibus editions of the first four volumes in the series. Most recent are

> *Rising Tides*. 2011. 432p. 9780451463333.
> *Firestorm*. 2011. 432p. 9780451464170.
> *Iron Gray Sea*. 2012. 421p. 9780451464545.

📖 **Banks, Iain M. *Transition*.** 2009. 416p. 9780316071987. The inhabitants of a parallel dimension discover that they can transport their consciousness into the bodies of unsuspecting hosts, and meddle with the development of alternate Earths.

🎗📖 **Chabon, Michael. *The Yiddish Policemen's Union*.** 2007. 432p. 9780007149827. One of history's forgotten possibilities: what if a Jewish homeland had been established on the Alaska panhandle? The "frozen Chosen" is the premise of this clever and moving murder mystery, speculative history, Jewish identity, noir chess thriller. Deserving winner of the 2008 Hugo, Nebula, Locus, and Sidewise Awards.

🎗 **Goonan, Kathleen Ann. *In War Times*.** 2007. 352p. 9780765313553. In an alternate version of World War II, the protagonist acquires a device that could change human nature, and time itself. Blends bebop, physics, molecular biology, politics, and ethics into a compelling story. Winner of the 2008 John W. Campbell Memorial and 2008 RUSA Reading List Awards.

Kenyon, Kay

Entire and the Rose Series. A mishap catapults pilot Titus Quinn and his family into a parallel universe called "the Entire." Quinn must protect his reality from the plans of its rulers, the cruel, alien Tarig, while rescuing his daughter from enslavement.

> *Bright of the Sky*. 2007. 451p. 9781591025412.
> *A World Too Near*. 2008. 423p. 9781591026426.
> *City without End*. 2009. 433p. 9781591026983.
> *Prince of Storms*. 2010. 389p. 9781591027911.

McAuley, Paul. J. *Cowboy Angels*. 2007. 400p. 9780575079342. A cross-time gate offers "Real America" the opportunity to bring freedom and democracy to alternative versions of the United States. A rogue agent embarks on a plot to change all realities, once and for all.

🎗 McDonald, Ian. *Brasyl*. 2007. 357p. 9781591025436. Characters in past, present, and future Brazil realize that their worlds are strands of an immense multiverse. Quantum entanglements result. Winner of the 2008 British SF Association Award.

Stross, Charles

Merchant Princes Series. Some humans have an ability to travel between parallel Earths. Miriam Beckstein discovers that she is the long-lost heiress to a family of "world-walkers," whose schemes wreak havoc on various versions of reality. Winner of the 2007 Sidewise Award.

> *The Family Trade*. 2004. 303p. 9780765309297.
> *The Hidden Family*. 2005. 303p. 9780765313478.
> *The Clan Corporate*. 2006. 320p. 9780765309303.
> *The Merchants' War*. 2007. 336p. 9780765316714.
> *The Revolution Business*. 2009. 320p. 9780765316721.
> *Trade of Queens*. 2010. 304p. 9780765316738.

Walton, Jo

Small Change Trilogy. Three traditional country-house-style mysteries, set against the background of an England sympathetic to Fascism, which has made peace with Hitler.

> *Farthing*. 2006. 320p. 9780765314215.
> 🎗 *Ha'penny*. 2007. 319p. 9780765318534. Winner of the 2008 Prometheus Award.
> *Half a Crown*. 2008. 320p. 9780765316219.

The Shape of Things to Come

For some contemporary writers, the real challenge of SF lies not in the distant galaxies and distantly evolved versions of humanity, but in what awaits us tomorrow, as we deal with challenges that were not foreseen by the technology-loving futurists of Pulp SF and SF's Golden Age. Modern SF writers have risen to the challenge of, what author Geoff Ryman (one of the founders of the Mundane Manifesto) calls, "privileging the likely over the unlikely"—that is, SF set on or near the Earth, using technology and science that is available to us today. Or as the online futurist magazine, *io9* puts it, "Good science fiction begins with the present, where the line between what's real and what's speculative grows fainter every day."

Bacigalupi, Paolo

🎗 📖 *The Windup Girl*. 2009. 300p. 9781597801577. Bangkok struggles to survive in a post-oil era of rising sea levels and out-of-control mutation. Western agribusinesses push for more extreme mutations to boost their profits. Winner of the 2010 Hugo, Nebula, John W. Campbell, and Locus Awards for novel and first novel, as well as the 2010 RUSA Reading List Award.

🎗 **YA** *Ship Breaker*. 2010. 336p. 9780316056212. On America's Gulf Coast, grounded oil tankers are broken down for parts. Nailer risks his life scavenging from the beached hulks. An unusual boat, beached in a storm, offers him the chance of a new life. Postapocalyptic companion novel *The Drowned Cities* (2012). NBA finalist and winner of the 2011 Printz Award.

Gibson, William. *Zero History*. 2010. 416p. 9780399156823. Gibson returns to familiar concerns: hacker culture, surveillance, paranoia, viral marketing, and the semiotics of fashion and celebrity. An almost mainstream Thriller that features characters from *Pattern Recognition* (2003) and *Spook Country* (2007).

Must Read

★ **Heinlein, Robert A.** The man accounted "the Master" by those in the know. In *The Moon Is a Harsh Mistress* (1966), 384p. 9780312863555, and *Stranger in a Strange Land* (1961), 438 p. 9780441790340, the future is infused with Heinlein's philosophy of self-reliance and free love.

MacLeod, Ken. *The Execution Channel*. 2007. 288p. 9780765313324. In McLeod's near future, 9/11 and the Iraq war were followed by war with Iran, a flu pandemic and terrorist attacks—and the nuclear bombing of Scotland.

McDonald, Ian

🏵 *The Dervish House*. 2010. 410p. 9781616142049. Turkey in 2027 is part of Europe that stretches from the Arran Islands to Ararat. In the age of carbon consciousness, fortunes can be made and lost in trade-offs over scarce resources. Winner of the 2011 RUSA Reading List Award.

🏵 📖 *River of Gods*. 2006. 597p. 9781591024361. A richly detailed mystery set in India in 2047 graphically illustrates the clash between technology and tradition, the public and the personal. Winner of the 2005 British SF Association Award.

Robinson, Kim Stanley

The Science in the Capital Trilogy. Politicians and scientists are forced to confront the impact of global warming. The author of the Mars Trilogy establishes a utopian "permaculture" closer to home in this plausible near-future narrative.

> *Forty Signs of Rain*. 2004. 359p. 9780007148868.
> *Fifty Degrees Below*. 2005. 520p. 9780007148899.
> *Sixty Days and Counting*. 2007. 400p. 9780553803136.

🏵 **Ryman, Geoff.** *Air: Or, Have Not Have*. 2004. 400p. 9780312261214. An experimental communications system changes the life of Chung Mae, middle-aged housewife in a Central Asian village that has changed little over the centuries. Winner of 2006 Arthur C. Clarke, British SF Association, and James Tiptree Jr. Awards.

Sterling, Bruce. *The Caryatids*. 2009. 304p. 9780345460622. A dazzling novel that proves that Near Future SF does not have to think small. Three clone sisters hold the key to saving the world from global warming, runaway pollution, and political intrigue.

Earth's Children

What lies ahead for the human race? SF stories almost always involve some version of The Other: characters who have motivations and response that are very like ours, who are nonetheless not human—clones, robots, cyborgs, and individuals who have been genetically enhanced or otherwise had their humanity "tinkered with." Not surprisingly, SF authors have also been ahead of their times in writing thoughtfully and sympathetically about individuals who are different in ways that are more familiar to us: classic examples of stories that deal with the possibilities available for those who are differently abled, and the ethics of the way society treats them, are Daniel Keyes' *Flowers for Algernon* (1966), Anne McCaffrey's *The Ship Who Sang* (1969), Elizabeth Moon's *The Speed of Dark* (2003), and Lois McMaster Bujold's <u>Miles Vorkosigan</u> novels.

Must Read

★ 📖 🎬 **Dick, Philip K. *Do Androids Dream of Electric Sheep?*** 1968. 244p. 9780345404473. and ***The Man in the High Castle***. 1962. 239p. 9780965018852. Two particularly fine examples of works that find their power in the oscillation between what is real and what is not. *Do Androids Dream of Electric Sheep* was made into the movie *BladeRunner*.

🎭 📖 🎬 **Ishiguro, Kazuo.** *Never Let Me Go*. 2005. 304p. 9781400043392. The students of an elite school in the English countryside discover their unconventional origins, and their shocking destiny.

McAuley, Paul. *Gardens of the Sun*. 2009. 448p. 9780575079366. Clash of cultures between the ecologists of 23rd-century Earth and the anarchic "Outers," who have fled to the solar system's outer worlds. Sequel to 2008's *The Quiet War* culminates in bloody carnage.

🎭 **Morgan, Richard K.** *Thirteen*. 2008. 560p. 9780345485250. (UK: *Black Man*). When an aggressive genetically manipulated human (variation "Thirteen") escapes from exile on Mars and goes on an insane killing spree, Carl Marsalis—himself a Thirteen—is hired to track him down. Winner of 2008 Arthur C. Clarke Award.

Morrow, James. *The Philosopher's Apprentice*. 2008. 432p. 9780061351440. A graduate student takes a job tutoring a brain-damaged teenager. This child—and others like her—represents the tip of a Dr. Frankenstein-style iceberg.

Robson, Justina. *Living Next Door to the God of Love*. 2005. 400p. 9781405021166. In a post-Singularity future, AIs are in charge. Genetic manipulation is so common that "unevolved" people are disdained.

🎭 **Sawyer, Robert J.** *Mindscan*. 2005. 304p. 9780765311078. Individuals being treated for terminal diseases are "mindscanned": during treatment, their consciousnesses are uploaded into an android body. Complications—legal, ethical, and emotional—result, as Sawyer asks how identity is defined. Winner of 2006 John W. Campbell Award.

🎖 **Stephenson, Neal.** *Anathem*. 2008. 960p. 9780061474095. In the far future, scientists, philosophers, and mathematicians safeguard knowledge from the irrational world. Extraterrestrial catastrophe looms, and a novice scholar must face reality to save the world. Winner of the 2009 Locus Award.

Aliens and Alien Invasions

They are bug-eyed monsters; they are blobs of gelatinous goo. They are pointy-eared logicians and dome-headed invaders with an unhealthy green tinge. They are vapors and liquids, insectoid and reptilian, blessed with a superfluity of limbs and heads. They are the ultimate "other," the Alien. Most unsettling, of course, when they are just like you and me. And ever since H. G. Wells first decided to populate our neighbor, Mars, with "intellects vast and cool and unsympathetic," watching us with envious eyes, our default position has been that they are out to get us. However, from its earliest days, SF writers have reflected an ironic awareness of the fact that, in their tales of human colonization of the stars, the ultimate Alien (and Invader) is Humankind itself.

Cherryh, C. J.

Foreigner Series. Human refugees, marooned by a long-ago starship accident, must compromise to survive on a planet where they are barely tolerated by the humanoid natives. Beginning with *Foreigner* (1994), there are 11 volumes in the series, so far. The most recent are

> *Deliverer*. 2007. 357p. 9780756404147.
> *Conspirator*. 2009. 370p. 9780756405700.
> *Deceiver*. 2010. 384p. 9780756406011.
> *Betrayer*. 2011. 328p. 9780756406547.
> *Intruder*. 2012. 384p. 9780756407155.
> *Protector* (forthcoming).

📖 **Di Chario, Nick.** *A Small and Remarkable Life*. 2006. 240p. 9780889953369. Young alien Tink Puddah's parents are killed on the family's first day on Earth, and Tink is stranded in the Adirondack Mountains of 1845 New York.

Flynn, Michael. *Eifelheim*. 2006. 320p. 9780765300966. Two scientists investigating a historical oddity—a medieval German village that vanished at the time of the Black Death and was never resettled—discover evidence of interstellar contact that ends in tragedy.

Kress, Nancy. *Steal Across the Sky*. 2009. 320p. 9780765319869. The Aton-ers, who claim they once wronged humanity, ask for human volunteers to visit other planets as Witnesses. What did these aliens do? What do they really want, and how far can they be trusted?

Must Read

★ 📖 **Le Guin, Ursula K. *The Left Hand of Darkness***. 1969. 320p. 9780 441007318 Beautifully written story of snow-bound world and its androgynous inhabitants: male or female as circumstances require. Contains the immortal line, "the King was pregnant."

Levy, Roger. *Icarus*. 2006. 432p. 9780575078598. When human colonists on a far-off world discover the remains of an orbital escape pod containing knowledge that contradicts everything they know, they become fugitives, determined to find another way of life.

Miéville, China. *Embassytown*. 2011. 345p. 9780345524492. In the far future, humans share a distant planet with enigmatic aliens, the Ariekei, sentient beings famed for a language unique in the universe. A novel about diplo-macy and conflict—and the power of language—in a vividly created alien society. Nominated for the 2012 Hugo for Best Novel.

Ness, Patrick

YA <u>Chaos Walking Series</u>. On New World, war with the natives has killed all the women and infected the men with "Noise"—aural chaos graphically represented in the text by scratchy fonts and sentence fragments that run into and over each other.

> 🎗 *The Knife of Never Letting Go*. 2008. 496p. 9780763639310. Winner of 2009 James Tiptree Jr. Award.
> *The Ask and the Answer*. 2009. 518p. 9781406310269.
> *Monsters of Men*. 2010. 624p. 9781406310276.

Traviss, Karen

<u>The Wess'har Wars</u>. Three alien societies claim Cavanagh's Star. But new ar-rivals from Earth threaten the delicate balance of power, in a series that com-bines action sequences with thoughtful consideration of morals, spirituality, and environmental concerns.

City of Pearl. 2004. 392p. 9780060541699.
Crossing the Line. 2004. 373p. 9780060541705.
The World Before. 2005. 388p. 9780060541729.
Matriarch. 2006. 387p. 9780060882310.
Ally. 2007. 388p. 9780060882327.
Judge. 2008. 391p. 9780060882402.

Watts, Peter. *Blindsight*. 2006. 384p. 9780765312181. A linguist with multiple-personality syndrome, a cyborg, and a spectral captain whose genetic code incorporates vampirism must deal with beings who may not even be sentient, as we understand the term.

Must Read

★ 📖 🎬 **Wells, H. G.** *The War of the Worlds* (1898). 250 p. 9781 590171585. One of the five novels from Wells' early career (with *The Time Machine* [1895], *The Island of Dr. Moreau* [1896], *The Invisible Man* [1897], and *The First Men on the Moon* [1901]) that established his reputation, and some of the most enduring tropes of SF.

Genreblending

The ongoing success of SF rests, in part, upon its ability to adapt and to use elements of other genres to add narrative variety to the futurist vision it was offering its readers. While for some years SF purists were resistant to the idea of "tainting" scientific rigor with any hint of romance, the increasing presence of women in SF, as writers and readers, has meant that this latest cross-genreblend goes from strength to strength.

SF Horror

The very first authors acknowledged as modern SF, Mary Wollstonecraft Shelley and Edgar Allan Poe, combined SF sensibility with dark elements of the Gothic. The xenophobic attitudes of much early SF meant that creatures from beyond our world were often presented as figures from our worst nightmares, with dark motives to match. Starting with the real-life horrors of World War II and the potential for ultimate Armageddon of the Cold War, SF authors have long considered the possibility that the monsters under the bed might just be of our own making. Two classic SF Horror stories that reflect this heightened awareness of the symbolic power of what we fear are John Wyndham's *The Day of the Triffids* (1951) and Jack Finney's *Body Snatchers* (1954).

Bear, Greg. *Hull Zero Three*. 2010. 320p. 9780316072816. A man wakes up in a starship, hurtling through the emptiness of space. He is wet, naked, and freezing to death. The dark halls are full of monsters, but can he trust the other survivors he meets?

Gregory, Daryl. *Pandemonium*. 2008. 304p. 9780345501165. Demonic possession is a carefully recorded plague, with recognizable strains and predictable symptoms. One victim undertakes a dangerous quest to exorcise his demon as it fights him for control.

King, Stephen. *Under the Dome*. 2009. 1074p. 9781439148501. A small town in Maine is enclosed in an impenetrable force field. Isolated from the outside world, the best and the worst in human nature emerge.

Sigler, Scott. *Infected*. 2008. 352p. 9780307406101. Alien seeds from outer space result in unusual symptoms: the infected become homicidal maniacs. CIA operative Dew Phillips and epidemiologist Margaret Montoya race to stop the spread of a mysterious disease.

Thomas. Jeffrey. *Deadstock*. 2007. 414p. 9781844164479. Mind-bending SF mixed with bone-chilling horror, from bleak Punktown. A private eye is hired to find a missing bio-doll—a toy that isn't quite as defenseless as its teenage owner thinks. The Punktown Universe includes *Voices from Punktown* (2008) and *Blue War* (2008).

Science Fantasy

According to Sir Arthur C. Clarke's Third Law, first proposed in his 1962 book *Profiles of the Future*, "Any sufficiently advanced technology is indistinguishable from magic." Early SF was certainly indistinguishable from fantasy: in Edgar Rice Burrough's Barsoom novels, interstellar travel happens with little or no sense of the laws of physics; habitable planets and the creatures that inhabited them have little regard for simple biology and ecology. However, some SF authors have built careers—and huge fan bases—in deliberately toying with the fringes of SF: narratives that seem to be pure fantasy, but are revealed to have good (or at least passable) foundation in science. Well-loved SF Fantasy includes Marion Zimmer Bradley's Darkover Series, Anne McCaffrey's Dragonriders of Pern Series, Robert Silverberg's Majipoor Series, and Sheri S. Tepper's series The Land of True Game.

🎗 **Gaiman, Neil.** *American Gods*. 2001. 480p. 9780380973651. Odin the All-Father roams America rounding up his forgotten fellow gods in preparation for an epic battle against the upstart deities of the Internet, credit cards, television, and all that is wired. Winner of the 2002 Locus Award for Fantasy Novel.

Hughes, Matthew

<u>Henghis Hapthorn Stories</u>. A futuristic blend of Bertie Wooster and Sherlock Holmes, featuring Old Earth's foremost "discriminator" (i.e., private detective). Hughes has been hailed as heir apparent to the Science Fantasy of Jack Vance for his <u>Luff Imbry Series</u>.

> *Majestrum*. 2006. 209p. 9781597800617.
> *The Spiral Labyrinth*. 2007. 256p. 9781597800914.
> *Hespira*. 2009. 233p. 9781597801010.

McDonald, Ian. *Ares Express*. 2001. 352p. 9780684861517. Sequel to 1988's *Desolation Road*. Sweetness Octave Glorious Honey-Bun Asiim Engineer the 12th sets off on an epic journey across a far-future Mars and a conflict that spans time and multiple realities.

Robson, Justina

<u>Quantum Gravity Series</u>. Cyborg agent Lila Black must deal with an entertaining fusion of SF and Fantasy spiced with sex, drugs, and rock 'n' roll elves. A quantum bomb has blown a hole in space-time, opening our reality to elementals, and Lila must deal with the fallout—personal as well as professional.

> *Keeping It Real*. 2006. 279p. 9780575078628.
> *Selling Out*. 2007. 363p. 9781591025979.
> *Going Under*. 2008. 337p. 9781591026501.
> *Chasing the Dragon*. 2009. 401p. 9781591027461.
> *Down to the Bone*. 2011. 352p. 9780575085657.

SF Mysteries and Noir

In 1954, in *The Caves of Steel*, Isaac Asimov set out to demonstrate that SF could incorporate the classic format of the murder Mystery. Since then, SF authors (and their readers) have taken great delight in "playing" with the expectations of Detective Fiction—and sometimes with the expectations of life itself.

A common trope of SF mystery is the possibility that individuals can upload their consciousness and, in case of premature death, start again in a cloned or cyber body. *Altered Carbon* (2002), first of Richard Morgan's <u>Takeshi Kovacs Mysteries,</u> is one example of a future where death has been rendered obsolete. This can lead to the interesting phenomenon of characters investigating—and avenging—their own murders.

Must Read

★ **Bester, Alfred.** ***The Stars My Destination***. 1956. 232p. 9781876963460. and ***The Demolished Man***. 1953. Two complicated SF thrillers that bridged the gap between the Golden Age Pulp and the altogether weirder and more complicated SF that followed. Interplanetary revenge and a would-be murderer in a future where telepathy makes secrets impossible.

Castro, Adam-Troy

<u>Andrea Cort Series</u>. When foul murder is done, it's Prosecutor Andrea Cort's job to round up the usual suspects for the galactic Confederacy. But, contrary to instructions, from both her Confederacy minders and from the millennia-old AIsource from whom she secretly takes orders, Andrea is determined to find the truth. A conflicted heroine with a dark past that makes for classic murder Mystery scenarios in good SF settings.

> 🎗 *Emissaries from the Dead*. 2008. 387p. 9780061443725. Winner of 2009 Philip K. Dick Award.
> *The Third Claw of God*. 2009. 384p. 9780061443732.
> *War of the Marionettes*. 2012. Audible.com.

🎗 **MacLeod, Ken.** *The Night Sessions*. 2008. 324p. 9781841496511. In the aftermath of the "Faith Wars," Western society has rejected religion. The millions who still believe and worship are a marginalized and mistrusted minority. When a bishop is killed, Detective Inspector Adam Ferguson must find a killer whose plans may affect believers and unbelievers. Winner of the 2009 British SF Association Award.

Martinez, A. Lee. *The Automatic Detective*. 2008. 320p. 9780765318343. Fast and funny mishmash of SF and Hard-Boiled Detective story. Mack Megaton drives a cab in the technotopia Empire City. It's a step down for a massive killing machine created for world domination, but Mack has a kind heart. When his neighbors go missing, he investigates.

Rajaniemi, Hannu. *The Quantum Thief*. 2011. 336p. 9780765329493. British newspaper *The Guardian* describes this as " . . . at heart, a Noir Thriller in cosmic drag. . . . Wild SF concepts come thick and fast." Third Place in the 2011 John W. Campbell Memorial Award.

Rusch, Kristine Kathryn

<u>Retrieval Artist Series</u>. Humans who break the laws of our alien allies could find themselves sentenced to death—or worse—for minor crimes. Retrieval Artist Miles Flint attempts to help those whose punishments far exceed their crimes. A solid Police Drama that asks hard questions about different concepts of justice and retribution. Eight volumes have appeared since *The Disappeared* (2002). The most recent volumes in the series are

> *Paloma*. 2006. 371p. 9780451461155.
> *Recovery Man*. 2007. 374p. 9780451461674.
> *Duplicate Effort*. 2009. 384p. 9780451462602.
> *Anniversary Day*. 2011. 465p. 9780615521794.

Stross, Charles. *Halting State*. 2007. 368p. 9780441014989. Edinburgh policewoman Sergeant Sue Smith investigates a scheme to steal vast amounts through virtual reality, supposedly robbery-proof, banks. Brilliantly conceived Techno-Crime Thriller, leavened by black humor, and a painfully plausible version of 2012 in which the United States has ceded economic dominance to China and India, and faces bankruptcy over its failing infrastructure.

SF Humor

However bleak the subject, there is a kind of black humor in the way that SF can turn our reality on its head. (Consider, for example, the absurdity of the Martian's easy conquest of one of the greatest powers on Earth, in *The War of the Worlds* [1898], or the "be careful what you wish for" quality of the hedonistic, amoral society in Aldous Huxley's *Brave New World* [1931].) Serious authors like Robert Sheckley and Philip K. Dick can be very, very funny.

But SF played for big laughs has also been a popular variation on classic themes: Poul Anderson's the <u>Hoka Series</u>, Harry Harrison's <u>Stainless Steel Rat</u> and—even more delightfully lowbrow—<u>Bill the Galactic Hero</u>, Larry Niven's <u>Draco Tavern Series</u>, and Mike Resnick's <u>Tales of the Galactic Midway</u>.

Must Read

★ **Adams, Douglas.** *The Hitch-Hiker's Guide to the Galaxy* 1979. 208p. 9780345418913. (Movie). Much contemporary SF humor owes its style and subject matter to this ragtag group, roaming the universe on a ship powered by Infinite Improbability Drive and relying upon the unreliable advice of the *Guide* of the title. Demonstrated that absurd humor, paired with a razor-sharp wit, could win a wide, appreciative audience.

Baker, Kage. *The Empress of Mars.* 2009. 304p. 9780765318909. Mary Griffith establishes the first bar on Mars, home to colorful characters who live on the fringes of Martian society. Not broad laughs, but social satire and wit, as well as an endless mine of amusing references to pop culture in general and the canon of Martian SF literature in particular.

Bisson, Terry. *Numbers Don't Lie.* 2005. 163p. 9781892391322. Wilson Wu, Renaissance man and mad scientist in the great tradition, solves mysteries in three linked stories filled with puns and inscrutable mathematical formulas. Fans of ludicrous premises, nutty incongruities, and outrageous irony will enjoy this.

Colfer, Eoin. *And Another Thing.* . . . 2009. 288p. 9781401323585. Authorized sequel to the late, and deeply missed, Douglas Adams and his Hitchhiker's Guide Series. Fans will appreciate a chance to visit again with Arthur Dent, a pantheon of unemployed gods, everyone's favorite Galactic President, and one very large slab of cheese.

Frost, Toby

Chronicles of Isambard Smith. Lighthearted interstellar adventures of Captain Isambard Smith—square-jawed, courageous, and somewhat dim—plucked from a desk job to save the 25th-century British Space Empire from its alien enemies, who are (naturally) bent on galactic domination and the extermination of all humanoid life.

> *Space Captain Smith.* 2008. 320p. 9781905802135.
> *God Emperor of Didcot.* 2009. 323p. 9781905802241.
> *Wrath of the Lemming Men.* 2010. 320p. 9781905802357.

Jablokov, Alexander. *The Brain Thief.* 2010. 384p. 9780765322005. Bernal Haydon-Rumi's boss discovered something about the AI she's been funding, and then disappeared. Her trail leads to a 30-foot fiberglass cowgirl, an antiques heist, and a close encounter with a cast-iron borzoi.

Rankin, Robert. *Retromancer*. 2010. 348p. 9780575078727. Sequel to 2008's *Necrophenia*. Hugo Rune, occult adventurer, and his minion, Rizla, awaken to a 1967 that's harrowingly different. Nazis rule the United Kingdom, the United States was nuked during World War II, and Rizla can't find a decent English breakfast anywhere. Rankin excels at madcap weirdery.

SF Romance and Erotica

SF writers—and readers—were for some time resistant to Romance. C. L. Moore's novella "Shambleau" (1933) is a classic demonstration of what happens when a nice young space cowboy gets involved with the Wrong Girl. John W. Campbell refused to publish Philip José Farmer's novella "The Lovers" (1952), claiming that this mild (by modern standards) story of interspecies passion made him sick. Individual authors chipped away at this prudishness and prejudice (which often took the form of immature misogynism that regarded women as, at best, distractions, and at worst, downright dangerous), until, with the New Wave, adult themes in SF became more commonplace.

Reflecting the growing influence of women in the genre, according to online magazine *io9*, SF Romance "has gotten more sophisticated—and closer to real science fiction. . . . After all, astronauts need loving too."

Asaro, Catherine

<u>**Saga of the Skolian Empire**</u>. Political intrigue between two interstellar empires is played out against the backdrop of individual struggle, conflict, and romance. There are 14 novels, to date, in the <u>Skolian Empire Series</u>, beginning with *Primary Inversion* (1995). In 2001, *The Quantum Rose* was the winner of the Nebula Award. *Aurora in Four Voices* (2011), edited by Steven Silver, is a collection of four Skolian novellas and an essay by Asaro about her work. The more recent novels in the series are

> *The Ruby Dice*. 2008. 392p. 9781416555148.
> *Diamond Star*. 2010. 512p. 9781416591603. Asaro released a CD recorded with indie rock group Point Valid as a soundtrack to this novel.
> *Carnelians*. 2011. 364p. 9781451637489.
> *The City of Cries*. 2012. eBook.

"Gini Koch" (Jeanne Cook)

The Alien Series. When Katherine Katt sees a man on the street turn into a winged monster, she reacts as any girl would: she uses her Montblanc pen to kill it dead. And thus she learns that she is, by birth, a human agent of the Alpha Centaurians fighting a devious alien menace. Handsome Jeff Martini, local representative of the aliens, enlists her aid tracking alien parasites—and wins her heart.

> *Touched by an Alien*. 2010. 400p. 9780756406004.
> *Alien Tango*. 2010. 439p. 9780756406325.
> *Alien in the Family*. 2011. 466p. 9780756406684.
> *Alien Proliferation*. 2011. 448p. 9780756406974.
> *Alien Diplomacy*. 2012. 448p. 9780756407162.

Lee, Sharon, and Steve Miller

The Liaden Universe. Beginning with *Agent of Change* (1988), Lee and Miller created a wide-ranging saga of the swashbuckling Clans of the Liad: warring families and star-crossed lovers in a fantastic, other-world galaxy. In addition to the eight novels of the "Agents of Change" sequence, there are also 15 anthologies of short fiction in the Adventures in the Liaden Universe. The most recent Liaden novels are

> *Local Custom* (originally *Pilot's Choice*). 2001. 311p. 9780441009114.
> *Scout's Progress*. 2001. 311p. 9780441009275.
> *I Dare*. 2002. 467p. 9781892065032.
> *Mouse and Dragon*. 2010. 368p. 9781439133811.

Sinclair, Linnea

Dock Five Series. Adventures and romance in the midst of rebellion against an oppressive Imperial force.

> *Gabriel's Ghost*. 2002. 314p. 9781553165590.
> *Shades of Dark* (previously *Chasidah's Choice*). 2008. 410p. 9780553589658
> *Hope's Folly*. 2009. 424p. 9780553592184.
> *Rebels and Lovers*. 2010. 448p. 9780553592191.

Shared Worlds and Expanded Universes

From the earliest days of Pulp and the Golden Age, SF was often written by pairs—or even teams—of authors blending their identities under pen names, to maximize their earning potential. It was a creative background that discouraged excessive territoriality; comic book superhero collaborations established a respectable template for multiple author, "shared universe" series. New Wave author and editor Michael Moorcock recognized the creative potential of encouraging other authors and artists to write about his character Jerry Cornelius, the Eternal Champion. Other examples of Shared Worlds include Robert Lynn Asprin's Thieves' World and C. J. Cherryh's Merovingen Nights.

The term "Expanded Universe" is used to describe a media franchise that is extended with other media (generally comics and original novels). Novels that extend the universe of popular SF TV series and movies, in addition to the examples below, are *The X-Files, Babylon 5, Battlestar Galactica, Buffy the Vampire Slayer*, the various elements of the *Stargate* franchise, and the DC and Marvel Multiverses of superheroes.

1632 Universe, or The Ring of Fire Series

Series began with Eric Flint's 2000 novel *1632*. The inhabitants and environs of Grantville, West Virginia, are catapulted back in time over 300 years to Central Germany . . . with no way back. Their motto: "Get your pickup truck and deer rifle—we're joining the Thirty Years' War." The series now consists of nine volumes by Flint and various other authors, with half a dozen more titles projected. The most recent additions to the series are

> **Weber, David, and Eric Flint.** *1634: The Baltic War*. 2007. 752p. 9781416521020.
> **DeMarce, Virginia.** *1635: The Tangled Web*. 2009. 368p. 9781439133088.
> **Flint, Eric**
>
> *1635: The Eastern Front*. 2010. 400p. 9781439133897.
> *1636: The Saxon Uprising*. 2011. 432p. 9781439134252.

Bolos Series

A Bolo is a fictional type of artificially intelligent superheavy tank. They were first imagined by Keith Laumer (1925–1993) in novels such as *Bolo: Annals of the Dinochrome Brigade* (1976) and *Rogue Bolo* (1986), and have since been featured in stories by authors such as David Drake, Mercedes Lackey, Barry N. Malzberg, Mike Resnick, and S. M. Stirling. Most recent Bolo novels are

Ringo, John, and Linda Evans. *The Road to Damascus*. 2004. 688p. 97 80743471879

Weber, David. *Old Soldiers*. 2005. 294p. 9781416508984

Davis, Hank, ed. *The Best of the Bolos: Their Finest Hour*. 2010. 352p. 9781439133750. Stories by Keith Laumer, David Drake, Mercedes Lackey, and S. M. Stirling.

Doctor Who

Novelizations of the televised adventures of *Doctor Who* first appeared not long after the Doctor's BBC television debut, on November 23, 1963. Up until 1991, the books were primarily novelized adaptations of broadcast episodes. With the revival of the series in 2005, BBC Books launched a new range of original stories, often fitting into the timeline of the TV episodes. There have been over 150 novels based on Doctors 1 through 8, and (as of Spring 2012) over 50 novels based on Doctors 9 through 11. The most recent volumes—all featuring Doctor #11, and assistants Any Pond and Rory Williams—are

Moorcock, Michael. *The Coming of the Terraphiles*. 2010. 320p. 9781 846079832.

Goss, James. *Dead of Winter*. 2011. 256p. 9781849902380.

McCormack, Una. *The Way through the Woods*. 2011. 256p. 9781849902373.

Finch, Paul. *Hunter's Moon*. 2011. 256p. 9781849902366.

Morris, Jonathan. *Touched by an Angel*. 2011. 256p. 9781849902342.

Mann, George. *Paradox Lost*. 2011. 256p. 9781849902359.

Alderman, Naomi. *Borrowed Time*. 2011. 256p. 9781849902335.

Abnett, Dan. *The Silent Stars Go By*. 2011.352p. 9781849902434.

Colgan, J. T. *Dark Horizons*. 2012. 309p. 9781849904568.

Halo

Novels based on the popular video game franchise, set at different points in the Human-Covenant War. A collection of Halo short fiction, *Halo: Evolutions*, was simultaneously released in 2009, containing work by long-time Halo author Eric Nylund, material Tobias S. Buckell, and Karen Traviss, among others.

Deitz, William C. *Halo: The Flood*. 2003. 352p. 9780345459213.

Nylund, Eric. *Halo: Ghosts of Onyx*. 2006. 383p. 9780765315687.

Staten, Joseph. *Halo: Contact Harvest.* 2007. 396p. 9780765315694.
Buckell, Tobias S. *The Cole Protocol.* 2008. 358p. '9780765315700.
Bear, Greg. *Halo: Cryptum.* 2011. 342p. 9780765323965.
Bear, Greg. *Halo: Primordium.* 2012. 384p. 9780-765323972.
Traviss, Karen. *Halo: Glasslands.* 2011. 400p. 9780765330406.

Star Trek

At a very rough count, since the first appearance of Captain James T. Kirk and Mr. Spock, on September 8, 1966, there have been over 400 novels set in the universe of <u>Star Trek</u>. This includes moves and TV episode novelizations, novels from all of the subsequent Star Trek franchises (*Next Generation*, *Deep Space Nine*, *Voyager*, and *Enterprise*), novels from computer games and animated series, as well as original series such as <u>Star Trek: Titan</u>, <u>Star Trek: Stargazer</u>, and <u>Star Trek: Vanguard</u>.

Since James Blish wrote *Spock Must Die* (1970), notable authors who have written novels in the <u>Star Trek Universe</u> have included Steven Barnes (*Far Beyond the Stars* [1998]), Greg Bear (*Corona* [1984]), Diane Carey (*Cadet Kirk* [1996]), Diane Duane (*The Wounded Sky* [1983]), David Gerrold (*The Galactic Whirlpool* [1980]), Joe Haldeman (*Planet of Judgement* [1977]), K. W. Jeter (*Warped* [1995]), Vonda N. McIntyre (*The Entropy Effect* [1981]), Kristine Kathryn Rusch (*Thin Air* [2000]), Pamela Sargent and George Zebrowski (*Heart of the Sun* [1997]), Melissa Scott (*Proud Helios* [1995]), and Robert Scheckley (*The Laertian Gamble* [1995]).

The most recent publications for all of the major Star Trek story lines are

Foster, Alan Dean. *Star Trek.* 2009. 288p. 9781439171257. Movie tie-in.

George III, David R. Deep Space Nine: *Rough Beasts of Empire.* 2010. 387p. 9781439160817.

Martin, Michael A. Enterprise: *To Brave the Storm.* 2011. 340p. 9781451607154.

McIntee, David A. Next Generation: *Indistinguishable From Magic.* 2011. 483p. 9781451606157.

Beyer, Kirsten. Voyager: *Children of the Storm.* 2011. 418p. 9781451607185.

Mack, David. Vanguard: *Storming Heaven.* 2012. 347p. 9781451650709.

Cox, Greg. Original Series: *The Rings of Time.* 2012. 374p. 9781451655476.

Ward, Dayton. Original Series: *That Which Divides*. 2012. 390p. 978145
  1650686.

Star Wars

Fiction based on the *Star Wars* universe predates the release of the first film,
with the 1976 novelization of *Star Wars* (ghost-written by Alan Dean Foster
and credited to director George Lucas). Since then, several hundred tie-in novels have been published. With the release of *Star Wars Episode I: The Phantom
Menace* in 1999, Lucasfilm divided Star Wars titles into different eras: the Old
Galactic Republic, or the Sith Era; the Rise of the Empire; the Rebellion; the
New Republic Era; the New Jedi Order; and the Legacy Era. Notable authors
who have written volumes in the Star Wars Universe include Kevin J. Anderson (*Champions of the Force* [1994]), Steven Barnes (*The Cestus Deception* [2004]),
Greg Bear (*Rogue Planet* [2004]), Terry Bisson (*Boba Fett: The Fight to Survive*
[2003]), Terry Brooks (*Star Wars Episode I: The Phantom Menace* [1999]), Elizabeth Hand (*Boba Fett: Pursuit* [2004]), K. W. Jeter (*Hard Merchandise* [1999]), and
R. A. Salvatore (*Star Wars Episode II: Attack of the Clones* [2002]).

The most recent volumes in each era of the series, in chronological order,
are

Luceno, James. New Jedi Order Era: *The Unifying Force*. 2003. 529p. 9780
  345428523.
Traviss, Karen. Rise of the Empire—Clone Wars: *Star Wars Imperial
  Commando: 501st*. 2009. 449p. 9780345511133.
Williams, Sean. The Old Republic (Sith Era): *Fatal Alliance*. 2010.
  448p. 9780345511324.
Zahn, Timothy. Rebellion Era: *Choices of One*. 2011. 366p. 9780345
  511256.
Windham, Ryder. Rise of the Empire Era: *The Wrath of Darth Maul*.
  2012. 224p. 9780545383271.
Grubb, Jeff. New Republic Era: *Scourge*. 2012. 302p. 9780099542667.
Denning, Troy. Legacy Era: *Apocalypse*. 2012. 480p. 9780345509222.

The Man-Kzin Wars

Larry Niven's 1966 story "The Warriors," which introduced the warlike, tech-
nologically superior Kzinti and humankind's first, disastrous encounter with

them, was the first of what would become his *Known Space* Universe and the start of a popular shared universe series. Since 1988, stories in the 12 <u>The Man-Kzin Wars</u> collections consider almost every aspect of the Kzinti history, culture, and biology, and include stories by Poul Anderson, Greg Bear, Gregory Benford, Donald Kingsbury, Jerry Pournelle, and S. M. Stirling.

> *Man-Kzin Wars XII*. 2009. 272p. 9781416591412. Stories by Hal Colebatch, Paul Chafe, and Michael Joseph Harrington.
> *Man-Kzin Wars XIII*. 2012. Ed. Alex Hernandez. 366p. 9781451638165. Stories by Jane Lindskold, Charles E. Gannon, and Hal Colebatch.

Short Story Anthologies

SF is a genre that is fortunate to have lively outlets for short fiction. In fact, some of the best work by classic SF authors has been in the short form (Philip K. Dick, James Patrick Kelly, Ursula K. Le Guin, Frederick Pohl, Mike Resnick, Lucius Shepard, and John Varley). Recent anthologies that would be worth looking at are

Adams, John Joseph, ed. *Wastelands: Stories of the Apocalypse*. 2008. 331p. 9781597801058. The end of the world, and after, as told by Paolo Bacigalupi, Tobias S. Buckell, Orson Scott Card, Carol Emshwiller, Nancy Kress, and George R. R. Martin.

Anderson, Kevin J., ed. *The Hugo Award Showcase*. 2011. 416p. 9780765328427. Includes stories by Kage Baker, Eugie Foster, Kij Johnson, and Paolo Bacigalupi.

de Vries, Jetse, ed. *Shine: An Anthology of Near-Future Optimistic Science Fiction*. 2010. 464p. 9781906735678. Alastair Reynolds, Kay Kenyon, and Jason Stoddard (among others) propose the interesting idea that a brighter future could be possible.

Dozois, Gardner, ed. *The Year's Best Science Fiction: Twenty-Seventh Annual Collection*. 2011. 704p. 9780312569501. Favorites chosen by a veteran editor. Includes stories by Robert Reed, Alastair Reynolds, Damien Broderick, Carrie Vaughn, Ian R. MacLeod, and Cory Doctorow.

Fowler, Karen Joy, Pat Murphy, et al., eds. *The Third James Tiptree Award Anthology*. 2006. 304p. 9781892391414. Authors such as Ursula K. Le Guin and Nalo Hopkinson explore gender roles.

Includes "Have Not Have," the opening chapter of Geoff Ryman's 2004 novel *Air*.

Gevers, Nick, and Jay Lake, eds. *Other Earths*. 2009. 320p. 9780756405465. Stephen Baxter, Alastair Reynolds, Benjamin Rosenbaum, Lucius Shepard, Robert Charles Wilson, and Gene Wolfe, among others, focus on the difference that changed circumstances—wild or subtle—could make to life on this planet.

Hartwell, David G., and Kathryn Cramer, eds. *The Space Opera Renaissance*. 2006. 944p. 9780765306173. An anthology that organizes classic and contemporary authors in categories that enlighten and challenge preconceptions about Space Opera. In 2002, the editors produced the equally good *Hard SF Renaissance*.

Hartwell, David G., and Kathryn Cramer, eds. *Year's Best SF 17*. 2012. 512p. 9780062035875. Includes stories by Elizabeth Bear, Gregory Benford, Neil Gaiman, Nancy Kress, and Michael Swanwick.

Kelly, James Patrick, and John Kessel. *Feeling Very Strange: The Slipstream Anthology*. 2006. 320p. 9781892391353. Work that charts the nebulous territory between literary and genre, by Michael Chabon, Ted Chiang, Jeffrey Ford, Karen Jay Fowler, Jonathan Lethem, Kelly Link, George Saunders, and Bruce Sterling. See also Kelly and Kessel's *The Secret History of Science Fiction* (2009).

🎗 **Kelly, James Patrick, and John Kessel, eds.** *Nebula Awards Showcase*. 2012. 416p. 9781616146191. Annual award winners chosen by the Science Fiction and Fantasy Writers of America.

Ryman, Geoff, ed. *When It Changed: "Real Science" Science Fiction*. 2010. 272p. 9781905583195. SF stories whose "big ideas" are rooted in the possibilities of current technology and credible scientific research.

📖 **Scalzi, John, ed.** *Metatropolis*. 2010. 288p. 9780765327109. Thoughtful stories about the evolution of future urban communities, by John Scalzi, Elizabeth Bear, Tobias S. Buckell, Jay Lake, and Karl Schroeder.

Turtledove, Harry, ed. *The Best Time Travel Stories of the 20th Century*. 2004. 448p. 9780345460943. Collection by the master of Time Travel and Alternative History. Includes classics by Poul Anderson, Ray Bradbury, Ursula K. Le Guin, Robert Silverberg, and Theodore Sturgeon.

VanderMeer, Jeff, and Ann VanderMeer, eds. *Steampunk*. 2008. 400p. 9781892391759. Includes a helpful Introduction, "The 19th Century Roots of Steampunk" by Jess Nevins. Features standout stories by James P. Blaylock, Michael Chabon, Ted Chiang, and Paul Di Filippo.

TOOLS AND RESOURCES

Encyclopedias and Histories

Aldiss, Brian W., and David Wingrove. *Trillion Year Spree: The History of Science Fiction*. New York: Atheneum, 1986.

Barron, Neil. *Anatomy of Wonder*. 5th ed. Westport, CT: Libraries Unlimited, 2004.

Bould, Mark, Andrew M. Butler, Adam Roberts, and Sherryl Vint, eds. *The Routledge Companion to Science Fiction*. New York: Routledge, 2009.

Clute, John, and Peter Nicholls, eds. *The Encyclopedia of Science Fiction*. Revised edition. New York: Orbit, 1999.

Gunn, James. *Reading Science Fiction*. New York: Palgrave Macmillan, 2008.

Heaphy, Maura. *100 Most Popular Science Fiction Authors*. Westport, CT: Libraries Unlimited, 2010.

Heaphy, Maura. *Science Fiction Authors: A Research Guide*. Westport CT: Libraries Unlimited, 2008.

Roberts, Adam. *The History of Science Fiction*. London: Palgrave Macmillan, 2005.

Websites

Alpha Ralpha Boulevard. Catch-22. http://www.catch22.com/sf/arb. Over 500 SF, fantasy and horror bibliographies, biographies, and links.

Fantastic Fiction. www.fantasticfiction.co.uk. Bibliographies for over 4,000 British and American authors, including SF. Some entries include portraits and biographical statements.

SciFan.com. Olivier Travers and Sophie Bellais. www.scifan.com. Comprehensive bibliographic database of SF and Fantasy writers.

SF Magazines

Fantasy & Science Fiction. http://www.sfsite.com/fsf/index.html. Table of Contents and the full text of reviews are available online.

Io9. Gawker. http://io9.com

Locus Online. www.locusmag.com/Links/Portal.html. Links to any and all websites the Sf and fantasy fan could possibly wish for: 'zines, blogs, forums, authors' websites, etc.

SF Signal. www.sfsignal.com. Excellent website, with reviews and features related to all SF things.

Strange Horizons. www.strangehorizons.com. Original speculative fiction and poetry, author interviews, and articles.

Worlds Without End. www.worldswithoutend.com/index.asp. "Designed to help you find the books you crave." Extensive database of the books, authors, and publishers, using the top 10 awards in the field as its criteria.

Major Awards

A comprehensive index to all major awards can be found at www .locusmag.com/SFAwards. This includes complete award and poll results, 1971 through 2010, and information about the awards themselves: who sponsors them, who is eligible to vote, as well as information about winners and nominees.

Hugo Awards. www.wsfs.org/hugos.html. Awarded by the World Science Fiction Society for best books, stories, dramatic works, professional, and fan activities.

Nebula Awards. www.sfwa.org/awards. Created in the mid-1960s by the Science Fiction Writers of America (SFWA). Annual ballot of SFWA members, for the year's best fiction.

Locus Poll Awards. www.locusmag.com/SFAwards/. *Locus Magazine*'s annual readers' poll. Established in the early 70s to provide recommendations and suggestions to Hugo Awards voters. The Locus Awards often draw more voters than the Hugos and Nebulas combined.

The James Tiptree Jr. Award. www.tiptree.org. "Science fiction or fantasy that explores and expands the roles of women and men . . . "A memorial to Alice B. Sheldon, the author James Tiptree Jr.

British Science Fiction Awards. www.bsfa.co.uk/bsfa/website/awards .aspx

Other prestigious SF awards (with date of inception) are

John W. Campbell Memorial Award: 1973—Best SF novel published in the US. Judged award. www.ku.edu/~sfcenter/campbell.htm

Arthur C. Clarke Award: 1987—Best SF novel published each year in the United Kingdom. Juried award, administered by the Serendip Foundation. www.clarkeaward.com

Damon Knight Memorial Grand Master Award: 1975—Science Fiction and Fantasy Writers of America award to a living author for a lifetime's achievement in SF and/or fantasy. www.sfwa.org/awards/grand.htm

The Philip K. Dick Award: 1983—Best original paperback published each year in the United States. http://ebbs.english.vt.edu/exper/kcramer/PKDA.html

The Skylark: 1966—The New England Science Fiction Association annual award for significant contribution to SF in the spirit of the writer E. E. "Doc" Smith.

FIVE FAN FAVORITES

- Paolo Bacigalupi. *The Windup Girl*—Shape of Things to Come
- "James S. A. Corey" (Daniel Abraham and Ty Franck). *Leviathan Wakes*—Space Opera
- Suzanne Collins. Hunger Games Trilogy—Dystopias, Utopias, and Armageddon
- Hannu Rajaniemi. *The Quantum Thief*—Genreblending—SF Noir
- Connie Willis. *Blackout/All Clear*—Time Travel

NOTES

1. Sherard, "Jules Verne Re-visited," *T.P.'s Weekly* (October 9, 1903).

2. Heinlein, "Ray Guns and Rocket Ships," *The School Library Association of California Bulletin* (November 1952).

3. Pratchett, "Terry Pratchett: Discworld and Beyond," *Locus Magazine* 43, no. 6 (December 1999): 4.

4. Dick, "Introduction," *The Golden Man*, New York: Berkley Books, 1980.

5. Gernsback, ed., *Amazing Stories* 1, no. 1 (April 1926).

6. Clute and Nicholls, eds., "History of SF," *The Encyclopedia of Science Fiction*, 570.

7. Sterling, "Slipstream," *SF Eye* 5 (July 1989).

8. *SFF Chronicles*, "Geoff Ryman Interview, in Four Parts," June 2006, http://www.sffchronicles.co.uk/forum/11294-geoff-ryman-interview-in-four-parts.html

9. *Locus Magazine*, "Geoff Ryman: The Mundane Fantastic," January 2006, http://www.locusmag.com/2006/Issues/01Ryman.html

10. Clute and Nicholls, eds. "Edisonade," *The Encyclopedia of Science Fiction*, 368.

Chapter 16

Mainstream Fiction

Hannah Jo Parker

What is a chapter about Mainstream Fiction doing in a classic guide to the genres? Isn't Mainstream Fiction, in fact, a "nongenre"? Wait, what is Mainstream Fiction, anyway?

DEFINITION

Mainstream Fiction, for the purpose of this guide, is popular fiction that does not adhere to genre conventions, such as the happy ending we expect at the end of a Romance novel, or the clipped pace of Suspense novels, or fit into genre classifications, such as Fantasy or Science Fiction. These "nongenre" or Mainstream Fiction books often make up the bulk of a public library's fiction collection. You might refer to Mainstream Fiction in your library as "Popular," "Commercial," "General," or "Literary" fiction.

Many popular authors are considered "Mainstream," of course, but write novels that fit into other chapters of this guide. For example, Lee Child, who writes a popular Suspense series featuring former military man Jack Reacher, and Janet Evanovich, who writes the bestselling Stephanie Plum Mysteries, both show up in other chapters in this work. Popular author Nick Hornby, though, who writes thoughtful, character-centered novels about contemporary life and pop culture, shows up here in the Mainstream Fiction section. His often-humorous work is widely read and appreciated, but does not fit into other genres. Sometimes Historical Fiction, such as works by Andrea Barrett, or Women's Fiction, such as Elizabeth Berg's novels, is considered "Mainstream"; but since those genres are covered in other chapters of this guide, we focus here on stories set in contemporary times and without the trappings of other genres.

Mainstream versus Literary Fiction

Nick Hornby's work fits into the Mainstream Fiction genre, but is it Literary Fiction? Maybe, maybe not. It depends on whom you ask. We have intentionally avoided using the term "Literary Fiction" for this chapter because it is generally a loaded term, often deemed elitist. Definitions of Literary Fiction vary, even among librarians, but tend to include a reference to language and a writing style that is original and, well, literary. Literary stories are often dense or multilayered, but the plot is usually less important than the characters and the distinct writing style (or "voice"). The action may occur just below the surface, with a focus on the interior life of a character, rather than the exterior. These novels can be thought-provoking and complex, and sometimes end in a way that leaves them open to interpretation, making them excellent choices for book group discussions.

Works of Literary Fiction frequently win awards and critical acclaim, but don't necessarily become bestsellers, with the noted exception of books championed by Oprah (and classics that fall into "required reading" for literature courses), or those made into award-winning films. Examples of Literary Fiction authors include Isabel Allende, Paul Auster, A. S. Byatt, Don DeLillo, Kazuo Ishiguro, Ian McEwan, Philip Roth, Salman Rushdie, and John Updike.

Mainstream fiction includes Literary Fiction, but is broader, encompassing popular works by such authors as Leif Enger, Anne Tyler, Alice Hoffman, and Philip Roth.

In this chapter, the focus is on works of popular, contemporary Mainstream Fiction—novels that have been published recently, within the past decade, generally picking up where *Now Read This III: A Guide to Mainstream Fiction* (2010) left off through 2011. Authored by Nancy Pearl and other readers' advisors, the three *Now Read This* guides are excellent resources for contemporary Mainstream Fiction, providing hundreds of descriptive annotations, subject headings, and reading suggestions.

A Note about Classics

Of course, classic novels like F. Scott Fitzgerald's *The Great Gatsby* (1925) and Harper Lee's *To Kill a Mockingbird* (1960) are still read by legions of people many decades after their original publications (and not just because they're assigned as mandatory reading in English Literature classes). As mentioned previously, though, the scope of this chapter is limited to more recently published novels—i.e., "contemporary mainstream literature." Resources that list, rate, annotate, and dissect classic novels abound online and in print. For example, Simon Mason's *The Rough Guide to Classic Novels* (2008) covers more than 230 classics from various genres and countries, starting with *Don Quixote* (1614).

Not surprisingly, opinions vary about which classics are the "best" and why certain types of novels seem to be ignored or undervalued. When in 1998 the Modern Library published its list of the best English-language novels of the 20th century as selected by its editorial board—the "Board's List of 100 Best Novels" (www.randomhouse.com/modernlibrary/100bestnovels.html)—heated debate ensued. A "Reader's List of 100 Best Novels" was published on the same Web page the following year, after more than 200,000 people voted for their favorites, and this list varied widely from the original list.

CHARACTERISTICS AND APPEALS

Mainstream Fiction isn't driven by plot formulas or limited to specific characteristics. It doesn't function within the confines of any genre. In fact, authors of Mainstream Fiction are generally more interested in breaking rules and overturning conventions than in abiding by them. It could even be said that its most notable characteristic is its lack of characteristics. Thus, its appeal is broad and wide-ranging, with adherents enjoying the twists and surprises it offers. So, it is difficult to pigeonhole Mainstream novels; but this doesn't mean we can't approach the body of literature in a systematic way that reflects popular reader interests.

The first edition of Nancy Pearl's *Now Read This* (1999) presented an innovative approach to organizing and classifying Mainstream Fiction books, based on the concept of using "appeal characteristics," rather than plot details, to describe "the feel" of a novel. Originally articulated by Joyce G. Saricks and Nancy Brown in *Reader's Advisory Service in the Public Library*, 2nd ed. (1997), Pearl modified the appeals approach for *Now Read This*, organizing titles into four categories based on each novel's primary appeal characteristic (or "appeal factor"): language, character, story, or setting.

This chapter follows the successful *Now Read This* approach, organizing titles by appeal factors. Titles could also be grouped by time periods, such as decades; or writing styles or movements, such as magical realism, postcolonial fiction, or postmodern American authors. Titles could also have been arranged under popular themes or subject headings, such as psychological fiction, coming-of-age, or family relationships; but, as Pearl and Saricks put forth in their books, fiction readers are not usually looking for a book on a specific subject or with particular plot details. Instead, readers are more interested in the feeling that a book invokes and the overall quality of the reading experience.

Assigning a primary (and in some cases, secondary) appeal factor to a book is not easy, nor is it an exact science. It takes a certain amount of personal analysis and subjective interpretation, which varies from reader to reader. One reader might value *Let the Great World Spin* (2009) by Colum McCann because of the rich details in its 1970s New York City setting, while another person might connect with the fascinating characters that populate the story. Those two readers might differ on which appeal is the primary appeal, but they both have a strong enough sense about what they liked about the novel to help lead them to other books they might enjoy by investigating other books with the same appeal(s).

BRIEF HISTORY

The history of the novel is beyond the scope of this chapter, but a few benchmarks are worth noting. Benjamin Franklin printed Samuel Richardson's *Pamela* first published in England in 1742, but the first novel believed to have been written in the United States came out in 1789, when William Hill Brown published *The Power of Sympathy*, a fictionalized account of his sister-in-law's seduction by a wealthy man who was never punished. In the early 1850s, Nathaniel Hawthorne and Herman Melville produced their greatest works, *The Scarlet Letter* and *Moby-Dick*. Washington Irving encouraged these writers, as well as Henry Wadsworth Longfellow and Edgar Allan Poe, and argued for stronger copyright laws so that writers could make a decent living from their books.

After the Civil War, realistic novels began to appear: Henry James' *The Portrait of a Lady* (1881), Mark Twain's *The Adventures of Huckleberry Finn* (1884), Stephen Crane's *Maggie: A Girl of the Streets* (1893), and Theodore Dreiser's *Sister Carrie* (1900).

Some critics say that the age of the "Great American Novel" came between 1925 and 1955, marking the dawn of Modernism, with F. Scott Fitzgerald's *The Great Gatsby* (1925), Ernest Hemingway's *The Sun Also Rises* (1926), Willa Cather's *Death Comes for the Archbishop* (1927), Thomas Wolfe's *Look Homeward, Angel* (1929), William Faulkner's *The Sound and the Fury* (1929), John Steinbeck's *The Grapes of Wrath* (1939), Richard Wright's *Native Son* (1940), Ralph Ellison's *Invisible Man* (1952), and James Baldwin's *Go Tell It on the Mountain* (1953).

Others would say that "The Great American Novel," a term that was first discussed in an article in *The Nation* in 1868, has still to be written. However, writing the Great American Novel seems to be a 19th-century phenomenon, during a time when America was desperate to define its own culture.

After the 1940s, we see the beginnings of Postmodernism. Postmodernist authors experimented with the novel's form, played with its language, relied less on the narrative or story, tried various points of view, did not depend upon traditional character development, and often wrote "metafiction," or fiction about fiction. Some of the novelists considered to be Postmodernists are Italo Calvino, Donald Barthelme, Jorge Luis Borges, John Barth, Salman Rushdie, Don DeLillo, and Thomas Pynchon. In 1989, Tom Wolfe called for a return to realism in fiction.

While Modernists considered plot a cop-out and Postmodernists experimented with convoluted or incoherent plots, critic Lev Grossman, the book review editor for *Time* magazine and an author with a degree in literature from Harvard, points out that contemporary "writers like Michael Chabon, Jonathan Lethem, Donna Tartt, Kelly Link, Audrey Niffenegger, Richard Price, Kate Atkinson, Neil Gaiman, and Susanna Clarke, to name just a few, are busily grafting the sophisticated, intensely aware literary language of Modernism onto the sturdy narrative roots of genre fiction: Fantasy, Science Fiction, Detective Fiction, Romance. They're forging connections between literary spheres that have been hermetically sealed off from one another for a century" (Grossman 2009). Perhaps he is right, and that the novel is undergoing another transition, this time back toward a literature of pleasure.

CURRENT TRENDS

Whether or not fiction is turning back to a literature of pleasure, it can be said with certainty that today's novelists are not afraid to experiment with genre boundaries. For example, Barbara Kingsolver's *The Lacuna* (2009), which won the Orange Prize for Fiction in 2010, can be considered a work of Literary Fiction, but because of the time period in which it is set—in the 1930s–1950s—and because it is based upon the author's research rather than personal experience, we place it in the Historical Fiction genre.

Or, how about an author like Margaret Atwood? She commonly appears on lists of Literary Fiction authors, and you'll typically find her books in the Fiction section, rather than the Science Fiction section of your local public library. Yet, her 2010 novel *The Year of the Flood* is set in a postapocalyptic future, qualifying it for the Science Fiction chapter of this guide.

Today, librarians and readers see a great deal of what is called crossover or "genreblending," which makes using appeal factors to help readers find good books even more useful than ever.

They're also noticing that novels representing various cultures and countries are more abundant and in greater demand. Multicultural Fiction, across the genres, exposes readers to diverse points of view and helps members of cultural communities find characters they can identify with. Multicultural titles within the Mainstream Fiction genre often relate to the immigrant experience, if set in the United States, or present a minority perspective, such as gay and lesbian lifestyles.

Popular multicultural Mainstream Fiction authors include Jhumpa Lahiri and Amy Tan (Asian Americans), Toni Morrison and Colson Whitehead (African Americans), Sandra Cisneros and Oscar Hijuelos (Hispanic Americans), and Sherman Alexie and Louise Erdrich (Native Americans). Books by these and other multicultural authors often make terrific book group choices, leading to engaging discussions about cultural differences and similarities.

Another interesting trend in Mainstream Fiction is the rising popularity of novels that are hybrids of novels and short stories. These novels consist of linked short stories that could probably stand on their own, but are connected to each other through characters or setting, creating a narrative arc that feels more like a novel, even if the connections aren't obvious at times. Elizabeth Strout's *Olive Kitteridge* (2008), Colum McCann's *Let the Great World Spin* (2009), Jennifer Egan's *A Visit from the Goon Squad* (2010), and Tom Rachman's *The Imperfectionists* (2010) are popular examples of this trend.

Working with Mainstream Fiction Readers

Readers' advisors working with Mainstream Fiction fans face some challenges. Without genres and subgenres to help readers find the books they will enjoy reading, where can they turn for guidance? Well, beyond using the appeals features approach—which is generally restricted to instances where you are conducting a readers' advisory interview and are working with titles that have been assigned appeals features, such as those in this chapter—there are some other ways to approach the genre and its readers. Book lists, including lists of award winners, as well as book discussion groups are proven methods for working with Mainstream Fiction readers.

Book Lists

Who doesn't love a good book list? Mainstream Fiction readers often use book lists to lead them to what they're going to read next. Whether it's a list of classics, bestsellers, author read-alikes, or award winners, you can use a list as a starting point and then journey from there.

Bestseller lists can be based on sales—*New York Times*, *Publishers Weekly*, *USA Today*, and Amazon are frequently cited—or library circulation, such as the *Library Journal* list of books most borrowed in U.S. public libraries. Independent bookstores who belong to the American Booksellers Association share their sales data each week to create Indie Bestsellers Lists in several categories, including one for trade paperback fiction, which commonly includes works of mainstream and Literary Fiction. The booksellers at those stores also contribute to the *Indie Next List*, which is essentially an annotated book list of recommended new releases for each month, available in print at independent bookstores nationwide and online (www.indiebound.org).

Many libraries and bookstores produce their own lists of books or authors as a way of helping direct readers to a variety of books. Or, they access reading lists in *NoveList Plus*, a popular subscription database. The lists might be organized by a theme, such as High Comedy Authors or Best Books for Book Groups. Or, they might be read-alike lists for popular authors or specific book titles, or books written by authors representing a certain culture or ethnicity, such as Asian American or African American. These can be a great way of introducing readers to authors or books they might not be aware of, or in the case of libraries, to tide readers over while the bestsellers are all checked out.

And now, of course, thanks to online social networking and tagging functionality, people are exploring all kinds of new ways to create and share lists of books that they've read or want to suggest to others. They're on *Amazon*, *Facebook*, library catalogs, blogs, and sites like *Goodreads*, *LibraryThing*, and *Shelfari*, which help readers keep track of what they've read and share their opinions.

Book Discussion Groups

No discussion of Mainstream Fiction would be complete without mentioning book discussion groups. Book groups have been around for ages, but it was TV personality Oprah Winfrey who made them part of mainstream popular culture when she announced the creation of Oprah's Book Club in 1996. Her announcement inspired millions of Americans to start their own book groups and to read and buy books, providing a huge boost to the publishing industry and making some previously under-the-radar authors famous (and rich).

By April 2002, when the original Book Club officially ended, Oprah had championed 48 books for reading and discussion, 44 of which were works of fiction for adults. In general, Oprah's Book Club selections were considered accessible Literary Fiction, covering a broad range of subjects and themes, but mostly telling stories about people (usually women) facing some kind of personal challenge or conflict and then growing in the process. A good example is Wally Lamb's *She's Come Undone* (1992), the story of a teenager overcoming rape and self-hatred. Other examples include Anna Quindlen's *Black and Blue* (1998) and Ursula Hegi's *Stones from the River* (1994).

Oprah reintroduced her Book Club in 2003, focusing on classics, making a new selection every few months or so. She had not lost her Midas touch (or the "Oprah effect"). When she chose *Anna Karenina* by Leo Tolstoy, an 864-page novel originally published in 1875, as her summer selection for 2004, it immediately soared to the top of the bestseller lists. By 2006, she moved away from classics and chose new Book Club titles only occasionally, from various genres, but continued to make them instant bestsellers. (For a complete list of Oprah's Book Club selections, see www.oprah.com/oprahsbookclub/Complete-List-of-Oprahs-Book-Club-Books.)

What makes a novel a good candidate for a book group discussion? You want books that have a main character whose actions can be interpreted or understood in different ways. It helps if the main character is forced to make a choice that incites a strong reaction from you as you read the book, or if the subject matter is controversial. You'll want to discuss what is happening just below the surface or between the lines, rather than focusing on specific actions, which is why novels that are described as Literary Fiction are chosen so often by book groups. Books with ambiguous or open endings are especially successful in book group settings, sparking stimulating debates.

Many of the novels in this chapter would work well for book groups. They are indicated with a special symbol. 📖 Look for them in other chapters also.

THEMES AND TYPES

Key to Mainstream Fiction

(Rather than arranging Mainstream Fiction by subgenre, the author has arranged the books by appeal factor.)

Language

Character

Story

Setting

What follows is a list of recently published Mainstream Fiction novels that are already proving to be reader favorites, representing a broad range of authors and reading experiences. As mentioned previously, this list generally picks up where *Now Read This III* left off and goes through 2011, with just a bit of overlap, and is organized by appeal factor.

Language

Novels noted for the appeal of language are those in which the style and construction of the writing are the most notable features. Sometimes the style is experimental or unusual. Sometimes it is poetic. Reviews of novels that have language as the dominant appeal are often described as "lyrical" or "evocative," or, on the other end of the spectrum, may be noted for being "spare" because of an elegant, minimal approach. Works described as Literary Fiction often fall into this category.

Alexie, Sherman. *War Dances*. Grove Press, 2009. 209p. 978080 2119193. Described by the author as a "mix tape" of a book, this bittersweet collection of short stories and poems, which won the PEN/ Faulkner Award, takes on intersecting themes of identity, race, love, betrayal, and family. Alexie is a Spokane/Couer d'Alene Indian who has won numerous awards, including the National Book Award for Young People's Literature for *The Absolutely True Diary of a Part-time Indian* (2007).

Amis, Martin. *The Pregnant Widow: Inside History*. Alfred A. Knopf, 2010. 370p. 9781400044528. Told primarily in flashbacks, Keith Nearing recalls the "erotically decisive summer" of 1970, when he was 20 and lived with friends in a castle on an Italian mountainside, spending his days reading, talking, and figuring out his place within the sexual revolution.

Auster, Paul. *Invisible*. Henry Holt and Co., 2009. 308p. 978080 5090802. As a 1967 undergraduate and aspiring poet at Columbia University, Adam Walker gets caught up in the lives of an unstable visiting professor and his girlfriend. Many of Auster's hallmark traits are on display: multiple narrators, stories within stories, themes related to memory and one's search for identity, and ruminations on writing and language. A *New York Times* Notable book.

Bakker, Gerbrand. *The Twin*. Archipelago Books, 2009. 343p. 9780 980033021. More than 30 years after the death of his identical twin brother, which forced him to leave college and return to the family farm in the Netherlands, Helmer contemplates how he ended up living the life that was supposed to be his brother's. Translated from Dutch. Winner of the International IMPAC Dublin Literary Award.

Banville, John. *The Infinities*. Alfred A. Knopf, 2010. 273p. 9780307272799. Gods and mortals intermingle in this story narrated by Hermes, messenger of the gods (but disguised as a farmer), about a theoretical mathematician who lies on his deathbed, surrounded by his family members who have assembled there. Banville won the Man Booker Prize for *The Sea* (2005), and also writes crime fiction under the pseudonym of Benjamin Black.

🎗 📖 **Barnes, Julian.** *The Sense of an Ending*. Alfred A. Knopf, 2011. 163p. 9780307957122. When Tony Webster, a middle-aged man living near London, is unexpectedly bequeathed a journal written by a former school friend who died more than 40 years ago, he finds himself questioning his memories of that time and of his relationships throughout his life. Winner of the Man Booker Prize, a *New York Times Notable* book, and an ALA Notable book. **Second Appeal**: Character.

📖 **Bender, Aimee.** *The Particular Sadness of Lemon Cake*. Doubleday, 2010. 292p. 9780385501125. Just before she turns nine, Rose Edelstein samples the lemon chocolate birthday cake that her mother baked for her and discovers she can taste her mother's feelings in each bite she takes. Is it a gift or a curse? **Second Appeal**: Character.

🎗 **Bolaño, Roberto.** *2666*. Farrar, Straus and Giroux, 2008. 898p. 9780 374100148. The five sections of this huge novel (which were originally intended to be published as separate novels) are connected by a series of crimes against women in Santa Teresa (a fictional stand-in for Ciudad Juárez) on the United States–Mexico border, where hundreds of young factory workers have disappeared. Winner of the National Book Critics Circle Award and a *New York Times* Notable book. Translated from Spanish.

📖 **Clinch, Jon.** *Kings of the Earth*. Random House, 2010. 393p. 9781400069019. Three elderly, illiterate brothers, who are dairy farmers in Upstate New York, have shared a bed all their lives. When one of the brothers dies in his sleep, the other brothers become murder suspects. Told from the viewpoints of alternating narrators and spanning 60 years, this novel is inspired by the real-life Ward brothers, who were featured in the 1992 documentary *My Brother's Keeper*.

Coetzee, J. M. *Summertime*. Viking, 2009. 266p. 9780670021383. Nobel laureate and two-time Booker Prize winner Coetzee completes his trilogy of autobiographical novels (after *Boyhood* [1997] and *Youth* [2002]) by looking back on the late John Coetzee's life in the form of journal entries and transcripts from interviews with five people who knew him.

🎗 **Cole, Teju.** *Open City*. Random House, 2011. 259p. 9781400068098. This debut novel by a Nigerian-born author delves into the innermost thoughts of Julius, a young Nigerian doctor, as he contemplates life during long walks through New York City and listens to the stories of fellow immigrants. Winner of the PEN/Hemingway Foundation Award and a *New York Times* Notable book.

📖 **Cunningham, Michael.** *By Nightfall*. Farrar, Straus and Giroux, 2010. 256p. 9780374299088. Soho art gallery owner Peter Harris and his wife Rebecca, an art magazine editor, live a comfortable life in Manhattan until Rebecca's beautiful but recovering drug-addict brother arrives.

🎗 **Dee, Jonathan.** *The Privileges*. Random House, 2010. 258p. 978140 0068678. A charming young couple marries immediately after college, quickly has four children, and then becomes impossibly rich after some high-stakes insider trading. Written in a prose-style reminiscent of John Updike, this novel confronts questions about whether money can actually make you happy and whether the way you make that money really matters. A *New York Times* Notable book.

DeLillo, Don. *Point Omega*. Scribner, 2010. 117p. 9781439169957. Documentary filmmaker Jim Finley follows Richard Elster, a disillusioned "defense intellectual" who helped plan the Iraq War, to the California desert so he can make a film about him, but the arrival of Elster's daughter alters his plans. DeLillo is known for his spare, understated prose and this brief, bleak novel is a good example.

🎗 **D'Erasmo, Stacey.** *The Sky Below*. Houghton Mifflin Harcourt, 2009. 271p. 9780618439256. A grim medical diagnosis prompts 37-year-old Gabriel, an artist who works as an obituary writer in post-9/11 Manhattan, to turn his back on his rich older boyfriend and flee to a Mexican commune in an attempt to transform himself. A *New York Times* Notable book. **Second Appeal**: Character.

Must Read

🎗 📖 **Egan, Jennifer.** *A Visit from the Goon Squad*. Alfred A. Knopf, 2010. 273p. 9780307592835. Highly original novel of interlocking stories that move back and forth in time, all of them linked in some way to Bennie Salazar, former bass player in a 1970s punk band turned record company executive and music producer in the near future. Winner of the Pulitzer Prize for Fiction, the National Books Critics Circle Award for Fiction, a *New York Times* Notable book, and an ALA Notable book. **Second Appeal**: Character.

📖 **Ferris, Joshua.** *The Unnamed*. Little, Brown and Co., 2010. 313p. 9780316034012. An uncontrollable compulsion to get up from whatever he's doing and walk for miles and miles repeatedly strikes Manhattan attorney Tim Farnsworth, inflicting a huge physical and psychological toll on Tim and his family. Ferris was recently named one of *The New Yorker* magazine's "20 Under 40" leading fiction writers. **Second Appeal**: Story.

🎗 **Goldman, Francisco.** *Say Her Name*. Grove Press, 2011. 350p. 978080 2119810. The author's own tragic experience of losing his young wife in a bodysurfing accident shortly before their second anniversary informs this highly personal novel about loss, grief, and love. A *New York Times* Notable book and an ALA Notable book.

Goldstein, Rebecca. *36 Arguments for the Existence of God: A Work of Fiction*. Pantheon Books, 2010. 402p. 9780307378187. Psychology of Religion professor Cass Seltzer achieves celebrity status and is dubbed "the atheist with a soul" after publishing a surprise bestselling book that lists and debunks 36 arguments for the existence of God. This is an erudite work of satirical fiction that intertwines religion, science, and philosophy, crafted by a MacArthur genius-grant recipient.

🎗 **Gordon, Jaimy.** *Lord of Misrule*. McPherson & Co., 2010. 294p. 97809 29701837. Horse trainer Tommy Hansel plans to get rich quick at Indian Mount Downs, a small-stakes West Virginia racetrack, but the sketchy folks who live and work there are on to him. Plus, the horses may not cooperate. Thick with the vernacular of the horse-racing world, this novel was a surprise winner of the National Book Award. **Second Appeal**: Character.

🎗 📖 **Harding, Paul.** *Tinkers*. Bellevue Literary Press, 2009. 191p. 9781934137123. Lying on his deathbed, George Washington Crosby hallucinates and travels back through memories of his life—his love of repairing antique clocks, his hardscrabble childhood, and, especially, his epileptic father, a traveling salesman and tinker who abandoned the family when George was 12. Winner of the Pulitzer Prize for Fiction and an ALA Notable book.

Hodgen, Christie. *Elegies for the Brokenhearted*. W. W. Norton & Co., 2010. 271p. 9780393061. In a series of five quirky elegies for people who have shaped her, Mary Murphy tells the story of her life, beginning with her erratic childhood spent in several different homes with her sister and an attractive mother who marries five times.

🎗 📖 **Hollinghurst, Alan.** *The Stranger's Child*. Alfred A. Knopf, 2011. 435p. 9780307272768. While visiting his Cambridge classmate's home outside

London in the summer of 1913, an aristocratic young man writes a poem that becomes an English classic after his death and links two families for generations. Hollinghurst won the Man Booker prize for *The Line of Beauty* (2004). A *New York Times* Notable book.

Hynes, James. *Next*. Little, Brown and Co., 2010. 308p. 9780316051927. Can you reinvent yourself when you're 50 and full of neuroses? Kevin Quinn gives it a shot, secretly flying from Michigan to Texas for a job interview. The next eight hours fill the rest of this bitingly funny, touching, and shocking novel. An ALA Notable book. **Second Appeal**: Character.

Ishiguro, Kazuo. *Nocturnes: Five Stories of Music and Nightfall*. Alfred A. Knopf, 2009. 221p. 9780307271020. Ishiguro, who won the Booker Prize for *Remains of the Day* (1989), presents five impeccably crafted, loosely connected stories that range from farcical to reflective. All told in the first person, by five different narrators, they share a common theme of music and an air of regret. A *New York Times* Notable book.

Kehlmann, Daniel. *Fame: A Novel in Nine Episodes*. Pantheon Books, 2010. 192p. 9780307378712. Bitingly clever, dark satire about the ups and downs of notoriety, which begins when a man buys a new cell phone and is accidentally assigned the number belonging to a movie star, igniting a giant case of mistaken identity. Translated from German.

Lee, Chang-rae. *The Surrendered*. Riverhead Books, 2010. 469p. 9781594489761. The lasting wounds of war permeate the lives of three people initially drawn together at a Korean orphanage: June, the 11-year-old whose family perished during the Korean War; Hector, an American GI who works at the orphanage as a handyman; and Sylvie, the missionary wife who runs the orphanage with her husband. An ALA Notable book and a *New York Times* Notable book. **Second Appeal**: Character.

Li, Yiyun. *The Vagrants*. Random House, 2009. 337p. 9781400063130. In the fictional town of China's Muddy River in 1979, 28-year-old Gu Shun, a former Red Guard leader, is sentenced to a horrific public execution. Her death affects the townspeople who witnessed it in different ways. Li was recently named one of *The New Yorker* magazine's "20 Under 40" leading fiction writers. An ALA Notable book.

Mandanipour, Shahriar. *Censoring an Iranian Love Story*. Alfred A. Knopf, 2009. 295p. 9780307269782. Stylishly innovative, Postmodern novel that simultaneously tells two stories: one about an Iranian author whose attempts to write a love story set in present-day Iran are censored by the government and the other containing the romantic story taking place within the censored novel, which centers on a young couple who fall in love at the library, despite their country's rules forbidding social interaction between young men and women. Translated from Farsi.

McCarthy, Tom. *C*. Alfred A. Knopf, 2010. 320p. 9780307593337. Inventive, Postmodern novel about Serge Carrefax, who is born in England at the beginning of the 20th century and grows up in a household where his inventor-father runs a school for the deaf and experiments with new methods of communication. As an adult, Serge serves in World War I and then works in Egypt, where communication and connection (perhaps the inspiration for the book's enigmatic title?) seem to surround him, but do not necessarily involve him.

🏶 **Means, David.** *The Spot: Stories*. Faber and Faber, 2010. 164p. 978086 5479128. In his fourth collection of short stories, Means continues to garner comparisons to Raymond Carver because of his spare writing style and his ability to convey what's going on in the minds of his characters, many of whom live on the edges of society. A *New York Times* Notable book.

🏶 **Mengestu, Dinaw.** *How to Read the Air*. Riverhead Books, 2010. 320p. 9781594487705. Jonas, the American son of Ethiopian immigrants, leaves his job and marriage in New York to retrace the honeymoon trip his parents took 30 years before, from Peoria, Illinois, to Nashville, Tennessee, in an attempt to understand his family's history. Mengestu was recently named one of *The New Yorker* magazine's "20 Under 40" leading fiction writers. A *New York Times* Notable book. **Second Appeal**: Character.

🏶 **Moore, Lorrie.** *A Gate at the Stairs*. Alfred A. Knopf, 2009. 321p. 9780375409288. Tassie Kelttjin, a smart but naïve 20-year-old college student in a Midwestern town, becomes a nanny for an affluent couple who wind up not being quite what they seem in this novel that looks at race, 9/11, and betrayal. A *New York Times* Notable book.

🏶 **Munro, Alice.** *Too Much Happiness: Stories*. Alfred A. Knopf, 2009. 303p. 9780307269768. Winner of the Man Booker International Prize for her overall body of work, Canadian author Munro presents another collection of short stories that helps cement her reputation as one of the finest living short-story writers. These 10 stories explore themes of grief and loss in a sometimes unsettling way, but always in vivid, spare prose. A *New York Times* Notable book.

🏵 📖 **Obreht, Téa.** *The Tiger's Wife*. Random House, 2011. 337p. 9780385343831. While traveling across the border of a war-torn Balkan country to vaccinate orphans, Natalia learns that her beloved grandfather died alone on a trip away from home. As she investigates the circumstances of her grandfather's death, she recalls his stories about a "deathless man" and an escaped tiger that lived above his childhood village. Obreht is the youngest writer to be named one of *The New Yorker* magazine's recent "20 Under 40" leading fiction writers. Winner of the Orange Prize for Fiction, the Indies Choice Award for Adult Debut, a *New York Times* Notable book, and an ALA Notable book. **Second Appeal**: Setting.

Ōe, Kenzaburō. *The Changeling*. Grove Press, 2010. 468p. 9780802119360. Kogito, a Japanese author in his early 60s, receives a trunk full of cassette tapes that contain a series of reflective monologues by his long-time friend and brother-in-law Goro, just before Goro commits suicide. Kogito desperately tries to piece together what happened and obsesses over the tapes, hoping they might provide a clue, as he ponders the nature of life and death. Ōe won the Nobel Prize for Literature in 1994. Translated from Japanese.

🏵 📖 **Ondaatje, Michael.** *The Cat's Table*. Alfred A. Knopf, 2011. 269p. 9780307700117. In 1953, an 11-year-old boy travels for 21 days aboard the *Oronsay*, a ship bound from Ceylon to England, and forms a fast friendship with two other boys also assigned to eat at the cat's table, the least privileged place in the dining room. Together, they go on adventures, exploring the floating universe of the ship, meeting fascinating characters, and learning life lessons. A *New York Times* Notable book and an ALA Notable book.

🏵 **Petterson, Per.** *I Curse the River of Time*. Graywolf Press, 2010. 233p. 9781555975562. In a spare prose style, Norwegian author Per Petterson (best known for 2007's award-winning *Out Stealing Horses*) follows 37-year-old Arvid Jansen during a few intense days in 1989 as his marriage ends and his mother is diagnosed with stomach cancer. Prequel to *In the Wake*, published in the United States in 2006. Translated from Norwegian. A *New York Times* Notable book. **Second Appeal**: Character.

🏵 📖 **Phillips, Arthur.** *The Tragedy of Arthur*. Random House, 2011. 368p. 9781400066476. Arthur Phillips and his twin sister Dana grow up in awe of their charming father, a man who loves Shakespeare, but also happens to be an incarcerated con artist with one last request of his son: publish "The Tragedy of Arthur," a stolen play he's hidden for years, written by the Bard himself. Or was it? A *New York Times* Notable book and an ALA Notable book.

Powers, Richard. *Generosity: An Enhancement*. Farrar, Straus and Giroux, 2009. 296p. 9780374161149. Powers, who won the 2006 National Book Award for *The Echo Maker*, returns to complex themes of science and technology in this novel about an Algerian refugee college student in Chicago who seems impossibly cheerful and the people who want to exploit the young woman because they think she might possess a gene that causes extreme happiness. An ALA Notable book and a *New York Times* Notable book.

Robinson, Marilyn. *Home*. Farrar, Straus and Giroux, 2008. 325p. 9780374299101. After 20 years away, prodigal son Jack Boughton returns home to Gilead, Iowa, in the 1950s to help his sister Glory care for their dying father in this follow-up to Robinson's Pulitzer Prize–winning novel, *Gilead* (2004). Winner of the Orange Prize for Fiction and a *New York Times* Notable book. **Second Appeal**: Character.

Roth, Philip. *The Humbling*. Houghton Mifflin Harcourt, 2009. 140p. 9780547239699. When Simon Axler, a leading American stage actor in his 60s, feels his acting skills decline and his confidence slip away, he eventually retreats to a farmhouse where an unexpected visit from a younger woman results in an all-encompassing sexual affair.

Spiotta, Dana. *Stone Arabia*. Scribner, 2011. 239p. 9781451617962. Two adult siblings live hopelessly intertwined lives in Los Angeles, while struggling with issues of authenticity, connection, and memory. Nik, a reclusive artist and musician, creates and documents a series of self-produced albums for an audience of one—his older sister Denise—complete with fictional critical reviews and interviews. Devoted Denise repeatedly bails out Nik financially, but suspects her support might be doing more harm than good. A *New York Times* Notable book. **Second Appeal**: Character.

Syjuco, Miguel. *Ilustrado*. Farrar, Straus and Giroux, 2010. 306p. 9780374174781. When the body of a famous Filipino writer is pulled from the Hudson River, the writer's protégé travels to Manila in search of answers, tracing 150 years of Philippine history, presented in a collage of formats, including poems, interviews, fragments of manuscripts, and e-mails. Winner of the 2008 Man Asian Literary Award as an unpublished manuscript and a *New York Times* Notable book.

🎗 📖 **Trevor, William.** *Love and Summer*. Viking, 2009. 211p. 9780670021239. Once again, Irish author Trevor displays his mastery of graceful prose in this *New York Times* Notable book about Ellie, a shy young farmer's wife raised by nuns, who lives a quiet life in the small Irish town of Rathmoye until she encounters a young photographer who cycles into town. **Second Appeal**: Character.

🎗 **Updike, John.** *My Father's Tears and Other Stories*. Alfred A. Knopf, 2009. 292p. 9780307271563. Posthumously published collection of the last stories written by highly lauded, award-winning writer John Updike. These 18 moving and melancholy short stories primarily deal with family dynamics and relationships, such as the title story, about a man recalling the only time he ever saw his father cry. A *New York Times* Notable book.

🎗 **Walbert, Kate.** *A Short History of Women*. Scribner, 2009. 239p. 9781416594987. Beginning with Dorothy Townsend, a suffragette who dies during a hunger strike in England in 1914, five generations of women from one family are linked not just by blood, but by feelings of uncertainty and discontent in these interconnected short stories that crisscross a century. A *New York Times* Notable book.

🎗 **Ward, Jesmyn.** *Salvage the Bones*. Bloomsbury, 2011. 261p. 9781608195220. As Hurricane Katrina threatens to destroy her family's Mississippi home, 14-year-old Esch already has her hands full, thanks to her brother Skeetah's fighting pit bull just delivering a litter of pups, her alcoholic father's inability to help her raise her brothers after her mother's death, and Esch's dawning realization that she's pregnant. Winner of the National Book Award. **Second Appeal**: Character.

Character

Novels that center on well-developed characters with whom readers can connect and empathize—or become fascinated with—are referred to as "character-based." The characters feel real to us—they are three-dimensional and stay with us more than their actions do. Novels that include a character's name or a reference to a character's role in life within the title are generally character-driven, such as Pete Dexter's *Spooner* (2009) and Julia Glass's *The Widower's Tale* (2010). People who read for character often enjoy memoirs and biographies, as well.

Adichie, Chimamanda Ngozi. *The Thing Around Your Neck*. Alfred A. Knopf, 2009. 217p. 9780307271075. Nigerian American author

Adichie, who won a MacArthur genius grant at 31 and the Orange Prize for Fiction for *Half of a Yellow Sun* (2006), presents a collection of 12 short stories set in the United States and Nigeria that examine the tension felt between Nigerians and Nigerian Americans. Adichie was also recently named one of *The New Yorker* magazine's "20 Under 40" leading fiction writers.

🎗 📖 **Baker, Nicholson.** *The Anthologist*. Simon & Schuster, 2009. 243p. 9781416572442. On the verge of a breakdown, poet Paul Chowder finds a myriad of ways to delay writing the introduction to an anthology of poetry (called *Only Rhyme*), including cleaning out his office and having imaginary conversations with poets like Theodore Roethke. An ALA Notable book and a *New York Times* Notable book.

🎗 **Banks, Russell.** *Lost Memory of Skin*. Ecco, 2011. 416p. 9780061857638. The Kid, a homeless 22-year-old sex offender who grew addicted to Internet porn at age 10 and now lives with other homeless sex offenders under a Florida causeway, becomes the research subject of a university sociologist who has a complicated past of his own. A *New York Times* Notable book and an ALA Notable book.

Bloom, Amy. *Where the God of Love Hangs Out*. Random House, 2009. 201p. 9781400063574. Two sets of linked short stories and four standalone stories delve into various expressions of love among memorable characters, including family members, a pair of middle-aged friends who are drawn to each other while married to other people, and a young woman who is haunted by her roommate's murder. **Second Appeal**: Language.

🎗 📖 **Cleave, Chris.** *Little Bee*. Simon & Schuster, 2009. 271p. 9781416589 631. Little Bee, a 16-year-old Nigerian refugee, and Sarah, a British fashion magazine editor, narrate alternating chapters of a story that begins with an act of unimaginable violence on an African beach, and then migrates to a London suburb where their two lives intersect. An ALA Notable book.

Conroy, Pat. *South of Broad*. Doubleday, 2009. 514p. 9780385413053. Alternating between 1969 and 1989, Leopold Bloom King narrates this occasionally melodramatic story about his diverse group of friends from Charleston, South Carolina, who rally together to help one of their own in San Francisco.

🎗 📖 **Dexter, Pete.** *Spooner*. Grand Central Pub., 2009. 469p. 9780446540 728. In this semiautobiographical novel, Warren Spooner lives a tragicomic life full of bad choices and misadventures—from his small-town Georgia childhood to his career as a journalist in Philadelphia—but is sustained by his relationship with his nurturing stepfather, Calmer Ottosson. An ALA Notable book. **Second Appeal**: Language.

🎗 📖 **Durrow, Heidi.** *The Girl Who Fell from the Sky*. Algonquin Books, 2010. 264p. 9781565126800. Rachel, the daughter of a Danish mother and African American father (like the author), survives a terrible childhood tragedy and goes to live with her paternal grandmother in Portland, Oregon, in 1982, where she must deal with issues of race, identity, and her painful family history. Told from multiple viewpoints, this debut novel won the Bellwether Prize. **Second Appeal**: Language.

Eberstadt, Fernanda. *Rat*. Alfred A. Knopf, 2010. 293p. 9780307271839. Fifteen-year-old Celia Bonnet, nicknamed "Rat," lives a scruffy life in the Pyrenees with her loving but flakey mom. Rat flees to London, though, after a disturbing incident involving her mother's boyfriend, and searches for her biological father, whom she's never met.

🎗 **Eisenberg, Deborah.** *The Collected Stories of Deborah Eisenberg*. Picador, 2010. 992p. 9780312429898. Four of Deborah Eisenberg's previous volumes of short stories, including *Twilight of the Superheroes* (2006), are contained in this hefty collection. Her stories offer a perceptive view of contemporary American life, thanks to fully realized characters and a good ear for dialog. Winner of the PEN/Faulkner Award.

🎗 📖 **Erdrich, Louise.** *Shadow Tag*. Harper, 2010. 255p. 9780061536090. Tragic story about the deteriorating marriage of an affluent Native American couple who live in Minnesota with their three children. While wife Irene tries to convince her volatile husband Gil to divorce her by keeping a faux diary full of fake sexual exploits that she knows he'll read (and also keeps a real diary in a safe deposit box at the bank), Gil paints increasingly humiliating portraits of Irene. A *New York Times* Notable book. **Second Appeal**: Language.

🎗 📖 **Eugenides, Jeffrey.** *The Marriage Plot*. Farrar, Straus and Giroux, 2011. 406p. 9780374203054. At Brown University in the early 1980s, it's time for English major Madeleine Hanna to stretch herself beyond the familiar world of Austen and James, so she enrolls in a semiotics course where she falls for Leonard Morten, a brilliant and mysterious loner, complicating the plans of religious studies student Mitchell Grammaticus, who is convinced that he and Madeleine are destined to spend their lives together. Eugenides won the Pultizer Prize for *Middlesex* (2002). Winner of the Indies Choice Award for Adult Fiction and a *New York Times* Notable book.

Evans, Danielle. *Before You Suffocate Your Own Fool Self.* Riverhead Books, 2010. 240p. 9781594487699. Debut collection of funny and heartbreakingly real stories, mostly about African American and mixed-race teen girls and young women who must make complicated choices.

Faulks, Sebastian. *A Week in December.* Doubleday, 2009. 392p. 9780 385532914. In contemporary London, various aspects of modern urban life are dissected when a formal dinner party brings together a diverse group of guests, including a ruthless hedge fund manager, a Polish soccer player, a nasty book critic, and a Pakistani couple whose son might be linked to terrorism.

🎗 📖 **Franzen, Jonathan.** *Freedom.* Farrar, Straus and Giroux, 2010. 576p. 9780374158460. Author Franzen takes another stab at writing the Great American Novel, nine years after publishing *The Corrections* (2001), winner of the National Book Award. This time he shrewdly examines modern American culture by dissecting the household of Walter and Patty Berglund, a politically correct couple whose marriage is unraveling in St. Paul, Minnesota. An ALA Notable book and a *New York Times* Notable book. An Oprah Book Club selection.

📖 **Glass, Julia.** *The Widower's Tale.* Pantheon Books, 2010. 402p. 97803073 77920. Retired Harvard librarian Percy Darling lives comfortably alone in a farmhouse outside of Boston, but is persuaded to disrupt his life and let a preschool move into his barn because of the job opportunity it provides for his struggling daughter, Clover. Glass, author of the National Book Award–winning *Three Junes* (2002), once again skillfully portrays the intricate dynamics of family relationships.

📖 **Goodman, Allegra.** *The Cookbook Collector.* Dial Press, 2010. 394p. 97803 85340854. Love, loyalty, competition, and greed all play roles in this smart story about two sisters—one a 28-year-old CEO of a Silicon Valley start-up about to go public during the dot-com heyday, and the other a 23-year-old Berkeley grad student who works part-time at an antiquarian book store. **Second Appeal**: Story.

🎗 📖 **Harbach, Chad.** *The Art of Fielding.* Little, Brown and Co., 2011. 512p. 9780316126694. A deep friendship and love for the game connect superstar shortstop Henry Skrimshander and his mentor, catcher Mike Schwartz, two members of a small liberal arts college baseball team in Wisconsin. They just might have a shot at a championship, but Henry begins to battle self-doubt after an unfortunate error that has lasting consequences for his gay roommate Owen. A *New York Times* Notable book and an ALA Notable book.

Hijuelos, Oscar. *Beautiful María of My Soul, or, The True Story of María García y Cifuentes, the Lady behind a Famous Song*. Hyperion, 2010. 340p. 9781401323349. A partial retelling and sequel, of sorts, to the Pulitzer Prize–winning *The Mambo Kings Play Songs of Love* (1989), told from the point of view of María, the dazzling Cuban woman who inspired the Mambo Kings' biggest hit song in the first novel. Now 60, Maria looks back on her life, recalling her experiences of passionate love, sex, and beauty.

Hornby, Nick. *Juliet, Naked*. Riverhead Books, 2009. 406p. 9781594488870. Annie wonders whether she's wasted her life by spending 15 years with Duncan, who seems to be more infatuated with reclusive rock star Tucker Crowe than he is with her, especially after *Juliet, Naked*, a stripped-down version of Crowe's masterpiece breakup album, is released.

Jacobson, Howard. *The Finkler Question*. Bloomsbury, 2010. 307p. 9781608196111. Three men—two are Jewish and one is not—grapple with issues of self-identity as they explore what it means to be Jewish in modern-day London. Winner of the Man Booker Prize.

King, Lily. *Father of the Rain*. Atlantic Monthly Press, 2010. 354p. Eleven-year-old Daley feels her loyalties pulled in two directions when her mother leaves her alcoholic father, a man Daley can't help adoring, even as she grows older and more aware of how damaged he is.

Krauss, Nicole. *Great House*. W. W. Norton & Co., 2010. 289p. 9780393079982. A massive old desk links generations of people, multiple continents, and the four novellas that make up this captivating novel about memory and loss, written by the author of *The History of Love* (2005). Krauss was recently named one of *The New Yorker* magazine's "20 Under 40" leading fiction writers. A *New York Times* Notable book.

Lamott, Anne. *Imperfect Birds*. Riverhead Books, 2010. 278p. 9781594487514. Beautiful 17-year-old Rosie appears to be the ideal daughter, great at school and sports, but Rosie's mother and stepfather discover that she has duped them and is, in fact, abusing drugs and alcohol. Rosie first appeared in Lamott's earlier novels, *Rosie* (1983) and *Crooked Little Heart* (1997).

Lipsyte, Sam. *The Ask*. Farrar, Straus and Giroux, 2010. 296p. 9780374298913. Very dark, satirical story about self-loathing cynic Milo Burke, who loses his job as a fund-raiser for a mediocre New

York university, then scrambles to make ends meet to support his family. He might get his university job back, though, if he can secure a major donation from "the Ask," a former classmate who is now a millionaire with some special requests. A *New York Times* Notable book. **Second Appeal**: Language.

McMillan, Terry. *Getting to Happy.* Viking, 2010. 375p. 9780670022045. Author McMillan revisits friends Bernadine, Gloria, Robin, and Savannah—now in their late 40s and early 50s, and still supporting each other as they face more big changes in their lives—in this sequel to *Waiting to Exhale* (1992).

🎀 **Nicholls, David.** *One Day.* Vintage Books, 2010. 437p. 9780307474711. On July 15, 1988, Emma and Dexter graduate from the University of Edinburgh, share a bed, and go their separate ways. Then, their lives are revisited every July 15 for the next 19 years in this novel that draws frequent comparisons to the work of Nick Hornby. A *New York Times* Notable book. **Second Appeal**: Story.

📖 **Patchett, Ann.** *State of Wonder.* Harper, 2011. 353p. 9780062049803. Marina Singh, a Minnesota pharmaceutical scientist, descends into the Amazon jungle looking for answers after her colleague travels there and dies under mysterious circumstances. She must also pick up where he left off—searching for the noncommunicative Dr. Annick Swenson, who hopes to create a lucrative new fertility drug while on a secret research project that investigates how local tribal women can give birth into their 60s and 70s. **Second Appeal**: Setting.

🎀📖 **Phillips, Jayne Anne.** *Lark and Termite.* Alfred A. Knopf, 2009. 254p. 9780375401954. Set during the 1950s and told from multiple perspectives, this novel travels from Korea, where a young U.S. soldier is serving a tour of duty, to a small West Virginia town, where 17-year-old Lark helps take care of her 9-year-old half-brother, Termite, who cannot walk or talk. A *New York Times* Notable book.

🎀 **Rachman, Tom.** *The Imperfectionists.* Dial Press, 2010. 272p. 9780385343664. Chronicles the 50-year history of a floundering English-language newspaper based in Rome and paints true-to-life portraits of the people who worked on it, published it, and read it. Funny and poignant debut novel by a former editor of the *International Herald Tribune*. A *New York Times* Notable book. **Second appeal**: Setting.

📖 **Schwarz, Ghita.** *Displaced Persons.* William Morrow, 2010. 340p. 9780061881909. Pavel, Fela, and Chaim, three Polish Jews who survived a World War II concentration camp, must carry around the traumatic events of their past as they search for surviving relatives and eventually attempt to forge new lives in the United States.

📖 **Simonson, Helen.** *Major Pettigrew's Last Stand*. Random House, 2010. 358p. 9781400068937. Retired British Army officer Major Ernest Pettigrew, a 68-year-old widower, lives a quiet, proper life in the English village of Edgecombe St. Mary until he bonds with Jasmina Ali, a local Pakistani shopkeeper who has also lost a spouse and shares a love of literature.

🎗 📖 **Soli, Tatjana.** *The Lotus Eaters*. St. Martin's Press, 2010. 389p. 9780312611576. During the fall of Saigon in 1975, a female American photojournalist, who arrived in Vietnam 12 years earlier to document the war that killed her brother, looks back at how she became seduced by the danger inherent in her work and caught up in an affair with her mentor. An ALA Notable book and a *New York Times* Notable book. **Second Appeal**: Story.

🎗 📖 **Film Stockett, Kathryn.** *The Help*. Penguin, 2009. 451p. 978039 9155245. In 1960s Mississippi, maids Aibileen and Minny risk everything by secretly sharing stories about their experiences with Skeeter, a young white woman who is writing an anonymous book about the experiences of black maids—women who run the local households and raise the children, but are mistrusted by their employers. *The Help* is also a popular, award-winning movie. Winner of the Indies Choice Award for Adult Debut.

Must Read

🎗 📖 **Strout, Elizabeth. *Olive Kitteridge*.** Random House, 2008. 270p. 9781400062089. Retired schoolteacher Olive Kitteridge is the common thread in these 13 linked stories that take place in a small coastal town in Maine. Multiple narrators help paint a picture of Olive that reveals her seemingly conflicting traits—likeable yet unlikeable, plainspoken but moody, and hopeful despite encroaching despair. Winner of the Pulitzer Prize for Fiction and an ALA Notable book. **Second Appeal**: Language.

🎗 **Tower, Wells.** *Everything Ravaged, Everything Burned*. Farrar, Straus and Giroux, 2009. 238p. 978037492195. Tower, who was recently named one of *The New Yorker* magazine's "20 Under 40" leading fiction writers, expertly meshes the details of people's daily existence and their emotional states into arresting stories, usually set in contemporary America. This volume's title story, however, is about a group of bloodthirsty Vikings. A *New York Times* Notable book.

Tropper, Jonathan. *This Is Where I Leave You*. Dutton, 2009. 339p. 9780525951278. Very funny dysfunctional family story narrated by Judd Foxman, who has just discovered that his wife is having an affair and now has to sit shivah for seven days with his three adult siblings after their father dies. **Second Appeal**: Story.

📖 **Truong, Monique.** *Bitter in the Mouth*. Random House, 2010. 282p. 9781400069088. Linda has always had a secret sense—she can "taste" words. When she hears the word "disappoint," for example, she tastes slightly burnt toast. Now, in her 30s, Linda begins a journey to uncover truths about her family and identity by returning to her childhood home of Boiling Springs, North Carolina.

Tyler, Anne. *Noah's Compass*. Alfred A. Knopf, 2009. 9780307272409. Liam Pennywell, a former schoolteacher who was forced to retire at 61, finds himself lying in a hospital bed with a head injury that he doesn't remember receiving, one day after moving into a condo on the edge of Baltimore. Like most of Anne Tyler's novels, this is a subtle character study that moves at a gentle pace.

🏵 **Udall, Brady.** *The Lonely Polygamist*. W. W. Norton, 2010. 602p. 9780393062625. Golden Richards, a polygamist Mormon with 4 wives and 28 children, feels increasingly isolated as he attempts to keep big secrets from his sprawling family. An ALA Notable book.

🏵 📖 **Waldman, Amy.** *The Submission*. Farrar, Straus and Giroux, 2011. 299p. 9780374271565. Uproar ensues when a jury selects a design for a Ground Zero memorial from thousands of anonymous submissions and discovers that the winning designer is Mohammed "Mo" Khan, a Muslim-American architect. A *New York Times* Notable book. **Second Appeal**: Story.

Story

When the plot and pacing of a novel are compelling, the appeal of the book is "story." People who enjoy books with story as the main appeal often say they like to read "page-turners" or books that make them feel like they can't wait to find out what happens next. Thriller readers, for example, usually read for story. Descriptions of story-driven books tend to emphasize events more than characters.

📖 **Bohjalian, Chris.** *Secrets of Eden*. Shaye Areheart Books, 2010. 370p. 9780307394972. When a woman and her abusive husband are found dead of an apparent murder-suicide in their Vermont village home just hours after the woman was baptized, the local minister is racked with guilt about his inability to save her, and seeks comfort from a woman who writes bestselling inspirational books about angels. Told from multiple points of view that reveal various opinions about how the couple died. **Second Appeal**: Character.

Bronsky, Alina. *Broken Glass Park*. Europa Editions, 2010. 221p. 9781933372969. Modern coming-of-age story about 17-year-old Sascha, a Russian girl who lives in a Berlin housing project with her two younger siblings and has two goals: to write a novel about her beautiful mother and to kill the man who murdered her mother, Sascha's stepfather Vadim. Translated from German. **Second Appeal**: Character

Caputo, Philip. *Crossers*. Alfred A. Knopf, 2009. 447p. 9780375411670. A widower who lost his wife on 9/11 moves to a family ranch on the Arizona–Mexico border to grieve and recover, but enters a dangerous situation involving drug runners, illegal immigrants, and the ramifications of his grandfather's violent past.

🎗 📖 **Chaon, Dan.** *Await Your Reply*. Ballantine Books, 2009. 324p. 9780345476029. Three different sets of suspenseful story lines weave through this novel about people who are running away from their lives without fully knowing where they're going or who they'll be at the end. An ALA Notable book and a *New York Times* Notable book. **Second Appeal**: Language.

📖 **Dai, Sijie.** *Once on a Moonless Night*. Alfred A. Knopf, 2009. 277p. 9780307271587. A French student of Chinese literature becomes obsessed with an ancient silk scroll that once belonged to China's last emperor. The scroll is inscribed with the beginning of a lost Buddhist sutra and written in the lost language of Tumchooq. By the author of *Balzac and the Little Chinese Seamstress* (2001). Translated from French.

Divakurni, Chitra Banerjee. *One Amazing Thing*. Voice/Hyperion. 2009. 220p. 9781401340995. To prevent panic after an earthquake traps nine disparate people in a basement office of the Indian consulate in an unidentified U.S. city, they each take turns telling the others a story about "one amazing thing" from their lives that they have never shared before.

🎗 📖 **Donoghue, Emma.** *Room*. Little, Brown and Co., 2010. 336p. 9780316098335. Five-year-old Jack, who narrates this riveting story, has never been outside of the 11' × 11' room where he was born, spending most of his time with this mother who has been held captive for seven years and wants to escape even though Jack is reluctant to leave. Winner of the Indies Choice Award for Adult Fiction, a *New York Times* Notable book, and an ALA Notable book. **Second Appeal**: Character.

📖 **Gruen, Sara.** *Ape House*. Spiegel & Grau, 2010. 303p. 9780385523219. Researcher Isabel Duncan shares a close relationship with a special family of bonobo apes at the Great Ape Language Lab until someone "liberates" the apes from the lab. By the author of book club favorite *Water for Elephants* (2007).

Helenga, Robert. *Snakewoman of Little Egypt*. Bloomsbury, 2010. 352p. 9781608192625. After Sunny spends five years in prison for shooting her pastor husband because he forced her to stick her arm into a box of rattlesnakes, she enters college and rents a garage apartment from Jackson, an anthropology professor who becomes fascinated with the Pentecostal serpent-handling church Sunny grew up in.

📖 **Kostova, Elizabeth.** *The Swan Thieves*. Little, Brown and Co., 2010. 564p. 9780316065788. Creative obsession is the theme of this novel about Robert Oliver, an artist committed to a mental hospital after he attacks a famous painting in Washington D.C.'s National Gallery, and Andrew Marlow, the psychiatrist who tries to uncover what motivated the attack. **Second Appeal**: Character.

Langer, Adam. *The Thieves of Manhattan: A Memoir Novel*. Spiegel & Grau, 2010. 259p. 9781400068913. Ian Minot is a struggling writer and barista who, after watching his girlfriend and others rise fast in the literary scene, is driven by jealousy to pass off someone else's work as his own. Full of narrative tricks and imaginative word play, this is a fun and clever take on Manhattan's publishing industry.

🎗 **Murray, Paul.** *Skippy Dies*. Faber & Faber, 2010. 672p. 9780865479432. On page five of this ambitious 672-page novel, 14-year-old Daniel "Skippy" Juster dies during a doughnut-eating contest—a tragicomic event that sets the dark but humorous tone for the rest of the story, which takes place in a murky stew of hormone-fueled adolescent boys and frustrated teachers at a private Catholic school in Dublin. An ALA Notable book.

🎗 **Oates, Joyce Carol.** *Sourland: Stories*. Ecco, 2010. 384p. 9780061996528. Oates explores familiar themes of how loss, grief, and violence shape people in this collection of 16 short stories, including one about a glamorous, but dangerous, librarian who is an amputee. A *New York Times* Notable book.

Parkhurst, Carolyn. *The Nobodies Album*. Doubleday, 2010. 313p. 9780385527699. Just as bestselling writer Octavia Frost finishes her latest novel, she learns that her estranged son, Milo, has been charged with murdering his girlfriend. Interweaving excerpts from Olivia's new book with the story of how Olivia reconnects with Milo and tries to determine who really killed his girlfriend, Parkhurst ingeniously blends genres and narratives. **Second Appeal**: Language.

Perrotta, Tom. *The Leftovers*. St. Martin's Press, 2011. 355p. 9780 312358341. The distressed residents of a suburban New Jersey community attempt to recover after losing many of their loved ones during the "Sudden Departure," a secular version of the Rapture. Why were certain people "taken," while others, including the now infuriated Reverend Jamison, left behind? A *New York Times* Notable book.

Reikin, Frederick. *Day for Night*. Reagan Arthur Book/Little, Brown and Co., 2010. 326p. 9780316077569. Dozens of people's lives intertwine in this wondrously complex and intellectually satisfying novel told from many points of view (all in first person), spanning several decades and continents, including Florida, Utah, New Jersey, and Israel.

Shteyngart, Gary. *Super Sad True Love Story*. Random House, 2010. 334p. 9781400066407. Frighteningly plausible dystopian satire set in New York in 2018 that manages to be both supersad and wildly funny, and does indeed include a love story. Shteyngart was recently named one of *The New Yorker* magazine's "20 Under 40" leading fiction writers. A *New York Times* Notable book.

Stuart, Julia. *The Tower, the Zoo, and the Tortoise*. Doubleday, 2010. 304p. 9780385533287. The Tower of London is the setting for this zany but touching story about Beefeater Balthazar Jones, who lives at the Tower with his wife and nearly 180-year-old tortoise, and becomes, by royal decree, the Keeper of the Menagerie—a collection of exotic animals that have been given as gifts to the queen and now live at the Tower. **Second Appeal**: Setting.

Tsiolkas, Christos. *The Slap*. 2010. Penguin Books, 2009. 482p. 9780143117148. A single rash act—one man slapping another man's child at a barbecue in suburban Melbourne—sets off a series of repercussions that draw attention to complex and varying beliefs held by different social groups and generations of Australians. Originally published in Australia in 2008 and winner of multiple awards there.

Umrigar, Thrity. *The Weight of Heaven*. Harper, 2009. 365p. 9780061472541. A grieving American couple moves from Ann Arbor, Michigan, to India to rebuild their lives after the death of their seven-year-old son, but become unhealthily attached to the young son of their Indian housekeepers.

Must Read

🏵 📖 **Verghese, Abraham.** *Cutting for Stone*. Alfred A. Knopf, 2009. 541p. 9780375414497. Epic story about Ethiopian twin brothers who grow up to become doctors after their mother, a devout nun, dies during childbirth and their father, a surgeon, rejects them. Winner of the Indies Choice Award for Adult Fiction. **Second Appeal**: Character.

Walter, Jess. *The Financial Lives of the Poets*. Harper, 2009. 290p. 978006 1916045. Bitterly funny story about Matt Prior, a 40-something family man who left his job as a journalist to start a website offering financial information in the form of poetry—poetfolio.com—but failed. He's not sure how he's going to save his house and marriage until he stumbles upon a possible solution during a late-night stop for milk at his local 7-Eleven. **Second Appeal**: Character.

Setting

Where and when a novel is set can carry readers away, immerse them. The place or time of the story plays a key role in understanding the novel. Sometimes, readers and reviewers describe the setting as seeming like a character, especially if the book is named for a specific setting, such as Colm Tóibín's *Brooklyn* (2009).

Aw, Tash. *Map of the Invisible World*. Spiegel and Grau, 2010. 317p. 9780385527965. During the political turmoil of 1960s Indonesia, Adam, a 16-year-old orphaned boy, searches Jakarta for his Dutch foster father who was dragged away from his remote island home by soldiers. Aw won the Costa Book Award for First Novel for *The Harmony Silk Factory* (2005).

De Robertis, Carolina. *The Invisible Mountain*. Alfred A. Knopf, 2009. 364p. 9780307271631. Uruguay is the setting for this lavish story about three generations of women, beginning with the miraculous reappearance of a lost infant on the first day of the 20th century.

Harrison, Jim. *The Farmer's Daughter*. Grove Press, 2010. 308p. 9780802119346. Collection of three novellas that each share a strong sense of place, dark themes, and a connection to Patsy Cline's country-and-western song "The Last Word in Lonesome is Me." The title novella tells the story of Sarah, a teenage girl who is sexually assaulted by a Montana cowboy and then plots revenge.

📖 **Lalami, Laila.** *Secret Son*. Algonquin Books, 2009. 291p. 9781565 124943. Modern Morocco is the setting for this story about a young man who grows up in the slums of Casablanca and discovers that his mother has misled him about the identity and whereabouts of his father.

🏅 📖 **Marlantes, Karl.** *Matterhorn*. Atlantic Monthly Press, 2010. 600p. 9780802119285. Extraordinary descriptions of combat—and the tedium of downtime—distinguish this powerful novel set in 1969 during the Vietnam War on a hill that the Fifth Marine Division's Bravo Company has dubbed "Matterhorn." Winner of the Indies Choice Award for Adult Debut, a *New York Times* Notable book, and an ALA Notable book.

Must Read

🏅 📖 **McCann, Colum. Let the Great World Spin**. Random House, 2009. 349p. 9781400063734. Tightrope walker Philippe Petit's daring 45 minutes of high-wire antics between the World Trade Center towers on August 7, 1974 forms the backdrop for this novel of intersecting stories, told by 10 different narrators. Winner of the National Book Award and International IMPAC Dublin Literary Award, as well as a *New York Times* Notable book and an ALA Notable book. **Second Appeal**: Character.

🏅 **Mueenuddin, Daniyal.** *In Other Rooms, Other Wonders*. W. W. Norton & Co., 2009. 247p. 9780393068009. In this collection of eight linked short stories (which was a finalist for the 2010 Pulitzer Prize for Fiction), Pakistani American author Mueenuddin reveals intimate details about the intertwined lives of feudal landowners in late 20th-century Pakistan and their servants. A *New York Times* Notable book. **Second Appeal**: Character.

🏅 📖 **O'Neill, Joseph.** *Netherland*. Pantheon Books, 2008. 256p. 9780 307377043. After losing his bearings following the devastation of 9/11, Hans van den Broek finds solace in playing the game of cricket and becomes friends with Chuck, a Trinidadian who introduces him to other immigrants in New York City's outer boroughs who believe in the American dream. Winner of the PEN/Faulkner Award and a *New York Times* Notable book. **Second Appeal**: Language.

❦ **Pamuk, Orhan.** *The Museum of Innocence*. Alfred A. Knopf, 2009. 535p. 9780307266767. In 1975, Kemal, a 30-year-old businessman from a wealthy family in Istanbul, begins a long-term obsessive affair with a beautiful salesgirl just as he is about to celebrate his engagement to a woman from another prominent family. This is Pamuk's first novel since winning the Nobel Prize for Literature in 2006. Translated from Turkish. A *New York Times* Notable book.

❦ 📖 **Russell, Karen.** *Swamplandia!* Alfred A. Knopf, 2011. 315p. 9780 307263995. In the swamps of the Florida Everglades, 13-year-old Ava Big-tree tries to save her family's alligator-wrestling theme park from going under after her mother dies of ovarian cancer, her father disappears, her brother Kiwi goes to work for World of Darkness (a competing tourist attraction), and her sister Osceola falls in love with a ghost. A *New York Times* Notable book and an ALA Notable book. **Second Appeal**: Character.

❦ 📖 **Sabatini, Irene.** *The Boy Next Door*. Little, Brown and Co., 2009. 403p. 9780316049931. In tumultuous, postcolonial Zimbabwe, an unlikely friendship develops between Lindiwe, a 14-year-old girl of mixed race, and her neighbor Ian, an older white "Rhodie" boy who is accused of murder. Winner of the Orange Award for New Writers. **Second Appeal**: Character.

❦ 📖 **Skyhorse, Brando.** *The Madonnas of Echo Park*. Free Press, 2010. 199p. 9781439170809. The Mexicans and Mexican Americans—people working as day laborers, cooks, and housekeepers—who live in the Los Angeles neighborhood of Echo Park attempt to retain their ethnic identity while struggling with increasing gentrification and the aftermath of a tragic accident that occurs early in the life of a young neighborhood girl. Winner of the PEN/Hemingway Foundation Award. **Second Appeal**: Character.

❦ 📖 **Tóibín, Colm.** *Brooklyn*. Scribner, 2009. 262p. 9781439138311. After World War II, Eilis Lacey travels from her small Irish hometown to work in an American department store in Brooklyn. As she begins to imagine a future with a charming Italian man who courts her, Eilis receives news from Ireland that forces her to make some difficult choices. This quiet story calls to mind *The Portrait of a Lady* (1881) by Henry James. Winner of the Costa Book Award and an ALA Notable book.

📖 **Van Niekerk, Marlene.** *Agaat*. Tin House Books, 2010. 581p. 9780 982503096. At 67, Milla, a white South African who runs a farm that has been in her family for generations, lies slowly dying, dependent on her black maidservant Agaat to be her caretaker. Translated from Afrikaans. **Second Appeal**: Language.

Wilson, Edward O. *Anthill*. W. W. Norton & Co., 2010. 378p. 9780393071191. As a young boy growing up in Alabama, Raff explores the old-growth forest surrounding nearby Lake Nokobee, becoming a self-taught naturalist who eventually tries to save the area from land developers after studying ants at Florida State University and law at Harvard. The author, a Harvard biologist, is a two-time Pulitzer Prize winner for General Nonfiction, for *On Human Nature* (1978) and *The Ants* (1990).

Yu, Hua. *Brothers*. Pantheon Books, 2009. 641p. 9780375424991. Bawdy satire about two stepbrothers who must rely on each other as China radically transforms from the period of the Cultural Revolution, which was dominated by communist ideology, to the modern era, fueled by capitalism. This sprawling epic, which includes plenty of crude (and sometimes obscene) humor, was a bestseller in China. Translated from Chinese. **Second Appeal**: Character.

TOOLS AND RESOURCES

Awards

American Library Association (ALA) Notable Books for Adults. http://www.ala.org/rusa/awards/notablebooks. Top 25 Fiction, Poetry, and Nonfiction titles for adults each year.

Costa Book Awards (formerly the Whitbread). http://www.costa bookawards.com. Awarded to works by writers based in the United Kingdom and Ireland in categories including Novel and First Novel.

Indies Choice Book Awards. http://bookweb.org/btw/awards/ICBA.html. Given by staff at independent bookstores in several categories, including Adult Fiction and Adult Debut.

International IMPAC Dublin Literary Award. http://www.im pacdublinaward.ie. Awarded to a work of fiction published in English or English translation from nominations made by public libraries worldwide.

Man Booker Prize. http://www.themanbookerprize.com. Goes to the year's best original novel published in English in the United Kingdom, written by a citizen of the British Commonwealth or Ireland.

National Book Award. http://www.nationalbook.org. Recognizes works of exceptional literary merit by American authors in categories of Fiction, Nonfiction, Poetry, and Young People's Literature.

National Book Critics Circle Award for Fiction. http://bookcritics.org/awards. This annual award goes to the best work of fiction that is published in English in the United States, as selected by the members of the National Book Critics Circle.

New York Times **Notable Books**. http://www.nytimes.com/pages/books/index.html. Annual year-end list of 100 notable works of Fiction, Nonfiction, and Poetry.

Nobel Prize for Literature. http://¿www.nobelprize.org/nobel_prizes/literature. Awarded annually by the Swedish Academy, usually for an author's entire body of work, rather than a specific title.

Orange Prize for Fiction and Orange Award for New Writers. http://www.orangeprize.co.uk and http://www.orangeprize.co.uk/archive_newwriters.html. Includes novels, short stories, and novellas written by women.

PEN/Faulkner Award for Fiction. http://www.penfaulkner.org. Presented for a distinguished work of published fiction by an American author.

PEN/Hemingway Foundation Award. http://www.pen-ne.org/news-noteworthy/penhemingway-award. Honors novels and short stories by previously unpublished American authors.

Pulitzer Prize for Fiction. http://www.pulitzer.org/bycat/Fiction. Awarded for fiction by American authors.

There are many other major literary awards, of course, from countries all over the world. Canada has the Governor General's Literary Award and Scotiabank Giller Prize, Australia has the Miles Franklin Literary Award, and France has the Prix Goncourt, for example. You can easily locate lists of international literary prizes by searching the Web.

Print Resources

Boxall, Peter, ed. *1001 Books You Must Read before You Die*. Universe Pub., 2010.
Mason, Simon. *The Rough Guide to Classic Novels*. Rough Guides, 2008.
Pearl, Nancy. *Now Read This: A Guide to Mainstream Fiction, 1978–1998*. Libraries Unlimited, 1999.

Pearl, Nancy. *Now Read This II: A Guide to Mainstream Fiction, 1990–2001.* Libraries Unlimited, 2002.

Pearl, Nancy. *Book Lust: Recommended Reading for Every Mood, Moment, and Reason.* Sasquatch Books, 2003.

Pearl, Nancy. *More Book Lust: Recommended Reading for Every Mood, Moment, and Reason.* Sasquatch Books, 2005.

Pearl, Nancy, and Sarah Statz Cords. *Now Read This III: A Guide to Mainstream Fiction.* Libraries Unlimited, 2010.

Saricks, Joyce G. *Readers' Advisory Guide to Genre Fiction.* American Library Association, 2009.

Zane, J. Peder, ed. *The Top Ten: Writers Pick Their Favorite Books.* W. W. Norton, 2007.

Review Journals

The following review journals include reviews for many different genres. They are not restricted to mainstream or Literary Fiction. Most of these are available in print and online, although the online versions sometimes contain less content than the print versions or require separate subscriptions. Don't forget the role that many popular magazines and newspapers play by publishing bestseller lists and book reviews, read by huge numbers of readers. These include *The New Yorker, Entertainment Weekly, O, The Oprah Magazine, People, Essence,* the *Wall Street Journal,* the *Guardian, USA Today, The Washington Post,* and your local newspaper.

Bookforum. Published five times a year. Online at http://www.bookforum.com

Booklist. Published by the American Library Association 22 times a year. Online at http://www.booklistonline.com

Bookmarks Magazine. Published six times a year. Online at http://www.bookmarksmagazine.com

Kirkus Reviews. Published 24 times a year. Online at http://www.kirkusreviews.com

Library Journal. Published 20 times a year. Online at http://www.libraryjournal.com

The New York Review of Books. Published 20 times a year. Online at http://www.nybooks.com

The New York Times Book Review. Published weekly. Online at http://www.nytimes.com/pages/books/review

Publishers Weekly. Published 51 times a year. Online at http://www.pub
lishersweekly.com

Online Resources

The following websites include a variety of book reviews, lists, and publishing information for works of Mainstream Fiction and other genres. You
can also check library websites and sites like Amazon, Slate, Salon, Barnes &
Noble, NPR, and Powell's, which often have author interviews and other articles. Websites for individual publishers provide helpful information about
current and upcoming titles. The EarlyWord site listed below includes an ex-
haustive set of links to publishers' catalogs.

BookBrowse. http://www.bookbrowse.com

EarlyWord: The Publisher|Librarian Connection. http://www.early
word.com

Fiction_L. http://www.mgpl.org/read-listen-view/fl/flmenu/

Goodreads. http://www.goodreads.com

Indie Bound. http://www.indiebound.org

LibraryThing. http://www.librarything.com

The Millions. http://www.themillions.com

NoveList Plus. Subscription database, check with your local library

Overbooked. http://www.overbooked.com

The Reader's Advisor Online Blog. http://www.readersadvisoronline
.com/blog/

Reading Group Guides. http://www.readinggroupguides.com

Shelfari. http://www.shelfari.com

Bibliography/Works Consulted

Carr, David. "Getting Up to Speed in Literary Fiction." *NoveList Plus*, January 13, 2009.

Grossman, Lev. "Good Books Don't Have to Be Hard." *Wall Street Journal*, August 29, 2009. http://online.wsj.com/article/SB10001424052970203706604574
377163804387216.html

Maata, Stephanie L. *A Few Good Books: Using Contemporary Readers' Advisory
Strategies to Connect Readers with Books*. Neal-Schuman Publishers, 2010.

"Modern Library 100 Best Novels." *Modern Library*, 2007. www.random-house.com/modernlibrary/100bestnovels.html

Moyer, Jessica E., Amanda Blau, et al. *Research-Based Readers' Advisory*. American Library Association, 2008.

Oprah Book Club Selections. http://www.oprah.com/book-list/Oprahs-Book-Club-The-Complete-List

Saricks, Joyce G. *Readers' Advisory Service in the Public Library*. 3rd ed. American Library Association, 2005.

Turley, Julie. "Literary Fiction: The Pleasure of the Complex Text." *Libraries Unlimited: Reader's Advisor News*, March 2010. http://www.reader sadvisoronline.com/ranews/mar2010/turley.html

FIVE FAN FAVORITES

- Emma Donoghue. *Room*—Story
- Karl Marlantes. *Matterhorn*—Setting
- Téa Obreht. *The Tiger's Wife*—Language
- Kathryn Stockett. *The Help*—Character
- Abraham Verghese. *Cutting for Stone*—Story

10

11

12

13

14

15

16

17

18

Chapter 17

Nonfiction

Sarah Statz Cords

This is a very exciting moment for nonfiction: its long-awaited debut in a *Genreflecting* volume. Finally, nonfiction has been invited to the genre ball, where all the other glamorous groups are hanging out: Historical Fiction in their masquerade ball masks, Romances in alluring ball gowns, and Fantasy novels wearing their swords and magical talismans. You may think that nonfiction will be the dowdy cousin at this wonderful party—but I invite you to imagine nonfiction after a movie montage makeover, with her glasses off and her hair down.

DEFINITION

Nonfiction is the sole literary category defined by what it is not—it is *not* fiction. Perhaps, the best way to discover what it is, then, is to discuss the ways in which it differs from its opposite. Nonfiction, unlike fiction, is not composed of imagined or made-up stories. It is based on real events and characters, often contains verifiable facts, and is assumed to be "true" (although, especially in the case of Memoirs, the extent of "truth" to be found in nonfiction titles can vary widely). It is assumed that nonfiction authors, even when they are telling compelling stories or painting fascinating character portraits, have researched, investigated, and verified the narratives they have created.

Nonfiction, particularly in public and academic libraries, is often catalogued and arranged according to its subject matter. (In bookstores, nonfiction is often categorized into slightly more nebulous "interest categories," as denoted by their publishers.) A further complication with nonfiction is that it varies widely on a continuum with regard to its "readability"—on one side of the spectrum are the purely information-based scholarly treatises and reference works, including cookbooks, science and math textbooks, car repair manuals, health manuals, scores, decorating books, and how-to books (among others); while at the opposite side are the narratives that don't contain indexes or references, or which tell stories of events or characters, plain and simple. These books are often referred to as "narrative," "recreational," and "readable" (or even "read like a novel") nonfiction titles, which are useful enough when distinguishing them from their academic ready-reference counterparts.

But if nonfiction titles do not consist solely of their subject matter (and they don't—the subject of Malcolm Gladwell's massively popular title *The Tipping Point* is "causality," and have you ever had anyone ask for a book on causality?) or their narrative, what else can we use to distinguish one group of nonfiction titles from another and how can we find ways to link them to similar fiction titles? The answer lies, as it often does with fiction, in a mixture of understood genre and subgenre conventions combined with an understanding of those genres' appeal factors. The nonfiction genre of True Adventure, which is where you will find Sebastian Junger's classic *The Perfect Storm*, helps us understand that that is a primarily story-driven nonfiction title and that its readers might enjoy other Survival and Disaster Stories—both nonfiction and fiction—in addition to books about storms and commercial fishing.

For the purpose of readability, this chapter offers slightly more genre and subgenre classifications than do the other chapters in this book. Classifying titles simply as "nonfiction" is too broad to be helpful (which is why we have subject classification schemes in the first place), so we have made an attempt here to break the category into more approachable groupings by subject matter and type of writing.

CHARACTERISTICS AND APPEALS

A large part of the appeal of nonfiction is its genesis in the real: not only the factual and the verifiable, but also the "truth" of personal stories, reminiscences, and feelings. Nonfiction readers often cite their desire to learn something about the world (and the people) around them as the main reason they enjoy the genre. Nonfiction works exist on a continuum from the very factual and nonlinear to the very narrative, with readers who enjoy the nonlinear books also enjoying the ability to read short bits of them whenever they have the time and readers who enjoy the more story-driven works loving the chance to lose themselves in the author's storytelling.

Different types of nonfiction offer a wide variety of appeal characteristics to readers. True Adventure titles are often thrilling narratives, offering exciting stories and "edge of your seat" pacing. True Crime titles, although they focus on stories that are less thrilling than horrifying, also feature quick pacing and cliffhanger-driven plotting; to that they also add the lure of strong characterization, although the characters described in such accounts are often criminals (which does not make them sympathetic characters but does tend to make them fascinating ones). Travel and Environmental writing both offer the reader a strong sense of place and feature unique descriptions of a variety of global settings.

Although subject matter is an important draw for all readers choosing nonfiction, it is particularly important in the areas of Science and History. Because both areas have long been popular ones for readers and publishers, however, it is often necessary to differentiate between types of Science and History writing. Although many Science titles are fact-driven works that place less emphasis on the crafting of stories, there are also many more "popular" Science titles that appeal to readers on the basis of the authors' literary style or the characters described therein. Likewise, History books tend to be very story-driven (as can only be expected in a genre with "story" in its very name), but many, particularly Historical Biographies, also offer strong characterization as well. Depending on what historical subject is being covered, they might also offer setting and frame details that readers specifically seek out, with Anglophiles searching for works on British history, Francophiles limiting their reading to French events, and so on.

Nonfiction also has a lot to offer to those readers who enjoy skillful prose and unique literary styles (those readers most drawn to the appeal factor Nancy Pearl refers to as "language"). Investigative (also known as Journalism or Current Affairs) Writing authors are often journalists and prose stylists by trade, as are authors of Big Think books, who synthesize investigative work with research to create an entirely new format of books, rich with their own theories and neologisms.

In short, regardless of what appeals most to readers, nonfiction has something to offer anyone.

BRIEF HISTORY

Nonfiction writing has existed, in many forms, since human beings first began to write. Arguably, tablets containing accounts of household stores, marked in cuneiform symbols, contain a nonfiction story all their own: the facts of how ancient people farmed, ate, traded, and lived. Relating a brief history of nonfiction is akin to saying a few words on how human culture has evolved over the last few thousand years, but a journey through some of the most well-known early nonfiction books might prove instructive.

Although epic poems such as Homer's *Iliad* and *The Odyssey* are not considered to be truly factual nonfiction accounts, historians have suggested that they may have been at least partially based in fact and on the exploits of real individuals. These poems and other legends that have been recounted throughout our culture are early examples and contain many of the characteristics of the quickly paced and story-driven True Adventure narratives that we enjoy today. Another somewhat adventurous nonfiction genre, Travel, also has a rich historical tradition. Herodotus, writing in the fifth century BCE (and who is also often credited as being one of the earliest history writers as well), described his journeys from Greece to Africa, through the Persian Empire, and throughout such locations as Syria and Egypt. Marco Polo produced the journal outlining his travels in the 13th century, and he started a trend that was particularly popular during the 19th century (the National Geographic Society was founded in 1888), when explorers and adventurers of all types set out to explore the last remaining unexplored places on earth, and then wrote about their travels. Travel writing met Environmental and Nature writing in the person of one very well-known historical figure: Charles Darwin combined those genres when he described his sea voyage and his collection of many biological specimens from far corners of the globe in his *The Voyage of the Beagle*, first published in 1845. Environmental and Nature writing thrived in 19th-century America as well, with such practitioners as Henry David Thoreau and John Muir popularizing it. The lure of Environmental writing is still strong today, particularly as our world faces more environmental challenges and we become more aware of our impact on the planet.

When it comes to the history of History, we are much in the debt of at least two Greek writers whose enduring classics scholars and readers still seek out. Herodotus, who we mentioned for his role in Travel writing, was a prolific fellow. Working in the fifth century BCE, he also produced something we now call *The Histories of Herodotus*, in which he recounts the events of the Persian invasion of Greece earlier in that era and in which, according to scholars, he was not afraid to recount battlefield and cultural gossip, or to offer his own opinions to fill factual voids. Nor can we ignore another Greek writer, working in same period: Thucydides, noted for his more stringent attention to factual detail and abhorrence of using hearsay in his accounts, who described the battles between Sparta and Athens in his *History of the Peloponnesian War*. You can see that the human impulse to record historical events as well as to record them in different styles (one a bit more, dare we say, loosey-goosey and opinionated) itself has a very long history. Science writing, likewise, has been around for a very long time, with no less an historical figure than Aristotle producing numerous works of what was then called "natural philosophy." Although many Science books still focus on natural history and observations of the natural world, the dawn of the Scientific Revolution in the early 17th century led to an emphasis on the recording of scientific experiments and precepts. As our understanding of the fields of biology, chemistry, physics, astrophysics, and many others developed, so did our curiosity to read about advances in scientific fields.

Life Stories such as Biographies and Memoirs, of course, have long and storied histories in their own rights. For those readers interested in those histories, both popular resources (Ben Yagoda's *Memoir: A History*) and more scholarly ones (Maureen O'Connor's *Life Stories: A Guide to Reading Interests in Memoirs, Autobiographies, and Diaries* and Rick Roche's *Real Lives Revealed*) provide thorough discussions and time lines of them. Suffice it to say that Autobiographical writing has been with us as long as people have written diaries (with some citing Augustine's *Confessions* as one of the earliest disseminated examples of the form, produced in the fourth century CE). Our compulsion to record the lives of others has also been around for a long time: in medieval times, the life stories most often told were those of saints; in more recent years, biographies of celebrities, political figures, inspirational individuals, and many others have broadened the field considerably. Although they are often considered together and even shelved together in many bookstores and libraries, it is important to note that Memoirs in particular reflect more personal, subjective stories, while Biographies often tend to be more rigorously researched and fact-checked life-story accounts.

In recent years, the emphasis has been on the development of narrative nonfiction and nonfiction that borrows heavily from the fiction writers' craft in its focus on character development, arrangement in "scenes," and attention to pacing plotting. This style has been called by such names as "creative nonfiction" and "the new journalism," and was popularized in the latter half of the 20th century by such practitioners as Truman Capote, Norman Mailer, and Joan Didion, among others.

CURRENT TRENDS

Nonfiction continues to grow in popularity, a trend that author and *GQ* columnist Chuck Klosterman first noted in 2004 when he wrote that the current generation was what he termed "the Suddenly and Deeply Engrossed with Nonfiction Generation" (Klosterman 2004, 194). Although its various subgenres wax and wane in terms of their popularity and number of titles published, more people than ever are discovering that nonfiction, particularly narrative nonfiction, has a lot to offer to readers who might previously have only read fiction.

The first decade of the 21st century belonged to Memoirs. Popular with readers due to their emphasis on characters and stylistic storytelling, a wealth of them has been published since 2000. In addition to becoming bestsellers, many of them also made appearances on annual "Best of . . . " book lists. However, controversy also followed in their wake, as when James Frey's bestselling (and Oprah-approved) Memoir *A Million Little Pieces* was exposed to contain many exaggerations by the author, if not outright lies and concoctions. In recent years, "memoir debunking" has become almost a contact sport, with critics, reviewers, and readers roundly slamming Memoirs they believe to be more fabrication than fact. A glance at the forthcoming titles lists for 2012, however, suggests that Memoirs continue to have high appeal for readers (and therefore for publishers as well), particularly Memoirs by celebrities and other famous, and sometimes infamous, personages.

When Malcolm Gladwell published *The Tipping Point* in 2005, he not only created a huge bestseller and his own brand, but a new classification for similar nonfiction books. These books, in which authors explore ideas on (often) esoteric subjects, draw their own conclusions regarding a variety of research findings, and often create neologisms and theories of their own, which have been labeled such things as "Big Think books," "Big Idea books," and "Making Sense of . . . books." They continue to be popular with readers, particularly dedicated nonfiction readers, who enjoy their mix of scholarly and popular writing. Their popularity has very little to do with their subject matters—the subject heading for *The Tipping Point* was "causality"—and more to do with their authors' flair for language and trendspotting.

Finally, a focus on accessible writing and storytelling continues to be seen throughout a wide variety of nonfiction subgenres, from such subject interest areas as science and history to more stylistically unique Memoirs, Biographies that offer new perspectives on popular subjects, works of investigative journalism, and essay collections on every topic under the sun, from food to women's rights. One of the most popular books of 2010 was Rebecca Skloot's *The Immortal Life of Henrietta Lacks*, in which Skloot combined complex biological and medical scientific terms and topics with a very personal approach to the reaction of Henrietta Lacks' family members regarding the use of her cells in medical research.

A Word about the Selection of Titles and Authors

Because this is the first time nonfiction titles have appeared in an edition of *Genreflecting*, an effort has been made to include both popular titles from the years 2006 (the date of the previous edition) to 2011 as well as more "classic" titles that remain perennial reader favorites and can and should be found in the majority of public library collections. In addition, some titles are shown as "Must Read" books. Any book designated as such would be a great book with which to start if you'd like to read widely known and representative nonfiction titles. It has also been my goal to include a wide variety of popular authors within their various genres and areas of subject expertise, although there was not room to comprehensively list each popular author's complete bibliography of titles.

NOTES

Klosterman, Chuck. "The Rise of the Real." *Esquire* 142, no. 6 (December 2004): 194, 195, 236.

THEMES AND TYPES

Key to Nonfiction

True Adventure
   War, Intrigue, and Espionage
Travel
   Expatriate Life
True Crime
Environmental Writing
Science and Math
History
   Microhistories
Biography
   Historical Biography
Memoirs
Investigative Writing
   Immersion Journalism
Big Think Books

True Adventure

True Adventure nonfiction titles often include stories of survival, intrigue and espionage, war, militias, sports, and other thrilling topics. They also often depict their characters as larger-than-life heroic types. They feature strong plots, heavy with action, and are usually page-turning or quickly paced reads.

Brandt, Anthony. *The Man Who Ate His Boots: The Tragic History of the Search for the Northwest Passage.* 2010. 441p. 9780307263926. Brandt relates the stories of the 19th-century explorers and adventurers who searched for the Northwest Passage.

Erickson, Carolly. *The Girl from Botany Bay.* 2005. 234p. 9780471271406. Erickson tells the story of the indomitable Mary Broad, who was convicted of robbery in England in 1786, and her voyage along with other convicts to a new colony in Australia.

Grinnell, George James. *Death on the Barrens: A True Story of Courage and Tragedy in the Canadian Arctic.* 2010. 281p. 9781556438820. Grinnell recounts his 1955 journey, with four friends, into the Canadian Arctic, where the group faced challenges for which they were woefully unprepared.

Must Read

★ 📖 🎬 **Junger, Sebastian.** *The Perfect Storm*. 1997. 227p. 978039 3040166. Junger details the October 1991 confluence of several storm fronts at Gloucester, Massachusetts, in which the crew of the swordfishing vessel *Andrea Gail* was killed.

🎬 **Krakauer, Jon.** *Into the Wild*. 1996. 207p. 9780385486804. Presents the story of Christopher McCandless, who set out to find a simpler life in the wild, but who was caught unprepared when he traveled into the Alaskan wilderness.

Must Read

★ 🎬 **Krakauer, Jon.** *Into Thin Air*. 1997. 293p. 9780679457527. In May 1996, two rival expedition companies (and the author) departed for the top of Mt. Everest; nine of the climbers died when caught in a sudden storm at the peak.

📖 🎬 **Kurson, Robert.** *Shadow Divers: The True Adventure of Two Americans Who Risked Everything to Solve One of the Last Mysteries of World War II*. 2004. 375p. 9780375508585. Deep-sea diving combines in this account of Bill Nagle's and John Chatterton's efforts to salvage artifacts from a World War II U-boat shipwrecked off the coast of New Jersey.

📖 **Ollestad, Norman.** *Crazy for the Storm: A Memoir of Survival*. 2009. 272p. 9780061766725. Ollestad describes the experience of surviving a 1979 plane crash when he was 11 years old (in which his father perished) and making his way alone to safety.

🎬 **Ralston, Aron.** *Between a Rock and a Hard Place*. 2004. 354p. 9780743492812. While hiking in Utah, Ralston's arm became pinned underneath a boulder. He was trapped for days before he made the decision to amputate his own arm in order to escape.

🎬 **Read, Piers Paul.** *Alive: The Story of the Andes Survivors*. 1974. 352p. 9780397010011. In October 1972, an Uruguayan rugby team flying to Chile crashed in the Andes Mountains. Readers should note this is a graphic story of survival through any means.

🎬 **Simpson, Joe.** *Touching the Void: The True Story of One Man's Miraculous Survival*. 1988. 218p. 9780060730550. Simpson and his friend Simon Yates were determined to survive a mountain-climbing expedition gone horribly wrong.

War, Intrigue, and Espionage

War, Intrigue, and Espionage stories are often suspenseful narratives in which authors tell the stories of their subjects' will and ability to survive, and their desire to serve their nations, sometimes through complex intrigue machinations. They create character portraits that emphasize the heroic qualities of some individuals during wartime, as well as the sense of camaraderie that develops among compatriots; many are set in foreign locales; and they offer quickly paced prose.

Blehm, Eric. *The Only Thing Worth Dying for: How Eleven Green Berets Forged a New Afghanistan*. 2010. 375p. 9780061661235. Blehm relates the heroic tale of the 11 members of the U.S. Army Special Forces team that was one of the first units into Afghanistan after 9/11.

🎬 **Bowden, Mark.** *Black Hawk Down*. 1999. 386p. 9780871137388. On a 1993 mission inside war-torn Somalia, 2 massive Army helicopters, known as Black Hawks, were shot down and 18 Army Rangers lost their lives.

Brey, Ilaria Dagnini. *The Venus Fixers: The Untold Story of the Allied Soldiers Who Saved Italy's Art during World War II*. 2009. 308p. 9780374283094. Brey describes the activities of the MFAA (Monuments,

Fine Arts, and Archives) group, appointed by the World War II Allies, to save Italy's many precious art masterpieces.

📖 **Conant, Jennet.** *The Irregulars: Roald Dahl and the British Spy Ring in Wartime Washington*. 2008. 393p. 9780743294584. During World War II, British author Roald Dahl and other members of the British Security Coordination worked within America to weaken opposition to the war.

📖 **Finkel, David.** *The Good Soldiers*. 2009. 287p. 9780374165734. Embedded reporter Finkel relates the experiences of Battalion 2–16, serving in Iraq during the height of the Iraq War and fighting in Baghdad, in this ALA and *New York Times* Notable title.

Must Read

★ 📖 **MacIntyre, Ben.** *Operation Mincemeat*. 2010. 400p. 9780307453273. In "Operation Mincemeat," two British intelligence officers concocted a plan to deceive the Germans by letting them find a dead man dressed as a British operative, complete with a suitcase of false documents.

Morgan, Ted. *Valley of Death*. 2010. 722p. 9781400066643. Morgan describes the French decision to try and hold the base of Dien Bien Phu from the local Vietminh in 1953, and how American forces became embroiled in Vietnam.

O'Donnell, Patrick K. *The Brenner Assignment*. 2008. 286p. 9780306815775. A team of World War II American operatives was parachuted into Italy to destroy parts of the Brenner Pass, through which Germany maintained their all-important supply lines.

📖 🎬 **Sides, Hampton.** *Ghost Soldiers*. 2001. 342p. 9780385495646. Sides tells the story of the American and British POWs who were held in a Japanese prison in the Philippines under appalling conditions during World War II. The movie *The Great Raid* was partially based on this book.

Zuckoff, Mitchell. *Lost in Shangri-La: A True Story of Survival, Adventure, and the Most Incredible Rescue Mission of World War II*. 2011. 384p. 9780061988349. When 24 American service people set out in 1945 for a sightseeing tour over "Shangri-La" (a valley in Dutch New Guinea), their plane crashed. The three survivors found themselves hunted by native tribes and the Japanese until their rescue.

Travel

Travel books feature their authors' descriptions of new and exotic locales, their stories of sometimes torturous or enlightening journeys, and tales of camaraderie with other travelers and residents. Like True Adventure nonfiction, they are often described as "nonfiction that reads like fiction," primarily due to their authors' emphasis on story and subjective writing styles, which make use of novelistic techniques such as the blending of fact and imaginative exaggeration. The following are not typically factual guidebooks, but rather showcase setting descriptions, compelling stories, and vivid character portraits.

Must Read

★ **Bryson, Bill.** *A Walk in the Woods*. 1998. 276p. 9780767902519. Bryson decided to walk the length of the Appalachian Trail and uses his trademark humor to relate his exploits on the trail, especially those with his friend Stephen Katz.

Cahill, Tim. *Hold the Enlightenment*. 2002. 297p. 9780375507663. Cahill's unique and sometimes curmudgeonly voice comes across strongly in this collection of Travel essays, which are quickly paced and include lots of dialogue.

Chatwin, Bruce. *The Songlines*. 1987. 293p. 9780670806058. Chatwin journeyed across Australia in the paths along which the Aboriginal peoples "sing up the country."

Coyne, Tom. *A Course Called Ireland: A Long Walk in Search of a Country, a Pint, and the Next Tee*. 2009. 311p. 9781592404247. Coyne combined a trip to Ireland to discover his roots with his own challenge to play many of its golf courses (after hiking to them first).

Fraser, Laura. *All Over the Map*. 2010. 271p. 9780307450630. Fraser describes her travels through Argentina, Peru, France, and Italy, as well as her hopes and attempts to find love (even after she suffers the trauma of an assault).

Gilman, Susan Jane. *Undress Me in the Temple of Heaven*. 2009. 306p. 9780446578929. Gilman's Memoir describes her travels (particularly throughout Asia), undertaken with her friend Claire, youthful enthusiasm, and vast ignorance about travel's challenges.

🎗 **Grann, David.** *The Lost City of Z.* 2009. 339p. 9780385513531. Grann set off to find out what happened to British explorer Percy Fawcett, who disappeared during a 1925 Amazon expedition, in this ALA and *New York Times* Notable title.

Herzog, Brad. *Turn Left at the Trojan Horse.* 2010. 307p. 9780806532028. Herzog set out to find out more about America (and also himself, as he faced a midlife crisis) in this Memoir that has been compared to Steinbeck's *Travels with Charley* (1962).

🎗 **Horwitz, Tony.** *A Voyage Long and Strange.* 2008. 445p. 9780805076035. Named an ALA and a *New York Times* notable title, Horwitz's narrative describes his travels to American historical sites that predate Columbus and the arrival of the Puritans.

📖 **Mahoney, Rosemary.** *Down the Nile: Alone In a Fisherman's Skiff.* 2007. 273p. 9780316107457. Mahoney was determined to take a solo trip down the Egyptian Nile in a small boat, even though civil unrest and local traditions conspired to create obstacles along the way.

Matthiessen, Peter. *The Cloud Forest: A Chronicle of the South American Wilderness.* 1996 (1961). 280p. 9780140255072. Matthiessen's story is the quintessential journey narrative; with no set destination or travel itinerary, he relates his travels through Central and South America in diary form.

Moore, Tim. *Frost on My Moustache.* 2000. 280p. 9780312253196. Moore re-created (with humor, this time) the Artic journey of Lord Dufferin, a Victorian explorer who went on to serve as both Governor General of Canada and Viceroy of India.

Schooler, Lynn. *Walking Home: A Traveler in the Alaskan Wilderness, a Journey into the Human Heart.* 2010. 262p. 9781596916739. Schooler, a longtime Alaskan resident, set out to explore his adopted home state by trekking cross-country, finding adventure, danger, and (strangely enough) comfort.

Shah, Tahir. *In Search of King Solomon's Mines.* 2003. 240p. 9781559706414. Shah's journeys throughout Ethiopia were inspired by his finding of a treasure map in a tourist shop in Jerusalem that made reference to the gold mines of King Solomon.

Stewart, Chris. *Three Ways to Capsize a Boat: An Optimist Afloat.* 2010. 178p. 9780307592378. Stewart, one-time drummer for the band Genesis, relates a travel tale from the 1980s, when he spent a summer working as a yacht captain around the Greek islands.

Theroux, Paul. *Ghost Train to the Eastern Star: On the Tracks of the Great Railway Bazaar.* 2008. 496p. 9780618418879. Theroux reenacts the

Europe to Asia train journey he originally wrote about in his travel classic *The Great Railway Bazaar* in 1975, showcasing his acerbic observational style.

Thompson, Chuck. *To Hellholes and Back: Bribes, Lies, and the Art of Extreme Tourism*. 2009. 322p. 9780805087888. Former *Maxim* editor Thompson set out to visit places he didn't want to go, including Mexico City, India, and Disney World, to prove (humorously) that he hasn't gone soft.

Must Read

★ **Troost, J. Maarten.** *Lost on Planet China*. 2008. 382p. 978076792 2005. Intrepid globe-trotter Troost set out to travel through and write honestly (and humorously) about China, so that readers might "get a sense of this vast and complex country."

Expatriate Life

Expatriate Travel narratives are less travel stories than they are lifestyle Memoirs that happen to be set in other countries and exotic settings. These stories feature evocative descriptions of different environments, communities, and cultural landscapes, and many are quite gentle in tone and plot.

Barker, Adele. *Not Quite Paradise*. 2010. 303p. 9780807000618. Barker relates her travels in Sri Lanka, describing both its urban centers and countryside, and describing the devastation in the wake of the 2004 tsunami.

Berendt, John. *The City of Falling Angels*. 2005. 414p. 9781594200588. Berendt traveled to Venice several times, and provides a perspective on the city's buildings and residents that feels like a local's.

Dalrymple, William. *Nine Lives: In Search of the Sacred in Modern India*. 2009. 275p. 9780307272829. Dalrymple combines evocative details about life in India as well as describing the country's wealth of religious beliefs through character portraits of its residents.

De Blasi, Marlena. *The Lady in the Palazzo*. 2007. 317p. 9781565124738. De Blasi recounts the story of moving to Orvieto to live with her Italian husband, to renovate and make a real home (both physically and emotionally) in a crumbling palazzo.

Hessler, Peter. *Country Driving: A Journey through China from Farm to Factory*. 2010. 438p. 9780061804090. After living in China for many years, Hessler describes his experiences driving on China's many old and new roads, and exploring the country's rural and urban landscapes.

Must Read

★ 🎬 **Mayes, Frances.** *Under the Tuscan Sun*. 1996. 280p. 9780811808422. Mayes tells a tale of purchasing a home in Tuscany and the process of her acclimatization to all things Italian, relating evocative vignettes of Italian community and cultural life.

Mayes, Frances. *Every Day in Tuscany*. 2010. 306p. 9780767929820. In this expatriate Memoir, Mayes describes a year of restoring a 13th-century residence in the mountains above Cortona.

🎬 **Mayle, Peter.** *A Year in Provence*. 1989. 207p. 9780394572307. Organized by months, Mayle's diary of his year in Provence, France, provides anecdotes about fixing up their temporary home, eating French food, and meeting the neighbors.

True Crime

True Crime narratives describe all manner of crimes, criminals, and law enforcement techniques. They may focus on violent crimes such as homicide, rape, kidnapping, and arson (among others), as well as a variety of crimes that are more fraudulent (cons, financial scams, theft, etc.) than violent. Because they are often based on horrific and abhorrent crimes, they can be quite graphic and disturbing in nature, as well as quite suspenseful. The genre originally developed during the Victorian era (latter half of the 19th century) when crimes were reported upon salaciously in newspapers and contemporary novels. Much of their appeal derives from their suspenseful plot lines, their compellingly drawn (good and bad) characters, and their subject matter, which fulfills humans' sometimes morbid curiosity about crimes and criminals.

Baatz, Simon. *For the Thrill of It*. 2008. 541p. 9780060781002. Baatz relates the story of the crime and trial of Nathan Leopold and Richard Loeb, who murdered the young son (Bobby Franks) of a Chicago family largely "for the thrill of it."

🎬 **Berendt, John.** *Midnight in the Garden of Good and Evil*. 2005 (1994). 388p. 9780679429227. Berendt spent years investigating the murder of Danny Hansford at the hands of Savannah resident Jim Williams, and insinuated himself into the city's society as well.

Blum, Deborah. *The Poisoner's Handbook: Murder and the Birth of Forensic Medicine in Jazz Age New York*. 2010. 319p. 9781594202438. Blum weaves a tale that is equal parts True Crime, Jazz Age history, and science reporting in this thrilling narrative of New York City's earliest forensic scientists and their work.

10

Brown, Pat, and Bob Andelman. *The Profiler: My Life Hunting Serial Killers and Psychopaths*. 2010. 285p. 9781401341268. Brown describes her career as a female criminal profiler and her work on some of America's highest-profile and most disturbing criminal cases.

11

12

Must Read

★ Capote, Truman. *In Cold Blood*. 2007 (1965). 343p. 9780375507908. Capote's novelistic account of the murder of the entire Clutter family in 1959 Kansas features as its two main characters the murderers: Richard Hickok and Perry Smith.

13

Carlo, Philip. *Gaspipe: Confessions of a Mafia Boss*. 2008. 346p. 9780061429842. Popular True Crime author Carlo details the life and work of mafia boss Anthony Casso.

14

Dobyns, Jay, and Nils Shelton-Johnson. *No Angel*. 2009. 328p. 9780307405852. ATF agent Dobyns describes his work infiltrating the Hell's Angels motorcyle gang, describing their role in drug production, gun running, rapes, and other crimes.

15

Gilmore, Mikal. *Shot in the Heart*. 1994. 403p. 9780385422932. The brother of executed murderer Gary Gilmore tells his sad family history, beginning with his mother Bessie's childhood in a large family with an abusive father, in a book that was named an ALA Notable and won the National Book Award.

16

Jentz, Terri. *Strange Piece of Paradise*. 2006. 542p. 9780374134983. In 1977, Jentz and a friend were camping when they were attacked by an axe-wielding man; 15 years later, Jentz tried to find her own attacker and bring him to justice.

17

Junger, Sebastian. *A Death in Belmont*. 2006. 266p. 9780393059809. Junger explores the 1963 murder of Bessie Goldberg, arguing that she may not have been killed by the man who was convicted for the crime, but rather by the Boston Strangler.

18

Must Read

★ 🏅 🎞️ **Larson, Erik.** *The Devil in the White City*. 2003. 447p. 97806 09608449. Larson describes (graphically) the activities of both the 1890s Chicago serial killer Henry H. Holmes and the 1893 World's Fair director and architect Daniel Hudson Burnham, in this Edgar Award–winning title.

🏅 📖 **Larson, Erik.** *Thunderstruck*. 2006. 463p. 9781400080663. Larson combines stories of Dr. Hawley Crippen's 1910 murder of his wife with the invention of wireless communication (and its controversial inventor Guglielmo Marconi).

🏅 🎞️ **Mailer, Norman.** *The Executioner's Song*. 1998 (1979). 1056p. 9780375 700811. In this Pulitzer Prize–winning blend of fiction and nonfiction, Mailer tells the story of Gary Gilmore, who killed two men in Utah and was later executed by firing squad.

Malcolm, Janet. *Iphigenia in Forest Hills: Anatomy of a Murder Trial*. 2011. 155p. 9780300167467. Malcolm describes the perplexing case of the murder of Daniel Malakov and the trial of his wife Mazoltuv Borukhova, a successful physician, for hiring an assassin to kill him.

Mustafa, Susan D., Tony Clayton, and Sue Israel. *Blood Bath*. 2009. 346p. 9780786021338. Serial killer Derrick Todd Lee was thought by all to be an upstanding family man until he was found guilty of two murders and suspected of seven more throughout Louisiana.

Olsen, Jack. *I: The Creation of a Serial Killer*. 2002. 365p. 9780312241988. Olsen tells the story of serial rapist and murderer Keith Hunter Jesperson, who was convicted of killing eight women during the 1990s.

Pappas, Kevin. *Godfather of Night*. 2009. 256p. 9780345512239. When Kevin Cunningham learned that his real father was crime boss Lukie Pappas, he decided to embrace a life of crime in order to win the approval of Pappas.

Preston, Douglas, and Mario Spezi. *The Monster of Florence*. 2008. 322p. 9780446581196. The authors relate the history of the crimes of the "Monster of Florence"—a serial killer who targeted couples near Florence, Italy, through the 1970s and 1980s.

Rodriguez, Teresa, Diana Montane, and Lisa Pulitzer. *Daughters of Juarez*. 2007. 316p. 9780743292030. The authors investigate the serial murders (more than 400 girls and women) taking place in the town of Juarez, on the Mexican side of the border near El Paso, Texas.

Rule, Ann

Green River, Running Red. 2004. 436p. 9780743238519. Rule alternates the stories of the victims of the Green River (Washington State) Killer with the narrative of the suspect's capture and sentencing.

🎬 *The Stranger Beside Me*. 2009 (1980). 625p. 9781416559597. Rule relates the chilling details of her friendship with serial killer Ted Bundy (before anyone knew he was a killer), whom she met as they worked at a crisis hotline service.

Schechter, Harold. *Deranged*. 2005 (1990). 288p. 9780671678753. Schechter uses a horrifying level of detail in this book about killer and cannibal Albert Fish (supposedly the real-life inspiration for the character Hannibal Lecter).

Must Read

★ 📖 🎬 **Summerscale, Kate.** *The Suspicions of Mr. Whicher*. 2008. 360p. 9780802715357. When three-year-old Saville Kent was found dead in his own backyard in June 1860, suspicion immediately turned to the house's servants and the Kent family members.

Environmental Writing

Environmental Writing includes works of landscape description, animal studies, and ecological/political treatises, as well as stories describing what it means to feel a "sense of place." They are not typically story-driven narratives, but are often appealing due to their authors' reflective and distinctive uses of language, as well as their evocative setting descriptions.

Abbey, Edward. *Desert Solitaire*. 1998 (1968). 337p. 9780345326492. Abbey spent several summers working as a park ranger in the Arches National Monument in Moab, Utah; he describes his life there and lamenting "industrial tourism."

📖 **Ackerman, Diane.** *Dawn Light: Dancing with Cranes and Other Ways to Start the Day*. 2009. 240p. 9780393061734. Popular science writer Ackerman explores a year of dawns as she experiences them, referring also to related topics such as meteorology, world religions, and poetry.

Bass, Rick. *Wild Marsh: Four Seasons at Home in Montana*. 2009. 375p. 9780547055169. Bass is well known for his natural writings. In this account, he relates the details of a year in his and his family's life in Montana's Yaak Valley.

Bell, Laura. *Claiming Ground*. 2010. 241p. 9780307272881. Undecided on what to do with her life in the late 1970s, Bell left her Kentucky roots and forged a new life as a rancher in the back country of Wyoming.

Bortolotti, Dan. *Wild Blue*. 2008. 315p. 9780312383879. Journalist Bortolotti traces the history of the majestic and often misunderstood blue whale, focusing particularly on the history of whaling and the biology of the animal itself.

Carroll, David M. *Following the Water*. 2009. 186p. 9780547069647. For 25 years, naturalist and author Carroll has been exploring the same stream in New England, charting its wildlife and patterns in both prose and drawings.

Carson, Rachel. *Silent Spring*. 2002 (1962). 378p. 9780618253050. Carson explains the effects of synthetic pesticides, particularly on animals and birds and their habitats, as well as in our own water and food supplies.

D'Agata, John. *About a Mountain*. 2010. 236p. 9780393068184. D'Agata describes the plans underway to place a federal nuclear waste storage facility on Yucca Mountain in a Nevada area very near Las Vegas.

Must Read

★ 🎖 📖 **Dillard, Annie.** *Pilgrim at Tinker Creek*. 2007 (1974). 290p. 9780061233326. Dillard describes her home in the Roanoke Valley of Virginia in this Pulitzer Prize–winning and sensory detail-rich narrative, describing herself as explorer in the natural spaces of her own neighborhood.

Ehrlich, Gretel. *In the Empire of Ice*. 2010. 319p. 9781426205743. Ehrlich traveled the circumference of the Arctic Circle, describing the stark landscape and its indigenous peoples in evocative detail.

Ellis, Richard. *On Thin Ice*. 2009. 400p. 9780307270597. Ellis profiles the habitat and life cycle of the polar bear, focusing on its role in Inuit culture and the endangerment of its continued survival.

Flannery, Tim. *Here on Earth*. 2011. 316p. 9780802119766. Flannery delves into world history and relates the natural history of the Earth, as well as providing an engaging look at the development of one of its most troublesome and innovative species—humans.

■ **Fossey, Dian.** *Gorillas in the Mist*. 2000 (1983). 326p. 97806 18083602. The result of 13 years of observing mountain gorillas in Rwanda, this narrative is an "ethology," which details species' specific and genetically encoded behavior.

■ **Gore, Al.** *An Inconvenient Truth*. 2006. 325p. 9781594865671. Comprised largely of full-color photographs, graphs and charts, and text written in a factoid style, this treatise makes a strident case for the severity of climate change.

Grandin, Temple, and Catherine Johnson. *Animals in Translation*. 2005. 356p. 9780743247696. Grandin, a prominent animal researcher, uses her own autism to connect with animals on a more primal level and describes their different ways of understanding the world.

🎗 **Heinrich, Bernd.** *Mind of the Raven*. 2006 (1999). 380p. 9780061136054. Heinrich's brand of animal observation often seems to involve forging intimate relationships with animals he is observing; for this story, he adopted four ravens.

Must Read

★ 🎗 📖 **Kingsolver, Barbara.** *Animal, Vegetable, Miracle*. 2007. 370p. 9780060852559. Kingsolver describes her family's move from Arizona to the Appalachians, where they vowed to eat only what they grew themselves or could purchase from their neighbors.

🎗 **Macfarlane, Robert.** *Wild Places*. 2008. 340p. 9780143113935. British author Macfarlane set out to discover whether there were any truly "wild places" still left in his native Great Britain and Ireland.

Must Read

★ 📖 **McKibben, Bill.** *Eaarth: Making a Life on a Tough New Planet*. 2010. 253p. 9780805090567. Popular environmental writer McKibben matter-of-factly lays out his argument that the future will contain many broad climate changes for our planet.

■ **Mowat, Farley.** *Never Cry Wolf*. 2001 (1963). 246p. 9780316881791. Mowat's classic (and humorous) work details his experiences as a field biologist in Canada, studying the behavior of the caribou and wolves of Manitoba.

Pollan, Michael. *In Defense of Food*. 2008. 244p. 9781594201455. Pollan suggests we reaffirm our joy in food and eating but being more careful about our food choices, spending more money on fewer food items.

Rinella, Steven. *American Buffalo*. 2008. 277p. 9780385521680. When Rinella, a longtime hunter and outdoorsman, won a lottery to hunt for and kill one buffalo in Alaska, he decided to explore the history and biology of the American bison.

🎗 **Streever, Bill.** *Cold: Adventures in the World's Frozen Places*. 2009. 292p. 9780316042918. Author Streever undertook the task of finding many-degrees-below-zero cold as his travel mandate, exploring many Arctic ecosystems (and challenges they're facing).

Thoreau, Henry David. *Walden*. 2004 (1854). 370p. 9780300104660. In 1845, at the age of 28, Thoreau took an axe into the woods in Concord, Massachusetts, and endeavored to live a completely sustainable life there.

Science and Math

Science and Math titles do not constitute a genre as much as they do a subject area of reading interest. These titles offer facts, theories, and stories on varied scientific topics from biology, geology, evolutionary theory, astronomy, mathematics, chemistry, and physics (among many others). They range in emphasis from deep to popular science, in subject from biographical stories to theoretical treatises, and in style from story-driven narratives of discoveries and breakthroughs to more slowly paced and scholarly.

🎗 **Angier, Natalie.** *The Canon: A Whirligig Tour of the Beautiful Basics of Science*. 2007. 293p. 9780618242955. Angier sets out to provide an understandable and lively tour through the basic scientific disciplines of physics, chemistry, biology, and astronomy, in this ALA Notable title.

Arthur, W. Brian. *The Nature of Technology*. 2009. 246p. 9781416544050. Arthur compares the development and use of new technologies, as well as their connections with certain cultures, to an evolutionary process.

Belfiore, Michael. *The Department of Mad Scientists: How DARPA Is Remaking Our World, from the Internet to Artificial Limbs*. 2009. 295p. 9780061577932. Belfiore provides a glimpse inside the high-tech and cutting-edge world of scientific research being performed at the Defense Advanced Research Projects Agency (DARPA).

Ben-Barak, Idan. *The Invisible Kingdom*. 2008. 204p. 9780465018871. Microbiologist Ben-Barak's engagingly written book provides an inside look at the world of genes, proteins, bacteria, and viruses.

Bryson, Bill. *A Short History of Nearly Everything*. 2003. 544p. 9780767908177. Bryson compiled this book of science history and factoids to answer his urge to find out more about both scientific matters and those figures who discovered or studied them.

🎖 **Cathcart, Brian.** *The Fly in the Cathedral*. 2004. 308p. 9780374157166. Cathcart relates the history of the discovery of the nature of the atom and the events of 1932, when John Cockcroft and Ernest Walton discovered how to split the atom.

Crosby, Molly Caldwell. *Asleep: The Forgotten Epidemic that Remains One of Medicine's Greatest Mysteries*. 2010. 291p. 9780425225707. Crosby describes the encephalitis lethargica—"sleeping sickness"—outbreak that accompanied the flu pandemic in the years following World War I.

Dawkins, Richard. *The Greatest Show on Earth: The Evidence for Evolution*. 2009. 470p. 9781416594789. Popular and provocative science author Dawkins provides a summary of the field of evolutionary biology.

Devlin, Keith J. *The Unfinished Game: Pascal, Fermat, and the Seventeenth-Century Letter that Made the World Modern*. 2008. 191p. 9780465009107. Devlin describes the correspondence between 17th-century math pioneers Blaise Pascal and Pierre de Fermat that foreshadowed the birth of modern probability studies.

Gates, Evalyn. *Einstein's Telescope: The Hunt for Dark Matter and Dark Energy in the Universe*. 2010. 305p. 9780393062380. Gates describes one of the physics field's most revolutionary tools: "Einstein's telescope," which is allowing scientists to see more of space than ever before.

Must Read

★ 🎖 **Greene, Brian.** *The Elegant Universe*. 2003 (1999). 448p. 9780393058581. Greene eloquently describes the search for a single theory that will describe all physical phenomena and illuminates the current opinion that "superstring" theory may do just that.

Greene, Brian. *Hidden Reality: Parallel Universes and the Deep Laws of the Cosmos*. 2011. 370p. 9780307265630. Greene explores new advances in various fields from cosmology to quantum mechanics that are increasingly pointing to the existence of parallel universes.

▇ **Hawking, Stephen.** *A Brief History of Time.* 1998 (1988). 212p. 97805 53109535. A treatise on the nature of science and time, there are no equations here, but rather a chronological discussion of theories regarding gravity, the universe, and infinity.

Horner, John R., and James Gorman. *How to Build a Dinosaur.* 2009. 246p. 9780525951049. Horner describes the advances in paleontology that are leading scientists to understand more about dinosaurs and raising the possibility of fostering the growth of a dinosaur.

Kaku, Michio. *Physics of the Future.* 2011. 389p. 9780385530804. Theoretical physicist Kaku discusses which scientific developments and discoveries will impact our lives in the coming century, based on interviews with hundreds of scientists.

Must Read

★ **Nuland, Sherwin B. *The Doctor's Plague*.** 2003. 191p. 9780393052992. Nuland's text illuminates the development of contagion theory, focusing on the work of Dr. Ignác Semmelweis, who sought to curtail deaths from childbed fever.

Petroski, Henry. *The Essential Engineer.* 2010. 274p. 9780307272454. Petroski makes an impassioned argument for recognizing the value of good engineering design and suggests that scientists and engineers must find new ways to work together.

Preston, Richard. *The Hot Zone.* 1994. 300p. 9780679430940. Using suspenseful foreshadowing, Preston describes how many filoviruses (such as Ebola) replicate themselves and cause death in their hosts.

Sacks, Oliver W. *Musicophilia: Tales of Music and the Brain.* 2007. 381p. 9781400040810. Neurologist Sacks explores the myriad connections between human beings and music.

Must Read

★ 📖 **Skloot, Rebecca. *The Immortal Life of Henrietta Lacks*.** 2010. 369p. 9781400052172. Skloot tells the story of Henrietta Lacks, a black woman who died of cervical cancer in 1951, but whose cells have been grown and used in medical research for years.

Must Read

★ 🎗 **Sobel, Dava.** *Longitude*. 2005 (1995). 184p. 9780802714626. Sobel describes the development of the marine chronometer instrument, the life of its inventor John Harrison, and how figuring longitudinal positions changed the world.

Tyson, Neil deGrasse. *The Pluto Files*. 2009. 194p. 9780393065206. Astrophysicist Tyson tells the history of the "planet" Pluto—from its discovery in 1930 through its more recent history and its controversial demotion.

Watson, James D. *The Double Helix*. 2001 (1968). 226p. 9780743216302. Watson's first-person tale of the discovery of the double helix of DNA describes the complicated procedures that led to the theory.

🎗 **Wilson, E. O., and Bert Holldobler.** *The Superorganism*. 2009. 522p. 9780393067040. Wilson presents an account of the lives of social insects that draws on more than two decades of research and offers insight into how insect societies thrive.

Zimmer, Carl. *Microcosm: E. Coli and the New Science of Life*. 2008. 243p. 9780375424304. Zimmer provides a closer look at the life and times of the bacteria *E. coli*.

History

History narratives can be told in a variety of ways: in chronological order, examining specific events or historical periods, through the stories of human relationships and lives, or through the description of specific things and their use or presence in the historical record. These stories are told primarily by historians and authors who seek to create a vivid story or evocative description from vast amounts of research and evidence. Their authors also use a variety of writing styles and story lengths, from the most objectively factual to more provocative, from epic to brief, or from rigorously sourced to more anecdotal, to name just a few.

Andress, David. *1789: The Threshold of the Modern Age*. 2009. 439p. 9780374100131. Andress offers a broad, scholarly, but very readable history of the worldwide events that took place around 1789.

Bauer, Susan Wise. *History of the Medieval World*. 2010. 746p. 9780393059755. Bauer provides a history of the time between the 4th and 12th centuries, focusing on the influence of religion on politics and world history.

Bradley, James. *The Imperial Cruise: A Secret History of Empire and War.* 2009. 387p. 9780316008952. Bradley describes the 1905 diplomatic mission designed by President Teddy Roosevelt and undertaken by William Howard Taft, in the form of a cruise through Asia.

Brokaw, Tom. *Boom!: Voices of the Sixties.* 2007. 662p. 9781400064571. Brokaw spoke with both famous and unknown people to compile this oral history of the tumultuous decade of the 1960s (and its continuing influence on our current culture).

◼ **Brown, Dee.** *Bury My Heart at Wounded Knee.* 2009 (1970). 544p. 9781402760662. Historian Brown re-creates the horrific history of the American Indian in the latter half of the 19th century, as politicians followed the ideal of Manifest Destiny.

Cambor, Kate. *Gilded Youth.* 2009. 323p. 9780374162306. Cambor tells the story of France's Belle Epoque period, from the late 19th century until the beginning of World War I, through the stories of its notable figures.

Chang, Iris. *The Rape of Nanking: The Forgotten Holocaust of World War II.* 1997. 290p. 9780465068357. Chang uses primary sources, oral histories, and previously classified documents to piece together the horrifying sequence of events that led to Nanking's 1937 fall.

Corbett, Christopher. *The Poker Bride.* 2010. 218p. 9780802119094. Corbett relates the history of Polly Bemis, a woman first sold by her Chinese family in 1872 into the American Wild West.

🕴◼ **Diamond, Jared.** *Guns, Germs, and Steel.* 2003 (1997). 518p. 9780393061314. Diamond's personable but still scholarly (and Pulitzer-winning) text describes the concurrent development of human societies over the course of the last 13,000 years.

🕴 **Dickstein, Morris.** *Dancing in the Dark: A Cultural History of the Great Depression.* 2009. 598p. 978039307225. Dickstein's *New York Times* notable title is a history of the Great Depression, focusing on the cultural offerings of the period and such entertainments as music, film, and other arts.

🕴 📖 ◼ **Egan, Timothy.** *The Worst Hard Time.* 2006. 340p. 9780618346974. Egan tells a straightforward history of the hardships endured by those residents of the Great Plains states that were referred to as the "Dust Bowl" during the 1930s, in this National Book Award winner.

🕴 📖 **Faust, Drew Gilpin.** *This Republic of Suffering: Death and the American Civil War.* 2008. 346p. 9780375404047. Faust tells a new history of the American Civil War by examining its aftermath, particularly how the American people dealt with death on such a massive scale, in this ALA and *New York Times* Notable title.

🎗 **Gilmore, Glenda Elizabeth.** *Defying Dixie: The Radical Roots of Civil Rights, 1919–1950*. 2008. 642p. 9780393062441. Gilmore provides a comprehensive (and ALA Notable) history of the fight for civil rights throughout the American South in the first half of the 20th century.

📖 🎬 **Goodwin, Doris Kearns.** *Team of Rivals*. 2005. 916p. 9780684824901. Goodwin provides a political Biography of Abraham Lincoln and four of his rival politicians: Edwin Stanton, Salmon Chase, William Seward, and Edward Bates. The movie *Lincoln* is based on this book.

🎗 **Gordon-Reed, Annette.** *The Hemingses of Monticello*. 2008. 798p. 9780393064773.Gordon-Reed traces the lives of the descendants of Thomas Jefferson, America's third president, and Sally Hemings, who was both his slave and the mother of his children. This book was named both an ALA and a *New York Times* Notable.

🎗 **Gourevitch, Philip.** *We Wish to Inform You that Tomorrow We Will Be Killed with Our Families*. 2004 (1998). 355p. 9780312243357. Gourevitch describes (in strangely haunting prose) the 1994 Rwandan massacre wherein 800,000 Tutsis were killed in 100 days by the ruling Hutus. This title won the National Book Award.

🎗 **Howe, Daniel Walker.** *What Hath God Wrought: The Transformation of America, 1815–1848*. 2007. 904p. 9780195078947. Howe offers a massive (and Pulitzer Prize–winning) history of the United States during the period between the years of 1815 and 1848.

📖 **Jenkins, Sally, and John Stauffer.** *The State of Jones: The Small Southern County that Seceded from the Confederacy*. 2009. 402p. 9780385525930. This narrative focuses on the pro-Union Jones County (in Mississippi) where a group of Southerners, led by farmer Newton Knight, seceded from the Confederate union.

Judt, Tony. *Thinking the Twentieth Century*. 2012. 414p. 9781594203237. Historian Judt engages in conversation with author Timothy Snyder, mixing Memoir and history in this thoughtful overview of the major events of the 20th century and their continuing effects on our world and culture.

Keegan, John. *The American Civil War*. 2009. 396p. 9780307263438. Military historian Keegan offers an in-depth history of the military tactics used by both the North and the South in the American Civil War.

📖 **Maraniss, David.** *Rome 1960: The Olympics that Changed the World*. 2008. 478p. 9781416534075. Maraniss offers a well-researched account of the events and athletes of the 1960 Olympic Games, held in Rome, Italy.

Must Read

★ 🎬 **McCullough, David.** *1776*. 2005. 386p. 9780743226714. McCullough focuses on contrasting the miserable conditions endured by many of those fighting in the Revolution in 1776 with studies of American and British politicians.

🎬 **Schama, Simon.** *A History of Britain Vol. 1: At the Edge of the World, 3000 BC-AD 1603*. 2000. 416p. 9780563384977. Schama's massive history of Britain continues in two additional volumes, *The Wars of the British, 1603–1776* and *The Fate of Empire: 1776–2000*.

🎖 📖 **Spiegelman, Art.** *Maus*. 1997 (1986). 295p. 9780679406419. Spiegelman uses a Memoir style of recording conversations with his father to provide a history of life in Poland during World War II in this Pulitzer-winning graphic novel.

Tuchman, Barbara. *A Distant Mirror: The Calamitous 14th Century*. 2002 (1978). 677p. 9780394400266. By detailing every aspect of the life of the unremarkable French knight Enguerrand de Coucy VII, Tuchman drops the reader directly into the 14th century.

Vowell, Sarah. *The Wordy Shipmates*. 2008. 254p. 9781594489990. Vowell tells the stories of the Puritans who sailed to America from England in 1630 (who were different in slight but important ways from the 1630 Mayflower Pilgrims).

Winchester, Simon. *A Crack in the Edge of the World*. 2005. 462p. 9780060571993. Winchester describes the San Francisco earthquake of 1906, as well as other violent natural disasters that took place worldwide in that year.

Microhistories

Microhistories are stories in which authors examine very specific people, places, or things, and relate their stories as a new way in which to view the grand sweep of history. They have been referred to by Nancy Pearl as "one-word wonders," because many of their titles consist of one word (e.g., *Coal, Cod, Salt, Spice*, etc.). They are story-driven narratives, and their authors often present a vast amount of historical detail more informally or even humorously than do their more scholarly historian counterparts.

Abbott, Elizabeth. *Sugar*. 2008. 453p. 9781590202975. Abbott explores sugar's role in food science and culture as well as in world history.

Appleby, Joyce. *Relentless Revolution: A History of Capitalism*. 2010. 494p. 9780393068948. Appleby provides a comprehensive history of the development of the capitalist economic system, with chapters on trade, industrialization, and its international development.

Chapman, Peter. *Bananas: How the United Fruit Company Shaped the World*. 2007. 224p. 9781841958811. Chapman combines business history with global history as he recounts the rise and influence of the United Fruit Company and its most infamous commodity, the banana.

Ferguson, Niall. *The Ascent of Money*. 2008. 441p. 9781594201929. British historian and author Ferguson provides a whirlwind tour of the history of money in all its forms, from the first coins to the most complex modern financial markets.

Florey, Kitty Burns. *Script and Scribble*. 2009. 190p. 9781933633671. Florey examines the history of handwriting and penmanship from the origins of writing through her own history of learning the Palmer Handwriting Method.

Gately, Iain. *Drink: A Cultural History of Alcohol*. 2008. 546p. 9781592403035. Gately provides a lively history of alcohol distillation, as well as a cultural history of alcoholic beverages and their role in human society and celebrations.

Harline, Craig. *Sunday: A History of the First Day from Babylonia to the Super Bowl*. 2007. 450p. 9780385510394. Harline examines the history of the day Sunday in chapters that focus on the day during different time periods.

Must Read

★ 📖 **Kurlansky, Mark.** *Salt: A World History*. 2002. 484p. 9780802713735. Kurlansky explores world history through the lens of different societies' production and use of salt.

Murdoch, Stephen. *IQ: A Smart History of a Failed Idea.* 2007. 269p. 9780471699774. Murdoch offers a quickly paced history of the development and use of IQ tests, from their development at the turn of the 20th century to their continued influence today.

📖 **Petroski, Henry.** *The Toothpick: Technology and Culture.* 2007. 443p. 9780307266361. Petroski examines the cultural and technological history of the humble toothpick, tracing its appearances in literature as well as in the fossil record and historical documents.

Stuart, Tristram. *The Bloodless Revolution: A Cultural History of Vegetarianism from 1600 to Modern Times.* 2007. 628p. 9780393052206. Stuart traces the roots of vegetarianism and its development over the past 400 years of cultural and social history.

📖 **Sullivan, Robert.** *Rats.* 2004. 242p. 9781582343853. Sullivan staked out Edens Alley in New York City to observe the comings and goings of the common brown rat, in this combined biology and cultural history of the city.

Biography

Biographies are the stories of lives. As any number and type of lives can be recorded, these narratives cut across all subject and reading interest areas. Their formats vary from individual to group stories, informal to formal and academic, narrowly focused to broadly encompassing of all aspects of an individual's life. They not only recount verifiable details of lives lived, but also typically feature their authors' more speculative and analytical opinions regarding their subjects' internal processes and motivations. Readers often request them based on their subjects' names and exploits, but Biographies also offer subject-related personal and historical stories.

Adams, Henry. *Tom and Jack.* 2009. 405p. 9781596914209. Adams presents a dual Biography of artists Thomas Hart Benton (whose paintings featured "Americana") and Jackson Pollock (Benton's former student, who eventually moved into Abstract Expressionism).

🎗 **Bailey, Blake.** *Cheever.* 2009. 770p. 9781400043941. Bailey tells the life story of writer John Cheever, who combined his literary talent with personal struggles with his bisexuality, alcoholism, and other deep-rooted anxieties.

Beyer, Kurt W. *Grace Hopper and the Invention of the Information Age.* 2009. 389p. 9780262013109. Beyer relates the life story of Grace Murray Hopper, whose career burgeoned along with the 20th century computer programming and engineering revolution.

Brown, Tina. *The Diana Chronicles*. 2007. 542p. 9780385517089. This dishy story represents celebrity on two levels: it's the life story of Diana, beloved Princess of Wales, written by Tina Brown, a celebrity journalist in her own right.

Hirsch, James S. *Willie Mays*. 2010. 628p. 9781416547907. Hirsch provides a definitive look at the life and record-breaking (and inspiring) baseball career of Willie Mays in this authorized Biography, rich with interview material.

Must Read

★ 🏃 **Isaacson, Walter.** *Steve Jobs*. 2011. 630p. 9781451648539. Isaacson's lengthy but quickly paced Biography of seminal businessman and technology innovator Steve Jobs was the bestselling book of 2011, and delves into all aspects of Jobs' design and business prowess, as well as the details of his personal life.

Kelley, Kitty. *Oprah*. 2010. 524p. 9780307394866. Kelley provides an unauthorized Biography of talk show host and cultural icon Oprah Winfrey, one of the most popular and influential women of the 20th century.

Kriegel, Mark. *Namath*. 2004. 512p. 9780670033294. Kriegel has written a larger-than-life story to match his larger-than-life subject: 1970s New York Jets quarterback "Broadway" Joe Namath.

Marable, Manning. *Malcolm X: A Life of Reinvention*. 2011. 594p. 9780670022205. Marable draws on new research to focus particularly on Malcolm X's singular charisma and ability to reinvent himself.

Marcus, Greil. *When That Rough God Goes Riding*. 2010. 195p. 9781586488215. Music critic Greil writes on the life and music of singer and songwriter Van Morrison.

Meyers, Jeffrey. *Samuel Johnson: The Struggle*. 2008. 528p. 9780465045716. Biographer Meyers relates the life story of one of the 18th century's most volatile, notorious, and influential thinkers and authors: Samuel Johnson.

★ 🏃 🎬 **Nasar, Sylvia.** *A Beautiful Mind*. 1998. 459p. 9780684819068. Nasar's National Book Award–winning Biography of Nash focuses on his mathematical triumphs in the fields of game theory and economics, as well as on his two-decades-long struggle with schizophrenia.

Spoto, Donald. *Enchantment: The Life of Audrey Hepburn*. 2006. 352p. 9780307237583. Prolific Biographer Spoto explores Hepburn's personal life and acting career.

Must Read

★ **Taraborrelli, J. Randy.** *The Secret Life of Marilyn Monroe*. 2009. 560p. 9780446580823. Taraborrelli relies upon newly released information and new interviews with a variety of Monroe's acquaintances to tell the icon's life story.

Teachout, Terry. *Pops: A Life of Louis Armstrong*. 2009. 475p. 9780151010899. This Biography of jazz legend Louis Armstrong focuses on Armstrong's musical innovations and mastery, although it doesn't stint on personal and interpersonal details.

Historical Biography

Historical Biographies are the life stories of people who remain noteworthy for both their achievements and their staying power across the ages. Although authors of these narratives often provide historical stories and contextual details, the main focus of these character-driven titles is the person whose life is being described. They can vary in focus from one individual to groups or related individuals.

Benson, Bobrick. *Master of War: The Life of General George H. Thomas*. 2009. 416p. 9780743290258. Benson explores the Civil War general's childhood, rise through the military ranks, and many strategic successes during the Civil War.

Brinkley, Alan. *The Publisher: Henry Luce and His American Century*. 2010. 531p. 9780679414445. Brinkley relates the details of 20th century publishing giant Henry Luce's childhood, education, marriage to Clare Boothe Luce, and political views.

🎗 **Browne, Janet.** *Charles Darwin: The Power of Place*. 2002. 591p. 97806 79429326. Opening in 1858, Browne's National Book Award winner follows Darwin through the second half of his life, which was consumed by authoring and defending his theories. A previous volume, *Charles Darwin: Voyaging*, describes his early life.

Fraser, Antonia. *Love and Louis XIV*. 2006. 388p. 9780385509848. Prolific Biographer Fraser explores the life of France's infamous "Sun King" (Louis XIV, who ruled from 1643 to 1715) by relating the life stories of the women closest to him.

🎗 📖 **Greenblatt, Stephen J.** *Will in the World*. 2004. 430p. 9780393050578. Greenblatt acknowledges that little verifiable information is available about Shakespeare; rather, he speculates on the bard's life and personality using quotes from his writings.

🎖 **Greer, Germaine.** *Shakespeare's Wife*. 2007. 406p. 9780061537158. Feminist Greer argues that Ann Hathaway, Shakespeare's wife, may have played a larger role in his life and development as an author than long thought.

🎖 **Holmes, Richard.** *The Age of Wonder*. 2008. 552p. 9780375422225. Holmes focuses on the lives of three 18th-century British scientists: astronomer William Herschel, his sister and assistant Caroline Herschel, and chemist Humphry Davy. This title was named both an ALA and a *New York Times* Notable.

Nasaw, David. *Andrew Carnegie*. 2006. 878p. 9781594201042. Nasaw describes both Carnegie's hardcore business methods (as a steel executive) and his latter career as a major philanthropist.

🎖 **Pakula, Hannah.** *The Last Empress: Madame Chiang Kai-Shek and the Birth of Modern China*. 2009. 787p. 9781439148938. Pakula relates the history of the beginning of the modern Chinese state by examining the life story of Madame Chiang Kai-Shek.

Sobel, Dava. *Galileo's Daughter*. 1999. 420p. 9780802713438. Sobel tells Galileo Galilei's life story, using for her primary source material the letters that he and his illegitimate daughter Maria Celeste wrote to one another.

🎬. **Starkey, David.** *Six Wives: The Queens of Henry VIII*. 2003. 852p. 9780694010431. Starkey relates the lives of the infamous Henry VIII's six very different wives.

🎖 **Stiles, T. J.** *The First Tycoon*. 2009. 719p. 9780375415425. Stiles provides a larger-than-life Biography about a larger-than-life character in the tumultuous business world of 19th-century America: Cornelius Vanderbilt.

🎬. **Ward, Geoffrey.** *Unforgivable Blackness*. 2004. 492p. 9780375415326. Jack Johnson, the first African American heavyweight boxing champion, was as well known for his relationships and his flamboyant personality as for his prowess in the ring.

Memoirs

Memoirs are life stories, told in the first person by the individual living the experiences described. In Memoirs, authors typically explore noteworthy and finite events or time periods in their lives, based largely on their own subjective memories and reactions (as opposed to Biographies and Autobiographies, which typically encompass the whole of their subjects' lives and are most usually organized chronologically). Although the primary appeal of Memoirs is that of character development, many of these titles also appeal due to their authors' powerful and innovative use of language and prose style. Many of them also focus on transformative stories from their authors' lives. This is another category of nonfiction that is often said to "read like fiction."

Athill, Diana. *Somewhere Towards the End.* 2008. 182p. 9780393067705. British editor extraordinaire Athill offers a brief but powerful Memoir on the process of aging, both physically and mentally.

Bartok, Mira. *The Memory Palace.* 2011. 305p. 9781439183311. The daughter of a famous piano prodigy, Bartok's childhood was marred by her mother's schizophrenia. After experiencing her own health challenges, she was able to reconcile with her previously estranged parent.

📖 **Beah, Ishmael.** *A Long Way Gone.* 2007. 229p. 9780374105235. Beah describes his life as a 12-year-old child soldier in his war-torn homeland of Sierra Leone.

Bernstein, Harry. *The Invisible Wall.* 2007. 297p. 9780345495808. Bernstein describes his childhood in an English mill town in the early 1900s, focusing on the "invisible wall" that divided the town's Jewish families from its Christian ones.

Bissell, Tom. *The Father of All Things.* 2007. 407p. 9780375422652. Bissell offers a personal Memoir about being the child of a Vietnam War veteran, and describes his and his father's 2005 trip to Vietnam.

🎬 **Bourdain, Anthony.** *Kitchen Confidential.* 2007 (2000). 312p. 9780060899226. Bourdain details his early experiences with food, his chef training, and his career in restaurant kitchens, in this sometimes shocking but always hilarious work Memoir.

🎬 **Burroughs, Augusten.** *Running with Scissors.* 2006 (2002). 315p. 9780312425418. Burroughs' childhood Memoir details his horrific relationships with both his dysfunctional biological family and his adoptive family.

🏅 **Cooper, Helene.** *The House at Sugar Beach.* 2008. 354p. 9780743266246. Cooper describes her childhood in Liberia, Africa, in the "House at Sugar Beach," until, due to civil war, the family fled to America (leaving behind a Liberian foster child).

Corrigan, Kelly. *The Middle Place.* 2008. 266p. 9781401303365. Corrigan struggled to hold her life together when she was diagnosed with cancer in her mid-30s, a time when she had 2 young children and an aging father to care for.

Crosley, Sloane. *I Was Told There'd Be Cake*. 2008. 230p. 9781594483066. Crosley's smart, funny essays describe her 1980s childhood experiences, as well as her adult life in New York City.

Must Read

★ 🏆 **Didion, Joan.** *The Year of Magical Thinking*. 2005. 227p. 9781400078431. Didion recalls the year following the death of her husband, author John Gregory Dunne.

Fey, Tina. *Bossypants*. 2011. 277p. 9780316056861. Hugely popular female comedian Tina Fey mixes stories about her work life, writing about *Saturday Night Live* and *30 Rock* with essays about marriage and motherhood.

Flynn, Nick. *The Ticking Is the Bomb*. 2010. 283p. 9780393068160. Flynn tries to make sense of news stories regarding the torture at Abu Ghraib prison, as well as of his own addiction history and worry about the impending birth of his daughter.

Fuller, Alexandra. *Don't Let's Go to the Dogs Tonight*. 2001. 301p. 9780375507502. Fuller describes her childhood in Rhodesia (now Zimbabwe) in the 1970s and early 1980s, and focuses on her complex relationship with both her family and Africa.

Must Read

★ 📖 🎬 **Gilbert, Elizabeth.** *Eat, Pray, Love*. 2006. 334p. 9780670034710. When Gilbert's marriage ends, she sets off on a world journey to find "everything": from food and fellowship to spirituality and self-actualization.

Gorokhova, Elena. *A Mountain of Crumbs*. 2009. 308p. 9781439125670. Gorokhova relates the stories of her childhood and coming-of-age in the Soviet Union during the second half of the 20th century.

Must Read

★ ■ **Grogan, John.** *Marley and Me*. 2005. 291p. 9780060817084. Grogan combines life lessons learned from Marley, a Labrador retriever with a loving but boisterous personality, with tales of newlywed and family life.

Handler, Chelsea. *Chelsea Chelsea Bang Bang*. 2010. 247p. 9780446552448. Outspoken comedian and essayist Handler mines the wealth of her hilarious and extensive personal experiences in her Memoir about sexuality, family, and friends.

Hodgson, Moira. *It Seemed Like a Good Idea at the Time*. 2009. 334p. 9780767912709. Growing up in such varied locations as Egypt, Lebanon, and Saigon, Hodgson not only formed impressions of different cultures, but also imbibed their varied foods and routines.

hooks, bell. *Bone Black*. 2007 (1996). 183p. 9780805055122. hooks offers a highly stylized rendering of her own experience as a young African American girl, and her memories of family, race, and education.

▱ **Karr, Mary.** *Lit*. 2009. 386p. 9780060596989. Popular memoirist Karr describes her struggles to overcome her troubled childhood and adolescence, her tempestuous relationship with her mother, and her alcoholism.

Lawson, Jenny. *Let's Pretend This Never Happened*. 2012. 318p. 9780399159015. Lawson, better known as "The Bloggess," dishes about youthful humiliations, life with her long-suffering husband, and other embarrassing "mostly true" tales.

🕯 ■ **McBride, James.** *The Color of Water*. 2006 (1996). 328p. 9781594481925. McBride describes his and his 11 siblings' upbringing by his mother, and relates the difficulties she faced in childhood and, later, as a white woman married to a black man.

🕯 ■ **McCourt, Frank.** *Angela's Ashes*. 2003 (1996). 363p. 9780684842677. Darkly humorous as only a horrible childhood Memoir can be, McCourt tells tales of his parents' contentious marriage and his poverty-ridden childhood in Ireland in this classic (which was an ALA Notable title and won the National Book Award and Pulitzer Prize).

Moehringer, J. R. *The Tender Bar*. 2005. 370p. 9781401300647. Moehringer describes his suburban Long Island upbringing, exploring his relationship with his mother, his largely absent father, and the uncle who worked at a nearby bar.

Pamuk, Orhan. *Istanbul: Memories and the City*. 2005. 384p. 9781400040957. Novelist Pamuk offers a lyrical consideration of not only his life, but also the life of his home city, Istanbul.

Perry, Michael. *Population 485*. 2002. 234p. 9780060198527. Perry explores his move back to his rural hometown (New Auburn, Wisconsin), his role as a volunteer EMT, and rekindled relationships with family and community members.

📖 🎬 **Powell, Julie.** *Julie and Julia*. 2005. 309p. 9780316109697. Looking for a challenge in a life, Powell found it in Julia Child's cookbook *Mastering the Art of French Cooking* and set out to cook all its recipes (and blog about her experience).

🎗 **Queenan, Joe.** *Closing Time*. 2009. 338p. 9780670020638. Queenan relates the story of his Catholic youth in 1960s Philadelphia, where his family struggled with both poverty and their abusive father, in this *New York Times* Notable.

📖 🎬 **Satrapi, Marjane.** *Persepolis*. 2003. 153p. 9780375422300. Satrapi's Alex Award–winning Memoir, in graphic novel form, is the story of her childhood spent in Iran during the Islamic Revolution and its aftermath in the 1980s.

Must Read

★ **Sedaris, David. Me Talk Pretty One Day**. 2000. 272p. 9780316777728. Sedaris provides stories from his completely unique existence, including childhood mishaps, his struggles moving to France, and his checkered career path.

Sedaris, David. *When You Are Engulfed in Flames*. 2008. 323p. 9780316143479. Sedaris describes such varied topics as his first apartment, his struggle to quit smoking, and his partner Hugh's preferred traveling style.

🎗 **Small, David.** *Stitches*. 2009. 329p. 9780393068572. Small relates the story of his horrific childhood, in which he was mistreated with radiation for minor ailments and ignored by his mother, in the form of a graphic novel.

🎗 📖 **Smith, Patti.** *Just Kids*. 2010. 278p. 9780066211312. Pioneering poet and musician Smith relates a nostalgic but never cloyingly sentimental tale of her coming-of-age in 1960s and 1970s New York City, as well as her love affair with photographer Robert Mapplethorpe.

♠ 📖 **Walls, Jeannette.** *Glass Castle*. 2005. 288p. 9780743247535. Walls' childhood was anything but typical; she and her three siblings spent the majority of it being moved from one community to another by their eccentric but loving parents. This title was named both an ALA Notable and an Alex Award winner.

Investigative Writing

Investigative Writing titles are those in which authors use standard journalistic techniques to relate the who, what, why, when, and where of various current affairs and other issues. These authors frequently use stylistic techniques more frequently seen in fiction, including scene-by-scene construction, dialogue, and the description of "everyday" gestures and manners.

📖 **Auletta, Ken.** *Googled*. 2009. 384p. 9781594202353. Auletta provides an in-depth look at the mammoth company and cultural force that Google has become, as well as describing its business model and its founders.

Caro, Mark. *The Foie Gras Wars*. 2009. 357p. 9781416556688. Caro describes the 5,000-year history of foie gras, its use in cuisines and restaurants, and the controversy over how it is produced.

♠ **Chang, Leslie T.** *Factory Girls: From Village to City in a Changing China*. 2008. 420p. 9780385520171. Chang followed the lives of two young Chinese women for more than three years, as they left their rural homes and sought work in the factories of the cities.

Conover, Ted. *The Routes of Man*. 2010. 333p. 9781400042449. Conover travels the globe and explores the ways in which governments, paramilitary groups, and corporations are creating roads and infrastructure for their own needs.

♠ **Cullen, Dave.** *Columbine*. 2009. 417p. 9780446546935. Drawing on interviews and police reports, Cullen delves into the details of the 1999 Columbine high school shootings, in this ALA and *New York Times* Notable.

♠ 📖 **Eggers, Dave.** *Zeitoun*. 2009. 351p. 9781934781630. Eggers tells the story of Abdulrahman Zeitoun, a Syrian immigrant, who was wrongfully imprisoned in New Orleans in the aftermath of Hurricane Katrina, in this ALA and *New York Times* Notable.

📖 **Ehrenreich, Barbara.** *Bright-Sided: How the Relentless Promotion of Positive Thinking Has Undermined America*. 2009. 235p. 9780805087499. Ehrenreich tackles what she refers to as America's "cult of cheerfulness" in this biting polemic against proponents of positive thinking.

Frank, Thomas. *The Wrecking Crew*. 2008. 369p. 9780805079883. Frank describes American government and democracy as a shambles after decades of mismanagement and corruption by American political conservatives.

Friedman, Thomas L. *The World Is Flat*. 2007 (2005). 660p. 9780312425074. Friedman's book is informed by his "flat world" analogy, which posits that technological advances have made the global marketplace an unstoppable reality.

Johnson, Marilyn. *This Book Is Overdue!* 2010. 272p. 9780061431609. Johnson interviewed numerous librarians, cybrarians, and all flavors of information specialists to provide this inside look at the profession.

Junger, Sebastian. *War*. 2010. 287p. 9780446556248. Junger spent more than a year embedded with a military unit fighting in one of the most dangerous regions of Afghanistan.

Kozol, Jonathan. *The Shame of the Nation*. 2005. 404p. 9781400052448. Kozol explores the reality of segregation still present in America's educational institutions. This narrative is based on his observation of 60 schools.

Must Read

★ **Langewiesche, William.** *The Outlaw Sea*. 2004. 239p. 978086 5475816. Langewiesche details the activities of modern pirates and lawlessness on the oceans.

Lewis, Michael. *The Big Short*. 2010. 266p. 9780393072235. Lewis tells the story of the 2008–2009 American (and global) financial crisis by relating the stories of individuals who saw the crash coming and profited from it.

Maass, Peter. *Crude World*. 2009. 276p. 9781400041695. Maass relates the dirty business of global oil dependence, and explores what that dependence is doing to environments, governments, and people all around the world.

🏃 **Mayer, Jane.** *The Dark Side: The Inside Story of How the War on Terror Turned into a War on American Ideals*. 2008. 392p. 9780385526395. In this ALA and *New York Times* Notable title, Mayer exposes the details of the war on terrorism that the United States has pursued since 9/11, focusing specifically on preemptive wars and the curtailing of civil rights.

📕 **Roach, Mary.** *Stiff: The Curious Lives of Human Cadavers*. 2003. 303p. 9780393050936. Roach offers unstinting research, interviews, and dark humor in her attempt to study the life of our bodies after death.

Robbins, Alexandra. *The Geeks Shall Inherit the Earth*. 2011. 436p. 9781401302023. Journalist Robbins interviewed several high school students over the course of a school year to learn how cliquish behavior affects students' lives in school and beyond.

🎗 🎬 **Schlosser, Eric.** *Fast Food Nation*. 2006 (2001). 383p. 9780061161391. Schlosser's investigative account of the state of fast-food preparation and consumption in America was a huge bestseller.

Sorkin, Andrew Ross. *Too Big to Fail*. 2009. 600p. 9780670021253. Sorkin provides a detailed and comprehensive history of the American financial collapse of 2008 and 2009.

Thornton, Sarah. *Seven Days in the Art World*. 2008. 274p. 9780393067224. Thornton, using her contacts in the art world and expertise in art history, provides a series of in-depth portraits of the lives and dealings of artists, dealers, and critics.

Immersion Journalism/"Shtick Lit"/Year in the Life

Immersion Journalism is what writers engage in when they go beyond the bounds of objectively researching a story and instead step directly into it, living whatever experience they're writing about and periodically injecting their own reactions and thoughts into their narrative. They are often researched over long periods of time, are firsthand accounts, and are sometimes referred to as "Shtick Lit."

🎗 **Buford, Bill.** *Heat*. 2006. 318p. 9781400041206. Buford set out to find what it means to become a chef by apprenticing himself to celebrity chef Mario Batali, and also traveled to Italy to learn pasta-making and butchering.

Carr, David. *The Night of the Gun*. 2008. 389p. 9781416541523. Carr applies his own investigative techniques to exposing the secrets of his own life, particularly the mysteries of his alcohol and drug addiction.

Must Read

★ 📕 🎬 **Ehrenreich, Barbara.** *Nickel and Dimed*. 2008 (2001). 244p. 9780805088380. Ehrenreich spent a year working in various minimum-wage jobs (including housecleaner, waitress, and Walmart associate), none of which were sufficient to live on.

Foer, Joshua. *Moonwalking with Einstein: The Art and Science of Remembering Everything*. 2011. 307p. 9781594202292. Foer combines his tales of scientific precepts and advances in neuroscience with his own experiences training for and winning the title of "U.S. Memory Champion."

Jacobs, A. J. *The Guinea Pig Diaries*. 2009. 236p. 9781416599067. Jacobs relates a year's worth of self-inflicted experiments, including outsourcing his own work to India and living under the code of Total Honesty.

🎗 **McDougall, Christopher.** *Born to Run*. 2009. 287p. 9780307266309. McDougall studied the world's great long-distance runners, Mexico's Tarahumara Indians, and participated in a 50-mile race between the Indians and other marathoners.

Taibbi, Matt. *The Great Derangement*. 2008. 269p. 9780385520348. Taibbi reveals his undercover experiences in what he refers to as the four "defining American subcultures" of the military, the "system," the "resistance," and the Church.

🎬 **Thompson, Hunter S.** *Fear and Loathing in Las Vegas*. 1998 (1971). 204p. 9780679785897. "Gonzo" journalist Thompson immersed himself in the story of his reporter's lifestyle and coverage of a Las Vegas–sporting event.

📖 **Venkatesh, Sudhir.** *Gang Leader for a Day*. 2008. 302p. 9781594201509. Venkatesh wandered into the apartment buildings of Chicago's Robert Taylor Homes projects, hoping to ask residents "how does it feel to be black and poor?".

Big Think Books

Big Think books are books in which new and big ideas are explored, often in new and personal ways. They are descriptive, reflective, and synthesizing works in which their authors address an infinite number of topics and subjects and weave together narratives about them using a combination of research, experience, and other sources, including personal theories.

Ariely, Dan. *The Upside of Irrationality*. 2010. 334p. 9780061995033. In Ariely's follow-up to his bestselling nonfiction title *Predictably Irrational*, he explains how people's irrational behaviors affect their work, relationships, and personal happiness.

Bishop, Bill, and Robert G. Cushing. *The Big Sort*. 2008. 370p. 9780618689354. Over the last several decades, Americans have increasingly "self-sorted" themselves into remarkably homogeneous neighborhoods.

Cain, Susan. *Quiet: The Power of Introverts in a World that Can't Stop Talking*. 2012. 333p. 9780307352149. Relying on extensive research studies, Cain makes the case that introverts are wrongfully undervalued in a culture that places a premium on being "outgoing."

Chabris, Christopher, and Daniel Simons. *The Invisible Gorilla*. 2010. 306p. 9780307459657. The authors describe a variety of experiments that have proven how easily peoples' attention and intelligence can be misdirected.

Dubner, Stephen J., and Steven D. Levitt. *Freakonomics*. 2005. 242p. 9780060731328. "Rogue economist" Levitt presents a number of economic, financial, and sociological studies and theories, making connections few other economists make. The authors have also written a sequel, titled *Superfreakonomics*.

Gilbert, Daniel. *Stumbling on Happiness*. 2006. 277p. 9781400077427. Gilbert lists findings from psychology, neuroscience, economics, and philosophy to make the point that what really makes us happy is seldom what we think will make us happy.

Must Read

★ **Gladwell, Malcolm.** *Blink*. 2005. 277p. 9780316172325. Gladwell suggests that we might actually make better decisions and choices in the blink of an eye; in other words, by following our instincts instead of overthinking things.

Gladwell, Malcolm

The Tipping Point. 2000. 279p. 9780316316965. Gladwell's popular book investigates the relationship among the main cultural and interpersonal forces behind events that pass the "tipping point" and become epidemics.

Outliers: The Story of Success. 2008. 309p. 9780316017923. Here Gladwell focuses on "outliers"—hugely successful people who may just have been in the right place at the right time (rather than imbued with special genius or talent).

Lanier, Jaron. *You Are Not a Gadget*. 2010. 209p. 9780307269645. Tech guru, visionary, and the computer scientist who pioneered virtual reality, Lanier argues that collaborative softwares might be stifling individual creativity.

Lehrer, Jonah. *How We Decide*. 2009. 302p. 9780618620111. Science writer Lehrer examines the processes behind humans' rational-thinking processes (or lack thereof) and procedures for making decisions.

Pink, Daniel H. *Drive: The Surprising Truth about What Motivates Us*. 2009. 242p. 9781594488849. Pink investigates the science of motivation and exposes the myth that the only way to motivate people and workers is by using external rewards like money.

Must Read

★ **Putnam, Robert D. *Bowling Alone*.** 2000. 541p. 9780684832838. Putnam posits in this sociological treatise that as Americans join fewer community-based organizations, their interest in their communities and the welfare of others also declines.

Shields, David. *Reality Hunger*. 2010. 219p. 9780307273536. Shields demands in this manifesto that any new art form or creative work now being made must reflect and match the complexities and nuances of 21st-century life.

📖 **Vanderbilt, Tom.** *Traffic*. 2008. 402p. 9780307264787. Vanderbilt explains how our driving behaviors mirror our personalities and psychologies, in this ALA and *New York Times* Notable title.

TOOLS AND RESOURCES

Adamson, Lynda G. *Thematic Guide to Popular Nonfiction*. Greenwood Press, 2006.

Alpert, Abby. "Incorporating Nonfiction into Readers' Advisory Services." *RUSQ* 46, no. 1 (2008).

Blanton, Casey. *Travel Writing: The Self and the World*. Twayne, 1997.

Bolles, Edmund Blair, ed. *Galileo's Commandment: 2,500 Years of Great Science Writing*. W. H. Freeman, 1997.

Bookslut. http://www.bookslut.com/.

Boynton, Robert S. *The New New Journalism: Conversations with America's Best Nonfiction Writers on Their Craft*. Vintage, 2005.

Burgin, Robert. *Nonfiction Readers' Advisory*. Libraries Unlimited, 2004.

Burgin, Robert. "Nonfiction Readers' Advisory Web Resources." http://www.rburgin.com/sites/ranf.html.

Citizen Reader. http://www.citizenreader.com/.

Cords, Sarah Statz. *The Real Story: A Guide to Nonfiction Reading Interests*. Libraries Unlimited, 2006.

Cords, Sarah Statz. *The Inside Scoop: A Guide to Nonfiction Investigative Writing and Exposés*. Libraries Unlimited, 2009.

Drew, Bernard A. *100 Most Popular Nonfiction Authors: Biographical Sketches and Bibliographies*. Libraries Unlimited, 2008.

Fraser, Elizabeth. *Reality Rules!: A Guide to Teen Nonfiction Reading Interests*. Libraries Unlimited, 2008.

Glass, Ira, ed. *The New Kings of Nonfiction*. Riverhead, 2007.

Halberstam, David. *The Best American Sports Writing of the Century*. Houghton Mifflin, 1999.

Hamilton, Nigel. *Biography: A Brief History*. Harvard University Press, 2008.

Lyon, Thomas J. *This Incomparable Land: A Guide to American Nature Writing*. Milkweed Editions, 2001.

The Millions. http://www.themillions.com/.

O'Connor, Maureen, *Life Stories: A Guide to Reading Interests in Memoirs, Autobiographies, and Diaries*. Libraries Unlimited, 2011.

Overbooked. http://www.overbooked.org/.

RickLibrarian. http://ricklibrarian.blogspot.com/.

Roche, Rick. *Real Lives Revealed: A Guide to Reading Interests in Biography*. Libraries Unlimited, 2009.

Rollyson, Carl. *Biography: A User's Guide*. Ivan R. Dees, 2008.

Sophisticated Dorkiness. http://www.sophisticateddorkiness.com/.

Wyatt, Neal. *The Reader's Advisory Guide to Nonfiction*. American Library Association, 2007.

Yagoda, Ben. *Memoir: A History*. Riverhead, 2009.

Zellers, Jessica. *Women's Nonfiction: A Guide to Reading Interests*. Libraries Unlimited, 2009.

Zinsser, William. *Inventing the Truth: The Art and Craft of Memoir*. Houghton Mifflin, 1987.

FIVE FAN FAVORITES

- Timothy Egan. *The Worst Hard Time*—History

- Walter Isaacson. *Steve Jobs*—Biography

- Patti Smith. *Just Kids*—Memoir

- Mitchell Zuckoff. *Lost in Shangri-La: A True Story of Survival, Adventure, and the Most Incredible Rescue Mission of World War II*—True Adventure

- Rebecca Skloot. *The Immortal Life of Henrietta Lacks*—Science and Math

Chapter 18

Other Popular Reading Interests

PART A

CHRISTIAN FICTION

Terry Beck

with *Rosy Brewer, Diane Brown, Becky Buckingham, Marie Byars, Chy Ross, Amy Smith,* and *Marin Younker* (The Sno-Isle Libraries Readers' Advisory Team)

Christian Fiction is not usually considered a genre, but rather an overarching theme or reading interest that encompasses many genres—Romance, Historical, Westerns, Fantasy, Science Fiction, Suspense, Thrillers, Mysteries. And each of these genres written for the Christian Fiction reader always contains explicit Christian values and morals.

DEFINITION

The best readers' advisory resource to date on Christian Fiction is John Mort's classic, *Christian Fiction, a Guide to the Genre* published in 2002 by Libraries Unlimited. But Christian Fiction is not what it was in 2002. At that time, it was safe to say that it could best be defined as stories with explicit Christian values and morals within a work of fiction. More importantly, back in 2002, Christian Fiction contained no sex, no profanity, and no violence. Strictly speaking, it was not Inspirational Fiction, a Gentle Read, Jewish Fiction, or New Age Fiction.

While the values and morals remain central to Christian Fiction, in recent years, elements of violence have been interjected in many contemporary Christian works—generally to demonstrate a point, and often as part of the spiritual warfare that is the ultimate battle of good versus evil where good will always triumph. Heroes and heroines have flaws, but they are seeking redemption. Alcoholism, spousal abuse, and divorce, which would never have been found in Christian Fiction back then, are now often used as challenges and/or tests for the characters. The Christian Fiction publisher expects a "sensitivity" of the author to the market, which can include younger readers as well as adults.[1]

Nonetheless, in Christian Fiction, values and morals are explicitly expressed and dominate the story, rather than being just images and themes. It's not enough to mention Christ or Christianity, the characters and plot must reflect Christian values and way of life. So, for the purpose of this book, the definition of Christian Fiction is still stories with explicit Christian values and morals.

CHARACTERISTICS AND APPEALS

Spiritual Element

The core of Christian Fiction is the spiritual center. The characters will struggle to remain true to their beliefs while dealing with the life issues and problems that challenge them. God, Jesus Christ, is the Savior, and living a life that honors and emulates Christ is the goal of every Christian. Christian Fiction is built on the spirituality of the hero and/or heroine and shows their struggle to remain true to their beliefs while dealing with the life issues and problems that challenge them.

Christian Characters

Physically, there are some differences between the Christian Fiction character and those found in other novels. Some Christian publishers generally discourage any descriptions other than above the chest on the male hero and above the shoulders on the heroine. The hero and heroine may meet at the same level of faith, but often they come to the story at different levels. One may be a nonbeliever who will find God during a spiritual journey. Characters can be sinners, but those who are must pay the consequences of the sin and be redeemed in the readers' eyes by the end of the book. A main character who is not a Christian must come to faith by the end of the novel.

Beyond its spiritual core and Christian characters, Christian Fiction can often be identified by what it is "not."

Lack of Violence

Some degree of conflict and violence is necessary to any good story, including Christian Fiction. However, the difference between secular and Christian novels lies in the level of detail. If violence is part of the story, it must include righteous justice or punishment for the criminal and justice and redemption for the hero and heroine who may have had violent tendencies in the past. Topics such as rape, adultery, and domestic violence can be found, but the details are generally communicated without a play-by-play detail and are portrayed as immoral and wrong. Dialogue, introspection, or nightmares are often used to provide the information to understand the event's impact on the character.

No Strong Language or Profanity

Use of profanity or blasphemy in Christian Fiction is unacceptable. Even euphemisms such as gee, geez, golly, dang, heck, and shoot are not used to replace offensive words. The reader must assume that any profanity takes place without being written in the novel, with rare exceptions.

Absence of Physical Sensuality and Explicitly Sexual Content

Christian Fiction stresses chastity for the unmarried and closed bedroom doors for married couples. There could be handholding, embraces, kissing, or gentle expressions of affection. However, Christian Fiction strives to touch the heart with the knowledge that the man and woman have connected on that spiritual plane, and only when they marry will they be physically intimate. Sexuality is always implied, not explicitly spelled out for the reader.

Working with a reader of Christian Fiction is like working with other readers who have preferences surrounding genres and styles. These individuals have chosen to read Christian Fiction because there is an aspect to this fiction that appeals to them. It could be the setting, character, plot, or a combination. What is critical to remember is that the Christian Fiction reader is expecting the same moral universe in which he or she lives. When "handselling" or "shelf talking" a book for a Christian Fiction reader, there are a few things to look at as the book is presented:

- *Who is the publisher?* Is it one of the major Christian publishing houses or imprints? See the list of publishing houses and imprints in the "Tools and Resources" section of this chapter. When working with customers, it's important to understand that they are usually looking for titles published by Evangelical Christian publishing houses—stories with a message of redemption.

- *What's on the cover?* Typically, the cover will convey some aspect of the plot or character. There won't be cleavage, short skirts, or bare-chested men.

- *What does the short description provided by the publisher say?* The word "Christian" is often part of this description. Other words to scout for include salvation, Savior, and Bible.

BRIEF HISTORY

Bible stories began as part of the oral tradition of passing along what was taught. Biblical scholars have argued that the first novels actually appeared in the first century BC. These "fictitious tales" often began as stories being told to the lower classes.[2] And there are many who consider works such as Bunyan's *Pilgrim's Progress from This World to That Which Is to Come* (1678) as classic Christian Fiction. However, for the purpose of this book, we are exploring contemporary Christian Fiction that was published from 1880 to present.

Lew Wallace, a Civil War general, published *Ben Hur: A Tale of the Christ* in 1880, and it has never gone out of print. Its staying power is rooted in the telling of a compelling tale of a young Jewish prince who converts to Christianity and spends the rest of his life supporting the new religion. Grace Livingston Hill emerged on the scene with stories bound in Christian values and morals, with a very light touch of romance, not love. She is considered to be the "mother" of Inspirational Romance with more than 100 titles published between 1877 and 1947. Most of her titles are out of print, but are available in libraries and used bookstores.

Published in 1967, *Christy* by Catherine Marshall is also considered to be one of the milestones of the Inspirational Romance genre, even though it is more about the heroine's coming-of-age than about her romantic interests. By the time *Christy* hit bookshelves, the mainstream Romance genre was exploding and the "sweet" or Inspirational Romance declined. But the market for moral and/or Christian-themed Romance did not disappear.

In the late 1970s, Bethany House Publishers acquired a book that was groundbreaking, not just for Inspirational Romance but also for the Christian Fiction industry: *Love Comes Softly* by Janette Oke. This "prairie romance" not only rejected the popular trend of overt, graphic sexuality in current Romance novels, but also included a complete presentation of the gospel message.

CURRENT TRENDS

As mentioned, Christian Fiction is now increasingly available in multiple formats, including large print, Spanish language, audiobook, downloadable audiobook, and e-book. The quality of writing continues to improve. Even in the midst of the recent recession, Christian Fiction continued to maintain a positive edge in the Christian book market.

Until the publication of *Left Behind* (1995), Christian Fiction publishers were working with a reader profile that appeared to be the Caucasian Evangelical

Christian woman, 18–60 years of age. The Christian Fiction reader no longer fits that mold. We have observed that there are now more middle-of-the road readers who are testing the Christian Fiction waters, including men and minorities. The demographics are changing as more readers discover intriguing plots, interesting settings, and well-drawn characters. Spanish-language translations of popular books are more readily available, as are large print and audio editions. Readership has broadened as Christian Fiction has diversified into new genres and types.

Although Christian Fiction has been "issue driven" in the past, there's a move away from this "to a more eclectic mix of novels"[3] in genres such as suspense, thrillers, and science fiction. Readers more commonly purchase Christian Fiction at mass market retailers or online, instead of at specialty Christian bookstores. This move is significant as it opens up the Christian Fiction market to a more mainstream audience. Ten years ago, it would have been unthinkable to find Christian Fiction at Walmart or Costco, but now it is well represented. And the influence of Christian-themed Fantasy films has also contributed to a resurgence of interest in C. S. Lewis.[4] Christian Fiction has also found a theme that has dominated much of adult and young adult fiction in the past few years: vampirism.

In the past 10 years, Christian Suspense has undergone more changes than any other Christian genre. Whereas it once needed high-redemptive elements, it is now all about the story. Christian Crime Fiction now focuses on human versus human conflict, even murder, which brings Christian Suspense closer to its secular counterpart. This has brought more male readers to Christian Fiction. Of all the genres, this seems to be the one that acts as an entry point for Christian Fiction for many new or secular readers.

Readers will find more female Christian Suspense authors today, and that means more female characters. In true Suspense, these are female protagonists with no romantic elements. However, Romantic Suspense is still considered to be the mainstay of the genre. More publishers are taking chances with Christian Suspense, and the potential for crossover reading continues to grow.

THEMES AND TYPES

Key to Christian Fiction Subgenres

Contemporary Christian Life
Christian Romance

(Continued)

10

11

12

13

14

15

16

17

18

> Amish Romance
> Contemporary Christian Romance
> Historical Christian Romance
> Christian Historical Fiction
> Christian Suspense/Thriller/Crime
> Christian Mystery

Contemporary Christian Life

Some of the most significant changes in Christian Fiction have happened in contemporary and issues-driven works that bring in abducted children, marriages under stress, the impact of the Iraq and Afghanistan wars, and even themes similar to those in Urban Fiction.

Fabry, Chris. *June Bug*. Tyndale House, 2009. 326p. 9781414319568. June Bug, a precocious 9-year-old, spots a photo of herself on a Walmart bulletin board of missing children and forces her father to confront his past demons.

Jackson, Neta. *Yada Yada Prayer Group*. Thomas Nelson, 2003. 388p. 978159554423. An assignment to a prayer group at a women's conference has long-lasting consequences for Jodi Baxter and 11 other women who find comfort within the group and each other.

Kingsbury, Karen

Ever After. Zondervan, 2007. 356p. 9780310247562. A young couple's love is tested by their differing viewpoints about the war in Afghanistan.

🎗 *Oceans Apart*. Zondervan, 2004. 350p. 9780310247494. Conner Evans, marriage looks perfect until his actions from seven years ago come back with a vengeance and test his family's faith. Winner of the 2005 Gold Medallion Book Award.

Shades of Blue. Zondervan, 2009. 333p. 9780310266945. Brad Cutler must go back to the shores of Holden Beach in search of his first love, and a forgiveness neither of them has ever known.

🎗 **Meissner, Susan.** *The Shape of Mercy.* Waterbrook, 2008. 305p. 9781400074563.Lauren Durough chooses to attend a state college rather than the prestigious university her family prefers. She also chooses to earn her own income by transcribing the 400-year-old diary of Mercy, a victim of the Salem Witch Trials.

🎗 📖 **Nicholls, Linda.** *In Search of Eden.* Bethany House, 2007. 443p. 9780764201670. A long-standing feud between two brothers is reignited when a tragic accident brings back the past.

Norman-Bellamy, Kendra. *For Love and Grace.* BET Publications, 2004. 261p. 1583145494. Two lifelong friends find their faith and their relationship tested when an automobile accident kills one's mother and the other falls in love with the driver believed to be responsible for the accident.

Parrish, Christa. *Watch Over Me.* Bethany House, 2009. 349p. 9780764205545. Afghanistan veteran and sheriff's deputy Ben hopes to reclaim his marriage when he brings home an abandoned baby found in a nearby field.

Peterson, Tracie

Dawn's Prelude. Bethany House, 2009. 335p. 9780764201516. Young widow Lydia Gray flees to Alaska seeking refuge from family strife and finds romance with an unexpected suitor.

House of Secrets. Bethany House, 2011, 309p. 9780764209222. Three sisters come together at the family summer house and work through their emotions as they remember what happened 15 years ago, when their schizophrenic mother was murdered.

Samson, Lisa

📖 *The Living End.* Waterbrook, 2003. 306p. 9781578565979. Pearly Laurel has just lost her husband of 35 years and cannot imagine how she will go on, until she finds a list in her husband's jacket pocket that begins "While I live, I want to . . . " and decides that she will accomplish these goals in his memory.

🎗 *The Passion of Mary-Margaret.* Thomas Nelson, 2009. 316p. 9781595542113. A young woman preparing to enter the convent is shaken to the core by the return of a former friend who has other plans for her future.

Must Read

★ 📖 **Young, William P.** *The Shack*. Windblown, 2007. 253p. 9780964729247. This was the self-published bestseller of 2007. Mackenzie Allen Phillip's youngest child was abducted four years ago and most likely murdered. He journeys to the shack where evidence was located and has a life-changing experience.

Christian Romance

Amish Romance

Currently the trend in one segment of Christian romance is Amish love stories or "Bonnet Books." The appeal of a closed religious group, such as the Amish, continues to grow, and publishers are beginning to include other groups such as Mennonites. Bonnet Books may be set in contemporary times or in the past.

Cameron, Barbara. *A Time to Love*. Abingdon, 2010. 302p. 9781426707636. A war correspondent returns to her grandmother's Amish community and meets a love of her past.

Lewis, Beverly

🎗 *The Brethren*. Bethany House, 2006. 349p. 9780764201073. This is the conclusion to Lewis' Annie Trilogy, which features a young Amish woman who is caught between her religion and her art.

Must Read

★ *The Redemption of Sarah Cain*. Bethany House, 2000. 316p. 9780 764204036. Modern woman Sarah Cain journeys to Lancaster County, Pennsylvania, to claim her newly orphaned nieces and nephews, convinced that her life will not change in the new community.

Miller, Judith. *Somewhere to Belong*. Bethany House, 2010. 364p. 978076 4206429. Set in 1877, Johanna Ilg learns a troubling secret, the world she thought she knew in Main Amana, Iowa, is shattered, and she is forced to make difficult choices, while teenage Berta Schumacher has trouble adjusting to life in Amana.

Perry, Martha. *Leah's Choice*. Berkley Books, 2009. 312p. 9780426230503. Leah Baker has nursed a broken heart ever since Johnny Kile left her and the Amish community, but he's back and now she must choose between the newly reformed Johnny and Daniel, the attractive widower.

Wiseman, Beth

An Amish Gathering: Life in Lancaster County, Three Novellas. Thomas Nelson, 2009. 388p. 9781595548221. Three seasons, three stories, all filled with the dialect, traditions, and recipes of the Amish world.

Plain Perfect. Thomas Nelson, 2008. 305p. 9781595546302. Lillian returns to her grandparents' home in Lancaster County, Pennsylvania, and finds inner peace and a new love.

Contemporary Christian Romance

This subcategory of Christian Romance is set in contemporary times and features heroines who face issues such as money problems, marital woes, and midlife crisis.

Carlson, Melody. *A Mile in My Flip-Flops*. Waterbrook Press, 2008. 330p. 9781400073146. Reality television enters the Christian Fiction romance world. Gretchen Hanover is nursing a broken heart and becomes a first-time home flipper with disastrous results until carpenter Noah enters the picture.

🎗 **Goodnight, Linda.** *Touch of Grace*. Harlequin Press, 2007. 247p. 9780373874262. The discovery of her sister's boy near a New Orleans mansion has a young journalist wondering just how involved the owner is in her sister's death. Winner of a RITA Award.

🎗 **Mills, DiAnn.** *Breach of Trust*. Tyndale House, 2009. 392p. 9781414320472. A librarian's former CIA life comes back to haunt her. A slightly suspenseful romance. Winner of the Christy Award.

🎗 **Schalesky, Marlo.** *Beyond the Night*. Multnomah, 2008. 298p. 9781601420169. A couple's life is challenged by both an automobile accident and a catastrophic illness.

🎗 **Warren, Susan May.** *Finding Stefanie*. Tyndale House, 2008. 357p. 9781414310190. Can a young Montana ranch hand find true love with a Hollywood action hero? Part of Warren's <u>Noble Legacy Series</u>.

18

Historical Christian Romance

The setting is paramount in these stories and the American West dominates this subgenre: log cabins, sweeping plains, majestic mountains, and rugged characters who maintain their faith in challenging environments.

Alexander, Tamera

Must Read

★ ♞ *From a Distance*. Bethany House, 2009. 381p. 9780764203893. Elizabeth Westbrook yearns to be a photographer and captures the true beauty of the Colorado Territory, but finds herself at odds with a Confederate war veteran who tries to keep his land, despite the mysterious images that she's photographed.

The Inheritance. Thomas Nelson, 2009. 374p. 9781595546326. McKenna Ashford makes a fresh start in Copper Creek, Colorado, but things become complicated with an "untimely inheritance" and the arrival of U.S. Marshal Wyatt Carden.

♞ *Revealed*. Bethany House, 2006. 330p. 9780764201097. Second in the Fountain Creek Chronicles Series, this can be read on its own. The heroine is a former prostitute who hires a guide to take her to Idaho to claim her deceased husband's land.

Klassen, Julie

The Maid of Fairbourne Hall. Bethany House, 2012. 414p. 9780764207099. Feeling pressured into marrying a man she does not love, Margaret Macy flees her upper-class world for the life of a housemaid in the home of Nathaniel Upchurch, whose attention she'd previously rejected.

♞ *The Silent Governess*. Bethany House, 2010. 442p. 9780764207075. Secrets kept by both a governess and a nobleman bind them together in this 19th-century romance.

Mitchell, Siri. *She Walks in Beauty*. Bethany House, 2010. 398p. 9780764204333. Clara Carter is a young debutante in 1890s New York and feels of the pressures from her family and fellow debutantes to marry a man whose family is more wealthy than her own.

Wick, Lori

The Yellow Rose Trilogy. Set in 1881, the stories of the Rawlings family of Texas Rangers.

Every Little Thing about You. Harvest House, 1999. 299p. 0736901043.
A Texas Sky. Harvest House, 2000. 286p. 0736901876.
City Girl. Harvest House, 2001. 278p. 0736902554.

Christian Historical Fiction

Although historical Christian Fiction is not as strong as it once was in the 1980s, it is still a significant portion of the publishing cycle. Readers still enjoy learning about other times in history, including biblical times, and find inspiration of the lives of others, even when fictionalized.

Anton, Maggie. *Rashi's Daughters—Joheved*. Banot Press, 2005. 359p. 0976305054. Set in Medieval France, Talmudic scholar Salomon Ben Isaac has returned to his hometown to take over the family wine-making business. Little does the town know, he also secretly teaches the Talmud to his three daughters.

Beazley, Jan. *King's Ransom*. Waterbrook, 2004. 371p. 9781578567782. Based on the true story of Tsar Boris III of Bulgaria, who tried to save Bulgarian Jews from Hitler's concentration camps.

Must Read

★ **Bunn, T. Davis, and Isabella Bunn.** *Solitary Envoy*. Bethany, 2004. 319p. 9780764228629. First in the Heirs of Arcadia Series, this takes place in Washington, D.C., as the British invade the capitol in 1812.

Bunn, Davis T., and Janette Oke. *The Centurion's Wife*. Bethany House, 2009. 378p. 9780764206542. About to enter into an arranged marriage with a power-seeking Roman centurion, Leah finds herself entangled in a mystery with far-reaching implications.

Card, Orson Scott. *Rebekah*. Shadow Mountain, 2001. 413p. 97815 70089954. Part of the Women of Genesis Series, this is a fictional re-telling of the story of Rebekah, the wife of Isaac and mother of Jacob and Esau.

Carie, Jamie

Angel's Den. Broadman & Holdman, 2010. 304p. 9780805448146. In 1808, Emma meets and marries Eric Montclaire, but her dreams of an idyllic marriage quickly sour. She accompanies her husband on an expedition that parallels Lewis and Clark's famous journey, and is filled with terror and deceit.

Duchess and the Dragon. Broadman & Holdman, 2008. 294p. 9780805445350. A disinherited duke flees his county and meets a young Quaker woman who knows nothing of his royal status.

Chaikin, Linda Lee. *Tomorrow's Treasure.* Waterbrook Press, 2003. 392p. 1578565138. Set in 1878 South Africa, Evy Varley has returned to her homeland to clear her mother's name, but first she must face her family's dangerous past to find the key.

Higgs, Liz Curtis. *Here Burns My Candle.* Waterbrook Press, 2010. 465p. 9781400070015. Set in the turbulent time of 18th-century Scotland with Highlanders and Lowlanders, two women are brought closer by their faith.

Lacy, Al, and Joanna Lacy. *Line in the Sand.* Multnomah, 2007. 306p. 9781590529249. First in the Kane Legacy Series, Alan and Adam Kane arrive in Texas in 1835 and fight against General Santa Anna at the Alamo.

LaHaye, Tim, and Jerry B. Jenkins. *John's Story.* Berkeley, 2007. 358p. 9780425217139. Part of a four part series The Jesus Chronicles that recounts the lives of the four Gospel writers: Matthew, Mark, Luke, and John.

Morris, Gilbert

Honor in the Dust. Howard, 2009. 314p. 9781416587460. Young Stuart Winslow joins the court of King Henry VIII and is asked to deliver William Tyndale for execution, an acquaintance of Stuart's who wishes to translate the Bible into common language.

White Knight. Bethany House, 2007. 316p. 9780764200281. Morris' House of Winslow Series begins with the arrival of the Mayflower in 1620 and finishes with this title, set in 1941. This is a sweeping family saga that touches every period in American history.

Parshall, Craig. *Crown of Fire.* Harvest House, 2005. 415p. 9780736912785. Set in the period of the Reformation, this is the story of a young man who follows John Knox after witnessing a reformer burnt at the stake.

Phillips, Michael. *Dream of Freedom.* Tyndale House, 2004. 506p. 9781414301761. Part of the series American Dream and set during the American Civil War, story recounts a family's decision to follow God's will and free their slaves.

Must Read

★ 🎗 **Thoene, Bodie. *The Key to Zion*.** Tyndale House, 1988. 385p. 9781 414301068. As Israel approaches statehood in 1948, the British government is preparing to turn over the legendary Key to the Gate of Zion, but Arab–Israeli conflicts threaten the hope for this new nation.

Thoene, Bodie, and Brock Thoene

First Light. Tyndale House, 2003. 395p. 9780842375061. Set in New Testament times, story follows the life of Christ, paralleling it with modern times.

🎗 *Warsaw Requiem*. Tyndale House, 2005. 503p. 9781414301129. Christians work to save Jewish families in the early days of World War II.

Wangerin, Walter. *Jesus: A Novel*. Zondervan, 2005. 391p. 9780310 266730. The life of Jesus, presented as a literary novel, yet true to the Gospels' accounts of his life.

Christian Suspense/Thriller/Crime

Christian suspense shares common suspense elements with secular suspense novels. There are crime, medical thrillers, and legal dramas. Violence, though more explicit than it might have been 20 years ago, it is still purposeful and not gratuitous. It is often performed as part of spiritual warfare, which is scary but not bloody. The pace is fast and the tension high.

The critical difference between Christian Suspense and other Suspense novels is the Spiritual Element. It's there, though not always front and center. As one publisher recently stated, "it's hard to work in the saving message of Jesus in a chase scene."[5] But at the same time, as another publisher stated, "suspense is actually a genre that can put the Gospel out there really blatantly."[6]

Bateman, Tracy. *Thirsty*. Waterbrook Press, 2009. 368p. 9780307457158. Recovering alcoholic Nina is fighting both her inner demons and the mysterious forces lurking in her hometown. Yes, vampire fiction has come to the Christian Fiction world.

18

Blackstock, Terri

Cape Refuge Series. The murder of Thelma and Wayne Owens in a Christian halfway house brings together their daughters and son-in-law to find both the killers and the motive. The Owens family continues in the rest of the series.

> *Cape Refuge*. Zondervan, 2002. 385p. 0310235928.
> *Southern Storm*. Zondervan, 2003. 374p. 0310235936.
> *River's Edge*. Zondervan, 2004. 363p. 0310235944.
> *Breaker's Reef*. Zondervan, 2005. 326p. 0310235952.

Newpointe 911 Series. Set in a small Louisiana town and focusing on the emergency services, the series grew to feature Jill Clark, an attorney.

> *Private Justice*. Zondervan, 1998. 375p. 0310217571.
> *Shadow of Doubt*. Zonderavan, 1998. 371p. 031021758X.
> *Word of Honor*. Zondervan, 1999. 361p. 0310217598.
> *Trial by Fire*. Zondervan, 2000. 341p. 0310217601.
> *Line of Duty*, Zondervan, 2003. 381p. 0310250641.

Dekker, Ted

Adam. Thomas Nelson, 2008. 388p. 9781595540072. An antireligious FBI agent stalks a serial killer and is nearly killed, only to learn that the only way he'll identify his assailant is to recreate his death.

BoneMan's Daughters. Center Street Publishing, 2009. 401p. 9781599951959. A serial killer kidnaps young women, breaks their bones, and leaves them to die. And now Intelligence officer Ryan Evans must find him to save his own daughter who has been kidnapped.

Books of History Chronicles: Circle Trilogy. Each time Thomas Hunter wakes up, he's in an alternate reality and fighting evil in his dreams and in his realities.

> *Green*. Thomas Nelson, 2009. 392p. 9781595542885. This is the prequel.
> *Black*. Westbow Press, 2004. 408p. 0849917905.
> *Red*. Westbow Press, 2004. 381p. 0849917913.
> *White*. Westbow Press, 2004. 370p. 0849917921.

Books of History Chronicles: Paradise Series. Often referred to as the Project Showdown novels. Marsuvees Black appears in Paradise, and while he knows a lot about the town and its secrets, he's also hiding his own secrets.

Showdown. Westbow Press, 2006. 366p. 1595540059.
Saint. Westbow Press, 2006. 363p. 1595540067.
Sinner. Thomas Nelson, 2008. 386p. 1595540083.

<u>Lost</u>. Part Fantasy, part Horror, part Suspense, this series for teens and adults is linked with Thomas Hunter, Dekker's hero from the <u>Circle Trilogy</u>.

Chosen. Thomas Nelson, 2007. 260p. 9781595543592.
Infidel. Thomas Nelson, 2007. 245p. 9781595543639.
Renegade. Thomas Nelson, 2008. 285p. 1595543716.
Chaos. Thomas Nelson, 2008. 261p. 1595543724.
Lunatic. Thomas Nelson, 2009. 304p. 9781595543738.
Elyon. Thomas Nelson, 2009. 287p. 9781595543745.

Obsessed. Thomas Nelson, 2006. 508p. 9781595543110. A serial killer waits 30 years for another try at someone who stands in his way.

Skin. Westbow, 2007. 395p. 9781595542779. A former cult member seeks refuge in a small town that is now the center of three tornados converging on it and a serial killer.

Must Read

★ *Thr3e*. Thomas Nelson, 2004. 352p. 9780849945120. A young seminarian receives a mysterious call, telling him that he has three minutes to confess his sins to the world, or else!

Thunder of Heaven. Thomas Nelson, 2005. 304p. 9780849945175. A young couple's love in the Amazon jungle brings them to the edge when confronted by evil and terrorists.

Dekker, Ted, and Erin Healy. *Kiss*. Thomas Nelson, 2009. 322p. 9781595544704. An automobile accident leaves a young woman with no memories of recent time, but with the ability to read others' memories.

Dickson, Athol

🎗 *The Cure*. Bethany House, 2007. 334p. 9780764201639. An alcoholic looks for a miracle in a small town in Maine.

🏅 *Lost Mission*. Howard Publishing, 2009. 350p. 9781416583479. The discovery of the relics of an old Spanish mission leads some to believe that evil is at the core.

🏅 *River Rising*. Bethany House, 2006. 303p. 9780764201622. Set in Louisiana during the great Mississippi River Flood of 1927, this story examines race, prejudice through the eyes of a poor black preacher.

Henderson, Dee. *True Courage*. Multnomah, 2004. 330p. 1590520823. Dedicated FBI agent Luke Falcon works a complicated case involving the disappearance of family members and possible murder.

Holton, Chuck, and Gayle G. Roper. *Allah's Fire*. Multnomah, 2006, 398p. 9781590524053. Set in Beirut, reporter Liz Fairchild tries to locate her sister who has been kidnapped by terrorists and meets Special Ops Sergeant John Cooper, whose team is searching for a lethal new weapon. Their missions intersect and they must work together to survive.

LaHaye, Tim, and Jerry B. Jenkins

Left Behind Series. What began in 1995 as a single novel is now part of a family of series, including the Main Series, Kids Series, and Military Series. The world is in chaos and only a group called the Tribulation Force is poised to defeat the Anti-Christ.

Must Read

🏆 *Left Behind: A Novel of the Earth's Last Days*. Tyndale House, 1995. 468p. 9780842329125

Tribulation Force. Tyndale House, 1996. 450p. 0842329137.
Nicolae. Tyndale House, 1997. 415p. 0842329145.
Soul Harvest. Tyndale House, 1998. 426p. 0842329153.
Apollyon. Tyndale House, 1999. 403p. 0842329161.
Assassins. Tyndale House, 1999. 416p. 084232920X.
The Indwelling. Tyndale House, 2000. 289p. 0842329285.
The Mark. Tyndale House, 2000. 400p. 0842332251.
Desecration. Tyndale House, 2001. 407p. 084233226X.
The Remnant. Tyndale House, 2002. 405p. 0842332278.
Armageddon. Tyndale House, 2003. 393p. 0842332340.
Glorious Appearing. Tyndale House, 2004. 399p. 0842332359.
Kingdom Come. Tyndale House, 2007. 471p. 9780786295982.

Left Behind: The Prequels. This trilogy is set 27 years earlier and takes a closer look at the characters in the Main Series.

> *The Rising*. Tyndale House, 2005. 380p. 0842360565.
> *The Regime*. Tyndale House, 2005. 391p. 9781414305769.
> *The Rapture*. Tyndale House, 2006. 351p. 9781414305806.

Olsen, Mark Andrew. *Ulterior Motives*. Bethany House, 2009. 317p. 9780764202759. A disgraced FBI agent who is now serving in prison ministry is the unlikely interrogator of a terrorist who resists divulging any information.

Parrish, Robin. *Nightmare*. Bethany House, 2010. 347p. 9780764206078. The daughter of two renowned ghost hunters sees the image of a lost friend in an amusement park's haunted house.

Peretti, Frank

House. Westbow (Thomas Nelson), 2006. 386p. 9781595541550. Two stranded couples find shelter in an inn, but find themselves trapped in a game with rules setting up a life-or-death situation.

Monster. Westbow (Thomas Nelson), 2005. 451p. 9780849911804. A well-trained camper learns that there is something sinister in the forest.

Rosenberg, Joel C.

Jon Bennett and Erin McCoy Series. Rosenberg's fast-paced plots seem eerily prophetic now, with secret deals, terrorist attacks on American cities, and a Middle East war of terrorism and mass destruction.

> *The Last Days*. Tom Doherty/Forge, 2003. 384p. 0765309289.
> *The Ezekiel Option*. Tyndale House, 2005. 413p. 9781414303437.

📖 **Singer, Randy.** *Dying Declaration*. Tyndale House, 2009. 393p. 9781414331553. When two fundamentalist Christian parents try to heal their son's illness through prayer and fail to heal him, they are charged with murder.

Wilson, Eric. *Fireproof*. Thomas Nelson, 2008. 284p. 9781595547163. "Never leave your partner" is the adage spoken by many firefighters, but it takes on new meaning as firefighter Caleb Holt must examine his disintegrating marriage and choose his actions.

Christian Mystery

Christian mysteries are often included in the Thriller/Suspense category. But there have been some recent series that demonstrate that traditional mysteries still have a loyal readership. Mysteries are less graphic in the description of a crime than Suspense or Thrillers; they are more about piecing together the solution to the crime.

Stanley, Jennifer (J. B.)

Hope Street Church Mysteries. Cooper Lee and her Sunrise Bible Study Group find crime and solutions through great detective work and prayer. And like many other Mysteries, these include recipes.

> *Stirring Up Strife*. St. Martin's, 2010. 338p. 9780312376857.
> *Path of the Wicked*. St. Martin's, 2010. 342p. 9780312376833.
> *The Way of the Guilty,*. Minotaur Books, 2010. 320p. 0312376847.

Viguie, Debbie

Psalm 23 Mysteries. Not quite a cozy, but close. A church secretary and rabbi join forces to solve local crimes in a quite ecumenical fashion.

> *The Lord Is My Shepherd*. Abingdon Press, 2010. 285p. 9781426701894.
> *I Shall Not Want*. Abingdon Press, 2010. 279p. 9781426701900.

Warren, Susan May

PJ Sugar Series. PJ Sugar returns to her hometown with hopes of becoming a private investigator. Crime seems to find her and her friends. Very Evanovich-like, but still very Christian.

> *Nothing but Trouble*. Tyndale House Publishers, 2009. 341p. 9781414313122.
> *Double Trouble*. Tyndale House Publishers, 2010. 335p. 9781414313139.
> *Licensed for Trouble*. Tyndale House Publishers, 2010. 375p. 9781414313146.

Wiehl, Lis. *Waking Hours*. Thomas Nelson, 2011. 329p. 9781595549402. The beginning of the **East Salem Trilogy** featuring forensic psychiatrist Dani Harris and security system business owner Tommy Gunderson. They investigate the death of a local teenager and are being thwarted by the local school administrators.

TOOLS AND RESOURCES

Awards

Christy Awards. www.christyawards.com. This award is bestowed by an independent group of judges who honor the best in many genres of Christian Fiction. It is named in honor of Catherine Marshall's novel and there are currently nine categories: (1) Contemporary Fiction, (2) Contemporary Fiction, (3) Contemporary Romance, (4) Historical (up to 1960), (5) Historical Romance (up to 1960), (6) Suspense, (7) Visionary, (8) First Novel, and (9) Young Adult.

Christian Book Awards, Fiction Category. http://www.ecpa.org/goldmedallion/index.php. The Christian Book Awards are among the most prestigious awards in the religious publishing industry, as well as the oldest. Formerly the Gold Medallion Book Awards, the Christian Book Awards have been awarded to Christian authors since 1978.

INSPYs. http://inspys.com. A new award that recognizes the need for a new kind of book award, the INSPYs were created by bloggers to discover and highlight the very best in literature that grapples with expressions of the Christian faith.

Romance Writers of America Best Inspirational Romance. http://www.rwa.org/cs/contests_and_awards/rita_awards. RWA's RITA Award has a category for Inspirational Fiction that honors romance novels in which religious or spiritual beliefs (in the context of any religion or spiritual belief system) are a major part of the romantic relationship.

Publishers

The major publishers of Christian Fiction have undergone the same changes as mainstream publishers. They've been merged and sold. And several have become imprints of the major publishing houses. It's important to explore the subtle differences between each publisher and imprint. Looking at their writing guides for authors can be a useful tool for learning more about what they're seeking and what restrictions they place on the author. There is now a website for authors who are trying to market their work to the various Christian publishing houses: http://www.christianmanuscriptsubmissions.com/. And there are more writing workshops and seminars for prospective Christian Fiction authors.

Abingdon Press. www.abingdon.com
B & H Publishing Group. www.bhpublishinggroup.com/fiction/
Bethany House. www.bethanyhouse.com
FaithWords. www.faithwords.com
Harvest House. www.harvesthousepublishers.com
Howard Books. http://christian.simonandschuster.com/howard
Steeple Hill. www.eharlequin.com
Thomas Nelson. www.thomasnelson.com
Tyndale House. www.tyndale.com
Waterbrook Multnomah. www.waterbrookmultnomah.com
Zondervan. www.zondervan.com

FIVE FAN FAVORITES

- Chuck Holton, and Gayle G. Roper. *Allah's Fire*—Christian Suspense/Thriller

- Julie Klassen. *The Maid of Fairbourne Hall*—Christian Historical Romance

- Siri Mitchell. *She Walks in Beauty*—Christian Historical Romance

- Tracie Peterson. *House of Secrets*—Contemporary Christian Life

- Lis Wiehl. *Waking Hours*—Christian Mystery

NOTES

1. "Analysis: Popularity of Christian fiction." *Talk of the Nation*, May 20, 2004. *Literature Resource Center*. Web, July 27, 2010.

2. Aune, David. *The New Testament in Its Literary Environment*. Philadelphia: Westminster, 1987, 150, 151.

3. Riess, Jana. "Christian Fiction Editors Talk Trends: Bonnets Multiply; Goodbye, Chick Lit." *Publishers Weekly* 257, no. 10 (2010): 1.

4. Rudder, Randy. "The Spirit of Christian Fiction Today: Publishers Are Looking for the Next Blockbuster Novel in This Successful Niche Market." *Writer* 122, no. 12 (2009): 46.

5. Winston, Kimberly. "Keeping Us in Suspense." *Publishers Weekly* 255, no. 22 (2008): S6 and "Questions and Answers on Ratings and Labeling Systems." *American Library Association*, April 6, 2006. http://www.ala.org/ala/issuesadvocacy/intfreedom/librarybill/interpretations/qa-labeling.cfm

6. Winston. "Keeping Us in Suspense."

PART B

URBAN FICTION

David Wright

The emergence of Urban Fiction from its underground roots to a thriving genre with dozens of publishers, hundreds of authors, and millions of avid readers is one of the most extraordinary publishing success stories of the past two decades. Its swift rise has caught many libraries unawares, who by learning about and serving the needs of Urban Fiction fans can engage new patrons and in many cases new readers.

DEFINITION

Urban Fiction is the most commonly used term for a genre that has been alternatively known by such labels as "Street Lit," "Ghetto Lit," "Hip-Hop Fiction," or "Gangsta Lit," and that has been enjoying a tremendous upsurge in popularity and visibility over the past several years. Essentially a marketing label, the term "Urban Fiction" as such is imprecise, being defined broadly or narrowly as needed. For this section, I am using it narrowly to denote books that portray the struggles, triumphs, and tragedies of African American characters living and dying in the city, told in the language of the streets.

The milieu of Urban Fiction is the highly charged and dangerous world of gangs, prostitution, and drugs, where incipient poverty is contrasted with the lure of easy money and fast living, and where the stakes are often life and death. Populated with dealers, gangsters, pimps, and players, the pages of Urban Fiction are replete with drug use, sex, and violence, often graphically depicted. In this world, crime is not viewed as a problem to be solved but as an ever present and largely inescapable fact of life. Here the heroes and victims are often one and the same, caught up in a game that is rigged from the start, destined to be predators or prey—to play or to get played. The name of the game is survival, and the rules follow their own logic and their own stark morality, a code of the streets.

It is not surprising that Urban Fiction has drawn controversy, with many calling into question both its explicit content and its unflattering portrayal of African American characters. The popularity of these very adult books with teen readers has been another source of concern. While it behooves us to be sensitive to these issues, reader's advisors cannot afford to remain in the dark about this dynamic genre, or fail to serve the avid and growing readership for whom urban fiction can represent a pleasing recreation, an exhilarating escape, or an important entryway into the world of books and reading.

APPEAL AND CHARACTERISTICS

From its very beginnings, Urban Fiction has striven to speak with an authentic voice and rhythm all its own, employing profanity and the latest street slang in ways that ring true and familiar with readers from their own conversations or from the refined parlance of hip-hop. Rap music is in many ways the soundtrack of Urban Fiction—the poetry to its prose—making Urban Fiction a natural choice for anyone interested in hip-hop music and culture.

That premium on authenticity extends to the authors themselves, some of whom have lived lives similar to those depicted in their books, and not a few of whom began their writing careers behind bars. For readers, that experience, be it shared or vicarious, lends credence to the implicit promise of Street Fiction to tell it like it is, with no preaching or apologies. In this way, Urban Fiction can be similar to fictional and true crime tales of crooks and mafiosi, giving the reader a glimpse of the glamour and deadly grandeur of the professional outlaw, or the daring and desperate wiles of tricksters, gold diggers, thieves, and con men and women. Many urban authors write trilogies or series featuring the ongoing adventures of a charismatic antihero and employing cliff hangers to draw the reader from book to book. Other series feature a large cast of characters, each playing the game in their own way, whose lives intersect in thrilling, amorous, and deadly ways.

Urban Fiction titles are often fast-paced and dialog-driven, with a high degree of suspense. Danger is omnipresent, and plots can be highly dramatic, hinging on a complex web of alliances and betrayals. Characters are sometimes tragically caught in the pull of addiction or obsession, or struggling desperately to survive, to dominate, or to escape a world that seems bent on their destruction. Here Urban Fiction shares many of the traits of crime noir, with its gritty tales of transgressors that range from darkly comic to grim and tragic. The streetwise attitude and assumptions of Urban Fiction fit what many crime readers would term "Hard-Boiled."

Even ghetto stories have their lighter side, and many titles celebrate the camaraderie of the streets or revel in the titillating drama of romantic intrigue or erotic gamesmanship, as friends and lovers cross and double-cross, indulging in the sheer pleasure of loose talk and bad behavior. In the Urban Erotica genre, the appeal is more blatantly physical, and the shameless sexual escapades of these stories arouse the interest of readers who may have scant interest in the harsh realities of the streets.

BRIEF HISTORY

Urban Fiction has roots and analogs that go back at least as far as *Moll Flanders* (1721), with nods along the way to Newgate novels; slave narratives, the bleak naturalism of Theodore Dreiser and Frank Norris; the noir of James M. Cain, Horace McCoy, and Jim Thompson; and the stark, racially charged novels of Richard Wright, Chester Himes, and Clarence Cooper Jr.—whose raw 1960 debut *The Scene* prefigured the hustlers, pimps, and players of today's Street Lit. The frank, unapologetic voice of Claude Brown's 1965 memoir *Manchild in the Promised Land* has also been a model for generations of urban authors.

The more immediate antecedents to today's Urban Fiction revival were the so-called "black experience" novels of the 1960s and 1970s, and especially two "old school" writers who are still widely read today: Robert "Iceberg Slim" Beck and Donald Goines. Slim's *Pimp* (1969), a shameless and spirited recollection of his days as one of Chicago's most ruthless pimps, is a seminal work of Street Literature. Goines, an ex-con and heroin addict who lived and died on the streets of Detroit, penned often bleak and unrelenting novels about hustlers, whores, and junkies—such as his 1971 debut *Dopefiend*, in which a pusher will stop at nothing to subjugate the object of his desire, or *Black Girl Lost* (1974), in which young streetwise Sandra teams up with a vicious dealer to ride it out or die trying. Long before the Internet, these gritty stories were distributed to an inner-city readership through channels totally outside those of mainstream publishing. Sold on street corners, in barbershops, and by mail, these books established a grassroots literary scene that would ultimately give rise to Contemporary Urban Fiction. Far from forgotten, the unvarnished authenticity of Goines' and Slim's narratives still captivates urban writers and readers today.

A couple of decades later, Street Fiction was still largely an underground phenomenon, with self-published titles sold alongside hip-hop music off card tables in the streets of Harlem, Queens, Oakland, and Detroit. In 1999, Simon & Schuster published *The Coldest Winter Ever*, the saga of a drug kingpin's ruthless and materialistic daughter, written by the outspoken activist and hip-hop artist Sister Souljah. The book was a huge success, alerting the publishing industry to a lucrative and largely untapped market.

Meanwhile, authors who had been unable to sell their works to mainstream publishers were having runaway successes of their own. Teri Woods' popular ghetto love story *True to the Game* (1994) began its life as a photocopied manuscript sold out of the back of her car, while Vickie Stringer's prison-penned cautionary tale *Let That Be the Reason* (2001) became a big seller as well, quickly recouping the $2,500 she'd borrowed to print the first thousand copies. With an independent entrepreneurial spirit that has become the hallmark of urban publishing, both authors quickly capitalized on their initial successes, signing up other authors and establishing publishing houses of their own, thereby setting off a veritable avalanche of publication that has continued to this day.

Another area of urban publishing arose not from the streets but from the suburbs. Kristina Roberts began publishing her popular erotic stories under the name Zane on the Internet, after putting her kids to bed. She experimented with selling print copies of her stories online, and within a few years, Zane had become her own publishing empire and the reigning queen of African American erotica, with many imitators.

CURRENT TRENDS

The past decade has seen a proliferation of new urban authors, with a commensurate rise in the genre's readership. Once the genre's flagship, Vickie Stringer's Triple Crown Publications has been joined by other independent houses such as Augustus, Cartel, Melodrama, Strebor, and Urban Books. This last a large publisher with multiple imprints of its own that include upscale Romance and Christian Fiction. Mainstream publishers such as Random House, St. Martin's Press, and Simon & Schuster have also gotten in on the game, resulting in a chorus of emerging voices, published by themselves or under independent or mainstream imprints (and sometimes all three), which can seem bewildering to readers and librarians alike. The rapidly evolving new marketplace has seen other trends, such as the increasing popularity of titles in series and a diversification of formats from trade paperback on to mass market, hardcover, and audio formats. Popular with readers young and old, Urban Fiction has also had a marked influence on young adult fiction, with many teen titles and series adopting an urban vibe.

The Urban Fiction scene is highly changeable and dynamic, with new authors appearing each month. A brief chapter cannot hope to provide more than a quick overview of this burgeoning genre, highlighting some of the most prolific and representative authors in the field. Fortunately, better and more complete resources are now appearing on the scene, and these are listed at the end of this section.

Who Reads Urban Fiction?

Urban Fiction readers are diverse. As with any genre, readers' advisors must take care not to stereotype or make assumptions about readers of Street Fiction, which appeals to an array of men and women from many different walks of life, from street kids to rural hip-hop fans, from young urban professionals to ex-cons. While it is fair to say that the majority of Urban Fiction readers are African American, this readership is anything but exclusive, and of course the converse is not true. It is hard to imagine a more embarrassing interaction than when a librarian assumes that a young African American patron seeks Urban Fiction, when in fact they want Science Fiction, History, or Romance.

It is important to not assume that your library lacks an audience for Street Fiction just because your patrons haven't specifically asked you for it. It is easy for readers to conclude that your library isn't equipped to serve their needs, and turn elsewhere. Until you've purchased Urban Fiction and displayed it prominently, you cannot know whether there is a readership for Street Fiction in your community.

THEMES AND TYPES

Key to Urban Fiction

Street Fiction
    Coming-of-Age
    Love Stories
    Gangster Sagas
    Bad Girls
    Short Stories and Novellas
Urban Erotica
    Erotica Short Stories
Urban Nonfiction

There are two main types of titles commonly referred to as Urban Fiction: Street Fiction and Urban Erotica.

Street Fiction

The gritty stories found in Street Fiction do not resolve into tidy subgenres, but among the genre's most popular themes are coming-of-age, love stories, gangster sagas, and misadventures of bad girls.

Coming-of-Age

These stories tend to focus on the individual and the challenges they must face and overcome, or not.

Anthony, Mark. *Lady's Night*. St. Martin's Griffin, 2005. 324p. 9780312340780. Young Tina flees an abusive home situation and tries to make it on her own, but when the dangerous and unpredictable pimp named Cream recruits her for his team of prostitutes, Tina is reborn as Lady, giving up minimum wage for the maximum wages of sin.

Baker, T. N.

The Sheisty Series. Back in high school, they used to be the best of friends, but life takes Ephiphany, Keisha, and Shana in very different directions. With friends like these . . .

> *Sheisty*. Triple Crown Publications, 2004. 170p. 9780974789590. They may not approve of her low down, dirty ways, but gold-digging Epiphany still holds sway over her more straightlaced friends, luring them into the nonstop drama of her life. The story unfolds from three points of view, each woman expressing her own attitude on the game and how it is played.
> *Still Sheisty*. Triple Crown Publications, 2004. 248p. 9780976234906

Blue, Treasure E.

Harlem Girl Lost Series. Blue takes a hard but hopeful look at the cycles of addiction as they play out from one generation to the next.

> *Harlem Girl Lost*. One World Ballantine Books, 2006. 332p. 9780345492647. Silver Jones has seen the very worst that life has to offer, and yet is determined to find a new path for herself and overcome the destructive pattern set by her mother Jesse.
> *Harlem Girl Lost 2*. Harlem World Pub., 2011. 312p. 9780615486864
> *Get It Girls: A Harlem Girl Lost Novel*. Cash Money Content, 2012. 336p. 9781936399246

Brown, Tracy. *Criminal Minded*. St. Martin's Griffin, 2005. 292p. 9780312336462. Curtis stood up to a high school bully and wound up going to prison. Now his cousin Lamin tries to choose from many dead-end paths before him the likeliest way through to the other side. Multiple voices highlight the difficult choices these Staten Island teenagers face.

The Snapped Series. Ex-model Camille, her man-crazy younger sister Misa, music executive Dominique, and glamorous realtor LaToya may have each other's backs, but their fronts still find plenty of trouble, often where least expected. Friends 'til the end, but when will that be?

> *Snapped*. St. Martin's Griffin, 2010. 368p. 9780312555214.
> *Aftermath*. St. Martin's Griffin, 2011. 464p. 9780312555221.

D. (Kenji Jasper)

Got Series. Jasper puts a fresh stylistic spin on urban fiction, writing this story in the powerful immediacy of second-person narration.

> *Got*. Akashic, 2007. 171p. 9781933354163. Within a few short hours, petty larceny turns into major felony, and you are there, feeling the pain and passing it on.
> *Cake*. Akashic, 2008. 139p. 9781933354545.

Endy

In My Hood Series. Endy's hard-hitting, unrelenting tales pull no punches, centering around the diverse characters living and dying on the blighted streets of Newark.

> *In My Hood*. Melodrama Publishing, 2006. 219p. 9780971702196. Knowing the stakes are life and death, Desiree has resolved to find a new path when she gets out of prison, but the streets are there waiting for her, and she learns that even though the bars are gone, she is not yet free.
> *In My Hood 2*. Melodrama Publishing, 2007. 256p. 9781934157060.
> *In My Hood 3*. Melodrama Publishing, 2009. 295p. 9781934157626.

Jihad. *Baby Girl*. Urban Books, 2005. 272p. 9781893196230. She may be young, but she ain't dumb: her streetwise junky uncle Shabazz sees to that.

Johnson, Keith Lee

Little Black Girl Lost Series. While much street fiction is set back in the 1980s, Johnson breaks new ground in this series that begins in 1950s New Orleans, and reaches back into the days of slavery.

> *Little Black Girl Lost*. Urban Books, 2005. 371p. 9780974702551. It was on Christmas Eve that devout young Johnnie Wise was sold by her own mother to a white man.
> *Little Black Girl Lost 2*. Urban Books, 2006. 372p. 9781893196391.
> *Little Black Girl Lost 3*. Urban Books, 2007. 294p. 9781893196780.
> *Little Black Girl Lost 4: The Diary of Josephine Baptiste*. Urban Books, 2009. 245p. 9781601621498.
> *Little Black Girl Lost 5*. Urban Books, 2010. 304p. 9781601622600.
> *Little Girl Lost: The Return Johnnie Wise*. Dare to Imagine Publishing, 2010. 300p. 9781935825005.
> *Little Girl Lost: Johnnie Wise in the Line of Fire*. Dare to Imagine Publishing, 2010. 280p. 9781935825012.

Lennox, Lisa

Crack Head Series. The gritty fall and rise of good girl gone bad Laci Johnson.

> *Crackhead*. Triple Crown Publications, 2005. 222p. 9780974789538. Laci enjoys slumming with her South Bronx friends, until they trick her into getting on the pipe, and her comfortable middle-class world comes crashing down.
> *Crack Head II: Laci's Revenge*. Triple Crown Publications, 2008. 271p. 9780979951794.

Souljah, Sister

The Coldest Winter Ever Series. One of urban fiction's defining voices, Souljah's evolving series includes elements of crime saga, coming-of-age, bad girl, and love story.

> *The Coldest Winter Ever*. Atria Books, 1999. 368p. 9780743499385. The daughter of a drug kingpin, material girl Winter Santiaga and her sisters (Lexus, Mercedes, and Porsche) are used to all the finest things;

but when her father's empire comes crashing down, Winter is forced to decide what matters most to her and what she's willing to do to get it. Sister Souljah herself appears in the pages of this sly cautionary tale, attempting to show our ruthless heroine the error of her ways, but to no avail. This hugely influential title is perhaps the most widely read street novel of all time.

Midnight: A Gangster Love Story. Atria Books, 2008. 512p. 9781 416545187. After a 10-year hiatus that saw scores of urban authors follow in her footsteps, Souljah began a series of sequels with this long-awaited follow-up to *The Coldest Winter Ever*, which presents the very different coming-of-age of Midnight, a Sudanese emigrant who rises to become one of Santiaga's most loyal and enigmatic lieutenants.

Midnight and the Meaning of Love. Atria Books, 2011. 624p. 9781439165355. Sudanese ninja Midnight travels to Japan to rescue his kidnapped bride, Akemi.

Stringer, Vickie

<u>**Let That Be the Reason Series**</u>. Stringer began this series during the final weeks of a seven-year prison stint, drawing on her own journey from bourgeois respectability to felony.

Must Read

★ *Let That Be The Reason*. Triple Crown Publications, 2001. 304p. 9781416570486. When her dealer husband's money and affection dries up, Pamela adopts an alter ego capable of almost anything. As the streetwise Carmen, she turns tricks, becomes a madam, and then gets into the drug game.

Imagine This. Atria Books, 2004. 256p. 9780743493475. Pamela's and Carmen's struggles continue.

The Reason Why. Atria Paperback, 2009. 291p. 9781439166093. The series prequel tells us what first brought Carmen to the brink.

Turner, Nikki. *Riding Dirty on I-95*. Ballantine Books, 2006. 306p. 9780345476845. Ever since Mercy Jiles watched as her father was gunned down on her seventh birthday, she's been determined to lead a straight life. So why is she running drugs from Miami to Richmond, and will she find some way out of the life?

18

Tyree, Omar. *Flyy Girl*. Scribner Paperback Fiction, 1996. 480p. 978074321 8573. Growing up in Philadelphia, spoiled little Tracey Ellis learns how to get what she wants through bad behavior. With unfettered and irreverent language that rang true for many African American readers, Tyree anticipated the Urban Fiction boom by almost a decade. The author himself was deeply ambivalent about having his novel crowned as a classic street novel, and his latter books, including the sequels to *Flyy Girl*, stay well away from the streets.

Love Stories

Unlike mainstream Romance, in Urban Love Stories, happy endings can be hard to come by, making them often more reminiscent of Romeo and Juliet, or Bonnie and Clyde.

Brown, Tracy. *Black*. Triple Crown Publications, 2003. 182p. 9780970247285. Kaia and Aaron are high school sweethearts, and he is prepared to give her anything her heart desires, including a baby. But what can he do from behind bars, and how will Kaia handle her abrupt transition from child to mother?

The Dime Piece Series. She knew her beauty salon would be a hot spot, but Celeste Styles gets more drama than she bargained for when she falls for married gangster Rah-Lo, and his lieutenant Ishmael falls for her. When Rah-Lo is sent upstate, criminal and romantic rivalries take center stage, and Celeste is left to pick up the pieces.

> *Dime Piece*. Triple Crown Publications, 2004. 187p. 9780974789576.
> *Twisted*. St. Martin's Griffin, 2008. 352p. 9780312336509.

Chunichi

A Gangster's Girl Saga. Urban Books, 2007. 440p. 9781601620248. For Ceazia Devereaux, it all started when she went to work for an escort service, putting a price tag on her body. A gangster named Vegas wants her all to himself, and has the money to make it happen. Ceazia is glad to be off the streets and living in style, but has she just jumped from the frying pan to the fire? Originally published as three titles: *A Gangster's Girl*, *The Naked Truth*, and *Married to the Game*.

Return of a Gangster's Girl. Urban Books, 2007. 198p. 9781601620279. The high life behind her, Ceazia thinks she is out of the game for good, but the sexual rivalry of her friend Diamond rouses the sleeping tiger within.

Clark, Wahida

<u>Thug Series</u>. Clark's popular, action-packed saga tells of the struggles of Angel, Kyra, Jaz, and Roz (aka Tasha) to survive and transcend life on the streets.

Must Read

★ *Thugs and the Women Who Love Them*. Kensington Books, 2005. 232p. 9780758212863. These ladies are devoted to their men, but will it wind up killing them in the end? The course of true love never did run smooth, but here love proves itself to be a dangerous and sometimes deadly addiction.

Every Thug Needs a Lady. Kensington Books, 2006. 312p. 9780758 212887.
Thug Matrimony. Kensington Books, 2007. 277p. 9780758212559.
Thug Lovin'. Grand Central Publishing, 2009. 342p. 9780446178099.
Justify My Thug. Cash Money Content, 2011. 288p. 9781451617092.

Diamond, De'nesha. *Hustlin' Divas*. Kensington Books, 2010. 320p. 9780758247551. In Memphis, where we lay our scene, two deadly gangs from ancient grudge break to new mutiny. Caught in the middle are LaShelle and Ta'Shara, sisters and star-crossed lovers to rival gangsters.

Ervin, Keisha

Chyna Black. Triple Crown Publications, 2004. 259p. 9780976234913. She had some ideas about love, but when she fell for Tyreik, young Chyna had no idea where it would lead and what she would sacrifice. Would she do it again? Probably not, but that's life.

Torn. Triple Crown Publications, 2007. 400p. 9780977880492. After almost a decade of mind-blowing sex, Mo needs something more from her lover Quan: commitment.

Material Girl. Triple Crown Publications, 2010. 288p. 9781601622808. Ervin leaves the grit of her earlier street novels for this upscale soap opera centering around the insatiable appetites of little rich girl Dylan Monroe and friends in their quest for love, lust, and lucre.

Hernandez, Treasure. *The Flint Saga*. Urban Books, 2011. 576p. 9781601624345. Although their hometown of Flint, Michigan, has seen its share of trials, high school sweethearts Halleigh and Malek seem to have everything in their favor. Then fate intervenes, sending the couple on a treacherous odyssey. Originally published in seven episodic volumes.

Holmes, Shannon. *B-More Careful*. Meow Meow Publications, 2001. 280p. 9780967224916. This early entry in the Street Lit revival tells the story of ruthless gold digger Netta who goes after a drug dealer's cash and winds up with his heart. One broken heart later, it's time for some payback.

Whitaker, Tu-Shonda L.

Flip Side of the Game Series. An Urban Love Story that transcends the streets.

> *Flip Side of the Game*. Triple Crown Publications, 2004. 180p. 978097478
> 9545. Born to trouble (her mother dropped her into a dumpster), Vera
> Wright-Turner has developed thick defenses, but Taj's love for her
> tunnels through her castle wall. Let the healing begin.
> *Game Over*. Triple Crown Publications, 2004. 308p. 9780976234920.

Woods, Teri

True to the Game Series. Over a decade after her first self-published title, one of Street Lit's original success stories, Woods penned a pair of action-packed sequels.

> *True to the Game*. Teri Woods Publishing, 1994. 330p. 9780446581608.
> Coming up in the Philadelphia projects, Gena's only way out seems
> to be hooking up with a man with money. Enter Quadir Richards,
> looking fine and carrying paper that he showers on his new lady
> love. It is a dream come true, until the bill comes due.
> *True to the Game II*. Grand Central Publishing, 2007. 232p. 9780446581660.
> *True to the Game III*. Grand Central Publishing, 2008. 224p. 9780446581684.

Gangster Sagas

The shifting fortunes and machinations of dealers, kingpins, and crime families played out in bloody detail.

Carter, Quentin. *Amongst Thieves*. Triple Crown Publications, 2007. 280p. 9780979951725. In the late 1980s, Ramon Delay was a prime gangster. Then came prison. All these years later, has he still got what it takes to regain his crown as the king of Kansas City? Ramon himself is surprised at how swiftly he rises back to the top, slinging millions and juggling women, but on the streets, things are never quite as simple as they seem.

CA\$H. *Bonded by Blood.* W. Clark Publishing, 2011. 307p. 9780982841433. As she lay dying, their mother made her sons promise to be loyal to each other, but with all of Atlanta at their feet, will Khalil, B-Man, and Quantavious remain true to their word?

Clark, Wahida

Payback Is a Mutha Series. Clark parlays her own experiences in prison into this high stakes Thriller that leads to a show down on the bloody streets of Detroit.

> *Payback Is a Mutha.* Kensington Books, 2006. 227p. 9780758212535. Brianna has always been a player with expensive taste in clothes and men, while her friend Shan is more down to earth, her straight-and-narrow path reinforced by her job working with prison inmates. But Brianna's scheming has unexpected consequences that reach behind bars and put her friend in peril.
> *Payback with Ya Life.* Grand Central Publishing, 2008. 320p. 9780446178082.
> *Payback Ain't Enough.* Cash Money Content, 2012. 268p. 9781936399116.

Coleman, JaQuavis

The Cartel Series. Crime families battle it out like modern-day pirates of the Caribbean, striving for dominance in the global trade of a substance more maddening than gold: cocaine.

> *The Cartel.* Urban Books, 2009. 278p. 9781601621429. When Carter Diamond, the ruthless "King of Miami," is gunned down on the courthouse steps by a rival Haitian gang, the Cartel's hard-won spot at the top of the drug trade seems precarious. Will the arrival of a Carter's bastard son break their once great empire apart or reunite them in their struggle?
> *The Cartel, Part 2.* Urban Books, 2009. 236p. 9781601622563.
> *The Cartel, Part 3: The Last Chapter.* Urban Books, 2010. 288p. 9781601622570.

10

11

12

13

14

15

16

17

18

The Dopeman's Trilogy. Twists and turns abound as rivals spar for control of the Midwestern drug racket.

The Dopeman's Wife. Urban Books, 2009. 230p. 9781601621597. Cousins Khia and Nautica are in cahoots, stripping in the club and then stripping their distracted victims of their cash. When things take a deadly turn, Nautica is caught in the middle, forced to play one stone-cold killer off against another.
Dopefiend. Urban Books, 2010. 230p. 9781601622662.
Dopeman: Memoirs of a Snitch. Urban Books, 2011. 288p. 9781601622884.

Gray, Erick S.

Crave All Lose All Series. Money changes everything, and getting all that you want may be the last thing you need.

Crave All Lose All. Augustus Publishing, 2008. 260p. 9780979281617. Vincent knows about hard luck, but when he gets a taste of easy money, he forgets that nothing lasts forever.
Love & A Gangsta. Augustus Publishing, 2009. 261p. 9780979281648.

King, Joy (aka Deja)

Stackin' Paper Series. The life of a drug dealer is seldom easy. King writes multiple interrelated series under her two names.

Stackin' Paper. Street Knowledge Publishing, 2008. 212p. 9780975581117. His last good act landed him in prison; now Genesis is reborn as a criminal with his mind on his money and his money on his mind.
Stackin' Paper II: Genesis' Payback. A King Production, 2009. 217p. 9780975581162.

K'wan

Gangsta: An Urban Tragedy. Triple Crown Publications, 2002. 198p. 97809 70247216. Long a ruthless killer for the L. A. Crips, Lou-Loc heads east to help his friend Gutter establish new territory in Harlem. Bullets fly, but the real danger may lie in his unhealthy fascination for Satin Angelo, the sister to the local boss for the rival Bloods. Lou-Loc tries to get out of the game, but the only way out may be feet first; will it be Romeo and Juliet, or Bonnie and Clyde? The first book published by Vickie Stringer under the Triple Crown imprint, K'wan's debut epitomizes the rough edges and streetwise swagger of the early urban revival. The sequel is *Gutter*. St. Martin's Griffin, 2008. 406p. 9780312360092.

Hoodlum. St. Martin's Griffin, 2005. 336p. 9780312333089. Poppa wants to keep golden boy Shai clear of the family business, but those streets keep calling. A crime family saga in the tradition of *The Godfather*.

The Hood Rat Series. The scandalous misadventures of a large cast of gangsters, rappers, players, and their ruthless, gold-digging women in Harlem.

Hood Rat. St. Martin's Griffin, 2006. 368p. 9780312360085. Billy, Reese, Rhonda, and Yoshi are four friends who will stop at nothing to get theirs.
Still Hood. St. Martin's Griffin, 2007. 340p. 9780312360108.
Section 8: A Hood Rat Novel. St. Martin's Griffin, 2009. 358p. 9780312536961.
Welfare Wifeys: A Hood Rat Novel. St. Martin's Griffin, 2010. 352p. 9780312536978.
Eviction Notice: A Hood Rat Novel. St. Martin's Griffin, 2011. 448p. 9780312536985.

Woods, Teri

The Dutch Series. In one of street publishing's most infamous feuds, inmate Kwame Teague has disputed the authorship of the Dutch books and published his own finale to the trilogy. A full trilogy has now come out under Woods' name.

Must Read

★ *Dutch*. Teri Woods Publishing, 2003. 231p. 9780967224947. All rise for The People vs. Bernard James, aka Dutch, who rose from the streets of Newark to become the King of New York City in a month-long massacre. Uneasy lies the head that wears the crown, but is Dutch's reign of terror truly over?

Dutch II: Angel's Revenge. Teri Woods Publishing, 2005. 290p. 97809672 24961.

Dutch III: International Gangster. Grand Central Publishing, 2011. 240p. 9780446551540.

The Deadly Reigns Series. The swashbuckling adventures of a family of international crime lords takes Urban Fiction far from the streets.

Deadly Reigns: The First of a Trilogy. Teri Woods Publishing, 2005. 333p. 9780967224978

Deadly Reigns II. Teri Woods Publishing, 2006. 298p. 9780977323418.

Deadly Reigns III. Teri Woods Publishing, 2009. 215p. 9780977323432.

Bad Girls

Many of Urban Fiction's spirited antiheroines just take on a life of their own.

King, Deja (aka Joy)

Bitch Series. The adventures of Precious Cummings, a spirited, indomitable antiheroine, who will stop at nothing to get her ends. Easily one of the most successful franchises in Urban Fiction.

Must Read

★ *Bitch*. Triple Crown Publications, 2004. 196p. 9780976234982. Determined not to become another sad statistic like her drug-addicted prostitute mother, Precious takes charge at an early age, learning how to use her assets to get ahead.

Bitch Reloaded. Triple Crown Publications, 2007. 201p. 9780977880478.

The Bitch Is Back. Triple Crown Publications, 2008. 239p. 9780979951763.

Queen Bitch. A King Production, 2008. 208p. 9780975581155.

Last Bitch Standing. A King Production, 2009. 254p. 9780975581186.

Bitch: A New Beginning. A King Production, 2011. 224p. 9780984332571.

Boss Bitch. A King Production, 2012. 224p. 9780984332540.

Mink, Meesha

Real Wifeys Series. High drama from women on the make.

Real Wifeys: On the Grind. Simon & Schuster, 2011. 272p. 9781 439173114. Kaeyla "Goldie" Dennis is tired of being wifey number two, and starts looking out for number one, even if it means grinding on a stripper's pole.
Real Wifeys: Get Money. Touchstone, 2012. 256p. 9781451640823.

Stringer, Vickie M.

<u>**The Dirty Red Series**</u>. Meet Raven "Red" Gomez, the nastiest, two-timingest, stop-at-nothingest b***h who ever drew breath, and one of Street Fiction's most prolific bad girls.

Dirty Red. Pocket Star Books, 2006. 384p. 9781439175699. There are two sides to every story, but can Red's troubled life justify her sheisty ways?
Still Dirty. Atria Paperback, 2009. 226p. 9781416563594.
Dirtier Than Ever. Atria Books, 2010. 287p. 9781439166116.
Low Down and Dirty. Atria Books, 2012. 312p. 9781451660869.

Swinson, Kiki

<u>**Wifey Series**</u>. Kira knows that deep down her husband wants what's best for her, so she doesn't hesitate to see that she gets what's best for herself.

Wifey. Dafina, 2004. 294p. 9780758229014. Kira's man Ricky is the most feared drug dealer of the South, but that puts a target on his head, and she's determined not to be collateral damage. Ride or die? No thanks.
I'm Still Wifey. Melodrama Publishing, 2005. 239p. 978075829021.
Life After Wifey. Melodrama Publishing, 2007. 279p. 9780758229038.
Still Wifey Material. Melodrama Publishing, 2008. 232p. 97819341 57107.
Wifey 4 Life. Melodrama Publishing, 2010. 248p. 9781934157619.

Turner, Nikki

<u>**Hustler's Wife Series**</u>. The journey of Yarni from inexperienced teenager to polished corporate lawyer mirrors the evolution of Street Fiction it has spanned.

A Hustler's Wife. Triple Crown Publications, 2003. 259p. 9780970247254. Yarni cannot resist Des, who seems to be a dream come true, but then she wakes up to the cold morning light.

Forever a Hustler's Wife. Ballantine Books, 2007. 266p. 9780345493859.

Heartbreak of a Hustler's Wife. Ballantine Books, 2011. 224p. 978034 5511089.

Relapse. Ballantine Books, 2010. 279p. 9780345511058. As a concierge at a posh hotel, Beijing has risen above her humble beginnings, but her street smarts come in handy when a man from her past comes knocking.

Williams, Karen

Dirty to the Grave. Urban Books, 2010. 216p. 9781601622693. Friends Goldie, Cha, and Red, three sheisty dames who own the streets of Long Beach, will stop at nothing to get what they want, until Red takes the game to a whole other level, and it's every woman for herself.

Short Stories and Novellas

Urban Fiction abounds in anthologies that present swift and satisfying novellas by a mix of established authors and new voices, all in urban settings. Here are three of the most popular.

Around the Way Girls Series. Brooklyn, New York, is the common denominator of these novellas.

Must Read

★ *Around the Way Girls*. Urban Books, 2004. 350p. 781893196803. Featuring Angel Hunter, La Jill Hunt, and Dwayne S. Joseph.

Around the Way Girls 2. Urban Books, 2005. 400p. 9781893196858. Featuring KaShamba Williams, Thomas Long, and La Jill Hunt.

Around the Way Girls 3. Urban Books, 2006. 300p. 9781601620538. Featuring Pat Tucker, Alisha Yvonne, and Thomas Long.

Around the Way Girls 4. Urban Books, 2007. 293p. 9781601620088. Featuring Dwayne S. Joseph, La Jill Hunt, and Roy Glenn.

Around the Way Girls 5. Urban Books, 2008. 305p. 9781601620552. Featuring Tysha, Erick S. Gray, and Mark Anthony.

Around the Way Girls 6. Urban Books, 2009. 313p. 9781601621535. Featuring Mark Anthony, Meisha Camm, and B.L.U.N.T.

Around the Way Girls 7. Urban Books, 2010. 288p. 9781601622747. Featuring Chunichi, Karen Williams and B.L.U.N.T.

Around the Way Girls 8. Urban Books, 2011.288p. 9781601624512. Featuring Tina Brooks McKinney, Meisha Camm, and B.L.U.N.T.

Girls from Da Hood Series

Girls from Da Hood. Urban Books, 2004. 314p. 9780974702520. Features stories by Nikki Turner, Roy Glenn, and Chunichi.

Girls from Da Hood 2. Urban Books, 2005. 283p. 9781893196285. Features stories by KaShamba Williams, Joy Turner, and Nikki Turner.

Girls from Da Hood 3. Urban Books, 2006. 300p. 9781893196834. Features stories by KaShamba Williams, Mark Anthony, and Madame K.

Girls from Da Hood 4. Urban Books, 2008. 294p. 9781601620439. Features stories by Asley, JaQuavis, and Ayana Ellis.

Girls from Da Hood 5. Urban Books, 2009. 294p. 9781601621528. Features stories by Keisha Ervin, Brenda Hamilton, and Ed McNair.

Girls from Da Hood 6. Urban Books, 2011. 288p. 9781601624444. Features stories by Ashley, JaQuavis, and Amaleka McCall.

Street Chronicles Series

Nikki Turner Presents . . . Street Chronicles: Tales from Da Hood. Ballantine Books, 2006. 282p. 9780345484017. Features stories by Nikki Turner, Y. Black Moore, Seven, The Ghost, and Akbar Pray.

Nikki Turner Presents . . . Street Chronicles: Girls in the Game. Ballantine Books, 2007. 286p. 9780345484024. Features stories by Chunichi, Lakesa Cox, Meisha C. Holmes, Joy, and Tysha.

Nikki Turner Presents . . . Street Chronicles: Christmas in the Hood. Ballantine Books, 2007. 302p. 9780345497802. Features stories by K. Elliott, D. Blackmon, Seth "Soul Man" Ferrante, Mo Shines, and J. M. Benjamin.

Nikki Turner Presents . . . Street Chronicles: Backstage. Ballantine Books, 2009. 272p. 9780345504296. Features stories by Harold L. Turley II, Kristah Johns, Allah Adams, Lana Ave, and Nikki Turner.

10

11

12

13

14

15

16

17

18

Nikki Turner Presents . . . Street Chronicles: A Woman's Work. Ballantine Books, 2011. 256p. 9780345504302. Features stories by Keisha Starr, Tyra, Lakesa Cox, and Monique S. Hall.

Urban Erotica

Street literature often contains explicit sex; but in this genre, sexual relations take center stage, sometimes against the background of street life, as with Noire, and sometimes not, as seen in the work of influential genre pioneer Zane. Although there are many novel-length works in this genre, the subject matter lends itself to short story anthologies.

Anthony, Mark. *Dogism*. Q-Boro Books, 2006. 361p. 9780977733507. Family man Lance Thomas seems to have it all together, but the charms of his comfortable bourgeois existence are no match for his rapacious sexual appetites. Will he stop at nothing to feed his nasty addiction? Yes.

Cairo. *Daddy Long Stroke*. Strebor Books, 2010. 400p. 9781593092788. The best job is one that doesn't feel like work at all. On that score, gigolo Alexander Maples would seem to have it made, or is there a downside?

Hobbs, Allison

Double Dippin Series. The erotic adventures of lady pimp Misty and her chief breadwinner Brick mixing business with pleasure with scandalous results.

> *Double Dippin.'* Strebor Books, 2006. 304p. 9781593090654. Twins Shane and Tariq walk different paths, the one responsible and loving while the other is forever on the prowl with his nasty crew, Misty and Brick.
> *Big Juicy Lips*. Strebor Books, 2008. 368p. 9781593092078.
> *Lipstick Hustla*. Strebor Books, 2010. 352p. 9781593092825.

Noire

Must Read

★ *Candy Licker: An Urban Erotic Tale*. Ballantine Books, 2005. 291p. 9780345486479. Trouble on the streets gives way to trouble between the sheets, as Candy Raye Montana discovers that law-abiding boyfriends can be downright criminal in the bedroom.

G-Spot: An Urban Erotic Tale. Ballantine Books, 2006. 301p. 978034 5486875. What to do when your man offers you everything your heart desires, but nothing that your body craves? Gangster's girl Juicy is going to get what she needs even if it kills her, which it just might if she doesn't watch her back.

Unzipped: An Urban Erotic Tale. Ballantine Books, 2010. 288p. 9780345508799. On the brink of becoming at FBI agent, Pearl is drawn back to the streets to enact revenge on the enemies of her family, and get her share of pleasure along the way.

Pynk. *Sexaholics*. Grand Central Publishing, 2010. 336p. 9780446179584. Brandi, Miki, Valencia, and Teela Raye are all trying hard to overcome their sexual addictions, but first they must make a clean breast of their past down-and-dirty deeds.

Zane

Addicted Series. Dr. Marcella Spencer helps women overcome their addiction to sex by delving to the root of the problem, while you listen in on their steamy confessions.

Addicted. Atria Books, 1998. 326p. 9780743442848.
Nervous. Atria Books, 2003. 320p. 9780743476249.
The Hot Box. Atria Books, 2010. 320p. 0743499271. Four men. Two women, one a prude and the other a temptress. Throw in some deceit and betrayal, some true love, and a whole lot of loving, and stir.

Erotica Short Stories

Flexin' & Sexin' Series. A variety of Street Fiction authors indulge their nasty side.

Flexin' & Sexin': Sexy Street Tales, Volume 1. Life Changing Books, 2007. 211p. 9781934230961. Featuring K'Wan, Erick S. Gray, Anna J., Brittani Williams, Juicy Wright, and Aretha Temple.
Flexin' & Sexin' Volume 2. Life Changing Books, 2010. 248p. 9781934230817. Featuring Ashley, JaQuavis, Erick S. Gray, J. Tremble, Nakea, Nichelle Walker, Dashawn Taylor, and Derrick King.

Zane

Sex Chronicles Series. Zane made her name with these erotic stories in which women take the upper hand.

> *The Sex Chronicles: Shattering the Myth.* Atria Books, 2002. 320p. 9780743462709. Sexual escapades that go from intense to outrageous.
> *Getting' Buck Wild: Sex Chronicles II.* Atria Books, 2004. 292p. 9780743457026.
> *Zane's Sex Chronicles.* Atria Books, 2008. 219p. 9781416584117.

Zane, ed.

Flava Series. These thematic anthologies feature steamy sexual encounters across the racial spectrum.

> *Chocolate Flava: The Eroticanoir.com Anthology.* Atria Books, 2004. 334p. 9780743482387. African American Erotica.
> *Succulent: Chocolate Flava II: The Eroticanoir.com Anthology.* Atria Books, 2008. 318p. 9781416548836.
> *Caramel Flava: The Eroticanoir.com Anthology.* Atria Books, 2006. 337p. 9780743297271. Latino Erotica.
> *Sensuality: Caramel Flava II: The Eroticanoir.com Anthology.* Atria Books, 2009. 336p. 9781416548843.
> *Honey Flava: The Eroticanoir.com Anthology.* Atria Books, 2008. 268p. 9781416548850. Asian American Erotica.

Urban Nonfiction

Although not a genre per se, many readers who appreciate Urban Fiction's emphasis on keeping it real will be interested in nonfiction titles that share the same qualities. Here is a small sample.

Jay-Z. *Decoded.* Spiegel & Grau, 2010. 336p. 9781400068920. Megastar rapper breaks down the story of his life and rhymes.

Must Read

★ **McCall, Nathan.** *Makes Me Wanna Holler: A Young Black Man in America.* Random House, 1994. 404p. 9780679412687. McCall's impassioned, outspoken story of his own anguished youth and crooked path dares you to understand.

Pearson, Felicia "Snoop," and David Ritz. *Grace After Midnight: A Memoir.* Grand Central Publishing, 2007. 217p. 9780446195195. Having played a gangster on HBO's *The Wire*, Pearson tells her own harrowing experiences on the streets and behind bars.

Shakur, Tupak. *The Rose that Grew from Concrete.* Pocket Books, 1999. 1766p. 9780671028459. Poems written by the legendary rapper in his youth offer an introspective look at street life.

Steffans, Karrine. *Confessions of a Video Vixen.* Amistad, 2006. 224p. 9780060892487. This erotic dancer's tell-all memoirs mirrors many of the journeys of Street Fiction's heroines.

TOOLS AND RESOURCES

Initially, resources for Urban Fiction were created by readers and authors themselves on a variety of homegrown fansites. These continue to be popular resources for Urban Fiction's audience, and are now augmented by growing coverage in the mainstream literary media.

Books and Articles

Barnard, Anne. "Urban Fiction Makes Its Way from Streets to Libraries." *The New York Times*, October 22, 2008. http://nytimes.com/2008/10/23/nyregion/23fiction.html. A look at the popularity of Street Fiction at the Queens Public Library and its role in readers' lives.

Honig, Megan. "Takin' It to the Street: Teens and Street Lit." *Voice of Youth Advocates* (July/August 2008). Tackles the thorny subject of younger Street-Lit readers, and how to support their interests and reading lives.

Honig, Megan. *Urban Grit: A Guide to Street Lit.* Santa Barbara, CA: Libraries Unlimited, 2011. 251p. 9781591588573. An extensive annotated bibliography of over 400 works of Street Lit divided into thematic sections, featuring an introduction to the genre and its appeal for readers, suggested core collections for school and public libraries, and resources.

Library Journal's "Word on Street Lit." Librarians Vanessa Morris and Rollie Welch review a wide range of Street Fiction and Nonfiction in this regular feature of *Library Journal*'s "BookSmack/LJ Reviews," helping to bring critical attention to this often overlooked area of publishing.

Morris, Vanessa Irvin. *The Readers' Advisory Guide to Street Literature*. Chicago: ALA, 2011. 144p. 9780838911105. Morris discusses Street Literature in a broader historical and cultural context, explores its appeals and how to work with street-lit readers in the library, and highlights subgenres and major authors—with a forward from bestselling author Teri Woods.

Websites and Podcasts

Green, Kisha, host."What Is Street Lit?" *Blogtalkradio: Writers Life Chats*, April 9, 2010. http://www.blogtalkradio.com/writerslifechats/2010/04/09/what-is-street-lit

"What Is Street Lit: The Good, The Bad, & The Ugly." *Blogtalkradio: Writers Life Chats*, May 19, 2011. http://www.blogtalkradio.com/writerslifechats/2011/05/20/what-is-street-lit-the-goodbad-ugly

Two lively (and sometimes profane) conversations over the nature of Street Lit, its relationship to life, and its suitability for younger readers, featuring various Urban Fiction writers and readers.

Street Lit Collection Development Resources. http://wikis.ala.org/professionaltips/index.php/Street_Lit_Collection_Development_Re sources. An extensive and frequently updated collection of relevant sites and articles.

Streetfiction.org. http://www.streetfiction.org/. Featuring views and reviews from corrections librarian Daniel Marcou.

Streetliterature.org. http://www.streetliterature.com/. The blog of librarian and Street Lit scholar Vanessa Morris shares reviews, resources, and research.

The Urban Book Source. http://theubs.com/main.html. One of many extensive fansites where Urban Fiction readers, writers, and reviewers gather.

Urban Fiction/Street Lit/Hip Hop Fiction Resources for Librarians. http://www.libsuccess.org/index.php?title=Urban_Fiction/Street_Lit/Hip_Hop_Fiction_Resources_for_Librarians. Another good clearinghouse for information and articles on Street Lit.

FIVE FAN FAVORITES

These five popular titles provide a good sense of the breadth of Urban Fiction:

- Sister Souljah. *The Coldest Winter Ever*—Street Fiction—Coming-of-Age
- Teri Woods. *True to the Game*—Street Fiction—Love Stories
- K'wan. *Eviction Notice: A Hood Rat Novel*—Street Fiction—Gangster Sagas
- Noire. *G-Spot: An Urban Erotic Tale*—Urban Erotica
- Zane. *Addicted*—Urban Erotica

10

11

12

13

14

15

16

17

18

PART C

GRAPHIC NOVELS

Abby Bass and Jack Baur

Over the past decade, graphic novels (GNs) have become one of the hottest trends in the publishing world, breathing new life into a faltering industry. Several factors have contributed to the growing popularity of the format, including the increasing number of feature films based on comic books, the explosive impact of *manga* (Japanese comic books) on American popular culture and the critical and commercial success of books like *Maus*, *Watchmen*, and *Persepolis*. For these reasons and others, more and more adults are seeking out this literary and artistic format that was once widely perceived to be "just for kids."

DEFINITION

But what are "graphic novels," anyway? Aren't they just comic books? No. Actually, yes! Both comic books and GNs are works of "sequential art," in which pictures and (usually) words tell a story through their arrangement in a deliberate order. Although libraries and publishers have embraced the term "graphic novel," it remains controversial among many comic book creators and fans. Legendary cartoonist Will Eisner popularized the term in 1978, when he adopted it to distinguish his seminal work *A Contract with God* from mainstream, traditional comic books. Since then, the term "graphic novel" has served two primary purposes: (1) to indicate works of sequential art originally published in a single long-form volume and (2) to distinguish that work's quality from the typical (and, by implication, "trashy") fare of comic books.

For libraries, both uses of the term are problematic. First, many so-called GNs are not original long-form publications, but were reprinted from pamphlet-like serial publications, aka comic books. This is true of *The Sandman*, *American Splendor*, *Jimmy Corrigan*, *Ghost World*, and many of the other best-known GNs.

514

As for the implication that GNs are somehow "better" than comics, readers' advisors are well aware of the dangers of placing value judgments on a book's contents. After all, the first rule of reader's advisory is to respect the tastes of readers. Finally, many acclaimed GNs, such as *Fun Home* and *Footnotes in Gaza*, are not "novels" but works of nonfiction.

It is easy to dismiss these concerns as mere semantics, especially since the term "graphic novel" is now firmly entrenched in the library literature. However, readers' advisors should be comfortable using both terms because readers may use either when requesting good books to read. This knowledge can help you avoid leaping to false conclusions when your patrons ask for a comic book instead of a GN and vice versa.

For our purposes, the term "graphic novel" refers to works of fiction or nonfiction created in the comics format and published in paper or hardbound volumes. Throughout this chapter, the terms "comic book," "comics," and "graphic novel" (or GN) are used interchangeably.

CHARACTERISTICS AND APPEAL

Readers of GNs enjoy reading comics titles for the same reasons readers enjoy prose books in their favorite genres. Pacing of plotline, details of setting, and/or nuances of character are just as important factors in selecting titles for GN readers as they are for any other reader. However, when helping GN readers find books they will enjoy, readers' advisors must consider an additional factor: visual style. For many GN readers, the artwork is just as important as the traditional appeal factors, so be prepared to discuss this aspect when recommending titles.

Some key visual elements to consider include drawing style, panel layout, and the balance between images and text. Although it may seem daunting to those unaccustomed to discussing the artistic qualities of visual works, a degree in art history is not required to provide great GN reader's advisory. Scott McCloud's *Understanding Comics* (Harper, 1994. 224p. 9780060976255) provides an accessible but thorough and absolutely captivating introduction and guide to the visual language of comics.

BRIEF HISTORY

Until recently, American comic books were generally thought to be synonymous with one thing: superheroes. It's true that superhero stories have dominated the American comics market since the 1950s, and that

10

11

12

13

14

15

16

17

18

comics are the main literary form used to tell superhero stories. Before the 1950s however, comics covered a diverse range of genres, from Romance to Detective Stories to Horror, and adult readers comprised a large portion of the audience. Comics content and readership changed dramatically with the creation of the Comics Code Authority in 1954. This code was a by-product of the U.S. Senate Subcommittee on Juvenile Delinquency hearings, in which psychiatrist Fredric Wertham and others vilified comics as a corrupting influence on youth. The Comics Code mandated draconian restrictions on comic book content and served as a de facto censor that put many publishers of nonsuperhero titles out of business.[1]

However, starting with the underground "comix" scene that arose amid 1960s counterculture with creators like R. Crumb and Harvey Pekar, a steadily increasing number of comic artists have used the medium to create works of autobiography and literary fiction. In the last 25 years, cartoonists have produced major works in genres as diverse as Mystery, Horror, Fantasy, Biography, and Historical Fiction. Superheroes remain the specialty of two biggest publishers, Marvel and DC Comics; but a number of independent comics publishing houses—such as Dark Horse, Fantagraphics, Top Shelf, First Second, and Oni Press—produce titles in a wide variety of genres. Mainstream publishers including Houghton Mifflin, W. W. Norton & Co, and Pantheon (a division of Random House) have also gotten in on the act, publishing a growing number of GNs aimed at a broad audience. This diversity assures that readers' advisors should be able to provide a GN to any patron willing to read one.

CURRENT TRENDS

Who reads GNs and why? The common (mis)perception is that comics readers are overwhelmingly young, white, male, and heterosexual. Libraries and librarians have perpetuated this stereotype by cataloging most of their GNs, especially superhero titles, as Young Adult, and principally promoting GNs as a tool to reach "reluctant readers," particularly boys. Although many boys and young men certainly do read and enjoy comics, they are not and never have been the sole audience.

As cartoonist and comics historian Trina Robbins has noted, girls and women have always read comics, sometimes in greater numbers than boys and men.[2] Robbins argues that female comics readership has fluctuated in direct proportion to the number of comics written by and for women, and points to the current popularity of *manga* among teenage girls and the increasing number of GNs produced by female cartoonists as indicators that the female audience for GNs is growing. Since negative cultural attitudes toward comics have only begun to shift in the past few decades, it's not surprising that older adults (60s and up) sometimes shy away from the format. Despite this, some of our colleagues who have read *Persepolis* or *Fun Home* with their book groups found that their older members came to enjoy the books immensely. With the ever-expanding variety of genres, increasing mainstream acceptance, and growing number of titles published, it is likely that the audience for GNs will continue to expand far beyond its traditional demographic.

THEMES AND TYPES

Key to Graphic Novels

Superheroes
Realistic Fiction
Historical Fiction
Memoir
Crime
Science Fiction
Fantasy
Horror
Nonfiction

GNs are unlike the other books discussed in *Genreflecting*, in that technically they constitute a *format*, not a genre. As such, terrific GNs can be found in every genre described in this book. In this section, you'll find GN representatives in nine genres of major significance in the American comics scene.

Superheroes

Comic books are the native literary form for stories about superheroes, some of the most widely recognized characters in American popular culture. Most superhero stories feature people with amazing powers, dressing in colorful costumes, and fighting evil, though you'll see from this list that that's not all the genre has to offer. There are some interesting variations on that theme and mature works of art that use the idea of a superhero to explore headier issues.

Aaron, Jason (auth.), and Steve Dillon (illus.)

<u>Punisher MAX</u>. Marvel, 2010–2012. 4 volumes. After his family is killed in a mob hit, a deranged Vietnam vet wages a one-man war against the master criminal the Kingpin and his twisted assassin Bullseye. A dark, violent story with strong characterizations. The series begins with *Kingpin* (2010. 120p. 9780785145967).

Bendis, Brian Michael (auth.), and Michael Avon Oeming (illus.)

<u>Powers</u>. Image/Icon, 2001–present. 14 volumes, ongoing. Detective Walker and his partner Deena Pilgrim investigate crimes involving superheroes in this police procedural with a twist. *Who Killed Retro Girl?* (2006. 207p. 978158240 6695) and *Supergroup* (2006. 184p. 9781582406718) are standouts, while *Forever* (2004. 272p. 9780785116561) takes the series in a cosmic new direction.

Benchmark

★ **Bendis, Brian Michael (auth.), Alex Maleev (illus.), and David Mack (illus.). <u>Daredevil</u>**. Marvel, 2010–present (orig. 2001–2006). 3 volumes. Noir sensibility and realistic dialogue mark fan-favorite writer Bendis' game-changing work on this long-running title. The blind vigilante must first deal with having his identity revealed to the world, and then fills a power vacuum after he brings down a powerful mob. Unavailable for several years, these stories are finally back in print, starting with *Daredevil Ultimate Collection Vol. 1* (2010. 480p. 9780 785143888).

📖 **Millar, Mark (auth.), and Dave Johnson (illus.). *Superman: Red Son*.** DC Comics, 2004. 160p. 9781401201913. What if instead of growing up in Kansas to fight for "truth, justice, and the American way," the Last Kryptonian's spacecraft had crash-landed in the Soviet Union? This twist on the Superman mythos is a chilling story of the ultimate dictator.

Benchmark

★ **Miller, Frank. *Batman: The Dark Knight Returns*.** DC Comics, 1997 (orig. 1986). 224p. 9781563893414. After a 10-year hiatus, an aged Batman comes out of retirement to reclaim a Gotham City gone to hell. A landmark of modern comics and a bold reinterpretation of the Batman mythos.

★ ♟ 📖 🎬 **Moore, Alan (auth.), and Dave Gibbons (illus.). *Watchmen*.** DC Comics, 1986. 408p. 9780930289232. An investigation into the murders of several costumed crime-fighters reveals a conspiracy that could be the end—or salvation—of mankind. *Watchmen*'s brilliant structure, serious ethical concerns, and realism make it a classic. Winner of the Hugo Award in 1988.

Morrison, Grant (auth.), and Frank Quitely (illus.)

★ 📖 **All-Star Superman**. DC Comics, 2007–2009. 2 volumes. A sabotaged rescue attempt in the Sun gives Superman incredible new powers, but a limited time left to live. He'll protect Metropolis until the day he dies, but can he say goodbye to those he loves? Beautiful art pairs with a story that is both surprisingly moving and gleefully loony.

Vol. 1. 2007. 160p. 9781845763262.
Vol. 2. 2009. 160p. 9781041218377.

Rucka, Greg (auth.), and J. H. Williams III (illus.). *Batwoman: Elegy*. DC Comics, 2010. 192p. 9781401226923. After getting thrown out of West Point for refusing to lie about her sexuality in the face of Don't Ask Don't Tell, Kate Kane becomes Batwoman, fighting against the horrific Church of Crime. A multifaceted story is complemented by gorgeously painted art from Williams.

Benchmark

★ **Vaughan, Brian K. (auth.), and Tony Harris (illus.). Ex Machina**. Wildstorm, 2005–2010. 10 volumes. Science Fiction meets politics when New York City's premier superhero becomes its first post-9/11 mayor. Now, Mitchell Hundred must navigate hot-button issues from terrorism to legalized marijuana while trying to unravel the mystery of his powers. Begins with *The First Hundred Days* (2005. 136p. 9781401206123).

Benchmark

★ **Whedon, Joss (auth.), and John Cassaday (illus.). Astonishing X-Men**. Marvel Comics, 2004–2008. 4 volumes. Buffy the Vampire Slayer creator Joss Whedon offers up a fun and accessible story starring the world's most famous mutants, including Wolverine, Cyclops, and Kitty Pride. Marked by strong character development and lots of humor, this title makes a good entry-point for X-Men novices. The first two volumes, *Gifted* (2004. 152p. 9780785115311) and *Dangerous* (2005. 152p. 9780785116776), are standouts.

Wood, Brian (auth.), and Becky Cloonan (illus.)

📖 **Demo**. Vertigo, 2008–2011. 2 volumes. These offbeat short stories about young people discovering they have superhuman powers focus on moments of introspection and decision rather than heroics.

Realistic Fiction

In sharp contrast to the fantastical world of superheroes, Realistic Fiction comics feature stories about the everyday lives of ordinary people in contemporary settings. Many of these GNs are character-centered and dialogue-heavy.

Benchmark

★ 🎬 **Clowes, Dan. *Ghost World***. Fantagraphics, 2001 (orig. 1997). 80p. 9781560974277. With pitch-perfect dialogue and elegant line drawings, Clowes portrays the slow disintegration of the friendship between Enid and Rebecca, recent high school graduates on the cusp of adulthood.

Hernandez, Jaime, and Gilbert Hernandez

★ **Love & Rockets**. Fantagraphics, 1981–present. This acclaimed, groundbreaking comic follows the lives of Latina women in two completely different worlds. Jaime's "Locas" stories center on Maggie and Hopey, best friends and sometimes lovers who haunt the barrios and punk clubs of Los Angeles. Meanwhile, Gilbert's "Palomar" stories take place in a fictional South American village populated by a number of remarkable women, including Luba, proprietress of the local bathhouse, and Chelo, the sheriff. Originally published side by side, these stories are now compiled separately in various trade and hardcover editions. A good entry point into the "Locas" stories is *Maggie the Mechanic* (2007. 272p. 9781560977841), which chronicles Maggie's early adventures as a pro-solar mechanic. *Heartbreak Soup* (2007. 288p. 9781560977834) introduces Palomar and its residents with Luba's momentous arrival in the village.

Benchmark

★ 📖 **Mazzucchelli, David.** *Asterios Polyp*. Pantheon Books, 2009. 344p. 9780307377326. After his wife leaves him and a fire destroys his home and possessions, a middle-aged architect heads to middle America to sort through his past. Mazzucchelli's inventive use of color, drawing, and panel layout brings depth to a tale that is layered with allusions to mythology, literature, philosophy, and art history.

★ **Modan, Rutu.** *Exit Wounds*. Drawn & Quarterly, 2007. 168p. 97818 97299067. In modern-day Tel Aviv, a young man seeks to learn the truth behind his father's mysterious disappearance: Was he truly the victim of a suicide bombing or did he vanish for other reasons?

Rabagliati, Michel

Paul Series. Drawn & Quarterly, 2000–present. 3 volumes, ongoing. Rabagliati fictionalizes stories from his own life through the character of Paul, a young man coming-of-age in 1970s Montreal. Readers first meet Paul in *Paul Has a Summer Job* (2003. 152p. 9781896597546), in which he quits his boring factory job to work at a camp for disadvantaged youth. *Paul Goes Fishing* (2008. 208p. 9781897299289) finds Paul reflecting on childhood memories of family vacations in the Quebec countryside as he approaches fatherhood.

Seth. *George Sprott: 1894–1975*. Drawn & Quarterly, 2009. 96p. 9781897299517. A complicated and melancholy portrait of a former television host emerges from the contradictory, fractured recollections of the man himself and those who knew him.

★ **Tomine, Adrian.** *Shortcomings*. Drawn & Quarterly, 2007. 104p. 97818 97299166. With expressive, clear lines and pitch-perfect dialogue, Tomine provides incisive portraits of Ben, Miko, and Alice, three young Asian Americans struggling to navigate the treacherous waters of identity politics and sexual desire in present-day Berkeley and New York City.

Wood, Brian (auth.), and Ryan Kelly (illus.). *Local*. Oni Press, 2008. 376p. 9781934964002. This collection of 12 interconnected short stories, each set in a different city, centers on a restless young woman in search of a place she can truly call home.

Historical Fiction

Historical fiction comics depict fictional characters (or fictionalized versions of actual historical figures) in a bygone era. The setting (both time and place) is a central appeal of these works, and careful attention to the visual accuracy of clothing, architecture, food, and other period details is a hallmark of this genre in the world of GNs.

★ **Abouet, Marguerite (auth.), and Clément Oubrerie (illus.)**

Aya. Drawn & Quarterly, 2007–present (orig. 2005–2010). 6 volumes. Inspired by Abouet's childhood memories of Cote d'Ivoire in the late 1970s, this light-hearted series follows the lives of Aya and her friends and family in the bustling working-class neighborhood of Yopougon (aka Yop City). Oubrerie's vibrant illustrations bring to life the sights, smells, and sounds of Yop City. Only the first three volumes of this series, which begins with *Aya* (2007. 105p. 9781894937900), are currently available in English.

Benchmark

★ 📖 **Cruse, Howard. *Stuck Rubber Baby***. Vertigo, 2010 (first published 1995). 224p. 9781401227135. Now happily settled in San Francisco with his boyfriend, Toland Polk recalls the turbulent, formative years he spent as a closeted young white man growing up in the South at the dawn of the Civil Rights era. Nuanced characters, complex story lines, and masterful, cross-hatched illustrations make *Stuck Rubber Baby* a powerful and enduring classic.

Benchmark

★ **Eisner, Will. *A Contract with God***. W. W. Norton & Co, 2006 (first published 1978). 208p. 9780393328042. Widely considered the first GN, Eisner's four interconnected stories recreate the joys and sorrows of everyday life in the tenements of early 20th century New York City.

Inoue, Takehiko

Vagabond. VIZ Media, 2002–present. 31 volumes, or 9 "VIZBIG" volumes, ongoing. A fictionalized account of the life of Miyamoto Musashi, the legendary 17th-century "sword saint" of Japan. Filled with swordfights, this samurai *manga* is particularly revered for the accurate historical details in Inoue's story and art. Currently available in oversized "VIZBIG" editions, starting with *Vol. 1*(2008. 728p. 9781421520540).

10

Lutes, Jason

📖 **Berlin**. Drawn & Quarterly, 2000–present. 2 volumes, ongoing. This gripping, poignant series chronicles the fall of Germany's Weimar Republic and the ascendance of the Third Reich through the lives of several Berlin residents. With his intricately rendered landscapes and sensitive portrayals of citizens from all rungs of the social ladder, Lutes presents a sweeping portrait of a city tottering on the edge of violent upheaval. Begins with *City of Stones* (2000. 212p. 9781896597294), which spans September 1928 to May 1929, and continues with *City of Smoke* (2008. 200p. 9781897299531), which goes through 1930. The final volume is in the works.

11

12

📖 **Sturm, James. *Market Day*.** Drawn & Quarterly, 2010. 96p. 9781897299975. In this brief yet quietly affecting tale of 19th-century *shtetl* life, Mendleman, a skilled rug-weaver nervously anticipating the birth of his first child, travels to market to sell his wares, never suspecting the crisis that awaits him there.

13

14

Memoir

Autobiographical, or "autobio," comics have been a robust subgenre since the early days of underground comics, but the trend of illustrating one's own personal history has exploded in recent years. The Graphic Memoir subgenre is now a thriving field with subgenres of its own (cancer, war, coming-of-age stories, etc). Most Graphic Memoirs are written and illustrated by the same person, and describe the author's life in candid and intimate detail.

15

16

★ 📖 **Barry, Lynda. *One Hundred Demons*.** Sasquatch Books, 2002. 224p. 9781570614590. Head lice, terrible boyfriends, dancing, and the 2000 U.S. presidential election are just a few of the personal demons cartoonist Lynda Barry exorcises in this quirky, hilarious, and heartbreaking work of "autofictionalography."

17

★ 📖 **Bechdel, Allison. *Fun Home: A Family Tragicomic*.** Houghton Mifflin Harcourt, 2006. 240p. 9780618477944. A moving and literate memoir that doubles as personal archaeology. Using her multifaceted illustrative skills to recreate artifacts from her family's past, Bechdel

18

wrestles with her dysfunctional childhood, her relationship with (and the apparent suicide of) her eccentric father, and her sexual identity. *Time Magazine*'s 2006 Book of the Year.

📖 **Brown, Chester.** *Paying for It: A Comic Strip Memoir about Being a John.* Drawn & Quarterly, 2011. 280p. 9781770460485. After breaking up with his live-in girlfriend in 1996, Brown decided to eschew romantic relationships and seek sexual satisfaction exclusively from sex workers. His straightforward, pragmatic, and meticulous account of his paid sexual adventures (and his friends' reactions to them) provides a unique perspective on prostitution.

📖 **Farmer, Joyce.** *Special Exits: A Graphic Memoir.* Fantagraphics Books, 2010. 200p. 9781606993811. In this unflinching look at the realities of aging and death, Farmer depicts the slow physical and mental decline of Lars and Rachel (fictionalized versions of her parents) as they approach the end of their lives.

🎗📖 **Peeters, Frederik.** *Blue Pills: A Positive Love Story.* Houghton Mifflin, 2008. 192p. 9780618820993. In this Graphic Memoir, Peeters presents a heartfelt and sensitively told account of his life with his girlfriend Cati and her toddler son, both of whom are HIV-positive.

Benchmark

★ 🎬 **Pekar, Harvey (auth.), and Various Illustrators.** *American Splendor.* Four Walls Eight Windows and Ballantine Books, 1994–2010. From 1976 until his death in 2010, Harvey Pekar wrote about the trials and tribulations of everyday life through comics illustrated by a number of renowned cartoonists, starting with R. Crumb. A good introduction to the series is *Best of American Splendor* (Ballantine Books, 2005. 336p. 9780345479389). Another volume of note is *Our Cancer Year* (Four Walls Eight Windows, 1994. 252p. 9781568580111), coauthored by his wife Joyce Brabner, chronicling the year Pekar was diagnosed with cancer.

Benchmark

★ 📖 🎬 **Satrapi, Marjane.** <u>Persepolis</u>. Pantheon Books, 2004–2005. 2 volumes. Growing up in postrevolutionary Iran, young Satrapi chafed under the strict regulations of the Ayatollah's regime.

The Story of a Childhood. 2004 160p. 9780375714573. Warm characterizations and simple illustrations evoke the turbulence of Satrapi's childhood and adolescence.

The Story of a Return. 2005. 192p. 9780375714665. This book describes the author's homecoming after several years abroad in Europe.

📖 **Small, David.** *Stitches*. W. W. Norton & Co, 2009. 329p. 9780393068573. Using spare prose and evocative watercolors, Small recounts his singularly traumatic childhood and his struggle to overcome the physical and emotional scars inflicted by his parents.

Benchmark

★ 🎗 📖 **Spiegelman, Art, <u>Maus: A Survivor's Tale</u>**. Pantheon Press, 1986–1991. 2 volumes. In this Pulitzer Prize–winning work, cartoonist Spiegelman deftly weaves together the story of his difficult relationship with his father Vladek, a Holocaust survivor, and Vladek's memories of life before and during his imprisonment at Auschwitz. Spiegelman's depiction of the Jews as mice and Nazis as cats is powerful and unsettling.

My Father Bleeds History. 1986. 160p. 9780394747231. This book chronicles Vladek's life in Poland from the early years of World War II until 1944.

And Here My Troubles Began. 1991. 144p. 9780679729778. This book describes Vladek's experiences at Auschwitz.

Crime

Crime stories have a long tradition in the comic book form; many of the earliest bestselling comic book titles featured hard-boiled tales of private eyes, murderers, and gangsters. Those titles became victims of the Comics Code in the 1950s; but starting with the success of Frank Miller's <u>Sin City Series</u> in the 1990s, crime comics have been coming back in a big way, resulting in a flood of excellent works of fiction and nonfiction being produced in the last two decades. Crime comics frequently borrow from the visual language of *film noir* to set the seedy scene.

Benchmark

★ **Aaron, Jason (auth.), with R. M. Guéra (illus.) and Other Illustrators. <u>Scalped</u>**. Vertigo, 2007–present. 9 volumes, ongoing. After running away 15 years ago, Dashiell Bad Horse is forced to return to the Oglala Lakota reservation where he grew up—this time as an undercover FBI agent

18

tasked with bringing down the tribe's crooked chief. This ongoing noir series starts with *Indian Country* (2007. 126p. 9781401213176), and gets bigger and bloodier with each volume.

Cooke, Darwyn. *Richard Stark's Parker: The Hunter*. IDW, 2009. 144p. 9781600104930. Based on the stories of Richard Stark (a pen name of Donald Westlake), this adaptation introduces a remorseless professional thief who is betrayed by his partners, wronged by his woman, left for dead, . . . and after revenge! The second volume, *The Outfit* (2010. 160p. 9781600107621), has Parker taking on the mob, with more volumes to come!

♟ **Hubert (auth.), and Kerascoët (illus.).** *Miss Don't Touch Me*. NBM Publishing, 2008. 96p. 9781561635443. In 1930s Paris, Blanche, a prudish French maidservant, takes an undercover job as a prostitute in a high-class brothel in order to find her sister's murderer. A sequel, *Miss Don't Touch Me 2* (96p. 9781561635924), was published by NBM in late 2010.

Jason. *Why Are You Doing This?* Fantagraphics, 2005. 48p. 9781560976554. A case of mistaken identity leads to a murder, which leads to a frame-up, which leads to a headlong run from the police and a desperate attempt to find justice. Jason's distinctive style and droll sense of humor give this timeworn plot a new lease on life.

Jensen, Jeff (auth.), and Jonathan Case (illus.). *Green River Killer: A True Detective Story*. Dark Horse, 2011. 240p. 9781595825605. The son of a lead detective on the Green River Killer case relates the torturous final days of the investigation and its impact on his father. A nail-biting Police Procedural that focuses more on the people than the crimes, as well as a deeply felt family story.

Kindt, Matt. *Super Spy*. Top Shelf Productions, 2007. 336p. 978891830969. Intricately connected vignettes tell the stories of ordinary people working as spies across Europe in the closing days of World War II. By tracing the personal damage caused by the large and small betrayals in spy work, the book deftly balances suspense with pathos.

Layman, John (auth.), and Rob Guillroy (illus.)

<u>Chew</u>. Image Comics, 2009–present. 4 volumes, ongoing. Detective Chu has the strange ability to receive powerful psychic messages from anything that

he eats—be that a bowl of illicit chicken stew or a nibble off a murder victim's corpse—making him an important (if not always respected) agent for the FDA. A wild ride marked by pitch black humor, the first volume is *Taster's Choice* (2009. 128p. 9781607061595).

Urasawa, Naoki

🔖 **Naoki Urasawa's Monster**. Viz Media, 2006–2008. 18 volumes. A sprawling tale of murder starring Kenzo Tenma, a brilliant Japanese neurosurgeon working in Germany, who risks his career to save a boy named Johan whose parents have just been killed. But Johan is not what he seems, and soon Tenma's kindness will come back to haunt him.

Science Fiction

As a genre, Science Fiction tells stories of humanity's future dreams and technological nightmares that are sometimes action-packed and sometimes meditative. Readers enjoy reading Science Fiction for its ability to use the world we know to extrapolate new worlds that are completely different, but still recognizable.

Ellis, Warren (auth.), and John Cassaday (illus.)

Planetary. Wildstorm, 2000–2010. 4 volumes. Three "Archaeologists of the Impossible" excavate the secret history of the 20th century, discovering lost technologies and keeping the world strange. The first two volumes, *All Over the World and Other Stories* (2000. 160p. 9781563896484) and *The Fourth Man* (2001. 144p. 9781563897641), are standalone, while further volumes take the story to a mind-boggling climax.

Hickman, Jonathan. *Pax Romana*. Image Comics, 2009. 144p. 97815 82408736. The Vatican discovers the secret of time travel and sends a team of modern mercenaries back to Constantine's Holy Roman Empire in order to secure the Catholic Church's present standing. Brilliantly designed and dense with historical detail.

LeMire, Jeff

Sweet Tooth. Vertigo, 2009–present. 5 volumes, ongoing. A young boy born with antlers partners with a jaded killer to travel across a wasteland to unlock the mystery of the plague that wiped out humanity. The story, which begins in *Out of the Deep Woods* (2009. 128p. 9781401226961), emphasizes surreal lyricism over action.

Morrison, Grant (auth.), and Frank Quitely (illus.). *We3*. Vertigo, 2005. 104p. 9781401204952. When three household animals transformed into cybernetic killing machines escape from captivity, the hunt is on to put them down! But are these twisted creatures beyond redemption, or does something remain of their former selves?

Benchmark

★ ♀ 🎬 **Otomo, Katsuhiro. <u>Akira</u>.** Random House, 2009–2011 (orig. 1982–1990). 6 volumes. In a city at the mercy of a restrictive government and roving motorcycle gangs, a group of powerful psychics await their friend Akira, whose return will have catastrophic effects.

Urasawa, Naoki

<u>Pluto: Urasawa x Tezuka</u>. Viz Media, 2009–2010. 8 volumes. Something is trying to destroy the most powerful robots in the world, and Detective Geischt must unravel the mystery. But will he be able to stop this threat when he is also a target?

Vaughan, Brian K. (auth.), and Pia Guerra (illus.)

♀ **<u>Y: The Last Man</u>.** Vertigo, 2003–2008. 10 volumes. A plague instantaneously kills every male on the planet except for Yorick Brown and his pet monkey, who must embark on a journey across the globe to save humanity and find Yorick's girlfriend. The series begins with *Unmanned* (2003. 128p. 9781563899805).

Fantasy

Though we think of the standard Fantasy fare as castles and unicorns, the genre really is limited only by the imagination. The visual element of comics gives creators an added tool as they work to flesh out their imaginary worlds.

Benchmark

★ ♀ **Gaiman, Neil (auth.), and Various Illustrators. <u>The Sandman</u>.** DC Comics/Vertigo, 1991–1997. 10 volumes. After being imprisoned for 70 years, the King of Dreams must rebuild his kingdom and confront a world that has changed in his absence. This epic Fantasy series mines the mythic traditions of many cultures to create a rich and literate story. Winner of multiple Eisners, it is also the only comic book to win the World Fantasy Award. Begins with *Preludes and Nocturnes* (1993. 240p. 978156389 0116). *Dream Country* (1991. 160p. 9781563890161) and *Fables and Reflections* (1994. 264p. 9781563891052) are comprised of standalone shorts.

Hartzell, Andy. *Fox Bunny Funny*. Top Shelf, 2007. 104p. 9781891830976. The secret desires of a young fox lead him to challenge the rigid social order of his world, where foxes casually hunt and kill bunnies, who meekly suffer and die. This wordless GN is a powerful allegory for various forms of oppression in human societies.

Kelso, Megan. *Artichoke Tales*. Fantagraphics, 2010. 232p. 978160699 3446. In a fictional land where two formerly warring regions now warily coexist, the consequences of civil war still resonate for three generations of women whose family was caught between both sides of the conflict.

Sfar, Joann

🕴 📖 ⛏ **The Rabbi's Cat**. Pantheon Books, 2005–2008. 2 volumes. When a mischievous cat gains human speech by eating the family parrot, his relationships with his master and mistress—the rabbi and his daughter—are irrevocably altered.

> *The Rabbi's Cat*. 2005. 152p. 9780375422812. Sfar introduces his quirky cast of characters and vividly depicts the Sephardic Jewish community of 1930s Algeria.
> *The Rabbi's Cat 2*. 2008. 152p. 9780375425073. Sfar chronicles the cat's further (mis)adventures across Africa as he and the rabbi search for an African Jerusalem.

🕴 **Tan, Shaun.** *The Arrival*. Arthur A. Levine Books, 2007. 128p. 9780439895293. A beautiful "silent" GN that elegantly captures the bewilderment and wonder of a newly arrived immigrant in a strange country, which bears a partial resemblance to the early 20th century United States. Tan won the World Fantasy Award for Best Artist in 2007.

Thompson, Craig. *Habibi*. Pantheon Books, 2011. 655p. 978037542414. In an ornate and richly detailed mythical Middle Eastern land, two young slaves forge a powerful bond that sustains them through a series of trials and prolonged separation.

Willingham, Bill (auth.), Mark Buckingham (illus.), and Various Illustrators

🎗 <u>Fables</u>. Vertigo, 2003–present. 16 volumes, ongoing. After their home worlds are overrun by powerful invaders, a group of classic fairy tale characters take refuge in New York City in a story that mixes magic, intrigue, and epic battle. The series starts with Vol. 1: Legends in Exile (2002. 128p. 9781563899423) and is at its best through Vol. 8: Wolves (2008 160p. 9781401210014).

Horror

Horror is like the dark side of Fantasy, a genre where the strange turns dangerous. Telling Horror Stories in comics poses a unique challenge. In prose, the person reading creates the scene entirely in their mind; and in film, the film-makers can control everything about the visuals, the mood, the sound, and the pacing. In comics, however, the reader may free linger, jump ahead, or speed through their reading in ways that would kill the tension in a film. Nonetheless, some talented creators have found comics to be a fertile ground for things that go bump in the night.

Benchmark

★ 🎗 **Burns, Charles.** *Black Hole*. Pantheon Books, 2005. 352p. 978037 5423802. A sexually transmitted disease that afflicts the infected with bizarre disfigurements spreads through a group of teenage friends in 1970s Seattle. Burns' art uses heavy patches of black to create an unsettling tone and bring this nightmarish allegory of the fears of adolescence to life.

Hill, Joe (auth.), and Gabriel Rodriguez (illus.)

<u>Locke and Key</u>. IDW, 2008–present. 5 volumes, ongoing. After their father is murdered, the three Locke children move with their mother to the Maine

manor house where their father grew up. There they discover a set of magical keys that grant incredible powers and an ancient evil that will infiltrate their family to get what it wants. This series, written by the son of Steven King, starts with *Welcome to Lovecraft* (2008. 152p. 9781600 102370).

Kirkman, Robert (auth.), Tony Moore (illus.), and Charlie Adlard (illus.)

<u>The Walking Dead</u>. Image Comics. 2004–present. 15 volumes, ongoing. This unique Horror Story chronicles the struggles of a small group of survivors in the months and years after civilization collapses under a zombie apocalypse. Available in trade paperback form (*Vol 1: Days Gone Bye*. 2006. 144p. 9781582406725), or as two-in-one hardcover compendium editions (*Vol. 1*. 2009. 304p. 9781607060765). The basis for a well-received television show.

Mignola, Mike (auth. and illus.), and Various Artists

<u>Hellboy</u>. Dark Horse, 1994–present. 12 volumes, ongoing. A demon summoned by Nazis during World War II now battles big monsters as part of the U.S. Army's Bureau of Paranormal Research and Defense. This series, beginning with *Seed of Destruction* (2003. 128p. 9781593070946), has spun off novels, a cartoon, and two feature films.

Ralph, Brian. *Daybreak*. Drawn & Quarterly, 2011. 160p. 9781770460553. In this unusual spin on the classic zombie tale, a gregarious young one-armed man guides the reader through a densely drawn postapocalyptic landscape as an unseen menace shambles closer.

Nonfiction

Just like in prose, creators can use comics to educate readers in a plethora of fields, from philosophy to history and even mathematics.

Crumb, R. *The Book of Genesis Illustrated*. W. W. Norton & Co., 2009. 244p. 9780393061024. In his inimitable visual style, underground comics legend, R. Crumb graphically retells the first book of the Bible using the complete text.

Benchmark

★ ✹ 📖 **Doxiadis, Apostolos (auth.), Christos Papadimitriou (auth.), Alecos Papadatos (illus.), and Annie Di Donna (color).** *Logicomix: An Epic Search for Truth*. Bloomsbury USA, 2009. 352p. 9781596914520. A biography of logician Bertrand Russell that features accessible, humorous explanations of key philosophical and mathematical principles, *Logicomix* presents an engaging account of the search for the logical foundations of mathematics in the early 20th century.

✹ 📖 **Neufeld, Josh.** *A. D.: New Orleans after the Deluge*. Pantheon Books, 2009. 208p. 9780307378149. The catastrophic devastation wreaked by Hurricane Katrina and its aftermath is recounted through the true stories of seven ordinary New Orleans residents from different racial and socioeconomic backgrounds who survived the storm.

✹ 📖 **Sacco, Joe.** *Footnotes in Gaza*. Metropolitan Books, 2009. 432p. 9780805073478. In a little-known incident in 1956, Israeli soldiers shot to death 111 Palestinians in the town of Rafah. Fifty years later, reporter Sacco attempts to uncover what really happened and document the continuing toll on the people of Rafah and nearby Khan Younis.

Benchmark

★ **Talbot, Bryan.** *Alice in Sunderland*. Dark Horse, 2007. 328p. 781593076733. In a kaleidoscopic fusion of drawing and photo-collage, Talbot tells the history of North East England and its multifarious literary connections, notably Lewis Carroll's *Alice In Wonderland*.

TOOLS AND RESOURCES

Literature Guides

Gravett, Paul, ed. *1001 Comics You Must Read before You Die*. New York: Universe, 2011.

Kannenberg Jr., Gene. *500 Essential Graphic Novels*. New York: HarperCollins, 2007.

McCloud, Scott. *Understanding Comics*. New York: HarperPerennial, 1994.

Pawuk, Michael. *Graphic Novels: A Genre Guide to Comic Books, Manga and More*. Westport, CT: Libraries Unlimited, 2007.

Serchay, David. *The Librarian's Guide to Graphic Novels for Adults*. New York: Neal v Schuman, 2010.

Review Journals and Websites

Comic Book Resources. http://www.comicbookresources.com. Reviews, articles, columns, and more with a focus on superhero, science fiction, and fantasy comics and mainstream publishers like DC, Marvel, Vertigo, and Image.

The Comics Journal. http://www.tcj.com. Established in 1977, *The Comics Journal* was the first magazine to approach comics as an art form. Includes reviews, industry news, interviews, and more. Starting in 2009, print publication became limited to three times a year.

The Graphic Novel Reporter. http://graphicnovelreporter.com. Another GN review and resource site with a focus on libraries. Their Core Lists are useful tools for librarians building GN collections.

No Flying, No Tights. http://noflyingnotights.com. One of the first in-depth online resources for librarians about comics and GNs, created by Brookline, Massachusetts, teen librarian Robin Brenner. Features reviews of GNs for kids, teens, and adults; resource lists; and a useful introduction to the format.

Awards

Harvey Kurtzman Awards. Named after *MAD* magazine founder and cartoonist Harvey Kurtzman, these are awarded annually through open voting among comics professionals. A list of nominees and winners can be found at http://www.harveyawards .org/awards_current.html

Will Eisner Awards. Named after legendary cartoonist Will Eisner, these awards for creative achievement in American comic books are announced annually at Comic-Con. A five-member panel nominates candidates for each category that are then voted on by professionals across the comics industry. For a complete list of past winners, see http://www.comic-con.org/cci/cci_eisners_pastwinners.php

---

FIVE FAN FAVORITES

- Allison Bechdel. Fun Home: *A Family Tragicomic*—Biography/ Memoir

- Jaime Hernandez and Gilbert Hernandez. *Love & Rockets*—Literary Fiction

- Robert Kirkman (auth.), Tony Moore (illus.), and Charlie Adlard (illus.). *The Walking Dead*—Horror
- Alan Moore (auth.) and Dave Gibbons (illus.). *Watchmen*—Superheroes
- Brian K. Vaughan (auth.) and Pia Guerra (illus.). <u>Y: The Last Man</u>—Science Fiction

NOTES

1. See David Hadju's wonderful book *The Ten-Cent Plague: The Great Comic-Book Scare and How It Changed America* (Picador, 2009. 464p. 9780312428235) for a seething introduction to this controversial period.

2. Trina Robbins, "Girls, Women and Comics," in *Graphic Novels Beyond the Basics: Insights and Issues for Libraries*, eds. Martha Cornog and Timothy Perper, 45–60 (Westport, CT: Libraries Unlimited, 2009). Robbins cites a 1948 survey that showed 52 percent of comics readers aged 21–30 were women (p. 47).

Name Index

NOTE: This index includes names of authors, characters, and other individuals cited in this guide.

Subject Index

Title Index

NOTE: Series titles in this index are underlined; book and journal titles appear in italics; and short story and article titles are presented in quotes.

About the Editors and Contributors

EDITORS

DIANA TIXIER HERALD is an author, readers' advisory consultant, workshop presenter, and speaker. She started her career as an avid reader long before she ever saw the inside of a classroom, and usually reads in excess of 400 books a year. At age 10, she began working as a library volunteer and has since been a bookseller, a library assistant, a library director, head of a public library popular materials center, and administrator for 38 school libraries. Her Master of Arts in Librarianship and Information Management was earned at the University of Denver. Today, she lives on the edge of a canyon at 7,000 feet altitude with her husband in a sustainable house they built from recycled materials. She is the author of several other readers' advisory guides, including *Teen Genreflecting*, *Fluent in Fantasy*, and *Strictly Science Fiction*.

CYNTHIA ORR has held various positions in public libraries, including reference librarian, department head, deputy director, library manager, collection manager, and interim technical services director, and has worked in two very large star-rated multibranch urban and suburban public libraries, as well as a smaller suburban library and an exurban system. Her Master's in Library Science is from Case Western Reserve University. She is currently a library consultant with over 30 years of experience in public libraries. She consults with libraries and vendors; speaks extensively on the subject of readers' advisory service, collection development, and technical services; teaches a class on readers' advisory service at Kent State University's School of Library and Information Science; and edits the monthly Collection Development columns in *Library Journal*. She is the editor of the *Reader's Advisor Online Blog*, and was the 2004 winner of the ALA/RUSA Margaret E. Monroe Library Adult Services Award.

***

CONTRIBUTORS

ABBY BASS is an adult services librarian in the Arts, Recreation, & Literature Department at the Central branch of The Seattle Public Library. She received her MLIS from the University of Washington and has also worked as a teen services librarian, reader's advisory librarian, and branch assistant manager at various locations at The Seattle Public Library. She has contributed to *Library Journal*, *Alki*, and *The Reader's Advisor Online*, and has given presentations on digital reader's advisory at WLA/PNLA and PLA. An avid comics reader, Abby frequently guest lectures on graphic novels in Nancy Pearl's Book Lust 102 class at the University of Washington Information School.

JACK BAUR has been a teen services librarian at the Berkeley Public Library since 2008, a position that has afforded him many opportunities to tap into his lifelong passion for comic books. Jack has written and lectured about comics in libraries many times over the past few years. He is a reviewer for the website *No Flying No Tights*, and has served as the president of BAYA: The Bay Area Young Adult Librarians since 2010.

TERRY BECK is Manager of Adult and Teen Services at Sno-Isle Libraries in the state of Washington. She's an MLIS graduate of Dominican University's Graduate School of Library & Information Science.

JOHN CHARLES is an adult services librarian for the Scottsdale Public Library. He reviews romances for *Booklist* and the *Chicago Tribune*. He is the coauthor of *Romance Today: An A to Z Guide to Contemporary American Romance Writers*, and was named Librarian of the Year by the Romance Writers of America in 2002.

SARAH STATZ CORDS has worked as an academic and public librarian, and is currently the associate editor of the *Reader's Advisor Online* blog. She is the author of the reading guides *The Real Story: A Guide to Nonfiction Reading Interests*, *The Inside Scoop*, and *Now Read This III* (with Nancy Pearl), as well as the nonfiction-lit blog *Citizen Reader*.

KELLY FANN is the director of the Tonganoxie Public Library and teaches part time for the School of Library and Information Management at Emporia State University. She is a regular workshop presenter across Kansas and Missouri on readers' advisory practices, trends, and topics—her specialty being the Horror genre and the incorporation of digital mediums for enhancing and invigorating library readers' advisory services. Glued to the Internet, her iPhone, video games, and audio books, she is constantly seeking out new avenues and methods for finding the ultimate readers' services guides.

MAURA HEAPHY is Senior Lecturer at The Ohio State University, teaching Science Fiction, Fiction Writing, Composition and Business Writing. She is the author of *Science Fiction Authors: A Research Guide* (2008) and *100 Most Popular Science Fiction Authors* (2010), published by Libraries Unlimited of Santa Barbara, California. Special interests: British Science Fiction, Dystopian Fiction, and Slipstream. Work in progress: a Science Fiction novel about redemption and reinvention, set on a generation starship.

LESA HOLSTINE is Public Services Officer for the Evansville Vanderburgh Public Library, Evansville, Indiana. She has been a library administrator for over 30 years. She reviews books for a number of publications as well as on her award-winning blog *Lesa's Book Critiques*, where she specializes in covering mysteries.

SARAH JOHNSON, Reference/Electronic Resources Librarian at Eastern Illinois University, is the author of *Historical Fiction: A Guide to the Genre* (2005) and *Historical Fiction II* (2009). She serves as Book Review Editor for the *Historical Novels Review* and blogs at *ReadingthePast.com*. In 2012, she won ALA/RUSA's Louis Shores Award for book reviewing.

SHELLEY MOSLEY is a retired library manager, former Romance Writers of America Librarian of the Year, and has cowritten four nonfiction books, including *Romance Today: An A-to-Z Guide to Contemporary American Romance Writers The Suffragists in Literature for Youth: The Fight for the Vote The Complete Idiot's Guide to the Ultimate Reading List*, and *Crash Course in Library Supervision: Meeting the Key Players*. She has written five romantic comedies and one novella with Deborah Mazoyer as Deborah Shelley. She has written hundreds of articles and reviews for professional journals, and, with coauthor John Charles, won the Romance Writers of America Veritas Award twice.

HANNAH JO PARKER is an adult services librarian at the Ballard Branch of The Seattle Public Library. After graduating with an MLIS degree from the University of Washington, she worked as a reader's advisory librarian in the Fiction Department at The Seattle Public Library's Central Library and as a branch manager. When she isn't reading, talking about, or writing about Mainstream Fiction, she reads every rock memoir she can get her hands on.

ANDREW SMITH gave up apologizing for his reading tastes a long time ago. Now the Readers Services Librarian at Williamsburg (VA) Regional Library, he loves working with readers in person and through the library's Looking for a Good Book online profile service.

REBECCA VNUK is the author of *Read On . . . Women's Fiction* and *Author Research Series: Women's Fiction Authors*. A national presenter on a variety of reader's advisory topics, she is currently the Reference and Collection Management Editor for *Booklist* magazine. In 2010, she was named a *Library Journal* Mover and Shaker and was the recipient of PLA's Allie Beth Martin Award for excellence in reader's advisory service.

LYNN WIANDT, when she is not serving her three canine masters, manages the Seville branch of the Medina County District Library in Ohio.

DAVID WRIGHT is a reader services librarian at The Seattle Public Library's Central branch. He has been a regular contributor to *Booklist* magazine, the *NoveList* database, and the library's blog *Shelf Talk*. He has presented on a variety of topics at ALA, PLA, BEA, and other conferences.